ALBERTA OIL
AND THE
DECLINE OF
DEMOCRACY
IN CANADA

ALBERTA OIL AND THE DECLINE OF DEMOCRACY IN CANADA

edited by

MEENAL SHRIVASTAVA & LORNA STEFANICK

AU PRESS
Athabasca University

Published by AU Press, Athabasca University
1200, 10011 – 109 Street, Edmonton, AB T5J 3S8
ISBN 978-1-77199-029-5 (print)   978-1-77199-030-1 (PDF)   978-1-77199-032-5 (epub)
doi: 10.15215/aupress/9781771990295.01
Cover design by Natalie Olsen, kisscutdesign.com.
Interior design by Sergiy Kozakov.
Printed and bound in Canada by Marquis Book Printers.

Library and Archives Canada Cataloguing in Publication

Alberta oil and the decline of democracy in Canada / edited by Meenal Shrivastava
and Lorna Stefanick.

Includes bibliographical references and index.
Issued in print and electronic formats.

1. Petroleum industry and trade—Political aspects—Alberta. 2. Petroleum industry
and trade—Social aspects—Alberta. 3. Petroleum industry and trade—Government
policy—Alberta. 4. Democracy—Alberta. I. Shrivastava, Meenal, 1971-, author, editor
II. Stefanick, Lorna, 1961-, author, editor

HD9574.C23A54 2015   338.2'7282097123   C2015-904346-8
                                                       C2015-904347-6

We acknowledge the financial support of the Government of Canada.

Canadian   Patrimoine
Heritage   canadien

Assistance provided by the Government of Alberta, Alberta Multimedia Development
Fund.

Government

The illustrations that open each part are reproduced courtesy of the artist, Sylvie
Roussel-Janssens, www.lsclight.com.

On page 29, Caribou. 2010. 10" x 10" polyester fabric, photocopy on acetate and silver
ink. Courtesy of the artist; on page 169, Bird and Helicopter. 2010. 10" x 10" polyester
fabric, photocopy on acetate and silver ink; and on page 293, Salamander. 2010. 10" x
10" polyester fabric, photocopy on acetate and silver ink.

CONTENTS

ACKNOWLEDGEMENTS

In the spring of 2012, we had the opportunity to teach an intensive six-week course on oil and democracy. Offered through the University of Alberta's Community Service-Learning program, Class lectures were supplemented by a series of lectures sponsored by the university's Parkland Institute, which conducts research into contemporary social and political issues from the standpoint of political economy. We had recently co-authored an article on the topic of oil's potential to undermine democracy, which appeared in the May 2012 issue of *New Global Studies*, and we were aware of a number of our colleagues at Athabasca University whose research looked at various aspects of democracy in Alberta, in Canada, and internationally. Given that the following year would mark the sixtieth anniversary of the publication of C. B. Macpherson's seminal work *Democracy in Alberta*, the time seemed ripe for a collaborative, in-depth, interdisciplinary exploration of liberal democracy in Canada, focusing on Alberta as the epicentre of an expanding oil-based economy. By the time this book was completed, in the spring of 2015, the world market for oil was markedly different, with the production of oil in the United States at all-time highs and the volatility of oil prices threatening the economies of oil-exporting countries. In addition, concerns about the state of democracy had become widespread. This volume represents an attempt to examine some of issues arising in this complex milieu.

We thank Sara Dorow, of the University of Alberta's Department of Sociology, for inviting us to teach this class, and our teaching assistant, Matt Dow, for helping us to make it a success. Perhaps above all, we are indebted to the students themselves, who tackled a very demanding course with interest and energy and allowed us to share our ideas and to refine them in the process. Our thanks, then, to Karissa VanderLeek, Ashley Thompson, Peter Selcuk, Heather Sawchyn, Lynsey Race, Maria Montenegro, Doug Lemermeyer, Julianne Layton, Garret Johnston, Tim Isberg, Keltie Hutchison, Liam Hudson, Akimi Fukaura, Mireille Chamberland, Jonathon Cartmell, Olivia Bako, Anneka Bakker, and Malaika Aleba. If the future of our society is in the hands of thoughtful, diligent, and considerate people such as you, we have much reason to be hopeful about the prospects for democracy, despite its many current deficits, as detailed in this book.

We are also grateful to the Parkland Institute for its work in organizing the Speaker's Series that accompanied the class and, in particular, its executive director, Ricardo Acuña, and director, Trevor Harrison. Our special thanks go to Lorraine Woollard, Angie Meyer, and Auralia Brooke, along with the many Athabasca University administrators who assisted us in figuring out how to persuade two university bureaucracies to work together in order to create a learning experience that students would remember with the same enthusiasm that they originally brought to the class.

With remarkable patience and good humour, our contributors met demanding deadlines and willingly engaged in a seemingly endless exchange of ideas, drafts, and revisions, for which we are profoundly thankful. It was a pleasure to work with such a stimulating and cooperative group of collaborators. We are grateful to Megan Hall, Connor Houlihan, and Kathy Killoh, at Athabasca University Press, for their support of this project. We especially appreciate the insights provided by the two anonymous reviewers for the press, as well as those offered by Alvin Finkel, our colleague and former chair of the AU Press Editorial Committee, and by Pamela MacFarland Holway, senior editor at the press, who read and reread chapters as they evolved. Our copy editor, Joyce Hildebrand, deserves special thanks for her close attention to the text and for catching errors and omissions. Their comments and suggestions have greatly strengthened this volume.

None of this would have been possible without the help and support of our spouses, Sanjiv Shrivastava and Jim Race, who accepted our preoccupation with the project as we grappled with the many demands of producing this book. Their unconditional support, intellectual companionship, and love have been the bulwarks against which we have tested and retested many incoherent ideas, sought solace from major frustrations, and celebrated minor victories. Our many dog-walking adventures with Appu, Gauri, and Cleo provided much-needed breaks, as well as cherished memories.

Finally, a special thanks to our departed mothers, Surekha Sinha and Millie Stefanick, who died a few days apart in 2010. Living on different continents, they were connected not only by their daughters but also by a world view that they shared across time and space. Even though they never met, these two remarkable women continue to remind us of the ways in which human experience unites us.

ALBERTA OIL AND THE DECLINE OF DEMOCRACY IN CANADA

INTRODUCTION

Framing the Debate on Democracy and Governance in an Oil-Exporting Economy

Meenal Shrivastava and Lorna Stefanick

In 1953, C. B. Macpherson's *Democracy in Alberta: The Theory and Practice of a Quasi-Party System* appeared. Much has changed in the sixty years since the publication of this influential work, which explores the nature of democracy in a jurisdiction dominated by one class of producers—the farmers. Today, more than ever before, Alberta can be seen as a one-industry economy, with agricultural interests having been replaced by those of the oil industry. Since Macpherson's analysis, Alberta's population has also grown dramatically as a result of both national and international migration. Calgary and Edmonton have become major urban centres, and economic and political power has incrementally and steadily shifted from central Canada to western Canada. What did not change until 5 May 2015—when the New Democratic Party (NDP) formed a majority government in Alberta, decisively ending nearly forty-four years of rule by the Progressive Conservative (PC) Party—was the dominance of one party in the provincial political system and the resultant concern for the health of democracy in this province. While the symbolic significance of the NDP electoral victory is enormous, it remains to be seen to what extent the NDP's traditionally social democratic stance will alter the course of provincial energy policy.

At the time Macpherson wrote, the state of democracy in Alberta might have been assumed to be of only local importance. This, too, has changed: it is now clear that contemporary trends in Alberta have significant national and international implications. Because of Alberta oil, Canada joined the list of the world's top ten oil producers in 2006, and it subsequently rose to number five on the list in 2014 (USEIA 2014, 2). The far-reaching ramifications of environmental damage caused by unconventional oil extraction and the intensification of neoliberal policies in the country have garnered interest in the health of democracy in both Alberta and Canada. In this context, it is worth exploring Macpherson's thesis that a society dominated by petit bourgeois producers tends to reduce politics to a single-minded focus on maximizing returns from sales of commodities for these producers. In such a society, in which there is an unequal distribution of wealth, inevitable conflicts of class interests, if they are recognized at all, are treated as irrelevant to political life (Macpherson 1953).

This collaborative project originated in an article that we co-authored (Shrivastava and Stefanick 2012). The article provides a survey of studies, most of them focused on countries in the Global South, that explore the relationship between oil dependence and liberal democracy. Reliance on oil exports can provide important revenue that might be used for development purposes, but it can also have negative economic and political effects. From the studies focused on the Middle East (e.g., Mahdavy 1970) to wide-ranging cross-national studies (e.g., Ross 2001, 2009; Tsui 2011), much of the vast literature under the banner of "oil and democracy" argues that reliance on oil exports is strongly associated with undemocratic, authoritarian rule (e.g., Bulte, Damania, and Deacon 2005; Karl 1997; Lowi 2004; Wantchekon 2002). This is not to suggest that "oil undermines democracy" is an unchallenged thesis, since some studies have also shown the pro-democratic effects, in varying degrees, of the discovery of oil wealth on countries such as Ecuador, Congo, Nigeria, Trinidad, and Venezuela (e.g., Herb 2005; Smith and Kraus 2005). Nevertheless, the bulk of the oil and democracy scholarship has found a negative relationship between natural resource dependence, particularly oil revenue, and democracy.

This negative relationship has been traced to phenomena such as the rentier state (that is, a country that derives a high proportion of its income from resource rents) and the "Dutch disease." The term *rentier state* is most frequently used to describe countries in the Middle East and in North Africa, along with characteristics of their national economies and state institutions and their governments' attitude toward their citizens. Using the revenue generated by the extraction and export of resources as the independent variable, theories of the rentier state draw causal links between the income derived from resource rents and poor economic governance as well as authoritarian rule (Ross 2001, 2006).[1] The term *Dutch disease*—which first appeared in *The Economist* (1977) to describe the decline of the manufacturing sector in the Netherlands after the discovery of a large natural gas field in 1959—refers to another causal mechanism, one that harms a country's non-resource sectors. A sharp rise in revenue from the export of primary commodities, such as oil, has the effect of strengthening the country's currency, which in turn drives up the cost of its other exports. This reduces the competitiveness of the country's agricultural and manufacturing sectors, which have already been weakened by the booming resource sector, and thus draws both capital and labour away from these sectors, thereby raising production costs (Gylfason 2001).

These mechanisms are part and parcel of what is often called the "resource curse." Sometimes described as the "paradox of plenty" thesis, the resource curse is used to explain why countries rich in natural resources—notably, petroleum-producing countries—have been unable to use that abundance to boost their overall economic growth—although recent studies have shown that it is the volatility in commodity prices, rather than abundance per se, that drives the resource curse paradox (e.g. , Cavalcanti, Mohaddes, and Raissi 2012; Leong and Mohaddes 2011). Simply put, the resource curse posits that the narrowing of a capitalist economy down to one commodity gives those with control of that commodity inordinate power. This skewed power is particularly evident when comparisons are drawn to economies in which the competition between different factions of capital creates opportunities for varied agendas on the part of both the state and civil society.

Our 2012 article applies measures of democracy (such as the principles of "good governance") used in the oil and democracy literature to assess the impact of oil wealth on fundamental elements of liberal democracy in Canada. Specifically, we set out to determine whether relationships between oil-dependence and democracy similar to those found in the Global South could be found in Alberta, a subnational jurisdiction in the Global North. We argue that the political influence of the powerful oil lobby in the province has led to a decline in political liberalism—which refers to the limited role of government, reduced to that of a neutral referee mediating among competing definitions of the public good (see Rawls 1993)—and that the result constitutes a democratic deficit that is fuelling political and economic inequality in the province and the country. Although our focus is subnational, the implications of our findings are national in scope.

In any given context, political, economic, and social variables, which are the product of a range of historical factors, mediate the relationship between resource management and political economic outcomes.[2] These contextual differences might explain, at least in part, the discrepancy in development outcomes in different resource-abundant countries. Most importantly, these contextual variables are strongly influenced by the prevailing political dynamics. In the Canadian context, the strident rhetoric that characterizes debates about whether Alberta oil is "ethical" or whether reliance on "dirty" oil is turning Canada into a petro-state tends to deflect the focus from the political system and the policy apparatus that is shaping the relationship between resource management and political economic outcomes—in particular, the role of neoliberalism.

The term *neoliberalism* most commonly refers to economic reform policies and measures such as eliminating price controls, deregulating capital markets, lowering trade barriers, and reducing state influence on the economy, especially through privatization, fiscal austerity, and financialization.[3] Additionally, neoliberalism can be a political ideology that explains and justifies a preferred economic and governmental order for society (Knight 2006). In Canada, neoliberalism entered the national scene under the regimes of Jean Chrétien and Paul Martin, which oversaw the first wave of rollbacks of the national welfare state. Changes they made to the Canadian Assistance Program, for example, enabled welfare restructuring at the provincial level; Alberta and Ontario were the first provinces to replace welfare with workfare (Herd 2002; Peck and Theodore 2010). The Conservative-led government under Stephen Harper has overseen what Jamie Peck and Adam Tickell (2002) characterize as "roll-out neoliberalism": strategies for restructuring the state characterized by authoritarian measures that rollback the welfare state while maintaining class privilege and market dominance. In Alberta, restructuring of the welfare state through privatization, deregulation, the tightening of eligibility requirements for assistance, and the devolution of welfare services to nonprofit and voluntary sectors, has a long pedigree but certainly reached its zenith under Premier Ralph Klein in the 1990s. The intensification of neoliberal policy provincially and federally has implications for both natural resource management and political economic outcomes.

Contributors to this volume, therefore, consider two sets of issues: the first pertains to broad questions about institutions of liberal democracy in Alberta and Canada, and the second concerns specific trends in an oil-exporting jurisdiction. Unsurprisingly, these issues often overlap and are guided by similar questions: What are the historical, socio-political, and political economic trends that have played a role in the evolution of governance, equity, and citizenship issues in Alberta? How are these trends being felt on the national level? How does political ideology affect provincial and federal public policy issues? What are the impacts of economic and political inequality on resource management and governance?

This collection takes a different approach from that of much of the oil and democracy literature. Instead of relying on quantitative measures of democracy, the volume provides a critical evaluation of the application of the principles of liberal democracy in Alberta, and in Canada generally, by investigating significant public policy areas, such as energy, Aboriginal issues, the environment, labour law, and urban planning. Additionally, the book includes a selection of largely qualitative studies of political ideology, political economy, national security, political activism, gender, labour, and the visual arts in the milieu of increasing oil dependence federally and provincially. While most chapters focus primarily on Alberta as the major oil-producing jurisdiction in Canada, others draw comparisons between Canada and oil-rich powers in the Global South—notably, Venezuela and Iran. The fourteen scholars contributing to this book are from nine different academic disciplines; this diversity of approach and method reflects the cross-disciplinary reach of this topic. These many perspectives on the nature and operation of democracy in Alberta, all informed by liberal democratic theory, have significant ramifications for the country as a whole.

Liberal Democracy in an Oil-Exporting Jurisdiction

Among the many aspects of the "oil impedes democracy" claim is the state of liberal democracy in oil-based economies, which we have chosen as the focus for this book. Consequently, the theme of democratic governance weaves its way through every chapter of our exploration of various features of liberal democracy. We recognize, however, that the term *liberalism* encompasses a diversity of often contradictory streams of thought. For instance, in the United States, liberalism is associated with the welfare-state policies of the New Deal program instituted by the Democratic administration of President Franklin D. Roosevelt, whereas in Europe, it is more commonly associated with a commitment to limited government and laissez-faire economic policies. In Canada, liberalism is most often associated with social liberalism, which ascribes to the state a legitimate role in addressing economic and social issues such as welfare, health care, and education, while simultaneously expanding civil rights. For the purposes of this book, we use the terms *political liberalism* or *liberal democracy* interchangeably. They refer to a system of governance characterized by civil liberties, more than one political party competing for election, separation of power, the rule of law, and a representative government based on majority rule with protections for minority rights (see, for instance, Cunningham 2002).

Combining democracy with liberalism creates an uneasy juxtaposition of the individualistic ideology of liberalism, which in its classical form concerns itself with limiting the power of the state over the individual, and the collectivist ideal of democracy, which is concerned with empowering the masses. Thus, liberal democracy may be seen as a negotiated compromise between liberal individualism and democratic collectivism. One way to achieve this fine balance is through economic freedoms, which are supposed to result in the formation of a significant middle class and a broad and flourishing civil society. Moreover, attributes such as the protection of civil liberties and human rights, political pluralism, equality before the law, the right to petition elected officials for redress of grievances, and due process are often seen as preconditions for liberal democracy (Beetham 1992). In a nutshell, freedom, equality, and democratic participation are considered the cornerstones of a liberal democracy. As the cycles of recession became more common and intense after the end of the Cold War, however, some scholars (e.g., Habermas and Rehg 1998; Tamas 2011) argued that the increasing state authoritarianism and income inequality were important signifiers of the failure of the liberal or representative democratic framework and that alternative models of democracy were needed. Some of these models, such as deliberative or participatory democracy, go beyond but do not discard the liberal tradition. Moreover, the resilience of the liberal democratic model is amply attested to in the continued use of the attributes of this framework in measures such as the Democracy Index or the Polity Project, which seek to assess the political health of countries around the world, including that of oil-exporting states.

Nonetheless, we do not accept the premise of liberal democratic theory uncritically. As many of the chapters in the book explain, more expansive definitions of democracy are needed to challenge the assumptions and rigid limitations of the liberal democratic model. For instance, liberal democracy typically implies a market-based economy that relies on supply and demand, with some regulation to prevent monopolistic behaviour. Much like C. B. Macpherson, who highlighted the tensions between possessive individualism and capitalist market relations in the liberal democratic model (see Macpherson 1977, 1985), many chapters in this book call attention to the problems associated with accommodating the utilitarian concerns of the market and with broader developmental liberalism, both of which are important underlying assumptions of liberal democratic theory.

In this context, the notion of "developmental liberalism" is particularly pertinent to our use of liberal democratic theory. Developmental liberalism emphasizes notions of political legitimacy, public reason, and respect for reasonable pluralism (Rawls 1993); the conceptualization of development in terms of capability expansion (Sen 1999); and the role of the state in governance issues such as the fair distribution of resources (Rawls 1971). With the recognition of the socio-economic failures of neoliberal financialization and deregulation, the developmental role of a democratic state has re-emerged not only in the burgeoning critique of neoliberal orthodoxy but also in governance discourse, where good governance is essentially equated with sound "development management" (Harriss 2005, 37).

As pointed out by Munck and Verkuilen (2002), even the most widely used democracy indices suffer from important weaknesses deriving from methodological issues. The normative, descriptive, methodological, and semantic limitations of theorizing democracy amply apply to the liberal democratic framework and are dealt with in some detail in the opening chapter, by Meenal Shrivastava. We acknowledge the limitations of this framework, but because most studies on the impact of oil dependence on democracy apply the liberal democracy model, we have chosen to use it as a limited but necessary framework upon which to build our assessment of the strength of democracy in Alberta. While this has provided our authors with a consistent set of indicators, their application actually reveals the restrictive and simplistic nature of the liberal democratic conceptualization. The limitations of the liberal democratic parameters stand out most noticeably in the chapters comparing Venezuela (Kellogg, chapter 5) and Iran (Fraser, Mannani, and Stefanick, chapter 6) to Canada, but they are also evident in the examinations of homelessness in Canada's richest province (Evans, chapter 12), the legal and human rights of the First Nations communities affected by the extractive industry (Slowey and Stefanick, chapter 7), and the gendered dimensions of resource extraction (Dorow, chapter 10). Furthermore, Karen Wall's analysis of the state of the visual arts in Alberta (chapter 13) challenges this reductive conceptualization and joins the ranks of writings that re-examine the social and cultural dimensions of oil extraction in an oil-exporting economy.

In a liberal democracy, supreme power is assumed to be vested in the people and is expressed through the institutions of the state. In this formulation, strong democratic institutions support the expression of a plurality of political perspectives such that the "winners" and "losers" of any contestation over state policy are neither predetermined nor consistent. In this context, a democratic deficit arises when certain members of the community are systematically disenfranchised—specifically, when their voices are consistently ignored or when political, social, and economic benefits regularly accrue disproportionately to one group of people. While Shrivastava (chapter 1) points to the role of inequality in creating a democratic deficit, other authors—such as Barnetson (on occupational safety, chapter 8), Foster and Barnetson (on temporary foreign workers, chapter 9), Dorow (on women in Fort McMurray, chapter 10), and Evans (on homelessness, chapter 12)—demonstrate how inequality plays out in particular sectors in Alberta. Such a deficit manifests itself in low voter turnouts, distrust in or hostility toward state institutions, a pronounced lack of social cohesion, and wildly disproportionate allocation of societal benefits, in both the political and the economic realms. As illustrated by Stefanick's discussion of Alberta's energy paradigm (chapter 4), Smith's analysis of petro-politics (chapter 3), and Slowey and Stefanick's look at First Nations in the vicinity of Fort McMurray (chapter 7), this hegemony marginalizes alternative framing of issues, causing dissenters to seek new spaces for political contestation. Additionally, Harrison (on the fate of progressivism in Alberta, chapter 2), Acuña (on the nature of political power in Alberta, chapter 11), and Stefanick (on accountability, chapter 14) pointedly reveal the history and mechanism of ideological and political hegemony in the province, which can be construed as a democratic deficit within a liberal democratic context. The theme of democratic governance can thus be found in every chapter of this volume; however, the uniqueness of this book is that it is framed within the context of an oil-exporting economy in the Global North.

Terminology, Staples Theory, and the Impact of Oil Wealth on Democracy

Another theme that provides a connective thread in the following chapters is the relationship between oil dependence and democracy. The debate over the impact of oil dependence has at times been conducted at a shrill pitch in drawn-out public battles, with "petro-state" and "ethical oil" characterizing the two extremes of the ideological spectrum. At one time, the petroleum industry's chosen term for the bitumen sands was *tar sands*. The oil industry, mainstream media, and government officials have since adopted *oil sands* as their preferred term because the word *oil* is perceived to have a less negative connotation than *tar*. In an effort to achieve a balanced perspective unburdened by the political polarization inherent in "oil" versus "tar" sands, authors in the book have chosen to adopt the term *bitumen sands*. The goal is to emphasize the analysis. After all, if causal links exist between oil revenue dependence and specific elements of liberal democracy in Alberta, they do so independently of terminology.

On a global scale, there appears to be considerable support for the assertion that oil-dependent economies in the Middle East, Africa, and Latin America are characterized by a democratic deficit within both quantitative and qualitative measures of liberal democracy (Feldman 2003; Ross 2001, 2009; Tsui 2011; Wantchekon 2002). There are many other factors, however, that inhibit the growth of democracy in the Global South, most notably the legacy of imperialism and colonialism that continues to affect internal and external relations of these countries. However, both the impact of this important historical context and the international system that created and perpetuates the North/South division are often overlooked within the rigid confines of the liberal democratic framework.[4] Furthermore, singling out oil as a "curse" to democracy may well overstate the case, as other commodities such as diamonds, gold, and other minerals have been shown to have similar antidemocratic effects (Corden and Neary 1982; Ross 2006; Van Wijnbergen 1984).

As mentioned above, nearly all of the studies on oil and democracy use the liberal democratic framework and related measures for their analyses. Associated indices, such as the Worldwide Governance Indicators of the World Bank, and other good-governance models, such as that of United Nations Development Programme, have been applied in their various iterations as key variables for the development of a functioning market economy, economic development, and democratic characteristics.[5] A discussion of the evolution and limitations of these indicators is provided in the opening chapter. However, the notion that democracy is alive and well in the Global North is becoming increasingly contentious, as is evidenced by the many global movements, such as Occupy Wall Street, that protest the austerity measures in Europe and North America. These movements seek to address what is seen as a rising democratic deficit in both the Global North and the Global South that is producing socio-economic inequities and environmental destruction.

In Canada, there is sporadic rhetoric of "petro-state," on the one hand, by critics who charge that the oil industry has an inordinate amount of influence on democratic governance in Canada (e.g., Nikiforuk 2010) and "ethical oil," on the other, by those who advocate the development of bitumen oil on "ethical" grounds (Levant 2011). There is scholarship on the impact of Alberta's oil dependence on the environment from a political economic perspective (see, for instance, Davidson and Gismondi 2011) and on socio-cultural dimensions of an oil economy: see, for instance, the special issue of the *Canadian Journal of Sociology* in 2013 on the petro-culture of the Fort McMurray region.[6] This collection provides an important complement to the existing research by exploring the intensification of many political and policy trends in Alberta that appear to be directly or indirectly influenced by the development of Canada's bitumen oil. In doing so, this book evaluates the political, policy, and cultural dimensions of economic practices associated with the rise of oil dependence in Alberta and Canada, rather than examining political economy and culture as distinct components. This approach is in keeping with many studies which argue that the oil industry does not just function as an isolated outpost of the export economy but broadly influences the formation of social and political values, labour practices, and notions of citizenship (e.g., Chomsky and Santiago 1998; Coronil 1997; Finn 1988; Klubock 1998; Putnam 2002; Salas 2009). After all, as Miguel Salas (2009, 238) notes in the context of past studies of Venezuela, "To only address economic factors associated with this extractive industry was to underestimate the power of oil to influence society, politics, and culture. Beyond monopolizing the economy, oil shapes social values and class aspirations, cemented political alliances, and redefines concepts of citizenship for important segments of the population."

While applying to the Global North the same lens that has been used to analyze the oil-rich nations of the Global South helps to unearth the many similarities in economic and political trends in the two hemispheres, it is not very useful in providing a cogent explanation for the political and economic outcomes of oil dependence. By explaining development performance solely in terms of the size and nature of the resource wealth, the oil and democracy literature often does not adequately account for the role of internal and external social, political, and economic environments in shaping development outcomes in resource-abundant countries. In response to the perceived reductionism of the oil and democracy literature, some recent studies have been questioning the validity of examining various political pathologies and poor development performance fostered by natural resource wealth (Rosser 2006; Meissner 2010). According to Rosser (2006, 3), the most pertinent question to ask is this: "What political and social factors enable some resource abundant countries to utilise their natural resources to promote development and prevent other resource abundant countries from doing the same?" While Rosser asks this question with reference to the countries in the Global South, it is equally applicable to economic, political, and social development in the Global North, when, for instance, we consider the vast difference between the management of oil wealth and its impact in Canada as compared to Norway.

In our examination of the political economy of Alberta and Canada, we use staples theory, a complementary articulation of the more recent "resource curse" literature, to bring political economic and institutional dynamics into the study of oil and democracy. Emerging in the early decades of the twentieth century, the staples theory of economic development explained the role of Canadian staple commodities (fish, fur, lumber, agricultural products, and minerals) in the creation of institutions that defined the political trends of the nation and its regions (Innis 1956; Mackintosh 1923). This theory was revived in the 1960s through Mel Watkins's work on resource capitalism, and the state-fostered backward and forward linkages in the supply chain. These linkages were credited for creating opportunities for innovation and economic growth. Watkins's expansion of the scope of the staples thesis pointed out some active directions for policy makers to pursue in staples production. His work inspired many other staples-oriented theories in a similar vein (e.g., Hirschman 1980; Kindelberger 1986).[7] Fundamentally, the staples thesis argues that while the export of raw materials can sustain economic growth, reliance on exporting natural resources has made Canada dependent on the international market. This dependence has resulted in periodic disruptions to economic life as the international demand for staples rose and fell, as the staple itself became increasingly scarce, and as technological change resulted in shifts from one staple commodity to another (see Watkins 1963, 1977).

Writing just as Western Canada's most recent resource boom started, Michael Howlett and Keith Brownsey (2008) question the continuing importance of staples in the Canadian political economy, arguing that the Canadian economy has evolved past its mature staples stage and that Canada is becoming a "post-staples" state. This post-staples state features severe cost and supply pressures that have led to the contraction of the once important natural resource industries, growth in metropolitan shares of employment and population, and economic diversification in both urban and rural areas. Although the authors acknowledge that resource development continues to be important in some regions, they suggest that resource governance is now more participatory and democratic than previous staples development because it incorporates multiple interests, such as those of environmentalists and the Aboriginal peoples.

Other writings during the same period (e.g. , Stanford 2008; Watkins 2007) emphasize the fact that the unprecedented resource boom led to foreign takeovers, currency overvaluation, and crises in the domestic automotive sector. These changes mark a shift away from the mature staples political economy theorized by Mel Watkins in which governments provided firms with access to natural resources in exchange for royalties, commitments to employment, and infrastructural development in rural areas, leading to economic diversification through expanded secondary manufacturing. Instead, during the most recent resource boom, which extended from the rise of global petroleum prices in 2007 to the drop in prices in late 2014, natural resource firms used highly mobile workforces to produce commodities for export rather than for domestic manufacturing, and fewer benefits accrued to local communities. Particularly in relation to oil and gas as extensions of staples production, Watkins (2007) raises issues such as the appropriate use of the "rent" and associated fiscal effects that may suggest regression to a staples economy. In light of the preceding, many scholars (e.g. , Drache 2013; Mills and Sweeney 2013; Stanford 2013) contend that Canada's political economy is better characterized as neostaples, with resource rents increasingly concentrated in the hands of foreign investors rather than governments, employees, and resource-dependent communities.

It is important to note that recent characterizations of the neostaples economy do not pay enough attention to internal colonial relations or to the increased participation of northern Aboriginal peoples in resource industries over the past three decades. This increased participation has come about through the successful push for recognition of proprietary interests over the territory of the First Nations, expansion of their jurisdictional authority, and the relocalization of employment benefits for northern populations through measures such as Impact and Benefit Agreements (IBAs; see Mills and Sweeney 2013). However, Suzanne Mills and Brendan Sweeney (2013) admit that in its extensive use of subcontractors and "fly-in, fly-out" work arrangements, the governance of employment in a neostaples stage of resource development deviates from the Fordist compromise of preceding eras of resource development.[8] Shaped by global mining trends, the resulting model of employment governance has had ambiguous outcomes for Aboriginal workers. The agency of Aboriginal actors is constrained by the internationalization of the industry and private capital, the lack of control of Indigenous peoples over significant dimensions of work and labour practices, and the neoliberalization of Aboriginal governance (MacDonald 2011; Mills and McCreary 2013; Slowey and Stefanick, this volume).

Nonetheless, in keeping with the nature of the neostaples political economy, while Aboriginal institutions are playing an increasingly important role in governing employment, the role of unions is much diminished, as evidenced by the increasing number of non-union mines and the widespread use of subcontractors. The declining local influence over resource development and employment is particularly problematic in the context of encroachments on worker wages, benefits, and collective representation in a neoliberal economy. Labour unions in the mature staples regime represented a large number of workers and enhanced their ability to capture increasing shares of resource rents in wages and benefits. In the neostaples regime, however, unions have been relegated to defending a smaller proportion of workers, since new operations are increasingly non-unionized.

Clearly, staples theory continues to be popular and relevant, not only to describe the ramifications of staples production for the evolution of the Canadian economy and society but also as an analytical tool to study the economies of countries that are dependent upon resource extraction and primary industries. As such, we use the staples theory to complement the liberal democratic model that underlies our analyses and provides insights into the efficacy of various policy choices in promoting and supporting institutions of democracy. In particular, the history of the social and economic characteristics of Alberta is not only useful for understanding political monopolies but also raises probing questions about the nature and operation of democracy itself, particularly with respect to democracy in oil-exporting countries in both hemispheres.

Alberta: The Epicentre of Canada's Oil Economy

The nature and strength of democracy in Alberta became a subject of scholarly interest long before oil lubricated the political economy of the region.

C. B. Macpherson (1953) analyzed the phenomenon of one-party rule in Alberta, exemplified by two parties that grew out of populist movements: the United Farmers of Alberta (UFA), which ruled from 1921 to 1935, and the Social Credit Party, which grew out of depression-ravaged Alberta and dominated provincial politics for the next thirty-six years (Finkel 1989). Unbeknownst to Macpherson in 1953, a provincial branch of the Progressive Conservatives would replace the Social Credit in 1971 and would lead the government for almost forty-four years. Nevertheless, Macpherson correctly notes the uniqueness of Alberta politics since its earliest days: the same party leads the government for many years and is eventually decimated when the electorate switches en masse to a new party, which then continues to dominate the political scene. Reducing the PC numbers to a paltry ten MLAs in May 2015, the rise of the NDP from a four-MLA party in the 28th legislative assembly of 2012 to a fifty-four-MLA majority government in the 29th legislative assembly fits this pattern. It is too early to say, however, how long the reign of the left-wing NDP will last, or if the NDP will be able to make substantial policy changes to address issues related to democratic deficits noted in this volume.

According to Macpherson, this one-party dominance, which the resource curse literature generally associates with oil-exporting states, produced a new species of democratic governance in Canada, a "quasi-party system" that emerged in the first half of the twentieth century. Macpherson describes this system as a deviation from the normal two-or-more-party system generally envisaged in a liberal democratic state. In the quasi-party system, strong opposition and party competition appear only periodically, thus enabling one party to monopolize political power. It is noteworthy that the lack of political plurality and strong opposition is a characteristic most often associated with oil-exporting states in the Global South. According to Macpherson, the political longevity of one party in Alberta during the first half of the twentieth century had two significant causes: (1) the traditional system of alternating parties was never popular among the petit bourgeois class of independent producers in Alberta, whose interests and particular conceptions of society dominated the political landscape, and (2) this same interest group rejected party-dominated parliamentary representation, advocating instead for a populist system of functional representation, whereby legislators see themselves as delegates of their constituents rather than as representatives bound by party discipline (Macpherson 1953).

Macpherson's critics argue that his view of the homogeneity of Alberta's population is simplistic (Richards and Pratt 1979). Indeed, as the recipient, at the turn of the century, of waves of immigration from Britain, Europe, and the United States that comprised a diverse cross-section of people, Alberta experienced large electoral majorities, partly as a result of the first-past-the-post electoral system. This system over-rewards the winning party in a multiparty situation that reflects a very diverse electorate. But Macpherson's larger point about Alberta being dominated by the petit bourgeois class of independent producers has some merit. Since Alberta has always had an economy dominated by a single staple, the producers of the dominant commodity (whether wheat or oil) have had inordinate influence on provincial politics. Historically, commodities from the West have fed Central Canada's industrial heartland. It was not until the 1930s, however, that the Western provinces gained parity with other Canadian provinces with respect to gaining control of their own natural resources. The deep-seated distrust of the federal system of government is a legacy of these pre-1930s "quasi-colonial" years when Western provinces perceived themselves as continually subservient to the capital interests of the industrial heartland. As Harrison (this volume) notes, this has remained a defining feature of Alberta's politics and culture, providing fertile ground for new political parties that experimented with new forms of governance. In addition, as Macpherson (1953, 247) puts it, "The quasi-colonial society in which independent producers are the predominant element appears peculiarly liable . . . to reject the regular party system."

The first manifestation of the functional representation phenomenon can be seen in the first governing party in Alberta, the Liberals, who ruled from 1905 to 1921. In 1913, the Liberals passed the Direct Legislation Act, which provided citizens with the ability to call for a referendum through petition (Barrie 2006, 9). Strands of anticorporatism and concern about the stifling power of party discipline can be seen in subsequent parties, such as the UFA. This populist party advocated for farmers, particularly around improving access to health care and education; it also supported the women's suffragette movement. It was during the so-called dirty thirties that two other populist parties were born in Alberta—the Co-operative Commonwealth Federation (the forerunner of Canada's left-wing New Democratic Party) and the Social Credit Party. All of these early populist parties supported public health care, something that is normally associated with left-leaning parties. As Richards and Pratt (1979) and Harrison (this volume) point out, a staples-based economy does not preclude progressive politics. The story of the conversion of Alberta's Social Credit Party from left- to right-wing populism is discussed in Harrison's chapter. Suffice to say here that by the 1940s, Social Credit had firmly entrenched a right-wing populist agenda in Alberta that opposed both the social welfare programs and the centralizing tendencies of the federal government of Canada (Finkel 1989). Long after Macpherson's analysis of the party system and Alberta's political structures and institutions, right-wing populism flourished in Alberta under the Alberta Progressive Conservatives and the official opposition, the Wildrose Party, earning for Alberta the redoubtable distinction of being ruled by two right-wing parties without interruption for eighty years.

Another constant in Alberta is the nature of its economy. For nearly a century, Alberta's economy has followed a pattern of primary-resource exploitation and dependence on external markets, moving from the export of fur prior to becoming a province, to wheat and beef, and finally to petroleum. Although the existence of vast bitumen pools had been recognized for decades, it was only with advances in extraction technologies and the rapid rise in international prices of oil since the last quarter of the twentieth century that the production of unconventional oil became financially viable. The pace of bitumen oil production picked up significantly beginning in 2004–5, coinciding with consistently high international oil prices. The resulting socio-economic changes to the province were immediate and profound, and quickly spread across Canada. Imbalances in provincial fiscal capacity, waves of internal migration, and political and income disparities are a few examples of these changes. The rapid expansion of the oil sector has been realized with significant government support for Alberta's oil industry in the form of investment, subsidies, and tax breaks at both federal and provincial levels. In particular, this government support has spurred the expansion and development of the unconventional oil industry, which in the past provided little profit because of the high cost of extraction and transportation. Alberta's extremely industry-friendly tax and revenue-sharing regime, along with the province's propensity to externalize the social and environmental costs of bitumen oil production, has led to handsome returns for private corporations (Campanella 2012). For instance, Royal Dutch Shell announced in 2007 that its Canadian bitumen oil division made an after-tax profit of $21.75 per barrel, nearly double its worldwide profit of $12.41 per barrel on conventional crude oil (Mortished 2007). As noted in a Pembina Institute report (Dobson and Asadollahi 2014, 2), while federal and provincial taxes fell between 2009 and 2012, subsidies to the oil sector rose simultaneously.

The growing economic and political might of Alberta has made this province the barometer of political economic change in Canada. The rising political influence of this landlocked province can also be construed as leading to the "Albertization" of Canada under the leadership of Stephen Harper and the Conservative Party, as exemplified by fiscally and socially conservative federal policies. This policy orientation includes government austerity, especially with respect to social programs; privatization of government services; and reductions in income tax for corporations and upper-income earners. The role of the province of Alberta within the larger Canadian federation has changed dramatically in the past decade. With 11 percent of the total population of Canada, Alberta accounts for 17 percent of its gross domestic product (GDP), 28 percent of which is derived directly from the energy sector (Alberta, Alberta Energy 2015). In 2014, the oil and gas industry produced one-quarter of Alberta's GDP, almost 70 percent of its exports, and 35 percent of Alberta government revenues, and the industry accounted for 146,000 direct and indirect jobs (Alberta, Alberta Energy 2015; CERI 2014, ix). It is important to note that although it is best known for the world's largest bitumen oil reserves, Alberta is also the largest producer in the country of conventional crude oil, synthetic crude, coal, natural gas, and gas products. Agriculture and food processing, forestry, construction, manufacturing, biotechnology, and services are the other major sectors of Alberta's economy, but they are much smaller in relation to the energy sector (Alberta, Alberta Innovation and Advanced Education 2015). Moreover, as of 2011, the cumulative natural resources sector represented 15 percent of Canada's nominal (i.e., not adjusted for inflation) gross domestic product (GDP), generating nearly 800,000 direct jobs, as well as a roughly equivalent number of indirect jobs, in the construction, manufacturing, transportation, financial, technology, and service sectors (Canada, NRC 2012).

While the figures above are significant, they do not reflect the actual scale of the direct and indirect impact of the oil industry at both provincial and national levels. These numbers do not account for important factors such as the volatility of the unconventional oil industry; the combination of fiscal and taxation policy leading to significant concerns related to revenue realization; the weakening of the various regulatory regimes under pressure from the short-term priorities of the oil industry; and the cost of several externalities, such as pollution and inflation, related to the rising costs of manufacturing.[9] While some analysts point to the declining contribution of oil and gas to Canada's GDP, from a high of 12 percent in 1997 to 10 percent in 2012 (Leach 2013), the assertion that the influence of oil vis-à-vis the Canadian economy is actually lessening does not account for issues such as the diminishing share of total corporate taxes, problems of oil revenue realization, the impact on frontier lands of the elimination of foreign ownership restrictions for production licences, or the issue of First Nations treaty violations.

The financial crisis of 2008–9 compressed and depressed the world economy, as well as oil prices. The fiscal impact of this ongoing crisis was compounded by the rapid rise of bitumen production costs in Canada, owing in part to shortages of labour and materials. Government policies in response to these challenges continue along a familiar trajectory by ceding more regulatory control to industry; opening new doors for foreign acquisitions; and increasing financial, social, and environmental subsidies. Given this scenario—along with the direct and indirect environmental costs of the expansion of bitumen oil production, such as water and energy use, release of greenhouse gases, destruction of the boreal forest, water pollution, and toxic tailings ponds—the contributors to this book have focused their attention on bitumen oil development as the most contentious beneficiary of government support, rather than on the wider energy sector.

By using the contemporary political and policy trends in Alberta as a snapshot of the larger Canadian political economy, we hope that the analyses in this volume will be relevant for the examination of liberal democracy in a myriad of contexts in the world. Despite our focus on Alberta, the general principles, issues, and institutions explored in this collection are common to resource-based jurisdictions around the world and are pertinent to concerns about democratic governance. As the diverse topics covered in this volume reveal, oil wealth not only impacts democratic governance; it has infused all aspects of life in Alberta.

Themes and Assumptions

The uniqueness of this book lies in critically examining the "oil inhibits democracy" thesis within a jurisdiction in the Global North by applying the liberal democratic parameters that are usually applied to explain the deficiencies of democracy in the oil-dependent economies of the Global South. Of course, Canada is not the only oil-exporting country in the Global North and is most frequently compared to Norway. Despite the recent rise of right-wing politics in Norway, the country's high taxes continue to fund its welfare model, while almost all government revenue from oil go into the Norwegian pension fund. In contrast to this approach of sharing the resource rent with future generations, Alberta's low tax rate means that it must use oil royalties to fund current government expenditures. Norway's state capitalism, then, is markedly different from Canada's increasing entrenchment of neoliberal policies and its retreat from social democracy. By avoiding a North-North comparison that often assumes the strength of democracy as a given, not only do we open the door for a much richer and wider analysis of democracy in a specific jurisdiction and of democracy in oil-exporting countries of the Global North more generally, but we also eschew the normalized North-South dichotomy that informs studies of oil and democracy.

The three sections of this book explore the "oil inhibits democracy" hypothesis by examining some critical aspects of liberal democracy in Alberta and Canada. The first section starts with a broad theoretical discussion as well as the contextualization of bitumen oil in the global oil market. It then provides a context for democracy in Alberta through historical, political economic, and sociopolitical perspectives. Starting from the local and the specific, and then moving to the international, the chapters in this section outline the political peculiarities of Alberta and highlight the similarities and differences between Alberta and jurisdictions in the Global South. Clearly, neoliberalism has become a global phenomenon, sparing few countries, resource rich or not. Within this context, we are concerned about how the predominance of a single resource may create special problems for creating or maintaining democratic norms. Alternatively, could it be that the threat to democracy in states dependent on the export of one commodity is another manifestation of a generalized corporate attack against democratic norms in a period characterized by a global capitalist crisis of overproduction and declining confidence in governments and institutions? In the wake of the electoral rout of the PC Party in Alberta in May 2015, this trend is manifested by the reaction of the energy industry in the media and the stock exchange (Hussain and Morgan 2015).

The second section of the book concentrates on rights claims in an oil-exporting economy, focusing on the most vulnerable groups: women, workers, Indigenous populations, and immigrants. This section underscores the similarities among vulnerable communities in both the Global North and the Global South, showing that "First and Third World" relations can be replicated within any country, particularly those with Indigenous populations. Despite being focused on Alberta, these chapters illustrate a worldwide neoliberal trend toward maximizing profit by undermining the rights of labour, sidelining marginalized communities, and downloading specific functions of the state on the family—and in particular, on women. The end result is class-based, gendered, and racialized economic structures wherein certain groups in society bear the brunt of the social, political, and economic burdens of oil extraction.

The third section of the book considers the impact of the trends identified in the previous sections on certain governance, equity, and citizenship issues in Alberta. Specifically, the chapters in this section look at current policies and institutions as reflections of particular political ideologies. Significantly, these chapters identify existing policies as the manifestations of neoliberal notions of citizenship and identity that are shared by corporate and state interests, effectively excluding those who have different understandings. The disciplinary role of government is explored, as is the impact of privileging the role of government in fostering favourable market conditions for business on the provision of social and economic justice in Alberta.

It is obvious that oil influences democratic participation and governance in Alberta; however, it is equally clear that its impact is shaped by other factors. As illustrated in many of the chapters in this volume, the fact that Canada is part of the Global North does affect the trajectory of the form and outcome of political economic trends. Moreover, it is also clear that while the particular manifestation of the democratic deficit may be different in Alberta and Canada than elsewhere, the general oil versus democracy theme has relevance in various parts of the world. Finally, we cannot ignore the fact that while many jurisdictions in the Global South have the additional burden of colonialism, which adds to the democratic malaise, Canada's own internal colonization of its Indigenous population dampens its claims to having healthy democratic institutions.

Certainly, these chapters point to a variety of factors that ultimately influence the nature and practice of democracy in an oil-exporting country. Some of these interactions are consistent with what has been reported in studies of oil-dependent countries in the Global South, while others are unique to Canada as an oil-exporting country in the Global North. Perhaps the most valuable lesson that can be taken from this study is that oil-rich jurisdictions in the Global North are not so categorically different from those in the Global South. Nor is the binary classification of "North" and "South" very helpful in exploring the dimensions of democracy in an interconnected world. The chapters in this volume highlight that the success of liberal democratic institutions in reflecting collective priorities and interests is complicated not only by the nature and history of an oil-exporting jurisdiction but also by the rapidly changing global political and economic dynamics. In Canada, the short-term priorities of the oil industry are shaping politics and policy provincially as well as federally. Many chapters in this book suggest that these policies will have a long-term impact on democracy in Alberta. Oil wealth may not be the only engine that works toward diminishing democratic structures, but it certainly serves as the fuel that helps to propel specific socio-economic and political forces and ideologies. What is indisputable is that oil has left an indelible stamp on democracy in Alberta and Canada.

Notes

1 Resource rent is the surplus revenue generated from the extraction of a natural resource. That is, it is the revenue that remains after all the costs of extraction and production, including the minimum return that investors need on the capital they have invested, have been deducted from the total revenue. Governments do not typically engage directly in extraction and production activities. Instead, as the holders of the rights to a country's natural resources, they levy a tax on the resource rents earned by businesses.

2 We use the term *political economy* in its broad sense to refer to the influence of political ideologies on economic life, particularly in relation to the development of public policy. Although specific political economic analyses inevitably reflect the disciplinary framework and theoretical orientation of the researcher, all begin from the fundamental insight that politics and economics are inextricably bound up with one another.

3 Financialization is explained in more depth in the next chapter. Briefly, it refers to changes in the structure and operation of financial market that lead to an increase in the size and importance of a country's financial sector relative to its overall economy (Krippner 2005).

4 As Slowey and Stefanick explain in chapter 7 in this volume, the legacy of internal colonialism has also had a huge impact on the relationship between Aboriginal and non-Aboriginal people in Canada. In this regard, the same forces that inhibit development in the Global South are at work in the Global North.

5 See World Bank, "Worldwide Governance Indicators," 2014, http://info.worldbank.org/governance/wgi/index.aspx#home; and United Nations Development Programme, "Democratic Governance," http://www.undp.org/governance/.

6 See *Canadian Journal of Sociology* / Cahiers canadiens de sociologie 38 (2), http://ejournals.library.ualberta.ca/index.php/CJS/issue/view/1380. The issue set out to revisit the concept of community in the context of Alberta's oil fields.

7 Watkins's theoretical interpretation did not go unchallenged. For instance, John Richards and Larry Pratt, in *Prairie Capitalism: Power and Influence in the New West* (1979),

argue that staples theory ignores the classical theory of comparative advantage. They also question the Canadian dependency thesis as proposed by staples theory.

8 Fordism relates to an economic and social system based on industrialized and standardized forms of mass production, mass consumption, and changes to working conditions of workers over time. The Fordist compromise guarantees employment at relatively good wages for a subset of (usually) unionized workers in return for acceptance of capital's exclusive right to run the company and its right to earn high profits in the process.

9 At the time we write, the human impact of the volatility of the energy sector has been brought home once again, owing to the recent downturn in international oil prices. According to a Statistics Canada analyst, from September 2014 to early January 2015, thirteen thousand jobs were lost in Alberta's energy sector, most of them in oil and gas. Moreover, in January, the Canadian Association of Oilwell Drilling Contractors predicted that the number of rigs operating in the field would decline by 167 in 2015, "resulting in the layoffs of 3,400 rig workers with the loss of another 19,500 indirect jobs" (Geddes 2015).

References

Alberta. Alberta Energy. 2015. "Facts and Statistics." *Alberta Energy*. http://www.energy. alberta.ca/oilsands/791.asp.

Alberta. Alberta Innovation and Advanced Education. 2015. *Highlights of the Alberta Economy 2015*. http://www.albertacanada.com/files/albertacanada/SP-EH_ highlightsABEconomyPresentation.pdf.

Barrie, Doreen. 2006. *The Other Alberta: Decoding a Political Enigma*. Regina: Canadian Plains Research Centre.

Beetham, David. 1992. "Liberal Democracy and the Limits of Democratization." *Political Studies* 40 (1): 40–53.

Bulte, E. H. R. Damania, and R. T. Deacon. 2005. "Resource Intensity, Institutions and Development." *World Development* 33 (7): 1029–44.

Campanella, David. 2012. *Misplaced Generosity: Update 2012—Extraordinary Profits in Alberta's Oil and Gas Industry*. Edmonton, AB: Parkland Institute.

Canada. NRC (Natural Resources Canada). 2012. "Defining the Opportunity: Assessing the Economic Impact of the Natural Resources Sector." Prepared in collaboration with Provincial and Territorial Governments. Energy and Mines Ministers' Conference, September, Charlottetown, PEI. http://www.scics.gc.ca/english/ conferences.asp?a=viewdocument&id=1907.

Cavalcanti, Tiago V. de V., Kamiar Mohaddes, and Mehdi Raissi. 2012. "Commodity Price Volatility and the Sources of Growth." IMF Working Paper No. 12/12. International Monetary Fund, Washington, DC.

CERI (Canadian Energy Research Institute). 2014. "Canadian Economic Impacts of New and Existing Oil Sands Development in Alberta (2014-2038)." Briefing Paper, November. Calgary: CERI.

Chomsky, Aviva, and Aldo Lauria Santiago, eds. 1998. *Identity and the Struggle at the Margins of the Nation State: The Labouring People of Central America and the Hispanic Caribbean*. Durham, NC: Duke University Press.

Corden, W. M., and J. P. Neary. 1982. "Booming Sector and De-industrialisation in a Small Open Economy." *Economic Journal* 92 (368): 825–48.

Coronil, Fernando. 1997. *The Magical State: Nature, Money, and Modernity in Venezuela*. Chicago: University of Chicago Press.

Cunningham, Frank. 2002. *Theories of Democracy: A Critical Introduction*. New York: Routledge.

Davidson, Debra J., and Mike Gismondi. 2011. *Challenging Legitimacy at the Precipice of Energy Calamity*. New York: Springer.

Dobson, Sarah, and Amin Asadollahi. 2014. *Fossil Fuel Subsidies: An Analysis of Federal Financial Support to Canada's Oil Sector*. Calgary: Pembina Institute.

Drache, Daniel. 2013. "'Rowing and Steering' Our Way out of the Staples Trap." *The Progressive Economics Forum: Staple Theory @ 50*. http://www.progressive-economics. ca/2013/10/30/staple-theory-50-daniel-drache/.

"The Dutch Disease." 1977. *The Economist*, 26 November.

Feldman, Noah. 2003. *After Jihad: America and the Struggle for Islamic Democracy*. New York: Farrar, Straus, and Giroux.

Finkel, Alvin. 1989. *The Social Credit Phenomenon*. Toronto: University of Toronto Press.

Finn, Janet. 1988. *Tracing the Veins: Of Copper, Culture, and Community from Butte to Chuquicamata*. Berkeley: University of California Press.

Geddes, Lisa. 2015. "Timeline: Tracking the Layoffs in Alberta's Oilpatch." *Global News*, 18 March. http://globalnews.ca/news/1889598/timeline-tracking-the-layoffs-in-albertas-oilpatch/.

Gylfason, Thorvaldur. 2001. "Natural Resources, Education, and Economic Development." *European Economic Review* 45 (4–6): 847–59.

Habermas, Jürgen, and William Rehg. 1998. *Between Facts and Norms: Contributions to a Discourse Theory of Law and Democracy*. Cambridge, MA: MIT Press.

Harriss, John. 2005. "Great Promise, Hubris, and Recovery: A Participant's History of Development Studies." In *A Radical History of Development Studies: Individuals, Institutions and Ideologies*, edited by Uma Kothari, 17–46. London, UK: Zed Books.

Herb, Michael. 2005. "No Representation Without Taxation? Rents, Development and Democracy." *Comparative Politics* 37 (3): 297–316.

Herd, Dean. 2002. "Rhetoric and Retrenchment: 'Common Sense' Welfare Reform in Ontario." *Benefits* 34 (10): 105–10.

Hirschman, Albert O. 1980. *National Power and the Structure of Foreign Trade*. Berkeley: University of California Press.

Howlett, Michael, and Keith Brownsey. 2008. *Canada's Resource Economy in Transition: The Past, Present and Future of Canadian Staples Industries*. Toronto: Edmond Montgomery.

Hussain, Yadullah, and Geoffrey Morgan. 2015. "Alberta Oil Industry Fear World's 'Lowest Royalties' Threatened by New NDP Government." *Financial Post*, 7 May.

Innis, Harold A. 1956. *Essays in Canadian Economic History*. Edited by Mary Quayle Innis. Toronto: University of Toronto Press.

Karl, Terry. 1997. *The Paradox of Plenty: Oil Booms and Petro-states*. Berkeley: University of California Press.

Kindelberger, Charles. 1986. "International Public Goods Without International Government." *American Economic Review* 76 (1): 1–13.

Klubock, Thomas Miller. 1998. *Contested Communities: Class, Gender, and Politics in Chile's El Teniente Copper Mine, 1904–1951*. Durham, NC: Duke University Press.

Knight, Kathleen. 2006. "Transformations of the Concept of Ideology in the Twentieth Century." *American Political Science Review* 100 (4): 619–26.

Krippner, Greta R. 2005. "The Financialization of the American Economy." *Socio-economic Review* 3 (2): 173–208.

Leach, Andrew. 2013. "Canada, the Failed Petrostate? Canada Hasn't Bet the Economy on the Energy Sector, Not Even Close." *Maclean's*, 4 November.

Leong, Weishu, and Kamiar Mohaddes. 2011. "Institutions and the Volatility Curse." Cambridge Working Papers in Economics 1145. Department of Applied Economics, Faculty of Economics, University of Cambridge, Cambridge, UK.

Levant, Ezra. 2011. *Ethical Oil: The Case for Canada's Oil Sands*. Toronto: McClelland and Stewart.

Lowi, Miriam. 2004. "Oil Wealth and Political Breakdown in Algeria." *Journal of North African Studies* 9 (3): 83–102.

MacDonald, Fiona. 2011. "Indigenous Peoples and Neoliberal 'Privatization' in Canada: Opportunities, Cautions and Constraints." *Canadian Journal of Political Science* 44 (2): 257–73.

Mackintosh, W. A. 1923. "Economic Factors in Canadian History." *Canadian Historical Review* 4 (1): 12–25.

Macpherson, C. B. 1953. *Democracy in Alberta: The Theory and Practice of a Quasi-party System*. Toronto: University of Toronto Press.

———. 1977. *The Life and Times of Liberal Democracy*. Oxford and New York: Oxford University Press.

———. 1985. *The Rise and Fall of Economic Justice, and Other Papers*. Oxford and New York: Oxford University Press.

Mahdavy, Hussein. 1970. "The Patterns and Problems of Economic Development in Rentier States: The Case of Iran." In *Studies in the Economic History of the Middle East*, edited by M. A. Cook, 428–67. Oxford: Oxford University Press.

Meissner, Hannes. 2010. "The Resource Curse and Rentier States in the Caspian Region: A Need for Context Analysis." GIGA Working Papers No. 133. German Institute of Global and Area Studies, Hamburg, Germany.

Mills, Suzanne, and Tyler McCreary. 2013. "Negotiating Neoliberal Empowerment: Aboriginal People, Educational Restructuring, and Academic Labour in the North of British Columbia, Canada." *Antipode* 45 (5): 1298–1317.

Mills, Suzanne, and Brendan Sweeney. 2013. "Employment Relations in the Neostaples Resource Economy: Impact Benefit Agreements and Aboriginal Governance in Canada's Nickel Mining Industry." *Studies in Political Economy* 91 (Spring): 7–33.

Mortished, Carl. 2007. "Shell Rakes in Profits from the Canadian Oil Sands Unit." *The Times* (London), 27 July.

Munck, Gerardo L., and Jay Verkuilen. 2002. "Conceptualizing and Measuring Democracy: Evaluating Alternative Indices." *Comparative Political Studies* 35 (1): 5–34.

Nikiforuk, Andrew. 2010. *Tar Sands: Dirty Oil and the Future of a Continent.* Revised and updated. Vancouver: Greystone Books.

Peck, Jamie, and Nik Theodore. 2010. "Recombinant Workfare, Across the Americas: Transnationalizing 'Fast' Social Policy." *Geoforum* 41 (2): 195–208.

Peck, Jamie, and Adam Tickell. 2002. "Neoliberalizing Space." *Antipode* 34 (3): 380–404.

Putnam, Lara. 2002. *The Company They Kept: Migrants and the Politics of Gender in Caribbean Costa Rica, 1870–1960.* Chapel Hill: University of North Carolina Press.

Rawls, John. 1971. *A Theory of Justice.* Cambridge, MA: Harvard University Press.

———. 1993. Political Liberalism. New York: Columbia University Press.

Richards, John, and Larry Pratt. 1979. *Prairie Capitalism: Power and Influence in the New West.* Toronto: McClelland and Stewart.

Ross, Michael Lewin. 2001. "Does Oil Hinder Democracy?" *World Politics* 53 (3): 325–61.

———. 2006. "A Closer Look at Oil, Diamonds, and Civil War." *Annual Review of Political Science* 9: 265–300.

———. 2009. "Oil and Democracy Revisited." Preliminary draft, 2 March. http://www.sscnet.ucla.edu/polisci/faculty/ross/Oil%20and%20Democracy%20Revisited.pdf.

Rosser, Andrew. 2006. "The Political Economy of the Resource Curse: A Literature Survey." Working Paper 268. Centre for the Future State, Institute of Development Studies, University of Sussex, Brighton, UK.

Salas, Miguel Tinker. 2009. *The Enduring Legacy: Oil, Culture, and Society in Venezuela.* Durham, NC: Duke University Press.

Sen, Amartya. 1999. *Development as Freedom.* New York: Knopf.

Shrivastava, Meenal, and Lorna Stefanick. 2012. "Do Oil and Democracy Only Clash in the Global South? Petro Politics in Alberta, Canada." *New Global Studies* 6 (1): article 5. doi:10.1515/1940-0004.1147.

Smith, Benjamin, and Joseph Kraus. 2005. "Democracy Despite Oil: Transition and Consolidation in Latin America and Africa." Paper presented at the Annual Meeting of the American Political Science Association, 1–4 September, Washington, DC.

Stanford, Jim. 2008. "Staples, Deindustrialization, and Foreign Investment: Canada's Economic Journey Back to the Future." *Studies in Political Economy* 82 (Autumn): 7–34.

———. 2013. "Why Linkages Matter." *The Progressive Economics Forum: The Staple Theory @ 50.* http://www.progressive-economics.ca/2013/12/23/the-staple-theory-50-jim-stanford/.

Tamas, Gaspar. 2011. *Big Ideas: Gaspar Tamas on the Failure of Liberal Democracy.* TVO video. http://ww3.tvo.org/video/167943/gaspar-tamas-failure-liberal-democracy.

Tsui, Kevin K. 2011. "More Oil, Less Democracy? Theory and Evidence from Crude Oil Discoveries." *Economic Journal* 121 (551): 89–115.

USEIA (US Energy Information Administration). 2014. *International Energy Data and Analysis: Canada.* 30 September. http://www.eia.gov/beta/international/analysis_ includes/countries_long/Canada/canada.pdf.

Van Wijnbergen, Sweder. 1984. "The 'Dutch Disease': A Disease After All?" *Economic Journal* 94 (373): 41–55.

Wantchekon, Leonard. 2002. "Why Do Resource Dependent Countries Have Authoritarian Governments?" *Journal of African Finance and Economic Development* 5 (2): 57–77.

Watkins, Melville H. 1963. "A Staple Theory of Economic Growth." *Canadian Journal of Economics and Political Science* 29 (2): 141–58.

———. 1977. "The Staple Theory Revisited." *Journal of Canadian Studies* 12 (5): 83–95.

———. 2007. "Staples Redux." *Studies in Political Economy* 79 (Spring): 213–26.

part one

The Context of Democracy in an Oil Economy

Liberal Democracy in Oil-Exporting Countries

A View from the Perspective of Staples Theory

Meenal Shrivastava

The Many Modes of Liberal Democracy

The political history of our world could well be written as a continuing struggle to define and refine democracy—from its limited beginnings in the republics of India and the city-states of Greece in the seventh and sixth centuries BC, to the Magna Carta and the French Revolution, and finally to the emergence of so-called liberal democracy, in its many iterations, as the predominant political system throughout the world in the twentieth century. Most often described as a representative form of government that operates according to the principles of liberty and equality first articulated by John Locke and other philosophers of the Enlightenment, liberal democracy seeks to protect basic human rights, civil liberties, and political freedoms for all persons, including minorities. It is characterized by attributes that include fair, free, and competitive elections between multiple distinct political parties, a separation of power into different branches of government, and the rule of law. Liberal democracies often rely on a constitution to delineate the powers of the government and to enshrine the social contract—the legitimacy of the authority of the state over the individual (see Beetham 1992; Macpherson 1977).

Although expressed in widely varying manifestations, first in different parts of Europe, then in the Americas, and finally in the former colonies in the Global South, notions of widespread social, economic, and political equality have formed the basis of the quest for democracy over the past two centuries. However, the path to democracy is fraught with many obstacles in all parts of the world, as is evident from growing income and political inequality in both hemispheres and from the rise of movements such as the Arab Spring in the Middle East, Occupy in North America, Indignados in Spain, Aganaktismenoi in Greece, Movimento dos Trabalhadores Sem Terra (MST) in Brazil, and Naxal in India, among others.

Indeed, historically the vast spectrum of democracy ranges from minimalist, electoral, and polyarchical to many direct and representative types of democracies (Schmidt 2002). Clearly, the term *democracy* is a highly contested one, and much has been written within the field of democratization studies to try to define it. In the twenty-first century, the global financial crisis that began in 2008, the wars in Iraq and Afghanistan, the economic success of authoritarian China, and increasing inequality in all parts of the world, among other trends and events, have rekindled the debate about threats to democratization and about the probability of a "reverse wave" bringing a revival of authoritarianism (Carothers 2007; Diamond 2008; Krugman 2009, 181–96). Interestingly, despite these global warnings, the vast majority of comparative studies of democracy continue to focus on the reasons for and quality of democratization in the Global South. A quick survey of the most influential journal in this area, *Journal of Democracy*, reveals a continuing focus on the trends and causes of the emergence or reversal of democratization in the regions of the Global South (e.g., Puddington 2010). This focus appears to presume that democracy and its institutions are sound in the Global North. As recently as 2013, Jørgen Møller and Svend-Erik Skaaning, in their comprehensive analysis of the three waves of democratization, challenged common assumptions about the reversal of democratization, describing the situation as a "trendless fluctuation" (Doorenspleet 2000, quoted in Møller and Skaaning 2013, 105). They correctly acknowledge the inaccuracy of Samuel Huntington's (1991) description of a "second reverse wave of democratization" occurring between 1958 and 1975, which does not take into account the rise of democratic regimes after the decolonization of Africa in the 1960s (Møller and Skaaning 2013, 105–7). However, Møller and Skaaning's analysis of democratization trends in the world suffers from a blind spot of its own by only focusing on the non-OECD regions of the world.

Yet the notion that the countries in the Global North are immune from a democratic deficit is questionable, given both growing inequality and restive protests against government austerity measures in various OECD countries (OECD 2008, 2011). Although it is too early to predict their impacts, the ongoing popular movements inspired by increasing income and political inequality are indeed challenging the "authorized" site of politics (political parties, the electoral system, and other formal mechanisms of government), questioning the limits of political representation, and shifting the question of the survival of the economic system to the survival of democracy itself, in both the North and the South.

Ironically, while there has been a steady stream of writing on the relationship between democracy and inequality (Savoia, Easaw, and McKay 2010), as well as on a perceived democratic deficit in OECD countries such as the United States, Canada, and countries in the European Union (Bexell and Mörth 2010; Krugman 2007; Lenard and Simeon 2012; Lindgren and Persson 2011; Norris 2011; Tamas 2011), the insights from these studies have been slow to inform large-scale comparative studies of democratization spanning various regions. This may be the consequence of a world view that continues to conceptualize the globe as divided into North/South silos that are perceived as static social, economic, and political spheres rather than as dynamic and uneven constructions that interact, collide, and overlap unpredictably in a deeply connected international system. Additionally, the tendency of comparative studies to focus on the Global South can be seen as a reflection of the discrepancy between liberal democratic theory and its application—in other words, as ignoring the disjuncture between the principles and the practice of liberal democracy in various parts of the world. In this context, the worldwide trend toward economism—the theoretical separation of economic activity from a social and political ensemble and, specifically, the reduction of this ensemble to its economic causes (Gramsci 1971, 369–84)—has emerged as a particularly significant paradox of liberal democracies, inasmuch as giving primacy to the economic over the political has marginalized issues of justice and equality.

As demonstrated by a number of studies (e.g., Herb 2005; Karl 1997; Lowi 2004; Mahdavy 1970; Ross 2001, 2009; Shaxson 2007; Shrivastava and Stefanick 2012; Tsui 2011; Wantchekon 2002), oil-exporting countries of the world are at a particularly crucial juncture of economism and politics, since the tensions between the two core assumptions of liberal democratic theory—capitalist market relations and developmental liberalism—are heightened further in a resource-driven economy. The role of the state in providing the conditions for and thus the possibility of economic development underlies the concept of developmental liberalism within a liberal democratic framework (Chan 2002). The financial crisis of 2008–9, in particular, not only accentuated the virtues of state regulation of financial sectors but also brought back focus on the role of equality in ensuring economic stability. A recent report (G20 2012) notes the growing disparities in earnings and working conditions in the G20 countries, inequities that are undermining social cohesion, economic performance, and political legitimacy. This joint report identifies labour market and social protection policies, tax policies, and regulatory measures as the tools needed to reverse income inequality and ensure sustainable economic growth (9–13). This re-emphasis of the role of state policies in ensuring economic development, which used to be a staple of development studies literature focused on the Global South, is now experiencing a global resurgence of sorts in the context of the growth and assertiveness of emerging economies and the slowing economic growth in the Global North (Cammack 2012).

In the context of oil and democracy, another set of literature has emerged that incorporates the concerns of developmental liberalism, highlighting that it is not oil but the vast wealth that it generates in a short span that depletes democracy by tipping the balance too far away from the principles of liberal democracy, such as economic and political equality (e.g., Boschini, Pettersson, and Roine 2007; Gylfason 2001, 2006; Mitchell 2011; Rosser 2006). These studies emphasize the crucial role of economic and political institutions in successfully appropriating rent gains and countering any negative effects of reliance on resource exploitation.

Consequently, for the purposes of analyzing the practice of democracy in Canada as an oil-exporting country, I will use the term *liberal democracy* to refer to a mode of governing economic and political institutions and *neoliberalism* to refer to a political ideology that affects the mode of governing by increasing economic and political inequality. As an OECD and G8 country ranking high on the Human Development Index, Canada is also among those industrialized countries in which inequality is growing even faster than in the United States (Conference Board of Canada 2011, 10), providing a compelling example of a country that manifests the contradictions of a complex international system. Not unlike most developed nations, the largest share of Canada's GDP is provided by the service industry. However, Canada is unusual among these countries in that the primary sector, particularly lumber, minerals, agriculture, and energy, constitutes a significant bulk of Canadian exports. Along with Norway and the United States, Canada is one of the few OECD nations that are among the top ten producers and exporters of oil (IEA 2013, 479–83). Therefore, I also consider in this chapter trends in global oil markets as they pertain to Canadian political economy, since staples or natural resources have been central to Canada's economy since its inception (Innis [1930] 1977).

I begin by contextualizing the debates on the nature and evolution of the liberal democratic model, noting the discrepancy between liberal democratic theory and its application. I delineate a relationship between economistic conceptions of liberal democracy and the entrenchment of neoliberalism, arguing that an economistic application of liberal democracy has directly contributed to decreasing democratic engagement and increasing inequality in many countries of the world. Additionally, I provide an overview of the energy sector in Canada and situate bitumen oil in the context of the shifting global oil market. While the so-called oil curse literature points the causal arrow from oil dependence to democratic deficit, the following discussion includes staples theory, a Canadian theory of political economy, in order to examine the possibility that it is actually the rise of political and economic inequality that is fuelling a democratic deficit in Canada. Ultimately, it is not the commodity of oil itself that is the culprit, but the exacerbation of the tension between the individualist and collectivist assumptions underlying liberal democracy, an amplification brought on by the great wealth generated in a short span of time in a neoliberal context. This tension between the core assumptions of democracy is evident in the theoretical debates on liberal democracy and is explored in the next section.

Liberal Democratic Theory and Application: Two Sides of Different Coins

The ongoing debate on the nature and components of liberal democracy appears to be happening on two largely unconnected planes. On one plane are the political theorists and social philosophers who have been assessing the failures of the liberal or economic models of democracy in order to do justice to the ideals of democratic legitimacy (e.g. , Beetham 1992; Benhabib 1996; Cunningham 2002; Macpherson 1985; Polanyi [1944] 2001). Theoretically, the contested boundary between the "economic" and the "political" in a liberal democratic system is the most critical issue in this discussion. According to Gramsci (1971), positing the existence of an apolitical economic sphere—the stance referred to as "economism"—is problematic in a number of respects. For one, the subjugation of politics to economics privileges the transformation of economic production over the transformation of the state as the lever for creating a democratic society. At the same time, the separation of the economic sphere from the political encourages a view of the economy as a self-regulatory space of individual enterprise immune to the interventions of the state.

Many critical international political economy (IPE) scholars have used the Gramscian position on economism to explore the constitution of such dichotomous boundaries and their impact on democracy in the context of transnational capitalism (e.g., Cox 1992; Gill 1998; Teivainen 2002; Wallerstein 1995). They have shown that both the economic/political boundary and the domestic/external boundary are socially constructed and interconnected in many ways. Moreover, since the economic rendering of issues and processes changes the boundaries of the political sphere, activities situated within a socially constructed "economic sphere" are defined as nonpolitical or private, which denies the possibility of democratic consultation to socially significant activities. According to these scholars, the late-twentieth-century redefinition of politics based on the metaphysical separation of politics and economy could well be seen as producing limits to democracy domestically and internationally. In Canada, this has manifested in the erosion of social citizenship rights through neoliberal governing practices, which has negatively affected national identity and social solidarity (Brodie 2002).

In sharp contrast to the critical IPE scholarship is the application-oriented group of scholars who focus on identifiable practices and quantifiable measurement of the tenets of liberal democracy (e.g., Alvarez et al. 1996; Cheibub, Gandhi, and Vreeland 2010). The approach of this group overlaps significantly with that of the prolific and influential "ranking industry," which comprises intergovernmental organizations (such as the World Bank, the United Nations Development Program, and the International Monetary Fund) and nongovernmental institutions (such as Freedom House, the Economist Intelligence Unit, and the Centre for Systemic Peace). These organizations generally support the application of both liberal and democratic principles of the state, but they only apply the principle of liberalism to what is defined as the "economy." This limited application of liberal principles is essentially an economistic solution to the dilemma of democratic liberalism, but it provides no coherent justification for the asymmetric treatment of the state and the economy. According to this solution, also referred to as neoliberalism, activities situated within the economic sphere should not be under democratic control since the "invisible hand" of the market will ensure (in varying degrees) that the pursuit of private needs leads to the common good. This disjuncture between democratic ideals and the economist context is largely ignored in studies informed by the neoliberal perspective. In the process, this separation justifies the transformation of public and political activities into a private and apolitical realm.

Therefore, at the same time that liberal democracy was emerging as the dominant political paradigm in the international system, we were also witnessing the rise of another political and economic ideology—neoliberalism, the prime belief system driving and justifying economic globalization as well as the financialization of the national and international economy. Neoliberalism is the discourse of governance that informs the economistic separation of democratic spheres and only allows for minimalistic conceptions of liberal democratic theory. In this discourse, key institutions operating in the economic sphere are represented as nonpolitical or beyond politics (Plattner 2013). In practice, of course, policies affecting economic institutions such as central banks and business corporations involve a combination of public and private power and have deep implications for questions of social justice, distribution, and economic performance, all of which are deeply political questions.

Neoliberalism, Financialization, and Inequality: A Causal Relationship

The meaning of the term *neoliberalism* has changed over time: it has at times meant something quite different from the free market radicalism with which it is usually associated today. An analysis of leading scholars who have written on neoliberalism—such as Friedrich Hayek (1960), Noam Chomsky (1999), David Harvey (2007), Milton Friedman (2008), and Gérard Duménil and Dominique Lévy (2011)—shows a range of differences in the meaning and application of the concept. In fact, according to the Boas and Gans-Morse (2009) study of 148 journal articles, the word *neoliberalism* is used to describe an ideology, an economic theory, a development theory, or an economic reform policy. In the contemporary era, the term most commonly refers to economic reform measures such as eliminating price controls, deregulating capital markets, lowering trade barriers, and reducing state influence on the economy, especially through privatization, fiscal austerity, and financialization.

For the purposes of this chapter, neoliberalism will be understood as a political ideology—that is, as a belief system that explains and justifies a preferred economic and governmental order for society, offers strategies for its maintenance or attainment, and helps give meaning to public events, personalities, and policies (Knight 2006). Specific ideologies crystallize and communicate the widely shared beliefs, opinions, and values of an identifiable group, class, constituency, or society. In response to the resurgence of ideologically inspired political conflict and polarization in the current era, John Jost, Christopher Federico, and Jaime Napier (2009) reviewed recent scholarship on political ideology as a social psychological phenomenon. Their analysis focuses primarily on liberal versus conservative ideology and the two core aspects of Left-Right ideology—resistance to change and acceptance of inequality. It shows ideology not merely as an organizing device or a shortcut for making experiential judgments about various political objects but also as a device for explaining and even rationalizing the way things are or, alternatively, how things should be different than they are. Jost, Federico, and Napier argue that "the power of ideology to explain and justify discrepancies between the current social order and some alternative not only maintains support for the status quo, but also serves for its adherents the palliative function of alleviating dissonance or discomfort associated with the awareness of systemic injustice or inequality" (313) For instance, in attempting to understand why conservatives report being happier than liberals, the authors found that the association between political ideology and subjective well-being was explained by the degree to which respondents rationalized inequality in society. In other words, conservatives were better at rationalizing inequality than liberals (326–27). These two aspects of political ideology, resistance to change and acceptance of inequality, are important to bear in mind as we explore the impact of neoliberal ideology on the liberal democratic system of governance.

Within a liberal democratic framework, then, the phenomenon of financialization can be considered as neoliberalism's most powerful tool to entrench the separation of the political and economic spheres. Financialization refers to the vastly expanded role of financial motives, market institutions, and elites in the operation of governing institutions (Epstein 2006) at the international, national, and subnational levels. According to Krippner (2005, 181–82), the finance industry, as it becomes increasingly dominant, takes over the primary economic, cultural, and political role in a national economy. This is manifested in the inflated roles of financial controllers, financial assets, and marketized securities in determining corporate strategies, as well as in the fluctuations of the stock market as a determinant of business cycles in an economy. The entrenchment of financialization is most evident in the United States, where the share of the financial sector in corporate profit rose from just a few percent in the 1960s to over 30 percent in 2004. Financial sector profits as a percentage of the total dipped to -10 percent during the crisis of 2008/9; however, with further deregulations and government support, by 2011, financial profits once again accounted for a third of all profits in the United States (Madigan 2011).

The consequences of financialization have not only led to national and international financial crises but have also had a deflationary impact on real economic activity, major social effects in terms of loss of employment, and more volatile material conditions for most citizens. This phenomenon is not confined to the Global South (Chomsky 2010), as exemplified by the Indignados movement in Spain, the Occupy movement in nearly eighty-two countries (Adam 2011), and the rising crescendo of anti-austerity protests in Europe (Lichfield 2012). Furthermore, the Organisation for Economic Co-operation and Development (OECD) report titled *Divided We Stand: Why Inequality Keeps Rising* highlights trends from 1980 to 2008, showing that most OECD countries carried out regulatory reforms to strengthen competition in the markets for goods and services and to make labour markets more adaptable. The report notes that during this period, nearly all OECD countries significantly relaxed anticompetitive product-market regulations, loosened employment protection legislation for workers with temporary contracts, reduced unemployment benefit replacement rates, and changed wage-setting mechanisms leading to a decrease in the share of union members among workers across most countries. Consequent to these regulatory reforms and institutional changes, minimum wages declined relative to median wages in a number of OECD countries, contributing to widening wage disparities (OECD 2011, 30–33).

Despite the sporadic revisions of neoliberal orthodoxy, many advocates of neoliberal macroeconomic reforms have argued that the welfare costs of higher volatility are negligible since the negative effect on income distribution is probably outweighed by its contribution to growth (Hoxha, Kalemli-Ozcan, and Vollrath 2009; Lucas 1987). However, this is not borne out by trends in the era of financialization. The United States, in particular, provides a good example of the parallel growth of financialization and extreme economic disparity. During the era of financialization, the top four hundred earners in the United States saw their income increase 392 percent and their average tax rate reduce by 37 percent from 1992 to 2007. The share of total US income going to the top 1 percent of American households (also after federal taxes and income transfers) increased from 11.3 percent in 1979 to 20.9 percent in 2007 and 22.5 percent in 2012 (Domhoff 2013).

There is overwhelming evidence that income inequality is bad for the individual, the society at large, and for the economy. For instance, income inequality has been shown to exert a significant drag on effective demand (Rajan 2010). Reducing inequality could reduce consumer debt; indeed, as Paul Krugman (n.d.) suggests, the Great Divergence—the period, beginning in the late 1970s, when inequality grew dramatically in the United States—may have helped cause the recession of 2008 by pushing middle-income Americans into debt.

Krugman shows that the growth of household debt has followed a pattern strikingly similar to the growth in income inequality and suggests that political shifts may have led both to rising inequality and to a more vulnerable financial system. Similarly, two recent OECD reports note that while rising income inequality creates economic, social, and political challenges, there is nothing inevitable about growing inequalities (OECD 2008, 2011). Arguing that the social contract is starting to unravel in many countries, the reports also note that tax and benefit systems have become less redistributive in many countries since the mid-1990s.

Ironically, income inequality has been rising in Canada even more rapidly than in the United States since the mid-1990s. The richest 1 percent of Canadians saw their share of total income increase from 7.1 percent in 1982 to 13.3 percent in 2011 (OECD 2011, table 9.1; Wolfson, Veall, and Brooks 2014, 10).[1] At the same time, the top federal marginal income tax rates saw a marked decline, dropping from 43 percent in 1981 to 29 percent in 2010 and 20.8 percent in 2012 (Grant 2013). According to the OECD study, prior to the mid-1990s, the Canadian tax-benefit system was as effective as those of the Nordic countries in stabilizing inequality, offsetting more than 70 percent of the rise in market income inequality. The effect of redistribution has declined since then: therefore, in 2011, taxes and benefits only offset less than 40 percent of the rise in inequality. This downward trend in redistribution can be directly linked to three factors: the entrenchment of the neoliberal view of the role of the state, which is manifested in the "reduced role of means-tested transfers, as benefit rates fell and benefits became less targeted" (OECD 2011, 37–40); the effects of institutional shifts such as dwindling unionization rates and stagnating minimum wages (Conference Board of Canada 2015); and falling top marginal tax rates (Yalnizyan 2010).

While the use of neoliberal policies for "fiscal consolidation" started under the Liberal Party regime in the 1990s (Posner and Sommerfeld 2013, 149–52), the Conservative Party regime in Canada, since its rise to power in 2006, has further emphasized the economistic conception of the role of government through the policies of fiscal restraint via social spending cuts and tax cuts. Furthermore, in terms of liberal democratic theory and its core assumption of the separation of the political system from its environment, Canada is experiencing an unprecedented wave of market values, norms, and ideals from the private sector successfully penetrating the state. The separation of powers (between different government agencies like the legislature, the executive, and the judiciary) in a liberal democracy is supposed to protect the governing elite and their institutions from societal encroachment, and vice versa, in the interest of both state and society. Yet the significant inroads of market interests into the very locus of the powers from which they are to be protected blurs the boundaries with respect to the exercise of political power.

Oil Versus Democracy?

The disconnect between the critical theorists and the quantitative analysts noted above is particularly relevant for studies of oil and democracy, since such studies are often at the cusp of the theoretical and applied approaches to liberal democracy. While most of the oil and democracy studies are concerned with the theoretical assumptions of liberal democracy—political legitimacy and broad-based economic development—they generally use the measures and indicators of those who apply the theory. For instance, Polity scores are frequently used in studies of regime change and the effects of regime authority to evaluate a country's degree of democracy. According to the Center for Systemic Peace, "The Polity conceptual scheme is unique in that it examines concomitant qualities of democratic and autocratic authority in governing institutions, rather than discrete and mutually exclusive forms of governance." Employing six measures that capture "key qualities of executive recruitment, constraints on executive authority, and political competition," the scheme evaluates countries along "a spectrum of governing authority that spans from fully institutionalized autocracies through mixed, or incoherent, authority regimes (termed 'anocracies') to fully institutionalized democracies."[2] The Polity approach has been criticized for relying on a minimalistic definition of democracy and for not offering a theoretical justification for the way the component variables are aggregated into a single regime index (Munck and Verkuilen 2002). Such indicators, which are based on subjective and narrow interpretations of democracy, could be considered uncertain and contested.

Nevertheless, Polity scores continue to be among the most widely used indices of democracy, as seen in the extensive cross-national studies by Ross (2001) and Tsui (2011), which examine the impact of oil wealth on democracy as measured by the Polity index. Both studies note the antidemocratic effect of oil wealth on states, even when other factors are accounted for. However, while Ross focuses on the role of dependence on oil and other minerals in an economy that fails to bring about the social and cultural changes needed to produce democratic government, Tsui proposes a theory of endogenous barriers to political entry to explain democratic deficits in oil-rich states. The quantitative measures of such studies, however, have not gone unchallenged. Questioning the validity of regressions centred on cross-sectional analysis, Haber and Menaldo (2011) show that resource dependence is not necessarily associated with the undermining of democracy. The authors do a thorough job of critically evaluating the quantitative parameters of studies like those of Ross (2001), Mahdavy (1970), Huntington (1991), and others who claim a causal relationship between natural-resource reliance and authoritarianism. Their analysis, however, uncritically accepts the indicators of democracy as proposed by the Polity index.

The debate around using these indicators continues, as is evident in Ross's "Oil and Democracy Revisited" (2009), where he responds to his critics by using a more exogenous measure of oil wealth, separating democratic transitions from democratic survival, adding new robustness tests, and employing a dataset that extends from 1960 to 2002 and covers 170 states. In this new study, Ross still finds evidence that, regardless of any possible countervailing pro-democracy effects, the net impact of the dependence on oil revenue on democratic transitions in authoritarian states is strongly negative. Additionally, he finds that undemocratic effects fuelled by oil dependence are uneven but are growing stronger over time, which he argues is due to the rising prevalence of state ownership. Nevertheless, much like his detractors, Ross does not concern himself with the limited application of the principles of democracy in "measuring" it.

Despite their narrow use of the liberal democratic framework, many of the studies on oil and democracy provide valuable insights into the dangers of an economistic conception of liberal democracy in oil-exporting economies. The most pertinent pattern noted in these studies is the "rentier effect," which suggests that resource-rich governments use low tax rates and patronage to dampen democratic pressures (Feldman 2003; Ross 2001, 2009; Wantchekon 2002). According to these studies, the explanation for the rentier effect lies in the loss of fiscal connection between the government and the people in a state that derives all or a substantial portion of its national revenue from the rent of resources rather than taxes. In this scenario, the incumbent elite's power over rent distribution enables it to use resource revenue to favour one or more groups in the society at the expense of others. Using the measures of Polity IV, this trend is clearly shown in the oil-exporting countries in the Middle East and North Africa and is regarded as evidence of the negative impact of oil dependence on democratic transition in oil-exporting countries in the Global South.

Considering the vast array of variants of democracy, the standardized measures of democracy are contentious in themselves; moreover, such measures fall short in exploring the health of democracy in countries in the Global North that are regarded as "established democracies."

For instance, Norway could be seen as the model of a highly functioning democracy despite being a major oil-exporting country. The fifth-largest oil exporter in the world (compared to the ninth position held by Canada), Norway is the fourteenth-largest producer of oil, compared to the sixth position held by Canada (Campbell 2013, 10). Norway is the world's largest producer of oil and natural gas outside the Middle East, and it also holds the top spot in the Democracy Index (EIU 2013, 3). However, narrowly defined democracy indices and categories such as "electoral process and pluralism; civil liberties; the functioning of government; political participation; and political culture" (EIU 2013, 1) are unlikely to explain the role of the egalitarian welfare-state model. Neither is this limited framework likely to explain the impacts in Norway of the adoption of soft neoliberal policies during the 1980s and 1990s; the extensive program of privatization and deregulation since 2000–2001; unpopular restructuring, commercialization, and privatization of the public sector, including health, pension, and labour law; weakening of the trade unions; rising social and income inequality; and the recent ascendance of an economically neoliberal and right-wing populist coalition (Wahl 2011; Wahl and Pedersen 2013). Despite the rise of right-wing politics recently, Norway's high taxes continue to fund its welfare model, while almost all of the oil revenue goes into the Norwegian sovereign wealth fund. In contrast to this approach of sharing the resource rent with future generations, Alberta's low tax rate ensures that it must use oil royalties to fund current government expenditures, enabling the entrenchment of neoliberal policies and the chronic boom-bust economic cycles.

These trends are much more central to critical theoretical debates on the nature and dilemmas of liberal democracy and are likely to raise questions such as these: Why is the political-economic impact of oil dependence different in Norway, compared to other oil-exporting countries? What is the relationship among neoliberalism, income inequality, and democratic engagement? How do these factors affect the political-economic outcomes in various oil-exporting countries? These are questions worth asking in the context of oil-exporting countries in not only the Global South but also the Global North, especially since the list of top twenty oil-producing countries in the world in 2014 already included eight OECD countries.[3] Additionally, the discovery of recoverable shale oil deposits of 4.8 trillion barrels (2010 estimate) in the western United States, China, the Russian Federation, the Democratic Republic of the Congo, Brazil, Italy, Morocco, Jordon, Estonia, and South Australia (WEC 2010, 97–99) is likely to fundamentally alter global oil supply and, consequently, the political economy of oil-producing and -exporting countries.

Returning our focus to Canada, the next section explores the political economy of Canada, as a country with a resource-exporting economy, through the most consistent theoretical lens used to examine the evolution of political and economic trends in Canada. Broadly defined as a theory of unbalanced export-led growth (Watkins 1977, 2007), staples theory is more than an approach to economic history. It emphasizes the longer-term developmental questions related to policy, infrastructure, and redistribution linkages. In other words, the application of staples theory goes into the realm of a policy-oriented approach that describes the likely developmental accompaniments, positive or negative, of alternative export "choices" (where choices exist) and a policy-oriented solution to the inherent deficiencies in these choices. Thus, staples theory is uniquely complementary to the vast literature on the resource curse that mainly focuses on the interplay of resource rents, overvalued currencies, and their economic and political manifestations.

Staples Theory and Canada's Resource Economy

The staples thesis of economic development emerged in the 1930s through the work of Harold Innis ([1930] 1977) and W. A. Mackintosh (1936) on the evolution of the Canadian state, and the relationship between the nation and its regions, on the basis of its staple commodities such as fish, fur, lumber, agricultural products, and minerals. While the trading links cemented Canada's cultural connections to Europe, the search for and exploitation of these staples led to the creation of unique regional economic and political institutions within Canada. In addition, Innis and Macintosh argued that the nature of the staples was responsible for the unique regional political and economic developments. For instance, according to Innis, the independent nature of wheat farming in Western Canada led to a history of distrust of government and corporations in that part of the country (386–93). In Central Canada, the main staple was fur, controlled by large firms such as the Hudson's Bay Company. The fur trade produced the centralized, business-oriented society in that region. Furthermore, Innis depicts the relationship between the nation and the regions of Canada as one of "heartland/core" and "hinterland/periphery," with the core seeking to gain economic and political power over the periphery, since the staples are located in the hinterland. While Mackintosh suggests that staples export could be the positive path to more diversified development (459–60), Innis emphasizes the significance of the characteristics of the commodity itself and cautions against the tendency toward wildly fluctuating economic activity (396–402).

In the 1960s and 1970s, the staples thesis was revived by Melville H. Watkins (1963, 1977) through his work on resource capitalism and Canadian political economy. Innis's analysis had pointed to the vagaries of international commodity markets, which tend to witness violent fluctuations and where any decline in demand or increase in supply can have drastic consequences for the staples-exporting economy. Watkins refers to this vulnerability to broader economic trends as the "staples trap," arguing that a resource-exporting economy is poorly placed to respond to the challenge of finding a new economic base. Watkins proposes creating linkages that produce economic spinoffs for the region and the country (backward, forward, final demand linkages) in order to plan for growth and economic stability and to avoid the staples trap. He argues that public policy could strengthen linkages and thus help to tame the volatility of a staples economy and change the "boom-and-bust psychology" of staples-export development. Watkins's analysis is supported by studies such as those by Peter A. Hall and David Soskice, which classify Canada as a successful "coordinated market economy" (2001, 8). According to Hall and Soskice, Canada's unique model of a growth strategy founded on the export of natural resources blended the dynamism of a powerful export sector with elements such as skilled human resources, a high-wage manufacturing sector, modern public infrastructure, a robust financial sector, macro-economic stability, and a relatively unionized workforce. Arguably, under the ongoing neoliberal economic restructuring in Canada, wages are declining, collective bargaining is being suppressed, and public investments in infrastructure related to education, health and social service are declining significantly—a pattern that is likely to fundamentally alter the basis of the Canadian resource economy model as perceived by Hall and Soskice.

On the basis of the declining percentage share of natural resources relative to other sectors in the GDP, however, some commentators contend that Canada has entered a "post-staples" political economy. Two decades ago, Thomas A. Hutton, in *Visions of a "Post-Staples" Economy* (1994), argued that some regions were showing signs of the emergence of a post-staples economy, signs such as industrialization and urbanization, resources depletion, the regionalization of markets, and industrial restructuring. At that time, these elements were seen by some as driving the Canadian political economy in a new, post-staples direction, as illustrated by the apparent importance of manufacturing and tertiary activities, the rise of social movements, the importance of knowledge elites, urbanization, and increasingly disconnected regional politics (Howlett and Brownsey 1996; Howlett and Ramesh 1992; Hutton 1994). However, Canada's enduring reliance on international trade, the consistently high interprovincial trade in natural resources and related sectors (Wellstead 2007), and the recent emergence of Canada as a major oil-exporting country confirm the continuing significance of the natural resources sector for the Canadian economy. In terms of the energy sector, Watkins (2007, 215) argues that Canadian "oil and gas in particular, which flows heavily to American markets, are much closer to being simple staples exports—which suggests a regression to a staples economy," or to a neostaples economy (Mills and Sweeney 2013, 7).

Undeniably, the most recent resource-commodity boom involving bitumen oil has been accompanied by neoliberal cutbacks and the shrinking of redistributive policies and programs, both provincially and federally. Moreover, many of these policies have effectively removed resource rents from the control of the state, workers, and resource-dependent communities. Without the earlier mix of goods and social programs for working families and individuals or the regulatory role of the state, "rowing and steering" the economy, the bitumen boom has led to an unprecedented degree of wealth creation for some and rising income inequality for the majority. Undoubtedly, this inequality further restricts the Canadian state's ability to attain an economic trajectory that is socially and environmentally sustainable, giving credence to the assertions of a regression into a neostaples economy made by analysts such as Stanford (2013), Drache (2013), and Mills and Sweeney (2013).

From this perspective, the staples theory of economic development remains critical to understanding questions of public policy in Canada, including those regarding resource development; industrial, fiscal, and social policy; and federal-provincial relations. Despite its limited use of the liberal democracy framework and its dominant focus on the transformation of economic and political institutions in the Global South, the oil and democracy literature provides many useful insights for oil-exporting jurisdictions. These insights can be complemented rather neatly by the staples theory of economic development, which has been used to study the economies of many nations that are dependent upon resource extraction and/or primary industries (e.g. , Helleiner 1994; Levitt 2004). Indeed, the theoretical frameworks of liberal democracy and staples theory can be seen as largely complementary: while the "oil versus democracy" analysis highlights the mechanisms through which resource dependence leads to a democratic deficit, staples theory points to policy mechanisms to avoid the resource curse and the staples trap.

Interestingly, the rise of the Conservative regime in the country has coincided with the rise of Canada as a major oil-exporting country. The upswing in oil prices that began in 2005 led to a peak of $147 per barrel in summer of 2008, heralding a phase of unprecedented profits of hundreds of billions of dollars for the oil industry (see Cattaneo 2013; Tertzakian 2013; Weiss, Weidman, and Leber 2012) and creating the opportunity for unconventional oil field expansions in North America. After spending most of the past few decades as one of the top ten consumers and producers of oil, Canada entered the list of top ten oil-exporting nations in the world at number eight in 2007 (while the United States was at number sixteen). Despite the short-term price setbacks of 2008–9, while the high oil prices enabled Canada to rise to number six in the list of oil-producing countries, across the border, the production of shale oil and other tight oil allowed the United States to climb to number one in 2014 (USEIA 2015; Lane 2015, 5–6). As Canada becomes firmly established in the list of the top ten oil-exporting nations in the world (while it is estimated that the United States will be energy self-sufficient within a decade and a net exporter of energy by 2035 [British Petroleum 2014, 23–50]), it is important to examine the nature and impact of what is repeatedly dubbed the "driver of Canadian economy"—the oil industry (see Canada, NRC 2010; Canadian Press 2013a; Krugel 2012). The next section, therefore, provides a broad overview of the complicated world of the global oil industry before we contextualize its role in the Canadian political economy.

Global Oil Deposits, Oil Markets, and the Canadian Context

To begin with, it is important to recognize the very complicated world of different types of crude oils. Hydrocarbons such as coal, petroleum, and natural gas—and their derivatives such as plastics, paraffin, waxes, solvents, and oils— are economically the most significant commodities since the late nineteenth century. Of these, petroleum in particular is used for producing petroleum-based fuels, including petrol, diesel, jet, heating, other fuel oils, and liquefied petroleum gas. The petroleum industry generally classifies crude oil by the geographic location where it is produced, its API gravity or measure of density, and its sulphur content. Crude oil is considered "light" if it has low density or "heavy" if it has high density; it is referred to as "sweet" if it contains relatively little sulphur or "sour" if it contains substantial amounts of sulphur (Alboudwarej et al. 2006). Light crude oil is more desirable than heavy oil since it produces a higher yield of petrol, while sweet oil commands a higher price than sour oil because it creates fewer environmental problems and requires less refining to meet sulphur standards imposed on fuels in consuming countries. The price per barrel is determined by these characteristics, in addition to the geographic location of the wells, which affects the cost of transportation to the refinery. The lighter grades of crude oil produce the best yields of petroleum products, but as the world's reserves of light and medium oil are depleted, oil refineries are increasingly processing heavy oil, bitumen, and tight oil, and use more complex and expensive methods to produce the required products. Because heavier crude oils have too much carbon and not enough hydrogen, processing them generally involves removing carbon from or adding hydrogen to the molecules and using the process of fluid catalytic cracking to convert the longer, more complex molecules in the oil to the shorter, simpler ones in the fuels.

The inflation-adjusted price of a barrel of light crude oil remained under $25 per barrel from 1980 to September 2003. In late 2003, the price rose above $30; it reached $60 in August 2005 and peaked at $147.30 in July 2008. Commentators attributed these price increases to many factors, including the falling value of the US dollar, reports of a decline in petroleum reserves, worries over peak oil, Middle East tensions, and oil price speculations (Sieminski 2012). Geopolitical events and natural disasters indirectly related to the global oil market also had strong short-term impact on oil prices, hiking demand and threatening oil supply until the onset of the global recession in late 2008. The 2008–9 financial crisis led to the ongoing global recession, causing demand for energy to shrink and oil prices to fall from $147 in the summer of 2008 to $32 in December 2008. Oil prices stabilized in 2009 and established a trading range between $60 and $80. At the time of writing, while the economic recession continues to affect the world economy and oil production in the United States has climbed to a twenty-year high, the price of oil per barrel has slid to below $50 per barrel, posing new challenges to the unconventional oil industry and leading to worldwide job losses for an estimated 100,000 oil workers.[4]

Although Canada consistently appeared in the list of top ten producers and consumers of petroleum because of its conventional oil reserves and high per capita consumption, it was the dramatic increase in oil prices, beginning in 2005, that made the production of bitumen oil economically viable for global export. Consequently, despite the high costs of extraction and transport of bitumen oil, estimates of which range from $30 to $80 per barrel, by 2007, 64 percent of Canada's petroleum production of 1.86 million barrels per day was from bitumen oil rather than conventional oil fields (ERCB 2008).[5] Total crude oil production in Canada rose by an average of 8.6 percent per year from 2008 to 2011 (Canada, NEB 2011a, 2011b), prompting the Canadian Oil Sands Industry Review (COSIR 2011) to proclaim:

> Once a footnote in the story of world oil production, Canada's oil sands are part of the solution to declining conventional oil reserves elsewhere in the world. Canada has approximately 175 billion barrels of oil that can be recovered with today's technology. Of that number, 170 billion are located in the oil sands. There are an estimated 2.5 trillion barrels of bitumen in the Canadian resources. That is more than enough to supply all of Canada's needs and make a significant contribution to America, China and other oil importers for generations to come.

By 2013, the share of bitumen oil in Canada's total oil production stood at 82 percent (see Canada, NEB 2013a), enabling Canada to emerge as the sixth-largest crude oil producer in the world. Canada has also become the largest source of crude oil for the United States, supplying more than 20 percent of the US's import volumes in the past decade. The world at large consumes 32 billion barrels of oil per year, and the United States is the top oil consumer, accounting for 24 percent of world consumption in 2004, dropping to 21 percent by 2007, and stabilizing at 22 percent for 2010 and 2011. The slowing of the US economy, as well as advances in energy-efficient technology, are possible reasons for the declining share of US consumption of oil between 2004 and 2011. However, this decline was more than offset by the nearly 12 percent per annum rise of consumption in China and the steady rise in oil consumption in other "emerging economies" (Rapier 2012; USEIA 2012).

Canadian bitumen oil certainly filled an important gap created by declining conventional oil production in all the major OECD producers—the United States, the United Kingdom, Norway, Mexico, and Canada—and by the national security rhetoric in the post-9/11 era. However, the dramatic rise of oil prices from 2005 to 2008 led not only to the expansion of bitumen oil in Canada but also to a rash of investments in shale oil and other tight oil projects in the United States.[6] Shale oil drilling intensity in the United States skyrocketed from a few hundred wells brought online (becoming productive) before 2011 to more than four thousand in 2012 (Maugeri 2013, 1). By April 2013, US crude production was at nearly 7.2 million barrels per day, higher than it had been in more than twenty years. The shale oil production boom, particularly from sites in North Dakota and Montana, has allowed the United States to further decrease its reliance on oil imports and to emerge as the third-largest producer of oil in the world, preceded only by Saudi Arabia and Russia (IEA 2013), and overtaking them by June 2014 (Smith 2014).

The success of horizontal drilling and multistage fracturing to exploit tight shale formations is expected to catapult the United States into energy self-sufficiency within this decade, probably making it a net exporter of oil by 2035 (IEA 2012). The likelihood of this trend is confirmed by the 12 percent decline in US crude oil imports since 2005 (USEIA 2015). In other words, although the United States is importing more crude oil from Canada, the total amount of crude oil imported from foreign suppliers is falling in that country. With the cost of developing the tight oil trapped in unconventional rock formations estimated to be dropping below $50 a barrel—making it more competitive than Canadian bitumen oil or ultra-deepwater crude—recent price levels are spurring substantial investment in tight oil explorations (IEA 2012). As the United States has traditionally absorbed 95 percent of Canada's crude oil exports, rising US shale oil production stands to jeopardize a significant portion of Canada's future potential exports.

A recent study by Leonardo Maugeri (2013, 25–26) mentions two main reasons for this scenario. First, Canadian oil exports already compete for transportation capacity, particularly via pipeline, with North Dakota's surging production. Furthermore, both producing areas rely on the same trading and storage hub, the already overburdened Cushing, Oklahoma. But while North Dakota is finding alternative takeaway options because of rail transportation, a significant part of future Canadian oil production risks being landlocked without the availability of new pipelines, such as the much debated Keystone XL. Second, marginal production costs for a substantial amount of Canadian crude are the highest in the world, with several oil sands projects presenting a breakeven of more than $90 per barrel. Conversely, the price for West Canadian Select, a large heavy crude oil stream and the benchmark for Canadian heavy crude derived from oil sands, hit a six-year low in March 2015 at $29.54 per barrel, or less than half of the price of Brent crude (Tuttle 2015), thus making bitumen oil the cheapest crude oil on the planet, even though it continues to be the most expensive oil to produce and transport. Maugeri's analysis does not bode well for the future of bitumen oil and is supported by the fact that several Canadian oil sands companies have slashed their investment budgets and are posting losses (Lewis 2015).

Although the unique characteristics of shale oil in terms of drilling intensity makes it extremely vulnerable to a drop in oil price, as well as to environmental opposition, the shale oil boom in North America is massive in scope. According to Leonardo Maugeri (2012), the United States averaged 1,919 active drilling rigs in 2012 alone, which is just below 60 percent of worldwide activity and vastly more intense than that of Canada, with 356 active drilling rigs. Moreover, in 2011, roughly 90 percent of the US drilling rigs were equipped for horizontal hydraulic drilling, significantly contributing to shale oil production and to the revival of production in mature conventional oil fields (Maugeri 2013, 21). Additionally, on the basis of a comprehensive field-by-field analysis of oil exploration and development projects in the world, Maugeri (2012, 1) suggests that an unrestricted production and supply capacity "is growing worldwide at such an unprecedented level that it might outpace consumption," leading to "a glut of overproduction and a steep dip in oil prices" in the near future.

Whereas exporting crude oil has always been a highly sensitive and heated issue both in the United States and Canada, increased production in the United States, largely from light tight oil in North Dakota and Montana, combined with steadily increasing imports from Canada has already led to a glut in the US Midwest. As this glut took hold, it led not only to a disconnection of the US mid-continent oil market from world markets but also to lower oil prices in Western Canada relative to both world prices and the price of West Texas Intermediate (WTI). Consequently, in the spring of 2012, "light oil at Edmonton was trading at a discount of almost $CDN 40 per barrel to Brent prices, and at a discount of almost $CDN 20/barrel to US mid-continent prices" (Leach 2013b). Moreover, Canada is the cheapest alternative destination for moving oil via vessel because of the effects of the Jones Act (1920), which makes it very expensive to ship goods between domestic ports.[7] Therefore, in 2012 all exports of US crude oil went to Canada, the only destination to which approval for exports is easy under existing US laws (Clayton 2013; USEIA 2015). However, the growing surplus of domestic oil will probably catalyze a reassessment of US policies that were created in an era when domestic production was in decline and energy security was a major concern. Clearly, the implications of the shale oil boom in the United States are likely to be significant for Canadian bitumen oil.

Within this complicated context of the unpredictable global oil market, let us now consider the Canadian oil sector. The energy sector in Canada is vast, comprising crude oil, petroleum, coal and coal products, natural gas, and electricity. Canadian energy exports alone contributed $107.6 billion to the economy in 2012, which amounted to 9.5 percent of Canada's GDP that year. Within the energy sector, the share of crude oil, petroleum, and coal products is indeed the largest and growing. They contributed 77 percent of net energy export revenue in 2012, compared to 60 percent in 2009 and 42 percent in 2006. (Canada, NEB 2013b).

However, the real contribution of the energy sector to the national economy is likely to be significantly higher when we consider the direct and indirect investments, manufacturing, construction, services, and other factors that are associated with this industry. Additionally, as pointed out by Erin Weir (2006), transborder trade in exports and imports of manufactures between Canada and the United States has increased considerably since the North American Free Trade Agreement (NAFTA) came into force, creating trade statistics that can be interpreted as showing manufacturing to be a rising share, and resources a falling share, of exports. Weir argues that this is an illusion that comes from relying on gross figures of exports and imports. The movement of components back and forth across the border is heavily concentrated in the manufacturing sector, which leads to an overestimation of the actual share of the manufacturing sector relative to exports of services and natural resources. While such a correction is beyond the scope of this chapter, it is indeed a useful reminder to bear in mind in an analysis of the nature of Canada's political economy.

Canadian energy production increased in 2012 by about 2 percent, with growth in petroleum production and a decline in natural gas production. As mentioned earlier, the glut of supply in the American Midwest caused oil prices in Western Canada to be discounted by nearly 20 percent, which is "estimated to have reduced annualized Gross Domestic Product (GDP) growth by 0.4 percentage points in the second half of 2012. Canadian GDP increased by 1.8 percent in 2012 after growing by 2.6 percent in 2011" (Canada, NEB 2013b, 3). The National Energy Board report confirms the pessimistic outlook due to the impact of the shale boom, noting that "after a very active 2011, the leasing of petroleum rights in Western Canada fell to its lowest level since 2002" (3). Additionally, "Alberta's revenue from the sale of petroleum rights fell from a record $3.59 billion in 2011 to $1.12 billion in 2012" (3). In 2013, the Alberta government blamed the "bitumen bubble" for the loss of $6 billion in royalties (Bennett 2013). Alberta's proposed solution is to get more of its oil to tidewater ports for shipment overseas, where it will potentially fetch a higher price. However, this strategy does not take into account the realities of oil supply, particularly in terms of the shale oil boom, which is likely to include other big oil exporters such as Russia, China, and possibly Australia, where the second-largest shale oil reserves have been identified (Linc Energy 2013; Maugeri 2012). Nor does it take into account the realities of demand in terms of the impending energy self-sufficiency of its biggest market, the United States, or the complexities of energy markets elsewhere. For instance, as the OPEC countries lose their shares of the US market, they are more likely to turn to Asian markets to offset potential losses. Given the high cost of production and transportation of bitumen oil, it is quite unlikely that heavy crude from Alberta will prove to be competitive with significantly cheaper conventional oil in regions where the markets and the suppliers are in closer proximity.

Despite the inevitable uncertainties and clear trends in the oil markets, the policy direction in Alberta appears to be driven by the short-term priorities of the bitumen oil industry, as evidenced by the premiers of Alberta travelling overseas to sell the virtues of bitumen oil (Canadian Press 2015; Lye 2013), the dismantling of the Environment Department to advance oil-industry activity (Pratt 2013), and the curtailment of union activity (CBC News 2013) in a province that already has the lowest minimum wage in the country and the highest income disparity in Canada (Gibson 2012, 7–8). Nationally, the federal government's position on climate change, the muzzling of scientists working on climate change, and the shutting down of research and scientific facilities related to the environment and other data collection are seen as examples of the oil industry's very significant influence over the government (Homer-Dixon 2013). Such trends have led to claims by commentators that both Alberta and Canada are beginning to exhibit the economic and political characteristics of a petro-state in terms of environmental consequences, boom-bust economic cycles, investment imbalances, and the undermining of the institutions and practice of democracy in Canada (Hoberg 2014; Homer-Dixon 2013; Nikiforuk 2010, 2012).

Typically, *petro-state* is a derogatory term for a state that relies on oil revenue rather than on taxes and has weak political and economic institutions, and where power is concentrated in the hands of an elite minority (Karl 2007,

279). Some critics object to using this term for Canada since only the province of Alberta has exceeded the 20 percent mark for oil revenue as a share of the GDP, while the national share for oil revenue remains under 10 percent of the GDP (Leach 2013a). Setting aside polemical and rhetorical statements, the significance of bitumen oil in the Canadian economy remains undeniable for two reasons: first, underestimating the real contribution of the energy sector to the national economy is a statistical possibility, as noted earlier, and second, despite vociferous environmental opposition domestically and abroad (Rabson 2013; Wotherspoon and Hansen 2013), the federal Conservative government (and not the oil industry) spent $40 million in 2013–14 to advertise the importance and environmental responsibility of Canada's resource sector (Canadian Press 2013b), and talk of pipeline politics has dominated the governing agenda (Canadian Press 2013a).

While most recent writing on the impact of bitumen oil extraction is concerned with the economic and environmental consequences (e.g., Davidson and Gismondi 2011; Marsden 2010; Nikiforuk 2010, 2012; Taft, MacMillan, and Jahangir 2012), there is also growing concern about the rising democratic deficit in Canada, along with the recognition that dependence on natural resource rents produces political problems (Homer-Dixon 2013). For instance, Trevor Harrison and Harvey Krahn, in *Governing Alberta: Citizens' Views* (2013), note high levels of public concern over issues such as reform to systems of taxation and royalty collection, economic diversification, and the need for environmental protection (18). In another survey, Harrison and Krahn (2014, 1–4) found a continuation of high levels of political alienation and a declining voting trend among Albertans. Even the electoral victory of the New Democratic Party (NDP) in May 2015, while being a symbolic shift of seismic proportions in Alberta politics, came about with only 53.7 percent of eligible voters casting their vote (Elections Alberta 2015). Indeed, political alienation that perpetuates over time is corrosive to democracy and the legitimacy of government institutions. Concerns regarding opportunities for and degree of citizenship engagement are not limited to the provincial level, where the long-ruling Progressive Conservative Party as well as the opposition Wildrose Party were perceived as beholden to the powerful bitumen oil lobby in Alberta (Campanella and Stunden Bower 2013, 3–6). Samara, a private think tank, conducted a national public opinion survey in 2013 asking politically disengaged Canadians about the barriers they face to being politically active. While the most frequently cited barrier was a lack of political role models, the research also indicates that two-thirds of Canadians believe that members of Parliament are not representing their interests in Ottawa (Samara 2013, 2–3). Additionally, regardless of province of residence, only 55 percent of Canadians reported being satisfied with the way democracy works in Canada, down from 75 percent in 2004 (Samara 2012, 1). These trends are undeniably critical in understanding the ongoing transformation of the economic and political institutions in Canada, since they significantly affect the practice of liberal democracy provincially and federally.

Inequality: The New Trap in a Staples Economy

Amartya Sen characterized liberal democracy in the twentieth century "as the preeminently acceptable form of governance" (Sen 1999, 4). While exceptions such as Islamic theocracy in the Middle East and the "China model" of growth-promoting authoritarian government with a partially marketized economy do exist, liberal democracy in its various manifestations appears to be the dominant political system in much of the world today. The creation of a vast middle class undermined the appeal of Marxism, and Marx's socialist scenario was largely bypassed in most post-industrial societies (Moore 2003). Moreover, the growth of electoral democracies in the latter half of the twentieth century coincided with the emergence of new middle classes in countries such as Brazil, India, Indonesia, Malaysia, and South Africa. Significantly, as the middle class has expanded considerably in countries of the Global South, particularly in Asia (and most impressively in populous China and India), it has shrunk in the OECD countries, especially in the aftermath of the financial crisis of 2008–9.[8] Given the experience of industrialized countries in the nineteenth and twentieth centuries, as well as that of "emerging economies" (with the possible exception of China) in more recent years, clearly there is a broad correlation among economic growth, socio-economic change, and the hegemony of liberal democratic ideology in the world today.

In this scenario, divorcing the measures of democracy from the theoretical underpinnings of the liberal democratic framework is particularly problematic since it undermines the role of the state in striking a fine balance between capitalist market relations and developmental liberalism. Even the World Bank has, for some time now, accepted the failure of the long-standing attempts to improve the prospects for development on the basis of econometric analysis of large cross-country data sets and the need to understand the role of state agency in the processes that drive economic growth (World Bank 1992). These technical and methodological arguments, which are often focused on development processes in the Global South, are increasingly coinciding with a broader struggle against global capitalism (Little 2003), the moral and practical requirements of global justice (Cammack 2012), and the analysis of the drivers and impacts of inequality in the Global North (Krugman 2007; Norris 2011).

John Dryzek (1996) argues that historical conditions in the Western world made possible the theoretical separation of democratic rules from the social outcomes of political economic decisions, since economic rationality was used to battle the forces of entrenched hierarchy and religious privilege. In contemporary times, economic rationality is giving rise to an exclusionary approach to participation in economic policy making, with restricted public scrutiny or public accountability, nationally and internationally. Stephen Gill (1998) refers to this as "New Constitutionalism," which, he argues, operates to confer privileged rights of citizenship and representation to corporate capital and large investors, serving to secure investor freedoms and property rights for transnational enterprises. "What is emerging within state forms (state and civil society complexes)," writes Gill, "is a pattern of authority in which capital has greater weight and representation, restraining the democratisation process that has involved centuries of struggle for representation—a development that is contested and contradictory" (23).

As shown by numerous studies, changing trade and tax policies inspired by the neoliberal prescriptions of political and economic organization have led to rising inequality. Particularly in the wake of the global financial crisis, it is now more widely acknowledged that inequality may promote inefficiency rather than growth. A recent IMF study noted:

> When growth is looked at over the long term, the trade-off between efficiency and equality may not exist. In fact equality appears to be an important ingredient in promoting and sustaining growth. The difference between countries that can sustain rapid growth for many years or even decades and the many others that see growth spurts fade quickly may be the level of inequality. Countries may find that improving equality may also improve efficiency, understood as more sustainable long-run growth. (Berg and Ostry 2011, 13)

The political effects of increasing inequality should be considered equally significant. The unchallenged entrenchment of neoliberalism in Canada is likely to reduce further the role of the state as the provider of public and social services to the general population and the marginalized, thus undermining one of the core assumptions of liberal democracy. Disturbingly, rather than contributing to a post-staples political economy, increasing social, political, and economic inequality has pushed Canada toward a neostaples economy functioning within a postdemocratic state, that is, one in which elected governments continue to operate within a framework of democratic processes, of the sort measured by indicators of democracy, while the application of the basic principles of democracy becomes increasingly limited, such that the apparatus of democracy serves to benefit a relatively small, but powerful, elite (Crouch 2004). Despite current talk of recession, Canada does not lack for wealth, but the concentration of this wealth in the hands of the few, consequent on the embrace of neoliberal policies, is only fuelling more inequality. Moreover, the spectre of unpredictable and widely fluctuating oil prices and the changing map of oil production in the world make the postdemocratic scenario even more problematic. Much is therefore at stake. We can work to revive the underlying principles of liberal democracy in Canada, or we can allow ourselves to be lulled into complacency by the apparent functionality of the democratic apparatus.

Notes

1 Compared to the United States, income inequality levels in absolute terms are certainly lower in Canada and the rate of change in the top 1 percent is comparable in the two countries. However, in terms of the distribution of income among the various income groups, the rate of change in inequality has been greater in Canada than in the US since the mid-1990s (OECD 2008). Canada's Gini index (measure of inequality) rose from 0.293 in the mid-1990s to 0.320 in the late 2000s. During the same period, the US's Gini index increased from 0.361 to 0.378 (Conference Board of Canada 2011).

2 "The Polity Project: About Polity," *Center for Systemic Peace*, 2014, http://www.systemicpeace.org/polityproject.html. For more information about the Polity IV data sets, see Marshall, Gurr, and Jaggers (2014).

3 This list includes Canada, Mexico, Netherlands, Norway, Singapore, South Korea, the United Kingdom, and the United States (IEA 2014, 11; OPEC 2014, 314–19).

4 The number of lay-offs is mentioned by Vanderbruck (2015) in the context of illustrating the capacity of nonconventional oil companies to use the price free fall as an opportunity for cheaper technology and automation.

5 Despite its headline, "Oil Sands Crude Not as Expensive to Produce as It Used to Be," a *Financial Post* article quotes Jean-Michel Gires, former chief executive officer with the Canadian unit of France's Total SA, stating that bitumen sands-derived crude is still "among the most expensive oil" in the world to produce. The article mentions

that the supply cost (i.e., recovery of costs, plus a 10% return on capital) for bitumen oil projects in the range of US$50 to US$90 per barrel. It is not clear if this estimate takes into account "a history rife with cost overruns on project expansions," often as much as 40 percent above earlier estimates (Lewis 2013).

6 "Tight" oil refers to conventional light oil, with low sulphur content, trapped in unconventional formations of low permeability, often shale or tight sandstone, which requires hydraulic fracturing and/or horizontal well technology for extraction. Shale oil (a type of tight oil) should not be confused with oil shale, which is unconventional oil containing kerogen and is found in deposits closer to the surface than those containing shale oil. Estonia, China, and Brazil are the largest producers of oil shale (WEC 2010, 93).

7 The Merchant Marine Act (also called the Jones Act) of 1920 regulates the maritime transport of cargo between various points in the United States. It is criticized for, among other things, raising the cost of coastal shipping and distorting trade flows (Kemp 2013).

8 See Homi Kharas (2010) for a discussion of the many definitions of the "middle class" and of its political and economic impact, as well as for a quantification of trends in the growth of the middle class in the world.

References

Adam, Karla. 2011. "Occupy Wall Street Protests Go Global." *Washington Post*, 15 October.

Alboudwarej, Hussein, Joao (John) Felix, Shawn Taylor, Rob Badry, Chad Bremner, Brent Brough, Craig Skeates et al. 2006. "Highlighting Heavy Oil." *Oilfield Review* (Summer): 34–53.

Alvarez, Mike, Hose Antonio Cheibub, Fernando Limongi, and Adam Przeworski. 1996. "Classifying Political Regimes." *Studies in Comparative International Development* 31 (2): 3–36.

Beetham, David. 1992. "Liberal Democracy and the Limits of Democratization." *Political Studies* 40 (1): 40–53.

Benhabib, Seyla, ed. 1996. *Democracy and Difference: Contesting the Boundaries of the Political*. Princeton: Princeton University Press.

Bennett, Dean. 2013. "Finance Minister Blames 'Bitumen Bubble' for Alberta's $2.8 Billion Deficit." *National Post*, 27 June.

Berg, Andrew G., and Jonathan D. Ostry. 2011. "Equality and Efficiency." *Finance and Development* 48 (3). http://www.imf.org/external/pubs/ft/fandd/2011/09/berg.htm.

Bexell, Magdalena, and Ulrika Mörth, eds. 2010. *Democracy and Public-Private Partnerships in Global Governance*. Basingstoke, UK: Palgrave Macmillan.

Boas, Taylor C., and Jordan Gans-Morse. 2009. "Neoliberalism: From New Liberal Philosophy to Anti-Liberal Slogan." *Studies in Comparative International Development* 44 (2): 137–61.

Boschini, Anne D., Jan Pettersson, and Jesper Roine. 2007. "Resource Curse or Not: A Question of Appropriability." *Scandinavian Journal of Economics* 109 (3): 593–617.

Brodie, Janine. 2002. "Citizenship and Solidarity: Reflections on the Canadian Way." *Citizenship Studies* 6 (4): 377–94.

British Petroleum. 2014. *BP Energy Outlook 2035.* http://www.bp.com/content/dam/bp/pdf/Energy-economics/Energy-Outlook/Energy_Outlook_2035_booklet.pdf.

Cammack, Paul. 2012. "The G20, the Crisis, and the Rise of Global Developmental Liberalism." *Third World Quarterly* 33 (1): 1–16.

Campanella, David, and Shannon Stunden Bower. 2013. *Taking the Reins: The Case for Slowing Alberta's Bitumen Production.* Edmonton, AB: Parkland Institute.

Campbell, Bruce. 2013. *The Petro-Path Not Taken: Comparing Norway with Canada and Alberta's Management of Petroleum Wealth.* Canadian Centre for Policy Alternatives, Ottawa, ON. https://www.policyalternatives.ca/sites/default/files/uploads/publications/National%20Office/2013/01/Petro%20Path%20Not%20Taken_0.pdf.

Canada. NEB (National Energy Board). 2011a. "Canada's Oil Sands—Opportunities and Challenges to 2015: An Update—Questions and Answers." *National Energy Board.* https://www.neb-one.gc.ca/nrg/sttstc/crdlndptrlmprdct/rprt/archive/pprtntsndchllngs20152006/qapprtntsndchllngs20152006-eng.html.

———. 2011b. Canadian Energy Overview 2010. NEB, Calgary, AB. http://publications.gc.ca/collections/collection_2011/one-neb/NE4-2-9-2011-eng.pdf.

———. 2013a. *Canada's Energy Future 2013: Energy Supply and Demand Projections to 2035.* NEB, Calgary, AB. https://www.neb-one.gc.ca/nrg/ntgrtd/ftr/2013/2013nrgftr-eng.pdf.

———. 2013b. *Canadian Energy Overview 2012.* NEB, Calgary, AB. https://www.neb-one.gc.ca/nrg/ntgrtd/mrkt/vrvw/2012/2012cndnnrgvrvw-eng.pdf.

Canada. NRC (Natural Resources Canada). 2010. "The Importance of Crude Oil." *Natural Resources Canada.* http://www.nrcan.gc.ca/energy/publications/markets/6505?destination=node/1223.

Canadian Press. 2013a. "Energy Sector Key to Economy, Poll Suggests." *CBC News*, 22 November. http://www.cbc.ca/news/business/energy-sector-key-to-economy-poll-suggests-1.2436431.

———. 2013b. "Oil and Gas Ad Campaign Cost Feds $40M at Home and Abroad." *CBC News*, 27 November. http://www.cbc.ca/news/politics/oil-and-gas-ad-campaign-cost-feds-40m-at-home-and-abroad-1.2442844.

———. 2015. "Alberta Premier Jim Prentice to Lobby Washington About Keystone XL Pipeline." *CBC News*, 7 January. http://www.cbc.ca/news/canada/calgary/alberta-premier-jim-prentice-to-lobby-washington-about-keystone-xl-pipeline-1.2892614.

Carothers, Thomas. 2007. "How Democracies Emerge: The 'Sequencing' Fallacy." *Journal of Democracy* 18 (1): 12–27.

Cattaneo, Claudia. 2013. "Canadian Natural Resources' Big Bet on Heavy Oil Is Paying Off." *Financial Post*, 7 November.

CBC News. 2013. "Alberta Accused of Stripping Workers' Rights with New Laws: Province Introduces New Legislation Aimed at Union Activity." *CBC News*, 27 November. http://www.cbc.ca/news/canada/edmonton/alberta-accused-of-stripping-workers-rights-with-new-laws-1.2442969.

Chan, Sylvia. 2002. *Liberalism, Democracy and Development*. Cambridge: Cambridge University Press.

Cheibub, Jose Antonio, Jennifer Gandhi, and James R. Vreeland. 2010. "Democracy and Dictatorship Revisited." *Public Choice* 143 (1–2): 67–101.

Chomsky, Noam. 1999. *Profit over People: Neoliberalism and the Global Order*. New York: Seven Stories Press.

———. 2010. *Hopes and Prospects*. Chicago: Haymarket Books.

Clayton, Blake. 2013. "The Case for Allowing U.S. Crude Oil Exports." Policy Innovation Memorandum no. 34. 8 July. Council on Foreign Relations. http://www.cfr.org/oil/case-allowing-us-crude-oil-exports/p31005.

Conference Board of Canada. 2011. "World Income Inequality: Is the World Becoming More Unequal?" *Conference Board of Canada*. http://www.conferenceboard.ca/hcp/hot-topics/worldinequality.aspx.

———. 2015. "Canadian Income Inequality: Is Canada Becoming More Unequal?" *Conference Board of Canada*. http://www.conferenceboard.ca/hcp/hot-topics/caninequality.aspx.

COSIR (Canadian Oil Sands Industry Review). 2011. "Oil Sands Mining in Canada." *Oil Sands InfoMine*. http://oilsands.infomine.com/commodities/soir/oilsands/.

Cox, Robert W. 1992. "Global Perestroika." In *The Socialist Register 28: New World Order?* edited by Ralph Miliband and Leo Panitch, 26–43. London: Merlin Press.

Crouch, Colin. 2004. *Post-Democracy*. Cambridge, UK: Polity Press.

Cunningham, Frank. 2002. *Theories of Democracy: A Critical Introduction*. London and New York: Routledge.

Davidson, Debra J., and Mike Gismondi. 2011. *Challenging Legitimacy at the Precipice of Energy Calamity*. New York: Springer.

Diamond, Larry. 2008. "The Democratic Rollback: The Resurgence of the Predatory State." *Foreign Affairs* 87 (2): 36–48.

Domhoff, G. William. 2013. *Who Rules America? The Triumph of the Corporate Rich*. 7th ed. New York: McGraw-Hill.

Doorenspleet, Renske. 2000. "Reassessing the Three Waves of Democratization." *World Politics* 52: 384–406.

Drache, Daniel. 2013. "'Rowing and Steering' Our Way Out of the Staples Trap." *The Progressive Economics Forum: Staple Theory @ 50*. http://www.progressive-economics.ca/2013/10/30/staple-theory-50-daniel-drache/.

Dryzek, John. 1996. *Democracy in Capitalist Times: Ideals, Limits, and Struggles*. Oxford: Oxford University Press.

Duménil, Gérard, and Dominique Lévy. 2011. *The Crisis of Neoliberalism*. Cambridge, MA: Harvard University Press.

EIU (Economist Intelligence Unit). 2013. *Democracy Index 2012: Democracy at a Standstill*. EIU, London, UK. https://portoncv.gov.cv/dhub/porton.por_global.open_file?p_doc_id=1034.

Elections Alberta. 2015. "Provincial General Election May 5, 1015: Winning Candidates—Provincial Results." *Elections Alberta.* http://resultsnew.elections.ab.ca/orResultsPGE.cfm.

Epstein, Gerald, ed. 2006. *Financialization and the World Economy.* London: Edward Elgar.

ERCB (Energy Resources Conservation Board). 2008. *Alberta's Energy Reserves 2007: Supply and Demand Outlooks, 2008–2017.* ERCB, Calgary, AB. http://www.aer.ca/documents/sts/ST98/st98-2008.pdf.

Feldman, Noah. 2003. *After Jihad: America and the Struggle for Islamic Democracy.* New York: Farrar, Straus, and Giroux.

Friedman, Milton. 2008. *Milton Friedman on Economics: Selected Papers by Milton Friedman.* Chicago: University of Chicago Press.

G20 (Group of Twenty). 2012. *Boosting Jobs and Living Standards in G20 Countries: A Joint Report by the ILO, OECD, IMF and the World Bank.* Geneva: International Labour Office; Paris: Organisation for Economic Co-operation and Development; Washington, DC: International Monetary Fund; Washington, DC: World Bank.

Gibson, Diana. 2012. *A Social Policy Framework for Alberta: Justice and Fairness for All.* Edmonton, AB: Parkland Institute and Alberta College of Social Workers.

Gill, Stephen. 1998. "New Constitutionalism, Democratisation and Global Political Economy." *Pacifica Review* 10 (1): 23–38.

Gramsci, Antonio. 1971. *Selections from the Prison Notebooks.* New York: International.

Grant, Tavia. 2013. "Canada's Top 1% Take Home 10.6% of Country's Income." *Globe and Mail,* 9 December.

Gylfason, Thorvaldur. 2001. "Natural Resources, Education, and Economic Development." *European Economic Review* 45 (4–6): 847–59.

———. 2006. "Natural Resources and Economic Growth: From Dependence to Diversification." In *Economic Liberalization and Integration Policy: Options for Eastern Europe and Russia,* edited by Harry G. Broadman, Tiiu Paas, and Paul J.J. Welfens, 201–31. Berlin: Springer-Verlag.

Haber, Stephen, and Victor Menaldo. 2011. "Do Natural Resources Fuel Authoritarianism? A Reappraisal of the Resource Curse." *American Political Science Review* 105 (1): 1–26.

Hall, Peter A. , and David Soskice, eds. 2001. *Varieties of Capitalism: The Institutional Foundations of Comparative Advantage.* Oxford: Oxford University Press.

Harrison, Trevor, and Harvey Krahn. 2013. *Governing Alberta: Citizens' Views.* Edmonton, AB: Parkland Institute.

———. 2014. *Less Exclusion, More Engagement: Addressing Declining Voter Turnout in Alberta.* Edmonton, AB: Parkland Institute.

Harvey, David. 2007. *A Brief History of Neoliberalism.* Oxford: Oxford University Press.

Hayek, Fredrick. 1960. *The Constitution of Liberty.* New York: Routledge.

Helleiner, Gerry, ed. 1994. *Trade Policy and Industrialization in Turbulent Times.* London and New York: Routledge.

Herb, Michael. 2005. "No Representation Without Taxation? Rents, Development and Democracy." *Comparative Politics* 37 (3): 297–316.

Hoberg, George. 2014. "Canada: The Overachieving Petro-State." *GreenPolicyProf* (blog), 20 January. http://greenpolicyprof.org/wordpress/?p=952.

Homer-Dixon, Thomas. 2013. "The Tar Sands Disaster." *New York Times*, 31 March.

Howlett, Michael, and Keith Brownsey. 1996. "From Timber to Tourism: The Political Economy of British Columbia." In *Politics, Policy and Government in British Columbia*, edited by R. Kenneth Carty, 18–31. Vancouver: University of British Columbia Press.

Howlett, Michael, and M. Ramesh. 1992. *The Political Economy of Canada: An Introduction*. Toronto: McClelland and Stewart.

Hoxha, Indrit, Sebnem Kalemli-Ozcan, and Dietrich Vollrath. 2009. "How Big Are the Gains from International Financial Integration?" National Bureau of Economic Research Working Paper 14636. http://www.nber.org/papers/w14636.pdf.

Huntington, Samuel. 1991. *The Third Wave: Democratization in the Late Twentieth Century*. Norman: University of Oklahoma Press.

Hutton, Thomas A. 1994. *Visions of a "Post-Staples" Economy: Structural Changes and Adjustment Issues in British Columbia*. Vancouver: Centre for Human Settlement, University of British Columbia.

IEA (International Energy Agency). 2012. "North America Leads Shift in Global Energy Balance, IEA Says in Latest World Energy Outlook." News release, 12 November, London. http://www.iea.org/newsroomandevents/pressreleases/2012/november/north-america-leads-shift-in-global-energy-balance-says-new-world-energy-outlook.html.

———. 2013. *World Energy Outlook 2013*. Paris: OECD/IEA.

———. 2014. *2014 Key World Energy Statistics*. Paris: IEA. http://www.iea.org/publications/freepublications/publication/keyworld2014.pdf.

Innis, Harold. (1930) 1977. *The Fur Trade in Canada: An Introduction to Canadian Economic History*. Rev. ed. Toronto: University of Toronto Press.

Jost, John T. , Christopher M. Federico, and Jaime L. Napier. 2009. "Political Ideology: Its Structure, Functions, and Elective Affinities." *Annual Review of Psychology* 60: 307–37.

Karl, Terry. 1997. *The Paradox of Plenty: Oil Booms and Petro-states*. Berkeley: University of California Press.

———. 2007. "How to Maintain State-Society Relations? The Case for a Transplant Fiscal Social Contract." In *Escaping the Resource Curse: Optimal Strategies and Best Practices for Oil and Gas Exporting Developing Countries*, edited by Macartan Humphreys, Jeffrey Sachs, and Joseph Stiglitz, 274–306. New York: Columbia University Press.

Kemp, John. 2013. "Jones Act Is Set to Stay." *Reuters*, 2 May. http://www.reuters.com/article/2013/05/02/column-kemp-us-shipping-idUSL6N0DJ38A20130502.

Kharas, Homi. 2010. "The Emerging Middle Class in Developing Countries." Working Paper No. 285. Organisation for Economic Co-operation and Development, Paris. http://www.oecd.org/dev/44457738.pdf.

Knight, Kathleen. 2006. "Transformations of the Concept of Ideology in the Twentieth Century." *American Political Science Review* 100 (4): 619–26.

Krippner, Greta R. 2005. "The Financialization of the American Economy." *Socio-economic Review* 3 (2): 173–208.

Krugel, Lauren. 2012. "Alberta's Oil Riches Driving Canada's Economy: BMO." *Financial Post*, 9 October.

Krugman, Paul. N.d. "Inequality and Crisis: Coincidence or Causation." Slide presentation. http://www.princeton.edu/~pkrugman/inequality_crises.pdf.

———. 2007. *The Conscience of a Liberal*. New York: W. W. Norton.

———. 2009. *The Return of Depression Economics and the Crisis of 2008*. New York: W. W. Norton.

Lane, Timothy. 2015. "Drilling Down: Understanding Oil Prices and Their Economic Impact." Bank of Canada presentation at a meeting of the Madison International Trade Association, 13 January, Madison, WI. http://www.bankofcanada.ca/wp-content/uploads/2015/01/remarks-130115.pdf.

Leach, Andrew. 2013a. "Canada, a Petrostate or Not?" *Rescuing the Frog* (blog), 3 September. http://andrewleach.ca/uncategorized/canada-petrostate-or-not/.

———. 2013b. "The Shifting Flow of Oil: Andrew Leach—Oil Flow Change Since 2008." *Canadian Business*, Blogs and Comment, 19 September. http://www.canadianbusiness.com/blogs-and-comment/the-shifting-flow-of-oil/.

Lenard, Patti Tamar, and Richard Simeon, eds. 2012. *Imperfect Democracies: The Democratic Deficit in Canada and the United States*. Vancouver: University of British Columbia Press.

Levitt, Kari Polanyi. 2004. "Independent Thought and Caribbean Community." *Canadian Journal of Development Studies* 25 (92): 225–37.

Lewis, Jeff. 2013. "Oil Sands Crude Not as Expensive to Produce as It Used to Be." *Financial Post*, 19 August.

———. 2015. "Suncor Swings to Loss as Record Output Fails to Offset Weak Oil Prices." *Globe and Mail*, 29 April.

Lichfield, John. 2012. "European Protests Show North-South Discrepancies." *The Independent* (London), 14 November.

Linc Energy. 2013. "Independent Reports Confirm Significant Potential for Linc Energy's Shale Oil in the Arckaringa Basin." Sapex Division, Brisbane, Australia. ASX Announcement, 23 January. http://www.lincenergy.com/data/asxpdf/ASX-LNC-458.pdf.

Lindgren, Karl-Oskar, and Thomas Persson. 2011. *Participatory Governance in the EU: Enhancing or Endangering Democracy and Efficiency?* Basingstoke, UK: Palgrave Macmillan.

Little, Daniel. 2003. *The Paradox of Wealth and Poverty: Mapping the Ethical Dilemmas of Global Development*. Boulder, CO: Westview.

Lowi, Miriam. 2004. "Oil Wealth and Political Breakdown in Algeria." *Journal of North African Studies* 9 (3): 83–102.

Lucas, Robert E., Jr. 1987. *Models of Business Cycles*. New York: Basil Blackwell.

Lye, Chandra. 2013. "Alberta Premier Alison Redford Heading to Washington to Push for Keystone Pipeline." *CTV Edmonton*, 10 November. http://edmonton.ctvnews.ca/alberta-premier-alison-redford-heading-to-washington-to-push-for-keystone-pipeline-1.1536322.

Mackintosh, W. A. 1936. "Some Aspects of a Pioneer Economy." *Canadian Journal of Economics and Political Science* 2 (4): 457–63.

Macpherson, C. B. 1977. *The Life and Times of Liberal Democracy*. Oxford: Oxford University Press.

———. 1985. *The Rise and Fall of Economic Justice, and Other Papers*. Oxford: Oxford University Press.

Madigan, Kathleen. 2011. "Like the Phoenix, U.S. Finance Profits Soar." *Wall Street Journal*, 25 March.

Mahdavy, Hussein. 1970. "The Patterns and Problems of Economic Development in Rentier States: The Case of Iran." In *Studies in the Economic History of the Middle East*, edited by M. A. Cook, 428–67. Oxford: Oxford University Press.

Marsden, William. 2010. *Stupid to the Last Drop: How Alberta Is Bringing Environmental Armageddon to Canada (and Doesn't Seem to Care)*. Toronto: Random House.

Marshall, Monty G. , Ted Robert Gurr, and Keith Jaggers. 2014. *Polity IV Project, Political Regime Characteristics and Transitions, 1800–2013: Dataset Users' Manual*. Center for Systemic Peace, Vienna, VA. http://www.systemicpeace.org/inscr/p4manualv2013.pdf.

Maugeri, Leonardo. 2012. "Oil: The Next Revolution—The Unprecedented Upsurge of Oil Production Capacity and What It Means for the World." The Geopolitics of Energy Project, Discussion Paper 2012-10. Belfer Center for Science and International Affairs, John F. Kennedy School of Government, Harvard University.

———. 2013. "The Shale Oil Boom: A U.S. Phenomenon." The Geopolitics of Energy Project, Discussion Paper 2013-05. Belfer Center for Science and International Affairs, John F. Kennedy School of Government, Harvard University.

Mills, Suzanne, and Brendan Sweeney. 2013. "Employment Relations in the Neostaples Resource Economy: Impact Benefit Agreements and Aboriginal Governance in Canada's Nickel Mining Industry." *Studies in Political Economy* 91 (Spring): 7–33.

Mitchell, Timothy. 2011. *Carbon Democracy: Political Power in the Age of Oil*. New York: Verso Books.

Møller, Jørgen, and Svend-Erik Skaaning. 2013. "The Third Wave: Inside the Numbers." *Journal of Democracy* 24 (4): 97–109.

Moore, Barrington. 2003. *Social Origins of Dictatorship and Democracy: Lord and Peasant in the Making of the Modern World*. Boston: Beacon Press.

Munck, Gerardo L. , and Jay Verkuilen. 2002. "Conceptualizing and Measuring Democracy: Evaluating Alternative Indices." *Comparative Political Studies* 35 (1): 5–34.

Nikiforuk, Andrew. 2010. *Tar Sands: Dirty Oil and the Future of a Continent*. Revised and updated. Vancouver: Greystone Books.

———. 2012. *The Energy of Slaves: Oil and the New Servitude*. Vancouver: Greystone Books.

Norris, Pippa. 2011. *Democratic Deficit: Critical Citizens Revisited*. New York: Cambridge University Press.

OECD (Organisation for Economic Co-operation and Development). 2008. *Growing Unequal? Income Distribution and Poverty in OECD Countries—Summary in English*. OECD Multilingual Summaries. http://www.oecd.org/els/soc/41527936.pdf.

———. 2011. *Divided We Stand: Why Inequality Keeps Rising*. Paris: OECD Publishing.

OPEC (Organization of the Petroleum Exporting Countries). 2014. *World Oil Outlook*. Vienna: OPEC Secretariat.

Plattner, Marc F. 2013. "Reflections on Governance." *Journal of Democracy* 24 (4): 17–28.

Polanyi, Karl. (1944) 2001. *The Great Transformation: The Political and Economic Origins of Our Time*. Boston: Beacon Press.

Posner, Paul L., and Matthew Sommerfeld. 2013. "The Politics of Fiscal Austerity: Democracies and Hard Choices." *OECD Journal on Budgeting* 13 (1): 141–74.

Pratt, Sheila. 2013. "75 Alberta Environment Regulators Now Paid by Oil Industry." *Edmonton Journal*, 23 December.

Puddington, Arch. 2010. "The Freedom House Survey for 2009: The Erosion Accelerates." *Journal of Democracy* 21 (2): 136–50.

Rabson, Mia. 2013. "A Guide to the Idle No More Movement, Treaties, and Legislation." *Winnipeg Free Press*, 26 January.

Rajan, Raghuram G. 2010. "Let Them Eat Credit." *New Republic*, 27 August. http://www.newrepublic.com/article/economy/77242/inequality-recession-credit-crunch-let-them-eat-credit#.

Rapier, Robert. 2012. "Canada Rises and Saudi Arabia Slides: Top 15 Sources for U.S Crude Oil Imports in 2011." *Energy Trends Insider*, 9 April. http://www.consumerenergyreport.com/2012/04/09/canada-rises-and-saudi-slides-top-15-sources-for-u-s-crude-oil-imports-in-2011/.

Ross, Michael Lewin. 2001. "Does Oil Hinder Democracy?" *World Politics* 53 (3): 325–61.

———. 2009. "Oil and Democracy Revisited." Preliminary draft, 2 March. http://www.sscnet.ucla.edu/polisci/faculty/ross/Oil%20and%20Democracy%20Revisited.pdf.

Rosser, Andrew. 2006. "The Political Economy of the Resource Curse: A Literature Survey." Working Paper 268. Centre for the Future State, Institute of Development Studies, University of Sussex, Brighton, UK. http://www.ids.ac.uk/files/WP268.pdf.

Samara. 2012. *Who's the Boss? Canadians' Views on Their Democracy*. Samara Democracy Report No. 4. Samara Canada, Toronto. http://www.macleans.ca/wp-content/uploads/2012/12/Samara_Whos_The_Boss_Final_EN.pdf.

———. 2013. *Lost in Translation, or Just Lost? Canadians' Priorities and the House of Commons*. Samara Democracy Report No. 5. Samara Canada, Toronto. http://www.samaracanada.com/docs/default-document-library/samara_lostintranslation-pdf.

Savoia, Antonio, Joshy Easaw, and Andrew McKay. 2010. "Inequality, Democracy and Institutions: A Critical Review of Recent Research." *World Development* 38 (2): 142–54.

Schmidt, Manfred G. 2002. "Political Performance and Types of Democracy: Findings from Comparative Studies." *European Journal of Political Research* 41 (1): 147–63.

Sen, Amartya Kumar. 1999. "Democracy as a Universal Value." *Journal of Democracy* 10 (4): 2–17.

Shaxson, Nicholas. 2007. *Poisoned Wells: The Dirty Politics of African Oil*. Basingstoke, UK: Palgrave Macmillan.

Shrivastava, Meenal, and Lorna Stefanick. 2012. "Do Oil and Democracy Only Clash in the Global South? Petro Politics in Alberta, Canada." *New Global Studies* 6 (1): article 5. doi:10.1515/1940-0004.1147.

Sieminski, Adam. 2012. *Global Oil Geopolitics*. Presentation by U.S. Energy Information Administration at Rio Oil and Gas Conference, Rio de Janeiro, Brazil, 17 September. http://www.eia.gov/pressroom/presentations/sieminski_09172012.pdf.

Smith, Grant. 2014. "U.S. Seen as Biggest Oil Producer After Overtaking Saudi." *Bloomberg Business*, 4 July. http://www.bloomberg.com/news/articles/2014-07-04/u-s-seen-as-biggest-oil-producer-after-overtaking-saudi.

Stanford, Jim. 2013. "Why Linkages Matter." *The Progressive Economics Forum: The Staple Theory @ 50*. http://www.progressive-economics.ca/2013/12/23/the-staple-theory-50-jim-stanford/.

Taft, Kevin, Melville L. MacMillan, and Junaid Jahangir. 2012. *Follow the Money: Where Is Alberta's Wealth Going?* Calgary: Brush Education.

Tamas, Gaspar. 2011. *Big Ideas: Gaspar Tamas on the Failure of Liberal Democracy*. TVO video. http://ww3.tvo.org/video/167943/gaspar-tamas-failure-liberal-democracy.

Teivainen, Teivo. 2002. *Enter Economism, Exit Politics*. London, UK: Zed Books.

Tertzakian, Peter. 2013. "Oil and Gas Revenue on Track for Second-Best Year." *Globe and Mail*, 28 May.

Tsui, Kevin K. 2011. "More Oil, Less Democracy? Theory and Evidence from Crude Oil Discoveries." *Economic Journal* 121 (551): 89–115.

Tuttle, Robert. 2015. "Canada Crude Falls Below $30 for First Time in Six Years as BMO Warns Oilsands Must Cut Costs." *Financial Post*, 16 March.

USEIA (United States Energy Information Administration). 2012. *Country Analysis Briefs: China*. http://www.eia.gov/countries/analysisbriefs/China/china.pdf.

———. 2015. "Petroleums and Other Liquids: U.S. Exports of Crude Oil." *USEIA: Independent Statistics and Analysis*. http://www.eia.gov/dnav/pet/hist/LeafHandler. ashx?n=PET&s=MCREXUS2&f=M.

Vanderbruck, Tobias. 2015. "Current Oil Prices Create Opportunities." *Oil-Price. Net*, 19 February. http://www.oil-price.net/en/articles/current-oil-prices-create-opportunities.php.

Wahl, Asbjørn. 2011. *The Rise and Fall of the Welfare State*. London: Pluto Press.

Wahl, Asbjørn, and Roy Pedersen. 2013. "The Norwegian National Election: Europe's Most Leftist Government Defeated by Right-Wing Coalition." *Social Europe Journal*, 27 September. http://www.social-europe.eu/2013/09/the-norwegian-national-election-europes-most-leftist-government-defeated-by-right-wing-coalition/?utm_source=dlvr.it&utm_medium=facebook.

Wallerstein, Immanuel. 1995. *After Liberalism*. New York: New Press.

Wantchekon, Leonard. 2002. "Why Do Resource Dependent Countries Have Authoritarian Governments?" *Journal of African Finance and Economic Development* 5 (2): 57–77.

Watkins, Melville H. 1963. "A Staple Theory of Economic Growth." *Canadian Journal of Economics and Political Science* 29 (2): 141–58.

———. 1977. "The Staple Theory Revisited." *Journal of Canadian Studies* 12 (5): 83–95.

———. 2007. "Staples Redux." *Studies in Political Economy* 79 (Spring): 213–26.

WEC (World Energy Council). 2010. *Survey of World Energy Resources*. London: WEC.

Weir, Erin M. K. 2006. "Lies, Damned Lies, and Trade Statistics: The Import Content of Canadian Exports." http://www.progressive-economics.ca/wp-content/uploads/2007/07/WeirImportContent.pdf.

Weiss, Daniel J. , Jackie Weidman, and Rebecca Leber. 2012. "Big Oil's Banner Year: Higher Prices, Record Profits, Less Oil." *Center for American Progress.* http://www.americanprogress.org/issues/green/news/2012/02/07/11145/big-oils-banner-year/.

Wellstead, Adam. 2007. "The (Post) Staples Economy and the (Post) Staples State in Historical Perspective." *Canadian Political Science Review* 1 (1): 8–25.

Wolfson, Michael, Mike Veall, and Neil Brooks. 2014. "Piercing the Veil: Private Corporations and the Income of the Affluent." http://igopp.org/wp-content/uploads/2014/06/wolfson-brooks-veall_-_incomes_of_affluent.pdf.

World Bank. 1992. *Governance and Development.* Washington, DC: World Bank.

Wotherspoon, Terry, and John Hansen. 2013. "The 'Idle No More' Movement: Paradoxes of First Nations Inclusion in the Canadian Context." *Liberello* 1 (1). doi:10.12924/si2013.01010021.

Yalnizyan, Armine. 2010. *The Rise of Canada's Richest 1%.* Ottawa: Canadian Centre for Policy Alternatives.

Petroleum, Politics, and the Limits of Left Progressivism in Alberta

Trevor W. Harrison

Until the election of 5 May 2015, which saw Alberta's left-progressive New Democratic Party elected to office with a majority, Alberta was widely—and not inaccurately—viewed as a conservative province, based on the province's formal political history. This chapter proceeds along two lines of examination to place brackets around this conventional wisdom. The first line traces the history of left progressivism in Alberta. An admittedly vague term, left progressivism, for the purpose of this chapter, is defined as a set of values consistent with social, political, and economic equality; the inseparability of the individual and society; and the necessary subservience of market institutions to the common good. The second line of inquiry highlights the role of specific historical events and socio-economic and political factors in shaping Alberta's political terrain. Specifically, this chapter traces the gradual transition of Alberta from a hub of democratic radicalism, to a quasi-democracy, to a corporatist state, to—as of the recent election—a province and society that has perhaps rediscovered its left-progressive and democratic roots. Ultimately, while stressing the particular problems of democratic governance in a resource-based economy, this chapter also shows that politics matter.

Political Power and Democracy in Resource-Based Economies

Conventional theories of political power, at least in North America and especially in the United States, have long adopted pluralist notions of a largely neutral state—an empty vessel filled with the competing interests of more or less equal social actors. While pluralist theorists recognize the greater influence of business, they argue that no one actor holds sufficient power to overwhelm all the others, thus creating a system of checks and balances (Neuman 2005, 86–89).

Pluralist theory has many critics (Orum and Dale 2009, 121–25). It is especially inadequate in describing the situation of single-resource economies. Consider for the moment company towns, where single industries often dominate the lives of citizens economically, politically, and culturally and where class relations are often felt as much as observed. The same is true, although at a larger scale and more opaquely, for states and provinces in which a single resource holds sway. A large body of scholarship going back to Harold Innis's work of the 1920s and 1930s argues that dependence upon a single industry such as fishing, mining, forestry, or agriculture has impacts that go beyond the economy to include social and political relations.[1]

Oil appears to be just another staple resource. Except that it isn't. There is something quite distinct about oil: it is, quite simply, the energy source that has made the modern industrial (and post-industrial) age possible. People can substitute salmon for cod, or rice for wheat. They can substitute, in terms of building materials, wood for brick or straw for wood. But, as yet, there is no obvious or effective substitute for petroleum as the energy source for civil and military transport, for industrial production, or for the day-to-day uses of private homes and public buildings.

This ubiquitous demand for oil means that its suppliers have enormous market and political power, as evidenced when OPEC decides to raise or lower prices. But the power of oil goes beyond that of monopoly control of the market. It is also political. Andrew Nikiforuk (2010, 172), a long-time critic of energy and environmental policy in Alberta, argues that the price of oil is negatively correlated with the quality of freedom. He cites Michael Ross (2001), who notes three ways in which oil impacts democracy: oil royalties, because they are used to lower taxes, sever the connection between citizenship and political accountability (i.e., no taxes = no representation); oil wealth creates a system of patronage; and oil wealth provides the state with a means of organized repression when patronage fails.

Many critics use observations such as these to argue that Alberta is a petro-state, as discussed in the first chapter of this book. Whether or not such a description is accurate, certain questions need to be asked: What has been the state of democracy in Alberta? What role has petroleum played within it? And which roads have been taken—or abandoned—in getting the province to where it is today? In this chapter, I seek answers to these questions, beginning with a brief historical review.

Left Progressivism in Early Alberta

At first glance, Alberta's inception as a province in 1905 seemed favourable for left-wing politics. Created under Canada's National Policy as a colony of central Canadian industrialists, Alberta contained a ready-made class of agrarians with legitimate gripes against big business (e.g., grain companies and the CPR) and eastern bankers. Alberta's economy also featured a number of extraction industries, especially mining, where the diverging interests of labour and capital were too often evidenced, as in June 1914, for example, when the town of Hillcrest suffered the largest mining disaster in Canadian history, killing 189 workers. Finally, Alberta—like much of the prairies—featured a difficult and precarious climate that encouraged collective solutions.

Indeed, left progressive forces were successful during Alberta's early decades. Amidst declining grain prices at the end of the First World War, the United Farmers of Alberta (UFA) formed government, one of a series of so-called farmers' parties elected throughout Canada at the time.[2] Alberta's labour movement, though small, also made itself known in the growing cities of Edmonton and Calgary and in resource-based towns throughout the province. The late 1920s also witnessed a major victory for women's equality when five Alberta women won the battle to have women recognized as "persons" under the law.

The material conditions for left-wing success accelerated during the Great Depression of the 1930s. Against a backdrop of growing human misery, strikes and marches ensued, often turning violent. As the middle ground disappeared and unregulated capitalism was discredited, some people turned to right-wing solutions to the crisis, but many more turned to the left. In the mid-1930s, the coal-mining town of Blairmore elected a Communist town council. During the same period, Alberta also witnessed the founding of two populist parties, the Co-operative Commonwealth Federation (CCF), begun in Calgary in 1932, and the Social Credit Party, founded in 1935 and soon thereafter, forming government.

In their infancy, the CCF and Social Credit shared common left-wing credentials. Though the former was more avowedly socialist, the latter—supported by small independent farmers, townspeople, and workers—also regularly championed some very progressive and anti-corporatist views, including toying with the idea of nationalizing key industries (Barr 1974, 83–119; Finkel 1989, 88). Quickly, however, the Social Credit, and the province, veered politically to the right. What happened?

The Early Roots of Alberta's Political Culture

Alberta is unique in Canada for having been governed by a series of political dynasties: the Liberals (1905–21), the United Farmers of Alberta (1921–35), the Social Credit (1935–71), the Progressive Conservatives (1971–2015), and today, the New Democrats. The province has never had a minority government; indeed, through most of Alberta's history, the ruling party has faced minimal opposition in the legislature. There are several possible reasons for what C. B. Macpherson (1953) described as Alberta's "quasi-party system," but the impact of populism provides a starting point.

It is impossible to overstate populism's importance to Alberta's political culture.[3] But what exactly is populism? I use the term populism to refer to an urgent and personal appeal by a leader to a mass audience, "the people," an imagined group defined by its historic, geographic, and/or cultural roots and threatened by a crisis emanating from another loosely defined group, a "power bloc" made up of elites and other elements viewed as physically or culturally external to "the people" (Harrison 2000, 108). But populism can occur any-where on the left-right continuum. In fact, during the early stages of Alberta's political development, two left-wing political activists, Henry Wise Wood and William Irvine, espoused populist ideals. Missouri-born Wise Wood was a keen observer of American populism. After relocating to Canada in 1905, he joined a farmers' organization. In 1914, he became the UFA's director and, soon after, its vice-president and then president. At the time, the UFA was under growing pressure to formally enter the political arena. Much of this pressure came from the Non-Partisan League (NPL), whose founders included Irvine, a Scottish-born Christian Socialist who had moved to Canada in 1907. In the provincial election of 1917, the NPL elected two candidates on a platform that joined social-ist policies of intervention in the economy with a belief in nonparty politics, a success that proved to many UFA supporters the efficacy of electoral politics (Monto 1989, 13; see also Mardiros 1979).

Though both men were populists inspired by the beliefs and values of the Social Gospel movement, Wise Wood and Irvine viewed politics differently. Wise Wood believed that society necessarily involved a conflict between differ-ent economic interests and that all should be represented within government, a notion he referred to as "group government." But he wanted the UFA to remain primarily a pressure group—and not a party—made up of farmers, while Irvine favoured a broader political movement, embracing farmers and workers alike. Additionally, Wise Wood firmly rejected the NPL constitution, which was radically socialist, endorsing "government ownership and control of all natural resources and fundamental industries," including "banks, flour mills, packing houses, and Crown lands" (Monto 1989, 14).

In the end, the UFA did opt for a formal political role, resulting in its winning the Alberta election of 1921. Wise Wood was successful in restricting UFA membership to farmers and in sidelining the NPL's more radical, socialist agenda, but his emphasis on group government, combined with the NPL's antiparty stance, also had a more long-term impact: it led to a political culture within Alberta that largely eschews competitive party politics. Political conflict, rather than occurring between parties, takes place between factions operating within the governing party tent. It is a system that enforces conformity: anyone who refuses to get inside the tent is ostracized. Such persons are outsiders. Ironically, the tradition of non-party politics emerged, in large part, out of left progressive ideas.

Two other characteristics emerged out of Alberta's early years that influenced the province's political culture in the long term. The first is a tradition of strong, sometimes charismatic, leadership. It is significant that the only times since 1935 when the dominance of Alberta's governing party has been threatened is when their leadership appeared weak, indecisive, out of touch with the people, or corrupt.

The second characteristic is a tendency to seek technocratic solutions for what are essentially political and social problems. By the early twentieth century, North America was awash in efforts to apply scientific principles to improve society, one prime example of which is the theory of social credit. Social credit theory (also referred to as the A + B theorem) suggested that economic problems were amenable to technocratic solutions applied by technocratic experts (Bell 1993, 37–60). The Social Credit's leader in Alberta, the Reverend William Aberhart, did not understand the theory any better than his followers did, but, as he famously told them, they did not have to understand social credit theory any more than they had to understand how electricity worked (Barr 1974, 84). They simply had to flip the switch—that is, vote for Social Credit—in order for their economic problems to be solved. In an admittedly contradictory fashion, the belief that there was "one right answer" that could be supplied by experts was at once deferential to elites and anti-intellectual in regard to those disciplines that did not offer ostensibly scientific solutions (i.e. , the social sciences and humanities).

These early influences continue to be constant and perennial elements of Alberta's political culture: appeals to populism; the insistence that there are no fundamental social differences, or bases for conflict, between people (see Flanagan 1995, 34, on "monism"); and the belief that any problems are amenable to technocratic solutions.[4] None of these elements necessarily originated in right-wing politics. Indeed, many elements in Alberta's early political culture—opposition to party discipline and to control by financial interests, for example—had left-wing support. Yet, in time, these same elements coalesced around a one-party corporatist state wedded to a single dominant industrial sector based in petroleum (Harrison 1995). How did this come about?

Oil and the Social Credit's Rentier Government

Why did Alberta elect a right-wing Social Credit government while Saskatchewan, only a few years later, turned to the socialist Co-operative Commonwealth Federation? This question, which has vexed observers for decades, has several not incompatible answers. Howard Leeson (1992, 11–12) argues the CCF's close association with the UFA "tainted" the CCF party brand in Alberta (see also Finkel 2012). He further contends that the CCF was damaged by infighting between those who wanted power and those who demanded ideological purity—a conflict not uncommon to left-wing movements everywhere, even today.

One popular explanation holds that different early settlement patterns divided the two provinces politically: that southern Alberta was primarily settled by arrivals from the United States, exemplars of Frederick Jackson Turner's "frontier thesis," who carried in their saddlebags a mix of egalitarian, democratic, and individualist values, while, by contrast, Saskatchewan and northern and central Alberta were settled by European immigrants who brought with them class-based orientations to politics (Wiseman 2007).

Another explanation, grounded in political economy, traces the provinces' distinctive politics to differences in their primary economic activities (Brym 1978). Farming, the basis of Saskatchewan's early economy, is an activity commensurate with cooperative action, but ranching, Alberta's economic base, is an enterprise that accentuates competitiveness and individualism.

Finally, the element of religion is worth considering: specifically, that the distinctive political orientations of the two provinces express different articulations of religious belief. The influence of the Social Gospel movement on Wise Wood and Irvine has already been noted. The CCF's leadership in Saskatchewan and Manitoba, Tommy Douglas and J. S. Woodsworth, also came out of this tradition, which emphasized the role of creating a heaven on earth. By contrast, the Social Credit's leadership—William Aberhart and his disciple, Ernest Manning—belonged to an evangelical tradition that had originated in the United States and that emphasized personal salvation through struggle and spiritual rewards in the hereafter.

Still, which populist form—left or right—would come to dominate was not immediately determined. When Aberhart died in 1943, Alberta's economic circumstances were not much different from those of neighbouring Saskatchewan, a province that only one year later elected Douglas's CCF. By this time, the Social Credit's policy agenda was in tatters, the federal cabinet and the Supreme Court having long since disallowed much of what the party had set out to do politically (Conway 1994, 122).[5] The CCF, however, seemed on the rise, as shown in electoral outcomes of the period.

In 1942, Elmer Roper, running for the CCF, won a provincial by-election in Edmonton. Roper—who somewhat later became Edmonton's mayor—subsequently led the party into the 1944 election, and the CCF gained nearly a quarter of the vote but only two seats; the first-past-the-post electoral system combined with rural overrepresentation worked to the disadvantage of a left progressive alternative.

Two other factors also played an important role in blunting left progressivism in Alberta. The first was the Cold War, beginning after 1945. Ernest Manning did not coin the term "Godless Communism," but he certainly promoted fears of it to great effect through his weekly religious broadcasts. For Manning, Marxism, communism, socialism, and even liberalism shared the common sin of leading individuals away from their spiritual rebirth. The second factor was the discovery of oil at Leduc, just south of Edmonton, in 1947. Since 1930, the provincial governments of Alberta and Saskatchewan had owned the mineral rights under the topsoil. But, as luck would have it, under Alberta's turf lay an abundance of conventional petroleum deposits, while Saskatchewan was home to only a trickle of oil along the shared border. What might Alberta and Canada look like today had the CCF been in power in Alberta when oil was discovered? Might Alberta have developed its own oil as a national resource? It is intriguing to speculate.

Instead, Alberta—headed by a conservative, business-oriented Social Credit government—opted to allow foreign (mainly American) oil companies to locate and extract the oil in return for three types of revenue: deposits on exploration, bids on drilling rights, and production royalties (Barr 1974, 139–43). In effect, Manning's government took a rentier approach to the development of the province's oil resources, renting the resources to external clients and using the new revenues to entrench its own political power.

By the mid-1960s, Alberta had become—as Robin Mathews (1966) described in an early article in Canadian Dimension—a largely one-party, totalitarian state, buttressed by a corporatist relationship between government and business, aided and abetted by a compliant media. Dissent was systematically squelched; worse, its suppression was internalized. Edmonton was the lone significant site for left-progressive resistance, its standard bearer being the CCF-NDP and its union affiliates—who, during this period, gave the party a tougher, more political edge—along with a few academics from the University of Alberta and liberal-minded church leaders.[6] Edmonton was a lone beachhead, however. Power remained with an entrenched, politically and ideologically conservative and rural elite. Predictably, when the Social Credit was defeated, it came not from left progressive forces but from a new segment of the capitalist class itself, located in Alberta's other major city, Calgary.

Lougheed's Bourgeois Revolution

By 1968, oil had changed Alberta in noticeable ways. Though it was still a have-not province, its economic circumstances were improving. Moreover, it was becoming increasingly urbanized. The signs of change were particularly evident in Calgary where—despite the strong presence of American capital, expertise, and ideology—a new indigenous class of entrepreneurs arose. Its leader was Peter Lougheed, a former Edmonton Eskimo and a lawyer with deep family ties to the province and personal ties to Alberta's corporate community. In 1971, as leader of the Progressive Conservatives, Lougheed defeated the Socreds, ending one era of single-party dominance and beginning another.

In politics, as in life generally, being in the right place at the right time is important. Alberta's economy had long been dependent on conventional oil production, but by the late 1960s, technological developments had made extracting oil from the province's northern oil sands feasible. In 1967, the Great Canadian Oil Sands project started up, and the small locale of Fort McMurray/Waterways began its boom. This was followed by the construction of the Syncrude plant north of Fort McMurray in 1973—the same year the OPEC crisis drove the price of oil to new heights, signalling profound changes in the world economy.

The Lougheed PC's coming to power coincided with the rise of activist provincial governments across Canada who engaged directly in developing their own resources. Often, these resources were located in the northern reaches: hydro in Québec, Manitoba, and British Columbia, uranium in Saskatchewan— and oil in Alberta. To many, Lougheed represented a new breed of politician: young, urbane, and, at least in terms of provincial rights, a nationalist. Indeed, to some on the Left, Lougheed appeared to be an economic nationalist who would use the powers of the state to develop Alberta's oil riches for all citizens and—as he promised—to diversify the province's economy away from resource dependency.

As economist Ed Shaffer (1979) argued, however, the Lougheed government's rise to power signalled not a genuine revolution but the rise of a new class, an indigenous "industrial bourgeoisie" that merely wanted its cut of the petroleum spoils and used the state for these ends. While the Lougheed government set royalty rates high compared to subsequent Alberta governments (Campanella 2012), it did not challenge the right of private capital—foreign or otherwise—to develop the province's oil. The closest it came to doing so was with the creation in the early 1970s of the Alberta Energy Company, which, while organized by the Alberta government, was operated by nongovernment personnel on a for-profit basis.

By contrast, in 1973, Saskatchewan's NDP government, headed by Allan Blakeney, created a Crown corporation, Sask Oil. Though later privatized by a Conservative government, Sask Oil during its time provided a positive contrast to the approach taken by Alberta's PCs, as related by John Warnock (2012): "By 1981 Sask Oil had assets of \$191-million, gross revenues of \$60-million, and paid \$26-million in royalties to the government. The Blakeney government also raised the oil royalties significantly. The share of the economic rent (excess profits) going to the general population rose from 13 per cent in 1972 to reach a high of 65 per cent in 1982." A left progressive government in Alberta might have followed a similar path, using the profits from petroleum to spur broader social and economic development—indeed, to further democratic participation more generally. But the Lougheed government did not do this.

When Lougheed stepped down as premier in 1985, Alberta's economy was well on its way to being economically dependent on oil. The consequences of putting all of the province's economic eggs in one basket were not long in coming, as Ed Shaffer had warned presciently in 1979: "It is certain that this industrialization will have all the evils associated with capitalist development—boom and bust, over-expansion in some sectors, under-expansion in others, urban blight and the degradation of the environment. The benefits will accrue to the new ruling class while the relative position of the workers, farmers and small businessmen will continue to decline" (45).

Alberta's rapid and intense growth throughout the 1970s depended on a continued rise in the price of oil. But, as with all staple products, its price was set on the world market, over which Alberta had no control. In early 1979, the Shah of Iran was deposed, setting the stage for another surge in world oil prices. At first, this seemed a boon to Alberta, but as quickly as the price of oil had risen, it also fell. The result was starkly negative for Alberta. The planned expansion of the oil sands stopped abruptly and conventional oil drilling was scaled back. With few other significant industries to fall back upon, Alberta's economy and its people faced hard times. Laid-off workers either left the province or sought unemployment insurance, many of them walking away from mortgaged homes whose value had dropped dramatically. Food bank use proliferated and social services costs increased, even as government revenues dropped sharply.

Predictably, the collapse of oil prices in the early 1980s set in motion a series of conflicts between Alberta's capitalist state and specific groups within Alberta as well as the federal government. Over the next few years, Alberta experienced labour unrest in both the public and private sectors, highlighted by the bitter and violent Gainers meat-packing plant strike in Edmonton in 1986. As efforts at diversification and development pushed further into Alberta's north, conflict with the province's traditional Aboriginal communities also intensified, and environmental concerns moved to the forefront of political debate.[7]

Throughout 1983 and 1984, Alberta's economy languished, leading to Lougheed's resignation and replacement as premier by Don Getty in early 1985. It seemed an auspicious moment for Alberta's democratic Left to make a breakthrough, but fate intervened. On 19 October 1984, a plane carrying NDP leader Grant Notley crashed in northern Alberta, killing him and five others. Though he was the NDP's lone legislative member, Notley was highly respected by all parties and many Albertans. As the title to Howard Leeson's 1992 book suggests, Notley was "the social conscience of Alberta."

What might have happened had Notley not met his untimely death? We will never know. But two years later, under its new leader, Ray Martin, the NDP captured sixteen seats and 29 percent of the vote, while the Liberals took four seats and 12 percent of the vote. The collapse of the Progressive Conservative Party's program of state capitalism continued in 1989, when the NDP captured sixteen seats and 26 percent of the vote and the upstart Liberals took eight seats and nearly 29 percent of the vote.

Alberta's economy continued to slide. Efforts to stimulate the economy through subsidies to the private sector proved ineffective. Government investments went poorly, with some enterprises in which the government had a stake going bankrupt. A whiff of scandal ensued. Politically, the provincial government also faced pressure from Preston Manning's nascent federal Reform Party, which had major support in Alberta, to lower taxes, cut government spending, and bring in balanced budgets. Ironically, the NDP suffered political damage from the Conservative government's practice of state capitalism, which many Albertans wrongly associated with socialism.

Facing declining poll numbers, Premier Don Getty announced in the fall of 1992 that he was resigning. Thus ended, for a time, Alberta's experiment in government-led economic development. In tandem with the Canada-US Free Trade Agreement of 1989, the result was the abandonment by Alberta's bourgeoisie of hopes for autochthonous development; instead, the province threw its fate in with its larger, corporate North American counterparts and the neoliberal agenda of laissez-faire capitalism. Low in the polls, the Progressive Conservative Party cast its net in search of new ideas and, more importantly, a new leader. In Ralph Klein—a former television reporter, Calgary mayor, and all around "man of the people"—the party found a champion around which to repackage its image.

The Klein Era and the Rebuilding of the Progressive Left

The spring election of 1993 was a standoff between the Klein-led PCs and the Alberta Liberals, led by Edmonton's former mayor, Laurence Decore. In fact, there was little difference between the two parties.[8] Both coalesced around a single definition of the problem: a debt crisis for which there was a set of particular solutions—deregulation, privatization, lower taxes, and cuts to government programs. The New Democratic Party was shut out of seats, and the voices of the progressive Left was nearly drowned out entirely.

Over the next few years, Alberta reverted to its authoritarian impulses. Verbal attacks on those referred to as "special interests"—such as union members, environmentalists, academics, and feminists (Harrison, Johnston, and

Krahn 2005)—combined with drastic cuts in spending to public services and a messianic zeal for privatization and deregulation became the order of the day. In the broader picture, the Klein years saw the final stage of Alberta's transition to being a right-wing corporatist state in which the interests of the state align with those of private corporations (Harrison 1995).

At the same time, however, the actions of the Klein government—and, more broadly, the neoliberal project everywhere—created the conditions for the emergence of its own opposition. As before, much of the opposition arose in Edmonton, the government centre and the site where many of the spending cuts had their greatest effect. The opposition involved not only those in the public sector, however, but also private sector unions under the umbrella of the Alberta Federation of Labour (AFL); a few courageous journalists; many professional organizations, such as the Alberta Teacher's Association (ATA), the United Nurses of Alberta (UNA), and the Alberta College of Social Workers (ACSW); and some members of the academic community. Public protests— marches in the streets and pickets at the legislative building—became common events.

Alberta's political culture was influenced at the time by externally based left-progressive organizations, such as the Canadian Centre for Policy Alternatives and the Council of Canadians, founded in 1980 and 1985, respectively, and both headquartered in Ottawa. In Alberta, the decade prior to Klein's arrival saw the founding, in 1985, of the Pembina Institute, an organization that conducts research on energy and environmental issues and remains a vital source of information. The advent of Klein had the effect of reinvigorating existing left-progressive organizations in Alberta, such as Friends of Medicare, founded in 1979, which became a central player in battling efforts to introduce private health care into the province, thereby creating a two-tier system. The actions of the Klein government also gave birth to new movements and organizations.

Among these, the case of Parkland Institute is particularly instructive. Out of a coalescing of opposition forces, *The Trojan Horse: Alberta and the Future of Canada* was published in 1995 and launched at a conference held at the University of Alberta. Co-edited by Gordon Laxer and me, the book merged academic and non-academic authors, political theorists and social activists, in a critical examination of what was going on in Alberta at the time and how those happenings were relevant to larger changes within Canada and the world. The book and conference led to Parkland's founding in 1996. The institute soon published a seminal text in the history of critical thought in Alberta—Kevin Taft's

(1997) *Shredding the Public Interest*. The book detailed unflinchingly the Klein government's deceptive depiction of Alberta as facing a fiscal crisis based on social spending. It sold over twenty thousand copies, making it a publishing success. In addition, the Progressive Conservatives' hostile response to the book ensured its political success and quickly put Taft and Parkland on the political map. Today, the institute remains a centre of critical left-progressive thought within Alberta.

In time, as opposition to the government's neoliberal agenda grew, other organizations also entered the contest of ideas, one of them being Public Interest Alberta, a nonprofit, nonpartisan, province-wide organization dedicated to education and advocacy that was founded in 2004. Yet despite these eruptions at the level of civil society, the Progressive Conservative Party and its neoliberal policies maintain their stranglehold on Alberta politics. Why is this the case?

The Contradictions of Oil Wealth

To briefly recapitulate, when Peter Lougheed and the PCs came to power in 1971, they had one manifest purpose—to grow and diversify Alberta's economy—and one more latent aim—to act in the role of patron for Alberta's nascent bourgeoisie who, at the time, wanted to garner more of the spoils of the developing oil and gas economy. In the end, the ruling PCs failed on both counts. The recession of the early 1980s, combined with the rise of neoliberal globalization, squeezed out Alberta's indigenous capitalist class, which was quickly replaced at the top of the food chain by large international petroleum companies and their directors. At the same time, Alberta's economy became increasingly dependent, both directly and indirectly, upon the petroleum industry.

At the political level, the Progressive Conservatives assured their political support by keeping taxes low, relying instead on royalties to fund the kind of programs (health, education, and social services) that established their legitimacy with the electorate. But the governing party itself, through a lax system of political contributions, also became increasingly captive to the petroleum industry and its demand that royalty rates be kept low. As a consequence, because the government was unwilling to raise either general taxes or resource royalties, its policy options became limited, even as Alberta's economic expansion required increased spending—even, moreover, as the uncertainties of oil markets made reliance upon royalties alone untenable.

The government after 1993 dealt with these contradictions (and the recurrent fiscal crises) in two ways: first, by ramping up development of the Athabasca oil sands so that, although royalty rates remained low, production levels—and hence the government's total take—increased, and second, by keeping a tight rein on government expenditures. But these two tactics did not resolve the contradictions; they merely altered their form. Increased production meant additional costs in the forms of heightened inflation, higher infrastructure costs, and escalating environmental damage. The accelerating economy also required additional social expenditures (e.g. , health care, education, social services) to service a growing population, although spending was kept low relative to the growing size of the economy (Taft 1997, 2012). Finally, increased production also intensified the impact of unstable oil revenues on the funding of government programs.

Amidst a growing crisis of legitimacy, Ralph Klein left office in 2006 and was replaced as premier by a rural MLA, Ed Stelmach. Stelmach's victory was unexpected since he defeated the perceived front-runner Jim Dinning, a Calgary-based former Alberta Finance minister and a favourite of the oil companies. During his leadership run, Stelmach had announced his support for higher royalty rates, and, true to his word, the following spring, he created the Royalty Review Panel to examine Alberta's oil royalties. The panel's subsequent report, released in September 2007, recommended a rate increase. This recommendation was attacked immediately—by the industry as being too aggressive and by others as being too timid. In the end, the Conservative government chose to adopt an increase smaller than that recommended by the panel and phased in over a longer period of time.[9]

Unfortunately for Stelmach and his supporters, the Great Recession had begun. Although Alberta seemed at first immune to the growing crisis, a resultant drop in global oil consumption soon led to a drop in Alberta's revenues. After years of surpluses, Stelmach's Tories announced in the spring of 2009 that the province would run a record deficit for the year. The deficit opened up divisions between the PC party's fiscal hawks and its Red Tory faction. At the same time, the raise in royalty rates, albeit modest, caused the petroleum industry to seek out a new political partner, quickly finding one in an embryonic political party, the Wildrose Alliance Party of Alberta.

Wildrose was formed in January 2008 from the merger of two small conservative parties, the Wildrose Party of Alberta (founded in 2007) and the

Alberta Alliance Party (founded in 2003). Both of these parties had strong connections to the earlier right-wing populist Social Credit and Reform parties.

The Wildrose iteration gained political traction in the spring of 2009 from the growing deficit, divisions within the governing party, and pressures from the oil industry. The party received a further boost, in September 2009, when Danielle Smith was elected as its leader. Smith is a media-savvy populist with a libertarian streak, a graduate of the Calgary School of conservative thought and a former Fraser Institute intern. Measured against Stelmach's less than charismatic personality, Smith definitely came out ahead. Over the next year, the Wildrose Alliance Party's membership and donations soared, much of the latter coming directly from the oil and gas industry. Faced with declining poll numbers and growing dissent within his party, Stelmach announced in January 2011 that he would step down as premier, staying only until a new leader was in place.

In October 2011, Alison Redford, a former human rights lawyer widely viewed as a Red Tory, became Alberta's premier. In April 2012, Redford led the PCs to electoral victory, taking sixty-one of the eighty-seven seats and defeating the nearest competitor, the Wildrose Alliance, which took seventeen seats and became Alberta's official opposition.

But victory did not address Alberta's continuing budget problems brought about in part by changes in the global politics of petroleum. First, environmental concerns tied to climate change can no longer be politically ignored. Second, new discoveries of oil and gas in the United States mean a possible decrease in demand from Alberta's major buyer at the same time as a glut of available oil worldwide has decreased the price of oil. And while demand from newly developing economies, notably China, could offset this loss, Alberta's previous efforts to deal with its economic contradictions have created a third difficulty: a misalignment among the supply of bitumen, the province's capacity to turn this raw product into usable oil, and the means of getting either bitumen or refined oil to market. This mismatch has intensified the politics in recent years surrounding pipelines designed primarily to ship raw bitumen to refineries in the American south or to China, politics in which the Alberta government has found a strident supporter in the current Conservative-led government in Ottawa. An obvious solution to the lack of pipeline capacity was to decrease production overall, while increasing royalty rates, and to build refinery capacity in Alberta. But this would have required that the PC government face up to the contradictions embedded in the province's political economy and stand up to the power of the petroleum industry. These actions, in turn, would have confronted Alberta's democratic deficit, to which the dominance of petroleum has contributed. The PCs, having become a captive of the petroleum industry, lacked the relative autonomy by which to save itself. The political space for a left-progressive revival slowly took shape.

Alberta's 2015 Election: This Changes Everything

Until the recent 2015 election, Alberta seemed a paradigmatic case of an ostensibly liberal, authoritarian, and corporatist state: liberal in its adoption of laissez-faire economics, minimalist democracy (i.e., restricted to voting), and respect for human and political rights; authoritarian in its practice of controlling information, buying off supporters, and threatening opponents; and corporatist in its almost seamless merging of state and party, social institutions, and the interests of the oil industry (see Stefanick, chapter 14, this volume).

The problem went even deeper, however. It was not just the Alberta state that lacked relative autonomy from the petroleum industry; the same was true of many Albertans who had grown dependent, psychologically as well as economically, upon the petroleum industry for their well-being and sense of identity. Many oil workers in Alberta earn enough money to be safely placed within the top 1 percent of income earners, making them unlikely recruits for a proletarian revolution; hence, also, many Albertans, tied either directly or indirectly to the industry, tend to go to the barricades to defend the oil companies when there is any sign of criticism from outside the province or, indeed, from internal naysayers.

This kind of enforced conformity and defensiveness does not elicit political enthusiasm. Albertans, when asked about politics, routinely expressed high degrees of alienation, cynicism, and apathy (Johnston, Krahn, and Harrison 2006, 165–82), with the result that electoral turnout steadily declined after Klein's victory in 1993 (just over 40% in 2008 before rebounding in 2012 to just over 50%). While voting has declined across many Western democracies, it is particularly pronounced in Alberta and is a pattern specifically found in petro-states (Nikiforuk 2010). Thus, the most deleterious impact of Alberta's oil wealth has not only been on its economy but also, until May 2015, on the health of its democracy.

In the spring of 2014, Premier Redford resigned. Her personal poll numbers were low, partly due to a series of scandals. More broadly, however, an austerity budget brought out the previous spring had alienated the progressive base that helped her get elected in 2012. Once again, an unwillingness and inability to free itself from its corporate masters put the governing party in jeopardy, with added pressure coming from the Wildrose Party on the right.

In an effort to save itself, the PC party's brain trust recruited Jim Prentice to run for the leadership. Prentice is a former Alberta MP and federal cabinet minister, and former senior vice-president with the Canadian Imperial Bank of Commerce, from which (after winning the leadership) he stepped down in September 2014. From the outside, the PC party seemed unbeatable, possessors of enormous financial resources, the levers of state, and tradition. But, after forty-three years in power, its social base was small and aging, and the party was out of touch with the changes occurring in Alberta society.

The party faced accumulating hostility from both the Left and Right, hostility that soon intensified. The floor-crossing of (ultimately) eleven members of the Wildrose Party (including its leader, Danielle Smith) to the PCs in the fall of 2014 in order to "unite the Right" at a time of falling oil prices seemed to some, at the time, a master stroke. In fact, it hardened the dislike of Wildrose supporters for the PCs, while also further alienating progressives. The discontent grew stronger when the Prentice government brought in a budget in spring 2015 that raised taxes for nearly everyone—except, notably, the corporations—at the same time as Prentice publicly rejected any thought of reviewing Alberta's royalty structure.

Heedless of all warning signs, Prentice called an election, believing there was no legitimate political alternative to which Albertans might turn. But alternatives did exist, particularly that of the New Democratic Party. In the fall of 2014, the party had elected a new leader, Rachel Notley, the daughter of Grant Notley. Rachel Notley is a lawyer who was first elected to the legislature in 2008. As the election went on, Albertans came to see in her a genuine leader whose voice echoed earlier populist traditions, a leader whose vision suggests a way forward beyond the uncertainties and contradictions of the petro-economy to a restored practice of genuine democracy.

When the votes were counted on 5 May 2015, the NDs had won over fifty seats with 41 percent of the vote; the Wildrose party had re-established itself under a new leader, Brian Jean, taking 21 seats; and the PCs had fallen to eleven seats. Although Prentice was re-elected in the Calgary Foothills district, he resigned immediately as PC leader and also gave up his seat in the legislature. After almost forty-four years, PC rule was ended.

Today, as this book goes to press, Alberta has embarked on a fundamental political change, the outcome of which cannot be predicted. But for the first time in a long while, there is hope. Politics, as the 2015 Alberta election proved, makes a difference—even in a petro-dominated, resource-based economy.

Notes

1 For a summary of staples theory, see "Innis: Staples Theory," Library and Archives Canada, 2007, http://www.collectionscanada.gc.ca/innis-mcluhan/030003-1020-e. html.
2 The United Farmers of Ontario were elected in 1919, and the United Farmers of Manitoba in 1922. In the federal election of 1921, the National Progressives, support primarily by farmers, gained sixty-five seats, the second most in the House of Commons.
3 The term political culture has many meanings and is somewhat contentious. My use of the term refers not only to political norms but also to those material forces, especially as possessed by the state (through voice, control of information, laws, policies and programs, and the public purse), that shape values and beliefs. In short, I argue that norms are not free-floating but are materially produced under circumstances of power and contestation (Harrison 2011).
4 It is worth noting that Preston Manning, in his early training, applied a systems approach to analyzing social and political problems. Indeed, Manning's style of leadership has been widely described as technocratic (e.g. , Harrison 2000; 111).
5 Of course, disallowance was also useful to the Social Credit in proving the threat to Alberta posed by external power blocs—in this case, the federal government. Likewise, the National Energy Program of the 1980s would prove to be immensely beneficial in mobilizing Albertans against the federal government, especially the Liberal Party.
6 Of particular note in the union movement at this time was Neil Reimer, an established social activist and trade union organizer who headed the NDP from 1962 to 1968. Reimer's legacy later continued through his daughter, Janice Reimer, who was Edmonton's mayor from 1989 to 1995.
7 It is worth noting that conflict with Aboriginal peoples also occurred in other parts of Alberta (the Oldman Dam) and Canada (Oka, Ipperwash, and Gustafson Lake) during roughly this same period. As highlighted in part 2 of this book, conflicts between the capitalist state and labour (Canadian and foreign workers alike), women, and Aboriginal peoples continues apace.
8 The 1993 election points out the problem of necessarily labelling any party or group as "left" or "progressive," or even "right" or "centre." Nothing is fixed. The Liberals under Decore moved to the centre-right for political purposes, but after being defeated, they spent the next few years attempting to redefine their place on the political spectrum.

9 On the decreasing trajectory of Alberta's royalty rates over time, see David
 Campanella's 2012 report for Parkland Institute.

References

Barr, John. 1974. *The Dynasty: The Rise and Fall of Social Credit in Alberta*. Toronto:
 McClelland and Stewart.

Bell, Edward. 1993. *Social Classes and Social Credit*. Montréal and Kingston: McGill-
 Queen's University Press.

Brym, Robert. 1978. "Regional Social Structure and Agrarian Radicalism in Canada:
 Alberta, Saskatchewan, and New Brunswick." *Canadian Review of Sociology and
 Anthropology* 15 (3): 339–51.

Campanella, David. 2012. *Misplaced Generosity: Update 2012—Extraordinary Profits in
 Alberta's Oil and Gas Industry*. Edmonton, AB: Parkland Institute.

Conway, John. 1994. *The West: The History of a Region in Confederation*. Toronto: James
 Lorimer.

Finkel, Alvin. 1989. *The Social Credit Phenomenon in Alberta*. Toronto: University of Toronto
 Press.

———. 2012. *Working People in Alberta: A History*. Edmonton, AB: Athabasca University
 Press.

Flanagan, Tom. 1995. *Waiting for the Wave: The Reform Party and the Conservative Movement*.
 Montréal and Kingston: McGill-Queen's University Press.

Harrison, Trevor W. 1995. "Making the Trains Run on Time: Corporatism in Alberta." In
 Laxer and Harrison, *Trojan Horse*, 118–31.

———. 2000. "The Changing Face of Prairie Politics: Populism in Alberta." *Prairie Forum*
 25 (1): 107–21.

———. 2011. "Government and State in the Making of Political Culture: The Case of
 Canada." In *Essays on Social Themes*, edited by Gregory T. Papanikos, 17–28. Athens:
 Athens Institute for Education and Research.

Harrison, Trevor W. , William Johnston, and Harvey Krahn. 2005. "Language and Power:
 'Special Interests' in Alberta's Political Discourse." In *The Return of the Trojan Horse:
 Alberta and the New World (Dis)Order*, edited by Trevor W. Harrison, 82–94. Montréal:
 Black Rose Books.

Johnston, William, Harvey Krahn, and Trevor Harrison. 2006. "Democracy, Political
 Institutions, and Trust: The Limits of Current Electoral Reform Proposals." *Canadian
 Journal of Sociology* 31 (2): 165–82.

Laxer, Gordon, and Trevor Harrison, eds. 1995. *The Trojan Horse: Alberta and the Future of
 Canada*. Montréal: Black Rose Books.

Leeson, Howard. 1992. *Grant Notley: The Social Conscience of Alberta*. Edmonton: University
 of Alberta Press.

Macpherson, C. B. 1953. *Democracy in Alberta: The Theory and Practice of a Quasi-party System*.
 Toronto: University of Toronto Press.

Mardiros, Anthony. 1979. *William Irvine: The Life of a Prairie Radical.* Toronto: James Lorimer.

Mathews, Robin. 1966. "Alberta: The Totalitarian Drift." *Canadian Dimension* 3 (5): 9–11, 19.

Monto, Tom. 1989. *The United Farmers of Alberta: A Movement, a Government.* Edmonton, AB: Crang.

Neuman, W. Lawrence. 2005. *Power, State, Society: An Introduction to Political Sociology.* Montréal: McGraw-Hill.

Nikiforuk, Andrew. 2010. *Tar Sands: Dirty Oil and the Future of a Continent.* Revised and updated. Vancouver: Greystone Books.

Orum, Anthony M. , and John G. Dale. 2009. *Political Sociology: Power and Participation in the Modern World.* 5th ed. Oxford: Oxford University Press.

Ross, Michael. 2001. "Does Oil Hinder Democracy?" *World Politics* 53 (3): 325–61.

Shaffer, Ed. 1979. "Oil and Class in Alberta." Canadian Dimension 13 (8): 42–45.

Taft, Kevin. 1997. *Shredding the Public Interest: Ralph Klein and 25 Years of One-Party Government.* Edmonton: University of Alberta and Parkland Institute.

———. 2012. *Follow the Money: Where Is Alberta's Wealth Going?* Calgary, AB: Detselig Enterprises.

Warnock, John W. 2012. "Remembering Sask Oil: It Can Be Done!" *The Bullet.* Socialist Project. E-Bulletin 672, 31 July.

Wiseman, Nelson. 2007. *In Search of Canadian Political Culture.* Vancouver: University of British Columbia Press.

Petro-politics in Alberta and Canada

A New Spatiality of Political Contestation?

Peter (Jay) Smith

In today's globalized world of risks and uncertainty, global realities are increasingly impinging on the options available to Albertans and Canadians with regard to the development and export of their energy resources, particularly the bitumen sands of northern Alberta. This has led to a contentious debate—evident in the conflict over the terms *oil sands* and *tar sands*—that is taking place at local, national, and global levels.

Clearly, in a globalized world, the spaces of politics are being transformed. No longer is politics solely centred around the institutions of the state. Thanks to digital technologies, there is a new spatiality, one that Manuel Castells (2010a, xxxii) describes as the "space of flows"—"the material support of simultaneous social practices communicated at a distance," made possible by "the production, transmission and processing of flows of information." This space of flows, with its ideas, politics, new transnational political actors, and advocacy, is now intersecting with provincial and national politics and public policy. The result is a new cycle of what Charles Tilly (2008, 5) calls "contentious politics," defined as "interactions in which actors make claims bearing on someone else's interest, in which governments appear either as targets, initiators of claims, or third parties." Contentious politics—in this case, surrounding energy development in Canada—means that the normal expression of politics no longer centres around traditional interaction with the state (letters to MPs, lobbying, personal contact) but takes more disruptive forms, such as demonstrations. There are two forms of globalization at work here: globalization from above, in which governments and corporations are the key actors, and globalization from below, in which social movements, nongovernmental organizations (NGOs), and citizens are the key actors.

In this chapter, I argue that globalization and neoliberalism have opened up new spaces for political contestation in Alberta. A shrinking state characterized by a reduction in expenditures and functions and a weakening of democratic institutions within a globally driven oil economy makes Alberta vulnerable to this type of contestation. I explore this new era of contentious politics over the development and export of Alberta's bitumen sands, arguing that this newly contentious approach is already having significant political effects, particularly in regard to relations with Canada's Indigenous peoples. Essentially, Indigenous groups argue that Canada and mining companies are ignoring their rights, titles, and interests and that further development threatens their survival and the environment on which they depend. Not having received satisfaction from either the provincial or the federal state, many Indigenous groups are taking their case to the global level, often in alliance with environmental organizations. The global scope of the struggle over bitumen development means that, today, it is the national government, with its responsibilities for external relations, that is mediating the conflict on the international and global levels, with the Alberta government, historically the primary advocate of the oil industry, playing a secondary role. This has already had two effects. First, the Conservative-led Canadian government has warmed its once cool relations with China, a potential market, and, second, Alberta is in a period of warming with regard to its relations with Ottawa.[1] What is uncertain, however, is the outcome of the cycle of protest explored in this chapter.

I begin this chapter by placing this cycle of contention in a global context, arguing that it features two conflicting ideas of "how the world should be organized": the neoliberal vision relegates political and economic power to the market, and the justice-oriented vision emphasizes democracy at all levels, including international institutions and the liberal democratic state (Smith 2008, 3). In this first section, I also consider the changing locus of power in the world, the rise of the garrison or security state, the emergence of new political opportunity structures, and the framing of political messaging. I move in the second section to a discussion of the development and export of bitumen as the latest example of Canada's dependence on staple products, noting both the uncertainty surrounding bitumen export and the concern of critics in civil society. The third section considers the cycle of contention within the Canadian context, examining the issue of bitumen sands development and export in general and profiling this contention not in terms of the Keystone XL pipeline to the United States but on other fronts of the battle, including Europe and

British Columbia, the site of the proposed Enbridge Northern Gateway pipeline. I discuss the major players—in particular, the governments of Alberta and Canada, allied corporations and governments in Europe, and the networked transnational opposition represented by a growing confluence of Indigenous and environmental movements across Canada, the United States, and Europe. I focus particularly on how the debate has been framed and how both sides take advantage of political opportunity structures to press their case. The final section is an attempt to assess the relative success of each side in this continuing drama. I conclude with thoughts about the possible future of political contestation in Alberta and Canada: Is transnational activism a harbinger of things to come, especially in the natural resource sector?

Neoliberalism, Dissent, and National Discourse

There is little doubt that Albertan and Canadian energy development and export is spurring a new cycle of protest, one that has become transnational. This cycle needs to be situated within the context of the waves of protest against neoliberal globalization that began in the 1990s and continue to the present. Protests, then, have become a staple of contemporary political life.

Neoliberalism represents the latest form of globalization. *Neoliberalism* can be defined as a social, political, and economic ideology according to which markets, not states, should be the fundamental allocators of values in a society. With neoliberalism has come a shift in the loci of political power. First, external to the state itself, markets are increasingly replacing states as allocators of societal values and are viewed by proponents of neoliberalism as the best means of improving the lives of most people; thus, the role of the state in society has become more limited in scope. Internally within states, as Donatella Della Porta and Sidney Tarrow acknowledge (2005, 2), "there has been a continuing shift in power from parliaments to the executive, and within the executive, to the bureaucracy and to quasi-independent agencies." This shift represents a clear de-emphasis of democracy. Moreover, as states have begun to lose their capacity and willingness to perform and to deliver what many citizens want, political alienation has risen worldwide. Governments, parliaments, and global corporations now rank very low in terms of public trust. All of this has led Manuel Castells (2010b, 414) to conclude that "political [i.e., liberal] democracy ... has become an empty shell." Castells may be too dismissive here. Democratic institutions, while weakened, are still worth contesting. However, the trend is toward a "leaner, meaner state" (Evans 1997, 85), sometimes referred to as a "garrison state," in which the welfare state—a critical means to the provision of social and economic justice (in the form of social security, equality of access to education and health care, and the equitable distribution of wealth)—is de-emphasized in favour of security, the military, the protection of property, and the building of prisons (Smith 2008, 71). Yet at the same time, as Foucault (1978, 94–95) notes, "where there is power, there is resistance." Those who are engaged in nonviolent resistance and protest against neoliberal globalization, though, are often seen as another threat "on par with terrorism, football hooliganism, and transnational organized crime," to which authorities must respond (Smith 2008, 73).

Thus, dissenters are perceived as a threat to security, another risk to be managed. Foucault (1991) argues that risk is socially produced and that groups deemed to be sources of risk are subject to surveillance and to discipline and control through the collection and application of knowledge. Today, according to the Canadian government, these threats are "environmentalists" and other "radical groups," such as Indigenous peoples. (Oliver 2012). Just how the Government of Canada has framed these threats shall be examined shortly.

Although global neoliberalism has contributed to the rise of the garrison state in Canada, globalization also facilitates resistance. In particular, it fragments authority and creates new political opportunity structures for social movements and other nonstate actors. As Hein-Anton van der Heijden writes (2006, 28), "Political opportunity structure refers to the specific features of a political system . . . that can explain the different action repertoires, organizational forms and impacts of social movements, and social movement organizations in that specific country." In other words, a political opportunity structure (POS) is where one goes within a state—its institutions and personnel—to find friends, mobilize allies, and draw political attention to one's concerns. Today, globalization provides POSs beyond the state.

POSs can either constrain or enable collective action. On the one hand, the more decentralized and "the more open the formal institutional structure and the more integrative the informal elite strategies, the larger will be the number of NGOs that try to influence the politics . . . by conventional means" (37). Thus, a nation-state that features competitive parties, a legislature with relative independence, an independent judiciary, and political and bureaucratic elites who listen is a preferred POS for social movements and NGOs. At the international level, the same principle of decentralization and openness applies.

The United Nations is a preferred POS because it offers social movement organizations both consultative status and an opportunity to be heard, although the UN has little formal power to implement decisions. The European Union is also relatively open and decentralized, with social movement organizations able to gain access to political and bureaucratic elites.

On the other hand, Van der Heijden argues that "the more closed the formal institutional structure and the more exclusive the informal elite strategies, the larger will be the number of unconventional . . . actions" such as protests (38). Under the influence of neoliberalism, Laurie Adkin (2009, 2) argues, the Canadian and provincial political systems are closing. In Alberta, this is exacerbated by a historically weak legislature, strong executive, and weak party competition (see Harrison, this volume). While in recent years, the Alberta government has initiated multistakeholder consultations on bitumen sands development, the process is cosmetic and produces little policy change. As a result, "the government's strategy has lost its legitimacy" (Hoberg and Phillips 2011, 524).

However, as political spaces close in one venue, they can open up in another. One option for social movements is to go to bodies such as the UN and EU. In addition, governing institutions, whether national or international, in which political spaces have closed can find themselves targets of political protests and transnational campaigns against their policies. Increasingly, social movements and NGOs are also creating their own POSs, within which people can meet and organize. In a globalizing world, then, political spaces are becoming reconfigured, more complex, and fragmented (Crack 2007; Mouffe 1999). Citizenship is also becoming more complex and is being practiced on a variety of domestic and global levels (Sassen 2003).

Globalization, moreover, has stimulated the creation of global Indigenous and environmental movements. The exponential growth of the global economy has led to a thirst for cheap energy and resources (Haluza-DeLay and Davidson 2008). According to Ken Coates (2004, 216), "The imperatives of the industrial world, which needed energy, minerals, wood and pulp . . . drove nations to move aggressively into remote regions. In very few instances . . . did the national governments take the concerns and needs of indigenous peoples very seriously." Since states proved unresponsive to Indigenous peoples, the United Nations became a preferred venue, not only for human rights advocacy but also for participation in climate conferences, often together with environmental groups (Powless 2012). The rapid expansion of the global economy, the externalization of environmental costs, and the fear of climate change spurred the rise of a global environmental movement. In particular, the 1992 UN Conference on Environment and Development (UNCED) in Rio de Janeiro served as a catalyst for the creation of this movement (United Nations Department of Public Information 1997).

Given that the grievances and claims of Indigenous and environmental movements cannot be taken for granted, framing is critical to the success of these movements. Frames provide meaning and the symbolic construction of collective identity for social movements; they also assist in articulating the nature of the problem and the call for action (Gamson 2004, 243). However, governments can also frame an issue in a particular way; thus, frames can clash, with both sides—social movements and governments—competing to shape public opinion.

The terms *tar sands* and *oil sands* provide an excellent example of competing frames. As Debra Davidson and Mike Gismondi (2011, 27) point out, the bitumen deposits of northern Alberta have been known by both terms since their discovery in the 1800s. Today, governments and media prefer to use the term *oil sands*, while critics prefer *tar sands*. According to Davidson and Gismondi, the Alberta Minister of Environment announced in 2001 "that the issue is closed, and oil sands is the officially sanctioned term" (27–28). This has had a significant effect on discourse in both the legislature and the mass media. At one time, there was only a marginal difference in the provincial legislature in the use of these competing terms. By 2007, however, the ratio was over three to one, with *oil sands* being the preferred term (Davidson and Gismondi 2011, 27, fig. 2.1). When I inserted the two terms into ProQuest's data system on 13 April 2015, Canadian Newsstand brought up 83,933 stories with *oil sands* and 13,435 stories with *tar sands*, a six-to-one ratio: clearly, most Canadians are exposed to the more benign term. Today, using the term *tar sands* risks inviting the wrath of governments and the mass media, which serves as a means of disciplining public expression.

Landlocked Oil: All Dressed Up and Nowhere to Go?

Once only a dream of Alberta governments and petroleum corporations, the development of Alberta's bitumen deposits has become a reality and, increasingly, a multifaceted problem. At one time too costly to pursue, bitumen production in Alberta is rising rapidly, with *The Economist* predicting an increase from

2 millions barrels a day, in 2012, to 3.3 million by 2020, or "from 58% to 72% of Canada's total oil output" ("Great Pipeline Battle" 2012). Canada is vaulting into the top ranks of global crude oil producers, fulfilling the Harper government's pledge to make Canada an "energy superpower" (Canwest News Service 2006). The problem is "there's too much oil and not enough pipe" (Vanderklippe 2012), which has made finding markets and building pipelines matters of great political importance.

In one sense, there is little new here. Canada has a history of fretting about access to markets for its staple products. According to political economist Harold Innis (1984), the exploitation of successive staple commodities accounts for the particular pattern of Canada's economic, political, and cultural development. Canada was part of a world economic system, the hinterland dependent on a more economically developed nation, the metropolis. At the heart of Innis's analysis is the belief that staple production has dominated Canadian history. According to Stephen McBride (2005, 30), "There is little new about market dependency: the intrusion of international factors and concerns into Canada's domestic political economy was the central concern of Canadian political economy long before the term 'globalization' was coined." Market dependency was also a factor in the negotiation of the North American Free Trade Agreement (NAFTA). At that time, the problem was "trapped gas": Canadian producers had a surplus of deliverable natural gas, which led to depressed prices. In brief, "NAFTA opened the way to new pipelines and a much deeper integration of the American and Canadian energy sectors" (Pratt 2007, 468). Today, the issue is bitumen, not natural gas, and the fear, once again, is depressed prices—hence, the urgency to build more pipelines.[2]

In addition, there is uncertainty about demand in the United States, which is now almost the only customer for Alberta's energy. Thanks to new production technologies that are allowing the extraction of once inaccessible oil and natural gas supplies, US demand for foreign sources of energy is declining rapidly (Lamphier 2012). Indeed, the bitumen targeted for the Gulf Coast in the future could end up being surplus to US needs. At present, because the US market cannot absorb all the gasoline and diesel produced in the United States from the crude oil that is imported from Alberta, the excess is being shipped to Latin American countries such as Mexico and Colombia, who, while producers of heavy oil, do not yet have their own upgrading capacities, a situation that is expected to be rectified (Cooper 2012). This leads to a critical question: "With North American and European consumer markets flat or declining, and

Latin American nations producing enough for their own needs, what is left?" (Cooper 2012). The end result is that shipping bitumen to Kitimat on the BC coast through the proposed Enbridge Northern Gateway pipeline, and then on to Asia (primarily China), takes on paramount importance for the governments of Alberta and Canada, both increasingly anxious to find secure markets for bitumen. This anxiety is compounded by escalating national and transnational resistance to bitumen development and export.

Bitumen Extraction and Pipeline Export: Resistance Goes Transnational

Resistance to bitumen extraction and export can be found in two social movements that are increasingly working in concert: the Indigenous and environmental movements. The emphasis here will be on the Indigenous movement. Both movements are transnational and networked, embodying what can be described as a "cultural logic of networking" based on the logic of global capitalism, itself a networked system (Juris 2012, 266). That is, the same means of Internet communication that permits businesses to operate on a global scale also allows social movements and organizations to organize against them through highly diverse networks. Rejecting the top-down command structure of political parties, networked organizations forge horizontal ties and emphasize inclusivity and autonomy in pursuit of common goals.

Participants in both movements agree that formal political institutions and channels in Canada are closing, which necessitates finding and using political opportunity structures (POSs) outside of Canada to try and influence domestic opinion and government policy. Margaret Keck and Kathryn Sikkink (1998, 12) call this the "boomerang effect": "when a government violates or refuses to recognize rights . . . domestic NGOs bypass their state and directly search out international allies to try to bring pressure on their states from outside." Through their activities abroad, NGOs frequently utilize a "mobilization of shame" (23) to bring visibility to their causes and to reframe debate at home and make their domestic governments more compliant.

Canadian Indigenous organizations have found a variety of receptive POSs beyond Canada's borders. According to Ben Powless (2012, 415), "A transnational, Indigenous movement really emerged during the 1970s largely in response to these closed doors at the national level and seemingly opening ones at the level of the United Nations." In addition to the UN, the European Union and the governments and legislators of Europe have been open POSs.

Representatives of Indigenous organizations also attend mass global conferences and meetings, such as the World People's Conference on Climate Change and the Rights of Mother Earth held in Bolivia in 2010, where they are welcome and have opportunities to network with others. Increasingly, Indigenous groups are participating in shareholder activism, whereby activist organizations purchase shares in corporations—in this instance, oil companies invested in the bitumen sands—and make their case at the annual general meetings of shareholders. In addition, cross-country speaking tours in Canada and Europe have been organized.

Of particular importance to the transnationalization of the Indigenous movement is the United Nations. Going to the UN was a logical step, given its willingness to grant consultative status to NGOs. As early as 1982, a Working Group on Indigenous Populations was created at the UN. In 1987, this group was tasked with creating a declaration of Indigenous human rights, which took twenty years to complete, culminating in the adoption in 2007 of the Declaration on the Rights of Indigenous Peoples. These rights have become part of what are known as "third-generation" rights, or solidarity rights, and they include the rights to self-determination, economic and social development, a healthy environment, food, and natural resources, as well as the right to communicate. Of particular importance here is Article 32(2) of the declaration, which reads:

> States shall consult and cooperate in good faith with the indigenous peoples concerned through their own representative institutions in order to obtain their free and informed consent prior to the approval of any project affecting their lands or territories and other resources, particularly in connection with the development, utilization or exploitation of mineral, water or other resources. (United Nations General Assembly 2007)

The above has come to be known as the right to "free, prior and informed consent" (FPIC). Initially, Canada was opposed to this language, along with other articles of the declaration, and refused to adopt it, fearing it could be used as a veto power over issues affecting not only Indigenous peoples but all Canadians. Being one of four holdouts—along with the United States, Australia, and New Zealand, all with significant Aboriginal populations—isolated Canada in world opinion, and on 12 November 2010, Canada finally adopted the declaration, noting, however, that it was not legally binding on Canada (Canada 2014).

While not legally binding, the declaration is an important development in the acknowledgement of human rights and is indicative of the direction that world nations should be taking. The concept of "free, prior and informed consent" has become instrumental to the framing of the Indigenous movement. Moreover, as one of the signatories to the International Convention on the Elimination of All Forms of Racial Discrimination, Canada *is* legally obligated to report to the UN Committee on the Elimination of Racial Discrimination (CERD) on its compliance with the terms of the convention.[2] In February and March 2012, CERD reviewed Canada's nineteenth and twentieth periodic reports and allowed Indigenous organizations to respond by submitting alternative reports. One such report was submitted by First Nations Women Advocating Responsible Mining (FNWARM), a coalition based in northern British Columbia, where any proposed pipeline would necessarily traverse Indigenous lands. The FNWARM report declares:

> Our very survival is threatened by resource developments being pursued in the absence of proper consultation and accommodation, under a regime of antiquated government legislation, standards and practices and in an environment marked by discriminatory practices, ignorance and willful destruction of our lands and way of life in the name of profit at any cost.[4]

Other First Nations reports echoed this refrain. One report, jointly submitted by a number of First Nations and Indigenous rights organizations, requested that CERD ask Canada's UN representatives what the country was doing to fully implement the principle of free, prior, and informed consent.[5] This report places considerable emphasis on the negative environmental impacts of the development of the tar sands, stating that "the results are devastating for Indigenous Peoples," and calls for a moratorium on tar sands extraction and pipeline construction.[6]

Similar concerns were voiced in a resolution adopted in August 2011 at a meeting in Manaus, Brazil, that was attended by representatives of Indigenous peoples from around the world, in preparation for the UN Rio + 20 Conference to be held in June 2012 in Rio de Janeiro. The resolution noted that tar sands extraction was "vastly destructive to the Indigenous Peoples of the region" and was "a major source of greenhouse gas emissions." Moreover, like the Keystone XL pipeline project, these projects were "being carried out without the free prior informed consent of the impacted Indigenous Peoples as affirmed in Article 32 of the UN Declaration on the Rights of Indigenous Peoples." The resolution also called for "for an immediate halt to the Tar Sands extraction," as well as to construction of the XL pipeline.[7]

These documents exemplify the activity of Canadian First Nations at the United Nations in opposition to bitumen sands extraction and pipeline construction, as well as the inclusion of Canadian First Nations in a global network of Indigenous peoples.[8] Yet the UN is only one venue for activity. Not only is the movement for Indigenous rights in itself global, but it now works in concert with a broad-based network of environmental groups and allied organizations.

In May 2012, organizations in this network engaged in intense lobbying in Europe over the possible approval of an addition to the European Fuel Quality Directive that would determine the acceptable level of carbon emissions produced by various types of oil, including bitumen oil, that might potentially be sold in Europe. The EU has calculated that the "well-to-wheels" emissions of oil from bitumen sands are 23 percent higher than existing EU standards allow (McCarthy 2012). Despite this finding, on 17 December 2014, the proposed requirement that oil from unconventional sources, such as bitumen sands, be labelled as such was defeated in the European Parliament, albeit by only twelve votes (Crisp 2014). Europe does not currently import oil from Alberta, but should such a labelling requirement ever become part of the EU Fuel Quality Directive, it could become a widely accepted standard in other countries as well, thereby lending force to the claim of environmental groups that bitumen oil is "dirty oil."

In making their case in Europe, environmental organizations worked closely with Canadian First Nations. Included in the collective-action repertoire were speaking tours, lobbying, and shareholder activism. For example, in 2011, several of the organizations in the network facilitated a week-long speaking tour of England by Beaver Lake Cree Nation youth from Alberta. Support for the action came from a number of NGOs in the UK, including the UK Tar Sands Network. The purpose of the UK Tar Sands Network is to campaign "in partnership with Indigenous communities affected by the Tar Sands oil developments in Canada," with campaigns targeting "governments, UK companies, banks and investors operating in the Alberta Tar Sands."[9] The speaking tour was organized by People and Planet, the largest student network in Britain, and was part of a solidarity exchange in which UK students travelled to Alberta to visit the Beaver Creek Cree Nation. On 11 July 2011, the students staged a theatrical protest outside the Alberta Environment offices, which was widely covered by major UK media outlets.[10]

In 2011, the UK Tar Sands Network, together with the Indigenous Environmental Network (IEN), sponsored a First Nations speaking tour in the

UK to campaign for divestment from British Petroleum following the company's decision to invest in the bitumen sands. The speakers who took part in the tour attended BP's annual general meeting, which was very contested and received considerable publicity in the British press.[11]

The IEN, a key link between groups in the UK and Canadian First Nations and civil society organizations, focuses on issues of environmental and economic justice from an Indigenous perspective. Founded in the United States in 1990, the IEN has developed strong Canadian and global connections, particularly in Europe. For example, in May 2011, working with Friends of the Earth Europe and Friends of the Earth France, the IEN sponsored a tour that targeted French investors, the French government, and members of the European Parliament. "We are calling for a higher standard on tar sands in the EU Fuel Quality Directive," said the IEN's Heather Milton-Lightening: "We hope this forces other countries to stop developing, investing and importing Canadian tar sands oil." Lionel Lepine, of the Athabasca Chipewyan First Nation, described tar sands development as tantamount to "slow genocide for First Nations living within the extraction zone" (quoted in Canada Newswire 2011).

In March 2012, the IEN—in cooperation with the Council of Canadians, Climate Action Network Canada, and Bill Erasmus, chief of the Dene Nation, and with the support of European allies—organized a tour that began with visits to EU embassies in Ottawa and proceeded to Paris, The Hague, London, and Berlin to meet with government officials in support of strengthening the European Fuel Quality Directive (Council of Canadians 2012). Finally, in cooperation with the UK Tar Sands Network, the IEN coordinated a visit to The Hague of a spokesperson for the Athabasca Chipewyan First Nation in May 2012, who presented grievances to the chairman, board, and shareholders of Shell.

The foregoing is hardly exhaustive. In cooperation with other participants in the Indigenous movement, the IEN, and environmental organizations from Canada, the United States and Europe, the Indigenous peoples of Alberta have developed a strong, complex support network that allows them to voice their claims within a wide variety of POSs at various political scales. How have the Alberta and Canadian governments and their allies in the oil industry responded?

Fighting Back: The Development of a Counter-frame

Given the range of national and international POSs within which the Indigenous and environmental movements operate, the development of an effective counter-frame by the Alberta government alone is not possible. Critics of bitumen extraction and, increasingly, pipeline construction can be found on every continent. It is the Canadian government that is responsible for external relations and that has the right of primary access to many international POSs. Alberta, therefore, must cooperate with and rely upon the leadership of the federal government in framing its response.

Figure 3.1. "The Milch Cow," a cartoon first published in the 15 December 1915 edition of the Grain Growers' Guide. Courtesy of the Glenbow Archives (NA-3055-24).

This is contrary to much of Alberta's history within Confederation. Roger Gibbins (1992, 70) writes of a political ideology of western alienation, defined as "the belief that the West is always outgunned in national politics and as a consequence has been subject to varying degrees of economic exploitation by central Canada." This conviction was famously illustrated in a 1915 cartoon (see figure 3.1), and, as Gibbins notes, it "enjoys deep historical roots and contemporary nourishment." Today, however, this is not the dominant narrative of the Alberta government: working together and cooperating with the other provinces and the federal government is.

On the international level, gone is the Harper government's truculent relationship with China. When Harper and the Progressive Conservatives first came to power in 2006, the Canadian government was noted for its chilly relationship with China (Goodspeed 2012). Only later did it become apparent that China was an important potential customer for energy from Alberta's bitumen deposits and could no longer be given the cold shoulder.

It was clear that Canada and Alberta, facing a growing reputational problem, had to cultivate friends and allies abroad. By 2008, the international environmental movement had bestowed upon Canada its third Fossil of the Year award.[12] In Europe, the framing by the environmental and Indigenous movements had been gaining traction in public opinion and at the EU, which in 2007 began proposing amendments to the 1998 Fuel Quality Directive that would reduce GHG emissions for transport fuels. Emails obtained under the federal Freedom of Information Act indicate an awareness that negative publicity could adversely affect billions of dollars of investment in the bitumen sands. Sushma Gera, a London-based Canadian diplomat, wrote in a confidential email in August 2010, "The oil sands are posing a growing reputational problem, with the oil sands defining the Canadian brand." Gera went on to say that, in view of the growing number of NGO campaigns aimed at the European public, "we anticipate increased risk to Canadian interests much beyond the oil sands" (quoted in Lewis, Ljunggren, and Jones 2012).

In fact, in 2009, Ottawa established a Pan-European Oil Sands Team consisting of representatives from the Alberta government, the Canadian Association of Petroleum Producers (CAPP), federal environment and natural resource ministries, European oil companies, and the Royal Bank of Scotland, as well as diplomats from major Canadian embassies in Europe (Lewis, Ljunggren, and Jones 2012). In January 2010, a number of these embassies launched the Pan-European Oil Sands Advocacy Strategy. The strategy uses the language of framing and is explicit in its targets and its repertoires of action. One intended outcome is described as a "reframing of the European debate on oil sands in [a] manner that protects and advances Canadian interests related to the oil sands and broader Canadian interests in Europe." The strategy acknowledges the effectiveness of the opposition, stating that the "oil sands have been the focus of many high profile NGO campaigns in Europe stressing their environmental and social impacts (in particular Aboriginal issues) which are actively framing the issue in a strongly negative light . . . in key European countries." There was a lot at stake, as "Canada's reputation as a clean, reliable source of energy may be put at risk."[13]

Some of the desired outcomes of the reframing strategy include improving Canada's image as a "responsible energy producer," maintaining the confidence of investors, and encouraging the dissemination of "positive/factual information" about Canada's bitumen development. Goals also include an "increased acceptance by Europeans" of the critical role of Canada's bitumen production in global energy security, an "increased and more balanced" understanding of the environmental impacts of bitumen development, and an increased understanding of Canada's and Alberta's approach to "consulting with First Nations and addressing their concerns."[14] The promotional tactics implicit in the strategy correspond closely to a repertoire of actions that Canadian government officials in Europe have pursued since 2010, which have included lobbying efforts directed at European officials and politicians, the hosting of tours of the bitumen sands for investors and corporate executives, outreach to corporations and banks, and the hiring of public relations firms to focus on obtaining a watered-down version of the Fuel Quality Directive.

The document then identifies the POSs of the strategy—Canada's allies and adversaries. The POSs, or targets, include national and European politicians and governments, the public, investors, and the EU Commission. The allies listed in the document include energy companies, energy industry associations, the Alberta government, and the National Energy Board.[15] Naming the NEB as an ally is curious given that the NEB is supposedly neutral, serving at arm's length from government and functioning in the public interest. Adversaries include NGOs, especially environmental NGOs and Aboriginal groups. Naming the latter as an adversary highlights a conundrum faced by the Canadian government—that is, how to seem sympathetic to Canada's Aboriginal peoples, knowing that Europeans are concerned about their welfare, health, and right to be consulted, and yet have an effective strategy in which they are in fact marginalized.

Indeed, the marginalization of adversaries has become a cornerstone of the Canadian government's political and framing objectives. This is evident in federal Minister of Natural Resources Joe Oliver's "Open Letter" to Canadians, of January 2012. It is written from the perspective of security and risk, in which threats to the export of bitumen are identified and a course of action recommended. Oliver starts by acknowledging that the United States is no longer a dependable market for Canada's oil. Instead, "we need to diversify our markets in order to create jobs and economic growth for Canadians across this country." This means that "we must expand our trade with the fast growing Asian economies," as this "will help ensure the financial security of Canadians and their families" (Oliver 2012). Although Oliver nowhere explicitly mentions Enbridge's proposed Northern Gateway pipeline, the inference is clear.

However, there "are environmental and other radical groups" who "threaten to hijack our regulatory system to achieve their radical ideological agenda." They "seek to exploit any loophole ... to ensure that delays kill good projects"—projects (such as the Northern Gateway pipeline) that would "create thousands upon thousands jobs for Canadians." Worse yet, these groups "use funding from foreign special interest groups to undermine Canada's national economic interest." Only the federal government can protect the interests of Canadians from these threats and restore the balance to its regulatory environmental review system, so that "unnecessary delays" will not put an end to projects that are "safe, generate thousands of new jobs and open up new export markets" (Oliver 2012).

To remedy the situation, the federal government passed into law Bill C-38, a 425-page omnibus bill. The many provisions included new restrictions on the status of charitable organizations perceived to be accepting foreign funds, changes to the Environmental Assessment Act to ensure that pipeline infrastructure is not unduly delayed, changes to the NEB Act put a two-year limit on the review process and permit the federal cabinet to set aside the recommendation of the NEB and insert its own, and, finally, a stripping away of the requirements of the Fisheries Act to protect fish habitat. The purpose? To see that nothing stands in the way of building future pipelines or other development projects.

The language of government officials is heavily confrontational focused on projecting strength, power, and dominance. While the federal government had pursued a confrontational approach, the approach of Alison Redford, who became Alberta's premier in October 2011, was more collaborative in tone, although she stuck with the position of both previous Alberta governments and the federal government in maintaining that the bitumen sands provide energy security, are a key economic driver for the province and country, and represent an environmentally conscious energy supply. Redford did not speak of adversaries but rather of the need for cooperation, unity, and the national benefits of energy development. "What we have understood, as a federal government and a provincial government," she said in May 2012, "is we want to work together to advance Alberta's interests. And we have had . . . since I became premier, a real focused effort on ensuring that we're working well with our federal colleagues" (quoted in Wingrove 2012). Similarly, newly elected NDP premier Notley signalled that she would also take a cooperative approach, one grounded in Alberta traditions (McLeod 2015).

Conclusion

At this time, we are in the midst of a great struggle with an uncertain outcome. The Keystone XL pipeline, for example, has been delayed, with the Obama administration facing strong lobbying both for and against. In Canada, the federal Conservatives have the majority to ensure that the Northern Gateway pipeline is approved, but the project is facing intense opposition, nationally and beyond Canada's borders, that may make its completion difficult. Today, some of that opposition may come from Alberta itself. In a stunning political development, the Alberta Progressive Conservative government was defeated by the Alberta New Democratic Party in the May 2015 provincial elections. While getting Alberta's oil and bitumen to market will necessitate that the provincial and federal governments work together, the new premier, Rachel Notley, has made it clear that her government will no longer champion the Northern Gateway and Keystone XL pipelines (McDiarmid 2015). Notley realizes that climate change is a pressing global issue and Alberta was in the global spotlight. According to Notley, in order to build Canada's energy section, we must "build bridges and . . . open markets instead of having a black eye" (quoted in McDiarmid 2015). Notley favours more domestic refining, as well as TransCanada's $12 billion Energy East proposal to ship oil to refineries in Québec and New Brunswick and Kinder Morgan's Trans Mountain project from Edmonton to Burnaby, BC (Lewis 2015). But controversy remains over any pipeline development in Canada. If these routes are not supported by the federal and other provincial governments, the NDP will face the same challenge as that of past Progressive Conservative governments in Alberta—how to get oil to the market.

The EU battle has been intense. The Canadian and Alberta governments pulled out all the stops to defeat the amendment to the European Fuel Quality Directive that could have negatively affect bitumen development. Indigenous and environmental groups have responded in kind. Even though the Canadian government has prevailed in its attempt to block the EU's proposal, Canada now has fewer friends in Europe. According to one BBC report (Mallinder 2012), "Canada's decision last year to walk out of the Kyoto Protocol caused concern around the world," particularly in Europe, where the Kyoto agreement has much popular support.

Clearly, Canada and Alberta are in the global spotlight: what was once an internal struggle has spilled beyond their borders. The United Nations, the United States, and the European Union and its member states are just some of the spaces for political advocacy for the Indigenous and environmental movements. Beyond these spaces, movements today are capable of creating their own POSs, meetings, and venues. It bears repeating that the local is becoming the global, and the global, the local. No longer are issues of natural resource extraction, the environment, and the treatment of Indigenous peoples solely Albertan and Canadian issues. Both the Alberta and federal governments are losing control of publicity and the exclusive ability to frame a story.

Yet this is by no means a novel occurrence. In fact, Indigenous peoples have become an inspiration for social movements around the world. The Zapatistas, named after Emilio Zapata, a hero of the 1917 Mexican revolution, are a group of indigenous Mayan farmers in Chiapas, Mexico, who rebelled in January 1994 to draw attention to their exploitation and impoverishment. Seeking relief from oppression, desiring control of their land and local resources, and fearing the consequences of the North American Free Trade Agreement, they rose in rebellion. Instead of being crushed, a well-coordinated communications and Internet campaign was successful in drawing considerable international support from NGOs and the general public, making the Mexican government pause in its use of force.

Today, Indigenous political struggles are "placed-based, yet transnationalised" (Atkinson and Mulrennan 2004, 469, quoting Arturo Escobar).[16] In Canada, this has been the pattern since the Lubicon Lake Cree from Alberta went to the UN in 1984 to draw the world's attention to the exploitation of their land and resources by foreign corporations. In the 1990s, the James Bay Cree in northern Québec waged a successful transnational campaign against the expansion of the huge James Bay hydroelectric project (Atkinson and Mulrennan 2004). The identities of Indigenous peoples, as well as those of other social movements, are being increasingly formed in opposition to neoliberal globalization.

Transnational advocacy thus represents the new normal in Canadian political life. In the late 1980s, Canadians concerned about Canadian sovereignty and social and economic justice, led in particular by the Council of Canadians, began making transnational alliances in efforts to stop the Canada-US Free Trade Agreement, NAFTA, the Multilateral Agreement on Investment (which was successfully blocked), and proposed trade and investment agreements of the World Trade Organization. The Council of Canadians is particularly interesting in this regard, having shifted its focus in 2010 "from one of national sovereignty to one of popular sovereignty—that is, democracy for all the peoples of the planet."[17] No longer do participants in movements of resistance view democracy as expressed solely by liberal or representative democracy. Manuel Castells (2010b, 414) argues that the state has been undermined by the informational flows of corporate globalization.

There is little doubt that citizenship and democratic activity have spread beyond the borders of the nation-state. In a sense, the Alberta (certainly prior to the election of an NDP government in May 2015) and Canadian governments and the oil industry have underestimated their adversaries by acting as if they could build pipelines with no or little opposition. Those opposed to the construction of huge mineral extraction projects and pipelines have their own complex networks, histories, and experiences, as well as an ability to work beyond borders and galvanize public opinion. This is evident in the rapid rise in late 2012 of Idle No More, an Indigenous-led movement, assisted by social media, that rose up in protest against Bill C-45, another omnibus budget bill passed in Parliament in December 2012 that removed the protected status of thousands of rivers and streams in Canada, all to facilitate natural resource development. Within days of the bill's passage, rallies, marches, flash mobs in malls, and protests spread from Alberta across Canada and internationally to Britain and the United States, catching the Alberta and Canadian governments off-guard. This is clear evidence that as Alberta and Canada open their doors to global market demand for Alberta's natural resources, they will be shadowed by transnational movements of resistance. We are at the beginning of a new era in Alberta political life, an era of contentious politics.

Notes

1 Whether this warming continues with the election of a New Democratic Party
   government in May 2015 is uncertain, but as a province, Alberta will still rely
   on Ottawa, in terms of interactions with other provinces and other states in the
   international arena, to get its oil to market.

2 For a useful illustration of the pipeline development associated with Alberta's bitumen sands, see Catherine Mann and Stacy Feldman, "Exclusive Map: The Tar Sands Pipeline Boom," *InsideClimate News*, 30 April 2012, http://www. insideclimatenews.org/news/20120430/exclusive-map-tar-sands-pipeline-boom.

3 The Committee on the Elimination of Racial Discrimination was created by this convention, the text of which is available at http://www.ohchr.org/EN/ProfessionalInterest/Pages/CERD.aspx. See, in particular, article 9. The convention went into effect in January 1969.

4 Report submitted by First Nations Women Advocating Responsible Mining (FNWARM), British Columbia, Canada, "To Canada's 19th and 20th Periodic Reports: Alternative Indigenous Shadow Report on Canada's Actions on the *UN Declaration on the Rights of Indigenous Peoples*, with a Focus on the Canadian Extractive Sector Operating Within Canada," January 2012, http://www2.ohchr.org/english/bodies/cerd/docs/ngos/FNWARM_Canada_CERD80.pdf, 2. This and other alternative reports were reviewed at CERD's 80th session, from 13 February to 9 March 2012, in Geneva.

5 "Response to Canada's 19th and 20th Periodic Reports: Consolidated Indigenous Alternative Report," 2011, http://cdn7.iitc.org/wp-content/uploads/2014/08/JointIPShadow-Final_web.pdf, 8. This was a joint report submitted to CERD by the International Indian Treaty Council, the Confederacy of Treaty 6 First Nations, the First Nations Summit, the Dene Nation and Assembly of First Nations Regional Office (Northwest Territories), the Assembly of First Nations, the Union of British Columbia Indian Chiefs, the Samson Cree Nation, the Ermineskin Cree Nation, the Native Women's Association of Canada, the Indigenous World Association, and Treaty 4 First Nations.

6 Ibid., 26. Indigenous peoples invariably use the term *tar sands*, and where they are explicitly referenced, I do the same.

7 "International: Resolution in Support of Indigenous Nations, Tribes, Peoples and Organizations in North America in Opposition to the Tar Sands Extraction in Alberta and Keystone XL Pipeline," August 2011, http://www.turtleisland.org/discussion/viewtopic.php?f=14&t=9025#p13725.

8 Despite this, it must be noted that Indigenous peoples have not historically been of one accord in terms of their activism. Members of the Athabasca Chipewyan and Mikisew Cree have found employment in the industry and have supported bitumen sands development. However, since 2006, that support has begun to fray, in part because of the increased amounts of water being withdrawn from the Athabasca River when the flow is low. In 2006, the Athabasca Chipewyan withdrew from an Alberta government environmental multistakeholder committee (Brethour 2006; see also Hoberg and Phillips 2011). Since then, strong resistance has come from members of the Athabasca Chipewyan and Mikisew Cree nations. In British Columbia, First Nations representatives strongly dispute Enbridge claims of strong Aboriginal support, arguing that only two Aboriginal groups along the proposed route support the Northern Gateway Pipeline (Canadian Press 2012).

9 "About Us," UK Tar Sands Network, 2015, http://www.no-tar-sands.org/about/.

10 "'Tar Sands: Don't Turn a Blind Eye,' Say Youth," *People and Planet*, 12 July 2011, http://peopleandplanet.org/navid12500.

11 For coverage of the event, see "Protestors Dragged from BP Annual Meeting," *The Independent* (London), 14 April 2011.

12 "Canada Wins Fossil of the Year Award in Durban," *Climate Action Network*, news release, 9 December 2011, http://climateactionnetwork.ca/2011/12/09/canada-wins-fossil-of-the-year-award-in-durban/.

13 "Pan-European Oils Sands Advocacy Strategy," March 2011, http://climateactionnetwork.ca/wp-content/uploads/2012/01/ATIPPan-EuropeanOilSandsAdvocacyStrategy.pdf, 1–2. See also "GEM Briefing for DMS' Oil Sands Call, May 26, 2011: Background and Key Points," 2011, http://climateactionnetwork.ca/wp-content/uploads/2012/02/2011-05-24-Pan-European-Oil-Sands-Team-Backgrounder.pdf.

14 "Pan-European Oils Sands Advocacy Strategy," 1–2.

15 Ibid., 3.

16 The authors quote from Escobar's "Beyond the Third World: Imperial Globality, Global Coloniality, and Anti-globalisation Social Movements," published in 2004 in *Third World Quarterly* 25 (1): 207–30 (quotation on p. 222).

17 The quotation is from a 2010 Council of Canadians document titled "Vision Statement: Backgrounder," which is no longer available online but is in the author's possession.

References

Adkin, Laurie. 2009. "Ecology, Citizenship, Democracy." In *Environmental Conflict and Democracy in Canada*, edited by Laurie E. Adkin, 1–16. Vancouver: University of British Columbia Press.

Atkinson, Miriam, and Monica E. Mulrennan. 2004. "Local Protest and Resistance to the Rupert Diversion Project, Northern Quebec." *Arctic* 62 (4): 468–80.

Brethour, Patrick. 2006. "Aboriginal Support of Oil Sands Fracturing over Water." *Globe and Mail*, 25 September.

Canada. 2014. "Canada's Statement on the World Conference on Indigenous Peoples Outcome Document." *Government of Canada: Permanent Mission of Canada to the United Nations*, 22 September. http://www.canadainternational.gc.ca/prmny-mponu/canada_un-canada_onu/statements-declarations/other-autres/2014-09-22_wcipd-padd.aspx?lang=eng.

Canada Newswire. 2011. "First Nation Tour Brings Truth to France on Tar Sands Development." *CNW Telbec: Une société PR Newswire*, 16 May. http://www.newswire.ca/fr/story/800015/first-nation-tour-brings-truth-to-france-on-tar-sands-development.

Canadian Press. 2012. "B.C. First Nations Dispute Enbridge Pipeline Claims." *CBC News*, 6 June. http://www.cbc.ca/news/canada/british-columbia/b-c-first-nations-dispute-enbridge-pipeline-claims-1.1260277.

Canwest News Service. 2006. "Harper Calls Canada 'Energy Superpower.'" *Canada. com*, 14 July. http://www.canada.com/story.html?id=59c9a6fd-5d35-4ab4-a1e9-b2de9d507697.

Castells, Manuel. 2010a. *The Rise of the Network Society*. 2nd ed. Vol. 1 of *The Information Age: Economy, Society, and Culture*. Malden, MA: Wiley-Blackwell.

———. 2010b. *The Power of Identity*. 2nd ed. Vol. 2 of *The Information Age: Economy, Society, and Culture*. Malden, MA: Wiley-Blackwell.

Coates, Ken S. 2004. *A Global History of Indigenous Peoples: Struggle and Survival*. New York: Palgrave Macmillan.

Cooper, Dave. 2012. "Alberta Upgraders an Option If Pipelines Blocked, Analyst Says." *Edmonton Journal*, 25 May.

Council of Canadians. 2012. "Canadian Civil Society Delegation Ends Tar Sands Lobbying-Busting Tour with High Hopes." *Council of Canadians*. Media release, 26 March. http://canadians.org/media/energy/2012/26-Mar-12.html.

Crack, Angela M. 2007. "Transcending Borders? Reassessing Public Spheres in a Networked World." *Globalizations* 4 (3): 341–54.

Crisp, James. 2014. "Canada Tar Sands Will Not Be Labelled 'Dirty' After All." *EurActiv. com*, 17 December. http://www.euractiv.com/sections/energy/canada-tar-sands-will-not-be-labelled-dirty-after-all-310910.

Davidson, Debra J., and Mike Gismondi. 2011. *Challenging Legitimacy at the Precipice of Energy Calamity*. New York: Springer.

Della Porta, Donatella, and Sidney Tarrow. 2005. "Transnational Processes and Social Activism: An Introduction." In *Transnational Protest and Global Activism*, edited by Donatella della Porta and Sidney Tarrow, 1–21. Lanham, MD: Rowman and Littlefield.

Evans, Peter B. 1997. "The Eclipse of the State? Reflections on Stateness in an Era of Globalization." *World Politics* 50 (1): 62–87.

Foucault, Michel. 1978. *An Introduction*. Vol. 1 of *The History of Sexuality*. New York: Pantheon.

———. 1991. "Governmentality." In *The Foucault Effect*, edited by Graham Burchell, Colin Gordon, and Peter Miller, 87–104. Chicago: University of Chicago Press.

Gamson, William. 2004. "Bystanders, Public Opinion, and the Media." In *The Blackwell Companion to Social Movements*, edited by David A. Snow, Sarah A. Soule, and Hanspeter Kriesi, 242–62. Malden, MA: Wiley-Blackwell.

Gibbins, Roger. 1992. "Alberta and the National Community." In *Government and Politics in Alberta*, edited by Allan Tupper and Roger Gibbins, 67–85. Edmonton: University of Alberta Press.

Goodspeed, Peter. 2012. "Canada's Increasingly Lucrative Policy Pivot on China." *National Post*, 6 February.

"The Great Pipeline Battle." 2012. *The Economist*, 26 May.

Haluza-DeLay, Randolph, and Debra J. Davidson. 2008. "The Environment and a Globalizing Sociology." *Canadian Journal of Sociology* 33 (3): 631–56.

Hoberg, George, and Jeffrey Phillips. 2011. "Playing Defence: Early Responses to Conflict Expansion in the Oil Sands Policy Subsystem." *Canadian Journal of Political Science* 44 (3): 507–27.

Innis, H. A. 1984. "The Importance of Staple Products." In *Approaches to Canadian Economic History*, edited by W. T. Easterbrook and M. H. Watkins, 16–19. Ottawa: Carleton University Press.

Juris, Jeffrey. 2012. "Reflections on #Occupy Everywhere: Social Media, Public Space, and Emerging Logics of Aggregation." *American Ethnologist* 39 (2): 259–79.

Keck, Margaret E. , and Kathryn Sikkink. 1998. *Activists Beyond Borders*. Ithaca, NY: Cornell University Press.

Lamphier, Gary. 2012. "Energy Industry Ignored; Troubled Sector Needs Attention Right Away." *Edmonton Journal*, 25 April.

Lewis, Barbara, David Ljunggren, and Jeffrey Jones. 2012. "Insight: Canada's Oil Sand Battle with Europe." *Reuters* (US edition), 10 May. http://www.reuters.com/article/2012/05/10/us-oil-sands-idUSBRE84900L20120510.

Lewis, Jeff. 2015. "NDP Majority Means It's Back to the Pipeline Drawing Board." *Globe and Mail*, 7 May.

Mallinder, Lorraine. 2012. "Viewpoint: Canada's Green Image Tarnished by New Policies." *BBC News*, 15 May. http://www.bbc.co.uk/news/world-radio-and-tv-18020931.

McBride, Stephen. 2005. *Paradigm Shift: Globalization and the Canadian State*. Halifax: Fernwood Publishing.

McCarthy, Shawn. 2012. "Alberta Fires Back at Proposed EU Fuel Rules." *Globe and Mail*, 9 May.

McDiarmid, Margo. 2015. "Albert Election Could Break Climate Change Logjam in Canada." *CBC News*, 8 May. http://www.cbc.ca/news/politics/alberta-election-could-break-climate-change-logjam-in-canada-1.3067073.

McLeod, Trevor. 2015. "McLeod: Energy Companies Need to Engage Early with NDP." *Calgary Herald*, 13 May.

Mouffe, Chantal. 1999. "Deliberative Democracy or Agonistic Pluralism?" *Social Research* 66 (3): 745–58.

Oliver, Joe. 2012. "An Open Letter from the Honourable Joe Oliver, Minister of Natural Resources." *Natural Resources Canada*, 9 January. http://www.nrcan.gc.ca/media-room/news-release/2012/1/1909.

Powless, Ben. 2012. "An Indigenous Movement to Confront Climate Change." *Globalizations* 9 (3): 411–24.

Pratt, Larry. 2007. "Pipelines and Pipe Dreams: Energy and Continental Security." In *Whose Canada? Continental Integration, Fortress North America, and the Corporate Agenda*, edited by Ricardo Grinspun and Yasmine Shamsie, 459–81. Montréal and Kingston: McGill-Queen's University Press.

Sassen, Saskia. 2003. "The Participation of States and Citizens in Global Governance." *Indiana Journal of Global Legal Studies* 10 (5): 5–28.

Smith, Jackie. 2008. *Social Movements for Global Democracy*. Baltimore: John Hopkins University Press.

Tilly, Charles. 2008. *Contentious Performances*. Cambridge: Cambridge University Press.

United Nations Department of Public Information. 1997. "UN Conference on Environment and Development (1992)." http://www.un.org/geninfo/bp/enviro.html.

United Nations General Assembly. 2007. *United Nations Declaration on the Rights of Indigenous Peoples*. http://www.un.org/esa/socdev/unpfii/documents/DRIPS_en.pdf.

Van der Heijden, Hein-Anton. 2006. "Globalization, Environmental Movements, and International Political Opportunity Structures." *Organization and Environment* 19 (1): 28–45.

Vanderklippe, Nathan. 2012. "Hidden Oil Sands Growth Bodes Ill for Crude." *Globe and Mail*, 18 May.

Wingrove, Josh. 2012. "Redford Opens Ottawa Office to 'Advocate Alberta's Perspective.'" *Globe and Mail*, 25 May.

Alberta's Energy Paradigm

Prosperity, Security, and the Environment

Lorna Stefanick

It's critical to develop that resource in a way that's responsible and environmental and the reality for the United States, which is the biggest consumer of our petroleum products, is that Canada is a very ethical society and a safe source for the United States in comparison to other sources of energy.

Prime Minister Stephen Harper, 7 January 2011

Stephen Harper was referring, of course, to Alberta's bitumen sands. These comments to the media were made on the heels of a declaration by Peter Kent, Harper's newly appointed minister of Environment, that Alberta was an "ethical" source of oil. The terms *ethical oil* and *dirty oil* have recently crept into the lexicon of energy-related politics. Critics of the bitumen sands such as Andrew Nikiforuk (2008) bemoan the environmental degradation associated with this industrial megaproject and point to the myriad of social problems associated with hyperdevelopment. In contrast, proponents such as Ezra Levant (2010) claim that the "dirty oil" moniker used by environmentalists and other critics of bitumen development do not do justice to the benefits of Canada's "ethical" oil: that is, oil that comes from a nation that safeguards its citizens' rights and freedoms. Six months after the 2010 publication of Levant's *Ethical Oil: The Case for Canada's Oil Sands*, Prime Minister Stephen Harper began to draw attention to Canada's liberal-democratic institutions in order to promote Canadian bitumen sands on the international stage, particularly in the United States. The questions driving this chapter are these: What explains the emergence of the dirty/ethical oil monikers in reference to Alberta's primary resource? And why has the use of these terms led to such a polarized debate?

This chapter makes two arguments. The first is that the dirty/ethical debate represents a dramatic shift in the trajectory of Alberta's energy regime. The debate stems from the connection of Canadian oil-driven economic prosperity to American national security, a connection that is both a result of the entrenchment of neoliberalism and a tool to consolidate it within the Canadian landscape. Both industry and governments cast resistance to the current rapid pace of bitumen extraction as opposition to economic prosperity and, more importantly, to national security conceived in continental terms. Points of view that are in opposition to government policy are construed as treasonous resistance to a continentalized border and economy, making critics unpatriotic at best and criminal at worst. While the trajectory of Alberta's energy regime is shifting once again with the collapse in the price of oil in 2015 and the subsequent election of an NDP government in the province, the negative view of those who question bitumen extraction policy lingers on.

Second, while Alberta's citizens are typically construed as a homogeneous bloc whose interests are tied inextricably to the energy sector, this chapter will demonstrate that this view is simplistic. A particular set of historical circumstances in Alberta's democratic development helped to downplay the diversity of interests in the province, in addition to providing fertile grounds for those who would later sow the seeds of neoliberalism. For those who seek to challenge Alberta's unbridled economic development strategy, seeking support outside Canada offers opportunities to materialize their concerns about negative outcomes of hypercapitalism. As Gattinger and others have observed, environmental groups, labour unions, associations, and other nongovernmental actors can take advantage of the transnational character of the energy sector to add progressive voices to the milieu of its development (Gattinger 2005). Yet the strategy of bitumen sands opponents of leveraging international pressure on domestic decision makers may also be short-sighted, given bitumen's precarious position in a rapidly changing and unpredictable global oil market.

Alberta Oil: Neoliberal Transformation, Consolidation, and Resistance

In "Neoliberal Transformation and Antiglobalization Politics in Canada," William Carroll and William Little (2001) explore the specificity of neoliberal transformation in Canada by focusing on its peculiar history, geography, and organization of the state. They argue that the adoption of neoliberal ideas has been facilitated by Canada's regional political identities. Because the control of most aspects of education, health, welfare, labour law, and resource development rests with the provinces, Canada's federal structure of divided sovereignty provided the base "for launching certain elements of the neoliberal project, well in advance of the trade agreements" (39).

Carroll and Little identify "neoliberal mentalities of political and economic rule" as being critical for both the transition to neoliberalism and its consolidation (46). A neoliberal mentality involves attitudinal changes about the role of the state and markets in social life. "Alongside the new economic regime of accumulation is a political culture or 'governmentality' in which market rationales and 'active citizenship' replace the social rationales and entitlements of the postwar era" (46). Political and cultural identity is transformed; Prime Minister Pierre Trudeau's "good and just society" embodied by the activist welfare state is replaced by a neoliberal understanding of the relation of public to private, citizenship, and the role of government in managing the economy in a global era. Individual responsibility is emphasized, while universal entitlements associated with the welfare state are diminished. The free choice and autonomy that underpin this discourse ultimately create "new circuits" of control that limit the possibilities of resistance to neoliberal globalization through industry deregulation, increased self-regulation, and disciplinary procedures (51–53).

Although all Canadian provinces have adopted neoliberalism to varying degrees, the ideology finds its most comfortable home in free enterprise Alberta (39). The widely accepted view in Alberta that the development of Canadian national sovereignty will be done at the province's expense made it easy to resist nation-building exercises in favour of a less active role for the state—a role that was perceived to fit more closely with Alberta's interests. While Canada was already following other industrialized nations down the neoliberal path through state restructuring and the signing of continental free-trade agreements, it was the 2006 installation of Stephen Harper's federal Progressive Conservative government at a time when oil prices were climbing to record-breaking levels that signified the final nail in the coffin of a nationally focused, federal government-directed energy policy that might in any way resemble Trudeau's National Energy Program (NEP). The NEP will be discussed later in this chapter; suffice to say at this juncture that most Albertans despised it and that it still figures prominently on their list of historic grievances. Harper's Conservatives are now using the same energy playbook favoured by Alberta's Conservatives—specifically, that "security" is attained by prosperity derived from Alberta oil, which fuels both American and Canadian free market economies (Canada, Department of Finance 2012, 101–2). In this context, "economic security" is defined by strong economic growth based on oil extraction, regardless of whether the benefits of this growth accrue to more than a small minority of the population.

The evolution of the oil economy in Alberta and Canada provides the context for understanding both the resistance to the security/prosperity discourse and attempts to restrain and contain this resistance. To illustrate why the energy debate is so polarized, the following section tracks energy relationships among Alberta's provincial government, Canada's federal government, and the US Administration in three critical periods. The first period comprises the energy sector's early development, and its later evolution in the era of both province and nation building, that provided the foundation for neoliberal transformation. The second period saw the consolidation of neoliberalism, punctuated by a sharp turn toward protection from international terrorism. The third period is characterized by the entrenchment of the security/prosperity nexus in the post-9/11 period of revved up economic growth and rapidly rising oil prices, followed by an economic crash, recovery, and shifting demand for Alberta's oil. In the third period, those who frame the energy discourse in terms of security and economic growth stand in stark opposition to those who frame it in social or environmental terms.

The Project of Nation and Province Building: The Context for Transformation

The British North American Act of 1867 (BNA Act) formalized the Canadian federation by establishing a unique regime that mixed provincial rights with parliamentary supremacy. Uslaner (1992, 42–43) summarizes the tension this can produce: "The BNA Act reserved all lands, mines, minerals, and royalties within a province's borders to provincial control. Yet the act also permits the federal government to regulate international and interprovincial trade and to control any provincial works that it 'declares' to be 'for the general advantage of Canada' or 'of two or more of the provinces.'"

The situation in the West was complicated by the fact that the Prairie provinces were created after Confederation. Prior to becoming provinces, the western territories provided the resources for the industrial machines of the central Canadian heartland. Canada's National Policy ensured that the terms of trade were favourable for protecting these nascent industries, preventing westerners from engaging in trade on more favourable terms with the United States.

Even after Manitoba, Saskatchewan, and Alberta became provinces (in 1870, 1905, and 1905, respectively), the federal government retained administrative control over their natural resources in order to advance the broader interests of the new nation. After protracted negotiations, the federal government finally transferred control of natural resources to the western provinces in 1930 (Canada, Parliament 1930). In Alberta, this struggle for control of its resources began the tug-of-war between the federal government and Alberta's political and economic elite, which became a defining feature of the new province's identity.

Other groups in Alberta also were concerned with property rights. Waves of immigrants came to Canada at the turn of the twentieth century, enticed by the federal government with promises of land. When WW I broke out, many of these non-Anglo Saxon immigrants had title to their property revoked and were imprisoned under the War Measures Act because they held passports issued by the Austrio-Hungarian and Turkish empires, with whom Canada was at war. Ironically, many of these migrants had fled those empires because they had become ethnic minorities when their homelands were annexed during various European conflicts. Disproportionate numbers of these same minorities were later sterilized under the eugenics program of the Alberta government in an attempt to control the "mentally feeble" (Christian 1974). During World War II, it was the Japanese who were imprisoned. In both wars, the internment camps were disproportionately located in Alberta and British Columbia, and many former inmates settled in the local area. This dark early history helps to explain why a distrust of government and a devotion to the protection of private property permeates all facets of Alberta society. As noted in chapters 2 and 14 of this volume, the various forces of populism, progressivism, and distrust of central Canadian political and economic forces coalesced in what C. B. Macpherson (1953) described as "business government," wherein the role of government is limited to fostering favourable conditions for economic development. While this conception of government is consistent with neoliberalism, it is also consistent with developmental liberalism within a liberal democratic framework. Fostering economic development only becomes problematic in the developmental liberalism context when its broad definition is replaced by the narrowly defined interests of a dominant industry—in Alberta's case, agriculture, followed by oil.

When Peter Lougheed and the upstart Progressive Conservative Party swept into power in 1971, the role of government changed. Lougheed promoted province building through purposeful economic development (Dyck 1986, 481), making large investments in infrastructure and education (Wood 1985, 100–105) and managing both the province's finances and its economy through the establishment of the Heritage Savings Trust Fund (Le Riche 2006, 172). At that time, the Canadian economy was centred in and around the profitable manufacturing hub in Ontario and Québec (Innis 1995), albeit tied deeply to the American market. Recognizing that a global energy crisis was developing, Lougheed set his sights on developing Alberta's vast oil and natural gas reserves by enticing large oil companies to invest in their development (Lougheed 1980). This strategy was not a break from the past; over 90 percent of oil and gas assets in the 1970s were foreign owned, primarily by American-based companies (Fossum 1997, 25). At the same time, however, Lougheed raised oil extraction royalty rates (Wood 1985, 141–42), earning him the title of "the blue-eyed sheikh" (Pratt 2012).

Internationally, major oil-producing countries formed the Organization of Peteroleum Exporting Countries (OPEC) in 1960, and by 1973, industrialized countries were reeling from escalating oil prices that resulted from price coordination. Because industry in Central Canada relied on imported oil, Canada was not immune to the ensuing price shocks. Prime Minister Trudeau, like US President Nixon and other national leaders, began crafting policies to ensure sovereignty, economic stability, and protection from fluctuating energy costs. The creation of the Crown corporation PetroCanada in 1975 and the NEP in 1980 was an attempt to ensure Canadian energy independence. These initiatives—in particular, the NEP—were bitterly unpopular in Alberta, reminding Albertans once again of previous institutional arrangements that had made their province a subordinate partner in the Canadian confederation. In the words of Lougheed, the NEP was received in Alberta as "an outright attempt to take over the resources of [the] province" (Lougheed 1980).

During the 1970s, the Americans were looking north to diversify their supply of oil and move it away from the politically unstable Middle East. Writing soon after the 1973 OPEC oil embargo, Ted Greenwood (1974, 695) observed that

> shortages of domestic oil and gas in the United States and rising world oil prices have caused an increased American demand for Canadian crude and calls by both American legislators and administration officials for a continental energy policy. . . . At the same time the combination of declining conventional reserves, disappointing results in frontier exploration, and rising Canadian nationalism has led to a Canadian rethinking of long-term strategy for oil and gas exports.

With respect to oil and natural gas, Canada-US relations were as complex in the 1970s as they are now. Canada's concerns centred on ensuring self-sufficiency in domestic supply for its manufacturing sector, Alberta's concerns focused on garnering foreign direct investment in its nascent industry, and American concerns revolved around ensuring access to Canadian supply at prices that were not disruptive to American domestic oil suppliers.

This was also the era when neoliberal thought began to be expressed in the policies of Margaret Thatcher in Britain and Ronald Reagan in the United States. In Canada, Prime Minister Brian Mulroney replaced Trudeau in 1984, and in Alberta, Premier Don Getty replaced Peter Lougheed the following year. The new leaders did not have their predecessors' appetite for government using the state for nation or province building, and thus the way was paved for the transition to neoliberalism at the national and provincial levels. At the federal level, Mulroney discontinued the NEP and privatized PetroCanada. In Alberta, the predilection for smaller government was supported by the fiscal woes brought on by the collapse of the price of oil, which dropped to a meagre $9 per barrel in 1986, shortly after Lougheed left office. Despite efforts to diversify the economy, Alberta was more dependent on oil revenue than ever before (Pratt 2012). With 40 percent of the provincial budget coming from oil revenue, Alberta was particularly susceptible to fluctuations in global oil prices. The new premier cut spending in a vain attempt to balance the budget, but he also used public funds in an attempt to shore up Alberta's failing businesses. By the time of Getty's departure from office, the provincial debt had reached $11 billion. The stage was thus set for a dramatic change in policy direction.

Consolidation: 9/11 and the Alberta Advantage

Neoliberalism leapt forward under the leadership of Ralph Klein, who became premier in 1993. A former mayor of Calgary, Klein believed that the financial management of the province should resemble municipal financial management; he adopted policies aimed at balancing the books. Klein reduced the debt and deficit through eliminating government jobs, contracting out services, downsizing government, and cutting education and health care expenditures. Most importantly, the Klein government reduced oil royalties in order to encourage investment in what was then a very depressed industry because of the low price of oil. It also reduced personal and corporate taxes to the lowest in the country and adopted the "Alberta Advantage" corporate brand.

Of these changes, the reduction of taxes has arguably had the most significant impact on the relationship between citizens and the state. Alberta is unique among provinces in that until 2015, it did not have a progressive income tax system; all citizens who earn above $17,787 paid a 10 percent flat tax. For middle- and high-income earners, this represents a huge tax saving. For low-income earners, however, there is little tax relief. Additionally, Alberta is the only province in Canada that does not have a provincial sales tax. When citizens pay very low taxes, the bond between citizens and their government is weakened. Politicians must be re-elected of course, but when little money is generated directly from citizens, the political focus is on those who make the largest contributions to government budgets. While Alberta boasts low corporate rates of taxation, the government's dependence on resource rents for its operating expenses provides high incentive to nurture the corporate-government connection. Very low participation rates in elections in Alberta, which dipped to 40.6 percent in 2008 (Leger Marketing 2008), give Albertans the distinction of being among the most apathetic citizenry in Canada. Even in one of the most exciting elections in recent memory, voter turnout in 2015 was less than 54 percent (Elections Alberta 2015). Neoliberal governments have repeatedly told citizens over two decades that the government's role in their lives should be minimal; it appears that many have begun to believe that the state truly is so irrelevant that they cannot be bothered to vote.

In addition to changing Alberta's tax structure, Premier Klein (and Stelmach after him) set Alberta on a path of deep integration with the United States with respect to energy policy. Both premiers made trips south to "pitch the Americans on the notion that Alberta's bitumen sands represent an energy source of strategic importance to the continent" (Byfield 2002). In the United States, the Clinton and Bush II eras led a global shift toward neoliberalism through a number of regulatory reforms such as dismantling the Glass-Steagall Act. During this time, Klein and Stelmach's promotion of bitumen development met little resistance—perhaps because the environmental degradation was perceived to be "remote" and of little consequence (Stefanick 2009). The global shift toward a neoliberal policy orientation at the international, national, and provincial levels did not occur without resistance, however.

Around the turn of the millennium, a number of massive protests took centre stage in cities like Santiago (1998), Seattle (1999), and Québec City (2001) to protest the excesses of capital and the entrenchment of neoliberalism as a policy framework serving the interests of transnational corporations and an emerging global elite. Labour union representatives, environmentalists, students, pro-democracy activists, and others marginalized by decades of government cuts, decreased access to services, job losses, and environmental strain took to the streets. Energy policy was a concern to the extent that it was tied to the activities of transnational corporations and the global elite who ran them; however, the issues associated with bitumen extraction were not yet top of mind. That said, the move away from energy conservation in this era was underscored by the opulent lifestyles of those who were benefitting from the new global order. When OPEC cut production to take advantage of increased consumption, oil prices rose, and those least able to afford the increased costs were hurt by the price inflation. By early 2001, these protests had disrupted a number of international meetings, capturing the attention of media, the general public, and law enforcement. The events of 11 September 2001, however, dramatically changed the framing of these protests from being a legitimate response to the policies of neoliberalism to being unpatriotic and even treasonous.

The September 11 terrorist attacks were pivotal for American foreign policy; the top priorities of the United States became ensuring security and curbing the spread of terrorism. Before 2001, the focus of the American public was on energy—specifically, how to ensure affordable energy from a reliable source in the face of increasing demand. Oil and gas shortages, rising prices at the gas pumps, and periodic electrical power blackouts in California heightened American anxiety about long-term energy supply. At US$2.50 per gallon, the price of gasoline became the dominant issue of the presidential election contested by Vice President Al Gore and Texas Governor George W. Bush. Since 9/11, however, concern for American national security has defined a number of continental policies, such as border security, drug trafficking, and, as this chapter contends, energy security.

A particularly poignant example of the difference between the pre- and post-9/11 American world view is demonstrated by the question posed by a Wall Street columnist just prior to 9/11: "While the U.S. imports 52 percent of its energy, it's not clear why that's a problem either. The producing countries will always have an incentive to sell the oil somewhere, and in a world market, the U.S. will always be able to buy its portion. Moreover, foreign producers also tend to be the low-cost producers. Why make U.S. consumers pay higher prices to drain domestic reserves?" (Taylor 2001). After 9/11, most Americans could answer this question: they have grave concerns about oil-producing nations holding their country hostage to threats of turning off the taps. Moreover, existing producers were unable to keep up with increased demand for energy caused by the global economic boom beginning in 2003. Upheavals such as Nigeria's civil war, the ongoing conflicts in Iraq, and hurricanes in the Gulf of Mexico further disrupted supply. Prices rose 300 percent, with some observers claiming that the price increase was a result of oil companies manipulating prices in response to disruptions (Smith, Carlisle, and Michaud 2003). Whatever the source of rising oil prices, the concern over America's energy security became that much more acute. Unconventional sources of crude oil that were previously prohibitively expensive (such as the bitumen and heavy oil found in Alberta and Venezuela, and the shale in mineral deposits in the US Rocky Mountains) now became an attractive alternative.

In the immediate post-9/11 world, the idea of increasing oil imports from its "friendly neighbour," Canada, became very appealing to Americans. With oil prices reaching unprecedented levels, Alberta's lucrative extraction of natural resources became an increasingly important component of the Canadian economy (Stanford 2008, 7). The new federal government elected in 2006 moved swiftly to cement the security/prosperity nexus.

The Entrenchment of the Security/Prosperity Nexus

The economic policy *Advantage Canada: A Strong Economy for Canadians* (Canada, Department of Finance 2006) outlined the top priorities of the new Conservative government led by Stephen Harper. As one might expect from a title so closely linked with the Alberta Advantage corporate brand, the five major components of the federal policy were the following: reducing personal and corporate taxes; eliminating government net debt; reducing "unnecessary regulations" and burdensome "red tape"; creating an educated, skilled, and flexible workforce; and building modern infrastructure as required (6). In terms of energy, the Harper government aligned itself with those of Premiers Klein and Stelmach: "Advances in technology have made the Alberta oil sands a viable alternative to conventional sources and are pushing down costs of production for renewable sources. In the oil sands alone investments could top $100 billion over the next decade" (61). Moreover, "the Government will support Canada's emergence as an energy superpower by making the needed investments in knowledge and people and creating the economic environment that will attract capital from home and abroad" (61).

With the economy red hot in 2007, including skyrocketing prices for energy and record profits for oil companies, growing public pressure in Alberta suggested that oil companies should be paying higher royalty rates, despite internal government reviews saying that royalty rates were appropriate. Premier Stelmach ordered an external review, and the resulting report not only recommended increasing royalty rates by nearly 20 percent for all three major resources (conventional oil, natural gas, and bitumen) but also noted that the government had failed to collect royalties already owed (Hunter et al. 2007). The government partially implemented the review panel's recommendations, although it then rolled back many of the royalty increases in 2010, after the economic downturn.

The nexus between security and economic prosperity at the provincial, national, and international levels remained strong after President Obama was elected in 2008. Obama's first foreign visit was to Canada to meet with Prime Minister Harper, and among the top priorities on their agenda were economic recovery, energy, and security (Canada, PMO 2009). These sentiments manifested in a number of ways through Canada's coordinated efforts with the United States on security and economic growth. Both governments jointly released *Beyond the Border: A Shared Vision for Perimeter Security and Economic Competitiveness* as a declaration for "a new long-term partnership" in order to "enhance our security and accelerate the legitimate flow of people, goods, and services between our two countries" (Canada, Foreign Affairs and International Trade 2011, iii, 34). A Canada-United States Regulatory Cooperation Council was established, aiming "to better align our regulatory approaches to protect health, safety, and the environment while supporting growth, investment, innovation and market openness" (v). In the area of security, *Beyond the Border* notes areas of cooperation as joint integrated threat assessments, a harmonized approach to screening cargo and travellers, and shared information on immigration. With respect to strategies to increase trade and bolster economic growth, the report cites as examples the free flow of goods and services, supply-chain connectivity, and the reduction of administrative burdens through streamlining (12–22).

In terms of the energy sector, the freer flow of goods causes deeper integration of Canada and the United States. Canada's export of energy products (including oil, natural gas, and electricity) had been steadily increasing since 2000–2001 (Canada, NEB 2011, 1). By 2010, almost all of Canada's oil exports were going to the United States, representing 22 percent of US oil imports (3). The bulk of US imports of natural gas was also coming from Canada, representing 14 percent of US consumption (4). The security/prosperity nexus encouraged this energy relationship, facilitated the consolidation of neoliberal reforms in Canada and the United States, and hindered resistance to its effects. This is not to suggest, however, that dissenting voices were silent. Indeed, it was the articulation of the negative effects of rapid resource extraction for export that led to both the "dirty oil" descriptor by opponents of bitumen extraction and the adoption of the "ethical oil" moniker as a counterpoint. The Canadian federal government subsequently adopted the notion of oil as ethical, using this as a tool to stifle opposition, particularly that pertaining to the environment.

Environmental Resistance and the Neutralizing of Dissent

The consolidation of neoliberal policy and the increasing intransigence of its opponents were occurring at the same time that challenges to the security/prosperity framing of bitumen development were assuming new and more powerful forms. The sheer scale of the project to extract oil out of the province's massive reserves strikes anyone who visits the bitumen sands industrial complex in northern Alberta. The bitumen lies under 140,200 square kilometres; as of 31 December 2012, 767 square kilometres had been cleared or disturbed for development (Alberta, Alberta Energy 2014). Bitumen oil extraction is criticized because of its heavy toll on the environment; for example, two tonnes of bitumen sands must be extracted to produce one barrel of crude oil. As discussed in chapter 7 in this volume, additional environmental impacts include the destruction of habitat and its impact on wildlife and birds; the removal of peatland, which in its intact state acts as a carbon sink; greenhouse gases that are emitted as part of the extraction process; the amount of water used (although estimates vary, according to one government source, three to four barrels of water are used to mine one barrel of oil [Canada, NRC 2013, 3]); and the storage of contaminated water in massive tailings ponds, now covering 176 square kilometers of land. Back in 1999, the environmental issues had sufficient profile that the Canadian Senate Subcommittee on the Boreal Forest wrote: "The world's boreal forest, a resource of which Canada is the major trustee, is under siege" (quoted in Burton et al. 2003).

When the sharp increase in oil prices in 2003 made extracting oil from bitumen cost effective, the environmental community in Alberta became seriously alarmed and began to look outside the province for support. In December 2005, twelve prominent, nationally focused environmental groups issued a declaration that urged politicians to institute a new bitumen sands "licence to operate." Two years later, 1,500 scientists from more than fifty countries petitioned the Canadian government to protect the boreal forest (CBC News 2007). Critics also pointed out the myriad of social concerns and complained that the low royalty paid for this nonrenewable resource results in a massive transfer of wealth from the people of Alberta to oil corporations (Campanella 2012). Yet despite the environmental damage of the bitumen sands operations, its social consequences, and its impact on local Indigenous groups, the critics failed to garner much media attention or to mobilize significant opposition within the province to bitumen extraction projects.

It was the deaths of 1,600 migrating birds that mistook a tailings pond for fresh water in 2008 that galvanized media attention (Nelson et al. 2015). That same year, Andrew Nikiforuk's book *Tar Sands: Dirty Oil and the Future of a Continent* appeared in bookstores, and the moniker of "dirty oil" became the tagline of opponents. The following year, Canadian activists made a presentation about the global impact of the bitumen extraction at a "green summit" in rural Virginia attended by top American environmental activists (McCarthy 2012). The National Energy Board's approval of the construction of TransCanada's 1,897-kilometre Keystone XL pipeline elevated American concern over Alberta oil. The $7 billion pipeline would carry hundreds of thousands of barrels of bitumen from Alberta to Nebraska daily; it had been under review since 2008, and the US Department of State concluded in the spring of 2010 that the impacts on the environment would be minimal. The conflict between proponents and opponents took the familiar form of "jobs versus the environment." Over 1,250 were arrested during a sit-in, and nine winners of the Nobel Peace Prize wrote President Obama urging him to reject the Keystone proposal and to pursue renewable and clean energy sources.

By the fall of 2011, President Obama had revoked approval, necessitating a reapplication to the US Department of the State for a Presidential Permit to allow the pipeline to cross the border. The president of Friends of the Earth, Erich Pica, responded to Obama's decision and captured the position of environmental opponents in the debate:

> Today's announcement is a welcome example of President Obama following
> through on his promise that corporate polluter lobbyists will no longer set
> the agenda in Washington.... The Keystone XL pipeline would have been
> dirty at both ends, dangerous in between, and certainly not in our national

interest. Big Oil and its bought-and-paid-for confederates in Congress couldn't drown this dirty reality despite all of their threats and bullying. (Friends of the Earth 2012)

Not to be outdone, the federal government in Canada countered with equally strong rhetoric. In an open letter to Canadians posted on the Government of Canada website, Minister of Natural Resources Joe Oliver claimed that

> there are environmental and other radical groups that would seek to block this opportunity to diversify our trade.... These groups threaten to hijack our regulatory system to achieve their radical ideological agenda. They seek to exploit any loophole they can find, stacking public hearings with bodies to ensure that delays kill good projects. They use funding from foreign special interest groups to undermine Canada's national economic interest. They attract jet-setting celebrities with some of the largest personal carbon footprints in the world to lecture Canadians not to develop our natural resources. (Oliver 2012)

Environment Minister Peter Kent went further, alleging that "some Canadian charitable agencies have been used to launder off-shore foreign funds" (Max Paris Environmental Unit 2012). These statements stake out the position of the federal government in the clearest of terms: those who oppose the promotion of economic interests have a radical agenda.

In 2011, thirty members of the House of Representatives (both Republicans and Democrats from eighteen states) wrote a letter to Secretary of State Hillary Rodham Clinton in support of the approval of the Keystone XL project. According to the members, "Dependence on foreign oil has created difficult geopolitical relationships with damaging consequences for our national security." They summarized the Keystone issue as being not only a matter of national interest but also a matter of national security and urged Clinton to approve the transport of Canadian oil in order to minimize the need for the United States to purchase oil from nondemocratic countries in volatile regions of the world (TransCanada 2011). The same year, Michigan's House of Representatives passed a bill that used similar language in support of the approval of the Keystone pipeline (Michigan, Legislature, House of Representatives 2011).

What is notable about the language used is that Canadian oil is seen as an alternative to "foreign" oil. This conceptualization of Canadian oil as a "domestic" source springs from Canada's position as a friendly liberal democratic ally of the United States: the choice for consumers is between purchasing fuel from liberal democratic countries or from regimes that violate basic rights and freedoms. Popularized by Ezra Levant in 2010, this view is based on the argument that the environmental critique of Alberta's bitumen sands is incomplete and that Canada's record needs to be compared to those of other oil-producing nations (Levant 2010, 53). A 2011 report from the Fraser Institute by Mark Milke picks up this theme. Using a variety of measures, Milke analyzes thirty-eight oil-exporting countries that produce 250,000 barrels per day. He concludes that "with the exception of Norway, Canada is the only major oil exporting country that scores highly on all measurements of civil, political, and economic freedom, including the rights of women to full career, medical and travel choices, media freedom, religious freedom, and property rights, as well as on other measurements such as judicial independence and relative freedom from corruption" (Milke 2011, ii). Ethical oil proponents conclude that the net effect of demonizing Canadian oil will be to drive consumers to buy their oil from states with far worse records, using any type of measure.

The billion-dollar question, of course, is, What are the "right" things to measure? The Fraser Institute's measures are confined to individual freedoms and government priorities that impact individual freedom, and the economic and social well-being of individuals. Freedom is defined as the ability to participate in democratic elections, judicial freedom, media freedom, religious freedom, and so on. The Fraser Institute report also includes property rights as an indicator of freedom (Milke 2011, 25). While the report does include measures of such things as literacy rates and access to education as proxy measures of freedoms that contribute to social well-being, it makes no attempt to assess the freedom of minority groups, freedom from poverty, or the health of the environment (31). This focus on individually defined freedom is consistent with the neoliberal emphasis on personal responsibility; however, it is in direct conflict with a view of the state as playing an important role in promoting a more generalized public good. Even the very notion of an identifiable Canadian identity with respect to ownership could be questioned, given that the majority of shareholders of Canadian companies (defined as located in Canada, traded on the Canadian stock exchange, and using Canadian accounting practices) are foreign nationals, and over half of oil and gas revenue goes to foreign entities (De Souza 2012).

While the debate raged on over whether Alberta oil is "ethical" or "dirty," both the federal and provincial governments began to dismantle the structures that had been set in place after WW II to provide both public and scientific input into environmental protection processes. The goal was to make the environmental review process more "efficient," with efficiency defined as the speed with which approvals can be made. Along with the 2012 budget, the federal government passed Bill C-38, a massive omnibus bill that included a completely new environmental assessment law, repealed the Kyoto Protocol Implementation Act, weakened protection of at-risk species, decreased opportunities for public participation in environmental decision making, weakened accountability by allowing more decisions to be made by cabinet and individual ministers, allowed cabinet to override decisions made by the National Energy Board, and contained an entirely new environmental assessment law that sets timelines for environmental assessment hearings and narrows the range of projects that will come under review (May 2012). Another omnibus bill was subsequently passed in 2012 with equally devastating consequences for environmental protection: Bill C-45 made major changes to the Navigation Protection Act and the Environmental Protection Act.

The changes to the environmental protection regime were profound, and since they were contained in massive omnibus bills, the opportunities for debate and deliberation was minimized. In the case of Bill C-38, the time frame was seven days (Whittington 2012). The amendments to the Navigation Protection Act and the Environmental Protection Acts followed cuts to and dismantling of advisory bodies such as the National Roundtable on the Environment and Economy and the Canadian Environmental Network, the latter of which comprises hundreds of environmental groups across Canada and, according to its website, now operates on a volunteer basis. Environment Canada was also dramatically cut, and almost twenty thousand public servants were notified that they would lose their jobs, including the cadre of scientists within government departments and agencies who provided policy advice based on their environmental expertise (CBC News 2012a). Given the Keystone controversy, it is ironic that these sweeping cuts included the Environmental Emergencies Program, the group that coordinated the clean up of oil spills. In 2013, Alberta experienced two particularly large and damaging environmental incidents involving bitumen extraction that together were named the fifth-top news-making story of the year by the *Edmonton Journal* ("Top Stories" 2013).

Alberta followed the lead of the federal government with respect to environmental deregulation, albeit using a very different strategy. In December 2013, seventy-five environmental officers who provided oversight of bitumen extraction companies left their government posts to take higher-paying jobs with the newly created, arms-length Alberta Energy Regulator, which is funded by the oil, gas, and coal industries. By eliminating the Energy Resources Conservation Board, which was funded by both government and industry, the government handed over responsibility to administer the Water Act, the Public Lands Act, and the Environmental Protection and Enhancement Act, with respect to issues pertaining to the energy industry, to the industry-funded regulator. Critics argue that having the regulator entirely funded by industry makes it vulnerable to regulatory capture, especially given that the chair of the new entity is one of the founders of a leading industry lobby group—the Canadian Association of Petroleum Producers (Pratt 2013; Valentine 2013).

Federally, the auditing of nonprofit groups to ensure that their advocacy activities amount to less than 10 percent of their overall budget was yet another tool to discipline dissenting voices (Canadian Press 2012). Under rules set out in the Income Tax Act and a Federal Court ruling, groups that have nonprofit status are allowed to pursue nonpartisan advocacy work that is directly related to their group's mission as long as these activities do not consume more than 10 percent of their budget. Maintaining charitable status is critical to the ability of nonprofits to raise funds, since donors can deduct donations from their income tax. The Tides Foundation provides grants to Canadian environmental and social justice groups and was among those organizations singled out for audit because it receives support from American charitable foundations. A Tides spokesperson opined, "I do think it's very likely . . . that the government is really looking at environmental charities, and looking for ways to limit the effectiveness of those charities as they try and stimulate discussion and public discourse around major public-policy developments relating to resource extraction and the like" (Canadian Press 2012). The federal budget of 2012 proposed other disciplinary measures, such as fines and limits on the amounts of money charities can give to other charities for advocacy work, in order "to ensure that charities devote their resources primarily to charitable, rather than political, activities, and to enhance public transparency and accountability in this area" (Canada, Department of Finance 2012, 189). This followed the announcement, by the MP for Athabasca-Fort McMurray Brian Jean, of plans to put forward a private member's bill "to make sure that these people that receive the benefit of a non-profit status are transparent" (Banman 2012).

Jean (who would become the leader of Alberta's official opposition, the Wildrose Party, in 2015) eventually introduced a bill; however, Bill C-526, "Cracking Down on Organized Crime and Terrorism Act," focused on "gang members, organized criminals and terrorists." While Bill C-526 was not passed, the federal Conservatives did introduce another bill that reflects that party's focus on security. Bill C-51 sought to facilitate information sharing within government (with little or no restraints on how information is used—or misused), give authorities the power to arrest and detain people suspected of terrorism, widen the scope of what is considered to be a terrorist act, and greatly enhance the power of Canada's spy agency, CSIS (Forcese and Roach 2015). One hundred academics (mainly law professors) signed an open letter criticizing the bill, and rallies were held across Canada protesting both the method of passing the bill (cutting off debate) and the substance of the bill—specifically, its threats to freedom of speech in the name of national security (Payton 2015).

According to Carroll and Little (2001), the significance of the neoliberal mentality is that it removes the space for meaningful political contestation. Branding a discussion "against the national interest" effectively moves it out of the arena of debate. Cutting government funding to charities such as the Canadian Environmental Network serves to silence potential dissenters. Threatening remaining charities with fines or a revocation of the charitable status that is critical to their ability to fundraise is yet another way of chilling the debate. Cutting support to agencies that solicit input or promote evidence-based decision making in the name of fiscal austerity serves the same purpose. As noted by Carroll and Little (2011, 52), "when the activity of government is refocused on questions of cost, priority, efficiency, accountability, and 'continuous improvement' in the delivery of services, the space for debate on substantial public issues concerning social justice and citizenship rights is severely restricted." The neoliberal conceptualization of the citizen's place in society focuses on the rights of the individual; it has little to say about the possibilities for either collective choice or collective responsibility. Describing dissenters to the ethical oil narrative as using funds from "foreign special interest groups" or as being "radical" (Oliver 2012), or accusing them of "'laundering' funds from offshore donors" (CBC News 2012b) disperses and neutralizes resistance, which, as Carroll and Little (2011, 52) argue, "minimizes the opportunities for collective resistance to form around a common demonized identity." Using the levers of the state to discipline those who challenge neoliberal policies and the continentalization project neutralizes dissent. Neutralized dissent, however, is not equivalent to provincial consensus. This point is underscored by the unexpected results of the 2015 provincial election, when the nearly forty-four-year rule of the hegemonic Progressive Conservative Party came to a dramatic end, replaced by the left-leaning NDP, who rose from a mere four seats to form government. As has been demonstrated in this chapter, the interests of Albertans are not static; nor are they homogeneous.

Dirty Oil, Ethical Oil, and the Public Interest

This analysis underscores the importance of American and Canadian national interests in the development of Alberta's energy sector. Recently, the ethical versus dirty oil debate entered the discussion, allowing the two camps to pitch simplistic but convenient flags. Through the neoliberalization of the provincial, national, and continental economies, there has been a dramatic shift from the province- and nation-building aspirations of the Lougheed-Trudeau era to a neoliberal agenda built on, and reinforced by, the security/economic prosperity nexus. With this shift, we see the transformation of both political and cultural identity. Pierre Trudeau's notion of a "good and just society" embodied by robust social programs and Loughheed's use of the state to build infrastructure and diversify the economy are being replaced by a neoliberal conceptualization of the relationship between the state and citizen, wherein the primary role of the state is to provide security defined in terms of physical safety as opposed to social well-being. In this view of identity, divergent views are framed as being in opposition to national security and economic prosperity.

Three distinct developmental periods of Canada's oil industry help to explain why neoliberalism found such a natural home in Alberta, and more recently, why the debate over resource extraction has become so bitter. The first period sets the stage for Alberta's democratic development; it provides the context for Alberta's "business government" during the era when oil was discovered. During the latter part of this period, Premier Lougheed's province-building strategies collided with Prime Minister Trudeau's nation-building strategies, leaving an indelible mark on the psyche of Alberta. The clash over the NEP is the defining moment of this period, congealing Alberta's identity as a political community alienated from the interests of Central Canada. The second period begins in the 1990s, when Ralph Klein became the premier of Alberta; this period saw the transformation and consolidation of neoliberalism in Alberta and, later, in Canada more generally. The result of this consolidation is a weakening of the bond between citizens and the state, as the state shrinks its range of activities to focus on economic development. The mid-point of this period saw the end of economic recession, the beginning of global resistance to the neoliberalization of post-industrial economies, and the emerging preoccupation with security as defined by the events of 9/11. The third period began in the early years of the new century; this was the era of hypergrowth in the oil patch as a result of a booming world economy punctuated by a spectacular crash. The province's rapid growth and economic development saw an equally rapid rise in Alberta's political importance on the national stage. With this came the entrenchment of the frame of Canadian oil extraction as domestic US supply within the context of American national security and Canadian economic prosperity.

Oil-based economic growth brings with it social and environmental problems, which have resulted in increasingly frustrated critics taking their concerns to the global arena. New inter- and intrastate relationships have been supported by the framing of Canadian oil as "ethical" and weakened by its portrayal as "dirty," while opposition to the continental energy regime has been construed as radical. With criticism marginalized, neoliberal globalization flourishes: industries operate in an increasingly deregulated or self-regulated environment. Ironically, however, the transnational nature of the oil industry, which has allowed governments to define the public interest from a continental perspective, is the very thing that makes transnational mobilization effective.

The economic downturn of 2008, pronouncements that the development of US shale deposits will position the United States to become energy self-sufficient by 2020, the discovery of shale oil in Australia and China, and the collapse of oil prices in 2014 signal the beginning of another era of global energy relationships. The rise in fortunes of the federal NDP after the election of their provincial counterparts in Alberta provides another interesting variable to consider. A regime change at both levels will change the playing field, as presumably more attention will be given to environmental considerations. Given that bitumen oil is much more expensive to produce than other sources of oil, these new developments will have a significant impact on the markets for Canadian oil and will renew concerns about Canada's energy security due to the continued reliance of Central Canada on imported oil. Canada will move from depending on American consumption of its oil to pursuing emerging markets. New possibilities for resistance present themselves through the globalized and splintered character of the oil industry; however, the "dirty oil" frame that has been effective in the past in focusing attention on the environmental and social costs of bitumen extraction and transport may be less so in the future if the primary consumers of Alberta oil are not American. Similarly, framing Canadian oil as "ethical" will probably become less useful in the future, considering the rapidly changing and complicated market for Canadian oil. The only certainty in all of this is that the debate within Alberta will continue to occupy centre stage, given the enormous economic impact that bitumen extraction has on the province—and the equally enormous social and environmental consequences.

Notes

1 Harper's remarks are quoted in Steven Chase, "Harper's Embrace of 'Ethical' Oil Sands Reignites 'Dirty' Arguments," *Globe and Mail*, 7 January 2011. Kent had just declared that the United States should give preference to Alberta oil on the grounds that it is "the product of a natural resource whose revenues don't go to fund terrorism." Quoted in Steven Chase, "Peter Kent's Green Agenda: Clean Up Oil Sands' Dirty Reputation," *Globe and Mail*, 6 January 2011.

2 See Canada Revenue Agency, 2014, "Alberta Tax and Credits," http://www.cra-arc. gc.ca/E/pbg/tf/5009-c/5009-c-14e.pdf.

3 In the proposed 2015 Alberta budget, Premier Prentice introduced the elimination of the flat tax, replacing it with a progressive tax that, among other things, would see the tax rate of those making over $131,000 rise 1.5 percent over three years. Those who make over $250,000 would pay 2 percent over three years, although in the fourth year, their taxable rate would decrease 0.5 percent (Bellefontaine and Estabrooks 2015). There was no change to the corporate tax or oil royalty rates. While the additional amounts that high-income earners would be paying were modest, Prentice claimed that "this will be the most significant budget in modern times in the province" and that, as such, "whoever is the premier had better have a mandate" (Bennett 2015). With that, the government, breaking its own recently passed law fixing election dates, called an election a year early. The result was the historic election of an NDP majority government, which promised even more significant changes: replacing the flat tax with one that is progressive, increasing corporate taxes, and reviewing royalty rates.

4 The 1933 US Glass-Steagall Act, or the Banking Act, sought "to provide for the safer and more effective use of the assets of banks, to regulate interbank control, to prevent the undue diversion of funds into speculative operations." In 1999, sections 20 and 32, which stated that banks could not be affiliated with securities dealers, were repealed, helping to deregulate the conduct of banks and securities dealers. Since the stock market crash of 2008, a number of policies have been developed in an attempt to regain some government oversight into operations.

5 See "Recovery or Extraction," *Alberta Energy*, 2015, http://www.energy.alberta.ca/ OilSands/1719.asp; see also "Oil Sands: Unlocking Untapped Energy," *Chevron*, 2015, http://www.chevron.com/deliveringenergy/oilsands/.

6 Canadian Association of Petroleum Producers, "Tailings Ponds," *Oil Sands Today*, 2015, http://www.oilsandstoday.ca/topics/Tailings/Pages/default.aspx.

7 See "Managing Oil Sands Development for the Long Term: A Declaration by Canada's Environmental Community," 1 December 2005, http://www.pembina.org/reports/OS_declar_Full.pdf.

8 Bitumen extraction is also criticized for its social impacts: the consequences of hypergrowth on the small city of Fort McMurray, such as severe housing shortages, escalating prices, strained public services, and increased crime and drug use; the declining health of individuals in nearby First Nations communities; the increasing reliance on temporary foreign workers as a solution to chronic labour shortages; the stress on families due to the boom-bust cycle of shiftwork; and the high rate of worker injury and death, including those incurred on the so-called Highway of Death between Fort McMurray and Edmonton, which has seen over 125 fatalities since 1990. (See chapters 7, 8, 9, and 10 in this volume, as well as Bartko and Mertz 2015.)

9 See, for example, "Check the Facts: Energy Security—Good for Nebraska, Good for America," *Nebraskans for Jobs and Energy Independence*, n.d. , http://www.jobsandenergy.org/Facts/EnergySecurity.html.

10 The letter from the Nobel Women's Initiative to the president, dated 7 September 2011, is available at http://nobelwomensinitiative.org/wp-content/uploads/2011/09/KeystoneXL_Obama_Sept2011_Final.pdf.

11 The first incident involved a spill in an in situ bitumen sands project on the Cold Lake Air Weapons Range, while the second incident involved containment ponds on the Athabasca River upstream of the province's largest bitumen site.

References

Alberta. Alberta Energy. 2014. "Alberta's Oil Sands: The Facts." http://www.energy.alberta.ca/OilSands/pdfs/AlbertasOilSandsFactsJan14.pdf.

Banman, Tim. 2012. "Foreigners Funding Anti-oilsands Activities." *St. Paul Journal*, 28 February.

Bartko, Karen, and Emily Mertz. 2015. "Update: 18 Charges Laid in Fatal Highway 63 Crash from October." *Global News*, 24 March. http://globalnews.ca/news/1641909/two-dead-after-bus-and-car-collide-on-highway-63/.

Bellefontaine, Michelle, and Trisha Estabrooks. 2015. "Alberta Budget Delivers Tax Increases for 1st Time in Years." *CBC News*, 26 March. http://www.cbc.ca/news/canada/edmonton/alberta-budget-delivers-tax-increases-for-1st-time-in-years-1.3010696.

Bennett, Dean. 2015. "Alberta Budget Will Be So Radical It Will Likely Trigger an Election, Says Premier Jim Prentice." *Financial Post*, 27 February.

Burton, P. J. , C. Messier, G. F. Weetman, E. E. Prepas, W. L. Adamowicz, and R. Tittler. 2003. "The Current State of Boreal Forestry and the Drive for Change." In *Towards Sustainable Management of the Boreal Forest*, edited by Philip J. Burton, Christian Messier, Daniel W. Smith, and Wicktor L. Adamowicz, 1–40. Ottawa: NRC Research Press.

Byfield, Mike. 2002. "Klein Is Right to Seek US Help Against Ottawa." *The Report Newsmagazine*, 2 December.

Campanella, David. 2012. *Misplaced Generosity: Update 2012—Extraordinary Profits for Canada's Oil and Gas Industry*. Edmonton, AB: Parkland Institute.

Canada. Department of Finance. 2006. *Advantage Canada: Building a Strong Economy for Canadians*. Catalogue No. F2-105/2006-3E. http://www.fin.gc.ca/ec2006/pdf/plane.pdf.

———. 2012. *Jobs, Growth, and Long-Term Prosperity: Economic Action Plan 2012*. Catalogue No. F1-23/3-2012E. http://www.budget.gc.ca/2012/plan/pdf/Plan2012-eng.pdf.

Canada. Foreign Affairs and International Trade. 2011. *Beyond the Border: A Shared Vision for Perimeter Security and Economic Competitiveness*. Catalogue No. FR5-61/2011. http://actionplan.gc.ca/grfx/psec-scep/pdfs/bap_report-paf_rapport-eng-dec2011.pdf.

Canada. NEB (National Energy Board). 2011. *Energy Facts*. https://www.neb-one.gc.ca/nrg/ntgrtd/mrkt/archive/2011nrgytrdfct/nrgtrdfct-eng.pdf.

Canada. NRC (Natural Resources Canada). 2013. *Oil Sands: A Strategic Resource for Canada, North America and the Global Market*. http://www.nrcan.gc.ca/sites/www.nrcan.gc.ca/files/energy/pdf/eneene/pubpub/pdf/OS-brochure-eng.pdf.

Canada. Parliament. 1930. *Alberta Natural Resources Act* (S.C. 1930, c.3). Ottawa: F. A. Acland, King's Printer.

Canada. PMO (Prime Minister's Office). 2009. "President Obama and Prime Minister Harper Vow Joint Effort on North American Economic Recovery: Leaders Establish Clean Energy Dialogue, Discuss Global Security Concerns." News release, 19 February. http://pm.gc.ca/eng/media.asp?id=2432.

Canadian Press. 2012. "Charities That Spend on Political Action a 'Tiny Fraction.'" *CBC News*, 25 April. http://www.cbc.ca/news/politics/story/2012/04/25/politics-charity.html.

Carroll, William, and William Little. 2001. "Neoliberal Transformation and Antiglobalization Politics in Canada: Transition, Consolidation, Resistance." *International Journal of Political Economy* 31 (3): 33–66.

CBC News. 2007. "Scientists Call for Canadian Boreal Forest's Protection." *CBC News*, 14 May. http://www.cbc.ca/news/technology/scientists-call-for-canadian-boreal-forest-s-protection-1.643495.

———. 2012a. "Federal Job Cuts: Tracking the Rollout." *CBC News*, 13 April. http://www.cbc.ca/news/politics/story/2012/04/12/pol-federal-job-cuts-tracker.html.

———. 2012b. "Environmental Charities 'Laundering' Foreign Funds, Kent Says." *CBC News*, 1 May. http://www.cbc.ca/news/politics/environmental-charities-laundering-foreign-funds-kent-says-1.1165691.

Christian, Timothy J. 1974. *The Mentally Ill and Human Rights in Alberta: A Study of the Alberta Sexual Sterilization Act*. Edmonton: Faculty of Law, University of Alberta.

De Souza, Mike. 2012. "Majority of Oil Sands Ownership and Profits Are Foreign, Says Analysis." *Financial Post*, 10 May.

Dyck, Rand. 1986. *Provincial Politics in Canada*. Scarborough, ON: Prentice Hall Canada.

Elections Alberta. 2015. "Provincial General Election May 5, 1015: Winning Candidates—Provincial Results." *Elections Alberta*. http://resultsnew.elections.ab.ca/orResultsPGE.cfm.

Forcese, Craig, and Kent Roach. 2015. "Canada's Antiterror Gamble." *New York Times*, 11 March. http://www.nytimes.com/2015/03/12/opinion/canadas-antiterror-gamble.html?_r=0.

Fossum, John Erik. 1997. *Oil, the State, and Federalism: The Rise and Demise of Petro-Canada as a Statist Impulse*. Toronto: University of Toronto Press.

Friends of the Earth. 2012. "President Obama Rejects the Keystone XL Pipeline." *Friends of the Earth*. News release, 18 January. http://www.foe.org/news/news-releases/2012-01-president-obama-rejects-the-keystone-xl-pipeline.

Gattinger, Monica. 2005. "From Government to Governance in the Energy Sector: The States of the Canada-U.S. Energy Relationship." *American Review of Canadian Studies* 35 (3): 321–52.

Greenwood, Ted. 1974. "Canadian-American Trade in Energy Resources." *International Organization* 28: 689–710.

Hunter, William M. , Evan Chrapko, Judith Dwarkin, Ken McKenzie, André Plourde, and Sam Spanglet. 2007. *Our Fair Share: Report of the Alberta Royalty Review Panel*. Submitted to the Hon. Lyle Oberg, Minister of Finance, 18 September. http://www.energy.alberta.ca/Org/pdfs/RoyaltyReviewPanelfinal_report.pdf.

Innis, Harold A. 1995. "The Importance of Staples Products in Canadian Development." In *Staples, Markets, and Cultural Change*, edited by Daniel Drache, 3–23. Montréal and Kingston: McGill-Queen's University Press.

Leger Marketing. 2008. *Elections Alberta—Evaluation of Voters and Non-Voters: Research Report*. http://www.elections.ab.ca/Public%20Website/files/Documents/Elections_Alberta_-_Voters.pdf.

Le Riche, Timothy. 2006. *Alberta's Oil Patch: The People, Politics, and Companies*. Edmonton, AB: Folklore.

Levant, Ezra. 2010. *Ethical Oil: The Case for Canada's Oil Sands*. Toronto: McClelland and Stewart.

Lougheed, Peter. 1980. Transcript of Premier Lougheed's Address to the Province of Alberta in Reaction to the Federal Budget [Speech]. Edmonton: Legislative Assembly.

Macpherson, C. B. 1953. *Democracy in Alberta: The Theory and Practice of a Quasi-party System*. Toronto: University of Toronto Press.

Max Paris Environmental Unit. 2012. "Charities Urge Peter Kent to Retract 'Laundering' Accusation." *CBC News*, 4 May. http://www.cbc.ca/news/politics/charities-urge-peter-kent-to-retract-laundering-accusation-1.1213026.

May, Elizabeth. 2012. "Bill C-38: The Environmental Destruction Act." *The Tyee*, 10 May. http://thetyee.ca/Opinion/2012/05/10/Bill-C38/.

McCarthy, Shawn. 2012. "The Day the Oil-Sands Battle Went Global." *Globe and Mail*, 6 September.

Michigan. Legislature. House of Representatives. 2011. "House Resolution 0136" (adopted 18 October 2011). http://www.legislature.mi.gov/documents/2011-2012/resolutionadopted/House/htm/2011-HAR-0136.htm.

Milke, Mark. 2011. In *America's National Interest—Canadian Oil: A Comparison of Civil, Political, and Economic Freedoms in Oil-Producing Countries*. Studies in Energy Policy Series. Vancouver: Fraser Institute.

Nikiforuk, Andrew. 2008. *Tar Sands: Dirty Oil and the Future of a Continent*. Vancouver: Greystone Books.

Nelson, Paul, Naomi Krogman, Lindsay Johnston, and Colleen Cassady St. Clair. 2015. "Dead Ducks and Dirty Oil: Media Representations and Environmental Solutions." *Society and Natural Resources: An International Journal* 28 (4): 345–59.

Oliver, Joe. 2012. "An Open Letter from Natural Resources Minister Joe Oliver." *Natural Resources Canada*, 9 January. http://www.nrcan.gc.ca/media-room/news-release/2012/1/1909.

Payton, Laura. 2015. "Anti-terrorism Bill C-51 'Dangerous' Legislation, 100 Academics Say." *CBC News*, 27 February. http://www.cbc.ca/news/politics/anti-terrorism-bill-c-51-dangerous-legislation-100-academics-say-1.2975233.

Pratt, Sheila. 2012. "Peter Lougheed Leaves Lasting Economic and Political Legacy for Alberta." *Edmonton Journal*, 14 September.

———. 2013. "75 Alberta Environment Regulators Now Paid by Oil Industry." Edmonton Journal, 23 December.

Smith, Eric R. A. N. , Juliet Carlisle, and Kristy Michaud. 2003. "Trust During an Energy Crisis." Energy Policy and Economics Working Paper Series No. 6. University of California Energy Institute, Berkeley. http://www.ucei.berkeley.edu/PDF/EPE_006.pdf.

Stanford, Jim. 2008. "Staples, Deindustrialization, and Foreign Investment: Canada's Economic Journey Back to the Future." *Studies in Political Economy* 82 (Autumn): 7–34.

Stefanick, Lorna. 2009. "Who Speaks for the Environment? Alberta's Oil Sands and the Boreal Forest Ecosystem." Paper presented at the biennial conference of the Association for Canadian Studies in the United States, 18–22 November, San Diego.

Taylor, James. 2001. "Supporters of Bush Energy Plan Deflect Criticism: Environment and Climate News." *Wall Street Journal*, 21 August.

"Top Stories of the Year, #5: Unusual, Remote Spills Trigger Environmental Concerns." 2013. *Edmonton Journal*, 25 December.

TransCanada. 2011. "TransCanada Welcomes More Bipartisan Congressional Support for Keystone XL Pipeline Project." News release, 11 February. http://www.transcanada.com/5644.html.

Uslaner, Eric M. 1992. "Energy Policy and Federalism in the United States and Canada." In *The Canada-United States Relationship: The Politics of Energy and Environmental Coordination*, edited by Jonathan Lemco, 41–63. Westport, CT: Praeger.

Valentine, Katie. 2013. "Alberta Tar Sands Will Now Be Regulated by Fossil Fuels–Funded Group." *Climate Progress*, 26 December. http://thinkprogress.org/climate/2013/12/26/3104571/alberta-energy-regulator-tar-sands/#.

Whittington, Les. 2012. "Federal Budget 2012: Tories Criticized for Using Majority to Limit Debate on Omnibus Budget Bill." *Toronto Star*, 3 May.

Wood, David. 1985. *The Lougheed Legacy*. Toronto: Key Porter Books.

The Political Economy of Oil and Democracy in Venezuela and Alberta

Paul Kellogg

The discussion of oil in Alberta is very politically charged. On 5 May 2015, Rachel Notley's New Democratic Party (NDP) won a stunning majority, ending nearly forty-four years of rule by the Progressive Conservatives (PCs). The next day, Canada's major stock exchange plummeted two hundred points, largely in reaction to Notley's campaign promise to review royalties paid by oil and other resource-based corporations (Gerson 2015). Four days before the election, in part prompted by the threat of rising royalty fees, five Edmonton businessmen—including Doug Goss, member of the board of governors of the University of Alberta—held what one commentator labelled a "highly unusual" press conference in which they "pilloried Rachel Notley's 'amateur' NDP policies and highlighted the 'solid' track record of Jim Prentice's Progressive Conservatives" (Kleiss 2015).

This kind of fear mongering has deep roots. In 2011, Paula Arab, a *Calgary Herald* columnist and editorial board member, asserted that when one is discussing Alberta's oil industry, using *tar* rather than *oil* as the adjective for *sands* is "inaccurate and pejorative. It has become part of the rhetoric of extremists who are anti-oil and who want to shut down the industry" (Arab 2011). Ever since, the province has seen a neat division between those who use the adjective *tar* and those who use the adjective *oil*. While on a tour of Alberta during the 2012 federal election campaign, NDP leader Thomas Mulcair very nearly deployed the now politically incorrect adjective *tar*. As he recovered from his near-tar faux pas, he suggested the adoption of a perhaps more neutral and possibly more acceptable adjective—*bitumen*. "They're bitumen sands," he said, "because the chemicals are neither oil nor tar." Mulcair indicated his willingness to forgo the use of *tar*, saying, "If removing that linguistic impediment can make the conversation easier, I'm not going to keep it in place intentionally." However, he added that "a linguistic cleanup doesn't change anything about what we're talking about in terms of the ecosystems" (Fong 2012).

The truth is that the *Calgary Herald*–initiated tempest over the use of *tar* is a distraction from the real issues at stake, one of which, of course, is that identified by Mulcair—the threat to ecosystems. This chapter has a different focus. Bitumen exploitation has two great centres—the nation of Venezuela and the Canadian province of Alberta. This chapter examines the intersection between oil and politics in each of these jurisdictions, with a specific focus on the 2012 provincial elections in Alberta and the confrontation, from 2001 to 2003, between the state-oil company in Venezuela and the Venezuelan government. While bitumen sands play a large role in the politics of both Alberta and Venezuela, they do so in quite different contexts and in quite different ways. Venezuela remains extremely poor, while Alberta is a centre of enormous wealth and entrenched corporate power. This wealth difference is rooted in the very different places occupied by Venezuela and Canada (and by extension, Alberta) in the world hierarchy of nations: Venezuela is a semi-peripheral member of the world economy's Global South, while Alberta, as part of Canada, is very much a core member of the world economy's Global North.

The relationship between oil and democracy in Venezuela has been marked by the desperate attempt to assert sovereignty over the oil industry, a struggle to shift the locus of power out of the hands of what one might call a state-capitalist comprador elite into the hands of the Venezuelan state. In Alberta and Canada, by contrast, the oil and gas industry that intersects with Canadian democracy is, for the most part, very Canadian. There may well be issues of accountability and popular control in Canada that need to be addressed. Indeed, this chapter documents the heavy corporate footprint left by the oil and gas industry in the 2012 Alberta provincial election. However, unlike Venezuela, Canada does not face a national task of wrenching control of the bitumen sands from forces outside of the country. The dilemmas posed by the exploitation of bitumen sands in Alberta cannot be outsourced. They are quintessentially Canadian dilemmas, to be grappled with and addressed (or ignored and allowed to fester) by our own institutions of democracy and governance.

The Two Worlds of Alberta and Venezuela

A 2001 study estimates that Venezuela and Canada together hold approximately 3.4 trillion barrels of "original oil in place" (OOIP) trapped within their bitumen-soaked mud (2.2 trillion in Canada and 1.2 trillion in Venezuela), accounting for between 55 percent and 65 percent of the known reserves of such oil in the world. In Venezuela, the heavy oil exists in the Faja Petrolífera del Orinoco deposits, also known as the Orinoco Belt. In Canada, this resource is located in the heavy oil belt of northern Alberta and Saskatchewan, with Alberta containing the vast majority (Dusseault 2001, 1–2). In 2013 the Energy Resources Conservation Board estimated that in Alberta, 177 billion barrels of this OOIP are recoverable using current technologies. However, since the science and technology is constantly evolving, the "ultimate potential" of this resource "using reasonably foreseeable technology" is thought to be 315 billion barrels (ERCB 2013, 2–10). Venezuela's slightly smaller heavy oil deposits, are somewhat more recoverable, one report estimating their potential at 267 billion barrels using current technologies (Dusseault 2001, 2). A 2010 estimate by the US Geological Survey was much higher, at 513 billion barrels (BBC News 2010). The world's greatest known reserves of easily recoverable oil are located in Saudi Arabia, which had an estimated 250 billion barrels of recoverable oil in 2001, a figure that had grown to 260 billion by 2010 (Dusseault 2001, 2; BBC News 2010). The Alberta potential of 177 to 315 billion barrels, and the Venezuela potential of 267 to 513 billion barrels, put both constituencies very much in Saudi Arabia's league. The bitumen-soaked deposits in Venezuela and Alberta are without question an extremely important source of oil for the world economy in the twenty-first century.

The intersection of oil and politics in the two societies is, however, quite different. In Venezuela, that intersection has, for years, occurred on a terrain that is volatile and sometimes violent. The year 1935 saw the end of the twenty-seven-year dictatorship of Juan Vicente Gómez, only to be followed by the emergence of another dictator, Eleazar López Conteras, in power from 1935 to 1941. Political liberties were restored in the 1940s, but military dictatorships returned for much of the 1950s. Two parties vied for office through the 1960s, 1970s, and 1980s—Acción Democrática (Democratic Action) and Partido Social Cristiano (Social Christian Party, or Christian Democrats). Recent decades have seen economic and political turmoil, including an uprising in Caracas against austerity in 1989, in which three thousand people died and a 1992 coup attempt led by the late Hugo Chávez (who was finally elected president in 1998; Heckel et al. 2012). In Alberta, the picture is very different. Without doubt, there *is* an intersection between oil and politics, as is demonstrated below, but the terrain on which it has occurred has always been much less volatile. One party, the

Social Credit, held office from 1935 until 1971, and the Progressive Conservative Party held power for almost the next forty-four years, until its 2015 meltdown. There have been no coups d'état or revolutions.

In large part, these differences reflect the different places that Venezuela and Alberta occupy in the world economy. If they are similar in terms of heavy-oil deposits, they are extremely dissimilar in terms of their positions and trajectories in the global economy. The Canadian province of Alberta is in the Global North, while the Latin American nation Venezuela is in the Global South. While by no means one of the poorest countries of the South, Venezuela's economic position is extremely far removed from that of Alberta and Canada. Many within the field of international political economy are more specific, classifying Canada as being in the core of the world system and placing Venezuela in the semi-periphery—that important zone of countries that functions as a buffer between the core and the periphery.[1]

Measuring gross domestic product (GDP) per capita provides a helpful snapshot of a country's place in the world's hierarchy of economies. Figure 5.1 displays GDP per capita in constant 2005 US dollars for Canada and Venezuela from 1960 until 2013 and for Alberta from 1981 to 2013. Interestingly, the two countries were not worlds apart in 1960, with Canada's GDP per capita sitting at $12,931 and Venezuela's at $5,940. There were some who, based on these kinds of statistics, placed Venezuela, along with countries like Canada, as a member of the core rather than the semi-periphery of the world system (Babones 2005, 52). Today, no one would make such a decision. Figure 5.1 shows that over a half a century, Venezuela's GDP per capita stagnated, by 2013 sitting at just $6,402— roughly the same as it was in 1960. Canada's, in contrast, increased steadily to $37,524. These kinds of comparisons between core countries such as Canada and semi-peripheral countries such as Venezuela are, however, considerably distorted by the weak exchange rates typical of the latter, whose usually undervalued currencies have the effect of seriously reducing GDP per capita when expressed in US dollars. The dashed line in figure 5.1 takes this into account, expressing Venezuela's GDP per capita between 1990 and 2013 (in constant 2011 international dollars) using "purchasing power parity" (PPP), a method that largely removes this distortion. But while GDP per capita in Venezuela does increase by this measure, so do comparable figures for Canada (the dotted line), and Venezuela still lags considerably behind GDP per capita in Canada and still displays long decades of stagnation, contrasting sharply with the steady increase in the Canadian figures.

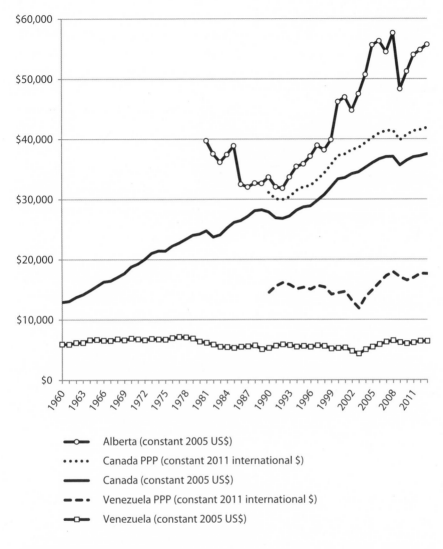

$60,000

$50,000

$40,000

$30,000

$20,000

$10,000

$0

1960 1963 1966 1969 1972 1975 1978 1981 1984 1987 1990 1993 1996 1999 2002 2005 2008 2011

—o— Alberta (constant 2005 US$)

••••• Canada PPP (constant 2011 international $)

——— Canada (constant 2005 US$)

— — • Venezuela PPP (constant 2011 international $)

—□— Venezuela (constant 2005 US$)

Figure 5.1. GDP per capita: Alberta, Canada, and Venezuela, 1960–2013. Source: Compiled from data available in World Bank (2014) and Statistics Canada (2014a, 2014b, 2015).

The most striking contrast, however, emerges from a comparison not of Canada to Venezuela but of Alberta to Venezuela. When Alberta's GDP per capita is expressed in 2005 US dollars, the picture that emerges is startling. Between 1981 and 1999, Alberta's GDP per capita, while greater than overall figures for Canada as a whole, tracked closely to that of Canada as a whole. But since 1999, it has greatly exceeded the Canadian average, surging by 2008 to $57,630, falling back considerably during the recession of 2009, but then continuing to increase again, until by 2013, it sat at $55,697, almost 50 percent higher than the figure for Canada as a whole and almost nine times greater than the US dollar figure for Venezuela. Without question, Alberta and Venezuela exist in extremely different places in the world hierarchy of economies.

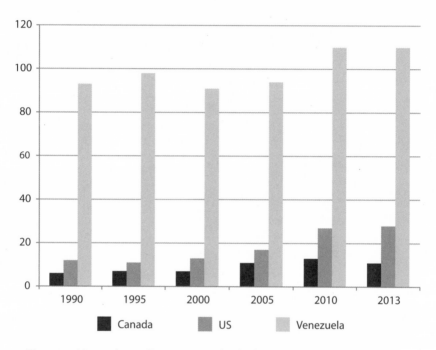

Figure 5.2. Maternal mortality per 100,000 live births: Canada, Venezuela, and the United States, 1990–2013. Source: Compiled from data available in World Bank (2014).

I am not arguing that there is a universal condition of wealth in Alberta and a universal condition of poverty in Venezuela. These kinds of aggregate figures are helpful at a very general level in placing different economies in the world system into appropriate categories (core, semi-periphery, etc.). By themselves, however, they tell us nothing about how the wealth within those economies is distributed. Travel to Calgary, and you will see ostentatious wealth existing side by side with the most extraordinary and visible poverty. A 2009 City of Calgary report observed that in the city, despite "enormous opportunities and socio-economic prosperity ... we are seeing growing income disparities and entrenching of poverty in racialized and Aboriginal populations" (Pruegger, Cook, and Richter-Salomons 2009, 1). Travel to Caracas and search for centres of support for the politics of the late Hugo Chávez, and you will inevitably end up in the neighbourhood of Petare, which Jonah Gindin (2004, 31) refers to as "an infamous epicentre of rebellion and politicization," noting that "Petare residents played a leading role in the *caracazo*—the popular uprising against the neoliberal policies of then President Carlos Andres Perez in February 1989." In 2002 after an attempted coup against Chávez, "Petare residents stormed the state television station, bringing it back on the air to inform the country of the coup, rallying Chávez's supporters to successfully demand his return" (31). Petare is extremely impoverished, leading many to see it as "the notoriously dangerous barrio of Petare" (Eulich 2010). By contrast, should you use the privileges that come with carrying a Canadian passport and visit the Embassy of Canada, you will find yourself in the Altamira neighbourhood of the city, a place of wealth and comfort on a Global North scale.

GDP per capita, in other words, is not a "lived" category, but rather an overall general indicator. Our lives are ordered according to more specific aspects of the economy—wages received from work, social wages received from government-provided services, access to education, access to fresh water and sanitation, and so on. For a complete picture of life in any society, all of these need to be examined. GDP per capita figures should be seen as just the beginning of an analysis, a preliminary window into the complex entities we call "economies"—an important beginning, often providing critical clues to what we will find when more specific categories are examined, but nonetheless, just a beginning. Here, we will look at just one such specific category. Figure 5.2 displays a key development statistic that is actually experienced—maternal mortality per 100,000 live births, from 1990 to 2013 in Canada, the United States, and Venezuela. In Canada, the figure was 6 in 1990. By 2010, it had more than doubled to a startling 13 per 100,000 live births, declining to 11 in 2013. The situation in the United States is worse. In 1990, maternal mortality was already at 12 per 100,000. In 2005 it jumped to 17, in 2010 it went to 27, and by 2013 it had reached the shocking figure of 28, more than twice what it had been in 1990. These figures reflect the shameful effects of neoliberal policies on one of the most basic indicators of development in two of the richest Global North states, Canada and the United States. Shifting our gaze to Venezuela, however, the figures are qualitatively higher. In 1990, maternal mortality rates were 93 per 100,000 live births, increasing to 98 in 1995. The rates declined to the low nineties in 2000 and 2005, reflecting the reforms implemented by Chávez and his successors, but in 2010, they shot back up to 110, where they remained in 2013—many times higher than rates in Canada and the United States. In Venezuela, in other words, it is far more risky for a woman to give birth than it is in Canada or the United States. For every other development indicator, these kinds of contrasts are visible. For example, in 1999, Chávez's first full year in office, mortality rates for infants per one thousand live births (i.e., the number of babies who would die before their first birthday) was a very high 18.8. This figure has been systematically lowered in the years since, by 2012 sitting at 13.1. Still, this is more than double the rate in the United States and almost triple the rate in Canada (6.0 and 4.7, respectively; World Bank 2014). The GDP per capita figures, in the case of these three countries, do not lie. Life is lived, on the whole, very differently in a Global South semi-peripheral country such as Venezuela compared to a Global North core country such as Canada.

Bitumen and Politics I: Alberta, 2012

How does oil intersect with politics in these two very different societies? In Alberta, the picture is somewhat opaque, but the 2012 provincial election provides a useful window. The surprising defeat of the Wildrose Alliance Party, despite its lead in every pre-election opinion poll, and the return to office of Alison Redford and the Progressive Conservatives is a story in itself. There had been a flight from the Tories toward Wildrose by a conservative base that saw new Tory leader Alison Redford as being too "liberal." This collapse of the Tories' conservative base, apparent to everyone in the province, seemed to point to a Wildrose victory. But to the surprise of many, there was an even bigger flight *to* the Tories driven by concern about the perceived pro-corporate and socially conservative politics of Wildrose. Commentators had anticipated a flight of this nature from the Liberal Party, but that in itself would not have been enough to stop Wildrose. What few predicted—and it proved to be the decisive factor—was the surge in voter participation, a surge clearly driven by an "anyone but Wildrose" sentiment (Kellogg 2014). Bitumen was part of this drama. The political economy of oil has many dimensions, but one of them is the relationship between bitumen sands development and climate change. Smith alienated many in the province when she argued, one week before the election, that the question of climate change was not yet settled (Canadian Press 2012). After the election, she acknowledged that controversial Wildrose statements including "her questions about climate change ... may have given undecided voters 'some pause' as they made up their minds. ... 'The fact of the matter is there are certain policies that clearly Albertans didn't want to see implemented,'" she said (CBC News 2012).

Many "oil-positive" media outlets had backed the election of Wildrose, including the editors of the *National Post*, who argued that "Alberta's government could use some fresh blood and vibrant new ideas" ("National Post Editorial Board" 2012). However, the fact that Smith, an oil company favourite, lost, in part because of her stance on climate change, does not mean that the oil companies themselves lost. The editors of the *Globe and Mail* differed from their colleagues in the *National Post*, backed the Tories because, in their eyes, Redford was a more positive voice than Smith for Alberta's oil industry. Redford's "Canadian Energy Strategy would facilitate the shipment of oil-sands oil to Asia, the US and Central Canada; she also promises to help fund oil-sands extraction technology" ("Time for Big Alberta" 2012). The *Globe and Mail* editors were reflecting the point of view of big sections of corporate Alberta. The key issue in the election was to put in place an oil-friendly government. The *National Post* editors gave a nod to Wildrose. The *Globe and Mail* editors gave a nod to the Tories. These two conservative media outlets were reflecting the thinking in the boardrooms of corporate Alberta, comfortable with a victory by either Wildrose or the Tories. Both parties received corporate donations running to hundreds of thousands of dollars—in the case of Wildrose, reaching almost $1 million. Table 5.1 lists all the corporations that made donations to both parties, beginning with those involved in the petrochemical and energy industries.

Table 5.1. Corporate support for both the Wildrose and Progressive Conservative parties

Petrochemical / Energy corporations	Wildrose	PCs
Cenovus Energy Inc.	$25,500	$10,001–30,000
Enbridge Pipelines Inc.	$5,000	$5,001–10,000
EnCana Corporation	$15,000	$10,001–30,000
Ensign Energy Services Inc.	$5,000	$5,001–10,000
Marathon Oil Canada Corporation	$5,000	$10,001–30,000
North West Upgrading	$7,000	$5,001–10,000
NOVA Chemicals	$12,000	$10,001–30,000
Penn West Petroleums Ltd.	$10,000	$10,001–30,000
Suncor Energy Services Inc.	$7,500	$5,001–10,000

Petrochemical / Energy corporations (cont'd)	Wildrose (cont'd)	PCs (cont'd)
Transalta Corporation	$12,500	$5,001–10,000
TransCanada Pipelines Limited	$5,000	$375–5,000
Other corporations	Wildrose	PCs
Axia Supernet Ltd.	$7,500	$5,001–10,000
Borden Ladner Gervais LLP	$10,000	$375–5,000
Brookfield Residential	$10,000	$375–5,000
CANA Construction Co. Ltd.	$15,000	$10,001–30,000
CCS Corporation	$5,000	$5,001–10,000
Deloitte Management Services LP	$10,000	$5,001–10,000
Don Wheaton Ltd.	$5,000	$10,001–30,000
Maclab Enterprises	$5,000	$375–5,000
Prairie Merchant Corporation	$30,000	$375–5,000
Ramsay Ranches Inc.	$6,000	$5001–10,000
Shane Homes Ltd.	$5,000	$375–5,000
Sherritt International Corporation	$10,000	$10,001–30,000
WAM Development Corporation	$5,000	$10,001–30,000
Witten LLP	$5,000	$375–5,000

Source: Compiled from data available in Wildrose (2012); Audette and PC Alberta (2012). Wildrose provided actual amounts; PC Alberta provided ranges of support: hence the difference in the presentation of data.

Significantly, twenty-five corporations gave cash to both parties—including many companies in the petrochemical and energy industries. For Cenovus, Enbridge, Encana, Marathon Oil, North West Upgrading, NOVA Chemicals, Penn West Petroleum, Suncor Energy, Transalta, and TransCanada Pipelines, there was a certain indifference. Smith or Redford would do. Either of them would be a good bet to allow the expansion of bitumen sands production into the foreseeable future.

Clearly, oil and gas corporations play a central role in Alberta politics. But whose corporations are they? When we turn to an examination of Venezuela, we will see how the entire oil-politics connection has been shaped by the presence of an oil industry controlled in an earlier age by non-Venezuelan oil multinationals—in the late twentieth and early twenty-first century, by an externally oriented state-capitalist comprador elite. This is not the case in Canada. What has emerged in the oil and gas industry as a whole, and in the bitumen sands in Alberta in particular, is a capital accumulation process with Canadian firms entrenched as dominant players. Elsewhere, I have examined this in some detail (Kellogg 2013). For the purposes of this chapter, we need only examine the highlights.

— Canada — US — Other non-resident

Figure 5.3. Country of control: petroleum and natural gas (percentage of capital employed, 1954–87); oil and gas extraction and support activities (percentage of assets, 1999–2012). Source: Compiled from data available in Statistics Canada (2000, 2014c).

Statistics Canada provides a breakdown for the control of the petroleum and natural gas industry in Canada, from 1954 until 1987, on the basis of percentage of capital employed (see figure 5.3). There is a break in the series, but from

1999 on, we have statistics showing control for the industry by assets, operating revenue, and profits. Of the three categories, the one for assets is the most comparable with the earlier series. Throughout the 1950s and 1960s, Canadian control was quite low, at less than 40 percent, while nonresident corporations controlled in excess of 60 percent every year until 1970. Of this, the vast majority comprised US control. Through the 1970s and 1980s, however, the situation changed markedly. By 1987, 60 percent of the industry was in Canadian hands, US control had declined to 26 percent, and the share of other nonresident corporations stood at 14 percent. When the story picks up in 1999 with the new series based on assets, we see that Canadian control of the industry remains above 60 percent, US control slips to just below 20 percent, and other non-residents represent the rest (in 2012, just over 17 percent). Three trends stand out here: first, the clearly visible Canadian corporate dominance in the field; second, the steadily declining portion of nonresident control represented by US corporations; and third, the steadily increasing portion of nonresident control represented by "other than US" corporations.

Let us switch from the general category of petroleum and natural gas to the subcategory of bitumen sands production. Clearly some of the corporations involved in bitumen sands exploitation in Canada are nonresident. Statoil Canada is owned by Statoil Norway, Imperial Oil Ltd. is 69.6 percent owned by Exxon-Mobil in the United States, and Murphy Oil Corp. is headquartered in El Dorado, Arkansas.[2] But there are some who claim that other, nominally Canadian corporations are in fact not Canadian. Since "71 per cent of all tar sands production is owned by non-Canadian shareholders," argues one influential report, it is justifiable to deny that what is going on in the tar sands is made in Canada (Skuce 2012, 1). On this basis, Husky Energy is considered to be non-Canadian as are the two biggest oil and gas producers in Canada (Canadian Natural Resources Ltd. [CNRL] and Suncor Energy Inc.), as well as the seventh biggest (Cenovus Energy Inc.), the thirteenth biggest (Canadian Oil Sands), and the thirty-third biggest (MEG Energy Corp.; Skuce 2012). A specific controversy over the Canadian bona fides of Husky Energy is due to the dual citizenship of the family members who control it, a controversy I have dealt with elsewhere (Kellogg 2013). As for the others, the method by which their corporate nationality has been determined is misleading. The fact that just over 50 percent of the shares of CNRL, Suncor, Cenovus, and Canadian Oil Sands are held outside of Canada says very little about who controls these companies. As noted in their 2011 annual reports, all of them are headquartered in Calgary, and none are subsidiaries of another corporation. Furthermore, the issue of a majority of shares being held outside of Canada is by no means indicative of control. According to the very standard understanding of corporate power provided by the Organization for Cooperation and Economic Development (OECD 2003), "control of a corporation occurs when a single institutional unit owning more than a half of the shares, or equity, of a corporation is able to control its policy" (2003). In other words, non-Canadian ownership of 50 percent or more of the shares of a corporation would only be significant if those shares were controlled by a single entity. The OECD goes further: "In practice, when ownership of shares is widely diffused among a large number of shareholders, control may be secured by owning 20 per cent or less of total shares."[3] With the OECD definition of ownership as a basis, Figure 5.4 provides a snapshot for 2012, the year of the Redford election, showing the twelve top-producing bitumen-extraction corporations operating in Alberta and ranking them by barrels of bitumen per day, current and planned. It makes very clear the physiognomy of the industry in Alberta.

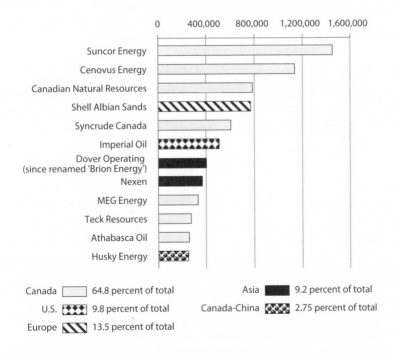

Figure 5.4. Top twelve bitumen-extracting corporations measured by barrels of bitumen per day (current and planned), Alberta, 2012. Source: Compiled from data available in Alberta (2013).

There are two Asian-based corporations on this top twelve list (Dover and Nexen, numbers 7 and 8), as well as one based in the United States (Imperial, number 6) and one based in Europe (Shell, number 4). Most striking, however, is the overwhelming Canadian presence on the list. The top three—Suncor, Cenovus, and CNRL—are all Canadian corporations, as are Syncrude (number 5) and MEG, Teck, Athabasca, and Husky (numbers 9, 10, 11, and 12). Even if we were to remove Husky from the list because of the dual citizenship of its principal owners, the key corporations are, without any question, Canadian. Overall percentage of control for bitumen extraction, current and planned, are given in percentages at the bottom of the figure. At 64.8 percent, Canadian corporations dominate the field. Far behind them are Europe (13.5 percent), the United States (9.8 percent), and Asia (9.2 percent).[4] We cannot outsource the problem of the bitumen sands—the problem is very Canadian, very Albertan.

Bitumen and Politics II: Venezuela, 2001–3

When we shift our gaze to Venezuela, we see a different political economy of oil, characterized in particular by a much more visible, volatile, and politically charged relationship of the oil industry with the state. This story has, for decades, been bound up with the Great Powers. Oil is the indispensable fuel that drives Great Power economies, a lubricant for their international rivalries and a source of incredible profit for their corporations. In the immediate aftermath of World War II, "Enrico Mattei coined the phrase 'the seven sisters' to describe the Anglo-Saxon companies that controlled the Middle East's oil" (Hoyos 2007). Several generations later, these remain very large and very powerful corporations. Table 5.2 lists the twelve biggest public corporations in the world, according to the 2011 figures compiled by Forbes.[5] Those highlighted in grey represent the former Seven Sisters, reduced to four through mergers. PetroChina and Petrobras (Petróleo Brasileiro) have recently risen to prominence and are oil companies from the Global South. Six, then, of the top twelve corporations in the entire world are involved in the oil industry, four of them being the consolidated continuation of the old Seven Sisters group. In 2011, the total sales of these contemporary six sisters amounted to $1.97 trillion, with net profits of $165 billion.

The economics of Big Oil, throughout the twentieth century, was inextricably linked with the politics of Great Powers. The premier of France, Georges Clemenceau, famously argued in 1917, that "gasoline was as necessary as blood in the battles of tomorrow" (Bérenger 1920, 60; my translation). In 1918, ten days after the armistice, Lord Curzon—former Viceroy of India and soon to be British Foreign Secretary—told the assembled guests at a British government dinner put on for the Inter-Allied Petroleum Conference that "the Allied cause had floated to victory upon a wave of oil" (Yergin 2008, 167).

Table 5.2. The twelve largest corporations in the world

Rank	Company	Country	Sales	Profits	Assets	Market value
1	Exxon Mobil	USA	$433.5	$41.1	$331.1	$407.4
2	JPMorgan Chase	USA	$110.8	$19.0	$2,265.8	$170.1
3	General Electric	USA	$147.3	$14.2	$717.2	$213.7
4	Royal Dutch Shell	Netherlands	$470.2	$30.9	$340.5	$227.6
5	ICBC	China	$82.6	$25.1	$2,039.1	$237.4
6	HSBC Holdings	UK	$102.0	$16.2	$2,550.0	$164.3
7	PetroChina	China	$310.1	$20.6	$304.7	$294.7
8	Berkshire Hathaway	USA	$143.7	$10.3	$392.6	$202.2
9	Wells Fargo	USA	$87.6	$15.9	$1,313.9	$178.7
10	Petrobras	Brazil	$145.9	$20.1	$319.4	$180.0
11	BP	UK	$375.5	$25.7	$292.5	$147.4
12	Chevron	USA	$236.3	$26.9	$209.5	$218.0
	TOTALS:		$1,971.5	$165.3	$1,797.7	$1,475.1

Note: Figures are in billions of US dollars. Corporations in shaded rows are the former Seven Sisters.
Source: DeCarlo (2012).

World War I was the cauldron from which the United States emerged as the world's dominant power; at the time, it was also the world's greatest producer of oil. As the US went abroad looking for sources of oil to import, Mexico was, at first, more important than Venezuela. That changed on 18 March 1938. In the context of a strike in the oil fields "against the appalling conditions in shanties and hovels," Mexican president Lázaro Cárdenas nationalized the foreign-owned oil companies So popular was this move, and so central to Mexican society, that 18 March was "proclaimed as a new day of independence." The response from the Great Powers was swift. A boycott of Mexican oil was organized by the United States, the United Kingdom, and the Netherlands. Even when the three governments lifted the boycott "to satisfy the demands of the Second World War," the Seven Sisters were busy looking for an alternative place to do business (Sampson 1991, 105).

Venezuela was a natural choice. There, too, oil workers had engaged in a strike against appalling conditions, this time in 1936, but the Venezuelan government took the side of the oil companies, using police force to suppress dissent (Prashad 2007, 189). On 22 January 1937, a wildcat strike by petroleum workers was settled through the granting of a small wage increase, but "in July of that year several labor leaders—dubbed as 'agitators' by the oil companies—were expelled from the Maracaibo area" (Baloyra 1974, 43). Venezuela was revealing itself as a more congenial place than Mexico for the oil companies to do business. Thus, while the Mexican people were left to "drown in their own oil," to use the words of US ambassador Josephus Daniels (Prashad 2007, 192), the Seven Sisters shifted their focus to the more compliant state of Venezuela. "In the 1950s, oil production doubled. . . . In 1957 alone the Seven Sisters made $828 million in Venezuela, whose regime allowed them to remit all their profits without restrictions. As one US banker noted, 'You have the freedom here to do what you want to do with your money, and to me, that is worth all the political freedom in the world'" (189, 191).

Beginning in 1958, the political and economic situation changed in form but not in substance. In 1958, a "new relatively progressive government led by Acción Democrática (AD)" took office (Prashad 2007, 192), and in 1960, the Venezuelan government created the Corporación Venezolana de Petróleo (CVP) "in an attempt to give the government more control over the oil industry within the country" (McNew 2008, 150). This was followed in 1976 by a nominal "nationalization" of the oil industry, in large part through the "creation of a new national company, Petróleos de Venezuela, S.A. (PDVSA)" (150). But the oil industry remained, in reality, in the hands of the Seven Sisters. The PDVSA did not do away with the oil concessions previously granted to the foreign transnational corporations. Instead, it "absorbed the fourteen existing entities and made them subsidiaries," which "left a substantial amount of power in the hands of transnational managing boards that had formerly controlled the oil industry in Venezuela" (151).

The oil industry in Venezuela became even more oriented toward the transnational oil companies in 1992 through what was called the "Apertura," or

"Opening." This is when the bitumen sands in the Orinoco Belt become a major factor. The Apertura involved the signing of "thirty-two operating agreements and . . . four joint ventures operating within the Orinoco Belt." These agreements involved "lower taxes and royalties to attract private enterprises under the premise that marginal oil fields were more risky and costly to operate" (152). The transnational corporations were in effect subcontracted by PDVSA and were, in legal terms, not considered producers of oil but service providers. This was very positive for the transnationals and very negative for the government of Venezuela:

> Classifying these companies as service providers . . . allowed for more than simple involvement in the oil industry; it also allowed for considerable tax and royalty breaks unavailable to "oil producers." Because these contractors were not oil producers, they did not pay the 67.7 percent income tax rate—the rate applicable to oil activities at the time they were created—instead, they only paid the 34 percent income tax rate applicable to non-oil activities. (153)

Because royalties were to be paid by the producer and because the transnational oil corporations were classified as "service providers," they were also able to avoid virtually all royalties. "The PDVSA capped the royalties to be paid by these projects at 1 percent, as opposed to the 16.6 percent maximum available at the time" (153).

Why would a government, and a government-run enterprise such as PDVSA, enter into such one-way contracts with foreign oil corporations? Perhaps they were in no position to bargain and so had little choice. But perhaps there are other, more complex class-related factors at work. In the dependency/ underdevelopment literature, the term *comprador* is used to describe an internal elite—economic and/or political—that works to enrich economic interests in the Global North at the expense of national economic development. The term originates in China and "refers to any national economic elite that enriches substantially itself through selling out its own country's assets and wealth to foreigners" (Dobbin 2007, 526). In an analysis of Egypt, Patrick Clawson (1978, 21) summarizes what he calls neo-Marxist understandings of the comprador bourgeoisie as "the large bourgeoisie based on trade and landownership . . . said to be tied to foreign capital, and totally reactionary." PDVSA is not "based on trade and landownership" and was not situated in the private sector. Nonetheless, until the 2001–3 strike wave (examined below), describing the company as a comprador is completely justifiable—a corporation based in the Venezuelan state but oriented toward the Global North, rather than toward national development in Venezuela. PDVSA, until the 2001–3 watershed, was a "state capitalist" comprador corporation. The upper levels of management at PDVSA were increasingly seen as being a "state within a state" representing "a parallel power to the elected president and the legislature. . . . PDVSA officials viewed themselves as part of a global managerial petroleum network, whose decisions reflected international concerns rather than primarily Venezuelan interests" (Tinker-Salas 2005, 52). This exactly corresponds to the term "comprador state capitalist elite." Between 1976 and 1995, according to an article entitled "El parasitismo petrolero" ("Petroleum Parasitism") by Uslar Pietri, this comprador oil elite "generated and largely squandered US$270 billion dollars from oil sales" (cited in Tinker-Salas 2005, 52).

This was the situation that Hugo Chávez, who took office as president in 1999, set out to change. By 2006, he would label his goal "full sovereignty over oil" (Carreño 2006; McNew 2008), with the aim of gaining 51 percent ownership of the thirty-two joint ventures with foreign companies, raise income taxes to 50 percent (O'Grady 2005), and increase "royalties payable to the government from as low as 1 percent to 33 percent" (Collier 2006). This process began in 2000 with much more modest goals, the National Assembly passing that year an enabling act allowing Chávez to rule by decree for one year. "In November 2001, shortly before the act was set to expire, Chávez enacted 49 decrees. These included the Hydrocarbons Law ("Venezuela—Chavez" 2007). Initially envisioning a 30 percent flat rate for royalties, the bill as introduced called for a "softer" royalty regime, "assessed on a sliding scale between 20% and 30%." Most controversial was the provision that "the state hold a majority stake in exploration, extraction, transportation, and initial storage of hydrocarbons" ("Venezuelan Strike" 2001).

The reaction from big business was one of outrage. On 10 December 2001, there was a twelve-hour national strike called by the "top business association, Fedecámaras, of which the Venezuelan Oil Chamber is a member." In an extraordinary development, this bosses' strike was also supported by "Venezuela's largest confederation of trade unions, the Workers' Confederation of Venezuela (CTV)—which includes oil workers" ("Venezuelan Strike" 2001). This initiated a "united front" between the bosses' organization, Fedecámaras (Federación de Cámaras de Comercio y Producción), and the trade union central, CTV (Confederación de Trabajadores de Venezuela)—a coalition that was to dominate the anti-Chávez, pro-PDVSA movement from that point until early 2003.

These pro-corporate actions by Venezuela's unions are why there is a literature analyzing some of these institutions as representing not labour as a whole but rather a "labour aristocracy" (Rutledge 2005, 95).

The December strike did not stop Chávez's attempt to reform PDVSA. In February 2002, Chávez fired the head of PDVSA and replaced him with Gaston Perra, a move widely seen as "intended to quash mounting resistance within the company to demands from the government for heavier fiscal contributions" (Webb-Vidal 2002). On 28 March, Fedepetrol (Federación de Trabajadores Petroleros, Químicos y sus Similares de Venezuela—the union representing oil and gas workers) launched a forty-eight-hour strike, ostensibly over wages (Webb-Vidal 2001). The real issue was the attempt to reform PDVSA. Chávez pushed ahead with these reforms, dismissing seven senior managers on 6 April. On Tuesday, 9 April, CTV leader Carlos Ortega and Pedro Carmona Estanga, the leader of Fedecámaras, "with the support of many other civil society organizations, called for a general strike" to stop the reforms at PDVSA (Encarnación 2002, 42). Initially, this was to be a twenty-four-hour strike, but it soon escalated into a mass confrontation with the regime itself (Lapper and Webb-Vidal 2002). On Thursday, 11 April, a massive march to PDVSA headquarters was redirected toward the presidential palace. In circumstances that remain extremely controversial, gunfire erupted and perhaps as many as twenty people, both pro- and anti-Chávez, were shot dead (Cannon 2004, 285). Over the next three days, Chávez was removed from office and a new government installed, headed by Pedro Carmona, but a massive pro-Chávez uprising made that new government unsustainable, and, with the support of a section of the army and mass demonstrations in the streets of Caracas, Chávez returned to office.

In and around this enormous social upheaval, a reconfiguration of class forces was taking place. At the base of society, new mass organizations were in formation, a process that had begun in 1999—the first full year of Chávez's presidency. With the official union movement deeply corrupted because of its privileged position inside the parasitic oil industry, Chávez had set out to establish new grassroots organizations "drawn mainly from the poorest sectors of Venezuelan society." These Bolivarian circles were in part social welfare institutions, delivering "healthcare, job-training and short-term credit" to the very poor in the country. They were also centres of political mobilization. "During the April coup, the members of the Bolivarian circles . . . took to the streets to demand the return" of Chávez (Encarnación 2002, 41). Marta Harnecker (2004, 39) notes that after the defeat of that coup, "Bolivarian Circles multiplied throughout the country, adopting more varied forms. New organizations emerged, such as urban land committees and specific middle-class groups of doctors, teachers, and lawyers. Further, union leaders from various industries, critical of the complicity of the CTV, accelerated their efforts to build an independent labor force to support the revolutionary process."

Chávez's return to office on 14 April 2002 did not end the dispute. In November and December, all the old issues re-emerged. A new general strike was launched in December: the hope was "to topple Chávez by reviving a military-civilian coup effort that overthrew Chávez for two days in April 2002." The situation, however, had evolved considerably since the spring. In April, when CTV leaders had called out their members, they had been relatively unchallenged from within the union ranks. By the autumn and winter, this was no longer the case. In October, Fedepetrol announced that it would not support a twelve-hour strike called against Chávez. Union official Rafael Rosales "said that he believed 85% of the federation's membership opposed the strike"; Rosales described the strike call "as a 'political ultimatum' by foes of Chávez" ("Fedepetrol" 2002). Nonetheless, the strike began on 2 December and was widely supported by the white-collar employees at PDVSA. About half of PDVSA's workforce, "executives, engineers, technicians and ship captains . . . went on strike and shut down almost all operations for three months" (Collier 2006). Unlike the earlier strike, however, many in the blue-collar unions were now supporting Chávez. In the end, this was to prove decisive (Toro 2002).

When the strike began, oil output was averaging three million barrels a day. The strike caused this to drop to almost nothing. By early January, production levels had crawled back up to 400,000 barrels a day, after the government was able to "restart production with loyal personnel" (EIU 2003). By the end of January, the strike was essentially over. Chávez officially ended it, declaring it unconstitutional and dismissing eighteen thousand PDVSA employees (International Business Publications, USA 2012, 98). Some put the figure at nineteen thousand ("Venezuela—Ali Rodriguez" 2005). The blue-collar workers supported Chávez. The more well-off workers, the white-collar "executives, engineers, technicians and ship captains," opposed him and were let go. The dismissed employees represented fully "90 percent of PDVSA's white-collar workforce" but only half of the company's entire workforce (Collier 2006).

The departure of the vast majority of the intelligentsia who had directed work at PDVSA has been extremely serious for the Venezuelan oil industry. Three years after the strike, one industry analyst put it this way: "The firing of over 50% of PDVSA's work force, over 19,000 employees, has had an irrecoverable impact on production" ("Venezuela—Ali Rodriguez" 2005). Anti-Chávista commentators have been quick to document these troubles. One blogger summarized it this way:

> PDVSA's effective crude oil production capacity has dropped to about 2.3 million barrels per day at best, compared with over 3.5 million barrels per day in 1998. . . . PDVSA's refineries—Amuay, Cardon, El Palito and Puerto La Cruz—are falling apart. All of PDVSA's programmed maintenance activities at three refineries have . . . suffered frequent delays and postponements over the past several years. And dozens of workers have been killed or injured in refinery accidents since 2005.[6]

All agree that there are problems at PDVSA, and these problems are certainly related to the dismissal of virtually the entire PDVSA intelligentsia. However, it is not clear what choice Chávez had. The flow of profits had to be redirected back into Venezuela, instead of out of the country and into the pockets of the corporations of the Global North. The strike could not have been allowed to go on much longer, as it had brought the country to its knees, "with real gross domestic product (GDP) contracting 29 percent in the first quarter [of 2003], and 9.2 percent for the entire year, after already contracting 8.9 percent in 2002" (International Business Publications, USA 2012, 97). The Spanish bank BSCH "described the situation as the 'biggest [example of] wealth destruction in Venezuelan history'" (EIU 2003). The choices were either to capitulate and leave the power of the comprador elite intact or to create PDVSA anew with a politically reliable workforce, since only such a workforce would agree to a PDVSA oriented toward Venezuelan development rather than toward corporate profits in the Global North.

Conclusion

This chapter opened with a survey of the somewhat silly linguistic polemic currently under way in Alberta, polarized around the use of the adjective *tar*. One of the difficulties confronting those who, with a kind of neoliberal political correctness attempt to vilify the use of the *tar* word, is that the pairing of this adjective with the noun *oil* is quite well-established in the industry itself. In early 2015, I searched for the term *tar sands* on the website OnePetro, which describes itself as "a unique library of technical documents and journal articles serving the oil and gas exploration and production industry" and is operated by the

Society of Petroleum Engineers.[6] At that time, the "library" contained 160,000 documents produced by eighteen publishing partners. The search resulted in 2,028 different hits related to research papers as varied as "Comparing Venezuelan and Canadian Heavy Oil and Tar Sands" (Dusseault 2001) and "Promising Approaches to Enhance SAGD Performance in Uneconomical Tar-Sands" (Akhondzadeh et al. 2012). Perhaps it is time to raise the level of discourse somewhat—to get beyond a dispute over adjectives and grapple with some of the real issues at stake. This chapter has outlined one such issue—the different ways in which the economics of processing bitumen impacts politics in Venezuela and Alberta, a difference shaped by the contrasting positions those economies occupy in the hierarchical world economy.

There is a deeply human side to this story. In the wake of the mass firings of 2003, hundreds of former PDVSA employees made their way to Alberta to put to use, in the bitumen sands of Alberta, heavy-oil skills developed in Venezuela. One of those is Pereira Almao, who, in 2006, estimated that there were "300 former PDVSA families in each of Calgary, Edmonton and Fort McMurray and more are on the way. Among the biggest employers of Venezuelans are Suncor Energy Inc., Syncrude Canada Ltd., Canadian Natural Resources Ltd. and Jacobs Engineering Group Inc." (Cattaneo 2006). According to Almao, "Canada is in a very privileged position. . . . Canada will expand its marketing of heavy oils and I don't think Venezuela is going to grow. . . . It could be 50 years before you see real activity and real growth in the Venezuelan oil industry again" (quoted in Harding 2006). The irony couldn't be more profound. The oil-related issue in the past for Venezuela was the flow of oil profits out of the country to the Global North. Chávez successfully reversed that flow, increasing taxes and royalties to keep the profits in Venezuela. But the price of that reversal has been a new flow out of the country—a flow into the Global North of talented, trained and experienced professionals.

Alberta is a subnational state within Canada, a member of the core of the world economy situated in the Global North. Venezuela is a semiperipheral country situated in the Global South. A comparative analysis of these two societies demands an approach sensitive to the complex relationship between classes, and between class, nation, and the world economy. Venezuela's oil economy began as an effect of Great Powers and corporate oil machinations (the need to punish Mexico and keep oil development under corporate, Global North control); it then continued, until 2002, to function under the direction of a comprador, state-capitalist elite. The effects were typical of resource development under neocolonialism—vast wealth removed from the country, leaving behind pools of stagnation and poverty. That stagnation has been evident for decades. Writing in 1973, Norman Gall documented that "Venezuela and West Germany had roughly the same per capita GNP in 1956. Since then, however, West Germany's per capita GNP increased from around $650 in 1956 to $1,300 in 1960 and $53,034 in 1970, while Venezuela's has remained largely stagnant" (Gall 1973).

By contrast, this chapter has documented the dynamic expansion of GDP per capita in Alberta. That province, like Canada as a whole, is one of the small number of places in the world that provides a home to the transnational corporations—among them oil corporations—that have over the years extracted enormous wealth from countries in the Global South. Oil corporations exert political influence in Alberta: the evidence from the 2012 provincial election makes this absolutely clear. The extreme reaction to the 2015 NDP electoral victory shows, by way of negative example, where their political loyalties lie. But they do not exert this influence as a "comprador elite" operating in a manner to frustrate capitalist development in Alberta. They do so as full partners with the provincial political elite, with both focused on establishing a self-sustaining cycle of capitalist accumulation in the province. Since the 1980s, a new, indigenous capitalist class has become entrenched at the apex of the Alberta economy, highlighting the prescience of John Richards and the late Larry Pratt, who in 1979 argued in *Prairie Capitalism* that "it would be absurd to conclude" that the Alberta government is "merely an instrument of external capital or that Alberta's new bourgeoisie is 'comprador' in nature—i.e., that its role is merely to facilitate the penetration of the local economy by foreign capital" (227). Their thesis was that the provincial intervention into the oil economy of the 1970s was laying the basis for an indigenous bourgeoisie in later years. This analysis has been completely confirmed. In 2005, in an interview with Jeremy Mouat, Pratt indicated that in the years since the now classic *Prairie Capitalism* was published, Alberta has become home to

> big world-scale Alberta companies . . . not just operating in Alberta, but internationally. Those are not foreign owned, they are Canadian-owned. . . .
> If you add them up, there's maybe 15 to 20 companies that are big enough to operate outside the country, and which also have significant operations inside the United States. In a sense, that is what we were getting at in *Prairie Capitalism*: the growth of an indigenous bourgeoisie, in Marxist terms, or an indigenous capitalist class. (Mouat 2005)

Oil development in Venezuela was dominated, until this century, by a state-capitalist comprador elite oriented toward non-Venezuelan external interests rather than Venezuelan economic development. Alberta, by contrast, has seen regional (provincial) state capitalism lay the basis for the development of what Richards and Pratt, years ago, called "a nascent regional bourgeoisie of substance and considerable power" (1979, 11), a development deeply rooted in the exploitation of mineral staples, particularly those associated with the bitumen sands. This reinforces a perspective being developed by a new generation of young Canadian political economists, who begin by situating Canada as a core economy, a mature capitalist country, actively helping to shape the policies of the Global North, the very policies that oppress and impoverish countries like Venezuela. (Two recent examples of this new scholarship are Klassen [2009] and Gordon [2010].)

This comparative framework can help us navigate Alberta's political terrain over the next few years. A clue as to what we might expect comes from the political biography of the new MLA for Lethbridge-West, Shannon Phillips, who is the NDP's minister of the Environment and minister responsible for the Status of Women. "As a policy analyst for the Alberta Federation of Labour, Ms. Phillips . . . steered the federation's opposition to the Northern Gateway pipeline," a position that clearly positions her against the oil elite. However, Phillips is also "a supporter of Enbridge's Line 9B proposal . . . 'because it established east-west connections, energy security for Canada and import substitutions for eastern Canada'" (Giovannetti 2015). This positions her and the Alberta NDP on side with the oil elite in Alberta and in opposition to the climate justice movements in Ontario and Québec, which have campaigned for years against the Enbridge proposal. There will be pressure applied to the new NDP administration by the powerful and entrenched oil elite in Alberta. There will be points of friction and tension. But Alberta is not Venezuela. We are not likely to see this scenario unfold through attempted coups and revolutions. The NDP is not likely to inspire equivalents to the Chávez-era Bolivarian Circles. We have many examples, in Global North countries, of social-democratic parties such as the NDP tapping into popular discontent with elite politics, but then adapting their policies, once in office, to the pressure of those very elites.

That, however, opens up a line of inquiry outside the scope of this chapter. There are many other such issues which require further investigation. This chapter has not focused on the deep inequities within Alberta's bitumen sands economy. It has not focused on the environmental devastation that accompanies bitumen sand exploitation. It has not raised the issue of Indigenous rights and land claims, which are inextricably intertwined with bitumen economies. Other authors in this volume take up many of these questions. All that is being said here is that the profound differences in the manner in which oil corporations have exerted political influence in Venezuela and Alberta are inexplicable without understanding the two economies' very different relationships to the world hierarchy of nations.

Notes

1 In recent years, a strand of Canadian political economy (CPE) has emerged that is influenced by world systems theory (WST) and takes a contrary view, conceptualizing Canada as a semi-peripheral rather than a core economy (Clarkson 2001; Clarkson and Cohen 2004; Glenday 2010; Ikeda 2004; Laxer 2004). The analysis offered by this strand of CPE is discordant with WST-influenced international political economy (IPE) literature, which almost universally conceptualizes Canada as a member of the core (Arrighi and Drangel 1986; Babones 2005; Boli-Bennett 1980; Chirot 1977; Kentor 2000; Kick and Davis 2001; Korzeniewicz and Martin 1994; Smith and White 1992; Van Rossem 1996). I find the latter school much more persuasive, and throughout this chapter, the terms *core* and *semi-periphery* are used, with IPE scholarship in mind. In chapter 2 of *Escape from the Staple Trap* (Kellogg 2015), I provide an overview and critique of both the CPE and IPE strands of WST-influenced approaches to Canada in the world system.

2 See "Company Overview of Statoil Canada Ltd .," *Bloomberg Businessweek*, n.d., http://investing.businessweek.com/research/stocks/private/snapshot. asp?privcapId=24402363; "2011 Summary Annual Report," *Imperial Oil Limited*, 2012, 29; and "2011 Annual Report" (El Dorado, AR: Murphy Oil Corporation, 2012), 1.

3 This does not by any means exhaust the issue of the influence of non-Canadian corporations on the trajectory of development in this country. The investment rules embedded in the North American Free Trade Agreement (NAFTA) give considerable scope for corporations to bypass the Canadian political and judicial processes and to seek redress through the dispute-settlement provisions of NAFTA (chapter 11). Using just this provision, for instance, the US-based oil and gas company Loan Pine Resources, on 8 November 2012, filed notice of intent to submit a claim for a quarter of a billion dollars in damages from the Government of Canada for what it saw as impediments to its fracking activities in Québec (Bennett Jones LLP 2012; Council of Canadians 2013). The point is to contrast the situation in Alberta with the situation in Venezuela.

4 The smallest category, Canada-China (2.75% of the total), is a one-company category, capturing the previously referenced controversy over the nationality of Husky Energy. How we resolve that controversy will be immaterial to the findings here.

5 It has become fashionable to highlight Apple as the world's biggest corporation. But this is true only if a single criterion is used—market value. The Forbes list is more accurate, as it avoids distortions that can arise when corporate size is "based on a single metric." When Forbes uses "an equal weighting of sales, profits, assets and market value to rank companies according to size," Apple falls to twenty-second place (DeCarlo 2012).

6 "Train Wreck at Pdvsa," *Caracas Gringo* (blog), 2 November 2009, http://caracasgringo. wordpress.com/2009/11/02/train-wreck-at-pdvsa/.

7 OnePetro, 2015, https://www.onepetro.org.

References

Akhondzadeh, Hamed, Ali Fattahi, Alireza Zare, Mohd. Derahman, and Ahmad Kamal Idris. 2012. "Promising Approaches to Enhance SAGD Performance in Uneconomical Tar-Sands." Paper presented at the North Africa Technical Conference and Exhibition, 20–22 February, Cairo, Egypt.

Alberta. 2013. *Alberta Oil Sands Industry, Quarterly Update: Winter 2013*. Edmonton: JuneWarren-Nickle's Energy Group. https://albertacanada.com/files/albertacanada/ AOSID_QuarterlyUpdate_Winter2013.pdf.

Alberta. Elections Alberta. Chief Electoral Office. 2013. *2012 Annual Report of the Chief Electoral Officer: The Election Finances and Contributions Disclosure Act for the 2012 Calendar Year.*

Arab, Paula. 2011. "Language Tars Debate over Alberta Oilsands." *Calgary Herald*, 21 April.

Arrighi, Giovanni, and Jessica Drangel. 1986. "The Stratification of the World-Economy: An Exploration of the Semiperipheral Zone." *Review (Fernand Braudel Center)* 10 (1): 9–74.

Audette, Trish, and PC Alberta. 2012. "PC Election 2012 Contributions." http://www. scribd.com/doc/91398014/PC-Election-2012-Contributions.

Babones, S. J. 2005. "The Country-Level Income Structure of the World-Economy." *Journal of World-Systems Research* 11 (1): 29–55.

Baloyra, Enrique A. 1974. "Oil Policies and Budgets in Venezuela, 1938–1968." *Latin American Research Review* 9 (2): 28–72.

BBC News. 2010. "Venezuela Oil 'May Double Saudi Arabia.'" *BBC News*, 23 January. http://news.bbc.co.uk/2/hi/8476395.stm.

Bennett Jones LLP. 2012. "Notice of Intent to Submit a Claim to Arbitration Under Chapter Eleven of the North American Free Trade Agreement." Lone Pine Resource Inc. v. Government of Canada. 8 November. http://www.international.gc.ca/trade-agreements-accords-commerciaux/assets/pdfs/disp-diff/lone-01.pdf.

Bérenger, Henry. 1920. *Le pétrole et la France*. Paris: E. Flammarion.

Boli-Bennett, John. 1980. "Global Integration and the Universal Increase of State Dominance, 1910–1970." In *Studies of the Modern World-System*, edited by Albert Bergesen, 77–107. New York: Academic Press.

Canadian Press. 2012. "Wildrose Leader Says Climate Science 'Not Settled.'" *CBC News*, 16 April. http://www.cbc.ca/news/canada/manitoba/wildrose-leader-says-climate-science-not-settled-1.1147604.

Cannon, Barry. 2004. "Venezuela, April 2002: Coup or Popular Rebellion? The Myth of a United Venezuela." *Bulletin of Latin American Research* 23 (3): 285–302.

Carreño, Rafael Ramírez. 2006. "Full Sovereignty Over Oil." Speech of the Venezuelan Minister of Energy and Petroleum at the Third OPEC International Seminar, "OPEC in a New Energy Era: Challenges and Opportunities," September. *PDVSA*. http://www.pdvsa.com/index.php?tpl=interface.en/design/biblioteca/readdoc.tpl.html&newsid_obj_id=2990&newsid_temas=110.

Cattaneo, Claudia. 2006. "A Chavez Loss Could Cost Oilpatch Skilled Workers." *National Post*, 23 November.

CBC News. 2012. "Wildrose May Reconsider Some Policies, Smith Says." *CBC News*, 24 April. http://www.cbc.ca/news/canada/edmonton/story/2012/04/24/albertavotes2012-smith-wildrose-reconsider-policies.html.

Chirot, Daniel. 1977. *Social Change in the Twentieth Century*. New York: Harcourt Brace Jovanovich.

Clarkson, Stephen. 2001. "The Multi-Level State: Canada in the Semi-Periphery of Both Continentalism and Globalization." *Review of International Political Economy* 8 (3): 501–27.

Clarkson, Stephen, and Marjorie Griffin Cohen, ed. 2004. *Governing Under Stress: Middle Powers and the Challenge of Globalization*. Black Point, NS: Fernwood Publishing.

Clawson, Patrick. 1978. "Egypt's Industrialization: A Critique of Dependency Theory." *MERIP Reports* (72): 17–23.

Collier, Robert. 2006. "Chavez Drives a Hard Bargain, but Big Oil's Options Are Limited." *San Francisco Chronicle*, 24 September.

Council of Canadians. 2013. "Lone Pine Resources Files Outrageous NAFTA Lawsuit Against Fracking Ban." *Council of Canadians / Le Conseil des Canadiens*. Media release, 3 October. http://www.canadians.org/media/lone-pine-resources-files-outrageous-nafta-lawsuit-against-fracking-ban.

DeCarlo, Scott. 2012. "The World's Biggest Public Companies." *Forbes*, 18 April. http://www.forbes.com/sites/scottdecarlo/2012/04/18/the-worlds-biggest-companies/.

Dobbin, Murray. 2007. "Challenging the Forces of Deep Integration." In *Whose Canada? Continental Integration, Fortress North America, and the Corporate Agenda*, edited by Ricardo Grinspun and Yasmine Shamsie, 501–28. Montréal and Kingston: McGill-Queen's University Press.

Dusseault, M. 2001. "Comparing Venezuelan and Canadian Heavy Oil and Tar Sands." Paper presented at the Canadian International Petroleum Conference, 12–14 June, Calgary, Alberta. http://www.onepetro.org/mslib/app/Preview.do?paperNumber=PETSOC-2001-061&societyCode=PETSOC.

EIU (Economist Intelligence Unit). 2003. "Venezuela Economy 'Faces Greatest Collapse.'" *Financial Times*, 14 January.

Encarnación, Omar G. 2002. "Venezuela's 'Civil Society Coup.'" *World Policy Journal* 19 (2): 38–48.

ERCB (Energy Resources Conservation Board). 2013. "ST9-2013: Alberta's Energy Reserves and Supply/Demand Outlook, 2013–2022." Calgary: ERCB.

Eulich, Whitney. 2010. "Slums: The Future." *Policy Innovations*, 16 March. http://www.policyinnovations.org/ideas/innovations/data/000161.

"Fedepetrol Won't Join Strike." 2002. *Oil Daily*, 21 October.

Fong, Petti. 2012. "Mulcair Has Near Slip Up During Tour of Oilsands: NDP Leader Corrects Himself on Technicality, Talks to Deputy Premier." *Toronto Star*, 1 June.

Gall, Norman. 1973. "Oil and Democracy in Venezuela—Part I: 'Sowing the Petroleum.'" American Universities Field Staff Report, January. *Norman Gall Publications*. http://www.normangall.com/venezuela_art1.htm.

Gerson, Jen. 2015. "Notley's Path to Power Beset by Many Challenges; 'You Don't Want to Become Bob Rae,' Analyst Cautions." *National Post*, 8 May.

Gindin, Jonah. 2004. "Possible Faces of Venezuelan Democracy." In *The Unexpected Revolution: The Venezuelan People Confront Neoliberalism*, edited by Carlos Torres, Marta Harnecker, Jonah Gindin, nchamah miller, Nicolas Lopez, David Raby, Marcela Maspero, and Greg Albo, 31–36. Toronto: Socialist Project.

Giovannetti, Justin. 2015. "Potential Cabinet Contenders in Province's Orange Wave." *Globe and Mail*, 19 May.

Glenday, Daniel. 2010. "Rich but Losing Ground: How Canada's Position in the World Economy Impacts Jobs, Social Choices, and Life Chances." In *The Shifting Landscape of Work*, edited by Ann Duffy, Daniel Glenday, and Norene Pupo, 15–35. Toronto: Nelson.

Gordon, Todd. 2010. *Imperialist Canada*. Winnipeg: Arbeiter Ring.

Harding, Jon. 2006. "Going Deep, Staying Deep." *National Post*, 3 April.

Harnecker, Marta. 2004. "After the Referendum Venezuela Faces New Challenges." *Monthly Review* 56 (6): 34–48.

Heckel, Heather D. , Edwin Lieuwen, John D. Martz, and Jennifer L. McCoy. 2012. "Venezuela." *Encyclopaedia Britannica Online Academic Edition*. Encyclopaedia Britannica Inc.

Hoyos, Carola. 2007. "The New Seven Sisters: Oil and Gas Giants Dwarf Western Rivals." *Financial Times*, 12 March.

Ikeda, Satoshi. 2004. "Zonal Structures and the Trajectories of Canada, Mexico, Australia, and Norway Under Neo-liberal Globalization." In *Governing Under Stress: Middle Powers and the Challenge of Globalization*, edited by Stephen Clarkson and Marjorie Griffin Cohen, 263–90. Black Point, NS: Fernwood Publishing.

International Business Publications, USA. 2012. *Venezuela Company Laws and Regulations Handbook*. Washington, DC: World Business Information Databank.

Kellogg, Paul. 2013. "Prairie Capitalism Revisited: Capital Accumulation and Class Formation in the New West." Paper presented at the annual meeting of the Canadian Political Science Association, 4-6 June, Victoria, BC. http://www.cpsa-acsp.ca/papers-2013/Kellogg.pdf.

———. 2014. "Democracy in Alberta: Political Transformations in North America's Energy Frontier." Paper presented at the annual meeting of the Canadian Political

Science Association, 27-29 May, St. Catharines, ON. http://www.cpsa-acsp.
ca/2014event/Kellogg.pdf.

——. 2015. *Escape from the Staple Trap: Canadian Political Economy After Left Nationalism.*
Toronto: University of Toronto Press.

Kentor, Jeffrey D. 2000. *Capital and Coercion: The Economic and Military Processes That Have
Shaped the World Economy, 1800–1990.* New York: Garland.

Kick, Edward L., and Byron L. Davis. 2001. "World-System Structure and Change:
An Analysis of Global Networks and Economic Growth Across Two Time Periods."
American Behavioral Scientist 44 (10): 1561–78.

Klassen, Jerome. 2009. "Canada and the New Imperialism: The Economics of a
Secondary Power." *Studies in Political Economy* 83 (Spring): 163–90.

Kleiss, Karen. 2015. "Tory Backers Rip 'Amateur' NDP Policies; Businessmen Point to
Prentice's Record in Appeal for PC Votes." *Edmonton Journal*, 2 May.

Korzeniewicz, Roberto P., and William Martin. 1994. "The Global Distribution of
Commodity Chains." In *Commodity Chains and Global Capitalism*, edited by Gary Gereffi
and Miguel Korzeniewicz, 67–92. Westport, CT: Praeger.

Lapper, Richard, and Andy Webb-Vidal. 2002. "Militaristic President Falls Victim to
Military Revolt." *Financial Times*, 13 April.

Laxer, Gordon. 2004. "Preface." In *Governing Under Stress: Middle Powers and the Challenge
of Globalization*, edited by Stephen Clarkson and Marjorie Griffin Cohen, x–xx. Black
Point, NS: Fernwood Publishing.

McNew, B. Seth. 2008. "Full Sovereignty over Oil: A Discussion of Venezuelan Oil Policy
and Possible Consequences of Recent Changes." *Law and Business Review of the Americas*
14: 149–58.

Mouat, Jeremy. 2005. "Thinking About Prairie Capitalism: Interview with Larry Pratt."
Aurora Online. http://aurora.icaap.org/index.php/aurora/article/view/1/1.

"National Post Editorial Board Endorses Danielle Smith and the Wildrose in the
Alberta Election." 2012. *National Post*, April 19. http://fullcomment.nationalpost.
com/2012/04/19/national-post-editorial-board-endorses-danielle-smith-and-the-
wildrose-in-the-alberta-election/.

OECD (Organisation for Economic Co-operation and Development). 2003. "Control
of a Corporation." *Glossary of Statistical Terms.* http://stats.oecd.org/glossary/detail.
asp?ID=445.

O'Grady, Mary Anastasia. 2005. "Americas: Oil Wells Refuse to Obey Chavez
Commands." *Wall Street Journal*, 20 May.

Prashad, Vijay. 2007. *The Darker Nations: A Biography of the Short-Lived Third World.* New
Delhi: LeftWord Books.

Pruegger, Valerie J., Derek Cook, and Sybille Richter-Salomons. 2009. *Inequality in
Calgary: The Racialization of Poverty.* Prepared for the City of Calgary, Community and
Neighbourhood Services, Social Research Unit.

Richards, John, and Larry Pratt. 1979. *Prairie Capitalism: Power and Influence in the New
West.* Toronto: McClelland and Stewart.

Rutledge, Ian. 2005. *Addicted to Oil: America's Relentless Drive for Energy Security*. New York: I. B. Tauris.

Sampson, Anthony. 1991. *The Seven Sisters: The Great Oil Companies and the World They Shaped*. Toronto: Bantam Books.

Skuce, Nikki. 2012. "Who Benefits? An Investigation of Foreign Investment in the Tar Sands." *ForestEthics*. http://www.forestethics.org/news/who-benefits-investigation-foreign-investment-tar-sands.

Smith, David A., and Douglas R. White. 1992. "Structure and Dynamics of the Global Economy: Network Analysis of International Trade 1965–1980." *Social Forces* 70 (4): 857–93.

Statistics Canada. 2000. "Table 3760047: International Investment Position, Capital Employed in Non-Financial Industries by Country of Ownership, Annually." Ottawa: CANSIM (database). Using CHASS (distributor).

———. 2014a. "Table 510001: Estimates of Population, by Age Group and Sex for July 1, Canada, Provinces and Territories, Annually (Persons Unless Specified)." Ottawa: CANSIM (database). Using CHASS (distributor).

———. 2014b. "Table 3840038: Gross Domestic Product, Expenditure-Based, Provincial and Territorial, Annually (Dollars Unless Specified)." Ottawa: CANSIM (database). Using CHASS (distributor).

———. 2014c. "Table 1790004: Corporations Returns Act (CRA), Major Financial Variables, Annually." Ottawa: CANSIM (database). Using CHASS (distributor).

———. 2015. "Table 3260021: Consumer Price Index (CPI), 2009 Basket, Annually (2002 = 100 Unless Specified)." Ottawa: CANSIM (database). Using CHASS (distributor).

"Time for Big Alberta." 2012. Editorial. *Globe and Mail*, 20 April.

Tinker-Salas, Miguel. 2005. "Fueling Concern." *Harvard International Review* 26 (4): 50–54.

Toro, Francisco. 2002. "White-Collar Oil Workers Key in Venezuela Crisis." *New York Times*, 30 November.

Van Rossem, Ronan. 1996. "The World System Paradigm as General Theory of Development: A Cross-National Test." *American Sociological Review* 61 (3): 508–27.

"Venezuela—Ali Rodriguez Araque." 2005. *APS Review Gas Market Trends*, 28 November.

"Venezuela—Chavez Background." 2007. *APS Review Oil Market Trends*, 3 December.

"Venezuelan Strike Poses Big Challenge." 2001. *Oil Daily*, 10 December.

Webb-Vidal, Andy. 2001. "Venezuelan Oil Workers Strike." *Financial Times*, 29 March.

———. 2002. "Venezuela Oil Company 'Ignores Meritocracy.'" *Financial Times*, 6 March.

Wildrose. 2012. "Redford PCs End Campaign Like They Began—with a Broken Promise." *Wildrose*, 22 April. http://www.wildrose.ca/redford_pcs_end_campaign_like_they_began_with_a_broken_promise.

World Bank. 2014. "World Databank." World Development Indicators (WDI) and Global Development Finance (GDF). Washington, DC: World Bank.

Yergin, Daniel. 2008. *The Prize: The Epic Quest for Oil, Money and Power*. New York: Simon and Schuster.

part two

Rights Claims
in an Oil Economy

Petroleum, Patriarchy, and Power

Women's Equality in Canada and Iran

Joy Fraser, Manijeh Mannani,
and Lorna Stefanick

The question of whether a country's economic dependence on oil has an effect on democracy has stimulated much debate, but analysis on the effects of oil-based economies on women remains relatively limited. While some scholars suggest that such economies hamper gender equality (Ross 2001, 2008; Sherk 2003), others argue that the roots of inequality for women are far more complex (Charrad 2009; Miller 2004). Using global indicators of gender equity (i.e., the degree to which people of different genders are treated with impartiality), we analyze the status of Canadian and Iranian women's equality (i.e., the state of being equal). These "snapshots" of women's equity and equality tell only part of the story, however. Therefore, we also employ the insights of Sylvia Walby on equality and human rights and of Erich Fromm and Michel Foucault on modernity to probe the issue of equality for women.

We begin this chapter by defining and exploring the concepts of "patriarchy" and "gender equality," as well as the utility of nationally based indicators of equity. Because of the shortcomings of these indicators in identifying sameness and evaluating difference, we provide a historical and cultural analysis of Iran and Canada as a context in which to evaluate the impacts of systems and structures on the status of women. Given both this book's focus on Alberta and the province's retrogressive status within Canada with respect to gender equality, we also consider the status of women in that province within the larger Canadian context. We show in our analysis that both Iran and Canada score well on some indicators of women's equity and equality relative to men and not so well on others. In both countries, women have not been able to build consistently on their achievements. This is largely because patriarchy is entrenched and reactive in both Canada and Iran, becoming even more pronounced in times of social dislocation. We conclude that giving primacy to oil dependency as a causal factor of gender inequalities is simplistic in societies where patriarchy is deeply embedded within political, social, cultural, and religious norms.

Patriarchy and Gender Equality in Iran and Canada

Sylvia Walby (2005, 20) defines patriarchy as "a system of social structures and practices in which men dominate, oppress and exploit women." Patriarchy is a system of power relations through which men control women's production, reproduction, and sexuality. Gender stereotypes are not only derived from patriarchy; they perpetuate it in that they reinforce inequality. Patriarchy is not static; gender relations are dynamic and complex, vary among societies, and are based in class, status, religion, region, ethnicity, and socio-cultural practices.

Concepts related to gender equality, as well as the routes to achieving it, are equally complex. Walby describes the three most common models used to define gender equality: "equality through sameness (equal opportunities or treatment), through equal valuation of difference (special programmes) and [through] the transformation of gendered practices and standards of evaluation" (374). She notes that while some progress can be made using the first two approaches, they tend to maintain the status quo by leaving uncontested the masculine norm as the standard against which equality is measured. De Bonfils et al. (2013, 8) observe that the "sameness" approach emphasizes women becoming equal to men, whereas the "difference" approach suggests that "women's physical difference from men results in different life patterns, psychology and moral values." Advocates of the latter approach (e.g. Cockburn 1991) tend to seek parity rather than sameness. The distinction between the first two approaches is particularly germane to this study, since the quest for equality in the Eastern context is frequently based on "complementarity" (equal but different) rather than on the rights-based notion of "sameness" through which feminism in the West is often expressed.

Walby (2005, 374) contends that for true gender equality and justice to occur, there must be transformation and social reorganization of institutions, standards, and gender relations, for "it is not possible to be 'different but equal' because differences are too entwined with power and resources." Other scholars and the European Commission argue for using a combination of all three approaches—sameness, difference, and transformation—in the attempt to achieve deep cultural changes, create new structures, and transform the gendered nature of society (Daly 2005; De Bonfils et al. 2013; Martin 2003; Verloo 2005).

We begin our analysis using parameters that measure equality through sameness, but we also examine gendered practices implicit in Walby's third model. With respect to sameness, we use the "freedom" indicators employed by human rights bodies to categorize countries along a spectrum, with democracy and dictatorship at opposite ends. Various government and nongovernment agencies regularly rank countries on civil, political, and economic indicators of freedom and democracy, progress on human development (e.g., fertility rates), and the gap between outcomes for men and women in terms of education and labour force participation (Freedom House 2012; Hausmann, Tyson, and Zahidi 2011; OECD 2012; UN Women 2011; World Bank 2011). There are arguments against using this approach. For example, in her discussion of the institutionalization of "gender" within governance discourse in South Africa, Linzi Manicom (2001, 18), suggests that "evaluating the status of the nation in terms of the status, or freedom, of its 'womenfolk' echoes a patronizing colonialist stance that moralises hierarchical inter-state relations. It positions women as objects of rescue rather than as agents and equal participants in the national transformation project." Nevertheless, we use such indicators because they help illuminate the sources of inequalities that exist in Canada and Iran when examined within a human rights framework. The norm of gender equity is central to the rights-based approach, "which resists, rather than accommodates, relativist approaches to the interpretation of human rights" (Goonesekere, n.d., para. 7). Resisting relativism is particularly important when studying two countries with significant differences in culture, religion, and history.

In many respects, Canada and Iran could be seen as complete opposites: Canada is considered a "free" state, whereas Iran is "not free." Canada is a federation in the Global North, and Iran is a unitary state in the Global South. What these two countries have in common is that they are both among the world's top ten energy producers and exporters of oil (IEA 2011). To complicate our analysis, oil is concentrated in the province of Alberta in Canada and in the province of Khuzestan in Iran. The equivalent of country-level statistics and indices are not always reported at the subnational level, and provinces in both countries vary linguistically and culturally. However, because provinces share common political and economic structures within their country, as well as a national identity, we use national measures as proxies for the oil-producing provinces. Given this book's focus on Alberta and the historical importance of Alberta women to gender politics in Canada, we also consider the state of women in Alberta, despite the methodological challenges.

Interestingly, Alberta and Iran both have reputations as socially regressive regimes. Within Canada, oil-rich Alberta is known as the "redneck"; the Alberta government has historically resisted attempts to promote the equality of minority groups (Harder 2003) and until 2015, has been dominated by conservative parties since the rise to power of the Social Credit in 1935 (Barrie 2006; Finkel 1989; Gibbins and Arrison 1995). Similarly, Iran is popularly seen as the maverick "bad boy" of the Middle Eastern states: governed by a fundamentalist Islamic theocracy, it is known as anti-Western and ultra-conservative, particularly with respect to the equality of women (Afary 2009). Could the country's economic dependence on oil be an important factor in explaining its conservatism, especially with respect to gender equality?

The Oil Curse: An Explanation for Women's Inequality in Oil-Rich States

Much of the limited literature on the impact of oil on women's equality suggests that oil reinforces patriarchal norms. With special reference to the Middle East, Michael Ross (2008, 120) maintains that "petroleum perpetuates patriarchy." According to Ross, during an oil boom, the number of women in the labour force shrinks for two reasons: first, because the "tradable goods" sector—the sector where women are more likely to be employed—decreases, causing a decrease in demand for women's labour, and second, because the size of household income (via the male earner) increases, causing women to be less willing to take low-paying jobs (109–10). In turn, decreased participation in the labour force reduces the political influence of women; thus, oil-producing countries end up with unusually strong patriarchal norms, laws, and political institutions. Ross concedes that the reduction of female participation in the economy or in politics is not seen in oil-rich countries such as Norway, New Zealand, and Australia, a point noted by Mounira Charrad (2009). Charrad points out that the strong patriarchal cultures and institutions in Saudi Arabia, Kuwait, and Libya that Ross attributes to oil predate the oil economies in the Middle East (548). In her view, the pre-existing patriarchal, tribal, and kinship structures (solidarities in the political system that rely on bonds among men) are the basis for the formation of political systems and social structures, onto which the oil economy was later grafted, especially in the Muslim Middle East.

A study by Gloria Miller (2004) of the experiences of women engineers in the Alberta oil industry suggests that the oil industry itself exhibits a particular kinship structure based on hypermasculinity, to which women must adapt. Predictably, this high-paying sector remains predominately male, reinforcing the powerful patriarchal networks that perpetuate gender inequality. Likewise, Susan Sherk's (2003) study of women working in the oil and gas sectors in Canada reveals male-dominated organizational cultures that discourage alternative perspectives that may be brought in by women; ultimately, these women are under pressure to conform. Other factors—such as the lack of alternative work schedules, including part-time work and job-sharing, as well as challenges with child care arrangements—bar women from participating equitably and advancing within petroleum industries. The barriers to employment and promotion in this lucrative field help to exacerbate the difference in earning potential between men and women, relegating women to jobs that pay much less. Sara Dorow (this volume) explores the gendered, hierarchical nature of the oil industry and its impact on both jobs and family. Dorow argues that the oil economy both benefits from and perpetuates these unequal configurations.

Particularly germane to our work is Mark Milke's 2011 Fraser Institute report, which uses Freedom House indicators to compare thirty-eight oil-producing nations from five continents on civil, political, and economic freedoms. Indices include electoral democracy; media, religious, and economic freedoms; the legal system; property rights; corruption; and judicial independence (22). Milke concludes that oil-producing countries are strikingly different. For example, women in Canada are "free," whereas women in Iran are "not free," and, this being the case, it is more "ethical" to purchase oil from Canada than from a country like Iran that suppresses the freedom of women. If we accept his conclusions at face value, we might conclude that oil production has a differential impact on the equality of women in various countries. In the next section, we examine the evidence for this assertion.

Women's Status Assessed: The Evidence from Canada and Iran

Indicators that measure the liberal-democratic rights of their citizens underscore stark differences between Canada and Iran. Canada scores very well in all areas (Milke 2011, 36, 53), while Iran has no electoral democracy, and no media, religious or economic freedoms. Iran scores moderately well with respect to its economic system, legal system, and property rights; however, in the areas of corruption and judicial independence, it receives particularly low ratings, especially compared to Canada (69–71).

With respect to freedoms specific to women, Milke reports that Canadian women are free to choose careers, to travel outside the country without a male guardian's permission, and to have surgery without a male guardian's permission (53). In contrast, Iran scores poorly (71). But while Canadian women enjoy superior basic freedoms compared to women in Iran, they perform at much the same level on other indicators, such as education (36, 53, 71). Recent data from the World Bank (2011, 60) paints an even more positive picture for Iran with respect to literacy and education:

> The female-to-male ratio in primary school is the world's highest, with 1.2 girls enrolled for every boy. The number of women in secondary school as a percentage of the eligible age group more than doubled from 30 percent to 81 percent, and in 2009, more than half of all Iranian university students, 68 percent of the students in science, and 28 percent in engineering were women.

With only 37 percent of Canadian women enrolled in undergraduate science and engineering (and declining) in 2008–9 (Research Council of Canada 2010, 11), the participation rate of Iranian women is significantly higher. In addition, Iran shows consistent improvements in human development indices for Iranian women, particularly with respect to the World Bank's key indicator: fertility rates. Iran has the world's fastest declining rate: in ten years the rate went from 6.9 children to 1.8 (World Bank 2011, 60). Moreover, Iranian women now enjoy better health due to better service delivery and new labour market opportunities. They now constitute 30 percent of the labour force (60).

It seems that that there are indeed differential equality outcomes for oil-producing nations, albeit in different ways than Milke predicted. What is vexing for those who maintain that oil suppresses women's rights is that the gains for Iranian women were achieved in the two decades following the 1979 Islamic revolution—a time when Iran's oil-dependent economy almost doubled in value (60). Despite Iran having both an oil-based economy and an authoritarian regime, human development outcomes among Iranian women have improved in terms of reproductive, education, and economic rights (Bahramitash and Kazemipour 2006; World Bank 2011). The next section explores these gains in more detail.

The Quest for Equality in Iran

For centuries, Iranian women have been suppressed physically by the convention of the veil and verbally by the conventions of public silence. Theirs was a private world, where self-expression was confined to the accepted family circle (Milani 1992, 46). The subordination of women was particularly evident in marital relations, where men have traditionally had the right to divorce at will, the ability to execute an adulterous wife, and the right (albeit rarely used) to a polygamous marriage. While clearly patriarchal, the family, the kinship networks, and the customs surrounding the marriage contract itself provided some degree of economic and social support for women in their clearly defined roles within the family.

Like women elsewhere in the world, however, modernization prompted a quest for equal rights. New rights for Iranian women came in the early years of the twentieth century at the time of the 1905–7 Iranian Constitutional Revolution. During this era, members of the Iranian aristocracy travelled extensively abroad and were greatly influenced by Western ideas. The discovery of oil in 1908 resulted in the formation of the Anglo-Persian Oil Company; the agreement struck between Iran and Britain entitled Iran to 16 percent of the net profits. The Anglo-Persian partnership marked the beginning of a protracted period of agitation for increased gender equality. In the private sphere, women began working toward the reformation of marriage laws and the right to vote. But the impetus for change came primarily from the top rather than the bottom; the installation of Reza Shah through a military coup saw the replacement of the Qajar dynasty with the Pahlavi dynasty. Maintaining the modernization trajectory of those who had preceded him, Reza Shah ambitiously reformed the judiciary and undertook major infrastructure, industry, transportation, health, and education projects. This era also saw the modernization of gender relations through the passage of a new marriage law that limited polygamy, the abolishment of extrajudicial divorce, and the prohibition of women wearing the veil in public (Goldstein 2010). Milani (1992, 157) describes this era as characterized by an "intense thirst" for anything Western, at least on the part of the new middle classes. As Warren Goldstein notes (2010, 53), "Many traditional women felt that not wearing a veil in public was like being naked. Consequently, they did not go outside."

During this period, equality came in the form of rights, but it also came in the form of laws that prohibited traditional cultural norms. Thus, while Reza

Shah embraced Western ideas, he did not embrace the notion of consensual rule. Suffice to say, his autocratic governing style did not sit well with intellectual and religious elites. In the public sphere, the agitation for change focused on capturing a more equitable share of profit from Iran's petroleum partnership. Internal and external tensions over profit sharing increased, culminating in the 1941 invasion of Iran in a combined British-Soviet effort to secure flowing oil for the Allied war effort; the Allies forced the Shah to abdicate to his son Mohammad Reza Shah, and a constitutional monarchy was re-established. A decade later, the populist, democratically elected government of Mohammad Mossadegh nationalized the Anglo-Iranian Oil Company. In reaction, the West used the CIA to overthrow the government in 1953, protecting Western control of an enormously lucrative oil infrastructure. The coup also transformed a constitutional monarchy into an absolutist kingship and induced a succession of unintended consequences, including the Islamic revolution of 1979 (Kinzer 2003, 120–21). Modernization continued, but the new government did not tolerate political dissent.

Repeated encounters with imperialism caused infatuation with the West to be replaced by animosity. Westomania—or more commonly, Westoxification, a term coined by Jalal Al-e Ahmad to describe "a contagious disease that [had] infested, infatuated, and stupefied Iranians"—captured the sentiments of the larger public in this era (Milani 1992, 156). This new anti-Western orientation had little effect on progressive thought, however, and the following decades saw achievements of all kinds, including many relating to the status of women. Female literacy improved, women gained the right to vote, and, in 1963, Iranians elected the first woman, Farrokhroo Parsa, to Parliament. In 1968, Parsa became the first woman to hold a cabinet post in the Iranian government. In addition, two new marriage laws expanded the equality rights of women. These initiatives were part of a larger worldwide trend to improve the status of women, but in Iran, the combination of oil revenue and the initial embracing of Western norms meant that change came with extraordinary speed. Dramatic change, however, also fuelled festering anti-Western sentiment.

The legal equality of women took a dramatic U-turn after the Iranian revolution of 1979 and the installation of an Islamic theocracy (Afary 2009). This populist uprising against an unpopular monarch was in part the result of many decades of resentment against Western political and economic interests. One outcome of the revolution—the revival of eighth-century Sharia law—caught many Iranians by surprise. As Janet Afary (2009, 265) notes, "The

1979 Islamic Revolution was not a wholesale return to the past; rather, the new state reinvented and expanded certain retrogressive gender and cultural practices and presented them . . . through modern technologies of power." Within a month of Ayatollah Khomeini's return from exile, the newly installed Supreme Leader of the country presided over the firing of all female judges, the compulsory veiling of women, the banning of co-education of males and females, the barring of married girls from attending high schools, the closure of workplace nurseries, and the systematic dismantling of the previous fifty years of reforms to family law (Afshar 1998, 50). Farrokhroo Parsa was executed, and women's participation in the labour force contracted (Afary 2009, 309). The preamble to the post-revolution constitution underscores the new orientation. Specifically, it states that the roles of mother and wife had eroded as a result of the drive to modernize and that seizing them back would be particularly empowering for women: "Such a position in the family removes women from being objects of pleasure or tools of production and frees them of the burdens of exploitation and imperialism and enables them to find once more their critical duties of motherhood and raising of humanity" (translated and quoted in Afshar 1998, 150).

Women in Iran resisted these policies through legal challenges, protests, and outright refusals (Afshar 1998; Milani 1992). Had it not been for external threats that galvanized popular support for the new republic, it is plausible that such regressive "reforms" would not have had quite the staying power that they did. Soon after the revolution, militant students took American diplomatic staff hostage, resulting in both a botched rescue attempt by the United States and the Iran-Contra affair. Shortly thereafter, Iraq, with whom Iran had had ongoing border skirmishes, took advantage of Iran's internal turmoil and invaded the country. In the ensuing eight-year war, an estimated 500,000 people were killed; the international community remained silent over the Iraqi use of chemical weapons in this conflict (Pelletiere 1992).

These events provide a backdrop for understanding why some Iranian women saw an Islamic government with its regressive policies toward women as tolerable in the face of foreign aggression. For Iranians, aggression took the form not only of invasion but also of cultural imperialism—namely, the Western commodification of women as sex objects. In her summation of this perspective, Afshar (1998, 15) explains that for many Iranian women, the veil "puts an end to the beauty myth and the relentless pursuit of fashion and beauty products. It is this view which, at the end of the twentieth century, has persuaded many women to abandon the mini-skirt for the veil, and has persuaded many Islamist groups and governments to adopt veiled women as the public emblem of Islamification."

Although the immediate post-revolutionary period saw a dramatic decline of women's rights, gender equality actually improved in the ensuing decades. For example, the share of women in the labour force rose from 20 percent in 1986 to 33 percent in 2011 (World Bank 2011, 60). A booming oil economy that resulted in a rapid rise in female education and a change in demographics accounts, to a large extent, for this progress. Moreover, some attribute the absorption of women into the education, health, and social services sectors to the fact that Iran does not rely on cheap female labour in the manufacturing export sector, as other Global South countries do (Bahramitash and Kazemipour 2006, 118–19). Thus, contrary to Ross's conclusion that oil production reduces the number of women in the labour force in the Middle East (2008, 1), the opposite appears to be true in Iran. In 2009, Shahla Haeri noted that Iranian women are now "working in various professions and pursuing different sociopolitical goals" (134).

Although some progress toward equality has been made, patriarchy is alive and well in Iran. In terms of labour force participation, oil stimulated the economy and provided the necessary funds to expand educational and employment opportunities for women. The primary causal factor in the inhibition of women's rights in contemporary Iran is not oil, but the installation of an Islamic theocracy that interprets the Koran in a paternalistic way.[1] Given the strategic importance of Iran to the industrialized world, this orientation can also be seen as a conscious rejection of the modern international political system. The next section illustrates that Canada has also not been immune to patriarchy, nor to the forces of change.

The Quest for Women's Equality in Canada

Since Canada's confederation in 1867, Canadian women have achieved many successes in attaining equal rights, among them the right to own property and to vote. Much of the pressure to grant these rights came from Western Canada—and in particular, from Alberta, where women were actively involved in politics. The election of Hannah Gale as alderman on Calgary's City Council in 1917 represented a first for women serving at any level of government in Canada—and indeed, in the British Commonwealth (Sanderson 1999, 28). Canada's Famous Five also lived in Alberta; they were among the first women in Canada to hold legal and political positions.[2] Their most well-known accomplishment was having women recognized as "persons," thus making women eligible for appointment to the Canadian Senate in 1929. Commenting on the fact that the two main political parties in Alberta in 2012 were led by females, Sylvia Bashevkin (2012) references the province's trail-blazing history in Canada: "This pattern is consistent with an international trend that saw women's rights move forward far more rapidly in frontier environments rather than traditional societies."[3]

Interestingly, the reinforcement of women's unequal status that enraged women across Canada also involved an Alberta woman. In 1973, the Supreme Court upheld an earlier decision in the Murdoch divorce case that denied an Alberta farm wife (Irene Murdoch, from Turner Valley) her rights to a share in the family cattle ranch that she had worked on and managed for twenty-five years. That same year, the Supreme Court of Canada made a second inequitable ruling that validated a section of the Indian Act that denied Native status to Indian women who married non-Natives. Native men who married non-Natives did not lose their status (CBC 2001). Thus, achieving equal rights for women has had an uneven trajectory, with race and class discrimination often embedded within gender discrimination. As is evident in chapter 10 in this volume, race- and class-based gender inequality in Canada, and in Alberta specifically, is still seen today.

The 1970s and 1980s saw the passage of the Canadian Human Rights Act (1977), the adoption of the UN Convention on the Elimination of All Forms of Discrimination Against Women (1979), and the entrenchment of the Canadian Charter of Rights and Freedoms (1982); all contained provisions prohibiting discrimination on the basis of gender. Additionally, the federal government was actively supporting feminist organizations, which where emerging in this era. Feminists in Alberta had the unenviable position of having to fight just to preserve earlier advancements, since this was also the era of a complex federal-provincial conflict over oil. The simple act of accepting money from the federal government, which was locked in a battle with the provincial government over the National Energy Program, demonized women's groups in the eyes of many Albertans (Harder 2003, 21).

Growing neoliberalism further exacerbated gender inequality in Canada by reducing the allocation of resources to alleviate gender inequities (Teghtsoonian 2005, 311). Adopting female-friendly conventions and funding feminist organizations do not mean much if the political will to promote equality is missing.

Neoliberal thought eschews using the state to effect progressive social change; by the mid-1990s, governments at all levels were dramatically reducing programs that benefited women. In 2008, the Canadian Feminist Alliance for International Action gave Canada "a failing grade on women's equality" because of its failure "to comply with its obligations to women under international human rights law" (CFAIA 2008, 9). The Alliance noted that Canadian women, and especially women from disadvantaged groups (including Aboriginal, and other nonwhite women, as well as the disabled, seniors, immigrants, and single parents), are disproportionately poor, leaving them particularly vulnerable to violence, precarious housing, political exclusion, poor health, and discrimination (CFAIA 2008). For many women in Canada, access to education, the justice system, and participation in politics is increasingly challenging. Moreover, cuts to public services do not acknowledge the value of unpaid labour and the sexual divisions of labour that reproduce inequalities based on gender. With particular reference to Alberta, New Zealand's Marilyn Waring observes that services are not devolved from the public to the private sector, but to the community, which "is usually mom or daughter or aunty or neighbour or some other woman" (quoted in Cavanaugh 1998; see also Waring 2012).

In the labour force, Canadian women remain overrepresented in sex-segregated lower-paying jobs. The Canadian Federation of University Women and the National Council of Women of Canada highlight the disparity in wages for Canadian women generally and have called on the government to follow through on its 2009 acceptance of the UN Universal Periodic Review's recommendation to "implement International Labour organization (ILO) and Convention on Economic Social and Cultural Rights (CERSC) recommendations to ensure remuneration for work of equal value in public and private sectors" (quoted in CFUW and NCWC 2012, 10). Instead, in February 2009, Stephen Harper's government introduced the Public Sector Equitable Compensation Act. The act changed the criteria used to assess whether jobs are of equal value and forces women to deal with pay equity at the bargaining table. More importantly, it makes pay equity claims more difficult by requiring a "female predominant" job group to comprise 70 percent women (10). The Public Service Alliance of Canada maintained that "the downgrading of pay equity as proposed in this bill is a violation of the constitutional Charter equality rights of working women" (PSAC 2009). According to Kathleen Lahey's analysis of Budget 2012, there appears to be no relief in sight for Canadian women, whose economic condition has remained virtually unchanged since 1997. She concludes that Budget 2012's cuts to taxes, public services, and Canada's old age security system, as well as its changes to Employment Insurance, benefit men and disadvantage women (Lahey 2012).

The labour situation for women in Alberta both reflects and deviates from the larger Canadian picture. A study by the Parkland Institute and the Alberta College of Social Workers (Gibson 2012) comparing Alberta to other Canadian provinces shows that the province leads the race to the bottom with respect to the social safety net, including such issues as maternity leave, child care, support for single mothers, and low-wage earners (who are overwhelmingly women in Alberta). Yet, according to statistics provided by the Alberta government, the province has the highest labour rate participation and highest employment rate of women in Canada. Moreover, while more women work part-time than men, over the ten-year period between 2004 and 2014, "the largest percentage increases in full-time employment were women in the 65 years and over and the 45-64 years age groups: 188.7% and 39.1% respectively" (Alberta 2015, 1). Alberta women also enjoy the highest average hourly wage ($24.63) compared to the overall average of $22.64 for Canadian women overall. Across all age groups, however, women's average wage is lower than men's ($31.21) in Alberta, and the difference increases with age (1). In the well-paid resource sector, women make up only 18.6 percent of the labour force, and only 1.4 percent of those who run the companies are women (Lahey 2015, 85). The gap between what women and men earn in Alberta has increased since the mid-1990s; in 2014, women in Alberta earned 63 percent of the earnings of their male counterparts (12). The wage differential between men and women is attributed to tax changes that increased the burden on low income earners in whose ranks women are concentrated (26) and to the rollback of social programs for ideological or budgetary reasons (89). Despite gains in some areas, women in Alberta are still lagging behind men in finding full-time employment, achieving pay equity, and escaping poverty. And, as explained by Sara Dorow (this volume), high wages, shift work, long commutes, and the lack of family support in Alberta's oil patch conspire to keep the lower-paid spouse (who typically is female) out of the workforce and taking care of children. As Lahey observes, Alberta's "paradox of plenty" produces a situation where women are "underdeveloped" in comparison to men "precisely because women's economic opportunities are more dependent on the adequacy of education, childcare, healthcare, transportation, housing, employment equality, skills training programs, and the vitality of value chain production. These are all the types of programs that will be the immediate focus of spending freezes and cuts when anticipated resource revenues suddenly vaporize due to market swings" (89).

It is evident that whether in the public realm of paid labour or in the private sphere, inequalities persist for Canadian women. Given the current government and its latest legislation on pay equity, Canadian women, in Alberta and elsewhere in the country, may be less likely today to achieve wage parity than they were in the past. In some ways, Alberta women fare better than their sisters in other provinces with respect to "sameness" indices like labour force participation, post-secondary education attainment, and hourly wage. But Alberta women are worse off than other women in Canada in terms of wage parity with Alberta men and government support for families. There appears to be an inverse relationship between the importance of Alberta's oil to Canada's economy and the federal government's concern with promoting equality for Canadian women; however, this deterioration could be the result of the entrenchment of neoliberal thought at the federal level. In the next section, we explore an alternative explanation of gender relations; we give primacy to pivotal historical events, fuelled by socio-economic dislocation, for understanding the suppression of women's equality.

Beyond the Indicators, Beyond the Oil Curse: Explaining the Retrenchment of Patriarchy

Sylvia Walby's idea introduced at the outset of this chapter, that women's equality comes through transformative social and institutional change, leads us to an examination of how public policy affects men and women's power, either reinforcing or challenging the existing forms of social organization (Paterson 2010). Foucault (1978, 110) argues that Western societies exercised increasing control over individuals, primarily through the family. Combined with urbanization, this control caused the role, function, and structure of the family to change. Change created stress, and subsequently, those individuals within the family who could not adapt to the new structure were deemed "abnormal." To address this dysfunction, professionals within the new disciplines of psychology and psychiatry emerged to assist individuals in adapting to the new boundaries set by society.

In a similar vein, Erich Fromm analyzed the psychological impact on individuals of the freedoms associated with liberalism. Fromm (1965, 123–29) argues that the negative impact of modernity on individuals was more acute than the impact of the retraction of the rigid class system and social norms that happened gradually in the Middle Ages. Freedom from social hierarchies and changes in the social order resulted in feelings of displacement, disconnectedness, and trauma within individual members of society who experienced economic instability and loss of identity in the new liberal order.

Fromm uses this crisis of identity in explaining why Germans joined the Nazi movement—they traded the anxiety associated with freedom for the security of an authoritarian regime. Similarly, Afary (2009) builds on Foucault's and Fromm's analyses to explain why Iranians embraced the ethico-political structure of the Iranian Islamist movement of the 1960s. She argues that in Iran in the 1960s and 1970s, people found themselves "caught between pre-modern and modern social values" (19) in the same way that people in Western societies experienced "cultural alienation and psychological trauma" as the result of the change in the social order (201). This trauma was particularly acute for a traditional Islamic society that was embracing modernity.

It is important to point out that with respect to Iranian public policy, the Islamic conception of female sexuality differed quite dramatically from the Western conception. Prior to the sexual revolution in the 1960s, the norm for Western women was to be passive in sexual relations, whereas women in Islamic culture typically have been seen as active participants in heterosexual relations. Female sexuality therefore cannot be left unrestrained; otherwise, chaos might ensue (Mernissi 1975, 31). Accounts of the awkwardness of male-female interaction after the forced unveiling of women by government decree in 1936 reflect this view and explain the high degree of psychological trauma both men and women experienced following the unveiling act (Milani 1992, 35).

While many Iranian women wanted more rights, freedoms, and opportunities in the years leading up to the 1979 revolution, they were uncomfortable with second wave feminism because of its association with imperialism, consumerism, and "free love" culture (Afary 2009, 234). Citing the work of Andrea Dworkin (1983) and Elinor Burkett (1999), American feminist scholars of second wave American feminism, Afray notes similar patterns of loss of identity and insecurity among right-wing American women's groups. Young Iranians reacted by embracing the regime's "third way" of understanding gender relations that rejected "the evils of Western imperialism, which turned women into sexual commodities, and Soviet communism, which destroyed family values" (Afary 2009, 234). Moreover, Islamism provided many Iranian women the opportunity to eschew oppressive familial and societal roles by committing themselves to new roles as revolutionaries. As Afary observes, "Their allegiance to a highly authoritarian and patriarchal movement that advocated women's subordination to men nonetheless allowed them to gain a measure of personal power, to exercise leadership over others, and to live more gratifying personal lives" (257).

Embracing radical Islamism was not just a quest for ideological and spiritual support, however. An added incentive for large numbers of rural Iranians who had "left the old hierarchical social order" of their villages to work or study in "urban industrialized environments" was the food subsidies, health care, and other services that were available to people with allegiance to local religious centres and mosques (201). A broad coalition of support, including more educated members of Iranian society, combined with the rural Iranians who had moved to urban environments and a host of international factors to bring the Islamic government into power in 1979. Islamic laws and policies implemented by the new regime further augmented the segregation of the sexes and the subjugation of women already in place in this millennia-old culture. While women made huge strides with respect to educational attainment in post-revolutionary Iran, this progress can be explained in part by the Islamic state's "programme for the 'purification' of the minds of its people" (Afshar 1998, 65), developed with the purpose of eliminating Western and imperialist ideas.

It is clear that the installation of an Islamic theocracy has had a huge impact on women's equality in Iran. The allegiance to religious fundamentalism can be interpreted as a reaction to the social, cultural, political, and economic displacement that resulted from urbanization and the transition to modernity. Oil revenue, of course, is an important component in these transformations, but so too are Iran's twentieth-century economic reforms, its geo-strategic importance, the influence of Western ideas, and Iran's place in the global economic order.

The loss of identity that comes with rapid change in the social order is also seen in Canada during this time. Canada was being transformed, first through immigration and then through urbanization. In Alberta, these changes were particularly dramatic. Successive waves of immigration from Asia and eastern and southern Europe challenged the hegemony of the white Anglo-Saxon Protestant elite. Adding Catholics, Slavs, and Chinese to a society that previously counted only Aboriginal people as outsiders threatened the social order. As Foucault might have predicted, one way in which provincial elites responded to this alienating and traumatic social transformation was to enact the Sexual

Sterilization Act 1928, which sought to prevent the province's "undesirables" from reproducing. More than 2,800 people in Alberta were involuntarily sterilized over a forty-three-year period ending in 1972, long after other jurisdictions had ended the practice. Timothy Christian (1974) concludes that the act was primarily used to exert control over the sexuality—and in particular, over the reproductive capacity—of those deemed to be immoral, delinquent, mentally deficient, or otherwise inferior. Women were overrepresented among those who were sterilized. Given that the legislation stipulated that one of the reasons for recommending sterilization was the vague criteria of being "incapable of intelligent parenthood," it is not difficult to see why Jana Grekul, Harvey Krahn, and Dave Odynak (2004, 365) conclude that "sterilization was essentially a medical solution for a variety of perceived social and behavioural problems."

A second dramatic social transformation in Alberta occurred after the discovery of oil in Leduc in 1947. This era saw rapid urbanization and dramatic population and economic growth, along with political changes. The thirty-four-year dynasty of the Social Credit Party came to an abrupt end in 1971, and with it ended the authoritarian, faith-based leadership (Finkel 1989, 58–60). For the first time, Albertans had a government wherein the number of representatives of urban ridings surpassed those of rural ridings. The rapid growth, social displacement, and growing inequalities experienced during the oil boom contributed to the province having the highest rates of divorce, suicide, teenage pregnancies, and abortion in the country. As Howard Palmer and Tamara Palmer note, "Many individuals and couples, lacking family support systems, could not stand the stress of a boom-bust economy that fostered big dreams, and produced confused values and identities" (1990, 336).

The provincial government's response to social injustice and dislocation was one of indifference. With respect to the oil boom in the 1970s, Lois Harder (2003, 21) suggests that the oil industry and the state had a symbiotic relationship that benefited the middle class but not those who were struggling:

> Those people subjected to the social displacements that emerged out of rapid population growth and economic expansion found their crises framed in terms of individual failings or were simply ignored. The seeming ease with which wealth was accumulated during this period could be used to support the view that systemic inequality could be alleviated by working harder, pulling up one's bootstraps, and taking advantage of the opportunities of a booming economy.

Despite the largesse that came from a booming economy, Alberta did not expand social entitlements, even though it was apparent that many Albertans were being left behind. As Harder points out, "In the context of an economic boom, the political costs of alienating groups perceived as marginal were minimal" (22). Women, of course, were the most marginal of the marginalized groups.

During this era, the plight of those who were struggling worsened even more during the 1980s world economic recession, which culminated in oil prices plummeting and Canada's biggest oil companies teetering on the brink of collapse. In Alberta, there was a dramatic rise in unemployment, outmigration, business closures, bankruptcies, and housing foreclosures (Gereluk 2012, 175). Provincially, government involvement in high-profile public investment failures and private sector bailouts led many to question the government's fiscal management (Gereluk 2012, 199; Harder 2003, 118). Pressure was increasing on already strained social services as public discontent and social hardship increased. In 1986, the opposition ranks swelled from four seats in the legislature to twenty-two (Elections Alberta 2015). The time was ripe for change: Albertans were rethinking the complex relationship between the state, markets, and civil society.

Albertans did not deal with the trauma of profound societal change by embracing a faith-based political movement in the 1990s as Iranians had in the 1970s. Rather, they embraced a radical restructuring of the state from activist welfare to limited laissez-faire. Alberta was the first jurisdiction in Canada to embrace neoliberalism, and other governments copied Alberta reforms, including the federal government. This new orientation meshed well with entrenched traditional Christian values, particularly as expressed by the Alberta Social Credit and Reform movements. The contraction of the welfare state affected women in many ways, including increased demands on the unpaid labour they performed within the family unit, and it also led to fewer opportunities for human rights and equality claims making. The entrenchment of neoliberalism in Alberta went hand in hand with the re-entrenchment of neoconservative ideology, which emphasized the traditional family and further decreased the range of possibilities for women. As Gurston Dacks, Joyce Green, and Linda Trimble (1995, 271) explain, "A central tenant of neoconservatism is a preference for hierarchical and authoritarian social relations. One of its most important expressions is its promotion of patriarchal social organization—the systematic domination by men of social, economic, and political power—and a social and family mythology emanating from and supportive of patriarchy." Sara Dorow (this volume) argues that the structure of the oil industry encourages the neo-conservative family mythology that supports patriarchy; women become "flexibilized" labourers, adjusting their paid work so that they can accommodate the demands of being the primary family caregiver. In this way, ideology and economic structures combined to give a particularly strong expression of patriarchy in Alberta.

With the emergence of Alberta as the economic powerhouse of Canada, and the election of the Harper Conservative government at the federal level in 2006, Canada as a whole began to follow Alberta's neoliberal path of major political and economic reorientation, a change in direction that has already led to profound societal change. The prospects for women's equality in Canada at the dawn of the new millennium are gloomy.

The Impact of Oil on Women's Equality

What emerges from this analysis is the recognition that the impact of the oil economy on women's equality status is complex and variegated. In Canada, women enjoy fundamental freedoms, many of which are now denied to women in Iran, specifically in relation to legal rights. During the postwar period, when oil was gaining economic importance in Iran and Canada, women's equality made steady strides forward. In both countries, however, progress toward equality has not been linear, with instances of sliding backwards.

A jurisdiction's economic dependence on oil may indeed work against women's equality in some instances, but the record is mixed. We suggest that many factors are critical in holding women back in Iran and Canada. Social dislocation has led to what many call "reactive patriarchy." This can be fuelled in part by oil, but it is also influenced by factors such as urbanization, population growth, modernization, neoliberal economic and social policies, and religion. In the first half of the century, immigration to western Canada resulted in a dramatic growth of non-Anglo-Saxon populations that threatened the existing pre-oil social order. The discovery of oil contributed to yet more social change in Canada, especially in Alberta. Similarly, the rush to modernize predated the discovery of oil in Iran. The development of an oil industry that encouraged British, Soviet, and American imperialism as well as pro- and anti-West ideologies caused yet more social changes in Iran. The identity crises brought about by social dislocations pushed the populations in both jurisdictions to embrace reactive ideologies that exacerbated existing patriarchal structures.

In the case of Iran, that ideology took the shape of religious fundamentalism steeped in patriarchy. In the case of Alberta, it took the form of eugenics in the early part of the century and neoliberalism in the latter part, both emphasizing patriarchal notions of the family structure that actively repress female sexual expression and cause women's equality in the social and economic realms to backslide. Neoliberalism would take hold federally in Canada somewhat later but with the same effect: not only was the quest for equality suppressed, but inequality was exacerbated.

In this chapter, we have demonstrated that while a country's economic reliance on oil clearly has some influence on women's equality, this is only part of the picture. Discrimination against women is pervasive, complex, and systemic in the world's oil-rich and non-oil economies. Moreover, the sources of discrimination are linked to deeply entrenched patriarchal systems and social structures that have a global reach and considerable staying power, particularly during times of social dislocation. The Iran-Canada comparison underscores the need to expand the horizon of the enquiry about the impact of oil wealth on political and ideological developments within a country. As noted by Sylvia Walby (2005), the lack of movement in the transformation and social reorganization of institutions, standards, and gender relations is the biggest obstacle in the quest for women's equality. In trying to understand how a resource economy operates, it is critical to pay attention to historical cultural phenomena that are embedded in a society. These phenomena play a significant part in preventing such a movement toward gender equality, be it in theocratic Iran or democratic Canada.

Notes

1 Interestingly, some Iranian feminists also anchor their equality demands in the Koran, with reference to a brief period of Shiite rule in the seventh century. As Afshar (1998, 19) notes, "in their pursuit of the golden age Iranian Islamist women are equipped with 50 years of history and 114 verses of a holy book—perhaps as good a resource as those offered by any other ideology or utopian vision."

2 The posts held by the Famous Five were significant even by today's standards: Emily Murphy was appointed magistrate in the British Empire; Louise McKinney and Roberta MacAdams were the first women to be elected to a provincial legislature; Irene Parlby was appointed Minister without Portfolio in the United Farmer's government, becoming the second woman in the British Empire to serve as a cabinet minister; and Nellie McClung was the third woman to sit on the Alberta legislature.

"The Famous Five Women," *Famous5Foundation*, 2012, http://www.famous5.ca/index. php/the-famous-5-women/the-famous-5-women.

3 As is noted later in this chapter, despite impressive progress early in its history, Alberta has garnered infamy for its egregious violations of human rights in this early period. While Alberta's most famous suffragettes fought for gender equality, they did not extend equality rights universally; in fact, they subscribed to the eugenics bio-social movement that promoted the involuntary sterilization of those deemed mentally, physically, or morally deficient. These included the indigent, single mothers, prostitutes, immigrants, and First Nations peoples (Christian 1974).

References

Afary, Janet. 2009. *Sexual Politics in Modern Iran*. New York: Cambridge University Press.

Afshar, Haleh. 1998. *Islam and Feminisms: An Iranian Case-Study*. Basingstoke, UK: Macmillan.

Alberta. 2015. *Alberta Labour Force Profiles: Women 2014*. March. http://work.alberta.ca/ documents/labour-profile-women.pdf.

Bahramitash, Roksana, and Shahla Kazemipour. 2006. "Myths and Realities of the Impact of Islam on Women: Changing Marital Status in Iran." *Critique: Critical Middle Eastern Studies* 15 (2): 111–28.

Barrie, Doreen. 2006. *The Other Alberta: Decoding a Political Enigma*. Regina, SK: Canadian Plains Research Centre.

Bashevkin, Sylvia. 2012. "Ms. Premier in Alberta? No Surprise." *Globe and Mail*, 6 September.

Burkett, Elinor. 1999. *The Right Women: A Journey Through the Heart of Conservative America*. New York: Simon and Schuster.

Cavanaugh, Cathy. 1998. "If Women Counted: Interview with Marilyn Waring." *Aurora Online*. http://aurora.icaap.org/talks/waring.htm.

CBC. 2001. "Equal Under the Law: Canadian Women Fight for Equality as the Country Creates a Charter of Rights." *CBC Learning*. http://www.cbc.ca/history/ EPISCONTENTSE1EP17CH2PA4LE.html.

CFAIA (Canadian Feminist Alliance for International Action). 2008. "A Failing Grade on Women's Equality: Canada's Human Rights Record on Women." Feminist Alliance for International Action Submission to the United Nations Human Rights Council, September. http://www2.ohchr.org/english/bodies/cedaw/docs/ngos/ FAFIAUPRSeptember8final_3.pdf.

CFUW (Canadian Federation of University Women) and NCWC (National Council of Women of Canada). 2012. "Joint Submission on the Occasion of Canada's Universal Periodic Review, 16th Session (22 Apr–3 May 2013)." http://www.fcfdu.org/Portals/0/ Advocacy/CFUW%20and%20NCWC%20Joint%20UPR%20Submission%20Final.pdf.

Charrad, Mounira M. 2009. "Kinship, Islam, or Oil: Culprits of Gender Inequality?" *Politics and Gender* 5 (4): 546–53.

Christian, Timothy A. 1974. *The Mentally Ill and Human Rights in Alberta: A Study of the Alberta Sexual Sterilization Act*. Edmonton: Faculty of Law, University of Alberta.

Cockburn, Cynthia. 1991. *In the Way of Women: Men's Resistance to Sex Equality in Organizations*. Basingstoke, UK: Macmillan.

Dacks, Gurston, Joyce Green, and Linda Trimble. 1995. "Road Kill: Women in Alberta's Drive Toward Deficit Elimination." In *The Trojan Horse: Alberta and the Future of Canada*, edited by Gordon Laxer and Trevor Harrison, 271–80. Montréal: Black Rose Books.

Daly, Mary. 2005. "Gender Mainstreaming in Theory and Practice, Social Politics." *International Studies in Gender, State and Society* 12 (3): 433–50.

De Bonfils, Laura, Anne Laure Humbert, Viginta Ivaškaite-Tamošiune, Anna Rita Manca, Ligia Nobrega, Jolanta Reingarde and Irene Riobóo Lestón. 2013. *Gender Equality Index—Country Profiles*. Vilnius, Lithuania: European Institute for Gender Equality.

Dworkin, Andrea. 1983. *Right-Wing Women*. New York: Perigee Books.

Elections Alberta. 2015. "Candidate Summary of Results (General Elections, 1905–2015)." *Elections Alberta*. http://www.elections.ab.ca/reports/statistics/candidate-summary-of-results-general-elections/.

Finkel, Alvin. 1989. *The Social Credit Phenomenon in Alberta*. Toronto: University of Toronto Press.

Foucault, Michel. 1978. *The History of Sexuality*. Vol. 1. New York: Vintage Books, 1990.

Freedom House. 2012. "Freedom in the World 2012." *Freedom House*. https://freedomhouse.org/report/freedom-world/freedom-world-2012#.VRlcQvnF9AI.

Fromm, Erich. 1965. *Escape from Freedom*. New York: Discus Books, 1941.

Gereluk, Winston. 2012. "Alberta Labour in the 1980s." In *Working People in Alberta: A History*, edited by Alvin Finkel, 175–204. Edmonton, AB: Athabasca University Press.

Gibbins, Roger, and Sonia Arrison. 1995. *Western Visions: Perspectives on the West in Canada*. Peterborough, ON: Broadview Press.

Gibson, Diana. 2012. *A Social Policy Framework for Alberta: Fairness and Justice for All*. Edmonton, AB: Parkland Institute and Alberta College of Social Workers. http://parklandinstitute.ca/research/summary/a_social_policy_framework_for_alberta/.

Goldstein, Warren S. 2010. "Secularization and the Iranian Revolution." *Islamic Perspective Journal* 3: 50–67.

Goonesekere, Savitri. N.d. "A Rights-Based Approach to Realizing Gender Equality." Paper prepared in cooperation with the UN Division for the Advancement of Women. http://www.un.org/womenwatch/daw/news/savitri.htm.

Grekul, Jana, Harvey Krahn, and Dave Odynak. 2004. "Sterilizing the 'Feeble-Minded': Eugenics in Alberta, Canada, 1929–1972." *Journal of Historical Sociology* 17: 358–84.

Haeri, Shahla. 2009. "Women, Religion, and Political Agency in Iran." In *Contemporary Iran: Economy, Society, Politics*, edited by Ali Gheissari, 125–50. Oxford and New York: Oxford University Press.

Harder, Lois. 2003. *State of Struggle: Feminism and Politics in Alberta*. Edmonton: University of Alberta Press.

Hausmann, Ricardo, Laura D. Tyson, and Saadia Zahidi. 2011. *The Global Gender Gap Report 2011*. Geneva, Switzerland: World Economic Forum. http://reports.weforum.org/global-gender-gap-2011/.

IEA (International Energy Agency). 2011. *World Energy Outlook 2011: Energy for All—Financing Access for the Poor*. Paris: OECD/IEA. http://www.iea.org/publications/freepublications/publication/weo2011_energy_for_all.pdf.

Kinzer, Stephen. 2003. *All the Shah's Men: An American Coup and the Roots of Middle East Terror*. New York: John Wiley and Sons.

Lahey, Kathleen A. 2012. *Canada's Gendered Budget 2012: Impact of Bills C-38 and C-45 on Women—A Technical Report*. Feminist Legal Study Queen's Working Paper, Queen's University, Kingston, ON. http://femlaw.queensu.ca/workingPapers/KLCanGenderedBudgetDc312012subm-printToPDF.pdf

———. 2015. *The Alberta Disadvantage: Gender, Taxation, and Income Inequality*. Edmonton, AB: Parkland Institute.

Manicom, Linzi. 2001. "Globalising 'Gender' in—or as—Governance? Questioning the Terms of Local Translations." *Agenda: Empowering Women for Gender Equity* 16 (48): 6–21.

Martin, Joanne. 2003. "Feminist Theory and Critical Theory: Unexplored Synergies." In *Studying Management Critically*, edited by Mats Alvesson and Hugh Willmott, 66–91. London: Sage.

Mernissi, Fatima. 1975. *Beyond the Veil: Male-Female Dynamics in a Modern Society*. New York: Wiley.

Milani, Farzaneh. 1992. *Veils and Words: The Emerging Voices of Iranian Women Writers*. Syracuse, NY: Syracuse University Press.

Milke, Mark. 2011. *In America's National Interest—Canadian Oil: A Comparison of Civil, Political, and Economic Freedoms in Oil-Producing Countries*. Studies in Energy Policy Series. Vancouver: Fraser Institute.

Miller, Gloria. 2004. "Frontier Masculinity in the Oil Industry: The Experience of Women Engineers." *Gender, Work, and Organization* 11 (1): 47–73.

OECD. 2012. "Gender, Institutions, and Development Database 2012 (GID-DB)." *OECD. Stat.* http://stats.oecd.org/Index.aspx?DatasetCode=GID2.

Palmer, Howard, and Tamara Palmer. 1990. *Alberta: A New History*. Edmonton: Hurtig.

Paterson, Stephanie. 2010. "What's the Problem with Gender-Based Analysis? Gender Mainstreaming Policy and Practice in Canada." *Canadian Public Administration* 53 (3): 395–416.

Pelletiere, Stephen C. 1992. *The Iran-Iraq War: Chaos in a Vacuum*. New York: Praeger.

PSAC (Public Service Alliance of Canada). 2009. "The End of Pay Equity for Women in the Federal Public Service: PSAC's Comments on the *Public Sector Equitable Compensation Act*." February. http://hunterofjustice.com/files/canada-pay-equity.pdf.

Research Council of Canada. 2010. *Women in Science and Engineering in Canada*. Ottawa: Corporate Planning and Policy Directorate, Natural Sciences and Engineering, Research Council of Canada.

Ross, Michael. 2001. "Does Oil Hinder Democracy?" *World Politics* 53 (3): 325–61.

———. 2008. "Oil, Islam, and Women." *American Political Science Review* 102 (1): 107–23.

Sanderson, Kay. 1999. *200 Remarkable Alberta Women*. Edited by Elda Hauschildt. Calgary, AB: Famous 5 Foundation.

Sherk, Susan. 2003. *Women in Canada's Oil and Gas Sector*. St. John's, NL: AGRA Earth and Environmental Ltd.

Teghtsoonian, Katherine. 2005. "Disparate Fates in Challenging Times: Women's Policy Agencies and Neoliberalism in Aoteara/NewZealand and British Columbia." *Canadian Journal of Political Science* 38 (2): 307–33.

UN Women (United Nations Entity for Gender Equality and the Empowerment of Women). 2011. *2011–2012 Progress of the World's Women: In Pursuit of Justice*. New York: UN Women. http://menengage.org/wp-content/uploads/2014/06/Progress_of_the_Worlds_Women_2011.pdf.

Verloo, Mieke. 2005. "Displacement and Empowerment: Reflections on the Concept and Practice of the Council of Europe Approach to Gender Mainstreaming and Gender Equality." *Social Politics: International Studies in Gender, State, and Society* 12 (3): 344–65.

Walby, Sylvia. 2005. "Measuring Women's Progress in a Global Era." *International Social Science Journal* 57 (184): 371–87.

Waring, Marilyn. 2012. "Making Visible the Invisible: Commodification Is Not the Answer." *50.50 Inclusive Democracy*, 7 May. http://www.opendemocracy.net/5050/marilyn-waring/making-visible-invisible-commodification-is-not-answer.

World Bank. 2011. *World Development Report 2012: Gender Equality and Development*. Washington, DC: World Bank.

Development at What Cost?

First Nations, Ecological Integrity, and Democracy

Gabrielle Slowey and Lorna Stefanick

Although the bitumen extraction industry in northern Alberta has been in operation for less than fifty years, it has already left a significant footprint, not only on the landscape but also on the lives of Aboriginal peoples living in the region.[1] For some First Nations who are proximal to bitumen sands development, neoliberal globalization diminished the heavy hand of the state and thus pried open some space for First Nation self-determination with the conclusion of land claims settlement (Slowey 2008). It did so, first, by providing the government with the impetus to settle unresolved land claims, a necessary step to achieve the goal of attracting and maintaining investment opportunities in the resource extraction sector.[2] Second, it provided the motivation for industry to forge impact and benefit agreements (IBAs, also known simply as benefit agreements, BAs) with local communities. These agreements—which have for the most part been concluded confidentially, outside the environmental and labour regulatory frameworks of government—provide a mechanism through which Aboriginal groups can secure local benefits (such as employment) from resource-extraction activities (Mills and Sweeney 2013, 8). As recently as fifteen years ago in the Aboriginal community of Fort Chipewyan, located a few hundred kilometres downstream of bitumen extraction sites, the enthusiasm was palpable for the new economic opportunities that oil provided.

As the pace of development accelerated, however, the concerns of local communities over environmental degradation amplified. Although hypergrowth since 2005 has fuelled wealth generation within local Aboriginal communities, it has also created alarm over the effects of pollution on both human and ecosystem health. The result has been deep divisions among an already diverse community; accusations that the government is failing in its fiduciary duty to consult communities with respect to bitumen sands development; and public relations campaigns by industry, governments, and leaders that seek to win the hearts and minds of the international public concerned with human rights and environmental integrity. As the stakes increase, the discourse becomes more heated. Indeed, some human rights observers now claim that Alberta is committing "slow industrial genocide" of Aboriginal peoples by failing to put the brakes on regional industrial development until outstanding issues are resolved (Huseman and Short 2012).

As Jay Smith sets out in chapter 3, liberal democratic processes require a public space for deliberation of policy issues, a space where a wide variety of citizens are engaged and special attention is paid to ensuring that minorities within the polity are not marginalized. This chapter considers the case of one such minority: the First Nations peoples of Fort Chipewyan. It investigates two questions: Does bitumen extraction come at the cost of treaty rights? What insights can be drawn from this case about democracy in Alberta specifically, and Canada more generally? We begin the chapter by providing the historical, geographic, and political context of the Mikisew Cree First Nation (MCFN) and the Athabasca Chipewyan First Nation (ACFN), with a particular emphasis on the relationship of people to the natural environment. We then investigate the contours of the debate about the environmental consequences of bitumen extraction from the perspectives of both scientific and traditional knowledge. Finally, we examine the consultations with First Nations that are informing regional oil extraction decisions, in order to assess whether the minority voice in northern Alberta is being heard within public spaces where bitumen development policy is deliberated.

This analysis reveals that the state is retreating from its traditional role as the instrument through which public interest and concerns are expressed. The new, truncated role of the state reflects a larger neoliberal conceptualization of citizenship that enhances economic efficiency through maximizing the role of the market and minimizing political negotiation. This market-based version of citizenship is a result of Alberta's and Canada's corporate and political elites leveraging their economic and political power to sideline public debate about the social and environmental consequences of bitumen development. In that process, democracy in Alberta and in Canada is diminished. Those who live closest to bitumen extraction sites—among them, Fort Chipewyan's First Nations—feel most acutely the consequences of this diminished brand of citizenship and debate.

Neighbours to Alberta's Bitumen Development

Alberta's bitumen extraction industrial complex is located in the Regional Municipality of Wood Buffalo. The second-largest of eight communities in this municipality, Fort Chipewyan lies approximately three hundred kilometres north of Fort McMurray, on the north shore of Lake Athabasca and on the boundary of Wood Buffalo National Park. About two hundred kilometres north of the bitumen sands development, the Athabasca River empties into Lake Athabasca and forms the Athabasca Delta, which surrounds the community with a landscape thick with boreal forests, wetlands, and swampy muskeg that nourishes numerous species. Until very recently, Fort Chipewyan's Indigenous peoples depended largely on the local animals, fish, and vegetation found in this diverse, cold-hardy boreal ecosystem. Thus, the natural environment figures prominently in their culture and identity in ways that at times converge but sometimes diverge with the interests of those seeking to protect the natural environment.

Founded in 1788, Fort Chipewyan is the oldest settlement in Alberta and was a key outpost for the Athabasca region during the fur trade era. While Euro-Canadians from the south typically think of this northern community as isolated, historically it has been an important site of economic and cultural convergence of people with different ethnic and linguistic backgrounds (McCormack 2010, 5). Today, the community is accessible by plane year round, by ice road in the winter, and by boat from Fort McMurray in the summer. With a population of only twelve hundred, Fort Chipewyan is a fraction of the size of the region's largest community, Fort McMurray, which boasts a population of over seventy-two thousand, including a "shadow population" of about two thousand: temporary residents who are employed by an industrial establishment and live in the community for more than thirty days. An additional forty thousand such temporary residents live in the surrounding service area (Alberta, Municipal Affairs 2012, 10). The hamlet of Fort Chipewyan is a plural society, consisting primarily of three Aboriginal groups: the ACFN, the MCFN, and Fort Chipewyan Métis Local 125.[3] In 2012, the MCFN had a total registered population of 2,841, of which 72 percent lived off-reserve, primarily in Fort Chipewyan, Fort McMurray, Fort Smith, and Edmonton. The ACFN had 1,071 registered members, with over 78 percent living off-reserve (Canada, AANDC 2012). The on-reserve MCFN population represents more than half the number of the residents of Fort Chipewyan; it is the largest and most affluent of the three Aboriginal groups living in the hamlet. Because of Fort Chipewyan's isolation, a subsistence lifestyle based on hunting and trapping persisted until the postwar period. The diet of local people still comprises a significant proportion of "country food" that is derived from the land (Wein and Sabry 1990, 188).[4]

For the inhabitants of the region, the sticky tar-like substance in the sand was well known historically: Indigenous peoples often used it to patch their canoes. Early Canadian geologists recognized the value of bitumen sands as oil; they also discovered natural gas, gold, silver, copper, and other valuable minerals in the region (Fumoleau [1975] 2004, 55–57). The influx of fifty thousand gold rush prospectors into the area, beginning in 1897, pushed the Canadian government to negotiate Treaty 8 two years later. This treaty, which covered 850,000 square kilometres of land (the largest territory of any treaty to date), guaranteed annuities of five dollars per person, provisions for health care and education, and exemptions from taxation and military service, as well as affirming the continuing freedom to hunt, fish, and trap (56, 69). The Government of Canada, however, did not formally allocate any land in the years following the signing of the treaty, although it did regulate all hunting and trapping in the area. In René Fumoleau's assessment, "Once the treaties had been signed, they were forgotten and disavowed by all levels of Government—the spirit of friendly co-existence of the Indians and non-Indians disappeared as soon as the ink dried up on the treaty documents" (413–14). The desire of Aboriginal groups to control the lands they traditionally inhabited is the basis of specific land claims relating to grievances regarding government obligations as outlined in specific treaties and of comprehensive land claims that have not yet been dealt with through legal means. As settlement increased, local Aboriginal groups asked for reserves. In 1921, the federal government responded with an amendment (rescinded only in 1951) to the Indian Act of 1876 that made it illegal to hire a lawyer to sue the government. The creation of Wood Buffalo National Park in 1922 further restricted Indigenous use of traditional lands. Parks are indeed symbolic of the divergent interests of Aboriginal peoples, who wish to use wilderness land to sustain life, and conservationists, who want to protect wilderness from human use.

After repeated ACFN requests, the government approved Indian Reserve 201 at the southeast end of Lake Athabasca in 1937 and allocated the land in 1940. The reserve would not be officially declared until 1954, however—almost fifty-five years after Treaty 8 was signed (ACFN 2003, 69). Nonetheless, a designated "Indian reserve" gave the ACFN the ability to control its own land and, well into the 1960s, ACFN members generated 30 percent of their income from trapping. In contrast, the MCFN gained control of its land comparatively recently. Over a period of sixty-four years, it made forty-one requests to acquire the reserve lands promised in Treaty 8. These requests were denied (Selin 1999, 13–16). Many MCFN members turned to wage labour; by the 1950s, many had moved from the bush into the community of Fort Chipewyan, which was developing infrastructure, social services, and, perhaps most importantly, schools (Slowey 2008; Tuccaro 1990, 239).

While the petroleum potential of the region long been known and its eventual development anticipated (see Fumoleau [1975] 2004, 26), technological limitations and the low price of oil and gas in the early 1970s did not make private sector investment worthwhile. During World War II, as part of its war effort, the federal government began identifying bitumen reserves, while the provincial government began testing processes to separate the bitumen from the sand. By 1962, the Great Canadian Oilsands Company (now Suncor) began extracting oil from sand (EUB 2000, 4). The stage was thus set for the development of Alberta's bitumen sands, a prospect that generated the political will to settle outstanding land claims with the MCFN. The First Nation reached a tentative agreement with the federal government in 1973; however, given the requirements of the 1930 Natural Resources Transfer Act, Alberta's consent was needed (Slowey 2008, 10). Although Alberta agreed to transfer land in 1975, the agreement was withdrawn in 1977 when the MCFN made it clear that it intended to lay claim to parcels of the bitumen sands in its overall settlement (Selin 1999, 16). After nine more years of trilateral negotiations with both levels of government, the MCFN agreed to take a much reduced amount of land in exchange for cash and, importantly, to drop its claims to bitumen-rich lands. As Gabrielle Slowey has argued elsewhere, the impetus for governments to come to the 1986 agreement, which clarified issues of land title and resource ownership, was to provide a stable environment conducive to investment in bitumen extraction (Slowey 2008, 10).

Settling the outstanding land claims associated with Treaty 8 paid handsome dividends to capital interests, as well as to the governments of Alberta and Canada. Over the past four decades, the political and economic value of bitumen has increased dramatically because of growing concerns over energy security, at the same time that new, sophisticated technologies have brought down the cost of production. Consequently, there has been a proliferation in the number of companies operating in the region, from British Petroleum to

China's Sinotec. The population of Fort McMurray has ballooned from 6,123 in the 1970 census to over 72,000 in 2012 (Alberta, Municipal Affairs 1970, 2; 2012, 10). Alberta became a key driver of the Canadian economy.

Treaty 8 has also been beneficial for the community of Fort Chipewyan. After the conclusion of the Treaty Land Entitlement (TLE) settlement in 1986, the MCFN began working with the oil company Syncrude to develop new businesses. The result is the Mikisew Cree Group of Companies, which is now the largest employer within the community; it comprises twelve companies ranging from oil field servicing to sport fishing. Other community members participate in oil companies' "fly-in, fly-out" work programs. The most renowned band member is Dave Tuccaro, who worked his way up from a heavy equipment operator to become a multimillionaire entrepreneur and the founding president of the Northeastern Alberta Aboriginal Business Association. Tuccaro estimates that companies run by the Mikisew Cree, Athabasca Chipewyan, and Fort McKay First Nations derive $1 billion in annual revenues from bitumen extraction (Vanderklippe 2012). The Fort McMurray–based ACFN Business Group, rebranded in 2013 as ACDEN, comprises seventeen businesses and joint ventures that specialize in oil and gas services. With 24 percent of its community members directly employed in resource-based industries, Fort Chipewyan is the most economically diversified of the ten communities of the Regional Municipality of Wood Buffalo (RMWB 2012, 99).

The benefits of bitumen development, however, have been uneven. For those who have a treaty right to resource-rich land or who live near resource-extraction projects, there is a solid basis from which to participate in the market economy. In Fort Chipewyan, the proximity to the bitumen development gives Treaty Indians a huge advantage over their Métis neighbours, who have certain rights to use land but do not actually own land. As Fumoleau ([1975] 2004, 107) observes about the Treaty 8 and scrip settlements, "As had been foreseen and feared, the Métis people were left in an unenviable position . . . between the white and the Indian world, not belonging to either." But even for those who have treaty status, a legacy of colonialism has exacerbated the cultural disconnection between them and the market economy into which they are expected to assimilate. Problems associated with influenza epidemics, racism, poverty, inadequate housing, inadequate medical care, substance abuse, and domestic abuse are documented elsewhere (Fumoleau [1975] 2004; Tuccaro 1990). Despite IBAs wherein oil companies have supported training initiatives in local communities, many Aboriginal people are limited by their lack of education.

Even basic qualifications such as a driver's licence can be an impediment: Fort Chipewyan's residents must travel to Fort McMurray for certification, which is accessible by air in the summer and by an ice road in the winter. Companies like Syncrude require that employees have a high school diploma, yet Aboriginal people who have post-secondary education are often limited to the lower rungs of the employment ladder and are hired as labourers, as dump truck drivers, or as part of shutdown maintenance crews (Taylor, Friedel, and Edge 2009). While for some Aboriginal groups, the benefits of development are huge, for others, the costs far outweigh the benefits.

Suzanne Mills and Brendan Sweeney (2013), who argue that employment of Aboriginal people in northern extractive industries represents a "neostaples" stage of development that is both locally empowering and divisive, pick up this theme of mixed effects on First Nations people. On the one hand, "by exerting political power and legal rights, Aboriginal governments have altered the trad-itional compromise among labour, corporations, and the government. Through IBAs, Aboriginal governments and organizations become influential actors in employment relations." On the other hand, "participating in economic develop-ment activities . . . limits Aboriginal leaders' ability to represent the interests of their worker members by pitting workers' interests against those of the broader constituency" (28). Accordingly, local agreements through IBAs pro-vide local benefits for some, but given the international nature of capital in this sector and the weak unions, even these beneficiaries lack significant control over important dimensions of their work lives. More importantly, the uneven benefits of employment undermine community solidarity.

The most urgent problem associated with bitumen development for Fort Chipewyan's residents, however, is its impact on the environment. Local con-cern that industry and government are ignoring Aboriginal concerns has escal-ated into a pitched battle in the international arena, as evidenced by the 2014 Neil Young "Honour the Treaties" concert tour. A comprehensive study that chronicles the transformation of the MCFN after its land claims were settled suggests that, as recently as 2003, the local community had a very good work-ing relationship with industry (Slowey 2008). What changed in the intervening decade? As one resident explained, people in the community generally point to the arrival of Dr. John O'Connor in 2000, a Fort McMurray physician who became one of Fort Chipewyan's family doctors.[5] Dr. O'Connor became alarmed at the number of cases of cancer he encountered in the small community, par-ticularly cases of cholangiocarcinoma, a relatively rare cancer of the bile ducts.

In 2003, O'Connor suggested to MCFN chief Archie Waquan that the high rates of cancer were anomalous and proposed that a baseline study be performed (CPSA 2009, 3). O'Connor suspected that upstream bitumen extraction might be the cause of environmental changes that some in the community had already noted, and he speculated that these might have implications for human health.

In 2006, O'Connor asked Health Canada to investigate, and, in response, a team of representatives from Health Canada and Alberta Health and Wellness travelled to Fort Chipewyan. O'Connor reports that one member of the team turned on a tap, took a drink from a mug, and told him, "See, there's nothing wrong with the water here" (O'Connor 2006). According to another resident of the area, O'Connor later described this incident as an insult to the local community. After a year of sparring, three physicians from Health Canada lodged a complaint against O'Connor, charging him with four counts of professional misconduct, including withholding data and causing harm to Fort Chipewyan residents because "they made lifestyle decisions based on concerns raised by Dr. O'Connor that were not in their best interests" (CPSA 2009). News of these charges generated such media attention, that O'Connor left his practice in Alberta and returned to Nova Scotia, much to the dismay of members of the local community who had become increasingly worried about observed changes to the environment. O'Connor's suspicions were underscored by a study conducted by Kevin Timoney, of Treeline Ecological Research, that documented unsafe levels of arsenic, mercury, and polycyclic aromatic hydrocarbons in the area's water, fish, and other wildlife (see CBC News 2007b). Early in 2008, the media reported that O'Connor had been "cleared" of the misconduct charges; an investigative report written for Alberta's College of Physicians and Surgeons subsequently denied that O'Connor had ever been formally charged or that efforts had been made to "muzzle" him (CPSA 2009, 6).[6] In any event, as former MCFN chief George Poitras explained in an interview, it was the sanction of O'Connor that led Poitras to launch an international campaign denouncing the impact that bitumen development was having on his community and, in particular, the social and health consequences that he claimed were the result of environmental degradation.

Poitras's "bloody oil" tour took him to London, Norway, Sweden, Denmark, Netherlands, France, and the United States. Poitras resigned his position as consultation coordinator for the MCFN's Government Industry Relations department in December 2009, fearing that the MCFN would suffer repercussions for his outspoken criticism. Shawn Bell, a reporter for the *Slave River Journal*, quotes from an email he received from Poitras:

> Because of this very successful campaign in the UK, one of the oil company's executives flew to Fort Chipewyan and attempted to force the hand of my First Nation to "silence or terminate" my employment with the Mikisew because they didn't like that I traveled internationally, on Mikisew time, and that by doing so I generated so much negative publicity on the tarsands industry.... Apparently we are not to speak publicly if we observe water quality issues, health impacts, or worse our people dying too frequently of cancers. This, they said, was not consistent with the company's "vision" and that if Mikisew didn't support their vision there would be repercussions. And there were repercussions. Many Mikisew employees lost their jobs on this particular company's site within weeks. (Bell 2010)

The chief at the time, Roxanne Marcel, responded to the controversy in a press release: "Every person in this country and province has the right to share and promote their feelings, the last time I checked this was still a democratic country where the right to speak and be heard was a fundamental cornerstone of citizenship right" (Marcel and Monaghan, n.d.). Nonetheless, Marcel also made it clear that Poitras was not speaking on behalf of the MCFN. Bell reported that the MCFN did eventually ask Poitras to refrain from publicly criticizing the bitumen sands after Syncrude cancelled millions of dollars in contracts with the Mikisew Group of Companies. At that point, Poitras decided to resign from his position with the MCFN in order to pursue his activism full time. Bell reports Poitras as stating, "I left because I would not be silenced" (Bell 2010). A year later, Poitras returned to the MCFN as its chief executive officer. As recently as October 2013, he was still raising concern in Europe, despite his employment with MCFN, which ended in the winter of 2015 (Wohlberg 2013b).

These events can be identified as the "tipping point" with respect to Aboriginal activism: community members began looking beyond Canadian borders to mobilize opposition to bitumen sands development based on the negative consequences for the environment. As mentioned previously with respect to the creation of Wood Buffalo National Park, while the interests of Aboriginal peoples often diverge from those of environmentalists, in this instance they converged. Moreover, members of the world's scientific community had also begun to sound the conservation alarm about the destruction of the boreal forest. In particular, Alberta scientists were beginning to garner negative publicity for the oil industry and the governments that are responsible for regulating them by providing evidence for habitat degradation and pollution caused by bitumen development. The result was the creation of a potent mix of scientists, environmental activists, and Aboriginal rights advocates.

The Intersection of Environmental and Aboriginal Concerns

Poitras's charge that development of the bitumen sands was negatively impacting local communities was a valuable addition to the toolkits of environmentalists, who had begun asking questions about pollution and habitat loss fifteen years earlier. In 1995, the Edmonton-based nonprofit Toxic Watch launched its "tar sands campaign." A dozen years later, fifteen hundred scientists from around the world were calling on Canada to provide better protection for the boreal forest (CBC News 2007a). Shortly thereafter, fourteen internationally renowned scientists—including David Schindler from the University of Alberta, who has earned worldwide recognition for his expertise on water quality and depletion—created the International Boreal Conservation Science Panel (borealscience.org) to conduct interdisciplinary studies for the purpose of providing policy advice to preserve the boreal forest habitat. Two Alberta-based think tanks and two national groups, the Canadian Centre for Policy Alternatives and Polaris Institute, also undertook research projects that examined the negative environmental externalities of bitumen production (Grant, Dyer, and Woynillowicz 2009; McCullum 2006). The catalyst for international attention was the death in 2008 of sixteen hundred ducks that mistook a Syncrude tailings pond for a lake because the company had failed to install, in a timely fashion, scarecrows and air cannons around the tailings pond to warn off wildlife (Weber 2010). Images of dead ducks covered in an oily substance caused an international uproar, and oil from the bitumen sands acquired the label of "dirty oil."

While the science community is divided over the environmental effects of the bitumen sands (see Gosselin et al. 2010), one fact that is not disputed is the sheer enormity of the bitumen extraction project. The bitumen is contained in an area covering nearly 142,200 square kilometres, roughly the size of the state of Florida (Alberta, Alberta Energy 2013). Alberta's total oil reserves are estimated to be 168.7 billion barrels, 99 percent of which are contained in the bitumen sands. In 2013, the production of oil from Alberta's bitumen deposits was over 1.98 million barrels per day (CERI 2014). These numbers are arresting when the resulting habitat disruption of the boreal forest is considered in a global context. The circumboreal forest covers about fourteen million square kilometres—about a third of the earth's forest cover. Canada is the world's second-largest country, and almost 60 percent of Canada's land base consists of boreal forest; this represents 40 percent of the world's total (Burton et al. 2003, 1). Although various industrial activities threaten the integrity of Canada's boreal forest, a key threat relates to the activities of the oil industry. Alberta's share of the boreal forest is 381,000 square kilometres, of which only 420 square kilometres had been touched by oil activity in 2008 (Alberta 2008, 2, 4). Five years later, this number had nearly doubled, to 767 square kilometres (Alberta, Alberta Energy 2013, 1). Bitumen sands deposits underlie an estimated 142,200 square kilometres, with the area that could potentially be surface-mined limited to 4,800 square kilometres in the vicinity of Fort McMurray (Alberta, Alberta Energy 2013, 1). While this represents only a fraction of the total area, the remaining habitat, covering 137,400 square kilometres, will be fragmented by the construction of roads, pipelines, transmission lines, and wells, if the entire area is developed. Over the long term, these activities will adversely affect flora and fauna that live on tens of thousands of square kilometres of boreal forest (Canada, Parliament of Canada, House of Commons 2007, 47). Owing to its harsh climate and short growing season, the human population in Canada's boreal forest region is less dense than in similar regions with more moderate climates, and, until bitumen extraction began to ramp up, this habitat was therefore less disturbed by human activity. In non-human terms, however, the area is populous indeed: its many lakes, rivers, and wetlands support large numbers of birds and mammals that are important for global biodiversity (Burton et al. 2003, 2). Given that Canada's boreal forest is the summer home for half of North America's bird species (CBC 2007a), Alberta's resource extraction activities could have far-reaching consequences for the continent's bird population.

The actual process of extracting oil from the bitumen sands is extremely destructive: it requires cutting down trees, disturbing peatlands that have built up over thousands of years, and draining wetlands. Two different processes are used in extracting bitumen, depending on how close to the surface the resource lies. Shallow deposits are accessed by digging up the land in a process that resembles open-pit strip mining. Two tonnes of bitumen sands must be dug up to produce one barrel of crude oil; trucks then move the oil-soaked ore to a cleaning facility, where it is mixed with hot water and diluent chemicals in order to remove the bitumen.[7] Deposits that are more than seventy-five metres deep are extracted in situ, largely through steam-assisted gravity drainage, which involves pumping steam into deep deposits to "melt" the bitumen so that it can be pumped out. Because of the heavy, viscous nature of bitumen, the in situ method requires even more water and energy resources than the excavation method. Roughly 80 percent of established reserves are too deep to be mined and so must be extracted using in-situ processes (Alberta, Alberta Energy 2013, 2); in 2008, 52 percent of bitumen production occurred through strip mining (Pembina Institute 2010).

While in situ extraction has much less obvious effects in its destruction of habitat than excavation does, critics claim that the in situ method also has major environmental impacts through the building of 3-D seismic lines, pipelines, well pads, and steam-generation plants (Leaton 2008, 10; Schneider and Dyer 2006). Licences to extract the bitumen are given with the condition that disturbed land will be reclaimed. As of the start of 2013, however, only 77 square kilometres of land were undergoing reclamation, and only 104 hectares (1.04 square kilometres)—that is, about 0.14 percent of the 767 square kilometres that had been disturbed to date—had been certified as reclaimed by the Alberta government (Alberta, Alberta Energy 2013, 1). In the plot that has been certified, the level of biodiversity in the reclaimed habitat has not been shown definitively to be equal to previous levels.[8]

Habitat destruction does not merely threaten wildlife and birds; it is also a source of greenhouse gas emissions. Temperate, tropical, and boreal forests store 1.146 billion tons of carbon; almost half of this is located in the boreal forest, making it the largest terrestrial carbon storage ecosystem (IPCC 2000, 4). Bitumen extraction often requires scraping up peatland that is acting as a carbon sink. When the peat is disturbed in the mining process, carbon is released into the atmosphere. Greenhouse gases are also produced in the process of energy production; the bitumen sands industry is one of the country's top producers of emissions. This is primarily due to the scale of its operations and to the fact that it takes three times more energy to produce oil from bitumen sands than from conventional sources (Leaton 2008, 11). Canada has the dubious distinction of being the world's leading greenhouse gas emitter on a per capita basis, and it failed to achieve its Kyoto targets. By 2006, its greenhouse gas emissions were 19 percent more than 1990 levels, despite its commitment to lower them by 8 percent (Canada, Environment Canada 2014).

The detrimental impact of industrial activities in Canada's boreal forest has been recognized for many years. Olla Ulsten, the co-chair of the World

Commission on Forests and Sustainable Development, observed in 1999: "New ways must be found to slow and ultimately reverse forest decline, and Canada has a special responsibility because it still has 20–25% of its primary forest" (WCFSD 1999). Despite these words of caution, the destruction of the boreal forest accelerated dramatically in the ensuing decade.

Another issue of concern is the amount of water that is used to separate the oil from the bitumen: about three to four barrels of water are needed for each barrel of oil (Canada, NRC 2013). According to data obtained from Alberta Environment in September 2008, existing licences for bitumen sands projects would entail the annual diversion of 550 million cubic metres of freshwater from the Athabasca River basin (Holroyd and Simieritsch 2009, 15). This represents the equivalent water consumption per year of a city of two million inhabitants—twice the annual amount used by Calgary, Alberta's largest city. Only 10 percent of the water taken from the Athabasca is returned to the river (Griffiths, Woynillowicz, and Taylor 2006, 3). After its use in bitumen extraction, much of the water is recycled, but it eventually becomes contaminated. This toxic water is then stored in huge tailings ponds comprising clay, sand, hydrocarbons, and heavy metals. As of January 2013, these ponds (more accurately described as lakes) collectively contained 830 million cubic metres of tailings and covered 176 square kilometres (Flanagan and Grant 2013, 3). Especially given present rates of reclamation, the question of what will happen to these tailing ponds in the future, when the bitumen runs out and the companies cease operations in the area, highlights a serious environmental concern. As Erin Flanagan and Jennifer Grant (2013, 3) point out, the 104-hectare area that has been certified as reclaimed "was never mined, did not include tailings, and is therefore not representative of the looming reclamation challenges that lie ahead." In the meantime, scientific studies (Frank et al. 2014; Kelly, Schindler et al. 2010; Kelly, Short et al. 2009; Kurek et al. 2013) showing leakage into the groundwater and into the nearby Athabasca River have fuelled even more pressing anxieties about the tailings ponds.

Until recently, the industry-funded Regional Aquatics Monitoring Program (RAMP) was responsible for water monitoring in the bitumen sands. In response to scientific studies that bitumen sands development was polluting the Athabasca River, RAMP claimed that toxins in the Athabasca River water were naturally occurring (CBC News 2010). RAMP was set up in 1997; its steering committee includes representatives from industry, both levels of government, Fort McKay and Fort McMurray First Nations, and Fort McKay Métis

Local No. 63. Because its funding has come in large part from oil companies, concerns have repeatedly been expressed about access to information and the scientific methods employed by the organization (see James and Vold 2010, 2). In 2010, a group of scientists, including University of Alberta biologists Erin Kelly and David Schindler, published a study that attributed toxins in the Athabasca River to bitumen extraction (Kelly et al. 2010). Schindler criticized RAMP's methods as having serious defects and advocated for an Environment Canada monitoring system (Schwartz 2010). These widely publicized statements caused an explosion of controversy that resulted in a polarized debate within both the scientific community and the public. A subsequent 2013 study by federal government scientists that built on Kelly et al.'s work found an even larger than expected footprint of the bitumen sands; it linked toxins to bitumen extraction in lakes ninety kilometres northwest of mining operations. As pointed out in this study, however, there are no benchmarks that can be used to assess the impacts of the bitumen extraction activities because there was little to no monitoring of air and water in the region prior to bitumen production (Kurek et al. 2013).

In response to the study by Kelly et al. (2010) and mounting international pressure, both the federal and provincial governments set up panels to investigate existing pollution-monitoring processes. The federal panel found that current monitoring systems produced limited useful data for decision makers because they lacked "consistency and coordination," while the provincial panel found that "new approaches" were needed (AEMP 2011, ii). In response, the governments of Canada and Alberta set up a joint federal-provincial water monitoring system (jointoilsandsmonitoring.ca). Later in 2012, the provincial government set up the Alberta Environmental Monitoring, Evaluation, and Reporting Agency as a new arms-length regulatory body that would control environmental monitoring. The minister responsible explained, "When it comes to resource management and the environment, Alberta recognizes the status quo is simply not enough to meet the challenges we face" (quoted in Gerein 2012). The membership of this agency is confined to scientific, regulatory, and academic experts; there is no Aboriginal involvement. While some critics of Alberta's water policy applauded the establishment of a regulatory agency as being a good first step, others wondered if the agency's reports and raw data would be made public, thus fulfilling its mandate to be independent from government. Rachel Notley, who at the time was an opposition MLA, argued that unless transparency is assured, the regulatory body will be used to assist the government in manipulating information to serve its own agenda (Gerein 2012). In the spring of 2014, the government appointed the first chairman of the agency—Lorne Taylor, a former Conservative MP who served as minister of the Environment from 2001 to 2004. Given that Taylor would be heading the agency charged with responding to criticisms of the environmental monitoring that was conducted during his tenure as minister of the Environment, Notley wryly observed, "Only in Alberta would the government not get the irony of that" (quoted in Weber 2014).

Meanwhile, in Fort Chipewyan, community members have also noted environmental changes. In the past decade, changes in water levels in the Athabasca Delta have made travelling across it a challenge. Although the drop in water levels has been attributed in part to the Bennett Dam in neighbouring British Columbia (Fuller 1990; Ladouceur 1990), local people suspect that the vast quantities of water needed to extract the bitumen is having a direct effect on water levels in the delta. Community members complain that muskrat and moose populations have decreased dramatically in the area and that the presence of deformed fish is a strong indicator that local fish are no longer edible (Candler et al. 2010). As one resident commented in an interview, "When we go out on the land, the most significant item hunters bring is a Gerry can filled—not with petrol—but with clean drinking water." Residents keep bottled water in their homes for drinking, and the local municipality is building an indoor water park because the delta is considered too polluted for children to swim in.

The problem for the residents of Fort Chipewyan who are convinced that the integrity of the local environment is declining is that traditional knowledge is not accorded the same status as scientific knowledge within decision-making circles. As discussed further in chapter 14, even though the previously respected status of scientific knowledge has come under attack in recent years, it still trumps traditional knowledge. Scholar Frances Abele (1997, iii) defines traditional knowledge as "knowledge and values which have been acquired through experience, observation, from the land or from spiritual teachings, and handed down from one generation to another." It is based on cumulative empirical observations gleaned from centuries of living close to nature in particular ecosystems and depending on the plants and animals found locally for everything from food to medicine. Knowledge is passed down orally and is not tested with Western scientific methods. Moreover, traditional knowledge infuses authority systems, traditions, culture, and religion. The lack of separation between the secular and the sacred within traditional systems of knowledge makes it easy to dismiss by those who are rooted in Western, rational ways of thinking. While the scientific community might be divided as to the reasons for environmental change in the area (Alberta, Alberta Environment 2011), the community is convinced that local environmental change is a negative externality of the bitumen extraction process. As MCFN chief Steve Courtoreille put it, "We depend on ... our livelihood, our way of life ... out in the land." He went on to say that the government is "supposed to protect our land, waters, air. Now it's giving industry open season to our territory" (quoted in Mackinnon 2013). MLA Notley agreed: "It's profit first; protecting people and the environment second" (quoted in Henton and Brooymans 2009).

As documented in chapter 3 in this volume, the marriage of environmental concerns with issues of Aboriginal rights has proven a potent mix in the court of international public opinion. Yet its effect on domestic political decision makers has been limited. The federal government has fiduciary obligations with respect to Aboriginal people, as well as responsibility for environmental regulations. It does not, however, have the political will to meet these obligations; responsibility for both consulting with Aboriginal peoples and for protecting the environment has been passed on to the Province of Alberta, which in turn has passed these responsibilities on to industry. In response, Aboriginal groups have increasingly looked to the courts for redress.

The Dishonour of the Crown

Section 35 of the Constitution Act, 1982 both recognizes and affirms Aboriginal rights, including treaty rights, in Canada. Decisions in a series of cases brought before the Supreme Court of Canada have resulted in a ruling that government has a "duty to consult" local Aboriginal communities whose rights may be affected by a proposed development project. No study of the consultation of Aboriginal peoples living in the Canadian North can ignore the example of the Berger Commission. In the 1970s, Justice Thomas Berger was asked by the federal government to tour northern Canada in order to determine whether a pipeline should be constructed through the Mackenzie Valley. Expected to take only six months, the inquiry took two years as Berger travelled to communities all over the North, consulting the people who would be most affected by development. As he recounted in a retrospective documentary, democracy requires more than voting government in or out, and consultation produces better projects (WCEL 2012). Indeed, consultative inquiries can be a critical part of the democratic process because they allow people to have a say about what their future might look like. In recommending a ten-year moratorium on the building of the pipeline, Berger recognized that the enormous wealth that would be generated by exploiting the resources in northern Canada might very well come at the expense of the rights and well-being of the Aboriginal peoples who live in those regions. According to Berger (1977, 33), "What happens in the North ... will be of great importance to the future of the country; it will tell us what kind of a country Canada is; it will tell us what kind of a people we are."

The importance of consultation to democratic processes was highlighted almost twenty-five years later in the "diversity model" developed by the Canadian Policy Research Network (CPRN). This model seeks to foster social cohesion when tension is created by competing values within society. In a discussion paper about the CPRN model, Jane Jenson and Martin Papillon (2001, 38) argue that attention must be paid to democratic spaces such as government consultation processes that structure state-society discussions:

> In a highly diverse society, such deliberation is essential for minorities' inclusion in the broad citizenry. It reinforces the legitimacy of public institutions and policies for groups that feel excluded from the classic democratic process, where the rule of the majority tends to obscure their voice. A strong and healthy public sphere is thus essential in a polity such as Canada where conflicts over the nature and boundaries of the political community are constantly negotiated and debated.

The popularity of such an approach can be seen by the proliferation of government-sponsored citizen engagement models to promote active citizenship. One might expect that resource-development planning in Alberta for a project as immense as the bitumen sands would include meaningful opportunities for citizens to provide input into decision making. The difficulty, however, is that the processes used reflect the deepening of the neoliberal institutional model in Alberta, which promotes the short-term interests of the oil industry over everything else.

Case law, however, is clear that the Canadian federal government and all provincial governments have a duty to consult with First Nations before taking any steps that might infringe on Aboriginal rights or on treaty rights, whether these are claimed or have already been established (Sanderson, Bergner, and Jones 2012). Beginning in 2004 with the Haida Nation's case against British Columbia, which was followed by the 2004 Taku River Tlingit First Nation case and the 2005 Mikisew Cree First Nation case, the Supreme Court set out the "duty to consult" doctrine.[9] As Dwight Newman (2009, 12) explains, these three cases extended existing case law "in elaborating the existence of a duty to consult Aboriginal communities potentially affected by government decision-making prior to final proof of an Aboriginal rights or title claim." Although the duty to consult is clear, the scope of the consultation is tied to the discretionary determination by government as to whether the infringement would be major or minor, with consultation processes mirroring the government's assessment.

It has further been established that the Crown cannot delegate its authority to consult. This means that corporations cannot negotiate agreements that effectively discharge the Crown's duty (Gibson and O'Faircheallaigh 2010, 30). Part of the problem, however, in Alberta as elsewhere, is that while the duty to consult is ultimately the responsibility of the federal and provincial Crown, certain procedural aspects of the consultation process can be delegated to the proponents of a planned project, according to the Supreme Court's decision in the Haida case (Ritchie 2013, 409). Indeed, as Ginger Gibson and Ciaran O'Faircheallaigh (2010, 30) note, "In practice, much of the obligation to consult falls to the industrial proponents." In other words, project proponents do play a procedural role in discharging the Crown's duty to consult and accommodate Aboriginal peoples whose rights or title may be infringed by development.

For its part, the Government of Alberta has preferred a remarkably hands-off approach to matters of consultation. As an August 2013 report on benefit agreements in northern Canada put it: "Currently, the Alberta government does not engage in socio-economic agreements/plans with resource development proponents directly, nor does it require industry proponents to develop BAs with First Nations' communities" (PPSRD 2013, 13). Moreover, historically, corporations that negotiate IBAs with Aboriginal groups have been under no obligation to disclose the content of these agreements to the Alberta government.[10] Thus, to date, only two IBAs are officially on record in Alberta (PPSRD 2013, 20). Gibson and O'Faircheallaigh (2010, 35) point to the political climate in the province, which has been "strongly supportive of resource development and antagonistic to Aboriginal rights." Concretely, this means that, as matters presently stand, the Alberta government does not directly discharge its duty to consult with Aboriginal communities, nor does it formally delegate procedural aspects by demanding that industry proponents engage in such consultation. Moreover, should an oil company voluntarily choose to negotiate with Aboriginal groups prior to development, the company is not routinely required to reveal the content of resulting IBAs, which therefore remain untracked and unrecorded.

When asked in an interview what recent consultation processes for new resource extraction projects look like, one resident of Fort Chipewyan explained that industry representatives typically show up with buckets of Kentucky Fried Chicken and spend an afternoon at the community centre, hoping that people will stop by for a few wings and a chat. The community has come to expect this type of flippant approach to consultation, and, as a result, the sessions are not well attended. If, per the Delgamuukw precedent, consultation is undertaken "with the intention of substantially addressing the concerns of the aboriginal peoples whose lands are at issue" (Delgamuukw v. British Columbia, [1997] 3 SCR. 1010 at 1113), it would appear that, to date, the goal has not been met with respect to the Aboriginal communities of Fort Chipewyan.

In the fall of 2012, the ACFN launched a $1.5 million lawsuit alleging that Shell had not complied with IBAs made with the ACFN regarding projects now underway within its territory. These agreements entailed mapping out traditional areas and analyzing the potential impact of Shell projects on sacred sites, in addition to setting up community monitoring programs (Wohlberg 2013a). The ACFN also challenged the Shell Jackpine mine expansion plan on the basis of Treaty 8 rights, arguing that the expansion project, which would see a hundred thousand more barrels of ore mined from its territory per day, would infringe upon the First Nation's treaty and Aboriginal rights. Recognizing the significance of the suit, ACFN chief Allan Adams declared: "Our rights are being overlooked, and that is a truth that cannot be denied. . . . If there is a violation of our constitutionally protected treaty rights, it should be dealt with before this project is found to be in the public interest" (quoted in Wohlberg 2012b). ACFN spokesperson Eriel Deranger elaborated, explaining that the chief and council

> repeatedly asked the government and Shell to engage in a new form of consultation that adequately looks at what our treaty rights really are, by working with traditional knowledge holders and implementing TK [traditional knowledge] and Western science to identify baselines for what our treaty rights are and how that adequately protects them. . . . There's been absolutely no support for that from the government or Shell to move forward in that direction. (Quoted in Wohlberg 2012a)

In response, ACFN chief and council declared a ban on development north of the Firebag River, about 150 kilometres north of Fort McMurray. They also promised to challenge any development projects that will operate on lands that various studies have identified as traditionally used by Aboriginal communities for hunting and trapping purposes.[11] Although the area is not currently under development, several project applications, including Shell's Pierre River Mine and Teck Resources' Frontier Project, involve land that is, and has been, integral to traditional Aboriginal economies (Wohlberg 2012a).

In December 2012, the federal government introduced Bill C-45, an omnibus budget bill that made changes to the Indian Act, the Navigation Act, and the Environmental Assessment Act. Opponents criticized both Bill C-45 and its predecessor, Bill C-38, as being antidemocratic because the sweeping changes contained within them were subjected to very limited legislative debate. These bills provided the impetus for the Idle No More campaign, a protest begun by four Aboriginal women in Saskatchewan (CBC News 2013). The campaign quickly spread through social media. In addition to the Aboriginal community, the campaign captured the interest of Canadians who were concerned about the bills' implications for both environmental regulation and capacity, as well as the potential for omnibus bills to stifle the debate that usually accompanies budgets.

A month later, in January 2013, the Mikisew Cree joined with the Frog Lake First Nation in a lawsuit to challenge the environmental provisions in C-38 and C-45 (MacKinnon 2013). They argued that the bills gutted environmental legislation and streamlined environmental review to facilitate rapid approvals of industrial megaprojects. Indigenous leaders claimed that Bill C-45 violated the federal government's duty to consult with First Nations. The Navigable Waters Protection Act, established in 1882 (and recently amended to the Navigation Protection Act), stipulated that any water that was deep enough to float a canoe could not be blocked, altered, or destroyed without federal government approval. While this act was cumbersome because of its scope, the new act only provided protection for major waterways. The two First Nations groups feared that the thousands of tributaries within the delta could be altered by bitumen sands development and said that government did not consult either band about development that might affect these lands and waters.

Bill C-45 makes additional changes to the Environmental Protection Act and alters the Indian Act to allow reserve lands to be leased by a majority vote of those attending the meeting as opposed to a majority of eligible voters. It also gives the Aboriginal Affairs minister the power to ignore resolutions from a band council that opposed the decision made by majority vote (CBC News 2013). These latter changes are of particular significance to Aboriginal peoples, and, perhaps because of this, the early environmental thrust of the Idle No More movement was eclipsed by concerns specific to Aboriginal communities. The overwhelming message of Idle No More is that current methods of doing business with Aboriginal groups are inadequate and that the failure to take their concerns into account is indicative of weak democratic processes.

Although, as mentioned above, no study of the consultation of Aboriginal peoples living in the Canadian North could ignore the Berger Commission, it appears that forty years later, Canadian governments are indeed ignoring this precedent-setting inquiry. The duty to consult is a legal requirement set out by the courts and tied to the potential infringement of Aboriginal rights. But it has broader application: consultation is recognized as an important component of the citizen engagement that is necessary for deliberations that represent diverse societal interests. Recent Canadian experience suggests, however, that the public space for such deliberations is contracting. As governments increasingly withdraw from their regulatory and mediation roles, these functions fall to industry or are simply eliminated. Industry, however, must respond to the demands of the marketplace. As a result, consultation processes are weakened, and along with them, so is democracy.

Resource Management and Bitumen: A Case of Spin and Dig

The dramatic changes within and around Fort Chipewyan reflect the dizzying pace and scale of industrial development and the subsequent speed and scope of change in the natural environment. This community illustrates both the diversity within Aboriginal communities and the competing perspectives on bitumen extraction. The presence of bitumen provided the impetus for governments to settle outstanding land claims and for industry to negotiate IBAs, which in turn has allowed some community members to take advantage of economic opportunity. Fear about the impact of bitumen extraction activities on traditional lands and the subsequent impact on human health was the spark that ignited Aboriginal opposition, which fanned the flames of environmental opposition that spread to the international arena. This battle coincided with an equally bitter debate between the government and environmentalists over the environmental consequences of large-scale bitumen extraction activities, particularly on natural habitat and water management.

These conflicts underscore different aspects of the same phenomenon: neoliberalism reducing the opportunities for input into decisions regarding resource development because of its systematic de-emphasis of the role of the state as the site for political discourse in favour of an emphasis on the market as the final arbiter of resource management decisions. The move toward market-based governance at both the national and provincial levels of government necessitated the settlement of land claims; land ownership has created economic opportunities that have produced increased prosperity, particularly for the First Nations peoples in Fort Chipewyan. But along with these benefits have come serious costs. Where once the governments of Canada and Alberta accepted their "responsibility" to protect First Nations peoples as wards of the state, now governments are neglecting their duty to consult by effectively relinquishing negotiations regarding project development and expansion to corporations. By dismantling existing environmental regulations and leaving industry to monitor such things as water quality, responsibility for the environmental commons is vulnerable to regulatory capture by industry. In the 1990s, in the neighbouring province of British Columbia, continuing to cut down the forest while competing interests argued over forest management was referred to as the "talk and log" approach to resource planning. In neoliberal Alberta, proceeding with industrial bitumen development while competing interests try to influence the markets for Alberta oil through public relations campaigns could be referred to as the "spin and dig" approach.

If democracy rests on the consent of the governed, then Aboriginal dissent caused by industrial degradation of treaty land implies that the institutions of governance in Alberta lack legitimacy. Both the ACFN and the MCFN spent many years asking for the land they were promised many years after signing Treaty 8 in 1899. The irony is that for members of the MCFN, just twenty-some years after the watershed moment in 1986 when this "oversight" was rectified, environmental concerns came to the forefront; self-determination was once again in jeopardy because of the inability of Aboriginal peoples to protect their treaty land from the negative environmental effects of industrial activities. Clearly, settling land claims will not enhance self-determination if those who now control the land have limited ability to maintain its integrity. A failure to protect the legal and human rights at both the federal and provincial levels is particularly problematic in Canada with respect to its First Nations minority, given the relationship of First Nations with the Crown, treaty rights, and the fiduciary responsibilities that have been recognized by courts. But Aboriginal people are not alone in their struggle. The loss of environmental protections affects the ability of all Canadians to protect the land, air, and water from which they derive their livelihoods—and their very lives. By neglecting their responsibility for protecting the larger public interest through the regulation of environmental externalities created by industry, governments not only fail in their duty to protect the interests of those most impacted by environmental contaminants; they also restrict the space where the debate over what constitutes the public interest occurs.

The democratic implications of dampening citizen engagement and debate by delegating that responsibility to industry are chilling, not only for First Nations communities but for all Canadians. This in turn suggests that the question posed at the outset of this chapter—Does bitumen extraction come at the cost of treaty rights?—is too restrictive. First, the words "bitumen extraction" could be replaced with "forest harvest" or "hydroelectric dams" or even "fracking." The impact of large-scale resource extraction activities on Indigenous peoples because of environmental degradation is a well-known theme worldwide; the players and the resource change, but the results are similar. In this regard, Mills and Sweeney (2013, 23) observe that "governance is being neoliberalized." The removal of the heavy hand of the state noted at the outset of this chapter has been replaced by the indifferent, invisible hand of the market. Second, with respect to bitumen extraction in Alberta, Aboriginal rights can be described as the proverbial canary in the coal mine. While Aboriginal rights are the first to be sacrificed at the altar of economic development, Canadians more generally will find their autonomy increasingly compromised with the ceding of control over bitumen extraction to corporate interests and with the concomitant contraction of public space to debate the environmental impacts of resource-extraction activities.

Notes

1 The term *Aboriginal* will be used in the context of section 35(2) of the Canadian Constitution Act, 1982, to include Indian, Inuit, and Métis peoples. The term *First Nations* has yet to receive legal definition; we will use it to refer to those communities that self-identify as such. The term came into widespread use in the 1970s to replace the word *Indian*, which many people found offensive, owing to its historical associations with the oppressive colonialism of the Indian Act. The term is still used for certain legal designations, such as "Treaty Indian." First Nations people form the largest Aboriginal group in Canada, comprising more than 850,000 people, out of an Aboriginal population of more than 1.4 million, and 4.3 percent of the total population (Statistics Canada 2013, 4).

2 The term *land claim* refers to the process introduced in 1973 whereby the federal and provincial or territorial governments negotiate treaty rights with Indigenous peoples with respect to land that they traditionally inhabited before the arrival of Euro-Canadians. There are two types of land claims: specific claims and comprehensive claims. Specific claims arise from the nonfulfillment of existing treaties and other lawful obligations, whether these involve lands or other promised goods. Specific claims deal with grievances of First Nations related to Canada's obligations under historic treaties or to the way in which the federal government managed First Nations' funds or other assets. To honour its obligations, Canada negotiates settlements with the First Nation and, where applicable, with provincial or territorial governments. Treaty Land Entitlement is a category of specific claims that refers to reserve lands that a band has not yet received as promised initially under treaty. Comprehensive claims occur in areas of Canada where Aboriginal title was never historically extinguished by means of treaty or other legal process. These claims produce agreements that are, in effect, modern treaties (Slowey 2008, 10).

3 The Métis Nation is organized into locals, which work on behalf of Métis communities in particular areas. Historically, because the Métis were not covered by treaty, they had no legal basis on which to claim land. In Alberta, decades of negotiation between the Métis and the provincial government culminated in the Alberta-Métis Settlements Accord of 1989. The following year, the Métis Settlements Act and associated legislation resulted in the transfer of 1.25 million acres of land to the eight Métis settlements represented by the Métis Settlements General Council. The legislation also ensures Métis communities a measure of local governance and provides for the comanagement of subsurface resources. In Forth Chipewyan, Local 125 represents local Métis who do not have their own territory. However, in its 2010 Métis Harvesting policy, the province recognizes Fort Chipewyan Métis as "both a historic and contemporary rights-bearing community." Because of the paucity of studies indicating Métis traditional land, 106 kilometres of land are "deemed traditional territory," giving Fort Chipewyan hunting and fishing rights. See the submission by the Fort Chipewyan Métis Local 125, Métis Nation of Alberta, to the Canadian Environmental Assessment Agency, 11 August 2012, https://www.ceaa-acee.gc.ca/050/documents/p59539/80937E.pdf.

4 For more on the MCFN, see "Who We Are," *Mikisew Group of Companies*, 2009, http://www.mikisewgroup.com/who-we-are.html.

5 In October 2012, Gabrielle Slowey interviewed members of Fort Chipewyan's First Nations communities. The discussion that follows draws on occasion from four of these interviews, all conducted on 16 October.

6 According to the 15 January 2008 issue of the *National Review of Medicine* (Lanktree 2008), the College of Physicians and Surgeons of Alberta (CPSA) contacted O'Connor in December 2007 with the news that he had been "cleared of three of the four professional misconduct charges Alberta Health and Wellness and Health Canada had brought against him." This provoked a letter from Howard May, of Alberta Health, who wrote that "Alberta Health and Wellness did not take part in filing any

complaint against Dr. O'Connor, nor did we try to stop him from coming forward. To the contrary, we have been trying for nearly two years (numerous phone calls, emails and letters) to get him to come forward with his clinical evidence." The editors responded that "although Alberta Health and Wellness is not officially listed on the complaint filed against Dr. O'Connor, their employees continue to assist Health Canada in pursuing action against him," adding that "Dr. O'Connor says he has never received emails, letters or phone calls" (see the "Letters" section, National Review of Medicine, February 2008, http://www.nationalreviewofmedicine.com/issue/2008/02/5_letters_2.html). The November 2009 CPSA report likewise attempts to shift the blame to O'Connor, accusing him of failing to respond to requests for information. For a perceptive analysis of the struggles of Fort Chipewyan First Nations with the oil industry, including the controversy surrounding O'Connor, see Brodie (2014, chap. 6).

7 "Recovery or Extraction," *Alberta Energy*, 2015, http://www.energy.alberta.ca/OilSands/1719.asp.

8 It is worth noting that "reclamation" does not mean restoration. Alberta's Environmental Protection and Enhancement Act regulations specify that the land must be returned to "an equivalent land capability" but that "individual land uses will not necessarily be identical." In the case of the first certification by the Government of Alberta of "reclaimed" land in the bitumen sands, a square kilometre of boreal forest and rare peatland that had developed over eight thousand years was replaced with a new forest with walking trails for humans that bear little resemblance to the complex ecosystem it replaced. Joyce Hildebrand, "Reclamation Illusions in Oil Sands Country," *Wildlands Advocate*, June 2008, 10–12.

9 The cases—sometimes referred to as the "Haida trilogy"—are Haida Nation v. British Columbia (Minister of Forests) 2004 SCC 73, [2004] 3 SCR 511; Taku River Tlingit First Nation v. British Columbia 2004 SCC 74, [2004] 3 SCR 550; and Mikisew Cree First Nation v. Canada 2005 SCC 69, [2005] 3 SCR 388.

10 This changed (at least to some extent) with the passage in May 2013 of Bill 22, now the Aboriginal Consultation Levy Act, which obliges companies that wish to develop on Crown lands to pay a fee, with the funds collected to be distributed to Aboriginal groups in order to assist them in participating in consultation. Section 8(1) of the act stipulates that, under certain circumstances, a project proponent may be required "to provide the Minister with information, including third party personal information, records and other documents, including copies of agreements relating to consultation capacity and other benefits pertaining to provincial regulated activities." The legislation provoked an outcry from Aboriginal leaders, given that the Alberta government hadn't bothered to consult with them prior to passing it.

11 These studies are listed in Shell Canada Limited's 2007 *Jackpine Mine Expansion and Pierre River Mind Project*, pp. 3-9 to 3-10.

References

Abele, Frances. 1997. "Traditional Knowledge in Practice." *Arctic* 50 (3): iii–iv.

ACFN (Athabasca Chipewyan First Nation). 2003. *Footprints on the Land: The Path of the Athabasca Chipewyan First Nation.* https://www.ceaa-acee.gc.ca/050/documents_staticpost/59540/82080/Appendix_D_-_Part_02.pdf.

AEMP (Alberta Environmental Monitoring Panel). 2011. *A World Class Environmental Monitoring, Evaluation, and Reporting System for Alberta: The Report of the Alberta Environmental Monitoring Panel.* http://www.environment.gov.ab.ca/info/library/8381.pdf.

Alberta. 2008. *Alberta's Oil Sands: Opportunity.* Balance. http://www.assembly.ab.ca/lao/library/egovdocs/2008/alen/165630.pdf.

Alberta. Alberta Energy. 2013. *Oil Sands Reclamation.* Fact sheet. http://oilsands.alberta.ca/FactSheets/Reclamation_FSht_Sep_2013_Online.pdf.

Alberta. Alberta Environment. 2011. "Scientists Call for Increased Water Monitoring, More Analysis: More Work Required Before Conclusions Can Be Drawn About Impacts, Says Committee." News release, 9 March. http://www.alberta.ca/acn/201103/300309B7C9208-C885-824C-D3C04D2D67FAEBF9.html.

Alberta. Municipal Affairs. 1970. "1970 Official Population." Local Government Advisory Branch, Information Support Services. http://municipalaffairs.gov.ab.ca/documents/ms/1970population.pdf.

———. 2012. "2012 Municipal Affairs Population List." Municipal Services Branch. http://municipalaffairs.gov.ab.ca/documents/msb/2012_pop.pdf.

Bell, Shawn. 2010. "Oilsands Company Attempts to Silence Former Mikisew Chief." *Northern Journal,* 23 March.

Berger, Thomas. 1977. *Northern Frontier, Northern Homeland: The Report of the Mackenzie Valley Pipeline.* 2 vols. Catalogue No. CP32-25/1977-1. Ottawa: Minster of Supply and Services Canada.

Brodie, Scott. 2014. "Greener Social Constructions: Marie Lake, Fort Chipewyan, and the Alberta Oil Sands." PhD diss. , School of Criminology, Simon Fraser University, Burnaby, BC.

Burton, Philip Joseph, C. Messier, G. F. Weetman, E. E. Prepas, W. L. Adamowicz, and R. Tittler. 2003. "The Current State of Boreal Forestry and the Drive for Change." In *Towards Sustainable Management of the Boreal Forest,* edited by P. J. Burton, C. Messier, D. W. Smith, and W. L. Adamowicz, 1–40. Ottawa: NRC Research Press.

Canada. AANDC (Aboriginal Affairs and Northern Development Canada). 2012. "Detailed Tables: Registered Indian Population by Sex and Type of Residence by Group, Responsibility Centre, and Region 2012—Alberta." *Aboriginal Affairs and Northern Development Canada.* http://www.aadnc-aandc.gc.ca/eng/1373986813464/1373986896953.

Canada. Environment Canada. 2014. "National Greenhouse Gas Emissions." *Environment Canada.* http://www.ec.gc.ca/indicateurs-indicators/default.asp?lang=en&n=FBF8455E-1.

Canada. NRC (Natural Resources Canada). 2013. *Oil Sands: A Strategic Resource for Canada, North America, and the Global Market.* http://www.nrcan.gc.ca/sites/www.nrcan.gc.ca/files/energy/pdf/eneene/pubpub/pdf/OS-brochure-eng.pdf.

Canada. Parliament of Canada. House of Commons. 2007. *The Oil Sands: Toward Sustainable Development.* Report of the Standing Committee on National Resources, 39th Parliament, 3rd Session, March. http://cmte.parl.gc.ca/Content/HOC/committee/391/rnnr/reports/rp2614277/rnnrrp04/rnnr04-e.pdf.

Candler, Craig, Rachel Olson, Steven DeRoy, and the Firelight Group Research Cooperative. 2010. *As Long as the Rivers Flow: Athabasca River Knowledge, Use and Change.* With the Athabasca Chipewyan First Nation and the Mikisew Cree First Nation. Edmonton: Parkland Institute.

CBC News. 2007a. "Scientists Call for Canadian Boreal Forest's Protection." *CBC News,* 14 May. http://www.cbc.ca/news/technology/scientists-call-for-canadian-boreal-forest-s-protection-1.643495.

———. 2007b. "Study Contradicts Earlier Findings on N. Alberta Water Quality." *CBC News,* 8 November. http://www.cbc.ca/news/canada/edmonton/study-contradicts-earlier-findings-on-n-alberta-water-quality-1.652529.

———. 2010. "Oilsands Water Toxins Natural, Monitor Says." *CBC News,* 31 August. http://www.cbc.ca/news/technology/oilsands-water-toxins-natural-monitor-says-1.939509.

———. 2013. "9 Questions About Idle No More." *CBC News,* 5 January. http://www.cbc.ca/news/canada/9-questions-about-idle-no-more-1.1301843.

CERI (Canadian Energy Research Institute). 2014. *Canadian Economic Impacts of New and Existing Oil Sands Development in Alberta.* Briefing paper, November. Calgary, AB: CERI.

CPSA (College of Physicians and Surgeons of Alberta). 2009. *Investigation Report.* File No. 070059. Report by Trevor W. Theman. 4 November. Edmonton, AB: CPSA.

EUB (Alberta Energy and Utilities Board). 2000. *Historical Overview of the Fort McMurray Area and Oil Sands Industry in Northeast Alberta.* Earth Sciences Report 2000-05. Edmonton, AB: EUB. http://www.ags.gov.ab.ca/publications/ESR/PDF/ESR_2000_05.pdf.

Flanagan, Erin, and Jennifer Grant. 2013. *Losing Ground: Why the Problem of Oil Sands Tailings Waste Keeps Growing.* Drayton Valley, AB: Pembina Institute.

Frank, R. A., J. W. Roy, G. Bickerton, S. J. Rowland, J. V. Headley, A. G. Scarlett, C. E. West et al. 2014. "Profiling Oil Sands Mixture from Industrial Developments and Natural Groundwaters for Source Identification." *Environment, Science, Technology* 48 (5): 2660-70.

Fuller, W. A. 1990. "Fort Chipewyan: The Fur Trade Since World War II." In McCormack and Ironside, *Proceedings,* 104–10.

Fumoleau, René. (1975) 2004. *As Long as This Land Shall Last: A History of Treaty 8 and Treaty 11, 1870–1939.* Calgary, AB: University of Calgary Press.

Gerein, Keith. 2012. "Alberta Takes Step Toward Improved Environmental Monitoring, but Questions Remain." *Edmonton Journal,* 17 October.

Gibson, Ginger, and Ciaran O'Faircheallaigh. 2010. *IBA Community Toolkit: Negotiation and Implementation of Impact and Benefit Agreements.* Toronto: Walter and Duncan Gordon Foundation.

Gosselin, Pierre, Steve E. Hrudey, M. Anne Naeth, André Plourde, René Therrien, Glen Van Der Kraak, and Zhenghe Xu. 2010. *Environmental and Health Impacts of Canada's Oil Sands Industry*. Report of the Royal Society of Canada Expert Panel, Ottawa. December.

Grant, Jennifer, Simon Dyer, and Dan Woynillowicz. 2009. *Clearing the Air on Oil Sands Myths*. Drayton Valley, AB: Pembina Institute.

Griffiths, Mary, Dan Woynillowicz, and Amy Taylor. 2006. *Troubled Waters, Troubling Trends: Summary Report*. Drayton Valley, AB: Pembina Institute.

Henton, Darcy, and Hanneke Brooymans. 2009. "Syncrude Charged over Dead Ducks." *Edmonton Journal*, 9 February.

Holroyd, Peggy, and Terra Simieritsch. 2009. *The Waters That Bind Us: Transboundary Implications of Oil Sands Development*. Drayton Valley, AB: Pembina Institute.

Huseman, Jennifer, and Damien Short. 2012. "A Slow Industrial Genocide: Tar Sands and the Indigenous Peoples of Northern Alberta." *International Journal of Human Rights* 16 (1): 216–37.

IPCC (Intergovernmental Panel on Climate Change). 2000. *IPCC Special Report: Land Use, Land-Use Change, and Forestry—Summary for Policymakers*. Geneva: Intergovernmental Panel on Climate Change.

James, D. R., and T. Vold. 2010. *Establishing a World Class Public Information and Reporting System for Ecosystems in the Oil Sands Region—Report*. OSRIN Report No. TR-5A. Oil Sands Research and Information Network, School of Energy and the Environment, University of Alberta, Edmonton.

Jenson, Jane, and Martin Papillon. 2001. "The 'Canadian Diversity Model': A Repertoire in Search of a Framework." CPRN Discussion Paper F19. Ottawa: Canadian Policy Research Networks.

Kelly, Erin N., David W. Schindler, Peter V. Hodson, Jeffrey W. Short, Roseanna Radmanovich, and Charlene C. Nielsen. 2010. "Oil Sands Development Contributes Elements Toxic at Low Concentrations to the Athabasca River and Its Tributaries." *Proceedings of the National Academy of Sciences* 107 (37): 16178–83.

Kelly, Erin N., Jeffrey W. Short, David W. Schindler, Peter V. Hodson, Mingsheng Ma, Alvin K. Kwan, and Barbra L. Fortin. 2009. "Oil Sands Development Contributes Polycyclic Aromatic Compounds to the Athabasca River and Its Tributaries." *Proceedings of the National Academy of Sciences* 106 (52): 22346–51.

Kurek, Joshua, Jane L. Kirk, Derek C. G. Muir, Xiaowa Wang, Marlene S. Evans, and John P. Smol. 2013. "Legacy of a Half Century of Athabasca Oil Sands Development Recorded by Lake Ecosystems." *Proceedings of the National Academy of Sciences* 110 (5): 1761–66.

Ladouceur, Frank. 1990. "The Impact of the Bennett Dam on the Peace-Athabasca Delta." In McCormack and Ironside, *Proceedings*, 99.

Lanktree, Graham. 2008. "Oilsands Whistleblower MD Cleared: Government Charge of 'Undue Alarm' from Cancer Warning Remains." *National Review of Medicine*, 15 January. http://www.nationalreviewofmedicine.com/issue/2008/01_15/5_patients_practice02_1.html.

Leaton, James. 2008. *Unconventional Oil: Scraping the Bottom of the Barrel?* Edmonton, AB: World Wildlife Fund.

MacKinnon, Leslie. 2013. "Native Bands Challenge Omnibus Budget Bill in Court." *CBC News*, 7 January. http://www.cbc.ca/news/politics/story/2013/01/07/pol-two-bands-duty-to-consult-court-challenge.html.

Marcel, Roxanne, and Dale Monaghan. N.d. "Mikisew Chief on Media Coverage of George Poitras." Press release. *Northern Journal*.

McCormack, Patricia A. 2010. *Fort Chipewyan and the Shaping of Canadian History, 1788–1920s: "We Like to Be Free in This Country."* Vancouver: University of British Columbia Press.

McCormack, Patricia A. , and R. Geoffrey Ironside, eds. 1990. *Proceedings of the Fort Chipewyan and Fort Vermilion Bicentennial Conference.* Edmonton: University of Alberta Press; Boreal Institute for Northern Studies.

McCullum, Hugh. 2006. *Fuelling Fortress America: A Report on the Athabasca Tar Sands and U.S. Demands for Canada's Energy.* Ottawa: Canadian Centre for Policy Alternatives and Polaris Institute; Edmonton, AB: Parkland Institute.

Mills, Suzanne, and Brendan Sweeney. 2013. "Employment Relations in the Neostaples Resource Economy: Impact Benefit Agreements and Aboriginal Governance in Canada's Nickel Mining Industry." *Studies in Political Economy* 91 (Spring): 7–33.

Newman, Dwight. 2009. *The Duty to Consult: New Relationships with Aboriginal Peoples.* Saskatoon, SK: Purich.

O'Connor, John. 2006. "Ethical Hypocrisy: Windmills, the Tar Sands and Human Health." *Rabble.ca*, 15 August. http://rabble.ca/news/2012/08/ethical-hypocrisy-windmills-tar-sands-and-human-health.

Pembina Institute. 2010. *Mining vs. In Situ: Fact Sheet.* Drayton Valley, AB: Pembina Institute.

PPSRD (Priority Project on Sustainable Resource Development). 2013. *Benefit Agreements in Canada's North.* Report prepared for the Northern Development Ministers Forum. http://www.nadc.gov.ab.ca/Docs/benifit-agreements-2013.pdf.

Ritchie, Kaitlin. 2013. "Issues Associated with the Implementation of the Duty to Consult and Accommodate Aboriginal Peoples: Threatening the Goals of Reconciliation and Meaningful Consultation." *UBC Law Review* 46, no. 2: 397–438.

RMWB (Regional Municipality of Wood Buffalo). 2012. *Municipal Census 2012.* http://www.woodbuffalo.ab.ca/Assets/Corporate/Census+Reports/Census+reports+Part+1.pdf.

Sanderson, Chris W. , Keith B. Bergner, and Michelle S. Jones. 2012. "The Crown's Duty to Consult Aboriginal Peoples: Towards an Understanding of the Source, Purpose, and Limits of the Duty." *Alberta Law Review* 49 (4): 821–54.

Schneider, Richard, and Simon Dyer. 2006. *Death by a Thousand Cuts.* Drayton Valley, AB: Pembina Institute; Edmonton, AB: Canadian Parks and Wilderness Society.

Schwartz, Daniel. 2010. "David Schindler: Five Decades of Doing Science, Advocating Environmental Policy." *CBC News*, 18 October. http://www.cbc.ca/news/canada/david-schindler-1.936809.

Selin, Ron. 1999. *Into the New Millennium, Our Story: The Mikisew Cree First Nation.* Edmonton, AB: Western Communications.

Slowey, Gabrielle A. 2008. *Navigating Neoliberalism: Self-Determination and the Mikisew Cree First Nation.* Vancouver: University of British Columbia Press.

Statistics Canada. 2013. *Aboriginal Peoples in Canada: First Nations People, Métis, and Inuit.* 2011 National Household Survey. Catalogue No. 99-911-X2011001. Ottawa: Minister of Industry.

Taylor, Alison, Tracy L. Friedel, and Lois Edge. 2009. *Pathways for First Nation and Métis Youth in the Oil Sands.* CPRN Research Report. Ottawa: Canadian Policy Research Networks.

Tuccaro, Therese. 1990. "Dealing with Social Problems in Fort Chipewyan." In McCormack and Ironside, *Proceedings,* 239.

Vanderklippe, Nathan. 2012. "In Oil Sands, a Native Millionaire Sees 'Economic Force' for First Nations." *Globe and Mail,* 13 August.

WCEL (West Coast Environmental Law). 2012. *Living Democracy from the Ground Up: Part 3.* Video. https://www.youtube.com/watch?v=n0bsqUlPEkM.

WCFSD (World Commission on Forests and Sustainable Development). 1999. *Our Forests, Our Future: Report of the World Commission on Forests and Sustainable Development.* Cambridge: Cambridge University Press.

Weber, Bob. 2010. "Syncrude Guilty in Death of 1,600 Ducks in Toxic Tailings Pond." *Toronto Star,* 25 June.

———. 2014. "Lorne Taylor, Former Tory Minister, to Head Alberta Environmental Monitoring Agency." *Huffington Post,* 20 March. http://www.huffingtonpost.ca/2014/03/20/lorna-taylor-alberta-_n_5001603.html.

Wein, Eleanor, and J. Henderson Sabry. 1990. "Contribution of Country Foods to Nutrient Intakes of Native Canadians in the Wood Buffalo National Park Area." In McCormack and Ironside, *Proceedings,* 181–89.

Wohlberg, Meagan. 2012a. "ACFN Launches Treaty Challenge Against Shell's Jackpine Mine Expansion Project." *Northern Journal,* 9 October.

———. 2012b. "Court Rules Against ACFN on Jackpine Oilsands Mine Decision." Northern Journal, 4 December.

———. 2013a. "Fort Chip First Nation Faces Tough Fight Against Oilsands." *Northern Journal,* 8 January.

———. 2013b. "Former Mikisew Chief Lobbies for Dirty Oil Label in Europe." *Northern Journal,* 14 October.

Worker Safety in Alberta

Trading Health for Profit

Bob Barnetson

Hundreds of thousands of Albertans are injured on the job each year (Barnetson 2012a). In part, this level of injury reflects inadequate enforcement of occupational health and safety (OHS) rules. Inadequate injury-prevention efforts, which result in unsafe working conditions, are symptomatic of successive Alberta governments' long-standing preferences for employer-friendly labour law, a preference that compromises workers' right to health.

Historically, Alberta's Conservative government has favoured employer interests in order to achieve electoral and economic goals. To achieve electoral success, the Conservatives privileged rural interests through public expenditures and limiting workplace rights. To achieve economic goals, the Conservatives enacted repressive labour laws to attract and retain investment, primarily in the oil industry. Such laws, operating in a boom-and-bust economy, have so weakened Alberta's labour movement that there are few political consequences for violating workers' freedom to associate and, ultimately, their right to a safe workplace.

Alberta's OHS regime exhibits classic symptoms of regulatory capture by employers. These include ineffectively regulating workplace safety, deeming employers to be "partners" in regulation, being reliant on employer funding of regulatory activity, allowing employers preferential access to policy making, enacting policies that reward the appearance of safety rather than safety itself, and promulgating a narrative that blames another stakeholder (i.e., workers) for workplace injuries.

In these ways, Alberta's regulatory climate undermines workers' freedom to associate and right to health, as well as the principle of the state acting in the public interest. These rights and principles are associated with democratic societies and constitute the main bulwark that workers have constructed against capital organizing work in an injurious manner, effectively trading worker health for profit. While employers have undermined such rights to some degree throughout Canada, Alberta's oil-driven economy appears to have facilitated much greater employer evasion and weakening of these rights.

Human Rights and Democracy in Alberta

Albertans possess a range of human rights characteristic of citizenship in liberal democracies. Despite widespread support around the world for human rights, they remain conceptually contested. For example, Gary Teeple (2005, 21) suggests that there is nothing particularly human or universal about civil, political, and social rights. Most of these rights have only existed for a few hundred years, and most humans have little ability to realize them. Rather, Teeple asserts, these "human" rights flow from a particular, and widely adopted, economic and political arrangement. Specifically, they are needed to legitimize capitalist propertied relations—the very relationship that gives rise to many of the problems some human rights seek to mitigate.

Furthermore, Teeple argues that these rights are often in conflict with one another and are accorded different weight (31). Most human rights are negative rights, in that they emphasize freedom from constraint. In this way, they are consistent with the tenets of classical liberalism. Yet the regulation and public provision associated with social rights often infringe upon civil rights and are a source of conflict between labour and capital. Given this conflict, social rights do not typically find expression in constitutional documents. Rather, they are voluntarily codified by the state in legislation or international agreements (53). Consequently, social rights are much easier to change over time than are political or civil rights and are more subject to particular political alignments and pressures.

Civil rights codify a set of relations between individuals based on the capitalist mode of production. The purpose of these rights is to protect individual liberty, property, security, and justice. Civil rights required by capitalism are embedded in Canada's Charter of Rights and Freedoms and are protected by (and from) the state. Also embedded in these constitutional documents are certain political rights—rights allowing direct or indirect participation in the establishment or administration of government, such as the right to vote and hold public office. These political rights legitimize liberal democratic government: the ruled choose the government of the day and its policies (42). Yet the political choices available to citizens do not typically challenge the underlying civil (i.e. , property) rights that structure relationships in society. Furthermore, the notional political equality of citizens is significantly undermined by the economic inequalities between various groups of citizens—most commonly, labour and capital.

Social rights, the last type of rights to be codified in Canada, seek to ameliorate the negative effects of capitalism. For example, when workers are unable to access the basic necessities of life, this threatens the availability of workers as well as workers' willingness to accept their subordinate position in society—both necessary components of reproducing the structures and relationships of contemporary society. For these reasons, the state may intervene in the operation of the labour market or workplace or may provide necessary services or supports (58). This may bring social rights (typically codified in legislation) into conflict with civil or political rights and result in weak or no enforcement as a result of political pressure on the state.

Repositories of human rights include various United Nations declarations and covenants, conventions of the International Labour Organization, the Canadian Charter of Rights and Freedoms, and various pieces of federal and provincial legislation. Typically, civil and political rights are treated quite differently from social rights. Consider the United Nation's Universal Declaration of Human Rights (United Nations 1948): Article 17 casts the right to hold property as an absolute, but the right to social security (Article 22) is conditional. This division is mirrored in the two associated covenants. The International Covenant on Civil and Political Rights outlines rights that are immediately enforceable and for which there is a mechanism (albeit weak) for enforcement. By contrast, the International Covenant on Economic, Social, and Cultural Rights has no complaint or enforcement mechanisms, and countries agree only to work toward fulfilling their commitments as resources allow (Normand and Zaidi 2008, 201). This is clear evidence that the imperatives of the market are given priority over at least some human rights.

Two rights important to workers include the freedom to associate (which is the basis of collective action in the workplace) and the right to health (which underlies injury prevention efforts). The freedom to associate finds protection in the Canadian Charter of Rights and Freedoms, as well as expression in provincial statutes, such as Alberta's Labour Relations Code. The degree to which the Charter protects workers' ability to unionize, collectively bargain, and strike is in significant flux, following a 2007 decision that significantly expanded the scope of the Charter protections (Fudge 2012). The right to health exists in the International Covenant on Economic, Social, and Cultural Rights, which includes the right to safe and healthy working conditions (United Nations 1966, 7[b]). This builds upon a more general right articulated in the Universal Declaration of Human Rights: "Everyone has the right to work, to just and favourable conditions of work and to protection against unemployment" (United Nations 1948, 23[1]).

Like most jurisdictions, Alberta has accommodated workers' desire to avoid workplace injuries by enacting a variety of statutes, including the Occupational Health and Safety Act. This act requires that "every employer shall ensure, as far as it is reasonably practicable for the employer to do so, the health and safety of workers engaged in the work of that employer" and empowers the government to regulate workplace safety (Alberta, Legislative Assembly 2000). There is, however, some question about the degree to which Alberta workers can realize and benefit from the freedom to associate and the right to health.

Workplace Safety in Alberta

By any measure, Alberta jobsites are unsafe places to work and among the least safe in the country (Gilks and Logan 2011). Each year, the Alberta government reports approximately 150 occupational fatalities and 50,000 serious injuries (Barnetson 2012a). While 50,000 serious injuries—injuries that prevent workers from doing some or all of their jobs the next day—is a lot of injuries, it is important to keep in mind that government statistics dramatically underreport the true level of injury in Alberta. Specifically, these "injuries" represent claims accepted by the Alberta Workers' Compensation Board (WCB), not actual workplace injuries (Ison 1986, 727).

In fact, there are approximately 500,000 injuries in Alberta workplaces each year—ten times the level of injuries the government likes to talk about. In 2009, Alberta reported approximately 149,167 accepted injury claims of all kinds (Barnetson 2012a). Correcting for the 13 percent of the workforce not covered by workers' compensation and the 40 percent of compensable injuries that are not reported brings the number of workplace injuries to approximately 285,760. Even this "corrected" number ignores most occupational disease and psychological injuries, as well as minor injuries where no treatment beyond first aid was required. These minor injuries include strains, contusions, lacerations, and burns of a degree that varies based upon a worker's ability to tolerate the injury without seeking medical treatment. Discussion among health and safety practitioners suggests that accounting for disease and minor injuries would push the number close to 500,000 injuries per year.

Injuries are primarily caused by hazards that exist in the workplace because of employer choices. Employers who organize work unsafely do so because it is in their economic interest to do so. That is to say, contrary to the popular maxim that "safety pays," it is in fact a lack of safety that pays (Cutler and James 1996; Health and Safety Executive 1993; Hopkins 1999; O'Dea and Flin 2003). Social disruption stemming from this conflict between profits and health is the reason that workplace safety laws and state enforcement mechanisms were first established (Tucker 1990, 81).

Research suggests that Alberta's high level of workplace injury is indicative of widespread employer noncompliance with Alberta's Occupational Health and Safety Code. In 2011, for example, the government announced a safety-inspection blitz in the residential construction industry. Despite knowing that government inspectors were coming, the majority of the 387 employers inspected had safety violations (Alberta, Human Services 2011). In ninety cases, these violations posed an imminent danger of injury or death. These results are broadly consistent with the results of other safety blitzes conducted by the government (Alberta, Employment and Immigration 2010, 2011a, 2011b).

This lack of compliance may reflect an expectation by employers that there is almost no chance they will be caught violating safety rules. On average, workplaces are inspected less than once every fourteen years in Alberta (Alberta, Employment and Immigration 2011c), and it can take safety inspectors up to eighteen days to respond to reports of unsafe workplaces (Alberta, Auditor General 2010). Employers also know that if they do get caught, there is almost no chance they will be penalized. Most commonly, inspectors simply order employers to make changes so that they are in compliance with the OHS Code—something that took employers an average of eighty-six days to do in 2010 (Alberta, Auditor General 2010). While Alberta changed its Occupational Health and Safety Act in 2004 and 2012 to allow inspectors to issue tickets for violations, the Province only enacted the regulation required for various forms of ticketing to commence in late 2013 (Alberta, Job, Skills, Training, and Labour 2013). No data were available at the time of writing as to how many (or indeed, if any!) tickets were handed out.

Alberta does prosecute a handful of employers each year—typically when a worker has been seriously maimed or killed because of employer negligence.

In 2013, Alberta levied fines in seven cases, less than one third the number of prosecutions undertaken by Alberta in 1985 (Alberta, Jobs, Skills, Training, and Labour 2014; Tucker 2003). In many cases, the fine was paid to a community group under Alberta's creative sentencing guidelines. Creative sentencing reduces the stigma attached to the conviction and often generates a tax deduction for the company—in effect, the taxpayer subsidizes the fine. Furthermore, some fines are paid to employer-controlled industry associations—in these cases, employers pay their taxpayer-subsidized fines to other employers.

The resulting health and safety dynamic is that ineffective enforcement encourages and facilitates noncompliance, which in turn compromises workers' right to health (Weil 2012). The former Conservative government's approach to enforcement developed over a number of years (Tucker 2003) and is consistent with its 1995 approach to regulatory reform in order to "promot[e] prosperity for Alberta through a dynamic environment for growth in business, industry and jobs" (Alberta, Regulatory Reform Task Force 1995, 2). "Necessary" regulations included those that "contribute significantly and positively to the competitiveness of the private sector" (2). Consequently, occupational health and safety in Alberta shifted away from state enforcement to self-regulation by employers (Alberta, Labour 1995) in order to create "greater workplace self-reliance in occupational health and safety" (Alberta, Labour 1996, 2). Employers have become increasingly involved in determining and monitoring workplace health and safety while state enforcement and monitoring activity has diminished. Workers are cast simply as recipients of employer safety programs, and, as Jason Foster (2011, 303) asserts, the role of organized labour has been reduced to tokenism.

Labour groups have complained about ineffective enforcement for decades, suggesting that it is a policy choice rather than an oversight. Supporting this notion of choice is the fact that Alberta also ineffectively enforces other employment laws, such as child labour laws (Barnetson 2009a, 2010a). An important consequence of widespread noncompliance is that employers can externalize some of the costs of production onto workers, their families, and taxpayers through workplace injury—the very outcome that statutory OHS laws were enacted to prevent. The inability of Alberta's unions to resist these changes reflects the weakness of Alberta's labour movement.

Organized Labour in Alberta

Organized labour is a weak presence in Alberta workplaces and is largely excluded from public policy making. A number of factors contribute to this situation. First, only 22.8 percent of Alberta workers (mostly in the public sector) were unionized in 2013, the lowest rate of unionization in Canada (Alberta, Innovation and Advanced Education 2015; Canada, HRSDC 2012). Second, the largest sectors in Alberta's economy (half of the GDP comes from energy, construction, and finance) are mostly non-unionized, while heavily unionized sectors are among the smallest contributors to GDP (health, public administration, and education contributed less than 13 percent of the GDP in 2011; Alberta, Innovation and Advanced Education, 2015; Alberta, Enterprise and Advanced Education 2012, 9). In this way, the dominant employment paradigm in Alberta is non-union. And third, the petroleum industry has developed sophisticated human resource practices that take wages out of competition and offer employees non-union forms of workplace representation (Ponak, Reshef, and Taras 2003, 282). While segments of Alberta workers periodically exhibit significant support for trade unionism, this has not translated into union members or political influence (Finkel 2012a, 144).

This may be partly explained as an impact of successive Alberta governments enacting employer-friendly labour laws. Labour laws enacted during the tenure of the Social Credit Party were designed to attract investment by (historically American) oil companies (Finkel 1989, 109). Laws enacted by subsequent Progressive Conservative governments have sought to retain investment via union suppression (Finkel 2012a, 144; Foster 2012, 224; Gereluk 2012, 182). Taken together, these policies aid employers to resist union organizing and collective bargaining. For example, Alberta's Labour Relations Code requires a union to win a certification vote in order to represent a group of workers. Other jurisdictions use the "card check" system, wherein a union which demonstrates that a certain proportion of workers are members is automatically certified as the bargaining agent. Certification votes result in fewer certification attempts and a lower success rate by giving an employer the opportunity to "chill" an organizing drive in a variety of (generally illegal) ways (Riddell 2004, 509; Slinn 2004, 299).

All Canadian jurisdictions identify as unfair labour practices (UFLPs) certain behaviours that undermine the intent of the legislation. For example, employer interference in the formation or administration of a trade union is prohibited, and some jurisdictions have given labour relations boards the power to automatically certify unions when the employer has attempted to illegally thwart an organizing drive. This reduces the incentive for employers to engage in this behaviour (Godard 2004; Lebi and Mitchell 2003; Slinn 2008). The Alberta Labour Relations Board does not have such remedial powers, which means, effectively, that there is no consequence for employers who commit UFLPs.

Alberta has resisted calls for first-contract arbitration (FCA) provisions. FCA facilitates the establishment of a collective agreement in a newly certified workplace via arbitration. Such provisions reduce the incentive for employers to use the first round of collective bargaining as an opportunity to refight the union's successful certification application by stalling and otherwise pressurizing the new union.[1] Six Canadian jurisdictions have first-contract arbitration provisions. While FCA is rarely used, its very presence has reduced first-contract work stoppages by up to 50 percent (Johnson 2010; Slinn and Hurd 2011).

Alberta has also limited the labour rights of several groups of employees. Public sector employees are governed by the Public Sector Employees Relations Act, which prohibits strikes and precludes arbitrators from making awards on a number of matters, although the arbitral preclusions may be unconstitutional. Similar alternative arrangements exist for police officers, as well as professors. Farm, ranch, and domestic employees are simply without any right to organize. Health care and construction workers have either no right to strike or face onerous requirements in order to strike.

Additionally, the former Conservative government frequently intervened directly in the labour market to the benefit of employers. It intervened in unionization to benefit "friendly" unions and punish combative ones. For example, in 2003, the government consolidated 480 health care bargaining units into 36 in a move widely seen as an effort to punish the Canadian Union of Provincial Employees (CUPE) for opposing the government's earlier (and ultimately unsuccessful) efforts to privatize health care (Fuller and Hughes-Fuller 2005). The outcome of this restructuring significantly advantaged the Alberta Union of Provincial Employees (AUPE), which was (at the time) favoured by the government and had been engaged in an ongoing dispute with CUPE.

In 2008, the government amended the Labour Relations Code to invalidate certification applications that have come about through union members seeking employment at a non-union firm to kick-start an organizing campaign (colloquially called "salting"). The amendment also prohibits unions from subsidizing contract bids by unionized contractors competing with non-union firms (colloquially called "merfing"). These changes were requested by the non-union Merit Contractors Association of Alberta, were rushed through the legislature in seventy-two hours, and were widely viewed as revenge for union-sponsored attack ads during the previous provincial election (AFL 2008; Gilbert 2008).

The government has expanded the labour force by increasing the use of international migrant workers in order to limit the labour market power of domestic workers and facilitate union avoidance tactics (Foster and Barnetson, this volume). And the government has intervened directly in collective bargaining, but only when it benefits employers (including itself). For example, Alberta's Labour Relations Code allows the government to prevent a strike by appointing a disputes inquiry board (DIB). Alberta labour-side practitioners view the imposition of DIBs as a means by which the government delays strike action to allow employers to prepare for the strike. During a 2002 teacher strike, the government passed back-to-work legislation after a public emergency declaration by cabinet was struck down by the courts as baseless (Barnetson 2010b; Reshef 2007). By contrast, the government refused to intervene in numerous labour disputes characterized by employer intransigence and, in some cases, violence, such as strikes at Palace Casino, the Calgary Herald, Lakeside Meat Packers, and the Shaw Conference Centre in Edmonton (Foster 2012).

Further explanation for the weakness of organized labour can be found within the labour movement itself. Since the Second World War, the movement has been markedly conservative (Finkel 1989; Foster 2012; Reshef and Rastin 2003; but see also Gereluk 2012). More recently, the movement has been divided between the Alberta Building Trades Council (with a business union orientation) and the Alberta Federation of Labour (with a social union orientation). Furthermore, the Alberta Federation of Labour has itself been the site of both interunion disputes and significant staff turnover, which has reduced its policy salience and capacity. Additionally, many Alberta workers do not see trade unions as useful. Practically speaking, there may be some truth to this. Alberta's energy-driven boom-and-bust cycles mean that workers have substantial personal labour-market power during the booms (i.e. , they do not need unions) while unions have difficulty protecting worker interests during the busts (Gereluk 2012; Taylor 1997). Furthermore, a significant portion of Alberta's workforce comprises migrants from other provinces, who may exercise exit options rather than resist unfavourable working conditions (Hiller 2009).

The upshot is that Alberta's labour movement, while not powerless, has not been a key player in provincial policy and is often unable to shape public policy.

Whether this situation will change under the recently elected New Democratic government is unclear. By contrast, there is significant anecdotal evidence that employers can shape public policy and that such favouritism has few political consequences for the government. For example, Lynette Shultz and Alison Taylor (2006, 436) note a loosening of child labour laws in 2005 to benefit the restaurant industry. Subsequently, Alberta introduced a two-tiered minimum wage for servers, again at the behest of employer lobby groups (Barnetson 2011).

The lack of effective class-based resistance is sometimes explained in terms of Alberta having a unique "quasi-party" political system (Macpherson 1962, 21) as the result of either single-member plurality electoral systems (Bell 1992) or a unitarist political culture that masks conflicts on the basis of class or race (Pal 1992). As suggested by Harrison (this volume), an institutionalized preference for non-class-based electoral politics (or at least the appearance of this) that emphasizes economic prosperity is certainly consistent with the seeming contradiction of a (notionally) free-market government repeatedly intervening in the labour market to benefit employers.

Impact of Oil and Agricultural Industries on Public Policy

While broad acceptance of a need for "non-partisan" government focused on economic matters may explain how legislators are able to advance employer interests, it does not really explain why they do so. Part of the explanation may be ideological: successive Alberta governments have embraced liberal—and more recently, neoliberal—capitalist values (Laxer and Harrison 1997). Yet it is also useful to examine the electoral benefits that politicians can gain by maintaining a repressive and injurious labour relations system.

Historically, agriculture was economically and politically important in Alberta (Leadbeater 1984, 63). Prior to 1945, the agricultural community supported limits on farm worker rights, including excluding farm workers from the ambit of employment legislation. Farmers colluded with the state to suppress farm worker wages, and the federal and provincial governments acted (often via law enforcement) to prevent union organizing among migrant farm workers (Barnetson 2009b). Despite the growing prominence of petroleum (which, as set out above, triggered anti-union legislation beginning in the 1950s), rural Alberta has retained political importance through the development of a symbiotic electoral relationship with the former Conservative government.[2] Over the past thirty years, as argued in Barnetson (2012b, 150), rural Albertans have sought to maintain their communities in the face of urbanization via significant government support programs (Tupper and Doern 1989, 134; Wilson 1995, 64). In return, rural communities almost always elect Progressive Conservative candidates to the legislature, and Conservative governments have ensured that electoral boundaries are drawn to ensure a disproportionately high number of rural ridings (Archer 1993, 185). In this way, rural Alberta was an important electoral base for the Conservatives, and rural-friendly public policy (funded by petroleum revenue) created a political reward for maintaining pro-employer labour laws. This arrangement has come into question following the 2015 election of a predominantly urban New Democratic government.

According to highly suggestive commentary, the former Conservative government used municipal grants to reward supporters and punish detractors. There are numerous examples of Conservative MLAs pressuring various groups and individuals to not complain about government policy or funding decisions by threatening to withhold funding or otherwise punish complainants. Recent examples include school boards, municipalities, and physicians (Kleiss 2012; Rusnell 2011; Rusnell and McKenna 2012). Furthermore, there is significant evidence that municipalities and public bodies, beholden to government for grants, have been using taxpayer money to contribute to the Conservative Party (CBC News 2012; Rusnell 2012a, 2012b; Rusnell and Russell 2012).

Revenue from oil-and-gas royalties also allowed the former government to fund significant (and often rural) public infrastructure and programming while maintaining low personal and corporate tax-rates (Harrison, this volume). In addition to the oil industry's direct contribution to the economy, the industry drives activity in a large number of other areas (e.g., construction, manufacturing, automotive sales and servicing, and the service and hospitality industries). When oil-industry production, exploration, and construction decline, the effects ripple through Alberta's economy (e.g., in 1986 and 2008), causing widespread job losses and a large reduction in tax revenue. One outcome of this dynamic is that the former government faced few political threats when it continued the province's long tradition of privileging employer interests in the oil and gas industry (Harrison, this volume). As noted above, during the 1950s and 1960s, Alberta's Social Credit government sought to maintain a weak labour movement to facilitate the development of the oil industry (Finkel 1988, 1989, 2012a). Warren Caragata (1979, 133) argues that workers in the oil industry are disinclined toward unionism. By contrast, Wayne Roberts (1990) indicates significant interest among oil-and-gas industry workers in unionization. The truth probably lies somewhere in the middle, with demand for unionization influenced by employer and state policies designed to prevent unionization, if at all possible.

Alberta's boom-and-bust cycle has also triggered state intervention to curtail workers' ability to resist employer demands for retrenchment. This includes legislative change in the 1980s to facilitate union avoidance (Gereluk 2012, 181), public sector wage rollbacks and job losses in the early 1990s (Foster 2012, 211) and 2010s (Alberta, Finance 2013c; Alberta, Legislative Assembly 2013b), and further changes to labour laws (Alberta, Legislative Assembly 2013a), as well as the expansion of child labour (Barnetson 2010a) and migrant worker populations (Foster and Barnetson, this volume) to loosen the labour market in the 2000s. There is voluminous evidence of favourable treatment for the oil industry in other areas, such as environmental regulation (Buzcu-Guven and Harriss 2012; Gosselin et al. 2010; Griffiths and Woynillowicz 2003; Kelly et al. 2010; Tenenbaum 2009) and resource taxation (Boychuk 2010, 7). The upshot of these circumstances is that the oil industry created pressures, opportunities, and inducements for Conservative politicians to continue, and to exacerbate, Alberta's tradition (found originally in agriculture) of privileging the interests of employers over workers. There is evidence that employers had effectively captured the regulatory system governing workplace health and safety issues and turned it to their own ends.

Regulatory Capture of Alberta's OHS System

Regulatory capture occurs when a state agency designed to act in the public interest instead acts to advance the interests of an important stakeholder group in the sector its regulates (Shapiro 2012). Regulatory capture occurs when groups with a significant stake in the outcome of regulatory decisions aggressively seek to gain advantageous policy outcomes. Focused efforts are often successful, because the public (who individually have only a small stake in the outcome) tend to ignore regulatory decision making.

Under a situation of regulatory capture, the dominant stakeholder group can then use the captured regulator to impose costs on other stakeholders, even if such costs are contrary to the public interest. Captured regulators may see themselves as partners of the captors they are supposed to regulate and may even find themselves financed by that group. It is important to recognize that regulatory capture is a contested concept (see Croley 2012) and that a number of new approaches to regulatory capture have emerged, such as soft capture via the provision of biased information (Agrell and Gautier 2012).

Alberta's OHS system exhibits several characteristics of regulatory capture. The ineffective enforcement of the province's OHS laws (thus negating the purpose of the regulation) is detailed above. The issue of who funds OHS in Alberta is trickier to unravel. Of the $23.3 million Alberta spent on OHS in 2009, roughly $21.7 million came from employer premiums transferred to the government from the Alberta Workers' Compensation Board, or WCB (Alberta, Auditor General 2010). Following a scathing series of newspaper articles about injury and death in Alberta during the summer of 2010, the government increased spending to $27.7 million in 2011–12 and has budgeted $43 million for 2015–16. This amount appears to be entirely offset by transfers from the WCB (Alberta, Finance 2015, 21). In this way, OHS is (indirectly) funded by employers. This funding is contingent upon continued approval by the WCB's board of directors, which is dominated by employer and government members. While it is unclear if aggressive enforcement would alter the willingness of the WCB to fund OHS activities, a number of labour- and employer-side practitioners privately suggest that this risk exists.

Since the 1990s, industry-funded safety associations have increasingly entered into "partnerships" with the government. These partnerships allow employers to play a formal role in determining policy and standards and to sponsor various safety-awareness campaigns and perform safety-auditing functions. A 1997 strategic plan for Alberta's Partnerships in Health and Safety framework explains the thinking underlying this approach:

> Partnerships is based upon the premise that more can be achieved through a cooperative, collaborative approach than by a one sided, dictatorial or interventionist approach. Leverage and synergy is possible without duplicating efforts and "re-inventing the wheel." Partnerships strives to promote a culture of increased proactive health and safety attitudes and behaviour in the workplace. These cannot be legislated! (Alberta, Labour 1997, 3)

This model prioritizes employer autonomy over safety and views government as a facilitator of employer-driven initiatives. Foster (2011, 294) notes that organized labour is offered the opportunity to collaborate with employers by encouraging workers to "take ownership" of their own safety. Workers have no role in the framework, other than that of passive recipients of new initiatives (Alberta, Labour 1997). In Alberta, the partnerships model divided the labour movement: the building trades unions opted to participate in the safety associations, while unions affiliated with the AFL declined to do so. The "collaborative" processes established by government to review standards created employer-dominated "working groups" deliberating over small changes for extended periods. This led to a "culture of compromise" among labour representatives on the groups, which undermined the effectiveness of labour's capacity to improve safety for workers (Foster 2011, 303).

In 2002, with employers facing rising workers' compensation premiums, the Government of Alberta challenged employers to reduce workplace injuries by 40 percent within two years. As part of the Partnerships in Injury Reduction (PIR) program, the government linked receipt of a Certificate of Recognition (COR) and employer claims costs to WCB premium reductions. Employers who passed an audit of their health and safety management system (performed by a certified auditor, generally from a safety association) received a COR (Alberta, Employment, Immigration, and Industry 2007). First-time COR recipients receive a 10 percent reduction in their WCB industry rate during their first year. Furthermore, by reducing WCB claim costs or maintaining claim costs at least 50 percent lower than the industry average for two consecutive years, employers can receive further discounts to an overall total of a 20 percent discount (WCB 2007). These incentives are in addition to incentives that exist under the WCB's own experience-rating system, which provided 9,264 employers approximately $77 million in WCB premium savings in 2010 (WCB 2011a, 2011c), up from $15.2 million saved by 2,233 employers in 2000. Additionally, the WCB issued $230 million in special employer premium rebates in 2011 (WCB 2011b). A 2010 audit questioned whether PIR has made workplaces safer, given that the employers with poor safety records continued to receive PIR rebates (Alberta, Auditor General 2010).

Alberta has promulgated the "careless worker" myth in its injury-prevention efforts. The careless worker myth explains occupational injuries as the result of workers being accident prone, careless, or even reckless. Historically, the careless worker myth has often been used in reference to workers of particular ethnicity and gender (Aldrich 1997, 139; Messing 1998, 24) to shift blame for injuries away from employers (Bale 1989, 35; Witt 2004, 119). Worker carelessness is a part of a broader narrative of "freedom of choice" that absolves employers and society of moral responsibility for worker injuries (Graebner 1984). In this narrative, workers choose the jobs they hold, and thus the level of risk they experience. As industrialization reduced worker autonomy and increased worker proximity to machinery, employers had a greater role in creating injurious working conditions, and the careless worker myth shifted blame back to labourers.

Blaming workers for their injuries is part of a broader employer strategy to evade liability and risk for workplace injuries. This strategy includes not only withholding evidence of harm but also requiring high standards of proof of causation and, when such proof is provided, requesting additional research, criticizing the methods, prohibiting publication of the research, misrepresenting the findings, and hiring a more compliant researcher to create evidence that there was no risk. It also includes blaming workers and consumers for their injuries and then arguing that the harm is simply an unavoidable (or otherwise acceptable) cost of doing business (Bohme, Zorabedian, and Egilman 2005; Michaels 2008). This is all consistent with a pervasive and negative view of workers. Consider the stigmatization of workers' compensation recipients as malingerers who exaggerate the extent of their injuries to maximize benefits from WCB and time away from work (Kirsh, Slack, and King 2012, 144). Compensation costs and duration are thought to be increased by the cheat in the same way that injury incidence and costs are caused by the careless worker. We see similar stereotypes elsewhere in the public policy literature, such as the "welfare mom" and the unemployment insurance "cheat" (Mirchandani and Chan 2008; Reutter et al. 2009). These stereotypes blame individuals for their circumstances while minimizing the contribution of other factors (e.g., employers organizing work unsafely and not providing real return-to-work options). Indeed, these negative perceptions of workers frame the employer as the victim, thus completing a reversal of blame.

In 2008, Alberta released Bloody Lucky, a gory workplace safety campaign. This campaign was sponsored by the Young Worker Provincial Advisory Committee, a collection of provincial safety associations. The videos that make up the campaign, as well as the text associated with each video, clearly and inaccurately portray workers as the cause of their own injuries.[3] Bloody Lucky is the culmination of a trend in Alberta safety campaigns of blaming workers for their injuries—a trend that intensified after 1995 (Barnetson and Foster 2012). An analysis of this campaign demonstrates that the bureaucrats involved with the campaign had difficulty identifying blaming behaviour and viewed such a messaging as important in securing political support for the campaign. Through this campaign, the state misinformed young workers about the nature of workplace hazards and appropriate mitigation strategies by publicly shifting blame for injuries away from employers.

Workplace Injury as a Bellwether for Democracy

There is substantial evidence that employers have had disproportionate access to and say in Alberta's OHS system. Indeed, Alberta's workplace health and safety system exhibits characteristics suggesting a significant degree of regulatory capture by employers—the very group it is supposed to regulate. The result of this arrangement is that Alberta workers face high levels of workplace injury due to ineffective state regulation. State facilitation of employers trading worker health for profit poses a significant impediment to workers realizing their right to health.

This special treatment of employers by the former Conservative government is also evident in Alberta's employment standards and labour relations regimes, as well as in the province's approach to immigration. Significantly limiting workers' freedom of association in order to attract and retain investment in the oil industry has created a weak labour movement. This, in turn, reduces the political cost of operating an ineffective injury-prevention system. Consequently, the costs associated with work-related injuries are externalized onto workers, their families, and society. This outcome broadly follows Teeple's 2005 analysis of the hierarchy of human rights, which predicts that social rights are subject to weak or nonenforcement due to political and economic pressure exerted upon the state by employers.

Alberta's decisions to limit workers' freedom of association and right to health reflect incentives, opportunities, and pressures caused or exacerbated by Alberta's oil-based economy. Alberta enticed foreign investment by limiting the power of trade unions, a pattern that continues to this day. Over the past thirty years, the revenue generated from the oil industry has allowed the government to ensure electoral success via public expenditures in rural Alberta. Employers have sought to minimize production costs via ineffective state enforcement of workplace safety measures, including regulatory capture of Alberta's OHS system. In these ways, this case supports the notion that there is a democratic deficit in Alberta that is at least partly related to the petroleum industry. Whether this arrangement will change substantially under the New Democrat government elected in 2015 is unclear.

The right to health and freedom to associate represent potentially potent legal counterweights to employers' common law right to organize work as they see fit, including organizing work in an injurious manner. While employers throughout Canada have undermined the effectiveness of these social rights since the 1970s, Alberta employers appear to have been unusually effective in doing so. Alberta's oil-based economy may be an important explanatory factor in both the historical creation and contemporary maintenance of this system. As noted by Trevor Harrison (this volume), oil revenue played an important role in allowing the Progressive Conservative party to maintain political power. In the case of workers, groups and rights that threaten either the economic or electoral basis of this power are constrained through a combination of state and employer action.

Notes

1 To elaborate, unions tend to be weakest immediately after they have successfully achieved the status of official bargaining agent for a unit of employees at their provincial labour board. The next step for a union is to enter into negotiations with the employer for a collective agreement. First collective agreements are often the most difficult to conclude, because virtually all of the provisions must be negotiated. Employers who continue to resist their employees' decision to unionize can stall such negotiations. This denies the union the opportunity to make good on the core expectations of its new members (i.e., that a collective agreement will be negotiated) and undermines their support. If no agreement is concluded, the workers then have an opportunity to revisit the unionization decision (often with covert encouragement and assistance by the employer) and may vote to decertify the union.

2 While outside the scope of this chapter, it is interesting to note that when the Conservatives came to power in 1971, they did so based upon urban support. By 1975, rural support had shifted to the Conservatives. This shift was lubricated by oil money, and rural support remained essentially "parked" with Conservatives until the 2012 Wildrose victories in southern Alberta.

3 The videos and associated text are available at "Bloodylucky," Alberta Jobs, Skills, Training, and Labour, 2014, http://work.alberta.ca/occupational-health-safety/bloodylucky.html.

References

AFL (Alberta Federation of Labour). 2008. "Alberta Braces for Protests After Making Anti-union Changes to Labour Code." *Alberta Federation of Labour*, posted from *The Energy News.com*, 11 June.

Agrell, Per, and Axel Gautier. 2012. "Rethinking Regulatory Capture." In *Recent Advances in the Analysis of Competition Policy and Regulation*, edited by Joseph E. Harrington and Yannis Katsoulacos, 286–30. Cheltenham, UK: Edward Elgar.

Alberta. Auditor General. 2010. *Report of the Auditor General*. April. http://www.oag.ab.ca/webfiles/reports/OAGApr2010report.pdf.

Alberta. Employment and Immigration. 2010. *Occupational Health and Safety (OHS) Focused Inspection Project: Commercial Construction. December.* http://work.alberta.ca/documents/ WHS-PUB-Commercial-Construction-Focused-Inspection-Report-2010.pdf.

———. 2011a. *Occupational Health and Safety (OHS) Focused Inspection Project: Powered Mobile Equipment.* 11 April. http://work.alberta.ca/documents/WHS-PUB-Powered-Mobile-Equipment-Focused-Inspection-Report.pdf.

———. 2011b. *Occupational Health and Safety (OHS) Focused Inspection Project: Young Workers.* 5 July. http://work.alberta.ca/documents/focused-inspection-project-young-workers.pdf.

———. 2011c. *Annual Report 2010–2011.* http://humanservices.alberta.ca/documents/2010-11-EI-annual-report.pdf.

Alberta. Employment, Immigration, and Industry. 2007. *About Worksafe Alberta: Fact Sheet.*

Alberta. Enterprise and Advanced Education. 2012. *Highlights of the Alberta Economy 2012.* August. http://www.albertacanada.com/SP-EH_highlightsABEconomy.pdf.

Alberta. Finance. 2013c. "The Government of Alberta Is Making Public Sector Pension Plans More Secure, Adaptable and Affordable."

———. 2015. *Budget 2015: Consolidated Expense.* March 30. http://finance.alberta.ca/ publications/budget/budget2015/fiscal-plan-consolidated-expense.pdf.

Alberta. Human Services. 2011. *Occupational Health and Safety (OHS) Focused Inspection Project: Residential Construction.* 7 November. http://work.alberta.ca/documents/ Focused-Inspection-Residential-Construction-Report.pdf.

Alberta. Innovation and Advanced Education. 2015. "Unionization Rates." 30 March. http://albertacanada.com/business/overview/unionization-rates.aspx.

Alberta. Job, Skills, Training and Labour. 2013. "Ticketing and Administrative Penalties." 10 September. http://work.alberta.ca/occupational-health-safety/ticketing-and-administrative-penalties.html.

———. 2014. "Summary of Prosecutions: Alberta OHS Prosecutions Penalties Summary 2004–2013." http://work.alberta.ca/occupational-health-safety/5538.html.

Alberta. Labour. 1995. *Alberta Labour Regulatory Reform Action Plan.*

———. 1996. *Occupational Health and Safety Business Plan, 1996/97 to 1998/99.*

———. 1997. *Partnerships Strategic Plan.* November.

Alberta. Legislative Assembly. 2000. *Occupational Health and Safety Act.* RSA 2000. C. O-2. s. 2(1)(a)(i). Edmonton: Alberta Queen's Printer.

———. 2013a. *Bill 45: Public Sector Services Continuation Act.* 28th Legis. , 1st Sess.

———. 2013b. *Bill 46: Public Service Salary Restraint Act.* 28th Legis. , 1st Sess.

Alberta. Regulatory Reform Task Force. 1995. *Alberta Regulatory Reform: Improving the Alberta Advantage Workplan.*

Aldrich, Mark. 1997. *Safety First: Technology, Labor and Business in the Building of American Work Safety, 1870–1939.* Baltimore: Johns Hopkins University Press.

Archer, Keith. 1993. "Conflict and Confusion in Drawing Constituency Boundaries: The Case of Alberta." *Canadian Public Policy* 19 (2): 177–93.

Bale, Anthony. 1989. "America's First Compensation Crisis: Conflict over the Value and Meaning of Workplace Injuries Under the Employer Liability System." In *Dying for*

Work: Workers' Safety and Health in Twentieth-Century America, edited by David Rosner and Gerald Markowitz, 34–52. Bloomington: Indiana University Press.

Barnetson, Bob. 2009a. "The Regulation of Child and Adolescent Labour in Alberta." *Just Labour* 13: 29–47.

———. 2009b. "The Regulatory Exclusion of Agricultural Workers in Alberta." *Just Labour* 14: 50–74.

———. 2010a. "Effectiveness of Complaint-Driven Regulation of Child Labour in Alberta." *Just Labour* 16: 9–24.

———. 2010b. "Alberta's 2002 Teacher Strike: The Political Economy of Labor Relations in *Education.*" *Education Policy Analysis Archives* 18 (3): 1–23.

———. 2011. "Two-Tier Minimum Wage." *Labour and Employment in Alberta* (blog), 2 June. http://albertalabour.blogspot.ca/2011/06/two-tier-minimum-wage.html.

———. 2012a. "The Validity of Alberta Safety Statistics." *Just Labour* 19: 1–21.

———. 2012b. "No Right to Be Safe: Justifying the Exclusion of Alberta Farm Workers from Health and Safety Legislations." *Socialist Studies* 8 (2): 134–62.

Barnetson, Bob, and Jason Foster. 2012. "Bloody Lucky: The Careless Worker Myth in Alberta, Canada." *International Journal of Occupational and Environmental Health* 18 (2): 135–46.

Bell, Edward. 1992. "Reconsidering Democracy in Alberta." In *Government and Politics in Alberta*, edited by Allan Tupper and Roger Gibbins, 85–108. Edmonton: University of Alberta Press.

Bohme, Susanna Rankin, John Zorabedian, and David S. Egilman. 2005. "Maximizing Profit and Endangering Health: Corporate Strategies to Avoid Litigation and Regulation." *International Journal of Occupational and Environmental Health* 11 (6): 338–48.

Boychuk, Regan. 2010. *Misplaced Generosity: Extraordinary Profits in Alberta's Oil and Gas Industry*. Edmonton, AB: Parkland Institute.

Buzcu-Guven, Birnur, and Robert Harriss. 2012. "Extent, Impacts and Remedies of Global Gas Flaring and Venting." *Carbon Management* 3 (1): 95–108.

Canada. HRSDC (Human Resources and Skills Development Canada). 2012. "Work-Unionization Rates." http://www4.hrsdc.gc.ca/.3ndic.1t.4r@-eng.jsp?iid=17.

Caragata, Warren. 1979. *Alberta Labour: A Heritage Untold*. Toronto: James Lorimer.

CBC News. 2012. "Alberta Doctors Bullied by Bosses, Panel Finds." *CBC News*, 22 February. http://www.cbc.ca/news/canada/edmonton/story/2012/02/22/edmonton-health-quality-council-report.html.

Croley, Steven P. 2012. "Beyond Capture: Towards a New Theory of Regulation." In *Handbook on the Politics of Regulation*, edited by David Levi-Faur, 50–69. Cheltenham, UK: Edward Elgar.

Cutler, Tony, and Phillip James. 1996. "Does Safety Pay? A Critical Account of the Health and Safety Executive Document: 'The Cost of Accidents.'" *Work, Employment and Society* 10 (4): 755–65.

Finkel, Alvin. 1988. "The Cold War, Alberta Labour, and the Social Credit Regime." *Labour / Le Travail* 21: 123–52.

———. 1989. *The Social Credit Phenomenon in Alberta*. Toronto: University of Toronto Press.

————. 2012a. "The Boomers Become the Workers: Alberta, 1960–1980." In Finkel, *Working People in Alberta*, 141–72.

————, ed. 2012b. *Working People in Alberta: A History*. Edmonton, AB: Athabasca University Press.

Foster, Jason. 2011. "Talking Ourselves to Death? The Prospects for Social Dialogue in North America—Lessons from Alberta." *Labor Studies Journal* 36 (2): 288–306.

————. 2012. "Revolution, Retrenchment, and the New Normal: The 1990s and Beyond." In Finkel, *Working People in Alberta*, 205–42.

Fudge, Judy. 2012. "Constitutional Rights, Collective Bargaining and the Supreme Court of Canada: Retreat and Reversal in the Fraser Case." *Industrial Law Journal* 41 (1): 1–29.

Fuller, Tom, and Patricia Hughes-Fuller. 2005. "Exceptional Measures: Public-Sector Labour Relations in Alberta." In Harrison, *Return of the Trojan Horse*, 313–27.

Gereluk, Winston. 2012. "Alberta Labour in the 1980s." In Finkel, *Working People in Alberta*, 173–204.

Gilbert, Richard. 2008. "Merit Alberta Vice-President Lauds Government's New Bill 26." *Journal of Commerce*, 11 June. http://www.joconl.com/article/id28204.

Gilks, Jaclyn, and Ron Logan. 2011. *Occupational Injuries and Diseases in Canada, 1996–2008: Injury Rates and Cost to the Economy*. Ottawa: Human Resources and Skills Development Canada.

Godard, John. 2004. *Trade Union Recognition: Statutory Unfair Labour Practice Regimes in the USA and Canada*. Employment Relations Series No. 29. London: Department of Trade and Industry.

Gosselin, Pierre, Steve E. Hrudey, M. Anne Naeth, André Plourde, René Therrien, Glen Van Der Kraak, and Zhenghe Xu. 2010. *Environmental and Health Impacts of Canada's Oil Sands Industry*. Report of the Royal Society of Canada Expert Panel, Ottawa. December.

Graebner, William. 1984. "Doing the World's Unhealthy Work: The Fiction of Free Choice." *The Hastings Center Report* 14 (4): 28–37.

Griffiths, Mary, and Dan Woynillowicz. 2003. *Oil and Troubled Waters: Reducing the Impact of the Oil and Gas Industry on Alberta's Water Resources*. Drayton Valley, AB: Pembina Institute.

Harrison, Trevor, ed. 2005. *The Return of the Trojan Horse: Alberta and the New World (Dis)order*. Montréal: Black Rose Books.

Health and Safety Executive. 1993. *The Cost of Accidents at Work*. Health and Safety Series Booklet. London, UK: HMSO.

Hiller, Harry. 2009. *Second Promised Land: Migration to Alberta and the Transformation of Canadian Society*. Montréal: McGill-Queen's University Press.

Hopkins, Andrew. 1999. "For Whom Does Safety Pay? The Case of Major Accidents." *Safety Science* 32: 143–53.

Ison, Terence G. 1986. "The Significance of Experience Rating." *Osgoode Hall Law Journal* 23 (2): 723–42.

Johnson, Susan J. T. 2010. "First Contract Arbitration: Effects on Bargaining and Work Stoppages." *Industrial and Labor Relations Review* 63 (4): 585–605.

Kelly, Erin N. , David W. Schindler, Peter V. Hodson, Jeffrey W. Short, Roseanna Radmanovich, and Charlene C. Nielsen. 2010. "Oil Sands Development Contributes Elements Toxic at Low Concentrations to the Athabasca River and Its Tributaries." *Proceedings of the National Academy of Sciences* 107 (37): 16178–83.

Kirsh, Bonnie, Tesha Slack, and Carole Anne King. 2012. "The Nature and Impact of Stigma Towards Injured Workers." *Journal of Occupational Rehabilitation* 22 (2): 143–54.

Kleiss, Karen. 2012. "Pork-Barrel Politics Over Municipal Funding? Not Us, Angry Conservatives Say." *Edmonton Journal*, 15 February.

Laxer, Gordon, and Trevor Harrison, eds. 1997. *The Trojan Horse: Alberta and the Future of Canada*. Montréal: Black Rose Books.

Leadbeater, David. 1984. "An Outline of Capitalist Development in Alberta." In *Essays on the Political Economy of Alberta*, edited by David Leadbeater, 1–76. Toronto: New Hogtown Press.

Lebi, Ron, and Elizabeth Mitchell. 2003. "The Decline in Trade Union Certification in Ontario: The Case for Restoring Remedial Certification." *Canadian Labour and Employment Law Journal* 10: 473.

Macpherson, C. B. 1962. *Democracy in Alberta: Social Credit and the Party System*. 2nd ed. Toronto: University of Toronto Press.

Messing, Karen. 1998. *One-Eyed Science: Occupational Health and Women Workers*. Philadelphia: Temple University Press.

Michaels, David. 2008. *Doubt Is Their Product: How Industry's Assault on Science Threatens Your Health*. Toronto: Oxford University Press.

Mirchandani, Kiran, and Wendy Chan. 2008. "The Racialized Impact of Welfare Fraud Control in British Columbia and Ontario." In *The Daily Struggle: The Deepening Racialization and Feminization of Poverty in Canada*, edited by Maria A. Wallis and Siu-ming Kwok, 167–82. Toronto: Canadian Scholar's Press.

Normand, Roger, and Sarah Zaidi. 2008. *Human Rights at the UN: The Political History of Universal Justice*. Bloomington: Indiana University Press.

O'Dea, Angela, and Rhona Flin. 2003. *The Role of Managerial Leadership in Determining Workplace Safety Outcomes*. Prepared by University of Aberdeen for Health and Safety Executive. Research Report 044. London, UK: HMSO.

Pal, Leslie A. 1992. "The Political Executive and Political Leadership in Alberta." In *Government and Politics in Alberta*, edited by Allan Tupper and Roger Gibbins, 1–29. Edmonton: University of Alberta Press.

Ponak, Allen, Yonatan Reshef, and Daphne Taras. 2003. "Alberta: Industrial Relations in a Conservative Climate." In *Beyond the National Divide: Regional Dimensions of Industrial Relations*, edited by Mark Thompson, Joseph B. Rose, and Anthony E. Smith, 267–305. Montréal and Kingston: McGill-Queen's University Press.

Reshef, Yonatan. 2007. "Government Intervention in Public Sector Industrial Relations: Lessons from the Alberta Teachers' Association." *Journal of Labor Research* 28 (4): 677–96.

Reshef, Yonatan, and Sandra Rastin. 2003. *Unions in the Time of Revolution: Government Restructuring in Alberta and Ontario*. Toronto: University of Toronto Press.

Reutter, Linda I. , Miriam J. Stewart, Gerry Veenstra, Rhonda Love, Dennis Raphael, and Edward Makwarimba. 2009. "'Who Do They Think We Are, Anyway?' Perceptions of and Responses to Poverty Stigma." *Qualitative Health Research* 19 (3): 297–311.

Riddell, Chris. 2004. "Union Certification Success Under Voting Versus Card-Check Procedures: Evidence from British Columbia, 1978–1998." *Industrial and Labor Relations Review* 57 (4): 493–517.

Roberts, Wayne. 1990. *Cracking the Canadian Formula: The Making of the Energy and Chemical Workers Union.* Toronto: Between the Lines.

Rusnell, Charles. 2011. "Councillor Alleged Intimidation by Tory MLA." *CBC News*, 14 October. http://www.cbc.ca/news/canada/edmonton/story/2011/10/14/edmonton-intimidation-johnson-shaw-allegations.html.

———. 2012a. "Alberta Colleges, Universities Made Illegal Donations to Tories." *CBC News*, 21 March. http://www.cbc.ca/news/canada/edmonton/story/2012/03/20/edmonton-college-donations-conservatives.html.

———. 2012b. "Alberta Art College Spent Thousands to Access Tory Government." *CBC News*, 6 November. http://www.cbc.ca/news/canada/edmonton/alberta-art-college-spent-thousands-to-access-tory-government-1.1255533.

Rusnell, Charles, and Niall McKenna. 2012. "School Board Gets Warning Letter from Tory MLA." *CBC News*, 2 March. http://www.cbc.ca/news/canada/edmonton/story/2012/03/02/edmonton-hector-goudreau-letter.html.

Rusnell, Charles, and Jennie Russell. 2012. "SAIT Exec Solicited Donations for Tories from Other College." *CBC News*, 7 November. http://www.cbc.ca/news/canada/edmonton/story/2012/11/06/edmonton-sait-political-dontations-conservatives.html.

Shapiro, Sidney A. 2012. "The Complexity of Regulatory Capture: Diagnosis, Causality and Remediation." *Roger Williams University Law Review* 17 (1): 221.

Shultz, Lynette, and Alison Taylor. 2006. "Children at Work in Alberta." *Canadian Public Policy* 32 (4): 431–41.

Slinn, Sara. 2004. "An Empirical Analysis of the Effects of the Change from Card-Check to Mandatory Vote Certification." *Canadian Labour and Employment Law Journal* 11: 259–307.

———. 2008. "No Right (to Organize) Without a Remedy: Evidence and Consequences of the Failure to Provide Compensatory Remedies for Unfair Labour Practices in British Columbia." *McGill Law Journal* 53: 687–740.

Slinn, Sara, and Richard W. Hurd. 2011. "First Contract Arbitration and the Employee Free Choice Act: Multi-jurisdictional Evidence from Canada." In *Advances in Industrial and Labor Relations*, vol. 18, edited by David Lewin, Bruce E. Kaufman, and Paul Gollan, 41–86. New York: Emerald.

Taylor, Jeff. 1997. "Labour in the Klein Revolution." In Laxer and Harrison, *Trojan Horse*, 301–13.

Teeple, Gary. 2005. *The Riddle of Human Rights.* Amherst, NY: Humanity Books.

Tenenbaum, David J. 2009. "Oil Sands Development: A Health Risk Worth Taking?" *Environmental Health Perspectives* 117 (4): A150–56.

Tucker, Eric. 1990. *Administering Danger in the Workplace: The Law and Politics of Occupational Health and Safety Regulation in Ontario, 1850–1914.* Toronto: University of Toronto Press.

———. 2003. "Diverging Trends in Worker Health and Safety Protection and Participation in Canada, 1985- 2000." *Relations Industrielles / Industrial Relations* 58 (3): 395–426.

Tupper, Allan, and G. Bruce Doern. 1989. "Alberta Budgeting in the Lougheed Era." In *Budgeting in the Provinces: Leadership and the Premiers,* edited by Allan M. Maslove, 121–42. Toronto: Institute of Public Administration.

United Nations. 1948. *Universal Declaration of Human Rights.* Geneva: United Nations.

———. 1966. *International Covenant on Economic, Social and Cultural Rights.* Geneva: United Nations.

WCB (Workers' Compensation Board). 2007. Partners in Injury Reduction. Brochure. Edmonton: Alberta Workers' Compensation Board.

———. 2011a. Partnerships in Injury Reduction: PIR Refund Results. Edmonton: Alberta Workers' Compensation Board.

———. 2011b. "Board of Directors' Meeting of April 26, 2011: Website Summary." Edmonton: Alberta Workers' Compensation Board.

———. 2011c. "Number of PIR refunds continues to grow!" 30 March. https://www.wcb. ab.ca/pdfs/employers/PIR_refund_growth.pdf

Weil, David. 2012. "'Broken Windows,' Vulnerable Workers, and the Future of Worker Representation." *The Forum: Labour in American Politics* 10 (1): article 9.

Wilson, Barry K. 1995. "Cultivating the Tory Electoral Base: Rural Politics in Ralph Klein's Alberta." In Laxer and Harrison, *Trojan Horse,* 61–69.

Witt, John Fabian. 2004. *The Accidental Republic: Crippled Workingmen, Destitute Widows, and the Remaking of American Law.* Cambridge, MA: Harvard University Press.

Exporting Oil, Importing Labour, and Weakening Democracy

The Use of Foreign Migrant Workers in Alberta

Jason Foster and Bob Barnetson

Rapid expansion of bitumen sands construction in Alberta during the 2000s led to an economic boom in the province. As in previous booms, rapid economic growth led employers to meet labour needs by seeking migrant workers. But the boom of the 2000s differed in that employers brought in workers from around the world rather than from across the country. The immediate cause of this unprecedented growth in the use of temporary foreign workers (TFWs) was federal policy changes to the Temporary Foreign Worker Program (TFWP) that made TFWs more accessible to employers. This policy change must, however, be viewed in the broader context of increasingly neoliberal politics in Canada. In this case study, we examine why the use of TFWs increased in Alberta, how the former Conservatives government of Alberta encouraged and justified the use of migrant workers, and how a petroleum-based economy affects labour markets and the democratic health of a region. This study also explores how Alberta's use of migrant workers is consistent with labour-market dynamics in an oil-exporting economy.

Increased reliance on migrant workers has multilayered consequences for employers, workers, government, and democracy. In the labour market, grow-ing reliance on foreign migrant labour disempowers both migrant and Canadian workers. Foreign migrant workers have limited ability to realize their rights because of their precarious employment and social isolation. At the same time, Canadian workers face competition from less expensive and more docile foreign migrant workers, thereby heightening the consequences of resisting employer demands. This pattern is useful to employers since it undermines the capacity of both domestic and foreign workers to resist the economic restructuring advocated by neoliberalism. The emergence of a permanent subclass of precarious foreign workers also weakens social and community bonds essential to democratic functioning and entrenches significant social inequalities.

Growing reliance on migrant labour also marks a significant shift in Canadian immigration policy away from multiculturalism and toward differential exclusion (Castles 2000, 61), facilitating the emergence of a second class of residents without full citizenship rights. It also raises serious questions about the consequences of shifting control over immigration to employers. This shift can be seen within a global context, where the growing use of migrant workers worldwide contributes to the weakening of workers' ties to and protection by the state, suggesting that consequences of foreign migrant labour extend far beyond Alberta's borders.

The use of migrant workers in Alberta cannot be disentangled from the context of an oil-exporting economy. The use of marginalized, vulnerable, and racialized foreign workers to create a conveniently docile workforce is both an outcome of politics in a petroleum-based economy and a part of the process of its construction, with significant implications for democracy.

Migrant Workers in Canada

Worldwide, approximately 200 million workers are employed outside of their home country (Crowley and Hickman 2008, 1225). Many migrants engage in employment-related geographic mobility (E-RGM), undertaking extended travel from places of permanent residence to work (Green 2004; Temple et al. 2011). The temporary nature of E-RGM differentiates it from immigration, although E-RGM may entail significant periods of temporary residency (Edmonston 2011, 194).

Alberta's oil boom has attracted tens of thousands of foreign and Canadian migrant workers to the province (De Guerre 2009; Hiller 2009; Mech 2011). Relatively few TFWs are directly employed in the oil industry. Most migrant workers are employed in related fields (e.g., construction) or in low-end service-sector jobs, many of which were opened up by Canadian workers moving to jobs in or associated with the petroleum sector (Foster 2012a, 36). In this way, Alberta's most recent oil boom intensified an existing trend toward greater use of foreign migrant workers (Foster and Taylor 2011).

Canadian provincial governments have facilitated E-RGM for citizens via interprovincial credential-recognition arrangements (e.g., the Red Seal program) and labour-mobility agreements (e.g., the New West Partnership Trade Agreement). The federal government also operates several programs permitting noncitizens to work. The TFWP, for example, allows employers to recruit TFWs if no qualified Canadian citizens are available. In 2002, the federal government extended the program to include lower-skilled workers (i.e., National Occupational Code classifications C and D). In 2006, the government established a list of "occupations under pressure" for Alberta and British Columbia, reducing employer requirements for acquiring Labour Market Opinions (LMOs), which grant permission to hire TFWs (Fudge and MacPhail 2009).

In 2012, the federal government dramatically reduced the turnaround time for processing LMO applications and amended wage rules in order to allow employers to reduce TFW wages (Foster 2012a). These changes include shortening turnaround time on LMO applications for high-skill occupations to ten business days; waiving the LMO process altogether for American TFWs in seven high-demand construction occupations; and allowing employers to pay up to 15 percent and 5 percent less than the regional median wage in high-skilled and low-skill occupations, respectively, if an employer can demonstrate that its Canadian workers also receive such wages. A series of public controversies involving the program forced the federal government to repeal the differential wage allowance policy a year later and to institute reforms to place added requirements on employers for acquiring LMOs (Canada, Employment and Social Development Canada 2013). These changes occurred at the same time as the federal government increased the age at which Canadians can receive Old Age Security payments and tightened the rules around Employment Insurance benefits. Critics charge that the series of reforms is an effort to make more workers available to employers in order to loosen the labour market (AFL 2012).

Following public outcry regarding misuse of the program by employers, in 2014 the federal government instituted a further set of reforms aimed at significantly reducing employer use of low-skilled TFWs (Canada, Employment and Social Development Canada 2014). The changes split the program into two pieces. Rules around higher skilled workers were loosened, making it easier for employers in construction, transportation, and bitumen sectors to hire TFWs. Meanwhile, a series of restrictions was added related to low-skilled TFWs found in retail, food, and hospitality industries, including a firm time limit for TFW residency in Canada of four years and phased-in quotas on employers' use of TFWs as a percentage of their workforce. As of the time of writing, the impacts of the reforms are unknown. The authors do not expect that the new rules will substantially reduce bitumen-related use of TFWs due to the skill requirements of these occupations. The relaxed rules for these occupations may lead to increased use of TFWs in the future.

The TFWP restricts the labour-mobility rights of TFWs by issuing work permits tied directly to employment status, requiring TFWs to receive formal permission to change employers or working conditions and prohibiting them from applying for work permits or changing immigration status from within the country (Abella 2006, 4–5; Martin 2003, 21; Sharma 2007, 167; Trumper and Wong 2011, 84; Wong 1984, 89). TFWs are permitted to remain in Canada for a maximum of four years. Restricted labour mobility compounds the effect of other characteristics of migrant foreign workers (e.g. , limited knowledge of the laws, institutions, and labour market; social isolation; language barriers; and limited financial resources) that make them vulnerable to exploitation by their employers or labour brokers. Such exploitation often manifests itself in unpaid wages, dangerous work, and inadequate housing (Otero and Preibisch 2010, 87; Pastor and Alva 2004, 105; Wilkinson 2012, 14). In Canada, workers report difficulty utilizing the labour rights they do have, although TFWs do sometimes exercise such rights, despite the risk (AFL 2009, 12; Foster and Barnetson 2012, 12–13; Nakache and Kinoshita 2010, 30; Valiani 2009, 7–8).

Rainer Bauböck (2011) differentiates among migrant workers on the basis of their freedom of movement and the extent of their equality with permanent residents and citizens, suggesting five "classes" of migrancy. TFWs fall primarily into Bauböck's guest-worker category: their controlled admission is conditional on their return to their home country. These workers typically have limited mobility and equality. TFWs selected for the provincial nominee program (PNP), the second category, transition toward permanent residence and fuller rights. Third, some migrants (e.g. , nannies) may be admitted as guest workers who have initial temporary status but who expect to eventually become permanent residents with full mobility rights and equality. A fourth group comprises TFWs who have stayed after their permits have expired are irregular migrants with no right to be in the country. They may experience greater (albeit illegal) mobility but are much less able to realize employment rights. Finally, Bauböck identifies migrants with citizenship status who have full movement and legal rights, such as interprovincial migrants.

The growth in TFWs can also be seen as a shift in Canada's postwar immigration policy, away from multicultural citizenship and toward differential exclusion (Castles 2000, 61) or partial citizenship (Vosko 2010, 10), where migrants are granted access to certain aspects of citizenship (e.g. , partial access to labour market) but excluded from other legal, political, and economic rights. Partial citizenship hearkens back to an earlier period in Canadian history when immigrants were afforded fewer rights than British-born residents (Whitaker 1987). This situation creates a class of "transnational" workers, who are full citizens of neither the source nor destination country. Nandita Sharma (2006, 7) notes that focusing on workers' citizenship status masks the racist nature of Canada's migrant worker programs. Migrant workers are predominantly from the Global South and are thus members of ethnic, cultural, and/or linguistic minorities. Providing migrant workers with fewer and/or different rights is a systematized form of racism that extends long-standing colonial practices of wealth appropriation by Western countries.

In addition to having limited labour mobility and difficulty realizing employment rights, many migrants also experience heightened labour insecurity "characterized by limited social benefits and statutory entitlements, job insecurity, low wages and high risks of ill health" (Vosko 2006, 4). Precarious employment may further limit the willingness of migrant workers to exercise workplace rights and may reduce direct and indirect labour costs (Bernstein et al. 2006, 210; Wilkinson 2012, 15–16). For example, employers in Alberta's bitumen sector have adopted a just-in-time model of staffing that offloads significant costs to workers (Ferguson 2011). The growth in migrant labour in Canada is linked to employer efforts to reduce labour costs and increase labour market flexibility.

Migrant Workers in Alberta

The growth in migrant labour, and therefore in the concerns associated with it, has been most noticeable in Alberta. While the province has a long history of domestic and foreign E-RGM in agriculture, railway construction, and domestic service (Danysk 1995; Holland 2007; Hsiung and Nichol 2010; Laliberte 2006; Laliberte and Satzewich 1999; Selby 2012; Thompson 1978; Thompson and Seager 1978), the emergence of oil exports as the dominant industry in the province has intensified and altered the nature of E-RGM. From 1975 to 1982 and beginning again in 1998, Alberta also saw significant E-RGM caused by oil-driven economic booms. The majority of migrant workers during these booms came from other Canadian jurisdictions, and when the booms ended, migrants often returned to their home province (Hiller 2009). The boom of the 2000s was different in a number of ways. First, while there was still significant inter-provincial migration of Canadian workers, net interprovincial migration began declining in 2006 and was effectively zero by 2009 (Alberta 2011a, 6). Second, this reduction in interprovincial migration of Canadian workers was offset by significant growth in both permanent immigrants and TFWs (Alberta 2011b, 15, 19).

From 2002 to 2012 (inclusive), approximately 250,000 TFWs were admitted to Alberta, with nearly 165,000 arriving between 2006 and 2010 (see table 9.1). Alberta's "stock" of TFWs (i.e., the number of TFWs on 1 December of each year; "stock" is the federal government's official term for the number of TFWs residing in Canada) rose from 15,714 in 2005 to 65,618 in 2009, before falling slightly in 2010 and then rebounding to 68,339 in 2012. Not captured by these numbers is the (according to anecdotal reports) growing number of nonstatus (i.e., illegal) foreign migrants in Alberta (Bouzek 2012). These include TFWs who stayed on after the expiration of their work permits, as well as other foreign nationals working without a permit.

Table 9.1. Alberta TFWs entries and stock, 2002–12

	2002	2003	2004	2005	2006	2007	2008	2009	2010	2011	2012
TFW stock	10,730	11,376	13,126	15,705	21,973	37,055	57,544	65,572	57,628	58,193	68,339
TFW entries	10,011	9,166	10,513	12,645	18,459	29,287	38,990	28,549	22,998	25,573	35,636

Source: Canada, Citizenship and Immigration Canada 2013.

This rate of increase in TFWs residing in Alberta has been much greater than in other Canadian provinces and includes a significant increase in the use of unskilled TFWs. Before the 2002 and 2006 policy changes, TFWs were found working as university teachers, scientists, specialist technicians, and entertainers. TFWs who arrived between 2005 and 2008 were more likely to be coming to work as cooks, clerks, cleaning staff, construction labourers, and truck drivers (Foster 2012a). In effect, there has been a significant downward shift in the skill level of the jobs to which TFWs are being recruited.

Employers and policy makers justified the growth in TFWs as necessary to address pressing labour shortages due to the economic boom. They also argued the program was highly elastic and closely linked to labour demand. A cooling off of the boom, predicted Immigration Minister Jason Kenney, would "translate into decreased number of temporary foreign workers" (quoted in "Interview" 2010, 13). This did not occur during the recession that began in the third quarter of 2008. From 2008 to 2009, unemployment climbed 36 percent (400,000 people). The provinces with the biggest booms—British Columbia and Alberta—witnessed the largest climb in unemployment rates (LaRochelle-Côté and Gilmore 2009, 5). While new entries of TFWs declined in 2009 and 2010, the overall number of TFWs remained relatively stable. One explanation, as seen in table 9.1, is that employers, while reducing demand for new TFWs, are retaining existing TFWs despite unemployment among Canadian workers (see remarks by former Minister of Employment and Immigration Hector G. J. Goudreau [Alberta, Legislative Assembly 2009a, 393–94, and 2009b, 964]). This shift may indicate an important structural change in Alberta's labour market: the addition of a permanent class of guest workers concentrated in the service sector with restricted labour mobility and other rights. With TFWs as a permanent part of Alberta's employment picture, there is a need to examine more critically their rights under Alberta employment law.

Worker Rights Under the TFW Program

TFWs legally possess the rights guaranteed to all employees by Alberta's employment legislation. As noted by former Minister of Human Resources and Employment Iris Evans:

> In our department we offer foreign workers the same protection that other employees have working in this province, not only in occupational health and safety but by making sure that deductions are properly taken from their cheques, that employment standard complaints are followed up on in the same fashion. We hold workshops for employers, so they know what our expectations are. (Alberta, Legislative Assembly 2007, 20)

These protections include minimum terms and conditions of employment under the Employment Standards Code, such as a minimum wage, maximum hours of work, overtime, and vacations. They also include the rights to know the hazards of the job, to participate in the control of hazards, and to refuse unsafe work under the Occupational Health and Safety Act and Code. TFWs are eligible for workers' compensation benefits if injured and possess the right to unionize under the Labour Relations Code. Despite possessing the same rights as Canadian workers, however, TFWs face at least two challenges to realizing these rights.

The first challenge (shared by all workers) is that enforcement of Alberta's employment laws is mostly complaint driven. Complaint-driven enforcement in Canada has been criticized for addressing only a minority of actual violations (Arthurs 2006, 191; Ontario, Auditor General 2004, 239). The literature also suggests that workers frequently do not complain when they perceive complaining to be ineffective (Weil and Pyles 2005, 63). Alberta has a poor record of enforcing its employment standards and occupational health and safety laws (Barnetson 2009a, 2010, and this volume), yet it generates statistics that convey the opposite impression (Barnetson 2008, 2012a). Consequently, as Bob Barnetson argues in chapter 8 of this volume, complaint-driven regulation has created a culture of noncompliance in Alberta, wherein workers routinely do not receive statutory entitlements.

The second challenge, unique to TFWs, is how TFWs' circumstances limit their ability to realize their rights. The knowledge that TFWs have of employment rights is limited and often provided by their employer. TFWs may also face significant language barriers and be socially isolated, making them unable to access support systems. TFWs are beholden to their employers for both their salary and their right to remain in the country, making complaining (which will probably be ineffective) a high-stakes proposition. All of these factors create additional barriers to TFWs accessing a complaint-driven enforcement system.

The increased use of TFWs in Alberta in the 2000s was soon followed by complaints of exploitation and violation of worker rights. The list of such violations includes substantial differences between promised and actual work; inadequate wages and working conditions; the requirement for unpaid overtime, as well as other breaches of employment standards; and substandard housing, often combined with excessive rent owed to the employer. TFWs also face racism and threats of deportation, illegal and exorbitant broker fees, and misleading promises about permanent residency and citizenship (AFL 2007, 2009). That said, TFWs are not entirely helpless, and some TFWs have successfully resisted these employment practices (Foster and Barnetson 2012). The overall picture is one of a workforce with restricted opportunity to advocate effectively for their employment rights, which can benefit employers.

The Utility of Migrant Workers

For employers, the attraction of TFWs is multilayered. Most employers say that TFWs are necessary to alleviate domestic labour shortages (Cook 2007;

Vanderklippe 2011), while others acknowledge that TFWs are more compliant (Foster and Taylor 2011). It is enlightening to probe when this domestic shortage arose and why. Harry Hiller's (2009, 58) analysis of previous booms—when labour demands were met via interprovincial migration—suggests that E-RGM reflects combination of "push" and "pull" factors: individuals must be motivated to both exit their home community and enter their destination community. Push factors included the need to seek employment and, more importantly, a sense of dissatisfaction with life in their home community (415). Pull factors included employment prospects in the destination community, as well as the desirability of the destination (e.g., ability to find and integrate into a social community, availability of housing) (425).

During the boom of the 2000s, there was a large surge in TFW entries beginning in 2006, reflecting employer recruitment efforts in the prior year (Alberta 2011a, 6). Net interprovincial migration began falling in 2007. This suggests that growth in TFW usage preceded declining interprovincial migration. Furthermore, interprovincial migration declined despite relatively high unemployment (between 7.9% and 14.8%) in traditional "sending" regions during this time—a situation that has historically been an important "push" factor (Statistics Canada 2015). This suggests that there was no absolute shortage of potential interprovincial migrants, particularly for unskilled jobs. Alberta's inability to attract interprovincial migrants may have been affected by deteriorating "pull" factors. While average weekly earnings in Alberta grew by 4.9 percent in 2006, down from 5.2 percent in 2005, inflation rose by 3.9 percent in 2006, up from 2.1 percent in 2005 (Alberta, Finance and Enterprise 2008, 6), significantly eroding wage gains by coming to Alberta. Alberta also experienced a severe housing shortage at this time, with workers in Edmonton living in tents in campgrounds and squatting in the river valley.

At the same time, the growing use of TFWs reduced job opportunities for domestic migrants. Easing labour shortage is, indeed, the main purpose of the TFW program. This dynamic broadly accords with neoclassical economic analyses of the TFW program, which conclude that the program distorts regional labour-market patterns by suppressing interregional labour mobility from provinces of higher unemployment to areas of low unemployment (Gross 2010; Gross and Schmitt 2010, 21–22). This analysis also suggests that employers may have viewed TFWs as a means of loosening the labour market and thereby containing wage demands. Canada has a long history of tapping into secondary sources of labour to loosen the labour market, including the use of women during both world wars (Crompton and Vickers 2000, 6), migrant labour in agriculture (Basok 2002), child labour in the service industry (Barnetson 2010), and forced labour of Japanese and enemy aliens during wartime (Daniels 1981; Farney and Kordan 2005). Further supporting the substitution hypothesis is a number of instances during the 2008–9 recession when Alberta employers continued to employ TFWs while laying off Canadian workers (Barnetson and Foster 2012). While it is not possible to prove that cost containment was the main reason employers increased their use of TFWs, the evidence is suggestive.

A slightly more nuanced employer explanation for the growing use of TFWs is that there is a skills shortage in Canada. There are two reasons to doubt this explanation. First, Foster and Taylor (2011) found several construction employers who openly admitted that they manipulate the LMO system in order to access lower-cost TFWs. This manipulation included conducting "paper" (i.e., insubstantial) recruitment campaigns for Canadian workers, as well as applying for an LMO only after a foreign worker had been successfully recruited. The Auditor General of Canada identified several shortcomings with the federal LMO system, including inadequate information to support an opinion and a lack of verification of the need for the worker (Canada, Auditor General of Canada 2009, chapter 2, 30–31). Second, the proportion of TFWs in skilled jobs is declining while the proportion of TFWs in unskilled jobs is increasing. According to neoclassical economic theory, it should be possible to engage any number of Canadian workers in unskilled work, provided that wages and working conditions are attractive. Rather than adjust to market conditions, Alberta employers have instead sought large numbers of low-skilled TFWs (Foster 2012a).

There is some evidence to suggest that employers find TFWs desirable for their compliance and willingness to cede to employer authority. Alberta construction employers viewed TFWs as harder working, more willing to accept overtime and additional work, less likely to question or challenge, and more appreciative of working conditions (Foster and Taylor 2011). These same employers reported that they were looking to TFWs as a long-term solution for their labour needs, in part because TFWs were seen as more compliant and also because they helped curb concerns about "high wages" in the sector.

Finally, hiring TFWs may be intended to reduce the labour-market power of domestic workers. The impact of the growing number of migrant workers on Canadian workers is largely unstudied. There has been very little research into the Canadian labour-market effects of a sizeable, long-term migrant-worker program reaching into multiple industry sectors. What research has been done examined the labour-market outcomes of TFWs themselves and shows that TFWs fare better than landed immigrants because they better fit employer needs (Warman 2009).

The availability of alternate sources of labour may undermine the militancy of organized labour to some degree. Historically, Alberta employers have regularly sought to displace unionized construction workers with non-union workers, as well as with workers who are members of employer-dominated "unions." This included a significant push to create "double-breasted" construction companies, with a union arm and a non-union arm, in the 1980s (Gereluk 2012, 181) and to develop non-union labour brokers and contract with employer-friendly "unions" in the 1990s and 2000s (Foster 2012b, 223). Included in the 2012 Progressive Conservative election platform was a promise to prohibit unions from fining members who work for non-union employers or for employers who sign contracts with nonsignatory unions, as well as a promise to allow employers to opt out of the existing trade-based construction labour-relations regime (PC Party 2012). Such provisions advantage employer-friendly unions as well as non-union labour groups. It is possible that TFWs serve as an additional alternative labour pool that facilitates employer efforts to undermine and avoid unions.

The labour-market experience of migrant workers broadly accords with neoliberal prescriptions of increasing efficiency and flexibility in the workforce. It is easier for governments to impose such an industrial restructuring on migrant workers than on Canadian workers for two reasons: migrant workers' lack of political power and the perception that being allowed to work in Canada is a charitable act for which migrant workers should be grateful (Sharma 2006). Once a low-cost workforce with minimal rights has been established, employers can use it to threaten the job security of Canadian workers and thereby undermine resistance to such restructuring. The threat posed by TFWs has the potential to cause significant resistance among Canadian workers, something the Alberta government has the foresight to manage.

Government Support for Migrant Workers

The government plays a role in the production and disciplining of the workforce. As noted by Eric Tucker (1990, 116), it is broadly accepted that government labour policy must mediate between the potentially conflicting demands of production and social reproduction (i.e., producing the structures and relationships of contemporary society). On the one hand, government must facilitate the capital accumulation process by allowing employers to produce goods and services in a profitable manner, thus encouraging private investment. On the other hand, government must maintain both its own legitimacy with the electorate and the legitimacy of capitalist social formation. The operation of capitalist systems often negatively affects workers, who compose the majority of the electorate. If enough workers experience low pay, poor working conditions, and workplace injury, they may lose confidence in a particular government or in capitalist social formation.

Between 1971 and 2015, the Progressive Conservative government of Alberta managed these competing demands by (marginally) accommodating the demands of workers while broadly continuing labour policies established by the former Social Credit government (1935–71). Many argue that these policies favour the interests of employers (in particular, oil and gas and related industries) by facilitating union avoidance and repression as well as minimal enforcement of the limited statutory rights granted to workers (Finkel 1989, 109). The growing use of TFWs supports production but may threaten social reproduction, which can pose a significant political risk to government. In Alberta, the government has managed the threat to social reproduction primarily by (incorrectly) framing TFWs as necessary, posing no threat to Canadian workers and facing no threat of exploitation (Barnetson and Foster 2012).

To accomplish this, government MLAs began by noting that Alberta was experiencing a labour shortage due to both an aging workforce and a hot economy. Migrant workers were mooted as the only solution to this shortage. While Alberta did experience a significant labour shortage during the 2000s, TFWs were not the only solution (Alberta 2011a, 6). The labour market may have returned to equilibrium as rising wages attracted more workers and/or employers reduced demand for workers (Anderson and Ruhs 2012, 39). The government also rejected moderating the pace of bitumen sands development and provincial infrastructure spending, both of which would have dampened labour demand (CBSR 2009, 5; Foster 2007, 12). That MLAs continued to advocate for TFWs during the recession of 2008 (despite rising domestic unemployment) further undermines this "there is no alternative" rationale and gives credence to the suggestion that the government supported loosening the labour market to dampen wage demands, thereby benefitting employers.

MLAs attempted to deflect resistance to importing foreign workers by positing that TFWs do not threaten Canadian jobs. Specifically, they asserted that the federal LMO system only allows TFWs when there are no qualified Canadian workers available, that TFWs are more expensive than domestic workers, and that TFWs will return to their home country when the demand ends (Barnetson and Foster 2012). There is, however, significant evidence that the LMO system can be gamed by employers (Foster 2012a; Foster and Taylor 2011). Evidence from 2009 and 2010 shows that the TFW program was not elastic and allowed employers to retain TFWs when laying off domestic workers (Barnetson and Foster 2014, 354; Foster 2012a, 38). Furthermore, it is not clear that migrant workers are more expensive than domestic workers. While recruitment costs may be higher for migrant workers, those costs are often offset through enhanced flexibility for the employer, higher productivity, and opportunity for cost recovery through employment standards violations, informal work arrangements, and excessive charges for accommodation. Facilitating union avoidance may further reduce the cost of migrant labour.

Of greater concern is that temporary workers do not appear to be temporary. They have largely displaced internal migrants as a source of workers, and a large, seemingly permanent class of unskilled migrant workers has emerged (Alberta 2011a, 6; 2011b, 15, 19; Foster 2012a). When critics raise this concern, the provincial government blames the federal government. This approach is politically convenient (and perhaps partially correct), but it ignores the province's responsibility for the results of a migrant-based labour market policy. If there had been more training of domestic workers and if employment regulation made Alberta workplaces more attractive to internal migrants and marginalized groups, TFWs might be less necessary. These options are, however, more expensive for employers than simply expanding the TFW program. Furthermore, there is mounting anecdotal evidence that a large number of foreign migrant workers (up to a hundred thousand) have not returned "home" and remain as nonstatus immigrants (Bouzek 2012).

Finally, Conservative MLAs sought to deflect criticism that the TFW program was resulting in exploitation of the TFWs by their employers by noting that TFWs have the same rights as Canadian workers (Barnetson and Foster 2014, 362). As set out above, migrant workers face a variety of barriers to realizing their rights, and an absence of complaints does not mean an absence of violations (Barnetson 2008, 46). Furthermore, there is clear evidence of widespread violations of Alberta employment law affecting TFWs (AFL 2009,

12; CBC News 2010; Foster and Barnetson 2012, 13). There is no evidence supporting MLAs' assertions that employee or employer ignorance lies at the root of these violations; an equally plausible explanation is that employers' economic interest creates an incentive for violations that are enabled by TFWs' dependence on employers for residency. Substantive response to criticisms of exploitation was limited to minor regulatory adjustments (e.g., restrictions on recruiting fees) and educational initiatives aimed at employers and TFWs (e.g., a TFW "hotline"; AFL 2009, 15).

Employer-friendly labour-market policies are consistent with past Alberta labour policy. It is also a common feature of oil-exporting economies elsewhere, which frequently use large numbers of guest workers (Karl 2007, 24–26). But using invalid narratives to justify employers' use of TFWs may entail political risk for a government that relies upon politically conservative voters for electoral support. It is difficult to substantiate the claim that Conservative Party supporters opposed growth in TFWs, in part because Conservative supporters are not a homogeneous group. Identifiable subgroups include the business community (which has actively supported growth in TFWs) and rural Albertans. Prior to its defeat in 2015, the Conservative Party went out of its way to cater to the interests of its supporters. For example, Conservative MLAs resisted including farm workers within the ambit of occupational health and safety legislation for decades (Barnetson 2009b, 2012b). This suggests that opposition to TFWs may be limited, muted, or both. Political considerations are insufficient for understanding the motivation for the government's strong advocacy for employer recruitment practices that substitute foreign workers for domestic. Further explanation is required.

One explanation is that Alberta's energy and construction sectors are very influential in Alberta politics. Energy is the single largest sector of the economy, responsible for 23.1 percent of GDP in 2013. When combined with finance and real estate and construction (sectors closely linked to energy), these three sectors constituted nearly half of Alberta's economic activity in that year (Alberta, Alberta Innovation and Advanced Education 2015, 6). These employers are some of the most supportive of increasing access to TFWs (Bouzek 2012). Leaders in these sectors have enjoyed direct access to policy makers, continue to have significant political clout, and were successful in ensuring that the Conservative government looked after their interests (Nikiforuk 2008, 159). For example, between 2004 and 2010, the Conservative Party received approximately $15 million in donations (excluding donations made directly to constituency associations). The largest corporate donors were oil and construction companies (Timmons 2012). Such a highly concentrated, organized, and influential capitalist class may be able to compel employer-friendly policy and leave politicians few options for maintaining legitimacy other than specious justifications.

An alternate (but not necessarily mutually exclusive) explanation is that Conservative MLAs viewed the migrant worker issue as relatively nonthreatening. Although there was substantial opposition to the use (and abuse) of TFWs, opponents of TFWs did not mount a credible political threat to the Conservative government. In 2005, petitions opposing expansion of the TFW program, with over five thousand signatures, were tabled in the Alberta legislature (Barnetson and Foster 2014, 355). Yet no meaningful opposition coalesced and the TFW issue played little role in the NDP's electoral success in 2015. Alberta's long-term oil boom meant that domestic workers had full employment and did not broadly view TFWs as a threat.

Research suggests that contradictory responses (particularly among the labour movement) diffused effective opposition (Foster 2014). Some labour leaders, especially those in construction unions, initially framed TFWs as "threats" to Canadian workers, since they undermined Canadians' "right" to "first" choice of jobs. By contrast, other labour leaders and many community groups framed TFWs as "vulnerable" workers needing government protection. These competing narratives and their importance ebbed and flowed over time, but appear to have undermined the political threat that Alberta's already weak and divided labour movement could mount. Prior to the New Democrats' unexpected victory in 2015, the only political threat that has emerged is from the right-wing Wildrose Alliance Party, which has a similar approach to the issue of TFWs as that of the Conservatives and thus is unlikely to raise concerns about the policies.

It may be, then, that the risks associated with increasing TFW numbers were low and the potential rewards were high, thereby emboldening the Conservative government to favour the interests of capital. Whether the New Democratic government will appreciably alter Alberta's approach to TFWs is unclear. Another factor is that those who are most affected (i.e., migrant workers) can't vote. One of the assumptions in the preceding analysis is that the growing use of TFWs reflects an important change in Canadian policy and employer behaviour. Sharma (2006) suggests that this assertion is only true in the short term; a historical examination of migrant labour suggests that Western governments have exploited the labour of noncitizens throughout history, and this may merely be the latest example.

Effects of Growing Migrancy on Democracy

Regardless of its historical origins, the current growth in TFW usage has a number of potentially negative effects for democracy in Alberta. Alberta's workforce was approximately 2.4 million in 2014 (Alberta 2014). There were approximately sixty-eight thousand TFWs in 2012, as seen in table 9.1 above, constituting approximately 3 percent of workers. Including other types of temporary workers (e.g., students and recent graduates, live-in caregivers, agricultural workers, and up to a hundred thousand nonstatus migrant workers) suggests that migrant workers might compose up to 8 percent of the workforce (Canada, Citizenship and Immigration Canada 2013). These workers have no political voice because they are not citizens, and few citizens are advocating for them. Consequently, there are both few political costs to allowing their exploitation and few political rewards for protecting them. As noted by Barnetson and Foster (2014), the Conservative government sought to mitigate the political risks associated with growing migrancy via careful messaging. The drop in oil prices in 2014 did not abate employer demand for TFWs. Changes announced by the federal government in 2014 that were aimed at reducing employer reliance on TFWs were roundly criticized by Alberta employers as not recognizing the significant and long-standing need for migrant labour in the province (Alberta Chambers of Commerce 2014). The reaction of Alberta employers, even during an economic downturn, suggests that Alberta will have a large, vulnerable, and growing group of workers with no political relationship to the state in which they work in the years to come.

Growing use of foreign migrant workers also creates a two-tiered labour market, populated by citizen workers and noncitizen workers. While citizenship forms the official basis of this division, Sharma (2006) suggests that the underlying distinction is racial and racist: those workers with the least labour mobility and the least ability to access employment rights are also disproportionately members of visible ethnic minorities. There are no definitive statistics about the ethnic or racial identities of TFWs and nonstatus migrant workers in Alberta, but large numbers of TFWs come from the Philippines, Mexico, India, South Korea, China, and Taiwan (Alberta 2011b, 16). The implications of this arrangement are troubling.

Justifying the negative experience of TFWs as being based upon their lack of citizenship undermines the notion that there are basic labour and human rights that all governments must meet and enforce. And creating tiers of workers (who bear different rights) opens the door to denying rights on other bases (e.g., cost effectiveness). Furthermore, the growth in TFWs also undermines the ability of Canadian workers to claim their rights. Loosening the labour market allows employers to credibly threaten with replacement any workers who resist employer demands or participate in legitimate union activities. While overt threats of termination for union organizing are illegal, subtle threats of plant closings and layoffs are much harder to police effectively. Indeed, simply the presence of a replacement pool may cause workers to behave in a more compliant manner. A docile labour force may also facilitate further weakening of worker rights. An example of disciplining the labour force by widening the pool of potential workers is the government's move to expand the secondary labour market by making child labour increasingly accessible to employers (Barnetson, this volume).

A subtler effect of growing migrancy is the state's increasing ceding of control over immigration to industry. The expansion of provincial nominee programs (wherein employers nominate workers for permanent residency) means that an increasing portion of newcomers are being selected based upon their utility to industry rather than other factors (e.g., refugee status, non-employment related characteristics, family reunification). Recent changes to the immigration system by the federal government to facilitate the transfer of TFWs to permanent residency and the creation of a new skilled trades class further entrench industry's influence over immigration (Canada, Employment and Social Development 2013). The structure of the TFW program (which restricts immigration applications from within the country and imposes a four-year limit on TFW permits) is consistent with how Gulf oil states and Asian tiger economies have sought to contain migration via programs that intentionally preclude long-term residency and family reunion (Abella 1995; Skeldon 2000). Castles (2006) observes that the long-term success of such policies is unclear, particularly given the historical difficulty governments have had compelling TFWs to leave the country when their work permits expire. Over time, such workers become enmeshed in society and may gain various political and social rights.

Beyond labour policy, the presence of significant numbers of differentially excluded residents weakens social cohesion important for healthy democratic communities. For the migrant workers, their contingent presence in the community and their conflicted community identities (for home and destination communities) weaken their connection to geographic community (Castles and Miller 2009, 3; Vergunst 2009, 264), and their ownership of only partial citizenship rights marginalizes them from important community participation, creating a form of "institutionalized uncertainty" (Anderson 2010, 311). Researchers into social cohesion have argued that this form of marginalization undermines the development of shared values, equal opportunity, trust, and reciprocity that is important in building cohesive communities (Green, Janmaat, and Han 2009; Jenson 2002). Indeed, the presence of TFWs as economic competitors to Canadian workers but without accompanying social and political commonalities can cause permanent residents to see migrant workers as part of the "other" whose interests are in competition to and in conflict with their own, thus undermining any potential for social solidarity (Gibbs 2008).

Conclusion

As expected, Alberta's most recent oil boom triggered a significant influx of migrant workers. Unlike previous booms, however, post-2000 migrants were increasingly likely to be foreign nationals rather than interprovincial migrants. Foreign migrant workers are vulnerable to exploitation because of restrictions on their labour mobility and access to employment rights. While the prevalence of foreign migrant workers has increased throughout Canada, the growth of TFW use in Alberta has been disproportionately high. Alberta's oil economy is at least partly responsible for that increase.

The former Conservative government managed the resulting exploitation of these workers primarily through messaging efforts and, to a lesser extent, by providing minor regulatory improvements. This suggests that the state had adopted the role of defender for employer staffing decisions that disempower and exploit migrant workers and indirectly undermine domestic workers. The creation of an underclass of guest workers has been rapid and has profound implications for democracy.

In a narrow sense, the presence of large numbers of migrant workers possessing only limited citizenship rights weakens the labour power of all workers in the province by thrusting into the labour market a group of highly vulnerable, contingent, and racialized workers. More broadly, the construction of a marginalized class of transnational workers undermines important social and community bonds that form an important part of the democratic fabric.

Furthermore, the use of TFWs, by softening labour shortages caused by rapid expansion of bitumen extraction capacity, deflects public attention away from more fundamental questions regarding Alberta's economic and political priorities. By focusing on TFWs as the "solution" to labour shortages and assuring the permanent population that TFWs pose no threat to Albertans, the former Conservative government neatly sidestepped the thornier debate about the pace of bitumen production and the desirability of building an economy around nonrenewable energy. There is, of course, a wide range of tools at the government's disposal to narrow political debate to issues amenable to the oil industry. The use of TFWs, and the narratives built around them, together serve as one mechanism to constrain public policy debate, at the expense of democracy in the province.

The extensive use of migrant workers in Alberta and the manner in which it was defended by the former Conservative government demonstrated the power and influence of energy corporations on Alberta's economy and politics. It is also an example of the processes employed by the energy industry to entrench, deepen, and solidify its grip on Alberta politics. The construction of a permanent class of contingent, marginalized, racialized migrant workers becomes a necessary part of ensuring docile, reluctant workers who perceive their interests as aligned with those of their multinational employers.

References

Abella, Manolo. 1995. "Asian Migrant and Contract Workers in the Middle East." In *The Cambridge Survey of World Migration*, edited by Robin Cohen, 418–23. Cambridge: Cambridge University Press.

———. 2006. "Policies and Best Practices for Management of Temporary Migration." 9 June. Paper prepared for the International Symposium on International Migration and Development, United Nations Secretariat, Department of Economic and Social Affairs, Population Division, 28–30 June, Turin, Italy.

AFL (Alberta Federation of Labour). 2007. *Temporary Foreign Workers: Alberta's Disposable Workforce*. Edmonton: Alberta Federation of Labour.

———. 2009. *Entrenching Exploitation: The Second Report of the Alberta Federation of Labour Temporary Foreign Worker Advocate*. Edmonton: Alberta Federation of Labour.

———. 2012. "Harper's Low-Wage Agenda Laid Bare with EI Changes." *Alberta Federation of Labour*. Press release, 24 May.

Alberta. 2011a. *2010 Annual Alberta Labour Market Review*.

———. 2011b. *Alberta Immigration Progress Report 2011.* http://work.alberta.ca/documents/immigration-progess-report-2011.pdf.

———. 2014. *Alberta Labour Force Statistics December, 2014.* https://work.alberta.ca/documents/labour-force-stats-Dec14-public-package.pdf.

Alberta. Alberta Innovation and Advanced Education. 2015. *Highlights of the Alberta Economy 2015.* http://www.albertacanada.com/files/albertacanada/SP-EH_highlightsABEconomyPresentation.pdf.

Alberta Chambers of Commerce. 2014. "Immediately Reinstate the TFWP in the Food Sector and Introduce an Effective Enforcement Mechanism Targeting Cases of Program Abuse." Policy brief. http://www.abchamber.ca/files/816.pdf.

Alberta. Finance and Enterprise. 2008. *Economic Spotlight: Measuring Wage Growth in Alberta.* Budget and Fiscal Planning. 21 May. http://www.assembly.ab.ca/lao/library/egovdocs/2008/altd/167225.pdf.

Alberta. Legislative Assembly. 2007. *Hansard.* 26th Legis. , 3rd Sess. 8 March.

———. 2009a. *Hansard.* 27th Legis. , 2nd Sess. 16 March.

———. 2009b. *Hansard.* 27th Legis. , 2nd Sess. 5 May.

Anderson, Bridget. 2010. "Migration, Immigration Controls and the Fashioning of Precarious Workers." *Work, Employment and Society* 24 (2): 300–17.

Anderson, Bridget, and Martin Ruhs. 2012. "Reliance on Migrant Labour: Inevitability or Policy Choice?" *Journal of Poverty and Social Justice* 20 (1): 23–30.

Arthurs, Harry. 2006. *Fairness at Work: Federal Labour Standards for the Twenty-First Century.* Ottawa: Labour Standards Review Commission.

Barnetson, Bob. 2008. "Performance Measures in Alberta's Labour Programming." *Canadian Political Science Review* 2 (1): 35–50.

———. 2009a. "The Regulation of Child and Adolescent Labour in Alberta." *Just Labour* 13: 29–47.

———. 2009b. "The Regulatory Exclusion of Agricultural Workers in Alberta." *Just Labour* 14: 50–74.

———. 2010. "Effectiveness of Complaint-Driven Regulation of Child Labour in Alberta." *Just Labour* 16: 9–24.

———. 2012a. "The Validity of Alberta Safety Statistics." *Just Labour* 19: 1–21.

———. 2012b. "No Right to Be Safe: Justifying the Exclusion of Alberta Farm Workers from Health and Safety Legislations." *Socialist Studies* 8 (2): 132–64.

Barnetson, Bob, and Jason Foster. 2014. "Political Justification of Employment-Related Geographic Mobility in Alberta." *Journal of International Migration and Integration* 15 (2): 349–70.

Basok, Tanya. 2002. *Tortillas and Tomatoes: Transmigrant Mexican Harvesters in Canada.* Montréal and Kingston: McGill-Queen's University Press.

Bauböck, Rainer. 2011. "Temporary Migrants, Partial Citizenship, and Hypermigration." *Critical Review of International Social and Political Philosophy* 14 (5): 665–93.

Bernstein, Stephanie, Katherine Lippel, Eric Tucker, and Leah Vosko. 2006. "Precarious Employment and the Law's Flaws: Identifying Regulatory Failure and Securing Effective Protection for Workers." In *Precarious Employment: Understanding Labour*

Market Insecurity in Canada, edited by Leah Vosko, 203–20. Montréal and Kingston: McGill-Queen's University Press.

Bouzek, Don. 2012. *The Truth About Alberta's Temporary Foreign Worker Project*. Edmonton: Alberta Labour History Institute.

Canada. Auditor General of Canada. 2009. *2009 Fall Report of the Auditor General to the House of Commons*.

Canada. Citizenship and Immigration Canada. 2013. *Canada—Facts and Figures: Immigration Overview, Permanent and Temporary Residents, 2012*. http://publications.gc.ca/collections/collection_2013/cic/Ci1-8-2012-eng.pdf.

Canada. Employment and Social Development Canada. 2013. "Harper Government Announces Reforms to the Temporary Foreign Worker Program—Ensuring Canadians Have First Chance at Available Jobs." News release, 29 April. http://news.gc.ca/web/article-en.do?nid=736729.

———. 2014. *Overhauling the Temporary Foreign Worker Program*. http://www.esdc.gc.ca/eng/jobs/foreign_workers/index.shtml.

Castles, Stephen. 2000. *Ethnicity and Globalization: From Migrant Worker to Transnational Citizen*. London: Sage.

———. 2006. "Back to the Future? Can Europe Meet Its Labour Needs Through Temporary Migration?" Working Paper No. 1. International Migration Institute, University of Oxford.

Castles, Stephen, and Mark J. Miller. 2009. *The Age of Migration: International Population Movements in the Modern World*. 4th ed. New York: Guilford Press.

CBC News. 2010. "Temporary Foreign Workers Treated Poorly, NDP Charges." *CBC News*, 17 March. http://www.cbc.ca/news/canada/edmonton/story/2010/03/17/edmonton-temporary-foreign-workers-ndp-reports.html.

CBSR (Canadian Business for Social Responsibility). 2009. *Stakeholder Relations in the Oil Sands*. Calgary, AB: Canadian Business for Social Responsibility.

Cook, Diane. 2007. "Piecing Together the Labour Puzzle." *Alberta Construction Magazine*, May.

Crompton, Susan, and Michael Vickers. 2000. "One Hundred Years of Labour Force." *Canadian Social Trends* (Summer): 1–13.

Crowley, Helen, and Mary J. Hickman. 2008. "Migration, Postindustrialism, and the Globalized Nation State: Social Capital and Social Cohesion Re-examined." *Ethnic and Racial Studies* 31 (7): 1222–44.

Daniels, Roger. 1981. *Concentration Camps, North America: Japanese in the United States and Canada During World War II*. Malabar, FL: R. E. Krieger.

Danysk, Cecilia. 1995. *Hired Hands: Labour and the Development of Prairie Agriculture, 1880–1930*. Toronto: University of Toronto Press.

De Guerre, Katherine. 2009. *Temporary Foreign Workers in Alberta's Oil Sector*. Brighton, UK: Sussex Centre for Migration Research, University of Sussex.

Edmonston, Barry. 2011. "Internal Migration." In *The Changing Canadian Population*, edited by Barry Edmonston and Eric Wai-Ching Fong, 190–206. Montréal and Kingston: McGill-Queen's University Press.

Farney, James, and Bohdan S. Kordan. 2005. "The Predicament of Belonging: The Status of Enemy Aliens in Canada, 1914." *Journal of Canadian Studies* 39 (1): 74–89.

Ferguson, Nelson. 2011. "From Coal Pits to Tar Sands: Labour Migration Between an Atlantic Canadian Region and the Athabasca Oil Sands." *Just Labour* 17: 106–18.

Finkel, Alvin. 1989. *The Social Credit Phenomenon in Alberta*. Toronto: University of Toronto Press.

———, ed. *Working People in Alberta: A History*. Edmonton, AB: Athabasca University Press.

Foster, Jason. 2007. "Labour, Climate Changes and Alberta's Oil Sands: In the Belly of the Beast." *Our Times* 26 (2). http://ourtimes.ca/Features/article_19.php.

———. 2012a. "Making Temporary Permanent: The Silent Transformation of the Temporary Foreign Worker Program." *Just Labour* 19: 22–46.

———. 2012b. "Revolution, Retrenchment, and the New Normal: The 1990s and Beyond." In Finkel, *Working People in Alberta*, 205–42.

———. 2014. "From 'Canadians First' to 'Workers Unite': Evolving Union Narratives Related to Temporary Foreign Workers." *Relations Industrielles / Industrial Relations* 69 (2): 241–65.

Foster, Jason, and Bob Barnetson. 2012. "Justice for Janitors in Alberta: The Impact of Temporary Foreign Workers on an Organizing Campaign." *Journal of Workplace Rights* 13 (1): 3–30.

Foster, Jason, and Alison Taylor. 2011. "Permanent Temporary-ness: Temporary Foreign Workers in Alberta's Construction Trades." Presentation at the annual conference of the Canadian Industrial Relations Association, 2–4 June, Fredericton, New Brunswick.

Fudge, Judy, and Fiona MacPhail. 2009. "The Temporary Foreign Worker Program in Canada: Low-Skilled Workers as an Extreme Form of Flexible Labour." *Comparative Labor Law and Policy Journal* 31 (1): 101–41.

Gereluk, Winston. 2012. "Alberta Labour in the 1980s." In Finkel, *Working People in Alberta*, 173–204.

Gibbs, Holly. 2008. "Social Cohesion, International Competitiveness, and the 'Other': A Connected Comparison of Workers' Relationships in Canada and Mexico." *Solidarity First: Canadian Workers and Social Cohesion*, edited by Robert O'Brien, 38–62. Vancouver: University of British Columbia Press.

Green, Andy. 2004. "Is Relocation Redundant? Observations on the Changing Nature and Impacts of Employment-Related Geographical Mobility in the UK." *Regional Studies* 38 (6): 629–41.

Green, Andy, Germen Janmaat, and Christine Han. 2009. "Regimes of Social Cohesion." Centre for Learning and Life Chances in Knowledge Economies and Societies. Research Paper No. 1. Institute of Education, London, UK.

Gross, Dominique. 2010. "Temporary Foreign Workers in Canada: Does a Policy with Short-Term Purpose Have a Long-Term Impact on Unemployment?" *Canadian Issues / Thèmes Canadiens* (Spring): 107–11.

Gross, Dominique, and Nicolas Schmitt. 2010. "Temporary Foreign Workers and the Persistence of Regional Labor Market Disparities." Metropolis BC Working Paper No. 09-05.

Hiller, Harry H. 2009. *Second Promised Land: Migration to Alberta and the Transformation of Canadian Society*. Montréal and Kingston: McGill-Queen's University Press.

Holland, Kenneth M. 2007. "A History of Chinese Immigration in the United States and Canada." *American Review of Canadian Studies* 37 (2): 150–60.

Hsiung, Ping-Chun, and Katherine Nichol. 2010. "Policies on and the Experiences of Foreign Domestic Workers in Canada." *Sociology Compass* 4 (9): 766–78.

"Interview with the Honourable Jason Kenney, Minister of Citizenship, Immigration, and Multiculturalism." 2010. *Canadian Issues / Thèmes Canadiens* (Spring): 10–13.

Jenson, Jane. 2002. "Social Cohesion in Canada and Europe: The Same or Different?" Presentation at Queen's University, Kingston, ON, 14 May. http://www.cprn.org/documents/28983_en.pdf.

Karl, Terry Lynn. 2007. "Oil-Led Development: Social, Political, and Economic Consequences." CDDRL Working Papers No. 90, Stanford University, January. http://cddrl.fsi.stanford.edu/sites/default/files/No_80_Terry_Karl_-_Effects_of_Oil_Development.pdf.

Laliberte, Ron. 2006. "The 'Grab-a-Hoe' Indians: The Canadian State and the Procurement of Aboriginal Labour for the Southern Alberta Sugar Beet Industry." *Prairie Forum* 31 (2): 305–24.

Laliberte, Ron, and Vic Satzewich. 1999. "Native Migrant Labour in the Southern Alberta Sugar-Beet Industry: Coercion and Paternalism in the Recruitment of Labour." *Canadian Review of Sociology and Anthropology* 36 (1): 65–85.

LaRochelle-Côté, Sébastien, and Jason Gilmore. 2009. "Canada's Employment Downturn." *Perspectives on Labour and Income* 10 (12): 5–12.

Martin, Philip. 2003. *Managing Labor Migration: Temporary Worker Programs for the Twenty-First Century*. Geneva: International Institute for Labour Studies.

Mech, Michele. 2011. *A Comprehensive Guide to the Alberta Oil Sands*. Green Party of Canada. http://www.greenparty.ca/sites/greenparty.ca/files/attachments/a_comprehensive_guide_to_the_alberta_oil_sands_-_may_20111.pdf.

Nakache, Delphine, and Paula Kinoshita. 2010. *The Canadian Temporary Foreign Worker Program: Do Short-Term Economic Needs Prevail over Human Rights Concerns?* Study No. 5, Institute for Research on Public Policy, Montréal.

Nikiforuk, Andrew. 2008. *Tar Sands: Dirty Oil and the Future of a Continent*. Vancouver: Greystone Books.

Ontario. Auditor General. 2004. *Annual Report of the Auditor General*.

Otero, Gerardo, and Kerry Preibisch. 2010. *Farm Worker Health and Safety: Challenges for British Columbia*. Research report for WorkSafe BC. http://www.sfu.ca/~otero/docs/Otero-and-Preibisch-Final-Nov-2010.pdf.

Pastor, Manuel, and Susan Alva. 2004. "Guest Workers and the New Transnationalism: Possibilities and Realities in an Age of Repression." *Social Justice* 31 (1–2): 92–112.

PC (Progressive Conservative) Party. 2012. *Alberta by Design: Election Platform 2012*. Edmonton: PC Alberta.

Selby, Jim. 2012. "One Step Forward: Alberta Workers, 1885–1914." In Finkel, *Working People in Alberta*, 39–76.

Sharma, Nandita. 2006. *Home Economics: Nationalism and the Making of "Migrant Workers" in Canada*. Toronto: University of Toronto Press.

———. 2007. "Freedom to Discriminate: A National State Sovereignty and Temporary Migrant Workers in Canada." In *Citizenship and Immigrant Incorporation*, edited by Godke Yurdakul and Y. Michal Bodemann, 163–83. New York: Palgrave Macmillan.

Skeldon, Ronald. 2000. "Trends in International Migration in the Asian and Pacific Region." *International Social Science Journal* 165: 369–82.

Statistics Canada. 2015. *Table 282-0086: Labour Force Survey Estimates (LFS), Supplementary Unemployment Rates by Sex and Age Group, Annual (Rate)*. CANSIM (database). http://www5.statcan.gc.ca/cansim/a26?lang=eng&id=2820086.

Temple Newhook, Julia, Barb Neis, Lois Jackson, Sharon R. Roseman, Paula Romanow, and Chrissy Vincent. 2011. "Employment-Related Mobility and the Health of Workers, Families, and Communities: The Canadian Context." *Labour / Le Travail* 67: 121–55.

Thompson, John H. 1978. "Bringing in the Sheaves: The Harvest Excursionists, 1890–1928." *Canadian Historical Review* 58 (4): 467–98.

Thompson, John H. , and Allen Seager. 1978. "Workers, Growers, and Monopolists: The 'Labour Problem' in the Alberta Beet Sugar Industry During the 1930s." *Labour / Le Travailleur* 3: 153–74.

Timmons, Lucas. 2012. "Political Donations from 2004 to 2010 or, Man, People Love Giving Money to the Tories." *Edmonton Journal*, 23 March.

Trumper, Ricardo, and Lloyd L. Wong. 2011. "Temporary Workers in Canada: A National Perspective." *Canadian Themes / Thèmes Canadiens* (Spring): 83–89.

Tucker, Eric. 1990. *Administering Danger in the Workplace: The Law and Politics of Occupational Health and Safety Regulation in Ontario, 1850–1914*. Toronto: University of Toronto Press.

Valiani, Salimah. 2009. "The Shift in Canadian Immigration Policy and Unheeded Lessons of the Live-in Caregiver Program." Independent research, Ottawa.

Vanderklippe, Nathan. 2011. "Gearing Up for a New Labour Crunch." *Globe and Mail*, 22 May.

Vergunst, Petra. 2009. "Whose Socialisation? Exploring the Social Interaction Between Migrants and Communities-of-Place in Rural Areas." *Population, Space, and Place* 15 (3): 253–66.

Vosko, Leah. 2006. "Precarious Employment: Towards an Improved Understanding of Labour Market Insecurity." In *Precarious Employment: Understanding Labour Market Insecurity in Canada*, edited by Leah Vosko, 3–42. Montréal and Kingston: McGill-Queen's University Press.

———. 2010. *Managing the Margins: Gender, Citizenship, and the International Regulation of Precarious Employment*. New York: Oxford University Press.

Warman, Casey. 2009. "The Earning Outcomes of Temporary Foreign Workers in Canada." Working paper. Kingston, ON: Queen's University, Economics Department.

Weil, David, and Amanda Pyles. 2005. "Why Complain? Complaints, Compliance, and the Problem of Enforcement in the US Workplace." *Comparative Labor Law and Policy Journal* 27 (1): 59–92.

Whitaker, Reginald. 1987. *Double Standard: The Secret History of Canadian Immigration.* Toronto: Lester and Orpen Dennys.

Wilkinson, Mick. 2012. "Out of Sight, Out of Mind: The Exploitation of Migrant Workers in Twenty-First-Century Britain." *Journal of Poverty and Social Justice* 20 (1): 13–21.

Wong, Lloyd L. 1984. "Canada's Guestworkers: Some Comparisons of Temporary Workers in Europe and North America." *International Migration Review* 18 (1): 85–98.

Gendering Energy Extraction in Fort McMurray

Sara Dorow

"You know us for oil," begins one of the advertisements. "Our story is one of production and money. But . . . there's a quality of life here that goes beyond money, giving people the confidence to build a future, to raise a family." Above the text, an image of a young boy high in a swing is superimposed over a line graph titled "Growth in Domestic Product." Another of the ads, with the heading "Fort McMurray, Indicators of Energy Performance," avers that "energy is more than a commodity; it's our way of life." The accompanying image superimposes a youthful female dancer over one section of a pie chart. In these two ads, in a few deft strokes, productive work and reproductive life are closely co-defined: oil wealth converts to familial and community riches, and energy translates as the "spirit of our people."

These advertisements were part of the Big Spirit campaign launched in fall 2007 by the Regional Municipality of Wood Buffalo (RMWB), the nearly seventy-thousand-square-kilometre municipality that sits atop the vast Athabasca bitumen sands formation in northern Alberta, at the centre of which lies the "urban service area" of Fort McMurray. The campaign's articulation of energy with community spirit echoes branding in the oil-rich province as a whole. In April 2010, for example, the Canadian Association of Petroleum Producers (CAPP) and a coalition of Alberta-based businesses announced Alberta Is Energy, "a community-building initiative to raise awareness about the important role the oil and gas industry plays in the lives of Albertans" (CAPP 2010).

Attempts to promote the quality-of-life benefits of the energy economy emanate from both public and private entities, reinforcing the importance of questions about oil, democracy, and the "resource curse" in the Global North. But these promotional discourses and representations also cry out for an analysis of the gendered infrastructure of a political economy built on oil. The Big Spirit campaign was, in part, a direct response to the negative reputation Fort McMurray had gained as a barely liveable boomtown of raucous single men who allegedly partied away money earned from plentiful work for the short time they were there, especially as the bitumen sands mega-program took off in the early years of the twenty-first century. Central to the message of the ad campaign was the notion that Fort McMurray is in fact a family-friendly place, a good place to raise kids, a place of multiple opportunities for leisure and community, and thus a place to which people might want to move. Central to the message of this chapter is the idea that feminized spaces of work and citizenship provide an important material and discursive link between oil energy and community energy (see also O'Shaughnessy 2011, and see Mercier and Gier 2009 for a historical overview of the gendering of resource extraction economies); in other words, gendered practices—along with assumptions of normative kinship—are integral to the extractive work that makes the bitumen sands region an economic engine of Canada.

Just as the term *energy* does double duty in public relations for the RMWB, so does the term *extraction* do double duty for my argument. First, it signals that the business of extracting northern Alberta bitumen—the tarry substance that is mined or coaxed (with pressure, steam, and chemicals) out of the third-largest known source of oil on the planet—is itself directly gendered. The male-dominated work of construction, mining, and engineering combines with a masculinized logic of northern development to shape a form of "frontier masculinity" (Miller 2004; O'Shaughnessy 2011). As one long-time oil industry administrator put it to me, "There really is an energy here and it's almost a male energy; it's kind of . . . I don't want to fall into any of the Alberta clichés but it is a place where you think that you can do anything and get things done." Second, extraction refers to how multiple forms of less visible gendered work both directly and indirectly supplement oil profits. In this view, gender inequities are not (only) side effects of the energy economy (Ross 2008) but are integral to the broad social arrangements that allow for wealth accumulation. Such an analysis is all the more urgent given the increased promotion of an active, self-sufficient citizenship that is touted as "gender neutral" in official Canadian discourse (Brodie 2008) even as it continues to rely on gendered hierarchies of labour, care, and family. A 7 January 2014 *Edmonton Journal* article on life for men and women in Fort McMurray, for example, highlights a gender-transcendent pioneering spirit while also celebrating "moms pushing strollers."[1]

By work, I mean to refer to all forms of work, paid and unpaid, and to the slippery relations between them. The ethnographic evidence I discuss in this chapter, drawn from dozens of interviews and a survey of more than fifty parents and nannies, all conducted in the bitumen sands region from 2007 to 2009, starts with the work of child care but connects and extends to examples of voluntarism, familism (a hyperemphasis on the social centrality of family), consumerism, and paid labour in multiple sectors.[2] A "social reproduction feminism" (SRF) framework understands these productive and reproductive activities to be of a piece and sees the logics governing these two arenas as integrally related (Ferguson 2008, 45). "Economy" and "work" are thus expanded to encompass not only the marketplace of paid work and production but also the social reproductive activities that provide individuals with the social and physical sustenance and care that they need (Luxton 2006). As Cindi Katz (2001, 710) puts it, "Social reproduction is the fleshy, messy, and indeterminate stuff of everyday life. It is also a set of structured practices that unfolds in dialectical relation with production, with which it is mutually constitutive and in tension."

The SRF approach has also emphasized the importance of intersectionality, the idea that unequal relations of race, class, age, and sexuality are not just relevant but crucial to the gendered dynamics of work (Arat-Koc 2006; Ferguson 2008). Rachel Simon-Kumar (2011, 458) even argues that "class, age, and ethnicity are more likely to throw light on the current modalities of gender relations within contemporary forms of Western democracy" than are dichotomies of male-female or masculine-feminine. In the context of the high levels of domestic and global labour mobility that mark the northern oil economy of Fort McMurray, seeing the various ways in which gender articulates with race, class, and age is imperative to understanding forms of inclusion and exclusion. Women and visible minorities, many of whom are noncitizens (most notably, participants in the Temporary Foreign Worker Program), are overrepresented in the feminized, precarious, and invisible work of service, retail, and care in Fort McMurray. And while this is true of the global division of labour more generally, bitumen extraction and production shape and sometimes intensify these inequalities in particular ways.

Indeed, the particular character of the bitumen sands region as a work destination is critical to understanding both intersectional modalities and gendered dichotomies. The population of the Regional Municipality of Wood Buffalo (RMWB) grew from over forty thousand to approximately a hundred thousand in the booming first decade of the century (RMWB 2012), and according to Statistics Canada, it had the highest median family income in the nation in 2010, at $169,790 (Statistics Canada 2012). Yet this is also a highly mobile population—the 2011 National Household Survey found that two-thirds of the sixty thousand permanent residents (an undercounted population) had lived somewhere else five years previous (Statistics Canada 2011c), and according to the 2012 RMWB municipal census, one-third of the total population in the region were mobile workers with permanent residence elsewhere (17). This mobility cannot be chalked up solely to the short-term need for high numbers of fly-in, fly-out construction workers. High housing costs, relative isolation at the "end of the highway," the uncertainties of oil boom and bust, and the social stresses and frenetic pace that accompany boom times all contribute to high levels of turnover and low levels of retention in the workforce. In short, while Fort McMurray is home to many people who have lived there for decades or generations, it is largely a place to *work*, a place to make money while you can. That "people are just working, working, working to make money, money, money," as one interviewee put it, was one of the most consistent themes in my interviews. The effect of this working frenzy on time and consumerism was a key concern for many interviewees, as they watched the relentless pursuit of the "good life" promised by high wages, overtime hours, and long shifts.

The gendered practices that supplement the production of oil are complicated by a combination of two factors: the burgeoning economy that makes Fort McMurray a place of employment opportunity for both men and women and the special premium that both government and industry place on family-oriented social life for attracting and keeping workers in the area. Alberta's brand of late neoliberalism contributes to this sharpened yet depoliticized set of gendered relations. As in the rest of Canada and other parts of the Global North, the devolution of social responsibility onto families and local communities contributes to the reproduction of gendered inequalities (Gazso 2009; Harder 2006), while the valorization of the productive entrepreneurial subject both de- and re-genders subjectivity (Simon-Kumar 2011). In some ways, the resource extraction economy of Alberta intensifies "the neoliberal and social conservative threads [in Canada] which simultaneously cast gender as being irrelevant and wives and mothers as critical to the reproduction of families, family values, and society" (Brodie 2008, 160–61). And this in a province with a history of political inattention to issues affecting women, as the Parkland Institute and the Alberta College of Social Workers reported in 2012: "Alberta is the only jurisdiction in Canada without a minister or advisory council responsible for the status of women. Alberta is alone in having no mechanisms for gender analysis of social and economic policy, or even a council acting in an advisory capacity to government" (2).

Gendered Work in Fort McMurray: A Snapshot of Paid Work

The gendered picture of paid work in the RMWB (more than 90% of whose residents are in Fort McMurray) during the boom that began in the early 2000s is especially pertinent, given the combination of high median incomes and high labour shortages that have marked this period. According to the 2011 National Household Survey, both male and female employment rates among residents in the RMWB were higher than in the province as a whole: 88.3 percent for males and 68.6 percent for females, compared to 74.6 percent and 63.4 percent for the province, and there is a higher percentage of women employed in trades and transportation than in Alberta or Canada (Statistics Canada 2011a, 2011b, 2011c).[3] These statistics seem to support Ross's finding (2008, 121) that in countries with large and diverse economies (like Norway and Australia), women are not as likely to be crowded out of employment in an oil and gas economy.

However, this story deserves further unpacking. First, consider that in 2011 nearly one-third of the resident labour force in the RMWB census area worked in "trades, transport and equipment operators and related occupations," and 90 percent of those workers were men (Statistics Canada 2011c).[4] Thus, the preponderance of images of women donning hard hats in oil industry ads and billboards is, ironically, more a reflection of the work that female bodies do to publicly produce the idea of inclusive economic participation than of the reality of work on the ground. Second, while women and visible minorities are overrepresented in the sales and service industry throughout Canada and much of the Global North, the percentage of these precarious jobs occupied by women was actually higher in the region than in Alberta or Canada as a whole. An increasing percentage of workers in this sector have come to Fort McMurray under the Temporary Foreign Worker Program, which, according to a 2011 provincial government report, grew sixfold between 2000 and 2010 (Woo-Paw 2011).[5]

These realities only begin to explain the gendered landscape of employment and income in Fort McMurray. The 2011 National Household Survey showed that among those over fifteen years of age with any income, the percentages of both men and women working full-year, full-time were almost double that in the province of Alberta (Statistics Canada 2011a, 2011c)—so, everyone is working more. However, income differences are striking. Median earnings for men in the RMWB were almost three times those of women, and were still more than twice as high when we consider only those individuals working full-year, full-time (see table 10.1). This is considerably more of a gap than in the province as a whole, which already has one of the highest gender wage gaps in Canada.[6]

Table 10.1. Median Earnings for Men and Women in RMWB and Alberta

		R.M. of Wood Buffalo		Alberta	
		Men	Women	Men	Women
Number of individuals	Persons 15 years and over with income	28,900	22,605	1,386,310	1,364,430
	Persons 15 years and over working full-year, full-time	25,410 (87.9%)	14,515 (64.2%)	670,880 (48.4%)	462,405 (33.9%)
Median annual income	Persons 15 years and over with income	$112,966	$39,648	$47,110	$27,769
	Persons 15 years and over working full-year, full-time	$137,422	$64,337	$63,635	$46,698

Source: 2011 National Household Survey profiles for the Regional Municipality of Wood Buffalo and for Alberta (Statistics Canada 2011a, 2011c).

These numbers underscore the almost mundane and tautological point that oil economies favour male employment because of the full-time, high-wage, male-dominated jobs available (cf. Ross 2008). However, that this is true even in an environment of work shortages and high housing costs demands that we look further. And looking further, we see how the political and cultural economy of the bitumen sands shapes gendered, raced, and classed arrangements of work in ways that supplement this extractive economy.

Child Care: A Window on Gendered Work

The work of child care, both paid and unpaid, is an instructive place to launch an examination of the arrangements of production and social reproduction—the gendered forms of "energy"—that supplement the oil economy. Like Alberta as a whole, Fort McMurray faces a child care shortage. And as in other boom-towns (Gillespie 2007), inadequate child care provision is further exacerbated by employment turnover and competition from attainable higher-paying work, driving up the cost of child care. Even though the province dedicated new funding to child care in Fort McMurray in 2009 and 2010, the municipality's website continued to advise that "child care in Fort McMurray is among the most expensive in the province" and that "it is important to plan ahead for child care before moving, as there are often waiting lists."[7] As one long-time resident put it during an interview in 2007,

> For all these families who come here, most of them have two people working. Where are the kids supposed to go? We need somebody to invest in daycare . . . And then how do you staff the daycare? . . . And then how can they [daycare staff] afford to live here when they make $14 an hour, let's say. They can't afford to live here. So you know it's a vicious circle of how do you meet the needs of these families and these individuals who are coming to Fort McMurray. There is so much pressure, it's like a pressure cooker.

This comment, like much of the data we gathered from dozens of interviews, as well as from a face-to-face survey of fifty-four parents and nannies at two sites of The HUB Family Resource Centre in Fort McMurray, suggests that gendered decisions and practices of child care include but go beyond the more general problem of limited provision and high cost of day homes and child care centres, to the very structures and cultures of the bitumen sands economy: pace, growth, overtime and shift work, ramped-up cost of living, and the promise of opportunity to live the good life.[8]

Time, "Good Jobs," and the Flexibilized Fort McMurray Woman

The frenetic and constant pace of bitumen production translates into round-the-clock shift work, work schedules like "ten days on and four off," lots of necessary and/or available overtime, and long commute times out to site and back. In this context, complained the spouse of an oil industry professional, "as much as the companies certainly say, 'Balanced life, that's what we want,' there's certainly that dichotomy between 'Make sure you're staying healthy and not working too much' but 'Could you come in and work tomorrow?'" These spatial-temporal particularities of paid work in the bitumen sands zone intensify the gendered experience of "flexibilization": women adjusting paid and unpaid work to accommodate the contradictory demands of economy and society in heteronormative, liberal democracies (Luxton 2006; Thorin 2001). First, time and distance between the city and the oil sites prompted some women to take jobs in town to be closer to home and children (see also Leach 1999).[9] This included women who at one point had worked in the oil industry. One woman, referring to commuting time, said,

> It started to get almost an hour now, each way. And I just felt that, you know, my time was best served in town. If one of us was working at the plant sites, that was fine: one could be in town with the son and one could be at the plant site. So I focused my careers, all my little careers, in town.

A second form of flexibilization entailed women taking a paid job that worked around a male partner's schedule in the oil patch. Often this was part-time work found in public, nonprofit, or service industry employment in town, given the relative dearth of part-time work with the oil companies themselves. One of these women told me, "I've been able to choose my hours and that has enabled me to work around my husband's schedule [at site]. . . . I'm able to work on one of the days that my husband has off."

These decisions were shaped in part by the lack of child care facilities and options. Indeed, half of the women we surveyed at The HUB in early 2009 who were not engaged in any kind of paid work indicated that a major contributing factor was that child care was unaffordable or unavailable; this included a lack of child care outside of standard work hours. With so much shift work and overtime and long commute times, this is an especially acute problem (Preston et al. 2000; O'Shaughnessy 2011). It is even more acute for people who do not have extended family in the area, which is typical because Fort McMurray is a relatively remote work destination. Several women we talked to counted themselves very "lucky" that their own mothers lived in town and could provide child care; in a couple of cases, older women had left their own lucrative jobs in the oil industry to look after grandchildren whose parents did not have such good jobs.

A "good job" in Fort McMurray usually translates as a job in the higher-paying oil industry, and this has further implications for the gendered distribution of child care in heterosexual families, especially given its cost. One young mother said that "things would be different"—namely, that her family would be able to afford the leeway for her to participate in some kind of paid work— if her husband had a job in the oil sands. Because he worked in less lucrative employment, when they weighed the cost of child care against the "extra" income she would make in a paid job, it made more financial sense for her to do the unpaid work of child care. Even when people who worked in nonindustry jobs (such as education, government, social services, etc.) began to receive an extra cost-of-living allowance (implemented in 2007 and 2008), their salaries were still not enough to cover the cost of housing and child care. A firefighter's wife told me that with the already high cost of housing, paying for daycare was just not a viable option, so she did the child care and then worked part-time on her husband's day off. "Lots of women are doing that," she said, and, with a shrug of her shoulders, added, "That's just the way it is."

This nexus of productive and reproductive work supplements the extractive needs of oil capital through both gendered and classed arrangements. To begin with, a "good job" is itself not just a matter of pay but also of time, and these were quite different for people in trades versus professional jobs in the oil industry. A retired professional summed up one class difference:

> [At the lower levels] you work fourteen hours, you get paid about six hours overtime, that's a lot of money... [Maybe] your wife is doing the same and you are working night and day, night and day. So it's the money is what is inviting that. To the professionals, they don't pay overtime so you go in the morning and you come [home] in the afternoon. That's it. So you are home every night and even if you are a little late, you're here at six or seven.

The desire and/or demand for overtime among men (and the limited number of women) who work in trades and construction combine with women's "flexibility" to deepen gendered arrangements. In many families where the father worked in the trades and the mother did part-time or no paid work, there was talk of adjusting to "daddy time"—when daddy returned for a few days after working out at site for a week or two, or longer. One long-time child care professional in the region noted that couples might not be able to find time together "because they can't afford child care or it's nonexistent, so somebody's doing a part-time job, so every second that daddy's off work he's at home because mommy's going to do something." One of the few fathers at The HUB with whom we spoke described a stressful transition each time he came off of five twelve-hour days in a row. "But what are you going to do, you have to work," he said.

"You have to work" becomes a masculinized ethos that contributes to seeing women's flexibilized labour as "just the way it is." In this instance, in this context, the gendering of social reproduction is seemingly naturalized by the demands of the particular political economy of paid work. But then, "you have to work" also attaches itself to the different versions of the "good life" promised by the neoliberal oil economy.

The Opportunity for the "Good Life": Family Values and the Fast Track

If neoliberalism valorizes the economic (productive-consumptive) citizen and at the same time reproduces the gendered norms of responsibility for family and community, this has particular effects on child care and other social reproductive work in Fort McMurray, where oil production promises opportunity. We might think of the promise of plentiful work in the energy economy and of the ability to translate it into the "good life" as a corollary to the "rentier effect" (Ross 2001)—that is, it may dampen not only broader political challenges but also challenges to gender inequities. In Fort McMurray, this translates into a network of gendered arrangements that variously support the opportunity to exercise family values and/or to get on the fast track to a handsome income.

The coupling of traditional family-based values and female-based community work constitutes one version of the good life promised by oil. Sometimes, this was narrated as a slowing down of the frenetic cycle of work, money, and consumption in which the oil boom catches people. As one long-time resident put it, "Some people sacrifice living a lifestyle where they have more stuff, I guess, where they do keep one parent home. Like, there are women here who stay home." A handful of women we interviewed and surveyed said that their families consciously had chosen to move to Fort McMurray because their husbands' jobs in the oil industry allowed them to be stay-at-home moms. In other words, the opportunity of high-paying jobs for men provided the opportunity to play out a conventional gendered division of labour.[10] Some of these same women were also active volunteers in the community. If in the late neoliberal state "there has been greater involvement of citizenship participation and community partnerships in the formulation and delivery of policy and services," this is still to some degree feminized work (Simon-Kumar 2011, 42; see also Luxton 2006). But in Fort McMurray, there is a particular premium on volunteer time: while voluntarism is essential to providing the "community energy" touted in the Big Spirit ads, the dominance of paid work and a relative shortage of retired people and women with "extra" time squeezes social reproductive time for volunteering, giving it all the more currency as a component of the good life.

While this first version of the good life sacrifices money for time, a second version, in which both male and female spouses participated in full-time (plus overtime) paid work to maximize the monetary benefits of the boom, sacrifices time for money. These benefits were often signalled through conspicuous consumption, such as investments in a home (and by default, an expensive one), sun-destination vacations, adult toys like a new truck or boat, and shopping trips to larger cities to acquire the latest consumer goods or children's toys. One source of social anxiety was the concern about overworked parents substituting hard cash or extravagant toys for quality time with children and family: as one interviewee recalled, "Our kids were telling us that among their peers, both of [their parents] work tremendous overtime and they get a lot of money and they don't spend time with the kids . . . [instead] they opened their wallet full of money."

This sacrifice of time for money seemed to apply whether the families of individual oil industry workers were in Fort McMurray or far away; in both cases, time spent in paid work was maximized to fast-track monetary provisions for family. For some, this meant deferring fulfillment of the first kind of "good life" (time for family and leisure) into some unknown time in the future, usually in some other place (Dorow and Dogu 2011). It also entailed the commodification of social reproductive work, revealing the globalized intersections of race, class, and gender that supplement the fast track to individual income and corporate profit.

Stratified Social Reproduction and the Global Service Economy

Exchanging earnings for paid child care is perhaps an obvious response for full-time dual-earner families, especially for people in middle- and upper-class forms of work. But these practices of stratified reproduction (Colen 1995) also highlight the reality that as highly educated women in liberal democracies find it easier to compete alongside men for better paid jobs (McDowell 2006) and as neoliberal governance places particular labouring bodies in differentiated global spaces (Ferguson 2008), we see new kinds of classed and raced divides among women. Life in the heart of bitumen production adds a couple of twists to this scenario. First, in a good number of well-off dual-earner families in Fort McMurray, two people are earning $30 or more an hour working in construction and other trades. Second, if one can afford child care at all, hiring a live-in nanny is especially attractive given not only limited and expensive day care but also exorbitant housing costs. In this context, the "savings" of an extra room in the house more than offset the $10 per hour wages for a live-in caregiver.

One-quarter of the fifty-four people we surveyed at The HUB were nannies, all of them Filipina. While exact numbers on live-in caregivers in Fort McMurray are hard to obtain, the number of Filipina nannies alone is in the hundreds. In almost all of their cases, one or both of their employers worked in the oil industry, with about half in administration or professional jobs and the other half in the trades. One of the mothers we interviewed at The HUB was on maternity leave but planned to hire a live-in caregiver when she returned to her engineering job—part of a larger plan to stay in Fort McMurray for another five years and save for her and her husband's early retirement.

This story highlights the ways in which live-in caregivers supplement the tradeoffs of time and money discussed above. Most poignantly, they absorb the social reproductive time that allows their employers to work odd and extra hours. One child care professional averred that shift workers preferred to hire nannies "because of their long hours. Because they don't have time for the housework when they get home so isn't it nice to come home and have some supper happening that somebody [else prepared] . . . Filipina nannies are the oil sands workers' solution because they'll clean the house, too." A subsequent survey conducted in 2014 with live-in caregivers in Fort McMurray corroborated that they work longer on average than local trades workers and often perform household duties outside of the scope of their contracts; long hours and extra duties are more pronounced among those caregivers whose employers work in the oil industry (Dorow, Cassiano, and Doerksen 2015).

This can turn into a gendered chain of increasing "surplus value," as described by two nannies interviewed together:

Vicky: [My] focus is on the child. And if you have time, you can cook, you can clean everything. But in my case my employer is a teacher, the lady. And because the guy is six days on, six days off [out at site], with the night shift and the day shift, so it's difficult . . . she doesn't have time so I will prepare supper for us because she's tired working . . .

Interviewer: It would be very difficult to have a family life working six days on, six days off and night shifts.

Vicky: So far I don't have [both of the parents doing] that.

Mia: Because if they [both] work six days on, six days off, you're
                working twenty-four hours.

Vicky: You're making good money for them.

Filipina nannies are part of the flexibilized and feminized global labour
force (Cohen 1994; Piper 2008) that articulates the reproductive and productive
sides of the oil economy. Many people on other types of foreign worker permits work in the local retail, service, and hospitality sectors of Fort McMurray
and in the outlying work camps, all of which have boomed because of oil. These
foreign workers do the commodified reproductive work of keeping industry
workers fed, housed, groomed, and entertained. They are largely visible minority and officially "unskilled" people, although many of them have degrees in
fields like human resources, accounting, or education. And while their wages
are often higher than in other places, this is offset by high housing costs and is
limited by contracts that tie them to specific employers and that prohibit many
of them from bringing families to Canada or applying for permanent residency
(Foster 2012). Also overrepresented in service jobs are other visible minority
groups, including people who came as refugees or immigrants to Canada.

Interviews with employers in restaurants, big box stores, and cleaning services in Fort McMurray revealed ways in which the particularities of the oil
economy intensify intersecting inequalities of race, gender, and class for this
global, flexibilized work force. To begin with, many such employers had begun
importing labour because of a lack of some of the usual labour pools, which,
combined with an abundance of better-paying work (such as in the bitumen
sands), created constant turnover and a desperate search for workers. A big box
store manager lamented that with so many fly-in, fly-out male workers, "you
don't have the stay-at-home mom or the teenagers or whatever to come to the
workforce. Just the dads. And they still want all the services in town but they
don't supply anything [to the sector by] bringing their families." Given these
shortages, this employer had instituted an extra-ordinary "mommy shift" cor-
responding to school and daycare hours in Fort McMurray in order to attract
mothers to apply; he had also hired many immigrant women.

While the plenitude of retail and service work in Fort McMurray creates
an employment "opportunity" for immigrant and foreign workers, the boom-
and-bust cycle creates its own hierarchical and racialized employment cycle.
One employer, for example, told us that the downturn of late 2008 allowed his
store the time to conduct proper screening and interviewing, which meant they

could hire more "locals" who spoke fluent English; some of these were people who had been laid off from the oil industry and were working in the store as a stop-gap measure until oil prices and investments rose again.

Gendered Energy and Democratic Equality

Globalization produces forms of inequality that make democratic ideals elusive, potentially dampening prospects for "thicker" and more inclusive forms of democracy—even in the most advanced democracies (Bayes and Hawkesworth 2006, 5–6). The case of Fort McMurray focuses these questions on an oil economy in the Global North and shows us how some of the material and discursive facets of that economy produce and normalize gendered, as well as raced and classed, arrangements of paid and unpaid work.

I have also tried to show how these arrangements supplement the ability of people who work in the oil industry to take advantage of its opportunities, and also, by extension, the ability of oil profits to proceed apace. While Hochschild (2000) has argued that global chains of care work supply "emotional surplus value," I argue that gendered chains of care work provide both emotional and material surplus value; in binding oil "energy" to community "energy," they allow the state to make good on the promises of the petroleum economy.

Neoliberal ideas of citizenship contribute to the feminizing of this relationship. Simon-Kumar (2011, 452–53) asserts that in late neoliberalism, the active citizen is a political actor "located in the intersections between the state, market, family, and community" (see also Sassen 2008); in this context, "citizenship is enacted through activities such as volunteering, and by participating in government-defined engagement strategies. . . . Citizenship, in this discourse, is ostensibly 'feminized,' mapped around feminist principles of relationships and mutual dependence" (Simon-Kumar 2011, 453).

At the same time, neoliberal ideologies contribute to the occlusion of gendered hierarchies. Brodie (2008, 161) has argued that in Canadian neoliberalism, "promise[s] of choice and self-sufficiency are . . . masculinist constructs" but are not named as such; gendered relations of power are thus rendered no longer visible "through the lens of social liberalism or the language of citizenship equality." In northern Alberta, the value put on both family/community *and* entrepreneurialism seems to narrow the political space for directly addressing gender relations as an issue of democratic equality.

The pressure cooker created at the social epicentre of the bitumen sands economy has been converted into a fraught form of strategic political capital. As Lauren Cutler reported in a 10 March 2009 article in *Fort McMurray Today*, new child care funding for Fort McMurray had come, in part, through political leveraging from the Oil Sands Secretariat, the provincial government unit charged with managing "sustainable" growth of the bitumen sands. And the three-term mayor of the RMWB, Melissa Blake, has effectively used the many social and infrastructural challenges in the region to press for cost-of-living allowance increases for essential services, including child care work. But then, these changes have often been made in the name of attracting workers to feed the labour needs of the oil economy. As a local child care professional told me, "I'm under no illusions that the provincial government cares about quality child care for children and I'm under no illusion that [industry] does. But I know they care about getting workers and so we'll use that, thank you very much." What continues to get lost is a series of issues that lie behind such political expedience: how women and visible minorities bear many of the social burdens of the pressure cooker, how both men and women are caught in the gendered structures of the oil economy, and how the oil economy both benefits from and reproduces these unequal configurations.

Notes

1 Jodie Sinnema's article, titled "Fort McMurray: It Is Manly and Moneyed . . . but Has a Soft Side That Might Surprise You," was part of a series of stories on life in the region.

2 Thanks to Goze Dogu for research assistance in the collection of interview and observational data. I also want to note that we did not have the opportunity to interview any parents or caregivers who identified as LGBT.

3 Because Statistics Canada only counts residents and not mobile workers, its numbers over represent workers with families and females in the region; the RMWB's own 2012 census report on project accommodations (work camps) found that its residents are 83 percent male and that just over 50 percent are married or common-law (RMWB 2012, 118–19).

4 The proportion of workers (men and women combined) in this category provincially and nationally was 17.4 percent and 14.1 percent, respectively (Statistics Canada 2011a, 2011b).

5 The *only* categories of mobility status in the RMWB in which women outnumbered men were for those who had lived outside the country (as opposed to census area or province/territory) one or five years ago (Statistics Canada 2011c), which would include both immigrants and foreign workers.

6 It is further worth noting that the earnings of lone parent families in the RMWB, most of whom are female-headed, equalled just half of the overall median family income (compared to 57% in Alberta as a whole)—a statistic all the more concerning when the very high cost of housing is taken into account.

7 "Child Care," Regional Municipality of Wood Buffalo, http://www.woodbuffalo.ab.ca/ living/Newcomers/Getting-Help-in-Wood-Buffalo/Child-Care.htm (accessed 31 December 2014).

8 While high housing costs in Fort McMurray are the result of a complex set of factors, the rapid growth of bitumen development, along with living allowances provided by oil companies, contributed to inflated housing costs during the boom years of the 2000s.

9 The 2011 National Household Survey profile of the RMWB shows a high average commute time overall, but more than this, finds that the commute time is twice as long for men as it is for women (Statistics Canada 2011c).

10 This isn't always necessarily an equally shared desire. One woman we interviewed felt pressure from her husband to enter paid work in order to even further extend his oil industry income, given the plentiful opportunities; another woman stayed home because an oil industry salary meant they could afford it, but she indicated that it wasn't necessarily her first choice.

References

Arat-Koc, Sedef. 2006. "Whose Social Reproduction? Transnational Motherhood and Challenges to Feminist Political Economy." In *Social Reproduction: Feminist Political Economy Challenges Neo-liberalism*, edited by Meg Luxton and Kate Bezanson, 75–92. Montréal and Kingston: McGill-Queen's University Press.

Bayes, Jane, and Mary Hawkesworth. 2006. "Introduction." In *Women, Democracy, and Globalization in North America: A Comparative Study*, edited by Jane Bayes, Patricia Begné, Laura Gonzalez, and Lois Harder, 3–28. New York: Palgrave MacMillan.

Brodie, Janine. 2008. "We Are All Equal Now: Contemporary Gender Politics in Canada." *Feminist Theory* 9: 145–64.

CAPP (Canadian Association of Petroleum Producers). 2010. "Alberta Is Energy." News release, 7 April.

Cohen, Marjorie Griffin. 1994. "The Implications of Economic Restructuring for Women: The Canadian Situation." In *The Strategic Silence: Gender and Economic Policy*, edited by Isabella Bakker, 103–16. London, UK: Zed Books.

Colen, Shellee. 1995. "'Like a Mother to Them': Stratified Reproduction and West Indian Childcare Workers and Employers in New York." In *Conceiving the New World Order: The Global Politics of Reproduction*, edited by Faye D. Ginsburg and Rayna Rapp, 78–102. Berkeley: University of California Press.

Dorow, Sara, Marcella S. Cassiano, and Chad Doerksen. 2015. *Live-in Caregivers in Fort McMurray: A Socioeconomic Footprint*. St. John's, NL: On the Move Partnership.

Dorow, Sara, and Goze Dogu. 2011. "The Spatial Distribution of Hope in and Beyond Fort McMurray." In *Ecologies of Affect: Placing Nostalgia, Desire, and Hope*, edited by Tonya Davidson, Ondine Park, and Rob Shields, 271–92. Waterloo, ON: Wilfrid Laurier University Press.

Ferguson, Susan. 2008. "Canadian Contributions to Social Reproduction Feminism, Race, and Embodied Labor." *Race, Gender, and Class* 15 (1–2): 42–57.

Foster, Jason. 2012. "Making Temporary Permanent: The Silent Transformation of the Temporary Foreign Worker Program." *Just Labour* 19: 22–46.

Gazso, Amber. 2009. "Reinvigorating the Debate: Questioning the Assumptions About and Models of the 'Family' in Social Assistance Policy." *Women's Studies International Forum* 32: 150–62.

Gillespie, Judy L. 2007. "Restructuring the Governance of Child Welfare in a Remote, Resource Based Community: Implications of Economic Crisis and Community Change." *Rural Social Work and Community Practice* 12 (1): 29–39.

Harder, Lois. 2006. "Women and Politics in Canada." In *Women, Democracy, and Globalization in North America: A Comparative Study*, edited by Jane Bayes, Patricia Begné, Laura Gonzalez, and Lois Harder, 51–76. New York: Palgrave Macmillan.

Hochschild, Arlie. 2000. "Global Care Chains and Emotional Surplus Value." In *On the Edge: Globalization and the New Millennium*, edited by Will Hutton and Anthony Giddens, 130–46. London: Sage.

Katz, Cindi. 2001. "Vagabond Capitalism and the Necessity of Social Reproduction." *Antipode* 33: 709–28.

Leach, Belinda. 1999. "Transforming Rural Livelihoods: Gender, Work, and Restructuring in Three Ontario Communities." In *Restructuring Caring Labour: Discourse, State Practice, and Everyday Life*, edited by Sheila M. Neysmith, 209–25. Toronto: Oxford University Press.

Luxton, Meg. 2006. "Feminist Political Economy in Canada and the Politics of Social Reproduction." In *Social Reproduction: Feminist Political Economy Challenges Neo-liberalism*, edited by Meg Luxton and Kate Bezanson, 11–44. Montréal and Kingston: McGill-Queen's University Press.

McDowell, Linda. 2006. "Reconfigurations of Gender and Class Relations: Class Differences, Class Condescension, and the Changing Place of Class Relations." *Antipode* 38: 825–50.

Mercier, Laurie, and Jaclyn J. Gier. 2009. "Introduction." *Mining Women: Gender in the Development of a Global Industry, 1670 to the Present*, edited by Jaclyn J. Gier and Laurie Mercier, 1–10. New York: Palgrave Macmillan.

Miller, Gloria E. 2004. "Frontier Masculinity in the Oil Industry: The Experience of Women Engineers." *Gender, Work, and Organization* 11: 47–73.

O'Shaughnessy, Sara. 2011. "Women's Gendered Experiences of Rapid Resource Development in the Canadian North: New Opportunities or Old Challenges?" PhD diss. , Department of Rural Economy, University of Alberta.

Parkland Institute and ACSW (Alberta College of Social Workers). 2012. *Women's Equality a Long Way Off in Alberta: Gender Gap Remains Among the Widest in the Nation.* Edmonton, AB: Parkland Institute and ACSW.

Piper, Nicola. 2008. "International Migration and Gendered Axes of Stratification: Introduction." In *New Perspectives on Gender and Migration: Livelihood, Rights, and Entitlements*, edited by Nicola Piper, 1–18. New York and Abingdon, UK: Routledge.

Preston, Valerie, Damaris Rose, Glen Norcliffe, and John Holmes. 2000. "Shift Work, Child Care, and Domestic Work: Divisions of Labour in Canadian Paper Mill Communities." *Gender, Place, and Culture* 7: 5–29.

RMWB (Regional Municipality of Wood Buffalo). 2012. *Municipal Census 2012: Count Yourself In!* October.

Ross, Michael L. 2001. "Does Oil Hinder Democracy?" *World Politics* 53: 325–61.

———. 2008. "Oil, Islam, and Women." *American Political Science Review* 102: 107–23.

Sassen, Saskia. 2008. "Two Stops in Today's New Global Geographies: Shaping Novel Labor Supplies and Employment Regimes." *American Behavioral Scientist* 52: 457–96.

Simon-Kumar, Rachel. 2011. "The Analytics of 'Gendering' the Post-Neoliberal State." *Social Politics* 18: 441–68.

Statistics Canada. 2011a. "NHS Profile, Alberta, 2011—NHS Data." *Statistics Canada: 2011 National Household Survey.* Ottawa: Statistics Canada.

———. 2011b. "NHS Profile, Canada, 2011—NHS Data." *Statistics Canada: 2011 National Household Survey.* Ottawa: Statistics Canada.

———. 2011c. "NHS Profile, Wood Buffalo, SM, Alberta, 2011—NHS Data." *Statistics Canada: 2011 National Household Survey.* Ottawa: Statistics Canada.

———. 2012. "Family Income and Income of Individuals, Related Variables: Sub-provincial Data, 2010." *The Daily*, 27 June. http://www.statcan.gc.ca/daily-quotidien/120627/dq120627b-eng.htm.

Thorin, Maria. 2001. *The Gender Dimension of Globalization: A Survey of the Literature with a Focus on Latin America and the Caribbean.* Serie comerci internacional 17. Comisión Económica para América Latina y el Caribe (CEPAL), Division of International Trade and Integration. Santiago: United Nations Publications.

Woo-Paw, Teresa. 2011. "Impact of the Temporary Foreign Worker (TFW) Program on the Labour Market in Alberta." Submitted to the Hon. Thomas A. Lukaszuk, Minister, Alberta Employment and Immigration, August.

part three

Governance, Identity, and Citizenship in an Oil Economy

A Window on Power and Influence
in Alberta Politics

Ricardo Acuña

The policy context in Alberta has changed significantly over the past forty years. A sharp move to the far right in the province's dominant political paradigm has been accompanied by a general disengagement by Albertans from politics and from a government whose hands are largely tied in terms of policy options. Although this shift has coincided with a similar process across North America over the same period, it would be a mistake to describe it as organic. The current state of affairs has actually been the direct result of a very strategic and purposeful set of actions undertaken by key players inside Alberta. This chapter uses Joe Overton's theory of the "window of political possibility" to explore how Alberta's corporate elites, and in particular the oil industry, have leveraged their economic and political power to support advocacy-based think tanks, the media, and well-placed political activists to purposefully shift Alberta's political paradigm in a bid to further increase their power.

As the political window moved in Alberta, the ideas being promoted by the province's elites worked their way into the government. The result is a government that is heading into a place of chronic financial crisis, with the scope of policy options at its disposal growing narrower and narrower, and an electorate that has disconnected almost completely from the public policy process and politics. This situation bodes poorly for the public interest, for democracy, and for the long-term well-being of the province as a whole. The deep entrenchment of the Alberta policy window on the far right of the spectrum has further damaged democracy by making genuine public dialogue on policy and alternatives unlikely, if not impossible. In the current reality, what were once seen as ideas that were debateable and questionable have come to be seen as something tantamount to objective truth, and there is no questioning objective truth.

The Overton Window

Joe Overton developed his idea of the window of political possibility (named the "Overton window" after his death in 2003) while he was vice-president of the Mackinac Center for Public Policy, a right-wing think tank based in Michigan. Overton originally used the theory to explain how think tanks can help change the course of public policy, but it is also useful in explaining shifts in the political context of a jurisdiction as a whole. The essence of the Overton window is this: if all of the possible policy choices for any issue are placed on a spectrum, there will always be a small window along that spectrum where those policies that are considered acceptable, sensible, and popular reside. At the very centre of that window is where public policy happens, and as one moves away from the window to the left or right of the spectrum, one finds the policies that are considered radical and unthinkable (Lehman, n.d.). If we use the example of gun control to explain how the Overton window works, we would find a policy of strong government regulation and the requiring of permits in the middle of the window. In the realm of the radical and unthinkable on one end of the spectrum, we would find the total outlawing and banning of guns. On the other end, we would find a policy of wide open gun ownership with no regulations, registration, or permit requirement. We would also find a broad range of policy options between the window and the unthinkable on either side.

Overton believed that the window can be moved or expanded by flooding the public discourse with ideas that are radical and unthinkable. The more people hear these ideas and see them represented in the media, the more likely they are to begin seeing them as acceptable and sensible—the ideas become normalized. Except for very rare instances, Overton observed, politicians don't lead, they follow. Once the window has moved to a new point on the spectrum or its boundaries have expanded to include new ideas, the politicians will follow, opting for the politically safe options inside the window rather than the electorally riskier options outside the window. They will all rush to occupy the Overton window (Lehman, n.d.).

One part of the analysis that Overton and his successors at the Mackinac Center did not fully integrate into the theory, however, is the idea of power and privilege. All public policies have winners and losers. The winners tend to build both economic and political power as a result of these policies. That power allows them to play an important role in filtering which ideas get a broad airing in the public discourse and which get shut out. Lewis F. Powell perhaps best articulated how this privileging of ideas could happen in a memo he wrote in 1971 to the director of the US Chamber of Commerce. In the memo, which has since come to be called the Powell Manifesto, Powell urges "pro-enterprise" conservatives to take control of public discourse by funding think tanks, using their influence in the media, reshaping universities, and using the judiciary (Powell [1971] 2015). The Powell memo is largely credited for sparking the birth of corporate-funded right-wing think tanks in the United States, and since those beginnings, their profile and visibility in the media has increased dramatically, largely because of the support of "some very wealthy people" (Lakoff 2004, 15–16). Powell recognized that corporations, the wealthy, and the mass media had significant impact over the direction of public discourse and that they could use that power to privilege ideas that would further their economic power. He also understood their ability to publicly delegitimize and discredit those ideas that pose a threat to their economic power and privilege (Powell [1971] 2015).

Although they do not use the same language as Overton, numerous other observers of think tanks and their influence have pointed to this same dynamic playing out in Canada since the mid-1970s. Donald Abelson identifies four waves in the development of think tanks, with the third wave being the rise of what he calls "advocacy think tanks" (Abelson 2000, 18). He dates the beginning of this wave in Canada to the early 1970s, when groups such as the Canada West Foundation, the C. D. Howe Institute, and the Fraser Institute were born. These think tanks, says Abelson, are not driven by a desire to advance scholarly research but by a deep commitment to impose their "ideological agenda on the electorate" (220). William Carroll and Murray Shaw (2001, 196) take this understanding one step further by asking on whose behalf this ideological agenda is being imposed on the electorate and identifying these right-wing advocacy think tanks as "embedded elements of a social network, within which neoliberal business activism has taken shape." Carroll and Shaw explicitly point out that the ties between the corporate elite and the world of think tanks enable "a continuing conversation in which political frames can be aligned and adjusted, effecting a moving consensus between functioning capitalists and their organic intellectuals" (196). They reach the conclusion that, particularly in the case of the Fraser Institute, what is more startling than the representation of large corporations on policy boards is the heightened level of business activism in the field of public policy since the 1970s, as witnessed in the formation, financing, and governing of right-wing think tanks (211).

In examining Overton's idea that the window can be moved by flooding the public discourse with radical ideas, Robert Hackett and Yuezhi Zhao (1998, 157–58) find that this is borne out in the case of the Fraser Institute and the popular media in Canada: the ideas promulgated by those institutions "shifted from a comic example of ultra-right hyperbole to the representation of reason." Hackett and Zhao also identify the degree to which mainstream media privilege these messages by publishing them uncritically and frequently—almost ten times as often as the messages of policy groups at the other end of the political spectrum.

One of the fiercest arguments for right-wing think tanks constituting a concerted effort by corporate elites to change the political fabric of Canada, and perhaps the argument most relevant to Alberta, comes from journalist, author, and researcher Murray Dobbin, who has dedicated much of his writing over the past twenty years to tracking the rise of the neoliberal right in Canada. Dobbin draws direct lines from Canada's most powerful corporations (including Alberta's oil companies) to groups like the Fraser Institute and the National Citizens' Coalition, to the birth of the Reform Party in Alberta and the elevation of Stephen Harper to national power. Through a detailed analysis, he also demonstrates the role of the communications strategies of these organizations and the impact these strategies have had on the public consensus (Dobbin 1998).

Andrew Nikiforuk (2012) brings all of this home to Alberta in his analysis of how neoliberalism has been advanced in petro-states. When jurisdictions are as economically dependent on oil and gas as Alberta is, the disproportionate share of economic and political power held by oil corporations makes it that much easier for them to fund the development and dissemination of ideas that will further privilege them as an economic and political elite (194–99). Nikiforuk points to how Texas oil money helped fund the rise of neoliberal fundamentalism in the United States by supporting right-wing radical candidates, founding and funding right-wing foundations and institutes, and ultimately building right-wing media empires dedicated to the spreading of the neoliberal gospel.

All of the literature referred to above explains how the move to neoliberalism has happened in North America over the past forty years and highlights the dangers and pitfalls it holds for democracy and the ability of citizens to impact or engage with public policy. It also confirms the validity of using Overton's window, combined with an analysis of power and privilege, to understand the changes in Alberta over the same period of time and the resulting implications for democracy and public policy in that province.

A Brief History of Power in Alberta

Alberta's economy has always been export driven, and public policy has always prioritized the needs of that export economy. Historically, these exports were agricultural, with the south and central parts of the province focusing on beef and wheat, respectively. Even after natural gas was discovered in Turner Valley in 1914, and oil in 1936, agriculture remained the most important contributor to Alberta's economy and therefore the focus of much government policy. All of this began to change after the discovery of oil in Leduc in 1947, and subsequent discoveries in the 1950s and 1960s. International oil companies began setting up shop in the province en masse, refineries and pipelines began to be built, and the importance of oil and gas to the Alberta economy quickly increased. By 1971, resource mining accounted for almost 20 percent of the provincial economy, while agriculture had been reduced to just over 7 percent (Anielski 2002, 31).

It is not surprising, therefore, that in the 1971 Alberta general election, energy policy occupied a prominent place in the platforms of all political parties. Peter Lougheed in particular ran on a platform advocating a greater role and profile for Alberta in Canada, but he was also highly critical of how the Social Credit had handled energy policy and proposed a fairly interventionist approach for ensuring that the province's natural resource wealth was developed in the long-term interests of Albertans. In particular, Lougheed argued that the provincial government had been complacent and irresponsible in its handling of the oil industry, that it had failed to maximize the revenue potential of the province's resources, that Alberta had become overreliant on the oil industry and needed to actively diversify the economy, and that the government had wasted an opportunity to put energy revenues to work for Albertans by creating secondary and value-added industries (Richardson 2012, 36).

The Socred's response to these accusations will sound very familiar to Albertans today. Their leader, Harry Strom, insisted that it had been harmony between the government and industry that had brought record profits to Alberta and that the Socred government had always preferred to influence industry in a quiet manner that would normally result in voluntary adjustments by private business than to enact legislation (Kennedy 1971). Beyond highlighting his preference for a laissez faire approach to the energy sector, Strom's position also highlights the degree of political power that the energy industry had already attained by 1971.

Despite only obtaining 5 percent more of the popular vote than the Social Credit, the combination of the first-past-the-post system and a strong showing in Alberta's cities resulted in Lougheed's Conservatives winning forty-nine out of seventy-five seats in the Alberta legislature. They moved quickly to enact policy based on their election platform. The government increased royalties from 16.6 percent to 25 percent to maximize the benefit Albertans were receiving from their resources and set a target of capturing 35 percent of the wealth generated by natural resources. Lougheed also moved quickly to establish the Alberta Heritage Savings Fund, where Albertans would save 30 percent of the province's nonrenewable resource revenues, plus any return on investments. Within the first ten years of its existence, the fund grew to $12 billion.

In addition, Lougheed acted on his belief that the long-term jobs and value lay not in mining and extraction but in upgrading and processing. He established a specific policy of diversifying the economy and encouraging value-added processing of natural resources. This facilitated the birth of Alberta's petrochemical industry and also the emergence and growth of a provincial forestry industry. Lougheed's increased interventionism in the economy coincided with the dawn of Alberta's first major oil boom. In 1973, the Yom Kippur War and the subsequent oil embargo resulted in the international price of oil almost quadrupling, from $3.29 to $11.58, within the space of a year. Prices increased further when the situation in Iran exploded in 1978 and 1979, so that by 1980 oil had reached $36.83 per barrel (ChartsBin 2014). These were generally good times for Alberta. The multinational oil companies were happy with the profits they were making, workers were happy with the jobs available, the population was growing significantly, Alberta's two major cities were booming, and Albertans felt that, overall, the government was doing a good job of balancing their interests with those of the energy sector.

Throughout Lougheed's tenure as premier, the Overton window of public policy was firmly planted slightly to the right of centre along the spectrum of possibilities. Public policy in Alberta during this time demonstrated a strong belief in the free market, free trade, and individualism, but it also included support for strong social services, government funding for economic diversification, strong public health care and education, and even some government ownership in key sectors like energy, petrochemicals, and telecommunications.

Although there was still a Social Credit presence in the legislature for at least part of Lougheed's tenure, the key opposition focus during that period was from the New Democratic Party and their leader, Grant Notley. Their critique of government came from the centre-left of the political spectrum, from a place just outside the limit of the Overton window of the time. Their focus was seeking to control the political and economic power of the big oil and gas companies, protecting workers and increasing their benefits and wages, and protecting and expanding social services and public services. Despite being a caucus of one for most of this period, Notley's opposition proved quite effective. It could be said that as a result of his articulateness and natural leadership ability, he was actually able to move the left boundary of the Overton window far enough to encompass many of his ideas. This is best exemplified by the fact that by the 1986 election, after Notley's death, the New Democrats captured close to 30 percent of the popular vote in the province and formed an official opposition of sixteen members.

The Move to the Right

At around this same time, two different dynamics came together to set the stage for a drastic shift in the public policy paradigm in Alberta: the growth of extreme right-wing think tanks in Canada and the global recession of the 1980s.

Public policy in Alberta was greatly impacted by the birth and growth of extreme right-wing think tanks in Canada, particularly the Fraser Institute and the C. D. Howe Institute. The latter had been in existence since the 1950s as the Private Planning Association of Canada, an institute dedicated to studying the bilateral relationship between Canada and the United States, but it rebranded itself as the C. D. Howe Institute in 1982. With the rebranding came a move to expand its operations and influence across the country and a broadening of its mandate to include all aspects of economic policy. Its messages strongly echoed the economic theories of Milton Friedman, with calls for reduced taxes, pension reform, decreased social spending and government intervention, privatization, free trade, and elimination of government deficits.

These same messages made up the core mandate of the Fraser Institute. Founded in 1974 by economist Michael Walker and a vice-president from forestry giant Macmillan Bloedel, the institute set out specifically to shift the prevailing consensus of the time (the Overton window) that governments had a key role to play in economic development because markets were flawed entities (Fraser Institute 1999, 4–5). Its primary focus was privatization and deregulation of all services, but the institute also made plenty of room for messages around reducing taxes, eliminating government deficits, and decreasing social spending. Although its first year operating budget was only $75,000, by 1988 its annual revenues exceeded $1 million (Fraser Institute 2004, 3). This growth is similar to the expansion of US think tanks following Powell's urging in 1971.

Likewise, through the support of corporate Canada, by the late 1970s and early 1980s, both of these institutes were beginning to have their messages and ideas privileged by Canada's media. By 1986, Michael Walker was doing more than 250 media interviews a year, was a regular contributor to newspapers across the country, and had a daily radio commentary in Vancouver that was syndicated to markets across Canada. At the same time, their messages of deregulation, privatization, and lower taxes were starting to generate considerable interest in Alberta, where corporate elites saw the possibility for greater profit and freedom than they were enjoying with the status quo at the time. This further contributed to the visibility and profile of these messages and to the fundraising efforts of the institutes (Fraser Institute 1999, 29).

This funding of right-wing think tanks and privileging of their messages in the right-wing media closely resembled similar dynamics that had taken place in the United States, the United Kingdom, and other countries around the world and that ultimately resulted in the elevation of the likes of Ronald Reagan and Margaret Thatcher, not only in their own countries but on the world stage. Their presence and constant repetition of similar messages internationally further helped privilege those messages domestically in Canada.

Alberta's drastic move to the right was also fuelled by Alberta's energy sector beginning to feel the impact of a global recession in the early 1980s, caused largely by an international oversupply of oil coming from OPEC and the falling prices that resulted. In 1982, Dome Petroleum, Canada's largest oil company at the time, was bailed out by the federal government and the banks (Doern 1983, 26). That same year, Lougheed's government announced a $5.4 billion package of royalty reductions and special grants and credits as a way of helping the industry. It didn't work. By 1984, unemployment in Alberta had more than doubled, people were starting to leave the province in droves, and foreclosures and bankruptcies were the order of the day. The situation grew worse through 1986, when the price of oil bottomed out at around $10 per barrel (Cameron 1986). In response, the government stopped putting money into the Heritage Fund, investment in economic diversification slowed significantly, and the government began running budget deficits and moving into an accumulated debt position.

In her book *The Shock Doctrine* (2007), Naomi Klein suggests that in times of crisis people tend to turn for solutions to the ideas that are lying around. In Alberta in the late 1980s, despite a brief electoral surge by the New Democrats, the ideas that were "lying around" were primarily those on the far right being promoted by the likes of the Fraser Institute, the C. D. Howe Institute, and the growing number of right-wing radio talk-show hosts and newspaper columnists. With a few minor tweaks, those voices were able to leverage the collective trauma that Albertans were experiencing because of the economic crash and to begin moving the Overton window to the right. Albertans were told repeatedly that the economic crisis came about because of government spending on unaffordable social programs, overpaid civil servants, and the growing debt and deficit. This need for government to live within its means resonated with Albertans who had just lost jobs, cars, homes, and vacation properties when the economy collapsed (Taft 1997).

Alberta's energy companies were also more than happy to spread the messages, coming from the same sources, that the bust was made worse by government intervention in the oil patch through the National Energy Program and that overregulation, high taxes, and high royalties were keeping new investment out of the oil patch. In 1981, the Fraser Institute had published the book *Reaction: The National Energy Program*, strongly criticizing the National Energy Program (Watkins and Walker 1981). Canadian energy companies helped disseminate this book across the country and used it extensively in their lobbying of government (Fraser Institute 1999, 28). These companies also joined with many others in the Canadian corporate sector to ensure that these messages continued to be developed by the Fraser Institute and aired as broadly as possible. The Fraser Institute's revenue base grew sixfold between 1988 and 1993 as a result of these efforts.

All of this effort paid off for Alberta's corporations: the Overton window began to move, as evidenced by the movement of politicians who followed the window to its new location. In 1988, former Edmonton mayor Laurence Decore was elected leader of the Alberta Liberal Party, and then to the Alberta legislature in the general election the following year. Decore used his position as leader of Alberta's third party to repeatedly and loudly push for eliminating the provincial debt and deficit, cutting spending on public services, reducing MLA pensions, and ending the government's direct involvement in the private sector (Kheiriddin and Hennig 2010). Four years later, Ralph Klein became leader of the Progressive Conservative Party of Alberta on a platform that contained virtually the same messages that Decore had espoused. The two faced off against each other in the 1993 Alberta election with almost identical policy platforms. The New Democrats ran on a traditional left-of-centre platform, which by this time was well outside the parameters of the Overton window and into the realm of the radical and unthinkable. Significant oil and corporate money flowed to both the Liberals and the Conservatives to help finance their respective campaigns, and both the media and the corporate sector worked hard to reinforce the New Democrats' positions as out of touch and unrealistic.

Ralph Klein's Conservatives won the election with 44.5 percent of the popular vote, which was enough to secure fifty-one of eighty-three seats in the legislature. The Liberals, with 39.7 percent of the vote, won the remaining thirty-two seats, and the New Democrats were totally shut out. With a comfortable legislative majority and the knowledge that 84.2 percent of voters had, in essence, supported the right-wing platform on which both he and Decore had run, Ralph Klein felt no qualms about beginning to implement policy that would have been considered radical in Alberta just a few years before. The Overton window in Alberta had moved, and Ralph Klein's election platform had been right in the middle of it.

The Klein government immediately implemented across-the-board cuts to all government departments and services, laying off thousands of public servants in all parts of the province. Those who got to keep their jobs were pressured to, and ultimately did, accept wage rollbacks. Alberta registries, liquor stores, and highway maintenance were privatized (Martin 2013). The government sold off its remaining stock in Alberta Energy Corporation, used the proceeds of the sale to eliminate the provincial deficit, and began the process of fully deregulating the provincial electricity market. Government investment in public infrastructure and the Heritage Fund stopped altogether, and the process of introducing greater private delivery of health care through Bill 11 and other measures began. The Conservative government also began providing public funds to private schools in the province—something that the Fraser Institute in particular had been advocating for years. As the flow of ideas from the far right continued to flood the realm of public policy dialogue, the Overton window continued moving to the right. Ralph Klein won even more convincing majorities in the general elections of 1997 and 2001 and felt even more emboldened in making sure that policy kept up with the window as it moved. This move in the late 1990s was further reinforced by examples from other Canadian provinces, like Ontario, and internationally in countries like New Zealand.

The Klein government proceeded to implement significant changes to Alberta's royalty regime, introducing inflation indexing and new tiers of royalties to reduce rates and establishing the 1 percent prepayout royalty rate for bitumen sands operations. The Conservatives also reduced Lougheed's target of 35 percent for revenue capture from the oil and gas industry to 25 percent, a target that they never met (Campanella 2012, 9–10). They then proceeded to drastically cut Alberta's corporate taxes and introduced a 10 percent single-rate personal income tax regime. Both of these were policy options that twenty years earlier would have been considered unthinkable and radical by Albertans, but, as a result of the moving Overton window, these changes were accepted and even applauded. These policies had a very significant impact on Alberta at the time they were implemented. They created significant job loss among government workers, reduced capacity in public services like education and health care, and initiated twenty years of serious neglect of the province's infrastructure.

Despite the clear policy wins for the neoliberal economic project, the flood of extreme right-wing ideas did not cease. If anything, these ideas appeared to gain momentum as a result of their proven ability to directly influence government policy. This combination of the ongoing flood of privileged ideas from the right and the severe economic restructuring of Alberta set in place by Ralph Klein's policies of the 1990s had two very significant long-term impacts that have largely determined where Alberta is today in terms of democracy and public participation in policy: the consolidation of the energy industry's power and the entrenchment of Overton window on the far right of the political spectrum. In the remainder of this chapter, I explore these two impacts in depth.

The Overton Window in Alberta Today

As a result of reduced tax revenue, infrastructure spending, and investment in diversification, Alberta's oil and gas industry became further entrenched as the only show in town, both politically and economically. A quick look at any of Alberta's provincial budgets, annual reports, or economic outlooks since 1993 is enough to demonstrate the degree of the province's dependence on the oil and gas industry. In the 2012–13 Alberta budget, for example, nonrenewable resource revenues accounted for almost 28 percent of total projected revenues (Alberta, Finance 2012, 13). In the 2014–15 fiscal year, even with the complete collapse of international oil prices, the Alberta government was still projecting that nonrenewable-resource revenues would make up fully one-fifth of provincial revenues (Alberta, Finance 2015, 6). In terms of the provincial economy, according to the Government of Alberta, the oil and gas sector accounted for 23.1 percent of Alberta's GDP in 2013 (Alberta, Alberta Innovation and Advanced Education 2015). Despite the drop in oil prices in 2014–15, that percentage is not expected to change drastically and will probably continue to grow. This number includes only extraction and rises significantly once those portions of the construction, manufacturing, and transportation industries that are directly or indirectly linked to oil and gas extraction are added. Of Alberta's approximately two million workers, about 7.7 percent are involved directly in oil and gas extraction, with a significant number of the province's 230,000 construction workers also engaged directly by the energy industry (Alberta 2014, 10). Again, those numbers do not include all those workers in transportation and service industries that are directly or indirectly linked to the oil and gas sector. The Pembina Institute's work on a genuine progress indicator for Alberta highlights how much less diverse Alberta's economy was in 2003 than it was in 1971, with natural resources playing a much more prominent role than ever before (Pembina Institute 2005).

When one sector of the economy accounts for anywhere from one-fifth to one-third of government revenues and GDP, and 10 to 15 percent of jobs in the province, it is also bound to have significant political power. One of the clearest manifestations of this political power came during the 2007 review of royalty rates in Alberta. One way in which Ralph Klein had justified reducing royalty rates in the 1990s was by asserting that because oil prices had dropped, industry needed the incentive in order to continue investing in Alberta. Beginning in 1999 with the publication of the report *Giving Away the Alberta Advantage* by the Parkland Institute, a number of Alberta-based groups including Parkland Institute, Pembina Institute, and the Alberta Federation of Labour began trying to move public consensus back to higher royalty rates. As the price of oil started to increase rapidly in the early 2000s, followed by record oil company profits, the repeated message from these groups that Albertans were not getting their fair share began to resonate, and the idea of increasing royalty rates began to move from the realm of the unthinkable to the realm of the reasonable and possible.

By the time of the 2006 Conservative leadership race to replace Ralph Klein, the Overton window on the royalty regime had moved enough that it became a leadership issue. During the leadership race, Ed Stelmach promised that if he were elected, one of his first orders of business would be a full review of the province's royalty structure. Once elected, he appointed a blue-ribbon panel to carry out the review and promised to implement changes based on their recommendations. Although the panel did not go as far in recommending higher royalties as had been suggested by groups like Parkland, it did ultimately recommend an increase in royalties and an overhaul of the system (Acuña and Gibson 2007).

In response to the recommendations, the oil and gas industry in Alberta launched a significant advertising and public relations campaign, including the funding and organizing of a sizeable rally at the legislature, to convince Albertans that increasing royalties would break the provincial economy. More importantly, however, industry representatives demanded and received closed door meetings with the premier and Energy minister to echo the veiled threats being issued publicly about the consequences of increased royalties (CBC News 2007).

In response to the industry's reaction, the new regime that Ed Stelmach announced in 2007, and implemented in 2009, was significantly weaker in terms of royalty collection than the review panel had recommended (Acuña and Gibson 2007). In the provincial election that took place between the announcement of the royalty regime and its implementation, the Conservatives actually increased their share of the popular vote from the previous election and won a convincing majority, but the industry was still not happy with the pending increase in royalties. The industry set out to send Ed Stelmach, and all future premiers, a strong message. Companies began throwing their political and financial support behind what had been a fringe start-up party until that point, the Wildrose Party. They supported the leadership campaign of an articulate and charismatic young woman, Danielle Smith, who also happened to be a graduate of the Fraser Institute's youth internship program (Canadian Press 2012). Corporate Alberta then ensured that the party was presented by the media as a viable option to the Conservatives—a process aided by her husband, an executive with Sun Media, and by her own past experience as a columnist at the *Calgary Herald* and the host of an interview show on Global Television.

The rise of the Wildrose Party on the right flank of the Conservatives caused significant division in the Conservative caucus, since many members felt that they needed to move further right to accommodate what they saw as a shift to the right among voters. This division in the party is what ultimately led to the secession of two Conservative MLAs in 2010 and the resignation of Finance

Minister Ted Morton and Premier Stelmach in 2011—just three years after Albertans had given him a clear mandate as premier. Alberta's energy industry had flexed its political muscle, thrown a government into disarray, and significantly influenced the leadership of the province.

The second impact of the political dynamic that has played out in Alberta in the past four decades has been an entrenchment of the Overton window on the far right of the political spectrum. Well-funded and well-connected groups like the Fraser Institute, the Canadian Taxpayers Federation, and the C. D. Howe Institute continue to flood the arena of dialogue and debate with extreme right-wing ideas. The danger here is that the Overton window has become so entrenched on the far right of the spectrum that what are actually ideologically based and political ideas are interpreted by the public as objective truths. These are the ideas at the heart of neoliberal economic theory that have been repeated across North America by right-wing think tanks and the mainstream media since the 1970s: that government is by nature inefficient, that markets can deliver services more effectively than government, that low taxes are objectively good, that quality public services are unaffordable, that politicians and public servants are self-interested and greedy, and that unions result in inefficiency and waste.

The impact of this, in terms of change, is twofold. First, acceptance of these market ideologies as unquestionable truths has moved a significant portion of the population to a place where we see ourselves first and foremost as consumers rather than as democratic citizens with rights and responsibilities. Second, a majority of citizens are no longer willing or able to consider or entertain anything that might contradict these "truths." That being the case, anything remotely to the left of the Overton window is discounted offhand not just as radical and unthinkable but also as contradicting basic sense and logic.

As John Ralston Saul (1995) suggests in *The Unconscious Civilization*, in its evolution as a "science," neoliberal economic theory has come to be considered economic law. In places like Alberta, therefore, you would have as much luck arguing for increased taxes or public ownership as you would arguing that $1 + 1 = 5$. Fraser Institute head Michael Walker reportedly once responded to the birth of a left-wing think tank in British Columbia by declaring that the laws of the free market can no more be resisted than the law of gravity (Klein 1998). Until these theories are removed from the realm of truth and brought back into the realm of ideas, there is no possibility of the Overton window moving anywhere but further right, if at all.

Conclusion

The implications for policy in Alberta of the consolidation of the oil and gas industry's power and the entrenchment of the Overton window are significant. It will be extremely difficult for any provincial government—regardless of political stripe, rhetoric, or the ideological leanings of its leader—to alter the provincial royalty regime, significantly raise personal or corporate taxes, or justify consecutive operating deficits that lead to a net debt position. This means that the range of real policy options in Alberta is severely limited by what the industry will allow without mounting a capital strike.

This inevitability was highlighted by the 2015 Alberta budget which, despite a $7 billion revenue shortfall and growing popular consensus that corporate taxes needed to be increased, included no increases to either royalties or corporate taxes, and only minor tweaks to the provincial income tax system (Howell 2015). The immediate reaction by the energy industry and financial investors to the election of a New Democrat majority in May 2015 provides further proof of the role of the energy industry in entrenching the Overton window. The day after the election, world oil prices rose to above $62 per barrel for the first time in months, yet the energy sub-index of the Toronto Stock Exchange saw a drop of 3 percent as the selloff began, and groups like the Canadian Federation of Independent Business warned of major job losses if taxes are increased (Johnson 2015).

When public policy is seen as inevitable and economic theories are seen as truth, people have no reason to engage with the political processes that impact their lives. This trend is reinforced by messaging from the far right that consistently labels government and politicians as irrelevant, inefficient, and self-serving. Voter turnout and participation in political parties in Alberta are both likely to continue dropping for the foreseeable future, further abandoning the realm of public policy to the energy industry and think tanks.

The rise of right-wing think tanks in Canada and their close connections to the country's corporate sector, and in particular the oil industry, were able to leverage Albertans' experiences of the economic bust of the 1980s to precipitate a significant shift to the right of Alberta's Overton window. This in turn led to the election of Ralph Klein. Klein's government enacted a set of public policies that consolidated the political and economic power of Alberta's energy sector, thus entrenching the Overton window on the far right of the political spectrum. As a result of these dynamics over the past thirty years, public policy in Alberta today has become subservient to corporate interests. The neoliberal logic of the market is the primary driver of policy change, and, such being the case, policies from the right are the easiest to implement. The unexpected election of a left-leaning majority government after nearly forty-four years of uninterrupted PC rule gives pause to the prediction that the prospects for significant change are slim. Yet even though the 57 percent voter turnout in the 2015 election was the highest in two decades, the reality is that almost half of all Albertans remain politically disengaged. While the end of Tory rule is significant symbolically, the constraints imposed by the shift in the Overton window to the right may preclude a dramatic change in policy direction. Then again, in Alberta stranger things have happened.

References

Abelson, Donald E. 2000. "Do Think Tanks Matter? Opportunities, Constraints, and Incentives for Think Tanks in Canada and the United States." *Global Society* 14 (2): 213–36.

Acuña, Ricardo, and Diana Gibson. 2007. "Stelmach Royalty Decision Shows It Will Be Business as Usual for Alberta." *Edmonton Journal*, 26 October.

Alberta. 2014. *Alberta's Labour Market Highlights, 2014*. http://work.alberta.ca/documents/labour-market-highlights.pdf.

Alberta. Alberta Innovation and Advanced Education. 2015. *Highlights of the Alberta Economy 2015*. http://www.albertacanada.com/files/albertacanada/SP-EH_highlightsABEconomyPresentation.pdf.

Alberta. Finance. 2012. *Fiscal Plan Overview: Budget 2012*. http://www.finance.alberta.ca/publications/budget/budget2012/fiscal-plan-overview.pdf.

———. 2015. *Alberta 2014–15: Third Quarter Fiscal Update and Economic Statement*. http://www.finance.alberta.ca/publications/budget/quarterly/2014/2014-15-3rd-Quarter-Fiscal-Update.pdf.

Anielski, Mark. 2002. *The Alberta GPI: Economy, GDP, and Trade*. Drayton Valley, AB: Pembina Institute.

Cameron, Peter. 1986. "Canadian-Owned Oil on Thin Ice." *Multinational Monitor*, 30 April.

Campanella, David. 2012. *Misplaced Generosity: Update 2012—Extraordinary Profits in Alberta's Oil and Gas Industry*. Edmonton, AB: Parkland Institute.

Canadian Press. 2012. "Wildrose Leader Releases Financial Platform." *CBC News*, 27 March. http://www.cbc.ca/news/canada/manitoba/wildrose-leader-releases-financial-platform-1.1254836.

Carroll, William K., and Murray Shaw. 2001. "Consolidating a Neoliberal Policy Bloc in Canada, 1976 to 1996." *Canadian Public Policy / Analyse de Politiques* 27 (2): 195–217.

CBC News. 2007. "Alberta Increases Royalties Charged to Energy Companies." *CBC News*, 25 October. http://www.cbc.ca/news/canada/calgary/story/2007/10/25/stelmach-response.html.

ChartsBin. 2014. "Historical Crude Oil Prices, 1861 to Present." *ChartsBin.com*. http://chartsbin.com/view/oau.

Dobbin, Murray. 1998. *The Myth of the Good Corporate Citizen: Democracy Under the Rule of Big Business*. Toronto: Stoddart.

Doern, G. Bruce. 1983. "The Liberals and the Opposition: Ideas, Priorities, and the Imperatives of Governing in Canada in the 1980s." In *How Ottawa Spends: The Liberals, the Opposition, and Federal Priorities, 1983*, edited by G. Bruce Doern, 1–36. Toronto: James Lorimer.

Fraser Institute. 1999. *Challenging Perceptions: Twenty-Five Years of Influential Ideas*. Vancouver: Fraser Institute.

———. 2004. *The Fraser Institute at Thirty: A Retrospective*. Vancouver: Fraser Institute.

Hackett, Robert A. , and Yuezhi Zhao. 1998. *Sustaining Democracy? Journalism and the Politics of Objectivity*. Toronto: Garamond.

Howell, Trevor. 2015. "Government Survey Reveals Strong Support for Hikes to Cigarette and Corporate Taxes." *Calgary Herald*, 24 March.

Johnson, Tracy. 2015. "Alberta Election 2015: Energy Sector Braces for Change with NDP Win." *CBC News*, 6 May. http://www.cbc.ca/news/canada/calgary/alberta-election-2015-energy-sector-braces-for-change-with-ndp-win-1.3062700.

Kennedy, Thomas. 1971. "Comment: Making an Issue of Alberta's Resources." *Globe and Mail*, 6 August.

Kheiriddin, Tasha, and Scott Hennig. 2010. "Alberta's 'Miracle on the Prairie.'" *National Post*, 6 April.

Klein, Naomi. 2007. *The Shock Doctrine: The Rise of Disaster Capitalism*. New York: Metropolitan Books.

Klein, Seth. 1998. "A Review of *The Myth of the Good Corporate Citizen: Democracy Under the Rule of Big Business* by Murray Dobbin." *The New Reader* (Summer). http://www.collectionscanada.gc.ca/eppp-archive/100/202/300/newreader/newreader.b03/Readers/Reader/1998Summer/dobbin.html.

Lakoff, George. 2004. *Don't Think of an Elephant! Know Your Values and Frame the Debate*. White River Junction, VT: Chelsea Green.

Lehman, Joseph. N.d. "A Brief Explanation of the Overton Window." *The Overton Window*. Mackinac Center for Public Policy. http://www.mackinac.org/12887#Explanation.

Martin, Sandra. 2013. "Obituary: Ralph Klein, 70: The Man who Ruled Alberta." *The Globe and Mail*, 29 March.

Nikiforuk, Andrew. 2012. *The Energy of Slaves: Oil and the New Servitude*. Vancouver: Greystone Books.

Pembina Institute. 2005. "Economic Diversity." GPI Indicator Summary No. 2. May. Drayton Valley, AB: Pembina Institute.

Powell, Lewis F., Jr. (1971) 2015. "Confidential Memorandum: Attack of American Free Enterprise System." *Reclaim Democracy!* http://reclaimdemocracy.org/powell_memo_lewis/.

Richardson, Lee. 2012. "Lougheed: Building a Dynasty and a Modern Alberta from the Ground Up." *Policy Options* (June–July): 32–37.

Saul, John Ralston. 1995. *The Unconscious Civilization.* Toronto: House of Anansi Press.

Taft, Kevin. 1997. *Shredding the Public Interest.* Edmonton: University of Alberta Press and Parkland Institute.

Watkins, Gordon Campbell, and Michael Walker, eds. 1981. *Reaction: The National Energy Program.* Vancouver: Fraser Institute.

The Paradox of Plenty

Ending Homelessness in Alberta

Joshua Evans

Homelessness is a prominent public policy issue in Canada, where an affordable-housing crisis has unfolded over the past two decades (Gaetz, Gulliver, and Richter 2014). This crisis is particularly acute in the country's biggest cities, where street homelessness has become an everyday feature of the urban landscape (Laird 2007). Alberta's prodigious prosperity has not exempted the province from these trends. In fact, Alberta has experienced some of the worst affordability problems and sharpest increases in homelessness in Canada, all in the midst of recent resource development booms (Calgary Homeless Foundation 2012). In the summer of 2007, the housing crisis became so severe that a large encampment of the homeless, which came to be called "Tent City," formed on a vacant lot in Edmonton's inner city (Ruttan 2007). Over several months, Tent City grew to a population of several hundred people. Although the encampment was initially tolerated, safety concerns and public pressure forced the hand of the City of Edmonton, and Tent City was dismantled. Camp residents were moved into emergency shelters and transitional housing units. But the encampment caught national media attention, exposing the underside of Alberta growth.

In October 2008, the Province of Alberta introduced an ambitious program to end homelessness in ten years (Alberta Secretariat for Action on Homelessness 2008). At the time of writing (April 2015), Alberta is the only province in Canada with such a plan; however, Ontario's poverty reduction strategy, initiated in 2014, includes "ending homelessness" as a long-term goal. The provincial strategy pledges investments to the tune of $3.316 billion, with the goal of moving eleven thousand individuals and families out of homelessness by 2019. Central to this strategy is the Housing First (HF) model developed in the early 1990s in New York City to meet the housing and health needs of chronically homeless populations (Falvo 2009). HF is based on the theory that rather than making permanent housing contingent on abstinence-based treatment in a shelter or transitional setting, permanent housing should be provided to chronically homeless individuals at the outset because this creates a better foundation for the recovery process (Tsemberis 2010).

The ambitious policy outlined in 2008 in *A Plan for Alberta: Ending Homelessness in Alberta in 10 Years* is no doubt made possible by Alberta's abundant resource endowments. Alberta's carbon-fuelled exceptionalism is the backdrop to rather bold social policy objectives in this regard, a pattern not uncommon in other oil-rich states (Karl 2004). But when it comes to what these policy developments say about the relationship between oil and democracy, it is imperative to scrutinize the type of democratic action they represent.

In this chapter, I examine democratic politics in the oil-rich province of Alberta through the lens of homelessness policy, employing a definition of democracy developed by philosopher Jacques Rancière. Here, rule (*kratos*) by the people (*demos*) is understood as action that springs from the realization that politics lacks any natural foundation capable of justifying oligarchic government—that is, the rule of a minority over a majority. Democracy is grounded upon an anarchic presupposition of innate equality: that we are all similarly capable and worthy of participating in the political community. Equality is *the* basic fact that we have in common. This radical presupposition of equality is perpetually at odds with hierarchical orders instituted along lines of gender, race, and class. It is the *mésentente*, the disagreement, between equality and hierarchy that constitutes politics. As Rancière (2007, 94) argues, there is politics because there is democracy. Democratic politics can thus be conceived as actions, taken by or on behalf of those who have no part—no share—in a prevailing order, that demonstrate how equality has been wronged by hierarchies. In Rancière's estimation (1999), democracy—and by extension, politics—very rarely occur, particularly in the industrialized world, which is increasingly dominated by approaches to government that Rancière pejoratively characterizes as "postdemocratic."

Rancière's view on democratic politics invites a particular examination of policies purporting to "end" homelessness. Can they be read as democratic, as actions that denaturalize prevailing hierarchies in the housing system and demonstrate how equality is fundamentally wronged by homelessness? Or are these policy developments better read as postdemocratic solutions to the collateral damage wrought by years of welfare state retrenchment and oil-fuelled economic booms and busts? In this chapter, I address these questions through a discursive examination of homelessness policy, using an approach that draws attention to how discourse shapes what can be said, and in turn understood, about homelessness. I argue that the discourse of "ending homelessness" is an economically rationalized, technocratic, and consensual mode of governing that aims interventions toward particular subpopulations of homeless people and, in doing so, neglects systemic problems in the housing system that perpetuate affordability problems. Such a policy environment effectively hampers democratic action around housing justice and thus invites comparisons to what Rancière calls postdemocracy.

Policy, Politics, and Democracy

Rancière's writings invite social scientists to think about politics and democracy differently. His novel political ontology rests on a distinction between the "police" and "politics," two contradictory logics. "Police," for Rancière (1999, 28), does not refer to law enforcement or the state apparatus; rather, it refers to a logic that "arranges that tangible reality in which bodies are distributed in a community." The police (or policy) is an order in which bodies are counted and assigned to a proper place. These hierarchical orders function as epistemological grids, systems of seeing and hearing, that establish the conditions for governance. Rancière (1999, 2010) discusses the establishment of a police order as one aspect of *le partage du sensible*, "the distribution of the sensible." The term *partage* refers to sharing out, dividing, or apportioning. Hence, the distribution of the sensible is simultaneously to make something common, to classify, and to allocate. Public policy is grounded in particular distributions of the sensible that—by rendering populations visible, problematizing them, and building a discursive world around them—evoke particular police orders (Dikeç 2005).

Politics also takes on a different meaning in Rancière's (1999, 2010) framework. Politics is the disruption of the police order by what is unaccounted for, by unnamed parts of the whole that have no proper place in the sensible field, parties outside of established orders rendered invisible within prevailing distributions. Their voices heard as noise, they are thus unrecognizable and unaccounted for. As Dikeç (2005, 176) puts it, politics "is the disruption of the police order—the sum of the *fully* counted, *rightly* named, and *properly* placed parts—by a part that has no part in this particular counting, naming and partitioning." Politics is the struggle for recognition by a party that has no part in an established police order, a struggle launched in the name of radical equality. In this sense, politics is conflict over who is recognized, whose voice is heard as speech rather than noise, and the divisions by which these relationships are established and changed. Politics is not a matter of recognizing an additional group that is not counted in society—this simply establishes another police order—but those moments that reveal the radical equality of anyone and everyone (for example, Edmonton's Tent City). It is the enactment of this equality, by identifying how it is systemically wronged within a police order, that functions as the (negative) ontology of politics (Rancière 1999).

Rancière's unique perspective on politics invites different ways of thinking about democratic politics. Rancière (2010, 50) views democracy as "neither a form of government nor a form of social life. Democracy is the institution of politics, of politics as a paradox." By paradox, he means that politics is the enactment of how equality is wronged. Politics "consists in blurring and displacing the borders of the political. This is what politics means: displacing the limits of the political by re-enacting the equality of each and all" (54). Rancière stresses how democracy implies this practice of displacement, a practice he calls "dissensus," which is continuously muted by budding police orders.

In Rancière's estimation, political dissensus is continuously thwarted in Western democratic politics by what he labels "consensus thinking": the "presupposition of inclusion of all parties and their problems that prohibits the political subjectification of a part of those who have no part, of a count of the uncounted" (1999, 116). Rancière calls the resulting postpolitical state of consensus building "postdemocracy," which he describes as "the consensual practice of effacing forms of democratic action" in the name of democracy. As he goes on to explain, "Postdemocracy is the government practice and conceptual legitimization of a democracy after the demos, a democracy that has eliminated the appearance, miscount, and dispute of the people and is thereby reducible to the sole interplay of state mechanisms and combinations of social energies and interests" (101–2).

Rancière contends that postdemocracy is itself a distribution of the sensible, a "regime in which the parties are presupposed as already given, their community established" (102). Postdemocracy is the evaporation of any gap between the excess that has no part and the order in which everyone is assigned to their proper place, the disappearance of any gap between politics and the police.

The Discourse of "Ending Homelessness"

Michel Foucault's (1972) archaeological approach to knowledge offers a useful means to examine the discourse of "ending homelessness." Foucault conceptualizes discourse as contingent formations of knowing and thinking that make up specific domains of knowledge and practice (Murdoch 2005). The archaeological method focuses on discursive discontinuities and ruptures that make possible the emergence of formal domains such as policy models (Scheurich 1994). The elementary unit of analysis when using the archaeological method is the *statement* (*enoncé*; Foucault 1972). Statements are not equivalent to sentences or propositions insofar as the meaning of the statement is not reducible to grammatical rules, logical formulations, or a single referent. Statements acquire their meaning on an enunciative level: "whatever it is that makes people at a certain period take certain speech acts seriously" (Dreyfus and Rabinow 1983, 58). Analyzing statements on an enunciative level involves describing those rules and conditions that enable or constrain what registers as sensible, comprehensible, or thinkable about people, relations, places, or experiences at a given point in time.

The discourse analysis on which this chapter is based focuses on major policy documents on the issue of homelessness at provincial and municipal levels in Alberta. This section identifies five statements—statistical, biographical, economic, planning, and philosophical—that together constitute Alberta's enunciative environment. This environment of speech acts and discursive events both enables and constrains what registers as thinkable (i.e. , Rancière's "the distribution of the sensible") with regard to homelessness in Alberta. This enunciative environment, established through the relations between statements, makes it possible to declare that an "end" to homelessness is within the realm of governmental possibility and responsibility. It is therefore pivotal for understanding the nature of policy shifts as well as their democratic relevance.

Statistical Statements

Statistical statements are indispensable discursive events when it comes to homelessness policy-making. Enumeration, tabulation, and categorization play constitutive roles in the social categorization of temporarily unhoused people as a distinct and measurable group: it is through statistical statements that people, united primarily by their lack of permanent housing, appear as a "homeless population." How many people are homeless? Who is homeless?

How long are people homeless? By answering these questions, a "homeless population" finds expression—in the form of tables, graphs, and pie charts—across research reports and policy documents. The conversion of people into a quantifiable population, in terms of their housing history and sociodemographic characteristics, is a noteworthy event insofar as it produces the objects of intervention for homelessness policy.

Statistical descriptions of homeless populations are central features of Alberta's policy discourse. As far back as the early 1990s, authorities in both Calgary and Edmonton formalized programs to enumerate the homeless using "point-in-time" (or "snapshot") census counts that collected data on the size and social characteristics of the homeless. Over time, these statistical statements evolved from simple charts and graphs to more complex population models, forecasts, and service utilization rates (see Sorensen 2010). These changes represent fundamental shifts in the enunciative environment. Two in particular are notable.

First, the "systems of classification" (Foucault 1972) used to define homeless persons became more complex over time. In Calgary and Edmonton, for instance, early counts drew upon the classic United Nations distinction between "absolute" and "relative" homelessness. Over time, classificatory schemes in both cities multiplied in terms of scope and specificity. In 2006, Calgary adopted the European Typology of Homelessness and Housing Exclusion (ETHOS). The ETHOS typology designates four conceptual categories—roofless, houseless, insecure, and inadequate—which are broken down into a total of thirteen different operational categories. These classification schemes permitted policymakers to speak about the homeless population with more precision and accuracy. Alberta's strategy to end homelessness, as laid out in *A Plan for Alberta: Ending Homelessness in 10 Years* (Alberta Secretariat for Action on Homelessness 2008, 7), identifies three major categories of homeless Albertans—the chronic homeless, the transient homeless, and the employable homeless.

A second shift occurred when the "authorities of delimitation" (Foucault 1972), those individuals and groups empowered by society as a whole to address homelessness, began to favour individuals and groups with professional expertise. In the early years, task forces, committees, and working groups were privileged speakers. These coalitions of elected politicians, appointed civil servants, private sector philanthropists, academics, and nonprofit representatives were granted authority over enumeration programs; however, over time social researchers, and social research units in particular, were accorded a special role in determining the size and characteristics of homeless populations. Today, research units coordinate the count of homeless populations, and it is common to contract out such research activities to professional research consultants and academics. Together, these shifts in systems of classification and authorities of delimitation reflect the consolidation of a research agenda, the adoption of more sophisticated data management systems, and the accumulation of additional research capacity and resources.

Biographical Statements

While statistical statements constitute one part of the enunciative environment for producing knowledge about the homeless as a population, homelessness policy is also replete with statements about homeless individuals. In this sense, another object, the homeless person, is constructed. But rather than offering objective statistics about housing status, age, or gender, biographical statements individualize the experience of homelessness through direct quotations, third-person narratives, and photographic images.

Biographical statements are relatively rare in early policy documents. For instance, the 1999 report of the Edmonton Task Force on *Homelessness, Homelessness in Edmonton: A Call to Action*, contains only a single direct quote from a "former homeless" person (5). This dearth of biographical information is addressed over time. More specifically, a new type of biographical statement—the case study—surfaces in later policy documents. Consider, for instance, the following statement from *A Place to Call Home*, a report written in 2009 by the Edmonton Committee to End Homelessness:

> Take Charles. He is 42 years old, HIV positive, and has spent most of the last 25 years sleeping on the street or in crack houses. But Charles' life changed the day he went into the Jasper Place Health and Wellness Centre for a cup of coffee and a shower: he developed a relationship with the staff at the Centre, who were able to give him the tools he needed to get an apartment of his own. They were there when Charles filled out the form for his lease, they helped him with the security deposit, and they assured the landlord that they would be responsible for the apartment if anything went wrong. The assistance and encour¬agement did not end there: a support worker went grocery shopping with Charles to help him stretch his dollar as efficiently as possible; he helped Charles out with furniture and learning to cook. Then when Charles decided to deal with his cocaine habit, the Centre gave him the resources he needed. The Housing First principle does work. (29)

Using third-person narratives, biographical statements tell a "success story" about interventions. These success stories represent a fundamental shift in the enunciative environment—namely, the formation of new "enunciative modalities" (Foucault 1972) governing who can speak, from where, and in what situation. Two aspects of these narratives are notable.

First, these biographical statements emanate from specific institutional sites in the community, including research and evaluation sites associated with Housing First programs (such as Calgary's Pathways to Housing or Edmonton's Jasper Place Health and Wellness Centre). Through biographical statements, these sites become embedded within broader multistakeholder policy processes. Second, biographical statements can be described in terms of the situations that bring a subject and object into a relationship. The success stories presented above evoke a new situation: "clients" are followed, monitored, and managed over time via highly synchronized case management approaches to mental health service delivery. The Edmonton report *A Place to Call Home* (Edmonton Committee to End Homelessness 2009, 64) defines case management as follows: "A collaborative process of assessment, planning, facilitation, and evaluation of the options and services required to meet an individual's health and human service needs. It is characterized by advocacy, communication, and creative resource management to promote quality, cost-effective outcomes." In this sense, relationships between subjects (such as the Alberta Secretariat for Action on Homelessness and the Edmonton Committee to End Homelessness) and objects ("Charles") in these stories are mediated by actual HF programs and their requisite case management orientations. In this way, biographical statements are no longer simple snapshot descriptions that personalize homelessness. Instead, they are narratives that tout the economic efficiency of the professional case management process. These homeless stories give a different inflection to "success."

Planning Statements
Statements referring to specific policy models and their procedures are prominent features of discourse surrounding homelessness policy. These planning statements diagram why and how interventions should work in practice. They presuppose a set of actors, each with specific roles and responsibilities, and prescribe a set of actions designed to achieve policy goals.

The planning statements that appear in early policy documents convey a particular set of policy goals. Foremost among them is rehousing the homeless. As late as 2005, Edmonton's community plan evoked this very premise:

> The Plan is built on the premise that Edmonton needs an integrated system that enables and encourages people to "move up" through various housing options, and ultimately, if possible, into the private housing market. This requires a sufficient supply of different types of housing units at each stage, along with support services that encourage and enable people to become as independent as possible. (Edmonton Joint Planning Council on Housing 2005, 2)

Planning statements at that time evoked a particular conceptual formulation: a service orientation called the "linear residential treatment" (LRT) continuum (Tsemberis 2010). Until 2007, the LRT continuum was a prominent feature of policy documents. This model of rehousing the homeless encompasses a range of services and supports, including street outreach and emergency accommodation, transitional housing, and independent housing. In this model, transitional and independent (and in some cases emergency) housing is provided on the condition that consumers participate in job training and psychological counselling and maintain sobriety. It is therefore sometimes referred to as the treatment first (TF) model (Tsemberis 2010).

Beginning in 2008, planning statements began to change with the adoption of an alternative model, the Housing First (HF) model, which calls for immediate access to permanent housing regardless of clients' commitment to treatment or sobriety. For example, Edmonton's *A Place to Call Home* (Edmonton Committee to End Homelessness 2009, 27) states: "The primary goal is finding a permanent home for people who are without a place to live, regardless of their past or present issues. This includes accessing rent subsidies and potentially negotiating leases with landlords, on behalf of the client."

Alberta's ten-year plan to end homelessness (Alberta Secretariat for Action on Homelessness 2008, 17) is even more explicit, stating: "Top priority is given to rapid re-housing of homeless Albertans into permanent housing. Permanent housing doesn't mean a shelter. It means a secure home using a housing option that's appropriate for the circumstances of the individual or family." This conceptual reformulation evokes a different style of reasoning. Rather than simply provide the opportunity to "'move up' through various housing options, and ultimately, if possible, into the private housing market" (Edmonton Joint Planning Council on Housing 2005, 2), as in the case of the TF model, these later planning statements direct service providers to house individuals immediately in the private housing market (Edmonton Committee to End Homelessness 2009, 27).

This conceptual reformulation reflects significant shifts in the enunciative environment. First, in the case of the HF concept, planning statements are organized around the presupposition that homeless individuals inherently deserve housing regardless of personal problems or behaviour. Housing is a human right and should be provided with no strings attached. *A Place to Call Home* (Edmonton Committee to End Homelessness 2009, 8) summarizes this basic premise of the HF concept:

> The Housing First approach says the first step in solving the problem is to find people permanent homes and give them the support they need to be successful in those homes. This philosophy represents a shift away from the theory that people have to be "prepared" or "transitioned" into housing by first dealing with mental health and addiction issues or finding a job. It recognizes that the best place to deal with those issues is not living on the street but in safe, secure housing.

In contrast, TF typically takes as its premise that homeless people are disproportionately sick or troubled and must be made "housing ready." The conceptual reformulation accomplished by planning statements in recent plans and reports is based on a recalibration of deservedness.

Second, this enunciative environment extends beyond Edmonton, Calgary, and Alberta to other places in the world. The Calgary Committee to End Homelessness cites specific studies on the effectiveness of the HF approach in US cities:

> The principles and strategies at the heart of Calgary's 10 Year Plan have been put to the test in other communities, with encouraging results:
>
> - In the short space of 18 months after the implementation of Portland, Oregon's 10-year plan, the city reduced its chronic homeless population by 70 per cent.
> - Denver, Colorado has seen an 11 per cent reduction in overall homelessness and a 36 per cent reduction in chronic homelessness since the city implemented its plan in 2005.
> - Hennepin County, Minnesota has seen a dramatic decline in family homelessness since it implemented its 10-year plan. From 2002 to 2004, the community saw family homelessness decline by 43 per cent, from 1,819 to 1,046. (Calgary Committee to End Homelessness 2008, 6)

When it comes to the HF concept, planning statements are constituted by flows of knowledge from sites around the world. These distributed sites serve as instrumental points of reference in legitimizing this particular style of reasoning.

Economic Statements

Economic concerns regarding housing systems have long been prominent features of policy discourses dealing with homelessness. Alberta research reports and policy plans contain numerous references to the hardships of poverty, the affordability of housing, and the costs associated with maintaining an adequate housing continuum. Questions and recommendations relating to funding levels for housing and support programs are prominent and generally take the form of a "gap analysis."

Over time, a different type of economic statement emerged, focusing on the indirect, or "spillover," costs of homelessness and the financial implications of different service models. *Calgary's 10 Year Plan* (Calgary Committee to End Homelessness 2008, 7), for example, points out some of the social and economic costs of homelessness:

> The social costs of homelessness are many and well understood. We know that people with mental illness or addictions get worse when they are un-housed and unable to receive treatment, and they often end up in ambulances and emergency wards. Citizens and visitors to Calgary are often disturbed by seeing so many people experiencing homelessness on our streets. Many don't feel safe downtown at night, particularly in and near the East Village and along the Bow River pathways. But we've also begun to realize that homelessness is exacting a terrible economic toll. Our own analysis shows it costs taxpayers more to manage homelessness than it would to end it. . . .
>
> If Calgary's current homelessness growth rate continues into the next decade, we estimate that the number of people homeless on any given night could reach 15,000 and cumulative spending could be more than $9 billion.

Statements such as these constitute the first half of the "business case" concept. This business case has also been taken up by the province and other cities. In a quintessential arrangement of economic statements, the provincial strategy (Alberta Secretariat for Action on Homelessness 2008, 8) enunciates it as follows:

If Alberta continues its current approach of simply managing our current homeless population, it's estimated that the Alberta government will incur costs of $6.65 billion over 10 years. This is because managing homelessness is extremely costly to taxpayers. The Alberta government incurs direct costs relating to homelessness, such as the emergency shelter system, services for homeless Albertans, and programming to homeless-serving agencies. The government also incurs expenses through indirect costs—that is, spending in other government systems such as the health system, corrections system, and justice system. Homeless Albertans utilize these systems in multiple ways that result in higher costs to the taxpayer.

Citing Steve Pomeroy's 2005 study for Canada's National Secretariat on Homelessness, the Edmonton Committee to End Homelessness (2009, 27) employs this same style of economic reasoning in *A Place to Call Home*:

> Studies across Canada have shown that institutional responses (detention, prison, psychiatric hospitals) for a person experiencing homelessness cost taxpayers between $66,000 and $120,000 each year. Emergency shelter costs average between $13,000 and $42,000 per person, per year. (In Edmonton, an average of $15,000.) The price of supportive housing for that person would be between $35,000 and $40,000 per year.

The last statement here is key: the business case not only accounts for the full societal costs of homelessness; it also employs a comparison of alternatives— in this case, supportive housing. This administrative style of cost-benefit reasoning is a prominent feature of economic statements.

This pattern of concept formation reflects additional shifts in the enunciative environment. First, as in the case of the HF model, it is clear that statements originating from outside Alberta are highly influential, particularly those emanating from the United States. Anecdotes such as the following, from *Calgary's 10 Year Plan to End Homelessness* (Calgary Committee to End Homelessness 2008, 44), are common:

> Into that atmosphere stepped Mr. Philip Mangano, Executive Director of the United States Interagency Council on Homelessness. Mangano spoke to a September 2006 breakfast meeting arranged by the Calgary Homeless Foundation. At that meeting, Mangano spoke passionately about the economic case for addressing chronic homelessness and about a new 10-year planning model that was showing some remarkable results south of the border.

Edmonton is no different. In *A Place to Call Home*, the Edmonton Committee to End Homelessness (2009, 24) observes that "where the Housing First model has already been fully implemented in the United States, evidence is emerging of social and financial benefits." Judging from these Alberta documents on homelessness, the United States Interagency Council on Homelessness (USICH) and the National Alliance to End Homelessness (NAEH) significantly influenced the genesis of the business case in Alberta.

Second, underlying the business case concept is the tacit assumption that not all policy is created equal. Within Alberta, the notion of "best practices" governs how the business case concept has been translated and rendered into local models for implementation. "Best practices" connotes the "expectation that an intervention has been successful according to some criteria and that it is better than something else" (Øyen 2009, 1). In Alberta, the translation of the US business case is underpinned by networks of policy learning spanning an ever-expanding evidentiary landscape of HF research in North America.

Philosophical Statements
A final statement constituting Alberta's policy discourse is the philosophical statement. Philosophical statements communicate broad-based, overarching policy themes. In Alberta, a new theme emerged, beginning in 2007. *A Plan for Alberta: Ending Homelessness in 10 Years* (Alberta Secretariat for Action on Homelessness 2008) was distinguished by a clear emphasis on putting a definitive end to homelessness. In a section titled "Setting the Vision," the report states:

> Homelessness is unacceptable in a province as prosperous as Alberta. No Albertan should be forced to live on the streets or remain in a shelter for an extended period of time. Albertans have the resources, the creativity and the compassion to effectively address homelessness in their communities. For a province built on great achievements and innovation, and a people who don't shy away from big challenges, the Secretariat has set a bold vision for its Plan: Homelessness is ended in Alberta by 2019. (14)

This emerging theme surfaces in the titles of other major policy documents as well. For instance, the titles of plans in Edmonton evolved from *Homelessness in Edmonton: A Call to Action* (Edmonton Task Force on Homelessness 1999), to *Edmonton Community Plan on Housing and Support Services* (Edmonton Joint Planning Council on Housing 2005), to *A Place to Call Home: Edmonton's 10 Year Plan to End Homelessness* (Edmonton Committee to End Homelessness 2009). A thematic pattern is discernible, moving from "taking action," to "managing accordingly," to "ending homelessness."

This pattern reflects a fundamental shift in the enunciative environment that was shaped by a number of conditions. First, these thematic choices derive from the coexistence of statistical, biographical, planning, and economic statements: together, they yield a particular theoretical option that was not possible before. In the late 1990s and early 2000s, advocates, policy-makers, and service providers were working within an enunciative environment that afforded a managerial style of reasoning focused on gaps in service. It was through the interrelationships established between new ways of representing homeless populations, portraying their lives, planning interventions, and rationalizing costs and benefits that previous policy approaches became subject to critique as "managerial" in a pejorative sense. The very opportunity to juxtapose "ending homelessness" with "managing homelessness" is itself a product of these emergent relations. The philosophical statement is the mode in which these strategic contrasts emerge.

Table 12.1. The discourse of "ending homelessness"

Rules of formation	Statement	Example	Conditions
Objects	Statistical	Homeless populations	Data management systems
Mode of enunciation	Biographical	Success stories	Professional case management
Concepts	Planning Economic	Housing First Business case	Evaluation studies Best practices
Strategy	Philosophical	Ending homelessness	Quasi-public planning process

In summary, a close examination of the shifts in Alberta's policy discourse reveals a significantly modified discursive formation (see table 12.1). The statements discussed above—statistical, biographical, planning, economic, and philosophical—are insinuated in the formation of new objects (a homeless population) and speaking positions ("success stories"), and they are mobilized together to form novel concepts ("Housing First" and the "business case") and strategic possibilities ("managing homelessness" versus "ending homelessness"). These statements, along with their conditions, constitute a renovated enunciative environment (or "distribution of the sensible") for homelessness policy-making in the province, one in which it becomes possible to declare "the end of homelessness."

A Refashioned Police Order

Following Rancière (1999), this enunciative environment can be theoretically interpreted as a new distribution of the sensible and, by extension, a refashioned police order. Policing encompasses the configuration of a perceptible field that functions as the basis for governing understood in the widest possible sense. As Dikeç (2005, 19) states:

> The police, therefore, is both a principle of distribution and an apparatus of administration, which relies on a symbolically constituted organization of social space, an organization that becomes the basis of and for governance. Thus, the essence of the police is not repression but distribution—distribution of places, people, names, functions, authorities, activities, and so on—and the normalization of this distribution.

"Ending homelessness," therefore, can be taken as a police order, a mode of perceiving predicated upon the identification of a whole (a homeless population) and the distribution of parts (homeless individuals) according to qualifications (recently homeless, periodically homeless, and chronically homeless), competencies (mental illness, substance use problems), and places (street, shelter, independent housing).

In tracing the discursive turn toward "ending homelessness," we are left with a clearer picture of Alberta's reorganized police order. This enunciative environment is constituted by the following:

- Evolving modes of classifying and categorizing homeless people (statistical statements);
- The substitution of new speaking positions, such as the "success story," from which homeless voices are heard (biographical statements);
- The introduction of new styles of reasoning such as "housing first" (planning statements) and the "business case" (economic statements);
- The deployment of new modes of critique (philosophical statements).

Within this new perceptual field, the homeless appear as a governable object of a different sort—a measurable population having particular social characteristics, personal problems, service utilization rates, and economic costs. As a network of statements that transform what can be said about, and done to, the homeless, the discourse of "ending homelessness" supplies a new police order for targeting the subpopulation representing the greatest costs—the chronically homeless.

It is vital to recognize that "ending homelessness," as a discourse and police order, is co-emergent with a number of enunciative conditions. For instance, statistical statements and the formation of homeless populations co-emerged with the consolidation of social research units, data-gathering activities, and increasingly complex data management and information systems. Biographical statements and the new speaking positions from which they emanate co-emerged with the formation of professionalized client-management systems. Planning statements and economic statements, along with the concepts of "Housing First" and the "business case," co-emerged with distended policy networks connecting sites of experimentation and evaluation around the world. Finally, philosophical statements, and thematic distinctions between "managing" and "ending" homelessness, co-emerged with technocratic public policy-making processes. The public expression of the goal of "ending homelessness" reflects not only a significant transformation in Alberta's policy discourse but also a reconfiguration of Alberta's institutional landscape. This marks a significant event with implications for democracy in the province.

(Post)Democracy in Alberta?

Drawing on Rancière's theoretical framework, Erik Swyngedouw (2009, 605) usefully describes the intrinsic link between politics and equality: "Politics is the arena where the principle of equality is tested in the face of a wrong experienced by 'those who have no part.' Equality is thereby axiomatically given and presupposed rather than an idealized-normative condition to move towards." Swyngedouw goes on to emphasize that equality is the necessary precondition of democracy:

> In other words, equality is the very premise upon which a democratic politics is constituted; it opens up the space of the political through the testing of a wrong that subverts equality. Equality is, therefore, not a sociologically verifiable concept or procedure that permits opening a policy arena which

will remedy the observed inequalities, but the ontologically given condition of democracy.

Distinguishing between "the police" and "politics"—and more specifically, between the "policing of homelessness" and the "politics of homelessness"—is useful when considering the democratic implications of Alberta's recent policy shift. Rancière's (1999) theoretical framework gives us pause when interpreting policy changes in Alberta. Housing First (HF), as a historical event, can be interpreted as more democratic than the treatment first (TF) approach in that HF challenges the hierarchy (i.e., deserving versus undeserving) that precludes access to housing under the TF model. In the HF model, equality (specifically in terms of the right to housing) is a presupposed given rather than a condition to move toward. In this sense, HF can be read as an expression of the politics of homelessness.

While recognizing this democratic impulse, it is hard to dismiss the wider characteristics of "ending homelessness" as a new police regime. Here, "ending homelessness" can be read as an economically rationalized, technocratic mode of consensual governing where power is centred outside of democratic accountability in the hands of experts and elites who target expensive subpopulations to minimize their "spillover" costs. Moreover, this new discursive formation circumvents systemic hierarchies in the housing system that precipitate housing crises. Thus, while taking extraordinary steps to house the chronically homeless, *this regime normalizes housing inequality*. This approach could be interpreted as an attempt to manage inherent contradictions in the housing system while keeping it tightly fastened to the marketplace.

What will authorities make of housing problems in 2019, after "homelessness" has been "eradicated"? In other words, what form will the politics of homelessness take after the supposed end of homelessness? If politics is a mode of action that enacts dissensus, then what form can politics take in the face of political consensus that a wrong no longer exists? In light of the inequalities that will still exist in the housing system, taking this policy turn—"ending homelessness"—at its word forecloses upon the properly political; it replaces dissensus with consensus, and in doing so, it imposes a type of closure on questions relating to housing justice. Paradoxically, therefore, "ending homelessness" can be read as a postdemocratic moment in the province.

In conclusion, one theoretical argument developed in this chapter is that democracy is stifled when issues of equality are subsumed within the realm of the police and out of the reach of democratic struggle. It is the stifling of dissensus through consensual practices that forecloses upon democratic action. If one accepts Rancière's definition of politics, then it is difficult to read Alberta's shift toward "ending homelessness" as a democratic move. While these policy developments have undoubtedly expanded access to housing and services for a subset of homeless people, they also constitute a strategy to end a specific type of homelessness (i.e., chronic homelessness) rendered perceptible in terms of economic spillover costs. Alberta's policy turn risks silencing conversations about homelessness as an expression of social injustice. The Alberta government's recent policy response to homelessness nicely illustrates the "paradox of plenty" as it relates to democracy: oil wealth provides states with extraordinary abilities to mute the social dissension and discord that is itself symptomatic of systemic social inequalities.

References

Alberta Secretariat for Action on Homelessness. 2008. *A Plan for Alberta: Ending Homelessness in 10 Years*. Edmonton: Alberta Secretariat for Action on Homelessness.

Calgary Committee to End Homelessness. 2008. *Calgary's 10 Year Plan to End Homelessness*. Calgary, AB: Calgary Committee to End Homelessness.

Calgary Homeless Foundation. 2012. *The State of Homelessness in Calgary in 2012*. Calgary, AB: Calgary Homeless Foundation.

Dikeç, Mustafa. 2005. "Space, Politics, and the Political." *Environment and Planning D: Society and Space* 23 (2): 171–88.

Dreyfus, Hubert, and Paul Rabinow. 1983. *Michel Foucault: Beyond Structuralism and Hermeneutics*. Chicago: University of Chicago Press.

Edmonton Committee to End Homelessness. 2009. *A Place to Call Home: Edmonton's 10 Year Plan to End Homelessness*. Edmonton, AB: Edmonton Committee to End Homelessness.

Edmonton Joint Planning Council on Housing. 2005. *Edmonton Community Plan on Housing and Support Services, 2005–2009*. Edmonton, AB: Edmonton Joint Planning Council on Housing.

Edmonton Task Force on Homelessness. 1999. *Homelessness in Edmonton: A Call to Action*. Edmonton, AB: Edmonton Task Force on Homelessness.

Falvo, Nick. 2009. *Homelessness, Program Responses, and an Assessment of Toronto's Streets to Homes Program*. Ottawa: Canadian Policy Research Networks.

Foucault, Michel. 1972. *The Archaeology of Knowledge*. New York: Pantheon Books.

Gaetz, Steven, Tanya Gulliver, and Tim Richter. 2014. *The State of Homelessness in Canada 2014*. Toronto: Homelessness Hub Press.

Karl, Terry L. 2004. "Oil-Led Development: Social, Political, and Economic Consequences." *Encyclopedia of Energy* 4: 661–72.

Laird, Gordon. 2007. *Homelessness in a Growth Economy: Canada's Twenty-First Century Paradox*. Calgary, AB: Sheldon Chumir Foundation for Ethics in Leadership.

Murdoch, Jon. 2005. *Post-structuralist Geography: A Guide to Relational Space*. Thousand Oaks, CA: Sage.

Øyen, Else. 2009. "A Methodological Approach to 'Best Practices.'" In *Best Practices in Poverty Reduction: An Analytical Framework*, edited by Else Øyen, 1–28. London, UK: Zed Books.

Pomeroy, Steve. 2005. *The Cost of Homelessness: Analysis of Alternate Responses in Four Canadian Cities*. March. Prepared for the National Secretariat on Homelessness.

Rancière, Jacques. 1999. *Disagreement: Politics and Philosophy*. Translated by Julie Rose. Minneapolis: University of Minnesota Press. Originally published as La mésentente: politique et philosophie (1995).

———. 2007. *On the Shores of Politics*. Translated by Liz Heron. London: Verso. Originally published as *Aux bords du politique* (1992).

———. 2010. *Dissensus: On Politics and Aesthetics*. Edited and translated by Steven Corcoran. London: Continuum.

Ruttan, Susan. 2007. "Option Eyed as Tent City Reaches 'Dangerous Size.'" *Edmonton Journal*, 31 July.

Scheurich, James. 1994. "Policy Archaeology: A New Policy Studies Methodology." *Journal of Education Policy* 9 (4): 297–316.

Sorensen, Marianne. 2010. *2010 Edmonton Homeless Count*. Edmonton, AB: Homeward Trust Edmonton.

Swyngedouw, Erik. 2009. "The Antinomies of the Postpolitical City: In Search of a Democratic Politics of Environmental Production." *International Journal of Urban and Regional Research* 33 (3): 601–20.

Tsemberis, Sam. 2010. "Housing First: Ending Homelessness, Promoting Recovery, and Reducing Costs." In *How to House the Homeless*, edited by Ingrid Gould Ellen and Brendan O'Flaherty, 37–56. New York: Russell Sage Foundation.

"The Sharpest Knives in the Drawer"

Visual Culture at the Intersection of Oil and State

Karen Wall

While perusing aerial photographs of the Athabasca bitumen sands, I hear the sounds of road construction outside. Turning from scenes of shining black flows attended by various machines, I look down from the second-storey window to road-resurfacing workers and machines pouring an oily river of black asphalt. The overlapping images serve as reminder of the reach of remote extraction sites into everyday life, of oil constituting not simply a resource but, as Imre Szeman notes, a part of the social ontology underlying industrial capitalism (quoted in Melathopoulos 2010). In Alberta, where the petroleum industry is deeply infused into the social and cultural imaginary, oil companies and provincial governments have together shaped discourses of prosperity, identity, and citizenship for generations. This chapter outlines ways in which oil money has sustained a conjunction of cultural, political, and economic power as it flows through networks of fine art, community entertainment, cultural institutions, and artistic practice. In that context, I inquire into how practices of visual arts "can be integral to political dialogue filling the vacuum left behind by the limitations of representative democracies" (Plessner 2012).

In a petro-culture, key characteristics of which are manifest in Alberta, our understanding of objects and events is deeply informed by oil energy, which shapes not only everyday life but also its representation and content.[1] At present, the entrenched association of the oil industry with a certain configuration of social power supports an adversarial rhetoric that posits critical analysis and challenge as being against the common good. The coincidence of government and industry interests raises questions about the limits to public political participation. If cultural expression is a dimension of democratic citizenship, what role can the visual arts play in both constructing and resisting dominant claims of the centrality of oil to the public interest and to provincial identity? Over the long integration of the oil industry into the complex social and environmental imaginary of the province, both the private and public sectors have supported the arts and cultural production, helping to shape a rich community capacity for critical thought and expression. However, the ongoing loss of public funding for cultural production at both federal and provincial levels, coinciding with steady surges of taxpayer-funded oil industry promotional materials, suggests that this potential wealth of voices is becoming increasingly muffled.

The following discussion first considers visual expression as potentially challenging the legitimation of oil as the central medium not only of energy but of regional identity, prosperity, and quality of life. Drawing on contemporary reportage, public relations statements, policy documents, and exhibition statements, the second section traces the relationship of Alberta governments and oil industry players to cultural development in the historical contexts of province building and the advent of neoliberalism. The analysis considers the potential for contestation and complicity in a province where culture remains integrated into the political and economic conditions of its production. Although a comprehensive survey of relevant cultural production is outside the scope of this chapter, I present representative examples of work in fields of visual arts, including installation and performance, in both institutional and everyday urban space and touch on the role of the Internet in expanding audiences and enabling participants in visual production. A central concern here is the instrumental role taken by the arts and cultural production.

Culture, Citizenship, and Consensus

The public sphere includes the cultural body of ideas informing public debate, as well as the media and spaces of public interaction. In practice, public influence on state decisions through debate is kept, through political institutions, in an orderly balance between social stability and change. When channels of communication fail, though, citizens no longer identify with the system and no longer give it legitimacy (Castells 2008). The understanding of visual cultural forms as part of these mediated networks of communication is particularly important as traditional spheres and spaces of citizenship shrink or vanish. Artists potentially fill a role that was previously taken by a political class involved in critiques of assumptions that steer public policy, helping to liberate thought from the status quo (Latour and Weibel 2005; Miller 2011). Szeman notes that art practices may activate a waning political will by "reminding publics that social life is something to be created and celebrated rather than feared or endured" (cited in Robertson 2006, 13). Commenting more straightforwardly on this potential role of artistic production, an Alberta rancher reportedly called the arts "the sharpest knives in the drawer" of creative democratic tools (quoted in Robinson 2012).

Visual culture, then, participates in discourses of everyday life that produce a set of common assumptions and tacit beliefs underlining public communication. Discourses are understood here in general terms as systems of ideas and practices that construct our understandings of the world and that mediate social and cultural identity, economic development, and social consensus around relations of power. Image-centred discourses and narratives, which Appadurai (1996, 35) calls mediascapes, shape notions of reality in this way and interact with ideoscapes, which are often directly ideological. However, visual imagery is so ubiquitous in our society that, like the network of pipelines under our feet, it can go unremarked as a vehicle of important social and cultural understandings. Creative visual production outside of political and commercial realms has the capacity to visualize or embody the absent or the invisible, whether metaphorical or literal. Such works can potentially break into systems of ideas that seem to be "matters of fact" and complement dominant claims to truth, intervening across boundaries of space—by bringing the far into the near, for example—and of time by reminding us of overarching values and long-term imaginaries.

Modern government arts policies have historically been based on ideals of the democratization of culture, whereby state arts funding, for instance, cannot support elite aesthetic tastes or political agendas but must serve the general public interest. All citizens have access to existing cultural resources and legacies; cultural programs and products are considered public goods. The concept of cultural democracy involves a more radical participation of citizens in cultural production and challenges the insistence of dominant powers that ordinary people remain passive consumers of the cultural status quo. Overwhelmingly, international neoliberal market economies have effectively defined cultural products as commodities and services labelled entertainment, tourism, and knowledge production (Mulcahy 1991). While citizenship historically emerges around civic rights, in the context of neoliberalism, a mass-mediated culture shapes notions of identity and subjectivity in terms of individual opportunity and commodity consumption. Arguments for cultural citizenship in this context broaden a concern with inclusion, belonging, and cultural identity to include potential for creative expression: that is, producing and manipulating dominant meanings of images in order to participate in the presence and volume of voices in public space (Miller 2011).

Critical theorists have called for devalued people and knowledge to engage in cultural participation to produce, as Horkheimer and Adorno (2002) put it, "authentic" art that emancipates citizens from the dominance of instrumental rationality that supports capitalist regimes. However, in practice, the knives usually don't travel far from the proverbial drawer for long. Revolutionary art movements have been repeatedly absorbed into established structures, the avant-garde tied to elite power with "an umbilical cord of gold" (Greenberg 1939, 38). Alternative cultural imaginaries are absorbed into mainstream systems of exhibition and marketing (Fisher 2009, 9).

Since Alberta governments have corralled culture into ministries also variously responsible for multiculturalism, sport, parks, recreation, tourism, and "community spirit," the visual and performing arts have their highest profile as a leisure consumption activity provided by oil wealth. As such, the arts, including visual representations and messages, serve as selling points for provincial destinations and align with economic discourses of creative commercial innovation and civic competition (Harvey 1990, 346–49; Robertson 2006, 12–14). In a petro-state, where state and corporate interests interlock to effectively shape the cultural imaginary, the impacts of oil on democratic society are usually sufficiently normalized as to be hidden in plain sight. Where government revenues accrue without requiring citizen legitimation through tax dollars, or even citizen political engagement, a political culture of "dependence, passivity, and entitlement" ensues (Karl 2007, 21). Alberta, where the Conservatives held power for over four decades, has historically had some of the lowest provincial voter turnouts in the country (Takach 2010, 154–58).[2] What political and economic relations rule the distribution of public funds to the creation of culture? What role, if any, have the visual arts played in the development of local cultural citizenship? As discussed in the following section, the state participates in an uneasy relationship with arts and culture, its support varying with changes in cultural and economic policies.

The Spirit of Alberta: Public Cultural Policies and Corporate Investment

Discourses and narratives are constituted not only of specific content but also of the externalized meanings of objects and phenomena. Oil extraction operations and sites such as the Athabasca bitumen sands have been framed in narratives that have effectively fossilized over several decades of capitalist political power. They are further embedded in histories of Canadian visual culture in naturalizing discourses of industrial capitalism since the late 1800s, with artists, governments, and industrialists connecting resource extraction and nation building in photography, paintings, and majestic murals (Hodgins and Thompson 2011, 394). In the 1970s, industrial images such as a giant bucket wheel used for bitumen extraction adorned postage stamps as a natural component of a collection also featuring hockey, wilderness, animals, and politicians (Davidson and Gismondi 2011, 65). When Stephen Harper, in 2006, compared the "epic" Alberta bitumen sands project with iconic structures such as the pyramids or China's Great Wall ("only bigger"), he placed oil extraction in the historical framework of established dynasties of power and public legacy (Canada, PMO 2006).

With respect to community and regional arts programs, Alberta governments have invoked cultural development as an instrument of province building since at least the 1920s. Goals of economic diversification rationalized related activity and infrastructure in the next decades. Associated ideals of social progress emphasized democratic access to culture, in part to counter stereotypes of the region as a frontier resource base (Whitson, Wall, and Cardinal 2011). The major oil strike of 1947 in Leduc launched a rapid expansion in cultural spending, and 1970s oil prosperity underwrote the Lougheed government's innovative funding programs on the principle "that the province's wealth had something to offer the spirit" (Knecht 2010, 21). Related cultural policies are largely responsible for the building of a significant community of artists and for nurturing audiences in both rural and urban areas (Fraser 2003).

State commitment to cultural funding has predictably risen during boom times and wavered during periods of economic recession in oil markets. However, as the influence of neoliberal ideas has expanded, cultural production that falls outside market processes, like other spheres of civil society, effectively draws power away from political toward economic frameworks. The state exists primarily to protect individual and commercial rights and must exert a minimum of power in a society that is driven by the pursuit of profit with the consequence of the commodification of all spheres of activity (Steinhauer 2009, 7–8; Thorsen 2011). In the economic downturn of the 1980s and early 1990s, described by former Edmonton city councillor Michael Phair as "a particularly dark period of benign neglect (bordering on hostility)" (quoted in

Babiak 2008b), the Klein administration slashed cultural and social program funding while paying large subsidies to the private sector and collecting the lowest oil royalties anywhere (Steinhauer 2009, 7–8).

Despite rising provincial revenues in the 2000s, the paths of oil wealth and cultural investment have diverged. In 2011, for example, funding for the Alberta Foundation for the Arts ($35 million) was less than 0.1 percent of the total $38 billion Alberta budget; the wealthiest jurisdiction in the country ranked sixth among provinces in its per capita funding in 2011 (Professional Arts Coalition of Edmonton 2011) However, in 2008 the province had the highest level of private sector support of the arts in the country (Alberta 2011, 49.) While neoliberalism assumes that economic, political, and cultural realms remain discrete, they are in fact inextricable from each other. Discourses of neoliberalism tend toward privatization, and rhetoric of family and community devolve cultural activity from the responsibility of the state or collective action to consumer activity. For example, the three-day provincial arts festival called "Alberta Arts Days" underwent a name change in 2012 to "Alberta Culture Days." The original focus on artists expanded to include "family-friendly" experiences such as heritage and multicultural events and performances by youth organizations (Hayes 2012; Kuhl 2012). Ideals of diversity, like those of family, align with the status of the arts as a medium for increasing cohesive community and quality of life. Government spending from general revenues tends to go to facility infrastructure such as museums, while lottery funds remain the source of arts funding for contemporary cultural production and critical voices (Wall 2013). Again, the amenities of entertainment and nonconfrontational activity are an unobjectionable perk of a comfortable society. Nevertheless, the trend reflects an ongoing pattern of the withdrawal of government from the provision of platforms for critical expression and for cultural citizenship as participation in production.

Although cultural funding directed to the arts is distributed on an arm's length basis, political strings tend to trail behind, as suggested by responses greeting state funding of films critical of the bitumen sands operations. In the name of economic diversification in 2008, the province increased the budget of the Alberta Mutimedia Development Fund (AMDF, now the Alberta Media Fund) from $20 million to $34 million (Gill 2006). Since that date, AMDF funds have contributed to the production of films including *Downstream* (2008, $67,000), *Dirty Oil* (2009, $54,000), and *Tipping Point: The End of Oil* (2011, $239,083) (Platt 2011). Controversy followed outrage that, in the words of a *Sun*

News columnist, Alberta pays millions to counter negative images of the oil sands while it funds directors "who don't even bother to hide their anti-oilsands agenda," with "every penny potentially damaging the province's economic engine" (Platt 2011). Leslie Iwerk, director of *Downstream*, argued that her work exposed the "province's own truths" and cost far less than efforts "to sugar coat and cover up far more than this film could ever reveal" (Christian 2010).

Shortly after the release of Iwerks's *Downstream*, Alberta's minister of Culture, Lindsay Blackett, awkwardly suggested that ministry investment should instead "show Alberta in a better light, to create an economic diversification" in order to avoid "a negative impetus on this province" (quoted in CBC News 2008a). A week later, he retracted comments about possible censorship in response to an outcry, asserting instead that his job was "to protect free speech, and [that] trying to exercise creative control over movies would be hypocritical" (CBC News 2008b). Three years later, Alison Redford, at the time campaigning for party leadership, emphasized that independent funding processes "protect our freedom of speech and protect our citizens from government-led propaganda," adding that she encouraged potentially fruitful debate toward "positive change" (Platt 2011).

The subject of censorship arose again in 2012 when Edmonton artist Spyder Yardley-Jones exhibited a collection of work, combining graphics and text, that critiqued the environmental impacts of the bitumen sands. Designed to provoke discussion about issues rarely raised in the mainstream media, the satirical work included images of Mother Earth being assaulted by the Harper government and an image with sexual innuendos of government complicity in the whims of Big Oil. Protesters objected, not to provocative challenges to the industry but to government funding of the exhibit, on the grounds that the metaphorical images, taken literally, offended taxpayers' social and moral standards (Di Massa 2012; Ramsay 2012). A year later, Fort McMurray residents protested singer Neil Young's assessment of the area as resembling Hiroshima, and a local radio station banned his music from their broadcasts (CBC 2013).

Similar charges have been regularly levelled at publicly funded art in the past, of course, but the points to consider here are that local cultural producers are explicitly associating their critique of the oil industry with democratic expression and that challenges to that process under the imprimatur of defending public coffers and morality are, at least briefly, considered to be acceptable by community members and leaders. Meanwhile, a 2011 provincial delegation to the Middle East to promote bitumen sands investment met with

Sheikha Hussah Al-sabah to plan the exhibition of her art collection at the new Art Gallery of Alberta (Alberta, International and Intergovernmental Relations 2011). International exhibition capacity was a selling point of the gallery design, but government use of the nonprofit facility to ameliorate oil industry partnerships is striking in a context of ongoing funding cuts for local artists and organizations. As international neoliberal market economies effectively define cultural products as commodities and services, the "Spirit of Alberta" cultural policy (Alberta, Culture and Tourism 2008) and the Alberta Chambers of Commerce (2014) called for greater private arts investment to supplement government funding. In its 2014 policy brief on the arts and creative industries, the Alberta Chambers of Commerce argued that the province's arts sector "can work in tandem with the economy" (1) and recommended that the government leverage existing funding through, for instance, an expanded system of matching grants to attract private donations (3).

As ideologies of neoliberalism have advanced since the late 1970s, arts organizations have increasingly fostered relationships with private donors. Oil industry money funds major Canadian institutions. As art historian and consultant Barry Lord puts it, "Where there's oil, there are museums. . . . *Where our energy comes from determines our values*"; it is surplus energy, he says, that "makes our culture possible" (Lauder 2012). An understanding of cultural expression and development in Alberta must include the seminal role of the oil industry from its early days in Alberta. Eric Harvie and Samuel C. Nickle, petroleum entrepreneurs of the 1940s, not only accumulated important art collections but later established key public cultural institutions, the Nickle Arts Museum and the Glenbow Museum, respectively. Following World War II, multinational oil interests increasingly collected and commissioned industrial images rather than more traditional fine art subjects. Pictures of golden grain fields dotted with drilling rigs, for instance, visually associated the oil industry with established mythic dimensions of Canadian and Albertan identity, much as had the public works and visual culture of an earlier era.

In the 1950s, the largely foreign-owned Imperial Oil, eager to associate itself with Canadian history and nationalism, not only collected Canadian art but commissioned public relations work by prominent artists, including prairie scenery untarnished by oil rigs (Lerner and Williamson 1991, 360; see also Art Gallery of Ontario 1959). In 1951, the Canadian Bank of Commerce, then as now invested in oil, commissioned a collection of Alberta artist Roland Gissing's paintings of oil extraction sites (Foran and Houlton 1988, 44). These and other collections were displayed in public galleries and corporate buildings, further helping to integrate the oil industry into the complex social and environmental imaginary of a progressive province. Such images reflected the merging of political and economic interests in that oil extraction activities were normalized as central to regional identity and prosperity. By the late 1980s, corporations were the fastest-growing sector of Canadian cultural support as neoliberal economic priorities shifted corporate involvement from direct patronage to influential partnerships with public institutions. Today, major oil companies hold professionally curated art collections that are regularly loaned to public institutions in return for promotional access, including facility and event-naming rights (Setterfield and Schabas 2006).

Benefits to the oil industry extend to public perception of industry providing amenities and infrastructure once accruing to the state, including access to culture and quality of community life. In 2000, when Petro-Canada found its large collection too expensive to maintain, the company reported that it would "unlock" its hold on some of the country's best art through donations to public institutions (CBC News 2000). Enbridge's support programs are motivated to provide communities with "inspiration and beauty," and Suncor has partnered with Fort McMurray area civic institutions to construct an eponymous performing arts centre.[3] Other corporations including Syncrude, British Petroleum (BP) Canada, Enbridge, Chevron, Imperial Oil, and Enmax sponsor prominent organizations such as the Alberta Ballet, the Royal Alberta Museum, the Glenbow Museum and Archives, and the Art Gallery of Alberta, as well as youth programs (Hunt 2014; Nestruck 2012).

There is no question that public benefits have accrued from such interventions and that artists and organizations have been enabled; the history of cultural development in Alberta would inarguably be bleaker without corporate involvement. At the same time, urgent questions about the future of oil dependency and environmental impacts demand a long-term view. As arts and culture associations provide oil companies with social legitimacy, symbolic capital, and established audiences, fossil-fuel dependency is normalized in contexts of pleasant aesthetic experiences in public spaces. The idea "that it is therefore normal to continue to burn fossil fuels subtly seeps into our imaginations" (Thomas-Muller and Smith 2012).

A recurring critique of government cultural funding is that its instability discourages long-term planning and the development of a thriving culture. But the distribution of corporate funds is often contingent on shifting commodity prices and competing claims to resources. In the wake of a global recession and spreading environmental concerns about the bitumen sands, some companies redirect public relations funding to higher-profile conservationist groups (Van Herk 2009). In 2008, Syncrude abruptly ended its substantial arts funding in Edmonton primarily in order to prioritize new marketing featuring conservation activities; diverted funds would have proved useful when, after hundreds of ducks died in its tailing ponds in 2008, it paid a $3 million fine in the form of donations to several environmental research and conservation organizations (CBC News 2010b; Saxe and Campbell 2012; "Syncrude Announces" 2012). Epcor and Enbridge stepped in to sponsor Syncrude's abandoned arts groups and Imperial Oil made an unprecedented donation of $300,000 to the Art Gallery of Alberta (Babiak 2008a). However, Epcor ended its agreement with Calgary's Epcor Centre in 2010, and provincial government funding was withdrawn in 2013, leaving the performing arts facility with a critical financial deficit (CBC News 2013, 2014.)

In 2008, Syncrude donated $1.8 million to Fort McMurray's Keyano College to begin the Aboriginal Trades Preparation Program, aimed at training First Nations people to work in the oil industry ("Canadian Oil and Gas" 2010, 3).[4] In 2012, the college abruptly laid off twenty faculty and staff from its arts programs, calling them "under-utilized" to the point that supporting them would undermine new engineering and business programs (Thomas 2012; see also Moher 2012). Low enrolments meant loss of government funding. Critics viewed the transfer of classroom space to new engineering technology and business degree programs as a provincial strategy to prioritize trades and industrial programs and a "devaluation of arts programs" (Yogaretnam 2012). The college's pledge to serve the broader interests of the community coincides with consistently falling support for arts education from a provincial government that bases its funding primarily on enrolment numbers and that increasingly stresses goals of job training. Programs to extend oil jobs to Aboriginal people will provide positive employment opportunities to individuals, but in this context, the consequent loss of other opportunities for artistic expression and employment further shuts down potential channels of cultural citizenship through critical creative training.

Meanwhile, oil companies continue to invest in high-profile professional Aboriginal artists, including Joane Cardinal-Schubert, George Littlechild, Alex Janvier, Bill Reid, and Jane Ash-Poitras, as well as in cultural artifact collections. Arts organizations and programs are also targeted: for example, Enbridge, at the same time that it is negotiating a controversial pipeline over Indigenous lands, is the sponsor of an Aboriginal youth writing program (Enbridge 2014), and Syncrude sponsors the Travelling Exhibition Program (TREX), an Alberta Foundation for the Arts program. Through TREX, professional and amateur painters from First Nations communities have exhibited their work. Two recent exhibitions, "Creator Paints the World . . . the Colour of Our Voice" and "Our Wilderness Is Wisdom," have focused on the human relationship to land and wilderness, through which Aboriginal artists can "speak our truth" amid louder voices (AFA 2011, 3; see also Arndt 2012; for "Our Wilderness Is Wisdom," see AFA 2012; Syncrude Canada Ltd. 2011, 23).

Despite the wide resistance to the bitumen sands project by some Aboriginal peoples (chapters 2 and 6, this volume), the corporate support of First Nations artists points to the fact that oil companies often sponsor or purchase art overtly critical of the status quo. One reason they do this is because "cutting-edge" art aligns with narratives of the sponsors' creative innovation and unbiased social responsibility (Giroux 2005, 31–32). Another is that in a relatively wealthy society, the accommodation of tolerated forms of social critique tends to undermine art's potential for social change since "the arts contribute less as a force for social change and more as a vehicle facilitating the reproduction of existing social formations" (Kenyon 1996, 33). In other words, cultural capitalism, whether underpinned by oil resources or other commodities, tends to absorb ideological conflict rather than give expression to it. As spaces of cultural citizenship come to exist primarily inside institutional walls, corporate cultural partnerships become the norm (Bewes and Gilbert 2000).

Together with the federal government, Enbridge sponsors Aboriginal Arts and Stories (formerly the Canadian Aboriginal Writing and Arts Challenge), a youth arts competition. Aboriginal Arts and Stories, a program of Historica Canada, has as its mandate to "build active and informed citizens through a greater knowledge and appreciation of the history, heritage and stories of Canada."[5] The project has widespread endorsement and participation by Aboriginal cultural leaders, but a group of opponents attending an Enbridge meeting in 2012 included Trevor Jang, a previous contest winner. Jang had appeared in Enbridge promotional material and renounced the corporation for using him as a "native poster boy" for the company (quoted in Healing 2013).

I now turn the discussion back to broader dimensions of visual culture and consider aspects of display and performance in public space and their implications for cultural citizenship through narratives of belonging and identity.

Associated at various times with images of wilderness scenery, agricultural abundance, and the Wild West, the notion of "being Albertan" resonates today with the oil and gas industry. In 2010, the Canadian Association of Petroleum Producers (CAPP) mounted a public relations campaign called "Alberta Is Energy," and the Alberta Enterprise Group likewise asserts that the energy industry is "what makes us Albertans" (Haluza-DeLay 2012, 2–3). Both the public and private sectors are deeply involved in the construction of meaning and consensus in these terms. In 2006, the Province of Alberta contributed a display to promote "Alberta's culture, quality of life and natural beauty" to the prestigious Smithsonian Folklife Festival in Washington, DC, an event conceived as an "educational exposition of living cultural heritage" featuring "community-based cultural exemplars" (Alberta, Alberta Community Development 2006).[6] Alberta displayed information on exports, investment, and tourism; innovation in oil extraction methods was linked to powerful motifs of historic frontier heroism. Looming in the midst of sideshows of cuisine and music, the central display featured a spectacular eighteen-foot-tall model of an oil sands haul truck parked on the Mall as part of the major section on the bitumen sands (Trescott 2006). In challenging the authority of the ministry to define cultural identity in terms of the energy industry in an international exhibition, the Canadian director for the Natural Resources Defense Council implied that the exhibit was a symbol of the "destructive environmental disaster" occurring in Alberta (quoted in Freeman 2006). In response to related criticism, the curator of the exhibit denied that the depiction of Alberta's living cultural heritage was, in essence, "an ad for the oil industry" (quoted in Freeman 2006).

CAPP and the federal Canadian Museum of Civilization announced a $1 million, five-year sponsorship deal in 2013 in support of the museum's planned exhibits celebrating the 150th anniversary of Confederation. The museum's president pointed out that inadequate government funding made such partnerships necessary, while the lobby group's president confirmed the oil industry's motivation of self-promotion. CAPP was previously involved in controversy after it was revealed that sponsorship of another federal museum exhibit had been accompanied by pressure to portray the industry in a positive light (Cheadle 2013).

Advertising and public relations are often indistinguishable in discourses of Alberta oil, as the provincial "brand" is contested and reconstructed. Contentious public debate carries on in what are essentially battles over discursive authority to associate cultural identity and expression with corporate activity in public spaces. Objecting in part to BP's investment in Alberta's "dirty oil," as well as to the 2011 Gulf of Mexico oil spill, the activist group Art Not Oil vehemently protested the corporation's long-standing sponsorship of the Tate Gallery in London. The group staged another protest event in early 2015 addressing Shell's sponsorship of a Rembrandt exhibit at Britain's National Gallery (Thomas-Muller and Smith 2012; Werth 2015).

In 2010, the American organization Corporate Ethics International, as part of its Tar Sands Campaign, launched multimedia advertisements under the tagline Rethink Alberta. The short videos contrast provincial tourism-campaign images of natural beauty "with disturbing images of oil-covered birds, contaminated tailings ponds, and industrial pollution" (CTV News 2010). Alberta retaliated in print and billboard media in the United States in an attempt to change "negative public perceptions of the oilsands" (CBC News 2010a). Corporate Ethics International, like Greenpeace and other activist organizations, relies on private donations, while the provincial government's international public relations campaigns are funded by taxpayers, rendered complicit by association. Those taxpayers did not manifest any substantial objections to the government's PR campaign, contrasting sharply with numerous complaints about government funding for a major new provincial art gallery in Edmonton around the same time (Wall 2011, 25).

Interventions in Petro-culture: Spectacle and Performance

To this point, I have suggested that oil capital has underwritten long, if capricious, state support of cultural production and consumption and has enabled decades of direct patronage and sponsorship of the arts by the private sector. Within this complex, the arts have, to varying extents, served instrumental purposes for both sectors. In the period of the late 1990s and early 2000s, art production increasingly supported neoliberal strategies. Defined as the creative or culture industries, the arts were economically viable resources to be exploited, and funding was provided according to instrumental outcomes (Robertson 2011). Art production also continued to challenge the status quo (Robertson 2006, 11–12), with visual art in particular providing powerful oppositional tools. As suggested above, visual disruptions of singular perspectives, whether visual or ideological, force us to rethink previously fixed meanings. A survey of the proliferating forms of artistic critique of the industry is beyond the scope of this chapter, but it is worth noting that the production of spectacle is particularly well situated at the intersection of art and politics (Boyd and Duncombe 2004; Debord [1967] 1995).

The spectacle experience is particularly powerful, both cognitively and emotionally, in art and performances that mingle elements normally opposed in social categories, such as the dirty, or contaminated, and the clean, or pristine. The concepts of "dirty oil" (i.e., unethical oil) and "clean" corporate patronage point to ideological associations, while sensory creative productions also effectively engage a range of physical senses. Tactical media strategies, including performance-based interventions and installations, have dramatized the eroding of protective boundaries between notions of "here" as pristine and under control and "there" as toxic and chaotic (Forkert 2008). Artists and activists, for example, have inundated the Tate Gallery entrance with gallons of oil-like molasses (Nayeri 2011), covered valuable wildlife paintings with pools of black oil paint (Fong 2008), installed binoculars on a Vancouver beach showing a 3D view of a catastrophic imaginary oil spill at the site (Vancity Buzz 2014), and staged a mock oil spill outside Vancouver pipeline company offices (De Souza 2012).

Mainstream gallery exhibits are typically more subtle and metaphorical in their approach to critique, but some do include overtly didactic pieces such as large immersive environments of slag, sand, and tar replicating oil extraction sites. Mitch Mitchell, for his 2009 installation in Edmonton, "Tar Plane Wayfarer," constructed forms out of newsprint, asphaltum, and carborundum from the bitumen sands to immerse viewers in remote visual and olfactory realities (Fung 2009). In Toronto, Allison Rowe's interactive gallery installation "Bringing Home the Tar Sands" and a mobile "Exploration Station" familiarized viewers with bitumen extraction substances, models, and information (Harbourfront Centre 2010). Canadian sculptor Mia Feuer exhibited an installation in Washington, DC, during political debates about the Keystone XL pipeline. Inspired by bitumen, the work includes an "ominous black skating rink" that "may or may not be a metaphor for oil's grip on Canadian politics" (Nikiforuk 2014).

Alberta artists Sherri Chaba, Lyndal Osborne, and Brenda Christensen, to name a few, have exhibited work, including installations, that brings home the impacts of oil on everyday life and landscapes (Peter Robertson Gallery 2012; Ryan 2012; Willerton 2011). Like the filmmakers noted above, Mitchell, Osborne, and Chaba have each received provincial funding in the form of purchase by the Alberta Foundation for the Arts, the government entity responsible for distribution of grants and support to artists. Such acquisitions, though, remain low profile, proceeding quietly without public discussion or regular display, and are rarely noted by anyone outside the arts community; the likelihood of controversy is remote. Public funding has also supported exhibitions with topical themes addressing the history, significance, and challenges of the oil economy. "Black Gold," an exhibition organized in 2013 by the Art Gallery of Alberta for TREX, featured six artists whose works "shine a spotlight on the oil industry in Alberta" and invited viewers to reflect on "the diverse and complex environmental and social issues associated with the extraction and use of 'black gold'" (AFA 2013, 4).

Artistic photography has possibly had the widest reach among viewers of work that merges documentation with aesthetic, emotional impact. Szeman and Whitehead (2012, 54) note the attempt by critical photographic realism to reveal the "largely hidden dynamic of globalization: the system of oil extraction and production that is the lifeblood of capitalism." Photographer Louis Helbig argues that art can provide "cultural touch stones" to help articulate our relationship to toxic spaces normally omitted from both industry narratives and from standard Canadian nature iconography (quoted in Gismondi 2012; see also Cezer 2012). Edward Burtynsky's renowned views of industry include a series of bitumen sands images in huge aerial views of the "big picture" and the stunning scale of a complex "landscape that cannot be comprehended from the ground" (Punter 2010). Burtynsky's body of work traces entire systems, including the cycle of oil from extraction to consumption, pointing to complicit links of consumers with production conditions and impacts (Shimshock 2008).

In contrast, focusing on the immediacy of a landscape with immediate material consequences for local life, photographer Andriko Lozowy's work constructs a roadside, shifting view of local environmental experience (Patchett and Lozowy 2011). Edmonton artist Brenda Christiansen has produced paintings of everyday oil culture in Fort McMurray. Anya Tonkonogy portrays the story of oil's impact "through the faces of those people whose livelihood depends on what the Great White North has coursing through its earthly veins."[7] Visual art by Susan Turcot and a 2013 film called *Oil Sands Karaoke*, directed by Charles Wilkinson, both take a holistic approach, addressing the nature of labour and daily life by industry workers ("Visual Arts" 2014; McGinn 2013). Kristopher Karklin of Fort MacMurray and Calgary creates large staged photographs based on his experiences in the "sensory-deprivation-like environment of oilsands work camps" (Hunt 2015).

Figure 13.1. Anya Tonkonogy, *I've Been Doing This for a Long Time*, 2010. Oil on birch panel, 20 x 30 in. Courtesy of the artist.

The subjective point of view has also proven effective for oil companies' public relations materials, which tend to feature close-ups of people flyfishing and canoeing on restored industrial lands, Aboriginal cultures and bison, community philanthrophic projects, and happy workers in the field or at gas stations (Friedel 2008). Aware of the public relations value of the personal scale, Shell Canada offered artists access to a refinery during a closure for maintenance to create works portraying individual workers' crafts and stories (Cooper 2013). Whatever their intrinsic merits, such products serve to domesticate extractive activities and integrate the benefits of toxic oil further into cultural imaginaries of the natural, pristine, and nurturing dimensions of Alberta landscapes.

One of the few Canadian collective actions by artists, as opposed to environmentalist groups, occurred when prairie artists and musicians appearing in the National Arts Centre's 2011 Prairie Scene! Festival opposed sponsorship by Enbridge Pipelines in light of the company's successive oil pipeline spills. The letter argued that "the National Arts Centre should choose sponsors that help to promote its values as an innovator in community programming" and that the Enbridge partnership "tarnishes that image with the company's disastrous environmental record."[8] One of the best-known public protests against oil industry cultural involvement in Alberta was mounted by the Lubicon Lake Cree in opposition to the Glenbow Museum's 1988 exhibition "The Spirit Sings: Artistic Traditions of Canada's First Peoples." Shell Oil, a major sponsor, was at the time conducting disputed drilling operations on Lubicon land. Another issue was lack of consultation with Aboriginal groups concerning the exhibit's production (Devine 2010).

As environmental impacts cross a "conceptual threshold . . . from slow change to slow catastrophe," some see a unique "opportunity for a social justice movement to truly articulate a different vision" (Doubleday 2008, 33). Underscoring a comparable lack of substantive influence on oil industry operations in areas directly affecting their lands, First Nations artists have acted outside mainstream cultural institutions. Raising awareness of, and funding for, opposition to the Enbridge pipeline project, West Coast artist Roy Vickers produced T-shirts bearing the slogan "Oolichan Oil Not Alberta Oil" and an oolichan fish—a mainstay of traditional West Coast cultural life—against a background of water darkening in layers to black (Drews 2012). In 2010, a group that included children and First Nations elders produced a painting for public exhibition in open spaces of protest; funds for this initiative were provided by Foreign Affairs, Trade and Development Canada. The canvas, measuring thirty-five by twenty feet, depicted a First Nations face enmeshed in a mosaic of images, including the BP oil spill, pipelines, dead ducks, deformed fish, and gashes in the earth (BC Council for International Cooperation 2010; Schambach 2010.). Cultural performance at marches and demonstrations—incorporating traditional ceremonial dress, drums, and chanting—remains the most visible public expression of collective Aboriginal direct action in the mainstream media (Postmedia News 2012).[9]

Activist interventions occurring in urban corporate and retail zones are a form of democratic representation that reclaims the space by redefining it as a more complicated narrative of public life and citizen activity. Artist Peter von Tiesenhausen, whose rural property displays scores of his earthworks and sculptures, exercised similar powers after fighting years of legal challenges from oil and gas interests determined to drill his land for its rich natural gas reserves. Taking the creative step of copyrighting his property as art in itself, which would make compensation costs for destruction much more prohibitive (Fung 2010; Jaremko 2006), he redefined the meaning and value of his land using legal discourse in an attempt to place it beyond the reach of the petroleum interests that have long had the upper hand in decision making. Presumably to avoid the risk of a drawn-out legal battle and bad publicity, natural gas companies have left Von Tiesenhausen and his land in peace (Goyal, n.d.).

In a framework of plural claims to truth, the production of meaning may be best democratized through dispersing understandings across enclaves of knowledge and practice: public and private, economic and aesthetic, literary and scientific (Gordon 2012; Stern and Seifert 2009, 33–34; Stevenson and Dryzek 2012). Opposition to the environmental effects of bitumen sands extraction, for example, links climate activists, audiences, scientists, Indigenous communities, and producers across continents (Fend 2001).[10] Kester (1999) suggests a "littoral art" or middle space between discourses of art and activism and across disciplinary bodies of knowledge, vaulting the sharp divide between official, institutionalized fine art and activist or amateur production. In this ethos, the artwork or project is not a discrete commodity, artifact, or object but a medium of socially engaged practice that can transgress dominant meanings.

Virtual Public Space

As Jay Smith puts it in chapter 3, "in a globalized world, the spaces of politics are being transformed. No longer is politics solely centred around the institutions of the state." Since new technologies of power cannot be identified with territory or centralized apparatus, the classic opposition of domination and resistance is also dispersed in a society which has become a .multitude of mobile subjectivities (Hardt and Negri 2009, xiii-cvi). As has been posited by a plethora of observers, the Internet has a demonstrated capacity to link oppositional, democratic interests as well as to connect imaginatively with distant sites and forms of knowledge. As new digital tools and technologies such as YouTube and social media are available for dissent, narratives expand and splinter in contact with a broader range of participants who are able to develop faster tactical responses and meanings of messages (Jenkins 2011). International artists steadily produce works in visual, cinematic, literary, digital, and performative media that critique and challenge the ecological impacts of the fossil fuel industry and its involvements with cultural institutions (Aidt 2013).

To illustrate, it was community members rather than oil companies who publicly objected to the 2012 Spyder Yardley-Jones exhibit of satirical images (Di Massa 2012). Responses are markedly different when very similar images make the leap from small gallery spaces to comparatively huge audiences online. In 2012, Enbridge released an animated video promoting its pipeline proposal with a series of pastel, romantic images of families, communities, and forests. Postmedia News cartoonist Dan Murphy adapted this utopian narrative by adding intermittent eruptions of oily black goo redolent of pipeline spills. After Enbridge reportedly threatened to withdraw advertising, the publisher pulled the piece off its website (CBC News 2012). Even more telling was the cancellation of federal government funding to Canadian artist Franke James, whose text-adorned graphics, which are very similar to those of Yardley-Jones, critique the oil industry and its political wingmen. In 2011, when Canada was negotiating a European trade deal while fighting European objections to "dirty oil," a federal grant supporting a European show of James's work was cancelled because her message was "not in sync" with government messaging (James, quoted in MacCharles 2011)—an event she documented in "Banned on the Hill (and in Europe!)" (James 2011). James reached a much larger audience by publishing an online series of pipeline images titled "What Is Harper Afraid Of?" (James 2012; see also LaFontaine 2012).

New media have inarguable value for cultural producers, whether amateur or professional, and thus expand the resources of cultural citizenship as they vastly expand audiences. However, dominant economic and political interests also adapt to new channels, and autonomous communication is under increasing stress. Sharp though the knives of virtual culture can be, those of other media need not become dull as means of dialogue. Public spaces, for example, can function as media for display and performance, as well as exhibition, in ways that enhance their potential for building social relationships and reimagining politics as part of everyday life. And conventional gallery spaces remain important media for exploring aspects of petro-culture, including the Athabasca bitumen sands. A few examples of recent international art exhibitions examining the impacts of oil include an Ontario show called "Perspectives on Canadian Tar Sands and the Northern Gateway Pipeline," a New York City exhibit titled "Petroleum Paradox: For Better or For Worse?" and a show in Texas called "Necrocracy" that examined fossil fuels in terms of our ongoing dependency on dead forms of life.[11] These and many more interventions in the visual discourses of oil energy across multiple media all have potential to contribute to a littoral public repository of knowledge and action.

Cultural Citizenship and "Peak Imagination"

The notion of a divide between a humanist approach to culture as having intrinsic value and a market-driven set of criteria for its existence has become blurred, if not collapsed, in the context of contemporary capitalist societies. Both the private and public sectors enable production at various levels, provide spaces of consumption, and legitimize the arts as commodity and as public goods, at least within certain boundaries of social cohesion, entertainment, and individual expression. A political culture that supports the arts benefits from association with long-term humanist values, including cultural identity, social cohesion, and free expression. Support by industry bestows direct and indirect public relations value amounting to economic strength. In practice, democratic values of cultural identity, cohesion, and free expression have been associated through the cultural realm with the needs of industry for deep embeddedness in political decision making. Cultural and corporate citizenship tend to overlap. At present, the emancipatory potential of cultural production is compromised by the steady withdrawal of public funding from individuals and organizations, along with a rise in public spending on the production of ubiquitous public relations imagery defending the oil industry.

Is oil wealth a positive force for democratic cultural development and expression? Is there any sign that art has successfully changed the course of politics or economic growth? Again, cultural production and citizenship are long-term processes, and it may be most useful to think about the arts not in terms of direct impacts of products or images but as a complex of practices and knowledge that are building or undermining consent to the status quo. On the one hand, government and corporate support of the arts in Alberta has produced not only a rich body of work but also several generations of artists and cultural activists questioning authority on a number of fronts. On the other hand, the fulcrum of effective change is the perceived legitimacy of the speakers. In a wealthy jurisdiction that is largely content with the status quo, the arts tend to be relegated to the status of entertainment, festival content, and cultural capital. They remain delegitimized both as serious occupations and as options for productive communication by nonprofessionals; funding cuts to arts education, as well as to practice, suggest the difficulty of collectively overcoming these stereotypes. With continually accelerating international attention to the impacts of Alberta's oil industry, however, the meaning of cultural citizenship in the province is perhaps less limited to its designated borders or to dependence on state or corporate permission. LeMenager (2012, 69) reminds us that, after all, we have not yet reached "peak imagination." The historic electoral victory of Rachel Notley and the New Democratic Party in 2015, displacing a four-decade political monopoly by the Conservatives, signals the determination of Alberta citizens to imagine new ways to reach that peak.

Notes

1 The study of petro-cultures is relatively new, but expanding. In 2011, the University of Alberta established the Petrocultures Research Group, which conducts and supports research into "the social, cultural and political implications of oil and energy use on individuals, communities, and societies around the world," in order to "observe, assess and analyze the multiple and complex impacts of the development and management of the oil industry and of energy more generally." "Petrocultures," 2015, http://petrocultures.com/about/.

2 Turnouts were especially low in the provincial elections of 2004 and 2008: 45.12 percent and 40.59 percent, respectively (Elections Alberta 2015).

3 See "Everyone's Community: Social, Cultural, and Educational Achievement," *Enbridge*, 2015, http://www.enbridge.com/InYourCommunity/CommunityInvestment/Community.aspx; and "Suncor Energy Foundation Partners to Build Fort McMurray Performing Arts Centre," news release, 1 October 2008, http://www.suncor.com/en/newsroom/5441.aspx?id=1088505.

4 "Syncrude Donates $5 Million to Keyano College," *Academica Group*, 15 October 2008, http://academica.ca/top-ten/syncrude-donates-5-million-keyano-college.

5 "About and Contact Us," *Aboriginal Arts and Stories*, Historica Canada, 2015, http://www.our-story.ca/about/.

6 "Mission and History," *Smithsonian Folklife Festival, Smithsonian Institution*, 2015, http://www.festival.si.edu/about/mission.aspx.

7 See Christiansen's artist statement for "The Fort McMurray Series" at http://www.brendakim.com/statement_ftmcmurray.html. Anya Tonkonogy's words are taken from her artist statement, 23 July 2012, at *Latitude 53: Contemporary Visual Culture*, http://blog.latitude53.org/post/27850079373/this-weeks-incubator-artist-anya-tonkonogy-is.

8 The group, calling itself Prairie Artists Against Enbridge, expressed their objections in a letter of 25 January 2011 to Christopher Dearlove and Rosemary Thompson, of the National Arts Centre. By accepting support from Enbridge, they argued, the NAC "associates itself with the company's irresponsible corporate behavior." The letter is available at http://pipeupagainstenbridge.ca/news/prairie_artists_against_enbridge.

9 For example, the fifth annual Tar Sands Healing Walk, sponsored by the Keepers of the Athabasca, took place on 27–29 June 2014 (http://www.healingwalk.org/home.html).

10 One example of an attempt to bring together "creatives, scientists, and informers" to produce an international "cultural response to the climate challenge" is the UK-based Cape Farewell project (http://www.capefarewell.com/about.html).

11 See "Perspectives on Canadian Tar Sands and the Northern Gateway Pipeline," Elora Centre for the Arts, Elora, Ontario, 17 May–8 July 2012, http://www.eloracentreforthearts.ca/index.cfm?page=Gallery_2012TarS_MED; "Petroleum Paradox: For Better or for Worse?" Denise Bibro Fine Art Inc., New York, 24 May–23 June 2012, http://www.denisebibrofineart.com/exhibitions/1256; and "Marina Zurkow: Neocracy," DiverseWorks, Houston, Texas, 17 March–21 April 2012, http://www.diverseworks.org/past-works/archive/marina-zurkow-necrocracy.

References

AFA (Alberta Foundation for the Arts). 2011. *Creator Paints the World . . . the Colour of Our Voice: Interpretive Guide and Hands-on Activities*. Alberta Foundation for the Arts Travelling Exhibition Program 2011–2013. Edmonton: AFA Travelling Exhibition Program. http://www.trexprogramsoutheast.ca/files/2012/10/Creator-Paints-the-World-ed-kit.pdf.

———. 2012. *Our Wilderness Is Wisdom . . . : Interpretive Guide and Hands-on Activities*. Alberta Foundation for the Arts Travelling Exhibition Program 2012–2014. Edmonton: AFA Travelling Exhibition Program. http://www.trexprogramsoutheast.ca/files/2012/10/Our-wilderness-is-wisdom...pdf.

———. 2013. *Black Gold: Interpretive Guide and Hands-on Activities*. Alberta Foundation for the Arts Travelling Exhibition Program 2013–2015. Edmonton: AFA Travelling Exhibition Program. http://www.youraga.ca/wp-content/uploads/2013/08/Black-Gold2.pdf.

Aidt, Mik. 2013. "Uprise Among Artists Against 'Dirty Oil Money.'" *Centre for Climate Safety*, 30 August. http://climatesafety.info/uprise-among-artists-against-dirty-oil-money/#sthash.wsxKegYy.dpuf.

Alberta. 2011. *Highlights of the Alberta Economy 2011*. http://www.slideshare.net/cambridgestrategies/highlights-of-the-alberta-economy-20111.

Alberta. Alberta Community Development. 2006. "Final Report: Mission to Washington, D.C. , June 24 to July 5, 2006." http://www.culture.alberta.ca/international_travel/Alberta_Week_in_Washington_and_the_Smithsonian_Folklife_Festival_Final_Report.pdf.

Alberta Chambers of Commerce. 2014. *Arts and Creative Industries Policy in Alberta*. Edmonton: Alberta Chambers of Commerce. http://www.abchamber.ca/accs-policies/.

Alberta. Culture and Tourism. 2008. *Spirit of Alberta: Alberta's Cultural Policy*. http://www.culture.alberta.ca/about/premiers-council/pdf/SpiritofAlberta.pdf.

Alberta. International and Intergovernmental Relations. 2011. *Final Report: Mission to Thailand, the Middle East, and the UK*. http://www.international.alberta.ca/documents/ThailandMiddleEastUK_January2011.pdf.

Appadurai, Arjun. 1996. *Modernity at Large: Cultural Dimensions of Globalization*. Minneapolis: University of Minnesota Press.

Arndt, Sandy. 2012. "Aboriginal Art Gives Vibrant Life to Culture, Tradition." *Alberta Sweetgrass*, 1 September. http://www.readperiodicals.com/201209/2770591101.html.

Art Gallery of Toronto. 1959. *A Canadian Survey: Selected Works from the Collection of Imperial Oil Limited*. Toronto: Art Gallery of Ontario.

Babiak, Todd. 2008a. "Oilsands Arts Funding Dries Up." *Edmonton Journal*, 21 February.

———. 2008b. "City Arts Plan: Not Just Smart, It's Essential." *Edmonton Journal*, 12 April.

BC Council for International Cooperation. 2010. "Tar Sand Art." *BCCIC*, 7 June. http://bccic.ca/event/tar-sand-art.

Bewes, Timothy, and Jeremy Gilbert, eds. 2000. *Cultural Capitalism: Politics After New Labour*. London: Lawrence and Wishart.

Boyd, Andrew, and Stephen Duncombe. 2004. "The Manufacture of Dissent: What the Left Can Learn from Las Vegas." *Journal of Aesthetics and Protest* 1 (3). http://www.joaap.org/new3/duncombeboyd.html.

Canada. PMO (Prime Minister's Office). 2006. "Address by the Prime Minister at the Canada-UK Chamber of Commerce." Prime Minister of Canada Stephen Harper. London, UK, 14 July. http://www.pm.gc.ca/eng/media.asp?id=1247.

"Canadian Oil and Gas: The First Nations—Building Successful Partnerships." 2010. *Profiler*, May. https://aboriginalhr.ca/sites/ahrc/files/attachments/Article%20--%20Profiler%20-%20Oil%20and%20Gas%20%20The%20First%20Nations.pdf May.

Castells, Manuel. 2008. "The New Public Sphere: Global Civil Society, Communication Networks, and Global Governance." *Annals of the American Academy of Political and Social Science* 616 (March): 78–93.

CBC. 2013. "Ft. McMurray Radio Station Bans Neil Young for Calling Their Town 'a Wasteland.'" *George Stroumboulopoulos Tonight*, 12 September. http://www.cbc.ca/strombo/music-2/fort-mcmurray-radio-station.html.

CBC News. 2000. "Petro-Canada Gives Away Its Art Collection." *CBC News*, 3 November. http://www.cbc.ca/news/canada/story/2000/11/03/petrocan_art001103.html.

———. 2008a. "Alberta Rethinks Film Funding Rules After Anti-Oilsands Doc Gets Cash." *CBC News*, 11 December. http://www.cbc.ca/m/touch/arts/story/1.721746.

———. 2008b. "I Won't Censor Films: Alberta Culture Minister." *CBC News*, 17 December. http://www.cbc.ca/news/arts/film/story/2008/12/17/blackett-recants.html.

———. 2010a. "Oil Sands Campaign Hits Times Square." *CBC News*, 11 September. http://www.cbc.ca/news/canada/edmonton/oilsands-campaign-hits-times-square-1.958781.

———. 2010b. "Syncrude to Pay $3M Penalty for Duck Deaths." *CBC News*, 22 October. http://www.cbc.ca/news/canada/edmonton/story/2010/10/22/edmonton-syncrude-dead-ducks-sentencing.html.

———. 2012. "Cartoonist Says Enbridge Spoof Pulled Under Pressure." *CBC News*, 26 June. http://www.cbc.ca/news/canada/british-columbia/story/2012/06/26/bc-cartoonist-enbridge-spoof.html.

———. 2013. "Calgary's Epcor Centre Faces Cash Crunch." *CBC News*, 4 September. http://www.cbc.ca/news/canada/calgary/calgary-s-epcor-centre-faces-cash-crunch-1.1396566.

———. 2014. "Calgary Arts Centre Drops Epcor from Name." *CBC News*, 24 June. http://www.cbc.ca/news/canada/calgary/calgary-arts-centre-drops-epcor-from-name-1.2686151.

Cezer, Julie Houle. 2012. "Louis Helbig's High Art Reflects Our Challenges." *Glebe Report*, 9 March.

Cheadle, Bruce. 2013. "Museum of Civilization Taps Oil Patch to Help Fund Canada's 150th." *Chronicle Herald* (Halifax), 25 November. http://thechronicleherald.ca/canada/1169896-museum-of-civilization-taps-oil-patch-to-help-fund-canada-s-150th.

Christian, Carol. 2010. "Dirty Oil Documentary Received Provincial Funding." *Fort McMurray Today*, 2 September.

Cooper, Dave. 2013. "Shell Seeks Artists to Capture Story of Scotford's 'Turnaround.'" *Edmonton Journal*, August 26.

CTV News. 2010. "Rethink Alberta Campaign Targets Tourists." *CTV News Calgary*, 15 July. http://calgary.ctvnews.ca/rethink-alberta-campaign-targets-tourists-1.532489.

Davidson, Debra J., and Mike Gismondi. 2011. *Challenging Legitimacy at the Precipice of Energy Calamity*. New York: Springer.

Debord, Guy. (1967) 1995. *Society of the Spectacle*. Translated by Donald Nicholson-Smith. New York: Zone Books.

De Souza, Mike. 2012. "Enbridge Can't Say If Federal Cuts Would Undermine Oil Spill Response." *Vancouver Sun*, 13 June.

Devine, Heather. 2010. "After the Spirit Sang: Aboriginal Canadians and Museum Policy in the New Millennium." In *How Canadians Communicate III: Contexts of Canadian*

Popular Culture, edited by Bart Beaty, Derek Briton, Gloria Filax, and Rebecca Sullivan, 217–39. Edmonton, AB: Athabasca University Press.

Di Massa, Michael. 2012. "Controversial Gallery to Stay Open." *Sherwood Park News*, 25 September. IU.

Doubleday, Nancy C. 2008. "Slow Catastrophes, Cumulative Impacts, Multiple Scales, and Resilience in the Oil-Tar Sands: A Case for Collaborative Communication and Communicative Planning?" Paper presented at Planning the Unthinkable: Symposium on Resilience Planning, 16–18 November, Virginia Institute of Technology, Blacksburg, VA.

Drews, Keven. 2012. "Renowned B.C. Artist Finds Political Voice of Proposed Enbridge Pipeline." *Global News*, 11 March. http://globalnews.ca/news/221350/renowned-b-c-artist-finds-political-voice-of-proposed-enbridge-pipeline-2/.

Elections Alberta. 2015. "Overall Summary of Ballots Cast and Voter Turnout, 1975–2015." *Elections Alberta*. http://www.elections.ab.ca/reports/statistics/overall-summary-of-ballots-cast-and-voter-turnout/.

Enbridge. 2014. "Promoting Perspectives: Enbridge Supports Emerging Aboriginal Artists Across Canada." *Enbridge*, 22 December. http://www.enbridge.com/Viewer?id=A6101BE9EBE945BE9D4AFFB967F3EBF0.

Fend, Peter. 2001. "H2Earth." *Mute* 1 (22). http://www.metamute.org/editorial/articles/h2earth.

Fisher, Mark. 2009. *Capitalist Realism: Is There No Alternative?* Blue Ridge Summit, PA: Zero Books.

Fong, Petti. 2008. "Robert Bateman Defaces Painting—on Purpose." *Toronto Star*, 20 March.

Foran, Max, and Nounie Houlton. 1988. *Roland Gissing: The People's Painter*. Calgary, AB: University of Calgary Press.

Forkert, Kirsten. 2008. "Tactical Media and Art Institutions: Some Questions." *Third Text* 22 (5): 589–98.

Fraser, Fil. 2003. *Alberta's Camelot: Culture and the Arts in the Lougheed Years*. Edmonton, AB: Lone Pine.

Freeman, Alan. 2006. "Alberta's Gift to Culture." *Globe and Mail*, 6 June.

Friedel, Tracy. 2008. "(Not So) Crude Text and Images: Stage Natives in 'Big Oil' Advertising. *Visual Studies* 23 (3): 238–54.

Fung, Amy. 2009. "Tar Plane Wayfarer: Kamikaze Tar Plane." *VueWeekly* (Edmonton), 15 January.

———. 2010. "An Alberta Sculptor Fights Oil Companies to Exhibit Art on his Own Land." *This Magazine*, 22 April.

Gill, Alexandra. 2006. "Alberta Arts on the Cusp." *Globe and Mail*, 9 December.

Giroux, Henri. 2005. "The Terror of Neoliberalism: Rethinking the Significance of Cultural Politics." *College Literature* 32 (1): 1–19.

Gismondi, Mike. 2012. "Aerial Photography, the Tar Sands, and Imagined Landscapes: Interview with Louis Helbig." *Aurora Online*. http://aurora.icaap.org/index.php/aurora/article/view/90/111.

Gordon, Jonathan. 2012. "Rethinking Bitumen: From 'Bullshit' to a 'Matter of Concern.'" *Imaginations* 3 (2): 170–87.

Goyal, Monica. N.d. "No, It's Not Copyright That Is Keeping a Natural Gas Pipeline off of Peter von Tiesenhausen's Farm." *Aluvion.* http://aluvionlaw.com/no-its-not-copyright-that-is-keeping-a-natural-gas-pipeline-off-of-peter-von-tiesenhausens-farm/.

Greenberg, Clement. 1939. "Avant-garde and Kitsch." *Partisan Review* 6 (5): 34–49.

Haluza-DeLay, Randolph. 2012. "Giving Consent in the Petrostate: Hegemony and Alberta Oil Sands." *Journal for Activist Science and Technology Education* 4 (1): 1–6.

Harbourfront Centre. 2010. "Too Cool for School: Art and Science Exhibition." Visual Arts Exhibitions 2010. *Harbourfront Centre.* http://www.harbourfrontcentre.com/visualarts/2011/too-cool-for-school-art-science-exhibition/.

Hardt, Michael, and Antonio Negri. 2009. *Multitude: War and Democracy in the Age of Empire.* New York: Penguin Books.

Harvey, David. 1990. *The Condition of Postmodernity.* Oxford: Blackwell.

Hayes, Scott. 2012. "Arts Days Becomes Culture Days." *St. Albert Gazette,* 4 July.

Healing, Dan. 2013. "Northern Gateway Foes Hijack Enbridge Meeting." *Calgary Herald,* 8 May.

Hodgins, Peter, and Peter Thompson. 2011. "Taking the Romance out of Extraction: Contemporary Canadian Artists and the Subversion of the Romantic/Extractive Gaze." In *Environmental Communication: A Journal of Nature and Culture* 5 (4): 393–410.

Horkheimer, Max, and Theodor W. Adorno. 2002. *Dialectic of Enlightenment.* Edited by Gunzelin Schmid Noerr. Translated by Edmund Jephcott. Stanford, CA: Stanford University Press.

Hunt, Stephen. 2014."Oil Companies See Value in the Arts." *Calgary Herald,* 12 December.

———. 2015. "Artist Kristopher Karklin Manipulates His Memories of Oilsands." *Calgary Herald,* 22 March.

James, Franke. 2011. "Banned on the Hill (and in Europe!)." *Franke James* (blog). http://www.frankejames.com/banned-on-the-hill/.

———. "What Is Harper Afraid Of?" *Franke James* (blog). http://www.frankejames.com/what-is-harper-afraid-of/.

Jaremko, Gordon. 2006. "Opposition to Drilling Elevated to an Art Form." *Edmonton Journal,* 27 February.

Jenkins, Henry. 2011. "The Revolution Will Be Hashtagged: The Visual Culture of the Occupy Movement." *Confessions of an Aca-Fan* (blog), 29 October. http://henryjenkins.org/2011/10/the_revolution_will_be_hashtag.html.

Karl, Terry L. 2007. "Oil-Led Development: Social, Political and Economic Consequences." CDDRL Working Paper No. 80. January. Stanford University, Center on Democracy, Development, and the Rule of Law.

Kenyon, Gerald S. 1996. "Corporate Involvement in the Arts and the Reproduction of Power in Canada." In *Art and Business: An International Perspective on Sponsorship,* edited by Rosanne Martorella, 33–46. Westport, CT: Praeger.

Kester, Grant. 1999. "Dialogical Aesthetics: A Critical Framework for Littoral Art." *Variant* 9 (Winter 1999/2000). http://www.variant.org.uk/9texts/KesterSupplement. html.

Knecht, Brigit M. 2010. "Government Imposition of Sustainable Business Practices in the Arts." *Stream: Culture / Politics / Technology* 3 (1): 20–32.

Kuhl, Nick. 2012. "Culture Gets Revitalized." *Lethbridge Herald*, 20 October.

LaFontaine, Peter. 2012. "An Artist's Take: Tar Sands and Canada's War on Mother Nature." *Wildlife Promise* (blog), 31 May. National Wildlife Federation, Merrifield, VA. http://blog.nwf.org/2012/05/an-artists-take-tar-sands-and-canadas-war-on-mother-nature/.

Latour, Bruno, and Peter Weibel. 2005. *Making Things Public: Atmospheres of Democracy.* Cambridge, MA: MIT Press.

Lauder, Adam. 2012. "Energy Trade: Where the Museums Are. An Interview with Barry Lord." *Canadian Art* (Summer): 102–4.

LeMenager, Stephanie 2012. "The Aesthetics of Petroleum, After Oil!" *American Literary History* 24 (1): 59–86.

Lerner, Loren R. , and Mary F. Williamson. 1991. *Art and Architecture in Canada / Art et architecture au Canada: A Bibliography and Guide to the Literature.* Toronto: University of Toronto Press.

MacCharles, Tonda. 2011. "Artist Sees Red Over Government 'Blacklisting.'" *Toronto Star*, 28 July.

McGinn, Dave. 2013. "Oil Sands Karaoke: A Rich Portrait of the People Who Work in Fort McMurray." *Globe and Mail*, 8 November.

Melathopoulos, Andony. 2010. "An Interview with Imre Szeman." With Brian Worley. *Platypus Review* 29 (November). http://platypus1917.org/2010/11/06/oil-and-the-left-an-interview-with-imre-szeman/#_foot2.

Miller, Toby. 2011. "Cultural Citizenship." *Matrizes* 4 (2): 57–75.

Moher, Frank. 2012. "Fort McMurray's Keyano College Sends Arts to Tailings Pond." *Back of the Book* (blog), 6 May. http://backofthebook.ca/2012/05/06/fort-mcmurrays-keyano-college-sends-arts-to-tailings-pond/6465/.

Mulcahy, Kevin V. 1991. "The Public Interest in Public Culture." *Journal of Arts Management, Law, and Society* 21: 5–25.

Nayeri, Farah. 2011. "Anti-BP Activists Stage Nude Lie-In, Pour Oil at Tate Britain." *Bloomberg Business*, 20 April. http://www.bloomberg.com/news/2011-04-20/anti-bp-activists-stage-nude-lie-in-pour-oil-at-tate-on-spill-anniversary.html.

Nestruck, J. Kelly. 2012. "The Oil Sands' Latest Byproduct: Cutting-Edge Theatre." *Globe and Mail*, 11 February.

Nikiforuk, Andrew. 2014. "The Oilsands-Inspired Creation That Looms in Washington." *The Tyee*, 23 January. http://thetyee.ca/ArtsAndCulture/2014/01/23/Oilsands-Art/.

Patchett, Merle, and Andriko Lozowy. 2011. "Reframing the Canadian Oil Sands." *Imaginations* 3 (2): 140–69.

Peter Robertson Gallery. 2012. "Brenda Kim Christiansen: The Premise of Nature." 10–27 March 2012. *Peter Robertson Gallery*. http://www.probertsongallery.com/component/exhibition/?task=exhibition_detail&id=56&year=2012.

Platt, Michael. 2011. "Oilsands Critics Taking Fool's Money." *SunNews*, 5 September.

Plessner, Daphne. 2012. "Political Activism and Art: A Consideration of the Implications of New Developments in Practice, Art, and Education." *Art and Education: Papers*. http://www.artandeducation.net/paper/political-activism-and-art-a-consideration-of-the-implications-of-new-developments-in-practice/.

Postmedia News. 2012. "First Nations Members Bring Pipeline Protest to the Steps of Alberta legislature." *Canada.com*, 2 May. http://www.canada.com/news/First+Nati ons+members+bring+pipeline+protest+steps+Alberta+legislature/6554237/story. html#ixzz1zqzKyWOd.

Professional Arts Coalition of Edmonton. 2011. "Artists 'Freeze' to Launch Advocacy Campaign." Media advisory, 15 February. http://www.pacedmonton.com/?p=508.

Punter, Jennie. 2010. "Bird's Eye View of the Oil Sands Rises Above the Spin." *Globe and Mail*, 22 January.

Ramsay, Caley. 2012. "Art Exhibit Causing Major Controversy in Strathcona County." *Global News*, 21 September. http://globalnews.ca/news/289394/art-exhibit-causing-major-controversy-in-strathcona-county/.

Robertson, Kirsty. 2006. "Tear Gas Epiphanies: New Economies of Protest, Vision and Culture in Canada." PhD diss., Department of Visual Arts, Queen's University.

———. 2011. "Dancing Mounties, Flamingo Pink Jackets, Culture and Elitism." *FUSE Magazine* 34 (2). http://fusemagazine.org/2011/04/dancing-mounties-flamingo-pink-jackets-culture-and-elitism.

Robinson, Mike. 2012. "Democracy's Sharpest Knives in the Drawer." *Troy Media*, 4 March. http://www.troymedia.com/blog/2012/03/04/democracys-sharpest-knives-in-the-drawer/.

Ryan, Janice. 2012. "Installations Explore Effects of Oil Industry on Landscape." *Edmonton Journal*, 18 July.

Saxe, Diane, and Jackie Campbell. 2012. "Getting Creative with the Law." *Water Canada*, 16 April. http://watercanada.net/2012/getting-creative-with-the-law/.

Schambach, Melanie. 2010. "Tar Sands Painting." *Community Arts Council of Vancouver*, 13 August. http://communityarts.ning.com/photo/tar-sand-painting/next?context=user.

Setterfield, Gwenlyn, and Ezra Schabas. 2006. "Funding, Patronage and Volunteerism." *The Canadian Encyclopedia*. http://www.thecanadianencyclopedia.ca/en/article/funding-patronage-and-volunteerism-emc/.

Shimshock, Ron. 2008. "Politicians Beware: Oil Photo Exhibit Opens in DC." *Chris Martenson's Peak Prosperity* (blog), 27 August. http://www.chrismartenson.com/forum/politicians-beware-oil-photo-exhibit-opens-dc/28659.

Steinhauer, Randy. 2009. "Born to Fail: Neoliberalism and the Meltdown." *Parkland Post*, Fall, 7–8.

Stern, Mark J., and Susan C. Seifert. 2009. "Civic Engagement and the Arts: Issues of Conceptualization and Measurement." January. Arts and Civic Engagement Impact Initiative, Americans for the Arts / Animating Democracy.

Stevenson, Hayley, and John S. Dryzek. 2012. "The Discursive Democratisation of Global Climate Governance." *Environmental Politics* 21 (2): 189–210.

"Syncrude Announces New Donations." 2012. *My McMurray*, 17 May. http://www.mymcmurray.com/syncrude-announces-new-donations/.

Syncrude Canada Ltd. 2011. "Artistic Impressions." *Pathways: Syncrude Canada Ltd. Aboriginal Review 2011*, 23. http://www.syncrude.ca/assets/pdf/Syncrude-Pathways-2011.pdf.

Szeman, Imre, and Maria Whiteman. 2012. "Oil Imag(e)inaries: Critical Realism and the Oil Sands." *Imaginations* 3 (2): 46–67.

Takach, Geo. 2010. *Will the Real Alberta Please Stand Up?* Edmonton: University of Alberta Press.

Thomas, Russell. 2012. "An Open Letter to the Editor." *Wood Buffalo Culture*. Posted from Keyano College, "News," 7 May. http://rmwbculture.blogspot.ca/2012/05/notification-about-keyanos-operational.html.

Thomas-Muller, Clayton, and Kevin Smith. 2012. "Social Licence: Cultural Complicity in the Age of Extraction." *Alternatives International Journal*, 30 March. http://www.alterinter.org/article3782.html?lang=fr.

Thorsen, Dag Einar. 2011. "The Neoliberal Challenge: What Is Neoliberalism?" *Contemporary Readings in Law and Social Justice* 2 (2): 188–214.

Trescott, Jacqueline. 2006. "The Truck Stops Here." *Washington Post*, 8 June.

Vancity Buzz. 2014. "Local Activists Create Illustration of Vancouver Beach Destroyed by Oil Spill." *Vancity Buzz*, 12 November. http://www.vancitybuzz.com/2014/11/local-activists-create-renderings-vancouver-beach-destroyed-oil-spill/.

Van Herk, Aritha. 2009. "How Arts Will Survive in a Down Economy." *Westworld*, September.

"Visual Arts: A Sneak Peak at the Montreal Biennial." 2014. *Montreal Gazette*, 26 September.

Wall, Karen. 2011. "The Gallery and the Inukshuk: Visual Art, 'Ordinary' People, and Mobile Exhibitions." *Leisure / Loisir* 36 (1): 17–35.

———. 2013. "Community Friendly but Still Strapped: The 2012–13 Alberta Budget from the Perspective of Arts, Culture and Heritage." In *Flat-Lined but Still Alive: Analyses of the Provincial and Territorial 2012–13 Budgets from the Perspective of Arts, Culture, and Heritage*, 142–49. Canadian Conference of the Arts, Centre on Governance, University of Ottawa.

Werth, Christopher. 2015. "For These Activists, Oil and Art Just Don't Mix." *The Guardian*, 2 January.

Whitson, Dave, Karen Wall, and Donna Cardinal. 2011. "Alberta." In *Les politiques culturelles provinciales et territoriales du Canada: Origines, évolutions et mises en œuvre*, edited by Monica Gattinger and Diane Saint-Pierre, 174–205. Laval, PQ: Presses de l'Université Laval.

Willerton, Alana. 2011. "Alberta's Apocalyptic Artistry." *The Gateway*, 9 March, 15.

Yogaretnam, Shaamini. 2012. "Keyano College Layoffs Spark Worries over Arts Education." *Edmonton Journal*, 7 May.

Blurring the Boundaries of Private, Partisan, and Public Interests

Accountability in an Oil Economy

Lorna Stefanick

Accountability regimes are recognized worldwide as crucial components of a democratic state because transparency helps to expose corruption, ensures due process in law, and encourages the citizen engagement that is central to citizen participation. In short, transparency aids in holding governments to account. As one democratic theorist observes, "Governance without accountability is tyranny. Few principles are as central to democracy as this" (Borowiak 2011, 3). For newly emerging democracies, the concept of "open government" challenges previously accepted notions that the interests of society (as expressed through the power of the state) take precedence over the interests of individual citizens. Institutions such as the World Bank and the UN Development Programme identify transparency as a critical component of good governance in all countries (Shrivastava and Stefanick 2012).

Studies of resource-rich countries that suffer from the "oil curse" underscore the importance of transparency as a bulwark against corruption. There are widely differing forms of corruption in the Global North and South; the oil-curse studies focus on the Global South. Since regulatory capture by financial and industrial lobbies is also a form of corruption, it is important to examine the effect on accountability regimes of the neoliberal notion of "governing without government" (Rhodes 1996). The economic meltdown in 2008 highlighted the decreased capacity of the hollowed-out state to safeguard the public good in a global market arena. These deficiencies have resulted in calls for the reaffirmation of the state in defining, pursuing, and protecting collective interests. As Martin Painter and Jon Pierre (2005, 1) note:

The events of the last decade have failed to prove the superiority of the market over the state in terms of fostering economic development and growth. Capital markets across Western Europe have generated massive losses, with consequent problems in respect of welfare, pensions and employment, while unregulated international capital movements coupled with liberalized domestic regulatory regimes were in large part responsible for the Asian financial crisis.

The new decentralized governance structures wherein the state shares functions with quasi-state, private, and nonprofit actors are here to stay. However, these structures—and in particular, the role of the state within them—must be continually scrutinized in order to ensure that the collective interest is promoted.

Even though Alberta was an early adopter of mechanisms to support government accountability, it has not escaped criticism.[1] During the nearly forty-four-year rule of the Progressive Conservative (PC) party in Alberta, the increasing shrinkage of the distance between the political and administrative systems in Alberta put a strain on democratic institutions. Ordinarily, this distance prevents the administration from becoming a tool to keep the government of the day in power. The merging of the political arm of government and the administrative apparatus that serves it is part of the legacy of the "business government" tradition in Alberta, which over the past few decades has been expressed by the merging of the interests of the oil industry with the public interest. Public sector accountability is compromised when a premium is put on market accountability, and a blended form of government is reduced to being an instrument for creating the most favourable climate possible for business interests. These trends are exacerbated by the ever shrinking role of the state and, in particular, by the reduction of government support for the creation and dissemination of information and knowledge that contributes to robust public policy debate.

This chapter evaluates democracy in Alberta through an analysis of accountability. It focuses on both political and administrative structures, and in particular, on the independent offices of the legislature that were established to be "watchdogs" of both the political and administrative arms of government. Embedded in the discussion is an analysis of the evolution of the administrative apparatus of Alberta's public service, with reference to the ways in which the oil-based economy has shaped it. Institutional structures that provide scrutiny of public sector activities will only be as strong as the political will that underpins them; both citizens and long-serving governments in a strong economy lubricated by resource rents become complacent about the need for democratic accountability, because it is assumed that interests of the governing party, the government, corporations, and the public are one and the same. While historians will no doubt have much to say about the toppling of the PC government in 2015 by the left-leaning New Democratic Party (NDP), a post-election survey overwhelmingly suggested that voting patterns did not reflect an ideological shift but were driven instead by a desire for change and by disappointment with PC leader Jim Prentice (Markusoff 2015). This chapter suggests that the anger expressed in the "Anyone but Conservative" sentiment evident in the campaign may have been fuelled by an implicit recognition that democracy rests on political accountability to citizens rather than to corporate interests.

Transparency, Democracy, and the Curse of Oil

A key dysfunction of political regimes that are not transparent is that secrecy can hide corruption. Corruption can be defined as "the misuse of public authority for private gains" (Shen and Williamson 2005, 327). Typically, corruption involves activities that are illegal. The United Nations Convention Against Corruption calls corruption "an insidious plague that has a wide range of corrosive effects on societies. It undermines democracy and the rule of law, leads to violations of human rights, distorts markets, erodes the quality of life and allows organized crime, terrorism and other threats to human security to flourish" (United Nations, Office on Drugs and Crime 2004, iii). The United Nations goes on to note that corruption is found in all countries, but it is in the Global South that its effects are most damaging, particularly with respect to the alleviation of poverty.

Researchers have noted that weak institutions that are vulnerable to corruption act as a hindrance to socio-economic development in resource-rich countries of the Global South (Kolstad and Wigg 2009; Mehlum, Moene, and Torvik 2006; Robinson, Torvik and Verdier 2006). The political elite in these countries has control of resources and resource rents, which leads to control over patronage and the distribution of resources. The private sector also recognizes corruption as a dysfunction in countries rich in natural resources and has instituted initiatives such as the Extractive Industries Transparency Initiative (EITI), which focuses on revenue transparency. According to Ivar Kolstad and Arne Wiig (2009, 521), this initiative reflects the popularity of transparency as a method of weeding out corruption. But, as they point out, an emphasis on transparency alone is insufficient, and, in particular, the emphasis of EITI on revenues is misplaced (529). Kolstad, Wiig, and Aled Williams (2009, 957) argue that negative behaviours are ameliorated by strong institutional structures that promote private sector efficiency and public sector accountability: the former helps to prevent private capture, while the latter prevents capture by government authorities. Regularized and transparent decision-making structures that produce administratively predictable outcomes provide strong protection from patronage.

While the obvious injustices associated with inequality and injustice may not be as visible in the Global North, this does not mean that corruption does not exist or that it does not constitute a problem with far-reaching implications. Corruption can be defined not merely as the abuse of power by a public official for the purpose of private gain but more broadly as patronage, or as "the distribution of rents for political purposes" (Kolstad, Wiig, and Williams 2009, 954). If corruption is defined even more expansively as a systemic dysfunction that causes certain interests to receive preferential treatment, which in turn creates or exacerbates inequalities, then the largest economies in the world may need the most scrutiny, given that preferential treatment within these economies results in economic, political, and social advantages that are felt around the globe. From this perspective, more insidious types of corruption exist in the realm of political practices, economic policies, and foreign policy that are not captured by the various corruption indices, which are slanted toward documenting the type of corruption that is most applicable to developing country institutions.[2]

While both efficiency and accountability are popularly used as normative markers of best practices in both the public and the private sector, little time is spent defining them. In his book *Accountability and Democracy*, Borowiak (2011) points out that while the notion of accountability is accepted as a *sine qua non* of democracy, its weakness is its conceptual ambiguity. He notes that accountability is a relational concept: "to be accountable is to be liable to be called to account, or to answer for responsibilities, positions, and conduct" (6). With respect to liberal democracies, Borowiak asks whether private sector efficiency requires accountability to anything beyond the market. Conversely, how is efficiency defined with reference to the public sector? From a neoliberal perspective, market efficiency replaces democratic accountability. And indeed, the blurring of boundaries that characterizes "governance" dictates that much of the state's policy capacity resides outside the domain of the state. But as Martin Painter and Jon Pierre (2005, 13) observe, "Private actors are not likely to support projects that do not directly cater to their interests, hence policy capacity in this approach is to some extent a capacity to formulate and execute certain types of policy rather than others." Accordingly, governance without some measure of democratic accountability will result in a public policy process that becomes captive to dominant coalitions of nonstate actors.

Democratic accountability can be broken down into two forms: political and administrative. While much emphasis is put on political accountability, the structure and activities of the administrative apparatus are equally important; this arm of government not only runs programs but translates the decisions of elected officials into program policy. The two arms of government are necessarily connected, but Western public administration theory has long lauded the merit of keeping some distinction between the two. When considering the call of President Woodrow Wilson over a century ago to keep administration outside the sphere of politics, Donald Savoie (2003, 4) notes that "to separate the two realms would constitute a powerful counterweight to 'centrifugal' democracy, since it would create an apolitical public service." An apolitical public service based on merit as opposed to patronage is important, because it provides the best chance that administration will be conducted in a fashion wherein all groups in society are treated equally, devoid of corruption and cronyism.

For the purposes of this analysis, democratic accountability can be seen as the public service being held to account by politicians, and politicians being held to account by the electorate. What is missing from this mix is that while the political and administrative components of democratic governance are held accountable to citizens, private sector actors have little accountability to the political community in which they operate, even though their actions arguably have far more impact on citizens in an era of globalization and a hollowing out of the nation-state. To say that private sector actors have no accountability to either governments or citizens is overstating the case: they are subject, of course, to regulatory regimes. But as mentioned earlier in this chapter, as well as in a number of other chapters in this volume, regulatory regimes can show evidence of regulatory capture, wherein industry co-opts the oversight mechanisms in order to promote its own interests. In the same way, the autonomy of legislative officers and public servants can be compromised by working in a political environment dominated by the same party year after year, where all-party legislative oversight committees are numerically dominated by the governing party, and the interests of the political party and government become indistinguishable. This chapter makes this case with reference to Alberta, beginning first with the institutional and political context of Alberta's officers of the legislature.

Democracy in Alberta: "Business Government" and Accountability

Alberta has had sovereignty over its internal affairs as defined in the Canadian constitution since the province was created in 1905. As in other Canadian jurisdictions, certain disadvantaged groups such as women and Indigenous peoples were not initially included in the franchise. Alberta stands among the first three jurisdictions in Canada to grant voting rights to women, despite the widespread belief that Alberta is the most conservative province in the country (Carroll and Little 2001, 39; Harrison, this volume). "Conservative" could refer to the market-based orientation of recent Progressive Conservative governments. But the vernacular usage of the term aptly describes the disinclination of Albertans to elect new governments on a regular basis. Prior to the NDP victory in 2015, Alberta had, in the first 109 years of its existence, seen only three changes in government. In the four elections in which the government changed, the new government won a decisive victory, and the number of seats held by the previous governing party was either reduced to less than half or the party was completely shut out of the legislature. Almost half of the elections in Alberta have produced very lopsided victories, with the winning party taking between 85 percent and 95 percent of the legislative seats (Elections Alberta 2015b).

But resounding electoral victories do not mean that there is a provincial consensus around how the public interest should be defined or how that interest should be promoted in policy. Even in elections in which the popular vote has been respectably close, the electoral results have been dramatically skewed in favour of the winning party because of the province's first-past-the-post system. This electoral system gives the advantage to parties that have regionally concentrated support as opposed to those that enjoy widespread but diffuse support in a given constituency. The former will produce sufficient voter support to elect a representative in particular ridings, while the latter will relegate political candidates to the "also ran" category in many ridings. Diffuse support can produce no elected members in the legislative assembly, even though support is fairly evenly divided between the winning and losing parties.[3]

In Alberta, diffuse progressive support has traditionally given the advantage to right-of-centre parties whose support is concentrated in rural areas.[4] The gap between the percentage of the vote the winning party takes and the seats awarded is wide, often as much as 30 percent. Doreen Barrie (2006, 57) notes that since 1905, the average of the popular vote received by the winning party "is right on 50%, not exactly a stampede towards a single party." Yet the winning parties have been awarded massive electoral victories. Once in power, often for very long periods of time, Alberta governments have been remarkably effective in controlling the definition of what constitutes the public interest.

It is thus not surprising that this unusual electoral history has produced ongoing concern about the ability of opposition parties (and, by extension, citizens) to hold the government members of the legislative assembly to account. C. B. Macpherson's *Democracy in Alberta* (1953) notes the virtual absence of opposition to the Social Credit government. Macpherson explained the lack of legislative opposition in terms of social homogeneity, arguing that, in a society made up of petit bourgeois farmers, class and redistributional conflicts were downplayed. In so doing, he overlooked the many divisions that in fact existed in early Alberta society: Canadian-born versus immigrant, Anglo-Saxon versus other ethnicities, industrial versus agricultural workers, farmers versus ranchers, Protestant versus Catholic, urban versus rural centres, to name just a few. Putting aside Macpherson's monolithic conception of Alberta society, however, his basic point is true: these long-serving governments, with large electoral victories, define the legislative debate, privileging some forms of conflict over others.

Ten years after Macpherson's book was published, the Social Credit held 60 of the 63 seats in the legislature. Ideas were floated for creating entities outside the legislature that "could do some of the chores ordinarily reserved for the House Opposition" (Keen 1963). One novel idea was the creation of an Ombudsman Office that would investigate administrative wrongdoing in order to ensure government accountability and fair practices. Even members of the ruling Social Credit Party promoted the idea, though perhaps their enthusiasm was less a concern for robust legislative debate and more a reflection of a government that had been in power for over thirty years looking for new ideas to refresh its "brand." Nonetheless, with the installation of the Ombudsman in 1967, the first independent officer of the Alberta legislature came into being.

With respect to administrative accountability, Alberta is unique in a number of other ways. As Edward LeSage Jr. (2000) and Trevor Harrison (this volume) explain, Alberta has been strongly influenced by turn-of-the-century western Canadian progressivism, as well as by agrarian populism. According to LeSage, populists shared the neoliberal distaste for the state, seeking to minimize and control its activities. Populists, however, recognized the need for Alberta's early governments to build the infrastructure necessary for commerce. Given the distaste for government activities beyond this basic function, the division between politics and administration was not critical, as it was thought best that the administrative arm remain under political control. In contrast, from the progressive point of view, the state was an instrument for social betterment. This meant that the division between the political and administrative apparatus *was* critical because an expert, merit-based administrative structure will act as a bulwark against patronage. Early Alberta was notable for an awkward truce between these two distinct political perspectives. "Progressivist and populist ideas do not mix especially well," notes LeSage, "and, in Alberta, these idea systems were uneasily joined under the 'business government' notion, wherein government serves as the interpreter and steward of the general community will" (399). One of the characteristics of business government is longevity: the government has considerable time to both define and shape the will of the community while suppressing dissent from the common vision. Even when governments in Alberta have only a slim majority of voters supporting them, repeated re-election gives them both the confidence and the legitimacy to claim that they represent the public interest.[5]

From the perspective of accountability, the notion of public interest is important. Politicians are accountable to the electorate (the public). Through elections, political parties can claim that they have a mandate to define the public interest through public policy implemented by public servants. While the winning party will dominate the legislature, at the very least the opposition MLAs can ask questions, present alternative perspectives, and engage in debate about what constitutes the public interest. As pointed out by a provincial commentator, "For there to be effective accountability, the opposition must be able to scrutinize and publicize government actions on an ongoing basis, even if we don't particularly like what the opposition had in mind" (Gunter 2009). Legislative officers provide an additional layer of scrutiny of both political and administrative activity. The functions of these officers differ, but ultimately it is their job to ensure that public and private interests are separated, that certain interests are not privileged during elections, that taxpayer money is spent appropriately, and that the administrative apparatus treats everyone the same and, in doing so, respects citizens' rights. In sum, these officers are vital to government accountability.

Administrative Accountability and New Public Management

There are six legislative officers in Alberta; all are chosen and report to an all-party standing committee. As noted, the Office of the Ombudsman was the first to be established, with the Chief Electoral Officer, the Ethics Commissioner, and the modern version of the Auditor General's Office following in subsequent years. The Office of the Information and Privacy Commissioner was created in 1994, and in 2012 the Office of the Child and Youth Advocate was established. The all-party Standing Committee on Legislative Offices develops the list of candidates for these offices; members of the legislature elect candidates by majority vote. Given that the membership of this committee reflects the distribution of seats in the legislature, it comes as no surprise that there are complaints that officers reporting to a PC-dominated committee are not highly critical of government.

While legislative offices in Alberta meet the requirements of independence, wide scope of purview, and accessibility (see Rowat 1985, 183–85), what is distinctive about Alberta with respect to their functioning is the province's enthusiastic commitment to neoliberalism in the early 1990s. Faced with a sluggish economy, large government deficits, and low oil prices, the PC government of Ralph Klein radically downsized government and adopted new public management (NPM) approaches to the public sector administration. While some aspects of NPM are attractive to parties of all stripes (value for money, efficiency and effectiveness, and outcome metrics), other NPM features are most consistent with free market, neoliberal political ideology. The NPM approach entails mimicking the private sector with respect to management practices, dramatically reducing or contracting out services to the private and nonprofit sectors, and decentralizing authority by transferring functions to regional authorities or community boards. In doing so, the government's role shifts from being the provider of services to being the body providing supervision of service provision.

Like other government bodies, the resources of the legislative offices were cut in the 1990s. The Office of the Ombudsman is illustrative of the ensuing challenges. Reorganization and the rapid rate of change from the government providing services to overseeing service provision left most people (including

Ombudsman Office staff) confused as to who should be held responsible for maladministration. Moreover, privatization often meant that the Office of the Ombudsman lost the authority to investigate complaints because the issue was outside its jurisdiction. As Ombudsman Johnson observed in 1995, "The privatization of government services is occurring without protective measures such as appeal mechanisms and/or ombudsman services. The lack of safeguards in the system erodes accountability" (Alberta, Office of the Ombudsman 1995, 2).

For those complaints in which the office maintained jurisdiction, investigations became more complex and time consuming, yet resources and training did not keep pace. Moreover, NPM places less emphasis on process and procedures, favouring the promotion of "results-based management." This is clearly apparent by the attention paid in annual reports to setting targets for the time taken to process complaints and then evaluating the success of the office in meeting these targets. As one long-time observer of Ombuds offices notes, "Results-based management has little regard for due process and for necessarily fair results. The challenges relating to attitude and practice are truly enormous" (Levine 2009, 295).

The difficulties for Ombuds offices in ensuring accountability with respect to privatized services and other by-products of NPM is a problem worldwide. However, the speed with which change happened in Alberta is unique. As will be illustrated in the next section, the confluence of neoliberal ideologies and NPM since the early 1990s, combined with the conflation of the governing party's interest with that of the government, has worsened the already tenuous ability of Alberta citizens to hold their politicians to account. The end result not only has implications for the ability of citizens to access government information using enabling legislation; it also reflects a more generalized trend of controlling and suppressing information that contributes to policy deliberations. Moreover, merging interests create a culture of entitlement that supports activities, sometimes illegal, that would not be tolerated in jurisdictions where the division between government and party is more distinct.

Information Management and "the Message": When Political and Administrative Interests Merge

In Alberta, the Information and Privacy Commissioner is the officer responsible for administering the legislation that ensures citizen access to information held by government. Critics have complained that the fees charged for access to information in Alberta are exorbitant, while delays ensure that, in the case of journalists, the "scoop" will be lost. So, for example, in the months leading up to the 2004 provincial election, two reporters and the opposition Liberals requested the release of the flight logs of airplanes used for government purposes. At issue were allegations that the premier and other PC members of the legislative assembly were making inappropriate use of taxpayer-funded planes. The reporter's request for information was filed in May 2004; the information was received three days after the provincial election in November (Simons 2007). The fee for the leader of the opposition's request to examine the same Alberta government flight log documents for the years 1996 to 2003 was estimated to be $4,671. In contrast, the fee for examining the much larger flight logs of the federal government was $5 (Taft 2007, 74–77).[6] Similarly, the Canadian Taxpayers Federation requested details regarding how much Alberta government departments were paying communications consultants, but since the bill exceeded $11,000 with less than half the departments reporting, the federation halted its investigation (75). The passing of amendments to the Freedom of Information and Protection of Privacy Act in 2006 gave the force of law to the trend of suppressing information. These amendments safeguard government internal audits from public scrutiny for fifteen years, as well as protecting ministers' briefing notes for five years. A leading access-to-information expert described the changes to the act as "noxious" (Alasdair Roberts, quoted in Baxter 2006). While access-to-information legislation is a useful tool to cut through bureaucratic layers, it is not particularly effective if the information is, for all practice purposes, inaccessible.

Some argue that the biggest issue with Freedom of Information and Protection of Privacy (FOIP) officers promoting access to information is that they are embedded in the government bureaucracy (Taft 2007, 72). In this case, however, the fundamental problem is larger than that of individual FOIP officers having close working relationships with the departments they oversee: it relates to departments not distinguishing between public and partisan interests. In the case of the flight logs, the reporter complained to the Information Access and Privacy Commissioner that Alberta Infrastructure and Transportation had purposely delayed the release of the flight logs until after the 2004 election. During the subsequent public hearing, a memo that had been altered was entered as evidence, prompting the RCMP to launch a criminal investigation. In other provinces, the falsification of evidence before a quasi-judicial body might precipitate a scandal that could bring down the government. In Alberta, however, this did not happen. As a reporter for the *Edmonton Journal* noted with considerable frustration, "We've so blurred the line between the Progressive Conservative Party and 'the government,' we can't even see it anymore" (Simons 2009).

Shifting to the issues that are under the purview of the Chief Electoral Officer, it is apparent that a similar problem exists with respect to the strong ties between corporate and political elites in Alberta. The province limits donations to political parties from an individual or corporation to $10,000 per year and $30,000 in any campaign period. As is demonstrated in Kellogg's chapter in this volume, this comparatively high limit has resulted in corporations donating hundreds of thousands of dollars to Alberta's PC Party over the years; almost half of these corporations are oil companies. In contrast, parties such as the Alberta Liberals receive comparatively little support and are chronically struggling financially (Timmons 2013). The 2012 provincial election was an anomaly in that corporations donated upwards of a million dollars to the Wildrose Party when it appeared that this party might topple the PC dynasty. Unlike the Wildrose Party, which publishes the exact dollar amount and source of the donations it receives, the PCs give only a range (e.g., from $10,001 to $30,000). The ability to make large donations to political parties without publicizing the exact amounts not only strengthens the ties between corporate and political elites; it also weakens the ability of the public to scrutinize the relationships.[7]

Donations from corporations, however, pale in the face of donations to the PCs made by billionaire Daryl Katz and his associates. The high-profile Katz is the owner of the Edmonton Oilers; he was accused of circumventing Alberta's Elections Finance Act, which prohibits donations over $30,000. Katz made a "bulk" donation of $430,000 to the PCs in one cheque, but an Elections Alberta report claimed that the money came from associates who "promptly and fully repaid" him (quoted in Walton and Wingrove 2013). In addition to this sum, representing almost a third of the total amount the PCs raised for the 2012 election, critics were concerned that the donation(s) violated conflict-of-interest guidelines, given that the Katz group was at the same time seeking $100 million from the provincial government in support of building a new arena for the Edmonton Oilers hockey team.

While Katz was eventually cleared of wrongdoing, the government passed the Election Accountability Act in response to these and other issues. The bill includes ninety recommendations from Alberta's Chief Electoral Officer; these did not include a limit on the amount parties can spend on an election, nor did the act prohibit donations from corporations or unions, as the comparable federal act does. The limit of $30,000 per individual donation remains and is among the highest in the country, compared to the federal limit of $2,400 per year, and $3,600 in an election year. The possibility of splitting a single donation still exists. As Bill Moore-Kilgannon of Public Interest Alberta puts it, "It's still the Wild West when it comes to campaign-finance rules" (quoted in Wingrove 2012).

The same pattern of blurring of the lines is evident in donations made to the PCs by postsecondary institutions over a period spanning 2004 to 2010. These publicly funded institutions paid for employees or members of their Board of Governors to participate in PC Party premier's dinners, golf tournaments, and policy conferences. This practice is illegal; Alberta law prohibits public institutions from directing taxpayers' money to a political party. Forty-five other organizations, including a school board, a department of Alberta Health Services, towns, and municipal districts engaged in this practice over a period of eight years.

Nonetheless, Alberta's Chief Electoral Officer Brian Fjeldheim did not pursue legal sanctions against any of the public institutions, prompting political scientist Duane Bratt to suggest that Fjeldheim's behaviour called his non-partisanship into question. "I don't want to say that he is working on behalf of the party," Bratt said, "as opposed to working on behalf of Albertans but there are some indications of that, or at least [of] not wanting to exercise his full role" (quoted in CBC News 2012). Bratt went on to speculate that perhaps Fjeldheim felt "chilled" by the fate of his predecessor, Lorne Gibson, who was fired after casting doubt on the fairness of Alberta's electoral process. After Alberta Justice did not pursue the prosecution in nine cases of illegal campaign donations, Gibson wrote two highly critical reports about the election processes in Alberta, which included a hundred recommendations for improving the province's laws. Gibson later sued the government for wrongful dismissal (Wingrove 2011). While the lines might be blurred between partisan and public interests, there can be no mistaking that in this instance, the lines were very clearly drawn between what independent officers of the legislature are and are not allowed to say.

The same blurring of lines can be seen with respect to the membership of quasi-governmental organizations. In 2007, the *Edmonton Journal* detailed the "disproportionately large percentage of card-carrying, high-profile Tories" among those who sit on government-appointed agencies, boards, and commissions in Alberta (Edmonton Journal 2007). A particularly egregious example was offered by the thirteen-member board of the Peace Country Health Region, each and every one of whom was a registered PC member. While these revelations did not appear to cause much concern in 2007, such partisan connections would become glaringly apparent in the 2015 election. A pivotal moment in the election was a press conference held by five CEOs four days before the election, at which they urged citizens to vote PC as opposed to NDP. Collectively, the group had donated nearly $95,000 to the PCs over the past five years, and several had garnered government contracts worth millions. One of the CEOs was Doug Goss, a trustee of the Stollery Children's Hospital and chair of the government-appointed University of Alberta Board of Governors. Goss explained, "We want to make sure that people are thinking—thinking straight—when they enter into the ballot box on May 5" (quoted in Kleiss 2015). Another cautioned that if the NDP raised corporate taxes, businesses might cease corporate donations to charities and worthy undertakings such as the Stollery Children's Hospital. The University of Alberta's faculty association demanded that Goss be removed from the board in view of his partisan stance. After the election, Goss said he regretted his comments and promised to work with the new government. He reflected, "You kinda go, geez, that maybe didn't come out quite the way it should have." But he insisted that "as a private citizen," he had a right to his opinions (CBC News 2015).

The preceding examples suggest an inability to distinguish clearly between public and private—to recognize that personal support (including financial support) for the party in power must not be allowed to influence the discharge of public office. This confusion is perhaps not surprising, given that, over the course of its extended reign in Alberta, the PC Party had become all but synonymous with "government" in the minds of most Albertans, especially younger ones who had never seen another party at the helm. Moreover, the provincial government defined the public interest as equivalent to corporate interests. Some analysts point to decades of government cutbacks to explain why citizens and public institutions are so deferential. Alvin Finkel (2012) describes this situation as a "culture of entitlement on the part of the governing party" that coerces various groups within Alberta into silence—a notable example being doctors who have reported that they were victims of intimidation after they engaged in advocacy on behalf of patients (see HQCA 2012, 154–57). While Premier Redford's sudden resignation in 2014 was depicted as the public's (and her caucus's) rejection of what commentator Don Martin (2014) called her "entitlement to perks," as exemplified in her expensive travel habits, it should be noted that the PCs have a long history of the very behaviour she exhibited. As Martin observed, Premier Klein used government planes "like a personal shuttle because he could smoke aboard."

The situation of postsecondary institutions in Alberta illustrates how reliance on government funding can silence opposition in a one-party system where critics can be ignored. In the spring of 2013, postsecondary institutions were anticipating a 2 percent increase in their operating grants but were instead hit with a 7 percent cut. Calgary's mayor, Naheed Nenshi, abandoned the usual diplomacy of mayors when dealing with the government that funds them, calling on Mount Royal's Board of Governors to push back on this "bad policy" (quoted in Dormer 2013). Edmonton's mayor at the time, Stephen Mandel, chimed in his opposition, worrying that the cuts would "shackle the creativity of our brightest people" (quoted in Wingrove 2013). Six months later, the provincial government reinstated a third of the money it had taken away. As Finkel would no doubt have predicted, the response from university presidents over this dramatic reversal of a policy that created huge system-wide disruption was one of subdued gratitude that the money had been restored (see, for example, Gerein and Howell 2013). The same phenomenon was observed in the 2014 budget and again in the budget that Premier Prentice proposed in 2015. Both budgets saw continued cutbacks to postsecondary education. Stephen Mandel, now a Tory Cabinet minister, had nothing to say about the 2015 cutbacks. As columnist Paula Simons lamented, "At this point, universities, colleges and technical institutions seem so resigned to playing whipping boy, they're just happy that no one's hitting them harder" (Simons 2015).

What could be construed as even more dangerous to postsecondary institutions, and in particular to the creation and dissemination of knowledge that could be deployed to promote dissent, is the government's desire to ensure that postsecondary institutions produce graduates whose skills will directly feed economic growth. In 2013, the government sent each of the province's twenty-six postsecondary institutions a draft "letter of expectation." In it, the minister of Enterprise and Advanced Education (since renamed Innovation and Advanced Education) directed the institutions to review their programs to determine whether they are "in demand by employers and students" and to enhance their collaborative work with "business and industry to maximize the responsiveness to community and regional economic and social needs" (Alberta, Enterprise and Advanced Education 2013, 2, 3). Two years later, the minister of Finance said in his budget address, "We will work with the post-sec-ondary institutions to preserve high-demand, high-value programs and, cor-respondingly, to identify and shed low-value programs that do not represent good return on investment" (Campbell 2015, 9). Such language clearly presup-poses a particular definition of "value." Many within the postsecondary sector and beyond have interpreted these pronouncements as evidence of the govern-ment's conviction that intellectual activities should be driven not by curiosity but by commercial potential.

The possibility that the government will dictate the direction of research and curriculum so that education serves economic interests is of concern not only to the academic community in Alberta but to those beyond its borders. As David Robinson of the Canadian Association of University Teachers put it, "It may sound romantic. . . . But I believe the university is the place where we are on a search for truth. Once we allow government control over that, we lose our way" (quoted in Simons 2013). This "truth" can be created collectively in a post-industrial society; in this way, education can be seen as a social right, one that allows citizens to participate in political decision making. With more involve-ment from citizens, governance becomes messy, leading some states to declare that this excess of democracy requires that the state exercise more control over both the creation and dissemination of knowledge and information (Harrison 2013).

The contraction of public space for debate is thus tied to the state's control over information, leading scholars to fear that as the state knows more and more about us, we know less and less about the state (see Harrison 2013; Stefanick 2011). Those who protest the effort to keep them silent about matters that they feel should be subject to democratic debate have responded by revealing infor-mation that governments are seeking to hide.[8] Individuals release information at enormous risk, but they often feel that they have no other choice, particularly when they are privy to information that reveals conflicts of interest.

Institutional Responses to Conflicts of Interest

Governments have responded in various ways to the charge that they are sup-pressing information that properly should reside in the public domain. Alberta created new political and administrative accountability positions and passed so-called whistle-blowing legislation. In 2012, Don Scott, the first occupant of the position of associate minister of Accountability, Transparency, and

Transformation, introduced Alberta's Public Interest Disclosure (Whistleblower Protection) Act. The newly created Public Interest Commissioner (a second function that was given to the provincial Ombudsman) will resolve complaints made under the auspices of this act. The legislation imposes fines for those who punish or intimidate public sector employees if they report wrongdoing, to the tune of $25,000 for the first offence and $120,000 for the subsequent offences (O'Donnell 2012). While the associate minister claimed that this legislation fulfilled the promise to Albertans for more open and transparent government, it did not include any of the many amendments proposed by opposition MLAs, who deemed it weak and ineffective.

Most troubling to its critics is the total discretion the legislation gives to the commissioner to "exempt any person, class of persons, public entity, information, record, or thing from the application of all or any portion of this Act or the regulations." According to Wildrose Party MLA Rod Fox, "This is the government saying 'trust us,' but from the pattern we've seen clearly over the past year, we can't" (quoted in Byfield 2013). One of Alberta's most famous whistle-blowers, Liberal MLA Dr. David Swann, cited his own case (that of going public with his concerns over climate change and air pollution) as an example of a situation that would not be helped by the new law (Larson 2012). Similarly, the nonprofit organization Federal Accountability Initiative for Reform (FAIR) issued a scathing report of both Canada's and Alberta's whistle-blowing legislation. The report's author says the new Alberta legislation "has fallen far short of the government's claims by ignoring modern best practice, copying outdated legislation from other provinces, and adding regressive measures that render the law essentially worthless" (Hutton 2013, 12).

Whistle-blowing often involves the reporting of conflict of interest; these matters fall under the jurisdiction of the Ethics Commissioner. In Alberta, many critics both within and outside the legislature have called for this legislative office to be abolished because of its ineffectiveness (Marsden 2013). Since the creation of the Ethics Office in 1982, there have been three commissioners. The first two commissioners appointed by the PC government were former Social Credit MLAs. In contrast, the third commissioner, appointed in 2003, has strong ties to the governing party. While the two previous commissioners conducted twenty-one investigations between 1993 and 2007, the commissioners have never imposed sanctions. More pointed criticism, however, is directed at the third commissioner, Neil Wilkinson. A newspaper columnist dubbed him

"Ethics Commissioner Neil 'What Happens in Vegas' Wilkinson," in reference to the perspective that "anything goes" (Byfield 2013).

The criticism of Wilkinson began with his appointment. A former chair of the now defunct Capital Health Region, Wilkinson was appointed as commissioner shortly after his previous job (to which he was appointed by the PC government) was abolished. Two opposition members of the all-party committee that appointed Wilkinson had serious misgivings about his selection. MLA Laurie Blakeman reported that the previous appointment committee she had sat on had sought an appointment with whom all MLAs would be comfortable. Blakeman not only voted against the appointment, but she made an impassioned speech to the legislature underscoring her concerns about Wilkinson's close ties to the PC Party: "I need to believe as a member of this Assembly, that I will be treated the same as any other member would be. I do not have that faith in this particular circumstance, and I'm saddened by that" (Alberta, Legislative Assembly 2008, 1518). Other critics pointed to Wilkinson's lack of ethical, legal, and financial experience. Rachel Notley, then an opposition MLA, noted that "based on the criteria we had set out . . . he was not anywhere close to being at the top of my list in terms of the person that was most qualified" (Alberta, Legislative Assembly 2008, 1522).

Criticism of the commissioner's bias ramped up after he took office. The most notable concern was Wilkinson's investigation of a former cabinet minister who was appointed, shortly after he was defeated in the 2012 provincial election, to the department that he had overseen as a minister. PC MLA Evan Berger had served one term, including five months as the minister of Agriculture; soon after his failed attempt at re-election, he was appointed an advisor to the deputy minister who had served under him. Normally, ministers are required to observe a one-year "cooling-off" period before they have dealings with the departments with which they were involved during their years in government. As Don Braid (2012) from the *Calgary Herald* quipped, "I can't recall another case of a defeated minister being directly hired by his own department while his office chair was still spinning." When this appointment was investigated by Wilkinson, he concluded that Section 31 of the Conflict of Interest Act that prohibits activity that might "create a conflict between a private interest of the former minister and the public interest" did not apply in this case because the hiring had occurred "within the family, the government family. . . . They can move within the government family. In the family there's no information to share. They know it all" (Bell 2012). While the former minister would have had to wait a year before being hired by a private sector firm in a position that involved his old department, there was no prohibition on him being hired by his own department during that time.

Braid (2012) complained that this decision followed a familiar pattern; he also noted that the commissioner had not produced a single ethics investigation report since taking office. Opposition critic Shayne Saskiw, a Wildrose MLA, put it more bluntly:

> The problem here is we don't have anyone who is independent or non-partisan because this PC government sets up a system where you basically have to be their lapdog. . . .
>
> He [Wilkinson] considers himself and (Conservative) MLAs to be insiders who are family.
>
> He is obviously not committed to upholding the separation between government and political parties, which is fundamental to parliament democracy, and he seems to believe as long as you're family you can do no wrong, so what else is he turning a blind eye to? (quoted in Dormer 2012)

While it could be argued that appointing a minister familiar with departmental issues and operations is efficient, the fact that the government did not anticipate or, at the very least, was not worried about the fallout from this symbolically nepotistic appointment speaks to its seeming invisibility.

A subsequent ruling created yet more controversy when Wilkinson found that PC MLA Peter Sandhu had violated conflict-of-interest guidelines by failing to disclose six lawsuits against his home-building company. Sandhu subsequently lobbied bureaucrats and politicians for legislative changes to the Alberta Builders' Lien Act (Rusnell and Russell 2013). Wilkinson refrained from sanctioning Sandhu. When Wildrose MLA Rob Anderson described legislative officers in the Commonwealth as "corrupt," Wilkinson lashed out at critics of his decision in the legislature, describing those types of comments as "hurtful" (Henton 2013). While Anderson later apologized for his remarks, it is useful to recall that the word *corruption* can be used to describe both illegal activities and systemic dysfunctions that cause some interests to be privileged over others. From this perspective, Anderson's charge of corruption may have been well founded.

Wilkinson's last investigation, the so-called Tobaccogate affair, also ignited heated debate. It revolved around the government's decision to give Premier Redford's ex-husband's law firm a contract to pursue a $10 billion legal action against tobacco companies. Redford had vacated the post of Justice minister shortly before the decision was taken. The Redford government successfully resisted efforts by Wilkinson to read a briefing note that would have shed light on the premier's role in the decision, claiming that making the contents public could damage the lawsuit. Moreover, Redford had written a communication to other government members the previous year while she was in the Justice portfolio saying that "the best choice for Alberta will be the International Tobacco Recovery Lawyers." Nonetheless, Wilkinson did not feel that Redford's activities constituted a conflict of interest. He ruled: "There is absolutely no evidence, nor even a suggestion, that the decision to engage ITRL on the tobacco litigation furthered, or might further, the private interest of Premier Redford, her spouse, or that of her minor child" (Alberta, Office of the Ethics Commissioner, 2013, 15). While Don Braid was more charitable than most critics in suggesting that an "error in political judgment did not prove a failure either of ethics or honesty," he mused that "perhaps she failed to see, like so many of ex-premier Ed Stelmach's crew, that the cosy old Alberta PC world was already wheezing and dying" (Braid 2013).

The suggestion that the Alberta PC Party was dying—or, indeed, even wheezing—was debatable prior to the election of 2015. But the bad optics of this situation once again underscore that long-serving governments that do not spend time on the opposition benches have little incentive to put much energy into creating institutions and practices that promote accountability beyond the symbolic level. The suspicion that the PC government has much to hide and little interest in transparency was underscored shortly after the 2015 election by whistle-blowers from within the public service. They complained to the Public Interest Commissioner and to the Information and Privacy Commissioner that ministerial documents were being illegally destroyed and that streams of shredded paper were flowing out of the legislature beginning the morning after the election (Giovannetti 2015). Indeed, in Alberta, it appears that, contrary to the tenets of NPM, the reflexive instinct is to centralize, control, and act upon information that is kept out of public forums where actions or policy can be debated. Governments that have been under the control of one party for extended periods of time are particularly vulnerable to this form of democratic dysfunction.

Transparency, Democracy, and Alberta Oil

Changing existing ideas about what is in the public's best interest and who is its champion is not unique to Alberta or to Canada. Not only do economic power and governance flow across sovereign boundaries in a globalized world; so, too, do ideas about leaving accountability to market forces. For decades, market efficiency was offered as a solution to political and administrative inefficiencies, including their extreme form—corruption. Democratic nation-states are increasingly unable to regulate global capital markets; if market accountability trumps political accountability, this is not seen as a problem. But as the 2008 financial crisis demonstrates, it is not only accountability *within* the market that is critical: so is accountability *of* the market. Actors who enter and exit contracts maintain accountability within the marketplace. Governments were compelled to intervene in 2008 because the scale of actors exiting the market created devastating social and political effects. As Borowiak (2011, 128) argues, "Proposals for enhanced government oversight can be seen as attempts to save the market system by re-embedding *market* accountability with the structures of *political* accountability." No one really anticipated the demise of the PC government in the 2015 election, despite the fact that Albertans consistently complained about government arrogance and polls accurately predicted that the NDP would win the election. The assumption was that, as Canada's "most conservative" province, Alberta had so firmly embraced neoliberal logic that very little appetite existed for demanding political accountability to citizens through the election of a left-leaning government. As such, even those critics who were most optimistic about citizen agency predicted that the inadequacies of market accountability would continue to allow political agency and administrative authority to be used for the short-term interests of the dominant industry rather than the pursuit of long-term collective goals.

While Alberta's PC government could point to such new positions as the associate minister of Accountability, Transparency, and Transformation as evidence of its commitment to accountability, its record was questionable with respect to providing access to information, providing an environment for legislative officers that would encourage scrutiny, and separating the public interest from political and economic interests. Like the Social Credit before it, these new positions reflected a desire to refresh a dated image rather than commitment to serious change.[9] The government's complacency was largely due to the longevity of its regime, which resulted in the conflation of the interests of the governing party with that of the government. The lack of electoral risk over an extended period allowed the state to diminish accountability regimes and control public perceptions of its performance through various political and administrative mechanisms. While this trend is arguably independent of the oil economy, it is certainly symptomatic of a resource- or staples-based economy.

The adoption of the neoliberal features of NPM exacerbated problems of accountability in the public service through the out-sourcing of public services, taking them out of the jurisdiction of legislative oversight. Government spending cuts also resulted in the downsizing of the government's intellectual capital that has traditionally produced fulsome public debate about policy direction. Without this, governments ceded control of the definition of the public interest to private sector interests. Encouraging publicly funded academics to seek private sector funds to undertake research that could serve commercial ends exacerbated the influence of the private sector in defining the public interest.

These trends combine to produce a politicized public service where policy emanated from the PC executive with little regard for input from public servants, legislative officers, opposition MLAs, or the public. The dominance of PC members on the all-party committee that oversees these officers promoted circumspect oversight of political and administrative activities; robust debate was not encouraged, dissenting voices were ignored. Electoral success and a strong oil-based economy gave the governing party the legitimacy to claim that its neoliberal logic is effective in promoting the public interest. Moreover, the business government tradition in Alberta legitimized the PC government both defining the public interest and executing policy to support it; the public interest was defined in market terms with reference to the commodity producers that fuel the economy. In twenty-first-century Alberta, there can be no doubt that the most important commodity is oil and that the interests of the oil industry are often conflated with the public interest. The oil economy creates great wealth but has a dark underbelly that is giving rise to troubling political and income inequality. While other chapters in this book discuss the problem of regulatory capture by industry, this chapter applies the concept of regulatory capture to the public service; institutional structures that are supposed to be apolitical identify closely with the interests of the PC Party. When the dominance of the governing party in both the administrative and political arms of government is combined with the dominance of one industry in the economy, accountability suffers and democracy is diminished. Whether a new government without strong ties to corporate interests will be able to chart a new course for Alberta remains to be seen. What is certain, however, is that, with a change in government after almost forty-four years, there is hope for the health of democracy in Alberta.

Notes

1 In 1967, Alberta became the third jurisdiction in the world to establish an administrative Ombudsman, and it established an access-to-information regime a decade before the United Kingdom, Switzerland, and Germany. While provinces in Canada followed Alberta's lead, the federal government still remains without an Ombuds office. ("Ombuds" has been proposed as a gender-neutral alternative to "Ombudsman." I use the latter when referring to the Alberta office.)

2 For example, a study of Atlantic Canadian retail gasoline price ceilings found that price ceilings were enacted to protect the public. However, these price ceilings became "focal points" that allowed gasoline companies to collude in order to sell their products at high prices (Sen, Clemente, and Jonker 2011, 534). This type of corruption in a Global North economy is not captured in the UN Convention Against Corruption or in the various corruption indices.

3 The best example of this phenomenon is the election in 1940. Liberals, Progressive Conservatives, and the United Farmers of Alberta worked together under the banner of the "independent movement" to run only one candidate against the Social Credit candidate in individual ridings. This resulted in a very close election, although this is not reflected in the seats awarded: the Social Credit captured 42.90% of the popular vote and the Independents 42.47%, with 11.11% going to the Co-operative Commonwealth Federation (CCF). The remaining 3.52% of the popular vote was divided among eight other parties (Elections Alberta 2015a). These shares of the popular vote translated into thirty-six seats for the Social Credit but only nineteen for the Independents, one each for the Liberal and Labour parties, with the CCF and the other parties shut out completely (Elections Alberta 2015b). Even though more people in Alberta voted against the Social Credit by a significant margin, the result was a Social Credit government with a strong majority.

4 The 2015 election was an anomaly in that the left-leaning NDP won in many rural northern constituencies (Elections Alberta 2015d).

5 Voter turnout in Alberta general elections steadily decreased between 1993 and 2008, from 60.2 percent to 40.6 percent (Elections Alberta 2015c), although it rebounded in 2012 to 54.4 percent, probably in the face of the threat posed by the Wildrose Party. Despite the fact that, in 2008, only 501,063 people—out of a provincial population approaching 3.6 million at the time (Alberta, Treasury Board and Finance 2013)— actually cast a ballot in support of the PCs, and despite the fact that the party's share of the vote declined from 52.72 percent in that year to 43.97 in 2012 (Elections Alberta 2015a), party leaders continued to assume that their policies reflected the will of the people.

6 The use of government planes would come to the fore again in 2014, culminating in the resignation of the premier halfway through her tenure and a pledge from the new premier to sell off the fleet of planes.

7 Corporate donations became a campaign issue in 2015, with both the Wildrose and the NDP parties promising that if they were elected, they would prohibit donations to political parties from corporations and unions. Shortly after being elected to office, the NDP made good on this promise.

8 Some of the notable public sector whistle-blowers in Alberta include Dr. John O'Connor, who raised concerns about the incidence of cancer downstream from the bitumen sands, former MLA Dr. Raj Sherman, who leaked information to the media about poor emergency room patient outcomes, and Health Canada's Steven Villebrun, who exposed the misuse of public funds (Hutton 2013, 20).

9 It is noteworthy that in 2013, the Government of Alberta spent $1.7 million of public money promoting its "Building Alberta" brand on such things as roadside signs—which featured the name of Alison Redford, premier at the time, and the PC Party colours (Wood 2014).

References

Alberta. Enterprise and Advanced Education. 2013. "Letter of Expectation Between the Minister of Alberta Enterprise and Advanced Education (as Representative of the Government of Alberta) and the Board of Governors of the University of Calgary (as Representative of the University of Calgary)." http://eae.alberta.ca/media/letters/U-of-C.pdf.

Alberta. Legislative Assembly. 2008. *Hansard*. 27th Legis. , 1st session. 23 October.

Alberta. Office of the Ethics Commissioner. 2013. *Report to the Speaker of the Legislative Assembly of Alberta of the Investigation by Neil Wilkinson, Ethics Commissioner, into Allegations Involving the Honourable Alison Redford, Q.C., Premier*. 4 December. http://www.ethicscommissioner.ab.ca/media/1063/final-ver-01-dec-03-13.pdf.

Alberta. Office of the Ombudsman. 1995. *Annual Report*.

Alberta. Treasury Board and Finance. 2013. "Quarterly Population Report: Second Quarter, 2013." http://www.finance.alberta.ca/aboutalberta/population_reports/2012-2013/2013-2ndQuarter.pdf.

Barrie, Doreen. 2006. *The Other Alberta: Decoding a Political Enigma*. Regina: Canadian Plains Research Center.

Baxter, James. 2006. "Tighter Control over Gov't Records Called 'Noxious.'" *Edmonton Journal*, 15 May.

Bell, Rick. 2012. "Alberta Ethics Commissioner Says Re-hiring Booted Ex-Tory Minister Evan Berger OK." *Calgary Sun*, 19 September.

Borowiak, Craig T. 2011. *Accountability and Democracy: The Pitfalls and Promise of Popular Control*. New York: Oxford University Press.

Braid, Don. 2012. "Berger's Case Needs Scrutiny." *Calgary Herald*, 21 August.

Byfield, Colman. 2013. "Alberta Whistleblower Legislation Is a Trap." *Edmonton Sun*, 24 May.

Campbell, Robin. 2015. "Budget 2015." Budget Address Delivered to the Legislative Assembly of Alberta. 26 March. http://www.finance.alberta.ca/publications/budget/budget2015/speech.pdf.

Carroll, William, and William Little. 2001. "Neoliberal Transformation in Canada: Transition, Consolidation, and Resistance." *International Journal of Political Economy* 31 (3): 33–66.

CBC News. 2012. "Alberta's Chief Electoral Officer Challenged over Illegal Donations: Fjeldheim Criticized for Downplaying Illegal Donations to Tories." *CBC News*, 17 April. http://www.cbc.ca/news/canada/edmonton/alberta-s-chief-electoral-officer-challenged-over-illegal-donations-1.1156621.

———. 2015. "Doug Goss to Remain U of A Chairman, Despite Pro-Tory Remarks." *CBC News*, 8 May. http://www.cbc.ca/news/canada/edmonton/doug-goss-to-remain-u-of-a-chairman-despite-pro-tory-remarks-1.3067080.

Dormer, Dave. 2012. "Opposition Cries Foul as Defeated MLA Nets $150K Government Gig." *Sun News Network*, 20 September.

———. 2013. "Calgary Mayor Naheed Nenshi Blasts Government of Alberta Cuts to Post-secondary Institutions." *Calgary Sun*, 17 April.

Edmonton Journal. 2007. "Tories Stack Alberta Boards." *Edmonton Journal*, 1 November.

Elections Alberta. 2015a. "Candidate Summary of Results (General Elections, 1905–2015)." *Elections Alberta*. http://www.elections.ab.ca/reports/statistics/candidate-summary-of-results-general-elections/.

———. 2015b. "Distribution of Seats by Party, 1905–2015." *Elections Alberta*. http://www.elections.ab.ca/reports/statistics/distribution-of-seats-by-party/.

———. 2015c. "Overall Summary of Ballots Cast and Voter Turnout, 1975–2015." *Elections Alberta*. http://www.elections.ab.ca/reports/statistics/overall-summary-of-ballots-cast-and-voter-turnout/.

———. 2015d. "Provincial General Election May 5, 1015: Winning Candidates—Provincial Results." *Elections Alberta*. http://resultsnew.elections.ab.ca/orResultsPGE.cfm.

Finkel, Alvin. 2012. "The Banality of Corruption in Alberta." *Troy Media*, 12 March.

Gerein, Keith, and Trevor Howell. 2013. "Province Restores $50 Million to Alberta Universities and Colleges." *Calgary Herald*, 6 November.

Giovannetti, Justin. 2015. "Watchdogs Investigate Document Shredding at Alberta Legislature." *Globe and Mail*, 13 May.

Gunter, Lorne. 2005. "Arrogance of Klein Tories as Bad as the Liberals." *Edmonton Journal*, 16 November.

Harrison, Trevor. 2013. "Who Controls Knowledge?" Op-ed, Parkland Institute, 15 November. http://parklandinstitute.ca/media/comments/who_controls_knowledge.

Henton, Darcy. 2013. "Retiring Ethics Commissioner Trades Barbs with Disgruntled MLAs." *Calgary Herald*, 1 December.

HQCA (Health Quality Council of Alberta). 2012. *Review of the Quality of Care and Safety of Patients Requiring Access to Emergency Department Care and Cancer Surgery and the Role and Process of Physician Advocacy*. February. Calgary: Health Quality Council of Alberta.

Hutton, David. 2013. *Shooting the Messenger: The Need for Effective Whistleblower Protection in Alberta*. Edmonton: Parkland Institute.

Keen, Eddie. 1963. *Edmonton Journal*, 19 June.

Kleiss, Karen. 2015. "Businessmen Attack NDP's 'Amateur' Policies." *Edmonton Journal*, 1 May.

Kolstad, Ivar, and Arne Wiig. 2009. "Is Transparency the Key to Reducing Corruption in Resource-Rich countries?" *World Development* 37 (3): 521–32.

Kolstad, Ivar, Arne Wigg, and Aled Williams. 2009. "Mission Improbable: Does Petroleum-Related Aid Address the Resource Curse?" *Energy Policy* 37 (3): 954–65.

Larson, Jackie L. 2012. "Critics Say New Alberta Whistleblowing Protection Laws Don't Go Far Enough." *Sun News Network*, 30 October.

LeSage, Edward, Jr. 2000. "Business Government and the Evolution of Alberta's Career Public Service." In *Government Restructuring and Career Public Services in Canada*, edited by Evert A. Lindquist, 399–440. Ottawa: Institute of Public Administration in Canada.

Levine, Gregory J. 2009. "Recapturing the Spirit, Enhancing the Project: The Ombudsman Plan in Twenty-First-Century Canada." In *Provincial and Territorial Ombudsman Offices in Canada*, edited by Stewart Hyson, 292–307. Toronto: University of Toronto Press.

Macpherson, C. B. 1953. *Democracy in Alberta: The Theory and Practice of a Quasi-party System*. Toronto: University of Toronto Press.

Markusoff, Jason. 2015. "Survey Says: Albertans Voted for Change, Anger and Dislike of Prentice—Less So for NDP, Hope and Notley." *Calgary Herald*, 17 May.

Marsden, David. 2013. "Marsden: Alberta Needs a New Ethics Commissioner (with Poll)." *Calgary Herald*, 23 October.

Martin, Don. 2014. "Don Martin: Albertans Rejecting Redford's Perceived Aura of Entitlement." *CTV News*, 14 March. http://www.ctvnews.ca/ctv-news-channel/power-play-with-don-martin/don-martin-albertans-rejecting-redford-s-perceived-aura-of-entitlement-1.1729871.

Mehlum, Halvor, Karl Moene, and Ragnar Torvik. 2006. "Institutions and the Resource Curse." *Economic Journal* 116 (508): 1–20.

O'Donnell, Sarah. 2012. "Alberta Government Approves New Whistleblower Act." *FAIR*, 29 November. http://fairwhistleblower.ca/content/alberta-government-approves-new-whistleblower-act.

Painter, Martin, and Jon Pierre. 2005. "Unpacking Policy Capacity: Issues and Themes." In *Challenges to State Policy: Global Trends and Comparative Perspectives*, edited by Martin Painter and Jon Pierre, 1–18. Basingstoke, UK: Palgrave Macmillan.

Rhodes, R. A. W. 1996. The New Governance: Governing Without Government. *Political Studies* 44 (4): 652–67.

Robinson, James A. , Ragnar Torvik, and Thierry Verdier. 2006. "Political Foundations of the Resource Curse." *Journal of Development Economics* 79 (2): 447–68.

Rowat, Donald C. , 1985. *The Ombudsman Plan: the Worldwide Spread of an Idea.* Rev. 2nd ed. Lanham, MD: University Press of America.

Rusnell, Charles, and Jennie Russell. 2013. "Ethics Commissioner's Decision Not to Sanction MLA Questioned." *CBC News*, 19 November. http://www.cbc.ca/news/ canada/edmonton/ethics-commissioner-s-decision-not-to-sanction-mla- questioned-1.2431375.

Savoie, Donald. 2003. *Breaking the Bargain: Public Servants, Ministers, and Parliament.* Toronto: University of Toronto Press.

Sen, Anindya, Anthony Clemente, and Linda Jonker. 2011. "Retail Gasoline Price Ceilings and Regulatory Capture: Evidence from Canada." *American Law and Economic Review* 13 (2): 532–64.

Shen, Ce, and John B. Williamson. 2005. "Corruption, Democracy, Economic Freedom, and State Strength: A Cross-National Analysis. *International Journal of Comparative Sociology* 46 (4): 327–45.

Shrivastava, Meenal, and Lorna Stefanick. 2012. "Do Oil and Democracy Only Clash in the Global South? Petro Politics in Alberta, Canada." *New Global Studies* 6 (1): article 5.

Simons, Paula. 2007. "Klein's Machine Undermined Civil Service." *Canada.com*, 28 June. http://www.canada.com/story.html?id=7bd8baf9-3e26-494a-b31f-7de0a426b54a.

———. 2013. "Maestro Lukaszuk May Want to Conduct, but Will Universities, Colleges, Play Along? *Edmonton Journal*, 8 March.

———. 2015. "Budget Attacks Intellectual Independence and Academic Autonomy of Post-secondary Schools." *Edmonton Journal*, 27 March.

Stefanick, Lorna. 2011. *Controlling Knowledge: Freedom of Information and Protection of Privacy in a Networked World.* Edmonton: Athabasca University Press.

Taft, Kevin. 2007. *Democracy Derailed: The Breakdown of Government Accountability in Alberta—and How to Get It Back on Track.* Calgary: Red Deer Press.

Timmons, Lucas. 2013. "Political Donations in Alberta, 2004 to 2010." *Edmonton Journal* (database). http://www.edmontonjournal.com/news/donations/database.html.

United Nations. Office on Drugs and Crime. 2004. *United Nations Convention Against Corruption.* New York: United Nations.

Walton, Dawn, and Josh Wingrove. "Katz Group's $430,000 'Bulk Donation' to Redford's Tories Cleared by Elections Alberta." *Globe and Mail*, 1 May.

Wingrove, Josh. 2011. "Fired Chief Electoral Officer Sues Province of Alberta." *Globe and Mail*, 8 March.

———. 2012. "Alberta Bill Fails to Clarify Rules on Single Large Political Donations." *Globe and Mail*, 20 November.

———. 2013. "Edmonton Mayor Calls Cuts to Universities 'Short-Term Thinking.'" *Globe and Mail*, 2 April.

Wood, James. 2014. "Redford Defends $1.7M Spent on Building Alberta Branding Campaign." *Calgary Herald*, 7 January.

CONCLUSION

Of Democracy and Its Deficits

Surviving Neoliberalism in Oil-Exporting Countries

Meenal Shrivastava

The substantial oil and democracy literature has contributed tremendously to understanding the relationship between oil dependence and liberal democracy in the Global South. Little effort, however, has been expended to analyze this question with reference to an oil-exporting country in the Global North. This book seeks to fill this gap by critically exploring the practice of liberal democracy and the impact of that practice on institutions of democracy at the subnational level in Alberta, as well as in Canada generally. On the back of Alberta oil, Canada has emerged as one of the top ten oil-exporting countries in the world. On the surface, it would appear that democracy is alive and well in Canada. After all, Canada is a jurisdiction that fares well in terms of all the attributes of liberal democracy measured by the influential ranking industry, through assessment tools such as the Democracy Index and Polity IV. However, a closer examination of the theory of liberal democracy reveals a growing rift between the two core assumptions of liberal democracy—capitalist market relations and developmental liberalism. This rift is not accounted for in the quantitative measurements of the practice of liberal democracy used by most oil and democracy studies. In order to broaden the narrow application of the liberal democratic framework in these studies, we suggest complementing it with the staples theory of economic development to examine the political economy of an oil-exporting country.

The oil and democracy literature contains valuable insights regarding the political and economic outcomes of resource dependence, such as the rentier effect and the resource curse. By pointing to policy mechanisms to avoid the resource curse, however, staples theory enters the realm of developmental liberalism, which is often a missing piece in the oil and democracy literature. Ignoring developmental liberalism within a democratic framework marginalizes the investigation and understanding of several characteristics of the process and outcomes of capitalism, including the source, dynamics, and effects of economic and political inequality, of relations of power, and of social upheavals and struggles. Consequently, the fourteen authors in this book examined significant public policy areas—such as energy, national security, Aboriginal issues, the environment, labour law, urban planning, gender, and the arts—in the context of the entrenchment of the neoliberal ideology in an oil-exporting jurisdiction. Observing the role of neoliberal political ideology on the liberal democratic mode of governing, we note an increase in economic and political inequality, as well as a decline in democratic accountability. The negative impact of these trends on the practice of liberal democracy can indeed be construed as a democratic deficit in Alberta, as well as in Canada.

Most studies define a petro-state as a political jurisdiction that depends on petroleum for at least 50 percent of its export, at least 25 percent of its GDP, and at least 25 percent of its government revenues. Oil and gas account for 18.5 percent of Canada's exports and roughly 8 percent of the country's GDP. Canada is also a major importer of oil, with Québec and the Atlantic provinces relying on foreign oil for more than 80 percent of their fuel needs (see Campbell 2012). Clearly, then, Canada falls well below the standard petro-state thresholds. In contrast, oil and gas account for 70 percent of Alberta's exports, 27 percent of its GDP, and 28 percent of its government revenues (Alberta, Alberta Energy 2015). Alberta's economic profile thus qualifies the province as a petro-province within the Canadian federation, which warrants a closer examination of the institutions of liberal democracy in the province. Moreover, it is telling that the rise of Canada as one of the top ten oil-exporting countries in the world has been accompanied by increasing income inequality nationally and a backward slide on many socio-political markers in comparison to its peer countries in the OECD. Undoubtedly, the impact of oil does not end at the Alberta border but affects the whole of Canada; therefore, how oil wealth is managed is a major national issue with substantial political, economic, social, and environmental consequences. A nuanced understanding of the political economic dynamics, at the national and subnational levels, of an oil-exporting economy in the Global North is likely to contribute to the burgeoning oil and democracy literature, which needs to expand beyond its focus on countries in the Global South, especially since the largest oil-exporting countries in the world now include several OECD countries with growing inequality. In this context, the health of liberal democracy can no longer be taken for granted, whether in the Global North or in the Global South.

Most of the chapters in this collection report that governance processes, policy, and institutions in Alberta are creating a democratic deficit through declining democratic accountability and increasing economic, political, and social inequality in the province. While the causal links between oil dependence and democratic malaise typically are not direct, it is well established in the oil and democracy literature alluded to in the introduction and in chapter 1 that significantly large oil extraction generates great wealth for some but also creates particular political and economic conditions that inhibit democracy for most of the population in an oil-exporting economy. The growing economic and political inequality in Canada (see chapter 1) and in Alberta (see particularly chapters 7, 8, 9, 10, and 12) not only raises moral questions about fairness; it also has implications for social outcomes such as quality of life and life satisfaction, as well as for long-term economic prospects.[1] Various chapters in this volume confirm the rising democratic deficit in Alberta (and Canada), as well as the mechanism through which it is rising—the entrenchment of the neoliberal state in an oil-exporting economy. The next section highlights themes within this volume with reference to the nature of the neoliberal state, particularly in terms of its application in the governance and administrative apparatus in Alberta. This chapter concludes with an analysis of the practice of liberal democracy in the context of rising inequality.

The Neoliberal State: Policies, Institutions, and Their Impact on Democracy

Neoliberalism can be defined as a political ideology or a discourse of governance that informs the economistic separation of democratic spheres and considers the economy as a nonpolitical self-regulatory space of individual enterprise immune to the interventions of the state. The minimalistic conception of liberal democratic theory in the neoliberal discourse has been fuelling economic and political inequality around the world through the vastly expanded role of financial motives, market institutions, and elites in the operation of governing institutions, an expansion that has occurred at the international, national, and subnational levels. As I point out in chapter I, practices and policies affecting economic institutions have significant ramifications for political issues such as social justice, distribution, and economic performance. Furthermore, the current focus on capitalist market relations at the cost of developmental liberalism is producing limits to the practice of liberal democracy, a process that is occurring through increasing economic and political inequality and decreasing democratic accountability.

It is important to note that the penetration of market values and instruments into the liberal democratic apparatus has not happened exclusively in oil-exporting jurisdictions such as Alberta. In particular, the new public management principle of administrative reform has spawned various forms of ".new governance" or "third-party government" models around the world. Many of these models redefine public roles and compromise the institutional integrity of the public sector at all levels, creating problems of political steering, control, transparency, and democratic accountability (see Peters and Pierre 2010; Stefanick 2009 and this volume). However, in an oil-exporting economy, the rentier effect further exacerbates the democratic deficit created by market-based structures, as shown by many of the chapters in this book.

Neoliberal formulations of political and economic organization began exerting their influence in the 1980s and found a fertile home in Alberta. Trevor Harrison, in chapter 2, and Lorna Stefanick, in chapter 14, note that while a large number of Albertans vote consistently for opposition parties that represent progressive sentiments, their diffuse distribution among parties and throughout Alberta, combined with a first-past-the-post system, has fragmented the vote, producing a reoccurring pattern. While May 2015 saw the unexpected election of an NDP majority government facing a sizeable opposition in the far-right Wildrose Party, it remains to be seen to what extent this electoral victory will translate into changing governance patterns established during the nearly forty-four-year rule of the PC Party. Midway through the province's history, Conservative governments in Alberta moved to the right of the political centre. This orientation—mixed with populism, western alienation, and commitment to individualism—made Albertans receptive to the neoliberal reforms implemented by the Progressive Conservative (PC) government of Ralph Klein in the 1990s. As Jay Smith points out in chapter 3, the neoliberal state has been referred to as the "garrison state," in which "the welfare state—a critical means to the provision of social and economic justice (in the form of social security, equality of access to education and health care, and the equitable distribution of wealth)—is de-emphasized in favour of security, the military, the protection of property, and the building of prisons."

The impact of neoliberal reform is evident in most chapters in this book. What is particularly noteworthy about neoliberalism in Alberta, however, is the interesting marriage it has had with another major strain in Alberta's socio-economic culture: business government. Coined by C. B. Macpherson (1953), the term *business government* refers to the important historical role that government has played in Alberta's economic development. Major infrastructure projects, such as building railroads, were undertaken by the federal government. Similarly, the provincial government was active in enticing commercial interests to Alberta through investments in infrastructure and social development (such as education and health care). These activities were an important feature of the first half of the PC tenure in Alberta, which began in 1971 and ended in 2015. In the past few decades, the dominance of neoliberal ideology is obvious; the PCs increasingly abandoned the role of the activist state and systematically dismantled the welfare state.

In chapter 4, Stefanick describes the neoliberal mentality, characterized by emphasizing "active citizenship" that focuses on emphasizing individual responsibility, dismantling the regime that regulates industry; enhancing measures for disciplining citizens, particularly those who oppose capitalist interests; and shrinking the space for public participation, advocacy, and contestation. These trends are linked to the neoliberal conception that the government's role is that of a facilitator for creating favourable market conditions for business. Many chapter authors discuss the disciplinary role of the government in terms of branding opposition as contrary to the public interest (chapter 4) and using tools of the state to limit and/or control the activities of civil society and advocacy groups (chapters 3, 6, 7, 10, 11, and 12), labour unions (chapter 9), workers (chapter 8), and those involved with the arts (chapter 13). In this disciplinary role, the Alberta government favours capital interests over the provision of social and economic justice, effectively limiting opportunities for public engagement with issues that relate to resource development and shrinking the public space for discussion and contestation of public policy. As Stefanick notes in chapter 4, the framing of Alberta oil as "ethical" oil normalizes the economic, environmental, and political risks associated with bitumen extraction, leading those who question this frame to be branded as "radical."

The distance between the two frames is telling. Ricardo Acuña, in chapter 11, describes how what is considered to be acceptable in Alberta's public policy realm has moved to the right of the political spectrum through a concerted effort to flood the public with radical neoliberal discourse. After a while, these radical ideas become normalized, and those whose ideas are slightly to the left of "normal" are portrayed as radical. The shrill responses to the NDP's recommendation of a hike in corporate tax from 10 percent to 12 percent is another indicator of how far to the right the policy window has moved in Alberta, and indeed in Canada. The rhetoric in the media continues to ignore the effects of increased oil production in the United States or of declining global oil prices, while vilifying the proposal in the NDP election platform to modestly revise the existing tax regime or review the energy royalty structures for potentially threatening the future of the oil industry (Penty, Tuttle, and Lam 2015).

The power of framing is seen most pointedly in the case of Aboriginal issues colliding with the extractive industry. Jay Smith, in chapter 3, and Gabrielle Slowey and Lorna Stefanick, in chapter 7, argue that the colonized Indigenous peoples in Canada are framed as outside of normal and are thus effectively ignored. The danger of this framing is evident in Bill C-51, which received Royal assent as the Anti-terrorism Act in June 2015 and which aims to grant exceptionally broad powers of surveillance to government agencies—seemingly targeting environmental and Aboriginal rights activists under the guise of "anti-terrorism" measures (Payton 2015). Under widespread public pressure, the Conservative government made a few amendments to Bill C-51, to ostensibly make it more palatable politically, while clearly denying the possibility of providing more oversight to protect civil liberties (Bronskill 2015).

The same phenomenon can be seen in chapter 12, with respect to the homeless. Josh Evans contends that "politics is conflict over who is recognized, whose voice is heard as speech rather than noise, and the divisions by which these relationships are established and changed." By seeking to "end" homelessness, the government puts the issue into the expert technocratic hands of public servants, thus removing the causes of homelessness from the realm of democratic debate or contestation. This new policy strategy of "ending" homelessness is good for business in that it removes the problem from public view while neatly sidestepping the issue of inequalities in an oil economy that causes some people to be left without shelter in the first place. According to Evans, the Alberta government's policy response to homelessness illustrates the way that "oil wealth provides states with extraordinary abilities to mute the social dissension and discord that is itself symptomatic of systemic social inequalities."

As the chapters above suggest, democratic struggle can take place in a variety of spaces and ways. But as spaces for this debate contract in an oil-exporting economy, and as governments increasingly abandon mechanisms for seeking public input into decision making, the dissenters turn to different arenas to affect political change. As a result, new circuits of resistance spring up, domestically as well as internationally. The chapters in this volume demonstrate the role that oil wealth has played in increasing political and economic inequality, while also providing a major incentive for marginalized groups to contest the distribution of that wealth.

Therefore, this book not only confirms the existence of deficits in the practice of democracy in Alberta but also explains the mechanism for the weakening of the bond of democratic accountability between the government and the majority of citizens. Conversely, the bond between the government and the corporate sector has been strengthening, nurtured by corporations assuming the regulatory functions of the government and through a more direct enmeshing of corporations and government, as Paul Kellogg notes in chapter 5 in relation to the corporate support for right-wing parties in Alberta. Kellogg highlights the differences between two oil-exporting countries, Venezuela and Canada, by virtue of their locations in two different hemispheres, as well as the nature of their corporations. He concludes that oil corporations exert significant political influence in both jurisdictions, although with vastly differential economic consequences. The difference, he argues, is tied more to the international hierarchy of nations than to the internal dynamics of a resource economy.

Considering the existence of the emerging democratic deficit as highlighted by several chapters in this volume, the internal dynamics of an oil-exporting nation could be seen to apply to Canadian political economy, albeit in varying measures. For instance, from the perspective of the democratic deficit, the issue of regulatory capture—allowing employers preferential access to policy making—is another critical dimension in a neoliberal conception. As Bob Barnetson observes in chapter 8, one of the consequences of a booming oil economy in Alberta has been an employer-friendly policy environment, where the basic rights of workers are compromised by weakening the labour movement and by regulatory capture.

In chapter 9, Jason Foster and Bob Barnetson explore policy changes to the federal Temporary Foreign Worker Program, one of the mechanisms through which an oil economy affects labour issues, noting in particular the impacts of that mechanism on the democratic health of a region. The Alberta government's justification and encouragement of the use of migrant workers in the oil industry had created an unprecedented growth in temporary foreign workers in Alberta. Foster and Barnetson note that not only is the growing reliance on foreign migrant labour creating a contingent, underpaid, racialized foreign workforce, but it is disempowering both migrant and Canadian workers by undermining the capacity of both to resist economic restructuring advocated by the powerful industrial lobby. Moreover, the TFWP could also be seen as shifting Canada's immigration policy away from the laudable objectives of multiculturalism to a policy of differential exclusions. The declining local influence over resource development and employment is not unique to Alberta; it is particularly problematic in the context of encroachments on worker wages, benefits, and collective representation across the board in Canada. As I pointed out in chapter I, the relegation of labour unions to defending a smaller proportion of workers and the curtailment of the role of the labour unions in their ability to capture increasing shares of resource rents in wages and benefits is definitely one of the characteristics of a neostaples economy.

Last but not the least, in terms of the nature of a neoliberal state, it has been suggested that the conceptual framework of neoliberalism goes beyond capital and class (see Cannella and Perez 2012; Hubbard 2004). The hegemony of neoliberalism reflects and reproduces a complex set of power relations that encompasses global capitalism, the neoliberal state, and the patriarchal family. In particular, there is a gendered dimension to the processes of excluding marginalized groups from political and policy spaces. In different ways, chapters 6 and 10 highlight how neoliberal policy serves to recentre masculinity in the political economy at the same time that it produces inequality. In examining the entrenchment of patriarchy in the political economy of oil-exporting countries, these chapters show how the oil economy both benefits from and reproduces these unequal configurations, not only in liberal democratic Canada but also in the Islamic Republic of Iran. Despite the best justifications of new public management, however, citizens are not just consumers of government services; they are members of political and social communities. These complex communities are context specific and are affected by social and institutional facets of the economy. Joy Fraser, Manijeh Mannani, and Lorna Stefanick, in chapter 6, Gabrielle Slowey and Lorna Stefanick, in chapter 7, and Sara Dorow, in chapter 10, highlight the gendered and racialized structures of the oil economy, showing that women and visible minorities bear many of the social and economic burdens of oil extraction.

Nevertheless, democracy in Alberta is more than just a textbook case of a neoliberal policy cauldron. As mentioned by Stefanick in chapter 14, Alberta was on the forefront of several progressive ideas, being among the first provinces, for example, to extend voting rights to women and to create an Office of the Ombudsman. Despite the historical lead on some issues, however, other elements of Alberta's history exacerbate the entrenchment of neoliberal formulations of a small state in contemporary times. Some of these elements include Alberta's alienation in its relationship with the federal power centre, the persecution of minority groups and the confiscation of their land, battles between levels of government for the control of natural resources, and finally, the battle over the control of oil wealth.

Far from being a provincial phenomenon, these trends pertaining to democratic accountability and developmental liberalism significantly impact the whole country. Indeed, Alberta's insatiable demand for workers from across Canada explains why it has been easy to conflate the best interests of the oil and gas sector with national interests, despite the oil industry reportedly contributing only 10 to 12 percent of Canada's GDP (Leach 2013). However, it is much more than that—it is the entrenchment of neoliberal ideology which is prompting a country that is statistically not a petro-state to behave like one in terms of its disregard for the basic tenets of liberal democracy and for sustainable economic and environmental objectives. A long list of actions related to this assertion have taken place under the leadership of Prime Minister Stephen Harper: centralization of power in the Prime Minister's Office and in unelected officials, arbitrary prorogation of Parliament for partisan ends, the Senate crisis, violation of the Access to Information Act (Janus 2013), undermining of unionized public service employers such as educational and medical institutions and postal services, and sustained attacks on scientific and research facilities and on data collection (CBC 2014; Linnitt 2013), and the revolving door between powerful industrial and mining sectors and high-ranking political officials, to name just a few. The marginalized sections of society bear the brunt of the resultant political apathy, which has led to record low voter turnouts and unprecedented levels of poverty in one of the world's richest jurisdictions (see Hudson 2013).

Inequality: The Stumbling Block in a Liberal Democracy

From early concerns with the issues of "underdeveloped" countries to considerations of international economic and political conditions of development, many development studies scholars have seen the complex legacy of "development" as involving ideological discourse and policy directed by the Global North toward former colonies in the Global South.[2] Much has been written about the ascendancy of neoliberalism in the 1980s, when the Washington Consensus was used to "roll back the state" in the Global South, a policy devised and pursued by governments in the Global North through bilateral aid programs and through interventions by international financial institutions. During the same period, however, the political course of neoliberalism as a program of state reform was also "squeezing and splitting" the state in the Global North, redefining what states should and can do (e.g. , less redistribution, more "security") and re-engineering the ways in which they do it (see Wuyts, Mackintosh, and Hewitt 1992, 61–63). Consequently, the earlier framework of state-led development—which included public investment and employment generation, strong provision of public goods, and redistributionist measures—was displaced by structures of incentives and competitive pressures of "efficiency" provided by the market and its price signals. The disastrous economic and political consequences of such "structural adjustment programs" subjecting countries in the Global South to market fundamentalism are very well documented. Interestingly, few studies see these trends in parallel with the trend of major welfare gaps created by squeezing and splitting the state in the Global North, leading to losses in formal employment and deteriorating provision of strategic public goods such as health care and education during the 1980s and 1990s. These developments can be directly linked to the unprecedented scale of inequality in countries in the Global North.

In 2011, the Occupy movement drew considerable attention to income inequality in the United States and globally and brought this issue back onto the political agenda. Inequality has been described both as irrelevant in the face of economic opportunity in a globalized world (Friedman 1999, 247–50) and as a cause of the decline in social mobility, particularly in industrialized economies (see Fukuyama 2012; Krugman 2007; Noah 2013). Politically, the impact of inequality can be seen in the declining influence of average citizens and mass-based interest groups on public policy, leading to economic elite domination and effectively transforming democracies into oligarchies where the wealthy elite wield the most power (Gilens and Page 2014).

While inequality has risen among most OECD countries, since the early 1970s it has grown the fastest in Canada and the most in the United States (OECD 2008). During the three decades after World War II, a "middle-class society" with a relatively low level of inequality emerged in the United States, the product of relatively high wages for the working class and political support for income-levelling government policies. The return to high inequality—or what Paul Krugman (2007, 125) calls the "Great Divergence"—began in the 1970s, leading to a trend of declining labour union membership rates and resulting diminishing political clout, decreased expenditure on social services, and less government redistribution. This period also saw the transformation of American politics away from a focus on the middle class, with a transition of the American elite from pillars of society to a special interest group, as aggressive and well-financed lobbyists and pressure groups effectively acted on behalf of upper-income groups in the power corridors. As a result, between 1979 and 2007, the top-earning 1 percent of households gained about 275 percent after federal taxes and income transfers, compared to a gain of less than 40 percent for the 60 percent in the middle of America's income distribution (United States, Congress, CBO 2011). From 1992 to 2007, the top four hundred earners in the United States saw their income increase 392 percent and their average tax rate decrease 37 percent. It is estimated that this continuing upward redistribution of income is responsible for about 43 percent of the projected Social Security shortfall over the next seventy-five years (Baker 2013).

Explanations for the "Great Divergence" of income levels in the United States include public policy and party politics, aside from the impact of race, gender, immigration, transformative technology, tax policy, the decline of labour, and the rise of globalized trade. Based on his synthesis of a number of studies, Timothy Noah (2013) concluded that the two biggest contributors to income inequality in the United States, each of which is responsible for 30 percent of the post-1978 increase in inequality, are the executive capture of corporate governance and various failures in the American education system. Most of the top earners in the United States work in finance, a sector of the US economy whose deregulated incentive structure relies on complex financial instruments increasingly divorced from traditional notions of value. The finance sector has seen its share of corporate profits rise from less than 10 percent in 1979 to more than 40 percent in the early 2000s, which has led to the top 0.01 percent of the population controlling 7.7 percent share of US national income (see also Saez and Piketty [2003] 2013).

The exception to these trends is Norway, which is often compared to Canada because of the two countries' many similarities, particularly as major oil-exporting nations in the Global North with high economic and political indicators. The eighth- and sixth-largest oil-producing countries in the world, Norway and Canada are both democratic constitutional monarchies ranking very high on the Human Development Index—numbers one and six, respectively (EIU 2013, 3). However, a number of underlying differences between the two countries shed light on the interrelationship of inequality and democracy, particularly in an oil-exporting economy. For instance, while Norway has maintained its second position as the world's most equal economy with a Gini coefficient of 0.25, Canada has slid to twelfth (out of seventeen peer countries), with a coefficient of 0.32 (Conference Board of Canada 2013).[3] Despite the petroleum industry accounting for nearly a quarter of Norway's GDP, the country has maintained its position in the five countries with the highest Human Development Index, as well as its top ranking in the Democracy Index (EIU 2013). An exemplary signatory of the Kyoto Protocol, Norway maintains a welfare model with universal health care, highly subsidized higher education, and a comprehensive social security system, all of which is funded by its high taxes (Holter 2012). The country generates money for its sovereign wealth fund from taxes on oil and gas, ownership of petroleum fields, and dividends from its 67 percent stake in Statoil ASA (STL), Norway's largest energy company. Of course, the management of the Norwegian oil wealth is not without problems, as evidenced by the criticism of its rate of crude extraction since the 1990s (Anderson 2012); the cynicism that met Norway's announcement to achieve emission cuts of 30 percent by 2020, which includes significant purchases of carbon offsets to achieve this goal (Rosenthal 2008); and the recent rise of right-wing parties to power (see Wahl 2011). Nevertheless, as illustrated by an Oxfam study (2013), despite the above problems, Norway has managed to counter increasing levels of income inequality through its efficient redistributive policies.

As an extreme example of the rise in inequality in Canada, in 2013 a story broke in the local media about cases of body lice in Edmonton's homeless population (CBC News 2013). Dr. Stan Houston, who first brought the story to the attention of the media, referred to this discovery as "a very powerful health indicator of the kind of poverty we are seeing (and creating) in this, one of the wealthiest political jurisdictions in the world. . . . Not only is body lice a marker of extreme, refugee camp-like conditions, it can transmit at least three potentially life threatening diseases" (pers. comm., 11 February 2013). Tax cuts in particular have stripped hundreds of billions from the public purse since the mid-1990s in Canada, squeezing public programs and support for necessities such as education, health care, housing, child care, and transportation. However, there was little acknowledgment of this bleeding of public funds in Alberta's "austerity budget" in March 2013, which included severe cuts to advanced education, human services, and the environment in the name of "fiscal necessity," despite record profits by oil companies and the growing crescendo of public opinion for meaningful revenue reforms related to taxation and oil rent (AFL 2013; Bower 2013).

Undoubtedly, the predominance of neoliberal beliefs has led to the growing concentration of income and wealth and to a new thrust in public policy—with ideology, rather than evidence, being the driver. Moreover, as Stefanick notes in chapter 14, as the role of the state as a producer or supporter of evidence-based research diminishes, there is little to hold back the tide of ideology. As pointed out in many of the chapters in this volume, in a neoliberal state, dependence on oil revenue is certainly playing a role in increasing income inequality and eroding institutions of liberal democracy, even if that oil-exporting country is in the Global North.

Oil and Democracy in the Global North

The timeliness of this book lies in wake of the recent surge in oil production driven by the discovery of massive shale oil reserves in the United States. The United States has the largest known deposits of shale oil in the world, although the estimates of recoverable reserves have been revised recently, raising uncertainty regarding the sustainability of such high levels of oil production (Ahmed 2014). Nevertheless, as of April 2013, US crude production was at a more than twenty-year high, at nearly 7.2 million barrels per day (USEIA 2014), with shale oil from the seven most prolific shale-producing regions of the country accounting for 95 percent of oil production growth from 2011 to 2013 (USEIA 2015). While shale oil and gas can be extracted by other methods, such as conventional drilling or horizontal drilling, hydraulic fracturing—the propagation of fractures in a rock layer by a pressurized fluid—is seen as the key method of extraction of shale oil and gas to make it commercially viable.

However, hydraulic fracturing, commonly called fracking, has raised environmental concerns such as groundwater contamination, risks to air quality, migration of gases and hydraulic fracturing chemicals to the surface, and other risks to public safety and health, challenging the adequacy of existing regulatory regimes (Jackson et al. 2014). Most troubling, according to the United States Geological Survey (USGS 2015), are earthquakes induced by hydraulic fracturing and the resulting waste disposal wells, which have been reported in several locations. Although the magnitude of these quakes has been small so far, the USGS says that there is no guarantee that larger quakes will not occur. Moreover, the frequency of the quakes has been increasing. In 2009, there were 50 earthquakes greater than magnitude 3.0 in the area spanning Alabama and Montana, and in 2010, there were 87. In 2011, in the same area, 134 earthquakes occurred, a sixfold increase over twentieth-century levels (Soraghan 2012). There are also concerns that quakes may damage underground gas, oil, and water lines and wells that were not designed to withstand earthquakes.

Canada has used fracking for decades, and many companies are exploring for and developing shale oil and gas resources in Alberta, British Columbia, Québec, and New Brunswick (CAPP 2012; Wood 2014). Fracking remains a popular technique despite the conclusion of a British Columbia Oil and Gas Commission investigation which found that a series of thirty-eight earthquakes (with magnitudes ranging from 2.2 to 3.8 on the Richter scale) that occurred in the Horn River Basin area between 2009 and 2011 were caused by fluid injection during hydraulic fracturing in proximity to pre-existing faults (BCOGC 2012, 6–8). The development of shale oil is going ahead with little regard for public outcry or scientific warnings. Indeed, several researchers and commentators have reported difficulty in conducting and reporting the results of studies on hydraulic fracturing due to pressure from industry and government and the censoring of environmental reports ("Documents" 2011; Elgin 2015; Urbina 2011; Wood 2014). It is not a coincidence that the extreme income inequality in North America has made it possible to ignore the democratic ideals of transparent public consultations, or political accountability, under pressure from politically powerful industrial interests.

On the other side of the planet, energy companies are celebrating the shale discovery bonanza in South Australia and Queensland, estimated to be nearly as large as the total expected oil deposit in Saudi Arabia. Australia is bracing for the rush of large multinational energy companies (Kaye 2013). With the significant rise of income inequality in the past fifteen years (Austrailian Social

Inclusion Board 2012), the spectre of unacknowledged environmental and public health concerns (Fraser 2013), the issue of Aboriginal land rights, and racial discrimination (e.g., Changarathil 2012; NLC 2013), Australia appears disturbingly similar to the other big unconventional oil producers—the United States and Canada.

The research of Andre Gunder Frank and Barry K. Gills (1992) on global economic systems reminds us that despite being the economic hegemons of the world economy for several millennia, China and India could not prevent being reduced to the poorest countries in the world after only two hundred years of colonization. The rise and fall (and the possible re-emergence) of these countries serve as an important reminder to not take for granted our perceived strengths in political and economic structures. For the countries in the Global North, it would indeed be a tragedy if the significant long-term gains of a liberal democratic system were sacrificed to the short-term priorities of the oil industry. While the causal relationship between an oil economy and a diminished democracy is too complex to prove unequivocally, the link between the rise of inequality through the institutionalization of unfettered neoliberalism in an oil economy and its detrimental impact on democratic institutions is undeniable. In this context, revisiting the basic assumptions of liberal democracy is very instructive. In particular, given the significant pitfalls of inequality, it is useful to bring back a focus on developmental liberalism, one of the consistently ignored assumptions of liberal democracy in a neoliberal context.

The staples theory of economic development has much to contribute to an exploration of the relationship between oil and democracy. In particular, it provides a useful framework for investigating the structural changes in the industrial landscape in an oil-exporting jurisdiction and for examining the governance of resource industries from the perceptive of workers, resource-dependent Aboriginal and non-Aboriginal communities, and governments. An intellectual and political process of both deconstruction and reconstruction is required to understand and reform the political, social, and economic institutions and practices in an oil-exporting country. We need a wider intellectual and political understanding of developmental liberalism as a process of redistributional conflict, and we must use the diverse intellectual resources that transcend binaries such as North/South in order to advance such an understanding. Moreover, removing the filters of the North/South dichotomy clarifies the global scale of comprehensive market reforms that rely on similarly comprehensive state reforms. Transcending the North/South binary also reveals the reasons for the pursuit of the narrowly defined "good governance" rather than the more expansive conceptions of liberal democratic framework. As Henry Bernstein (2005, 119) reminds us, the hegemony of neoclassical economics, which supports the neoliberal discourse, "is as good an example as any of a theoretical model achieving supremacy as a world view, and global progamme, owing to political and ideological conditions rather than intrinsic intellectual authority."

In the introduction to this volume, Lorna Stefanick and I noted that neoliberalism has become a global phenomenon, with few exceptions. We wondered if the predominance of a single resource creates special problems for creating or maintaining democratic norms, or if threats to democracy in resource-exporting countries are simply manifestations of a generalized corporate attack against democratic norms in a global capitalist era facing a crisis of accumulation and legitimacy. The evidence in this volume suggests that economies dominated by commodity production, and particularly fossil fuel production, do indeed pose particular challenges for proponents of liberal democratic norms—especially for unabashed proponents of economic democracy as a necessary complement to formal political democracy. The short-term society-wide prosperity created by oil allows dominant interests to perpetuate a mythology of social solidarity in which environmentalists, along with proponents of social and economic justice, are enemies of a supposedly unchallengeable "progress" and should not be permitted to conduct research and disseminate information and ideas that challenge the hegemony of a petroleum-based economic and political elite. But, as this book illustrates, movements of resistance have arisen within states dependent on petroleum wealth; the potential of such movements should not be discounted. It is equally important, however, not to discount the particular problems that these groups face in countering the dominance and power of neoliberal capitalist ideology when it is married to a commodity that dazzles huge segments of the population in countries or in subnational entities that house the commodity.

The picture that emerges in this volume of the relationship between oil and democracy in Alberta and Canada is suggestive of many themes that are global in nature. How these themes play out in a variety of jurisdictions will vary depending on the political, economic, and institutional contexts; they will diverge in unexpected ways that transcend antiquated binaries. Our hope is that by exploring the nature of the interaction of oil and democracy in Canada, we can contribute to a sophisticated analytical discussion of these increasingly important political economic issues.

Notes

1 A meta-analytical study (Doucouliagos and Ulubaşoğlu 2008) associates liberal democracy with higher human capital accumulation, lower inflation, lower political instability, and higher economic freedom. The researchers found that while democracy has no direct effect on economic growth, it has strong and significant indirect effects that contribute to long-term economic growth. The findings of this study are in stark contrast to the entrenchment of neoliberal orthodoxy that relies on the economic argument that equality and efficiency are trade-offs.

2 Although the United States had far fewer colonial possessions than did the European nations, it has substantial historical experience of policy making and intervention in its "informal empire," notably in South America.

3 The Gini coefficient measures income inequality by calculating the extent to which the distribution of income among individuals within a country deviates from a perfectly equal distribution—a Gini coefficient of 0 represents exact equality, while a Gini coefficient of 1 represents total inequality—that is, one person has all the income and the rest of the society has none.

References

AFL (Alberta Federation of Labour). 2013. "Albertans Reject Austerity: Nurses, Teachers, Health Sciences Professionals, and Public Employees Urge Government to Listen to Majority of Albertans." *Alberta Federation of Labour*. News release, 4 March.

Ahmed, Nafees. 2014. "Write-Down of Two-Thirds of U.S. Shale Oil Explodes Fracking Myth." *The Guardian*, 22 May.

Alberta. Alberta Energy. 2015. "Facts and Statistics." *Alberta Energy*. http://www.energy. alberta.ca/oilsands/791.asp.

Anderson, Mitchell. 2012. "The Mistake That Cost Norway Huge in Oil Wealth." *The Tyee*, 26 September. http://thetyee.ca/News/2012/09/26/Norway-Oil-Mistake/.

Australian Social Inclusion Board. 2012. *Social Inclusion in Australia: How Australia Is Faring*. 2nd ed. Canberra: Commonwealth of Australia, Department of the Prime Minister and Cabinet. http://ppcg.org.au/dev/wp-content/uploads/2011/08/HAIF_ report_final.pdf.

Baker, Dean. 2013. "The Impact of the Upward Redistribution of Wage Income on Social Security Solvency." *Centre for Economic and Policy Research*. http://www.cepr.net/index. php/blogs/cepr-blog/the-impact-of-the-upward-redistribution-of-wage-income- on-social-security-solvency.

BCOGC (British Columbia Oil and Gas Commission). 2012. *Investigation of Observed Seismicity in the Horn River Basin*. www.bcogc.ca/node/8046/download?documentID=1270.

Bernstein, Henry. 2005. "Development Studies and the Marxists." In *A Radical History of Development Studies: Individuals, Institutions and Ideologies*, edited by Uma Kothari, 111–37. London, UK: Zed Books.

Bower, Shannon Stunden. 2013. "Alberta's Budget Another Lost Opportunity." *Troy Media*, 13 March.

Bronskill, Jim. 2015. "Elizabeth May, Greens Say Bill C-51 Still Dangerous Despite Tory Amendments." *Huffington Post*, 30 March. http://www.huffingtonpost.ca/2015/03/30/federal-anti-terrorism-bi_n_6969434.html.

Campbell, Bruce. 2012. "Norway Manages Its Oil Wealth Much Better Than Canada Does." Part 1 of "A Tale of Two Petro-States." *Canadian Centre for Policy Alternatives*, 1 November. http://www.policyalternatives.ca/publications/monitor/tale-two-petro-states-part-i-iii.

Cannella, Gaile S., and Michelle Salazar Perez. 2012. "Emboldened Patriarchy in Higher Education: Feminist Readings of Capitalism, Violence and Power." *Cultural Studies Critical Methodologies* 12 (4): 279–86.

CAPP (Canadian Association of Petroleum Producers). 2012. "Shale Gas." *CAPP*. http://www.capp.ca/canadaIndustry/naturalGas/ShaleGas/Pages/default.aspx.

CBC. 2014. "Federal Programs and Research Facilities That Have Been Shut Down or Had Their Funding Reduced." *The Fifth Estate*, 10 January. http://www.cbc.ca/fifth/blog/federal-programs-and-research-facilities-that-have-been-shut-down-or-had-th.

CBC News. 2013. "Body Lice Found Amongst Edmonton Homeless." *CBC News*, 13 February. http://www.cbc.ca/news/canada/edmonton/story/2013/02/13/edmonton-body-lice-homeless.html.

Changarathil, Valerina. 2012. "Aboriginal Groups to Challenge SA Government's Legislation on Oil and Gas Licenses on Constitutional Racial Discrimination Grounds." *The Advertiser*, 8 October.

Conference Board of Canada. 2013. "Income Inequality." *Conference Board of Canada*. http://www.conferenceboard.ca/hcp/details/society/income-inequality.aspx.

"Documents: Natural Gas's Toxic Waste." 2011. *New York Times*, 26 February.

Doucouliagos, Hristos, and Mehmet Ali Ulubaşoğlu. 2008. "Democracy and Economic Growth: A Meta-analysis." *American Journal of Political Science* 52 (1): 61–83.

EIU (Economist Intelligence Unit). 2013. *Democracy Index 2012: Democracy at a Standstill*. London, UK: Economist Intelligence Unit, Economist Group.

Elgin, Benjamin. 2015. "Oil CEO Wanted Quake Scientists Dismissed: Dean's Email." *Bloomberg Business*, 15 May. http://www.bloomberg.com/news/articles/2015-05-15/oil-tycoon-harold-hamm-wanted-scientists-dismissed-dean-s-e-mail-says.

Frank, Andre Gunder, and Barry K. Gills. 1992. "The Five Thousand Year World System: An Interdisciplinary Introduction." *Humboldt Journal of Social Relations* 18 (2): 1–80.

Fraser, Andrew. 2013. "Suddenly Shale Oil Stakes Up." *The Australian*, 20 February.

Friedman, Thomas L. 1999. *The Lexus and the Olive Tree: Understanding Globalization*. New York: Farrar, Straus, and Giroux.

Fukuyama, Francis. 2012. "The Future of History: Can Liberal Democracy Survive the Decline of the Middle Class?" *Foreign Affairs* 91 (1): 53–61.

Gilens, Martin, and Benjamin I. Page. 2014. "Testing Theories of American Politics: Elites, Interest Groups, and Average Citizens." *Perspectives on Politics* 12 (3): 564–81.

Holter, Mikael. 2012. "Norway Oil Fund Made $29 Bln Last Quarter as Stocks Rose." *Bloomberg Business*, 2 November. http://www.bloomberg.com/news/2012-11-02/norway-oil-fund-made-29-billion-last-quarter-as-stocks-rose-1-.html.

Hubbard, Phil. 2004. "Revenge and Injustice in the Neoliberal City: Uncovering Masculinist Agendas." *Antipode* 36 (4): 665–86.

Hudson, Carol-Anne. 2013. *Poverty Costs 2.0: Investing in Albertans—A Blueprint for Reducing Poverty in Alberta*. Calgary: Vibrant Communities Calgary and Action to End Poverty in Alberta.

Jackson, Robert B. , Avner Vengosh, J. William Carey, Richard J. Davies, Thomas H. Darrah, Francis O'Sullivan, and Gabrielle Pétron. 2014. "The Environmental Costs and Benefits of Fracking." *Annual Review of Environment and Resources* 39: 327–62.

Janus, Andrea. 2013. "Problems with Access-to-Information System Put 'Canadian Democracy at Risk': Legault." *CTV News*, 17 October. http://www.ctvnews.ca/canada/problems-with-access-to-information-system-put-canadian-democracy-at-risk-legault-1.1501069#ixzz2q3jwTM3M.

Kaye, Tom. 2013. "Our Energy Future Is Cast in Stone." *The Australian*, 16 March.

Krugman, Paul. 2007. *The Conscience of a Liberal*. New York: W. W. Norton.

Leach, Andrew. 2013. "Canada, the Failed Petrostate? Canada Hasn't Bet the Economy on the Energy Sector, Not Even Close." *Maclean's*, 4 November.

Linnitt, Carol. 2013. "Harper's Attack on Science: No Science, No Evidence, No Truth, No Democracy." *Academic Matters: The Journal of Higher Education* (May). http://www.academicmatters.ca/2013/05/harpers-attack-on-science-no-science-no-evidence-no-truth-no-democracy/#sthash.BSshGq4L.dpuf.

Macpherson, C. B. 1953. *Democracy in Alberta: The Theory and Practice of a Quasi-party System*. Toronto: University of Toronto Press.

NLC (Northern Land Council). 2013. *Annual Report for 2011–12: Our Land, Our Sea, Our Life*. Darwin, NT: Northern Land Council.

Noah, Timothy. 2013. *The Great Divergence: America's Growing Inequality Crisis and What We Can Do About It*. New York: Bloomsbury Press.

OECD (Organisation for Economic Co-operation and Development). 2008. *Growing Unequal? Income Distribution and Poverty in OECD Countries—Summary in English*. OECD Multilingual Summaries. http://www.oecd.org/els/soc/41527936.pdf.

Oxfam. 2013. *The True Cost of Austerity and Inequality: Norway Case Study*. Oxfam Case Study, September. Oxford: Oxfam.

Payton, Laura. 2015. "Anti-Terrorism Bill C-51 'Dangerous' Legislation, 100 Academics Say." *CBC News*, 27 February. http://www.cbc.ca/news/politics/anti-terrorism-bill-c-51-dangerous-legislation-100-academics-say-1.2975233.

Penty, Rebecca, Robert Tuttle, and Eric Lam. 2015. "How Alberta's NDP Election Victory Could Spark a Stock Selloff and Stall Investment in the Oil Patch." *Financial Post*, 6 May.

Peters, Guy B. , and Jon Pierre. 2010. "Public Private Partnerships and the Democratic Deficit: Is Performance-Based Legitimacy the Answer?" In *Democracy and Public Private Partnerships in Global Governance*, edited by Magdalena Bexell and Ulricha Morth, 41–54. Basingstoke, UK: Palgrave Macmillan.

Rosenthal, Elisabeth. 2008. "Lofty Pledge to Cut Emissions Comes with a Caveat in Norway." *New York Times*, 22 March.

Saez, Emmanuel, and Thomas Piketty. (2003) 2013. "Income Inequality in the United States, 1913–1998." *Quarterly Journal of Economics* 118 (1): 1–39.

Soraghan, Mike. 2012. "'Remarkable' Spate of Man-Made Quakes Linked to Drilling, USGS Team Says." *Energy Wire*, 29 March. http://eenews.net/public/energywire/2012/03/29/1.

Stefanick, Lorna. 2009. "Alberta's Ombudsman: Following Responsibility in an Era of Out-sourcing." In *Provincial and Territorial Ombudsman Offices in Canada*, edited by Stewart Hyson, 27–52. Toronto: University of Toronto Press.

United States. Congress. CBO (Congressional Budget Office). 2011. *Trends in the Distribution of Household Income between 1979 and 2007*. October. http://www.cbo.gov/sites/default/files/cbofiles/attachments/10-25-HouseholdIncome.pdf.

Urbina, Ian. 2011. "Pressure Limits Efforts to Police Drilling for Gas." *New York Times*, 3 March.

USEIA (United States Energy Information Administration). 2014. "U.S. Crude Oil Production Growth Contributes to Global Oil Price Stability in 2013." *USEIA: Today in Energy*. http://www.eia.gov/todayinenergy/detail.cfm?id=14531#.

———. 2015. "Petroleum and Other Liquids: Drilling Productivity Report." *USEIA: Independent Statistics and Analysis*, 9 March. http://www.eia.gov/petroleum/drilling/.

USGS (United States Geological Survey). 2015. "Coping with Earthquakes Induced by Fluid Injection." *USGS Newsroom*, 19 February. http://www.usgs.gov/newsroom/article.asp?ID=4132&from=rss_home#.VOjQyfnF-ao.

Wahl, Asbjørn. 2011. *The Rise and Fall of the Welfare State*. London: Pluto Press.

Wood, Chris. 2014. "Fracking." *The Canadian Encyclopedia*. http://www.thecanadianencyclopedia.ca/en/article/fracking/.

Wuyts, Marc, Maureen Mackintosh, and Tom Hewitt. 1992. *Development Policy and Public Action*. Oxford: Oxford University Press.

CONTRIBUTORS

Ricardo Acuña has been the executive director of the Parkland Institute at the University of Alberta since 2002. He has a degree in political science from the University of Alberta and has over twenty years' experience as a volunteer, staffer, and consultant for various nongovernment and nonprofit organizations around the province. Acuña has spoken and written extensively on issues of water, commodification, politics, energy, and economic policy in Alberta. He is a regular media commentator on public policy issues and writes a column on Alberta politics for *Vue Weekly* in Edmonton.

Bob Barnetson is an associate professor of labour relations at Athabasca University. His research focuses on the political economy of workplace injury as well as on child, farm, and migrant workers. He is the author of *The Political Economy of Workplace Injury in Canada* (Athabasca University Press, 2010), and his articles have appeared in *Journal of Workplace Rights, Just Labour, Socialist Studies, International Journal of Occupational and Environmental Health,* and *Canadian Political Science Review.* Prior to joining Athabasca University, Barnetson worked for a trade union, for the Alberta Labour Relations Board, and for the Alberta Workers' Compensation Board.

Sara Dorow is an associate professor of sociology at the University of Alberta, where she teaches and conducts research in the areas of globalization, race and culture, gender and family, qualitative methods, and the concept of community. She is currently writing an ethnographic account of Fort McMurray, the "urban service area" for the bitumen sands, and is serving as Alberta team lead for the national research project On the Move: Employment-Related Geographical Mobility in the Canadian Context. These projects follow a decade of research on adoption as a form of transnational migration. Dorow is the author of *Transnational Adoption: A Cultural Economy of Race, Gender, and Kinship* (New York University Press, 2006).

Joshua Evans joined Athabasca University as an assistant professor in 2010. He is a human geographer by training, with broad interests in health, space, and power. He has published in academic journals such as *Progress in Human Geography*, *Health and Place*, *Social and Cultural Geography*, and *Social Science and Medicine*. Evans is currently involved in two projects funded by the Social Sciences and Humanities Research Council of Canada: the first investigates how social enterprises attempt to create accommodating work environments for people with serious mental health problems; the second maps the rise of Housing First policies and programs in Canada.

Jason Foster is an assistant professor of human resources and labour relations at Athabasca University and holds a PhD in management from Saint Mary's University. He was previously the director of policy analysis with the Alberta Federation of Labour. His research interests include migrant workers, union renewal, labour history, and diversity and equity in unions. His work has been published in a wide range of industrial relations and labour studies journals, including *Labor Studies Journal*, *Just Labour*, *Journal of Workplace Rights*, and *Relations industrielles / Industrial Relations*. He is also a contributor to *Working People in Alberta: A History* (Athabasca University Press, 2012). His current research focuses on the response of Canadian unions to the influx of migrant workers into Canada.

Joy Fraser is a professor in the Faculty of Humanity and Social Sciences at Athabasca University. In addition to her academic teaching and research, she has been a consultant on educational program planning and evaluation with the World Health Organization since 1999, focusing on social justice, human rights, and cultural competency. She is currently participating in the WHO Global Consultation on developing a midwifery and nursing workforce, with a view to achieving equity for women in low- and middle-income countries. Fraser has been active on many nongovernmental and governmental boards related to human rights and gender equity and was involved in the Canadian Human Rights Commission's efforts to develop a Human Rights Report Card for Canada (2011).

Trevor Harrison is a professor of sociology at the University of Lethbridge and cofounder and director of the Parkland Institute. Born and raised in Edmonton, Harrison studied at the University of Winnipeg before going on to earn his MA at the University of Calgary and his PhD at the University of Alberta. He is best known for his studies in political sociology, political economy, and public policy and for his research into populist politics in Canada and the Canadian West, in particular. He is the author, coauthor, or co-editor of eight books (including several on Alberta politics), as well as numerous journal articles and book chapters, and is a frequent contributor to public media.

Paul Kellogg is an associate professor in the Centre for Interdisciplinary Studies at Athabasca University, teaching in the Master of Arts in Integrated Studies program, and holds a status-only appointment at the University of Toronto as an associate professor in the Department of Political Science. He completed his MA at York University and his PhD at Queen's, and, prior to joining Athabasca, was an assistant professor in the Department of International Development Studies at Trent University. His research and teaching interests include political economy, social movements, and global governance, and his articles have appeared in a variety of scholarly journals, including *Canadian Journal of Political Science*, *International Journal of Žižek Studies*, *New Political Science*, and *Political and Military Sociology: An Annual Review*. He is the author of *Escape from the Staple Trap: Canadian Political Economy After Left Nationalism* (University of Toronto Press, 2015).

Manijeh Mannani is an associate professor of English and comparative literature at Athabasca University and an adjunct professor of comparative literature at the University of Alberta. Her research and teaching interests include Persian literature, comparative literature, autobiography, and cultural studies. In addition to numerous scholarly articles and book chapters, she is the author of *Divine Deviants: The Dialectics of Devotion in the Poetry of Donne and Rumi* (Peter Lang, 2007) and *Najvā: Selected Poems of E. D. Blodgett in Persian* (Nasl-i Nuvīn, 2006). She is also the co-editor of *Selves and Subjectivities: Reflections on Canadian Arts and Culture* (Athabasca University Press, 2012) and of *Familiar and Foreign: Identity in Iranian Film and Literature* (Athabasca University Press, 2015).

Meenal Shrivastava is an associate professor of political economy and global studies at Athabasca University. She holds an MPhil and PhD in international studies from Jawaharlal Nehru University, New Delhi, and taught for nearly a decade in South Africa before moving to Athabasca University. Her research and teaching explore the political processes affecting the conceptualization and manifestation of globalization, which she sees as a process along a historical continuum of global movement of humans, ideas, institutions, commodities, and technologies. She has published in *Politikon, New Global Studies, South Asian Survey,* and *South African Journal of International Affairs* (among others) and is the author of many book chapters, media pieces, and policy reports.

Gabrielle Slowey is an associate professor in the Department of Political Science at York University, where she specializes in Aboriginal affairs and Arctic studies. She holds a PhD from the University of Alberta and has worked with Indigenous communities in northern Québec, Alberta, the Northwest Territories, and the Yukon, as well as in New Brunswick and southwestern Ontario. Her research, which adopts a community-driven approach, focuses on the political economy of resource exploration and development and on land claims and self-government. She is especially concerned about the impact of current pressures to exploit shale oil reserves on the well-being of local communities. She is the author of *Navigating Neoliberalism: The Mikisew Cree First Nation* (University of British Columbia Press, 2008), in addition to numerous articles and book chapters.

Peter (Jay) Smith is a professor of political science at Athabasca University. His articles on new communications technologies, globalization, trade politics, transnational networks, democracy, and citizenship have appeared in such journals as *Journal of World-Systems Theory, Journal of Information Technology and Politics, Globalizations,* and *Information, Communication and Society.* He is among the authors of *Global Democracy and the World Social Forums* (Paradigm Publishers, 2007; 2nd ed., 2014) and contributed two chapters to the *Handbook on World Social Forum Activism,* edited by Jackie Smith, Scott Byrd, Ellen Reese, and Elizabeth Smythe (Paradigm Publishers, 2011): "The Road to the World Social Forum: The Case of the Dalit Movement" and, with Elizabeth Smythe, "(In)Fertile Ground? Social Forum Activism in Its Regional and Local Dimensions."

Lorna Stefanick is a professor at Athabasca University and the head of the Governance, Law, and Management program. She has a PhD in political science with a specialization in public administration from Queen's University, as well as degrees from the University of British Columbia and the University of Calgary. Stefanick's research interests are wide ranging: she has published on e-governance, accountability, environmental activism, and public engagement processes. She is the author of *Controlling Knowledge: Information Access and Privacy Protection in a Networked World* (Athabasca University Press, 2011). Born in Edmonton, she has spent much of her life in Alberta, thinking about the state of democracy in the province.

Karen Wall is an associate professor of communication studies at Athabasca University. She teaches and develops courses in the areas of cultural policy, heritage management, and media studies. Her interest in the history and culture of Alberta is reflected in several published articles and in *Game Plan: A Social History of Sport in Alberta* (University of Alberta Press, 2012). She has also held nonacademic positions in provincial and municipal heritage research and administration. Her current research interests include aspects of residual media, transmedia, and mobility in the contexts of tourism and everyday urban life.

INDEX

Aboriginal peoples: and bitumen oil production, 98–100, 108n8, 195, 198, 199, 200–203, 209; democratic consultation with, 210–11, 219n10; effect of neoliberalism on, 195, 196; and employment, 14–15, 200, 201; in Fort Chipewyan, 197–98; and land claims, 162, 195, 198, 199, 201, 216, 218n2; and neostaples economy, 14–15; and regulatory capture, 215–17; relations with big oil through art, 342–43, 349–50; relations with Canadian government, 86n7, 103, 198–99; and traditional knowledge, 209–10; use of courts to secure rights, 211–12, 213–14; use of political opportunity structures, 93–94, 96–100; use of transnational advocacy, 90, 106–7, 202–3

access to information, 372–74, 377–78

accountability: and access to information, 372–74, 377–78; of Alberta administration, 367–68, 370–72, 375–77, 384; Alberta government record of, 364, 369–71, 383–84; and corruption, 365–66; defined, 366–67; and conflict-of-interest investigation, 379–82; and financial crisis of 2008-9, 363–64, 383; and government-corporate ties, 374–75, 386n7; importance of, 363; and whistle-blowing legislation, 378–79, 386n8

agriculture, 234–35

Alberta democracy: and Aboriginal peoples, 216; and access to information, 372–74; and bitumen oil production, 93, 114, 196; effect of inequality on, 10; effect of migrant workers on, 255–56, 264–66, 397–98; effect of neoliberalism on, 79, 80, 119–20, 188–89, 394–96, 399; enforcement of workplace safety rules, 225–26, 228, 229–30; and conflict-of-interest investigation, 379–82; extent of citizen engagement in, 54–55, 84, 120, 295, 309, 310, 385n5; and functional representation, 17–18; government attitude toward consultation, 212–13; government control of postsecondary education, 377–78; and homlessness, 329–30; international effect of, 3–4; lack of workers' rights in, 230–34, 240–41; one-party rule, 3, 16, 72, 76, 368–69; and the public interest, 383–84; quasi-party system, 16–17; range of future policy options for government on, 309–10; roll of culture in, 12, 333–34, 345–53; whistle-blowing legislation, 378–79

Alberta economy (*see also* oil-dependent economies): compared to Venezuela, 143–45; dependence on oil, 18–20, 24n9, 76–77, 78, 81–84, 119, 235, 305–6, 392; and homelessness, 313, 317–27; importance of bitumen to, 52–53, 140–41, 149–51; inequality in, 403; and

Husky Energy, 150–52
hydraulic fracturing, 403–4. *See also* shale oil

impact and benefit agreements (IBAs), 195, 200, 201, 212–13
Imperial Oil, 149: art collection of, 340, 342
Indigenous Environmental Network (IEN), 99–100
Indigenous peoples (*see also* Aboriginal peoples): Article 32 of the UN Declaration, 97–98; Indigenous Environmental Network (IEN), 99–100; Zapatistas of Mexico, 106
inequality: and bitumen oil production, 46; in Canada, 38, 40, 57n1, 402–3; effect of financialization on, 39–40; and financial crisis of 2008-9, 33–34; health effects, 402–3; link with efficiency, 56–57; and neoliberalism, 181–82, 400; social movements fight against, 31, 32–33; as threat to liberal democracy, 10, 31–33, 328–29; in United States, 57n1, 400–402
Iran, 173–80, 185–86, 190n1
Irvine, William, 72, 73

Kent, Peter, 113, 126, 133n1
Keystone XL pipeline, 50, 98, 105, 125–26, 346
Klein, Ralph, 79–81, 82, 119–20, 303–5, 377

liberal democracy (*see also* Alberta democracy): and arts policy, 335; conflict between civil and social rights within, 226–28; and consultation, 210–12, 215; and corruption, 365–66; defined, 8–9, 31, 314; and economism,

35–36; effect of losing control of economy on, 55–57; effect of migrant workers on, 249–50, 252–53, 264–66; effect of neoliberalism on, 56–57, 91–92, 130, 393–94; and globalization, 288–89; hope for the future, 405–6; and importance of accountability, 363; limitations in assessing, 9–12; measure of in Norway, 43; and oil dependence, 4–5, 70, 406–7; Polity scheme for judging, 41–42; and protection of minorities, 196, 211–12, 216–17; rift between capitalism and developmental liberalism in, 391–92; and separation of government and administration, 367–68; and think tanks, 297–98, 301–2; and threat of growing inequality, 10, 31–33, 328–29; worldwide growth of, 55
liberalism, 7–8, 184–86
Lougheed, Peter, 76–78, 117–18, 299–300, 302
Lubicon Lake Cree, 106, 346

Manning, Ernest, 75
Manning, Preston, 86n4
manufacturing, 52
maternal mortality, 144–45
May, Howard, 218n6
media, 146, 351, 354n8, 373–74
Métis peoples, 200, 218n3
Mexico, 106, 152, 153–54
migrant workers: conditions of, 250–53; Conservative government support for, 260–64; effect of on democracy, 264–66, 397–98; implications of, 249–50, 266–67; numbers of, in Alberta, 253–55; rights of, 255–56, 261–62; why they are hired, 256–59
Mikisew Cree First Nation (MCFN), 197–98, 199, 200, 202–3, 214, 216
Mulcair, Thomas, 139–40

nannies, 285–87

National Energy Board (NEB), 103, 104

National Energy Program (NEP), 115, 118, 303

national security: and Bill C-51, 130, 396; and closer Canada-US ties, 123–24; effect of September 11th on, 121–22; as factor in bitumen oil debate, 114, 115–16; proposed Alberta bill for, 129

Navigable Waters Protection Act, 214

New Democratic Party (NDP) (Alberta): future policy options of, 310; and oil industry, 105, 162, 309, 396; as opposition party, 78–79, 300–301, 304; reaction of Conservative supporters to, 376; and 2015 election, 85, 365, 383, 385n4

New Democratic Party (NDP) (federal), 132

neoliberalism: and accountability, 363–64, 371–72, 383–84; in Alberta, 79, 80, 119–20, 188–89, 394–96, 399; and anti-democratic beliefs, 130, 196, 395–96; and bitumen oil production, 46; in comparison to nation-building agenda, 131; definition, 91, 393–94; development of in Canada, 6, 114–16; and economism, 35–37; and effect of financialization, 38–40; effect on Aboriginal land claims, 195; effect on liberal democracies, 56–57, 91–92, 130, 393–94; emphasis on security in, 92, 114, 123, 124; and gendered practices, 278–79, 288–89; and Harper government, 122, 399; and inequality, 181–82, 400; and migrant workers, 250, 259; and patriarchy, 398–99; as political ideology, 6, 37–38; and Progressive Conservative government, 6, 79, 115–16, 394–95; protests against, 92, 120–21; restricting democratic rights over resource projects, 215–16, 217; and rise

of think tanks, 297–98, 308, 309–10; view of culture, 335, 338, 340, 341, 345; view of education, 377–78

neostaples economy, 14–15, 57, 201

new public management (NPM), 371–72

Nikiforuk, Andrew, on neoliberalism in petro-states, 298

nongovernmental organization (NGOs), 96–100, 103–4, 129

Non-Partisan League (NPL), 72, 73

North American Free Trade Agreement (NAFTA), 95, 107, 163n3

Northern Gateway pipeline, 104, 105, 108n8

Norway, 20–21, 43, 402

Notley, Grant, 78, 300–301

Notley, Rachel: as MLA, 208, 209, 210, 380; and oil industry, 105, 139; and 2015 election victory, 85

Obama, Barack, 123, 125–26

occupational health and safety (OHS), 225–26, 228–30, 236–39, 255–56: Bloody Lucky campaign, 239

O'Connor, John, 201–2, 218n6, 386n8

oil-dependent economies (*see also* Alberta economy): and accountability, 365; and arts funding, 341; defined, 392; and democratic challenges, 406–7; and developmental liberalism, 34, 391–92; difficulties in assessing, 12–13; effect on liberal democracy, 4–5, 70, 406–7; evidence of Alberta as, 76–78, 81–82, 84, 305–6; and gendered employment, 280; and gender equality, 174–75, 176, 183–84, 189, 190, 398; and Iran-Alberta political comparison, 173–74; and lack of civic engagement in Alberta, 54–55; and Norwegian example, 20–21; Polity scheme for judging democracy of, 41–42; and problem of great wealth, 34; and staples theory, 13–14, 46–47,

405–6; use of migrant workers in, 250, 262; and workers' rights, 240–41

oil industry (*see also* bitumen oil production; oil-dependent economies): attitude toward consultation on projects, 212–14, 219n10; control of, in Canada, 90, 116–17, 140, 148–49, 152–53, 161, 163n3; and corruption, 385n2; criticism of by the arts, 336, 343, 345–52; discovery of oil in Alberta, 75–76; effect of September 11th on, 121–22; effect on citizenship, 12, 384; "ethical" v. "dirty oil" debate, 6, 11, 12; funding of visual arts, 334, 340–43; and gender equality, 398; history of control in Venezuela, 153–59; impact on Alberta economy, 18–20, 24n9, 76–77, 78, 81–84, 119, 235, 305–6, 392; importance of in Canadian economy, 52, 54; influence on Canadian government, 53, 129; influence over Alberta citizens, 84; international effect of, 3–4; and Klein government, 119, 305; and Lougheed government, 118, 299–300; and migrant workers, 250, 262, 267; in 1980s Alberta, 78, 119, 302; and oil glut, 51, 83, 95–96; post-2005 boom in, 47, 48–49; reaction to NDP government, 105, 162, 309, 396; and regulatory capture, 215–17; role in Alberta government accountability, 364; role in Alberta's social transformation, 187–88; role of in 2012 Alberta election, 146–48; role of in modern Iranian politics, 177, 178, 180; and royalty review in Alberta, 81–82, 85, 118, 123, 302, 305, 306–8; and shale oil boom, 49–50, 403–4; and think tanks, 298, 303; tie to PC Alberta governments, 82, 83–84, 104–5, 160–61, 187–88, 236, 262–63, 295, 299–300, 306–8; types of crude oil, 47–48; and

unions, 235–36; use of visual arts for branding, 344, 349; Venezuelan workers move to Alberta, 159–60; and Wild Rose Alliance, 83, 307

oil sands, 11, 94. *See also* bitumen oil production

oil shale, 58n6

Oliver, Joe, 103–4, 126

Organization of Petroleum Exporting Countries (OPEC), 118

organized labour. *See* trade unions

Overton window: definition of, 296;

Pahlevi, Reza Shah, 177–78

paradox of plenty. *See* resource curse

Parkland Institute, 80–81, 306

Parsa, Farrokhroo, 178, 179

patriarchy, 172, 188–90, 398–99

Petróleos de Venezuela, S. A. (PDVSA), 154–60

petro-states, 53–54, 84, 333, 336. *See also* oil-dependent economies

pipelines (*see also* Keystone XL pipeline, Northern Gateway pipeline): and Bill C-38

pluralist theory, 69–70

Poitras, George, 202–3

political opportunity structures (POSs), 92, 93–94, 96–100, 102–4, 105–7

Polity scheme of judging democracy, 41–42

populism, 17–18, 72, 370

postdemocracy, 316, 328–30

postsecondary education: cutbacks to funding, 375, 377–78

post-staples economy, 45–46

Powell, Lewis F. , 296–97

Pratt, Larry, 161

Prentice, Jim, 85, 133n3

private sector (*see also* bitumen oil production; oil industry): and control over immigration, 265; and homelessness, 323–25; negotiation on behalf of government, 212–13; and right-wing think tanks, 297–98, 301–3; ties to Alberta Conservative government, 374–75; and transparency, 365–66

privatization, 371–72

Progressive Conservative government (Alberta): and access to information, 372–74; anti-union bias of, 231–34, 259; arts funding, 342, 346–47; attacks environmental protection laws, 128–29; and illegal campaign donations, 374–75; and conflict-of-interest bodies, 375–82; creation of bitumen oil monitoring panel, 208–9; and defending bitumen internationally, 101, 104–5; and enforcement of workplace safety rules, 229–30; and gender equality, 180–81, 183–84; under Getty, 78, 79, 118, 119; government support for migrant workers, 260–64; and homelessness, 314; influence of oil industry on, 82, 83–84, 104–5, 160–61, 187–88, 236, 262–63, 295, 299–300, 306–8; and international oil politics, 90; under Klein, 79–81, 82, 119–20, 303–5; lobbying for bitumen oil production, 93, 101, 104–5, 339–40; under Lougheed, 76–78, 117–18, 299–300, 302; and neoliberalism, 6, 79, 115–16, 394–95; and postsecondary education, 375, 377–78; under Prentice, 85, 133n3; under Redford, 83, 84–85, 104–5, 145–46, 381–82; regulatory capture of occupational health and safety, 236–39; response to critical art, 337–39; rural bias of, 234–35, 241n2; under Stelmach, 82, 83, 120, 123, 306–7; and 2012 election, 145–48; and 2015 election loss, 84–85, 365, 382, 383

public interest, 81, 370, 383–84

racism, 253, 264

Redford, Alison: on arts funding, 339; becomes premier, 83; political style, 104–5; resignation, 84–85, 376–77; and Tobaccogate, 381–82; and 2012 election, 145–46

regulatory capture: and accountability, 363, 367–68, 384; of energy industry, 129; enforcement of Occupational Health and Safety laws, 225–26, 236–39, 240; of oil development, 212–13, 215–17, 397

religion, 74–75

rentier state, 4, 23n1, 42, 76

resource curse, 5, 11

Saskatchewan, 74, 75, 77

Saskiw, Shayne, 381

Saudi Arabia, 141

Scott, Don, 378–79

September 11th terrorist attacks, 121–22

shale oil, 49–51, 52, 53, 403–4; as compared to "tight oil," 58n6

shareholder activism, 97

Shell, 18, 100, 213–14, 345, 349

single-resource economies, 70

Smith, Danielle, 83, 85, 146, 307

Social Credit Party: creation of Ombudsman Office, 369, 371–72; early years of, 17–18, 71, 385n3; and eugenics, 187, 191n3; favors technocratic solutions, 73; and oil policy, 299; political success of, 75–76; and unions, 231

social movements, 31, 32–33, 39, 93–94, 105–7, 120–21; Idle No More, 107, 214, 215; Occupy movement, 400; People and Planet, 99

social reproduction feminism (SRF) framework, 277

social rights, 226–28

spectacle, 345–47

staples theory: and Alberta government, 384; and developmental liberalism, 392; explained, 13–14, 23n7; and market dependency, 95; as method of explaining Canadian economy, 44–47, 161; and neostaples economy, 14–15, 57, 201; and relationship of oil and democracy, 405–6; "staples trap," 45

Stelmach, Ed, 82, 83, 120, 123, 306–7

sterilization, 187, 191n3

Suncor, 148, 150–52, 160, 199, 341

Syncrude: and Aboriginal peoples, 200, 201, 203; and arts funding, 341–43; donation to Keyano College. 342; as early oil developer, 76–77; environmental criticism of, 204; share of Alberta oil industry, 150

tailings pond, 125, 207

tar sands. *See* bitumen oil production

Temporary Foreign Worker Program (TFWP), 251–52, 257–58, 261

temporary foreign workers: conditions of, 250–53; Conservative government support for, 260–64; effect of on democracy, 264–66, 397–98; in Fort McMurray, 279–80; implications of, 249–50; numbers of, in Alberta, 253–55; rights of, 255–56; why they are hired, 256–59

think tanks, 297–98, 301–2, 303, 308

Tobaccogate, 381–82

Tonkonogy, Anya, 347, *348*

trade unions: and migrant workers, 249, 255–56, 259, 263; and neostaples economy, 15; and oil industry, 235–36; and right to strike, 233; and safety partnership model, 237–38; weakness of in Alberta, 230–34, 241n1

traditional knowledge, 209–10

transnational advocacy, 90, 96–100, 105–7, 114, 132, 202–3

transparency, 363, 365–66. *See also* accountability

Treaty 8, 198–99

Trudeau government, 118

UK Tar Sands Network, 99–100

United Farmers of Alberta (UFA), 72–73

United Nations (UN), 93, 97–99

United States: effect of financialization on, 38, 39–40; focus on security in, 121–22, 123; and homelessness, 324–25; inequality in, 57n1, 400–402; and Keystone XL, 125–26; maternal mortality figures for, 144–45; as prime market for bitumen, 95; role in Alberta oil production, 118–19, 120; role in control of Canadian oil, 148, 149–50, 151; and shale oil boom, 49–50, 51, 403–4; as top oil exporting nation, 47; trade ties to Canada, 49, 52, 123–24; and US Glass-Steagel Act, 133n4

Usten, Olla, 206–7

Venezuela: the Apertura agreement, 154–55; *caracazo*, 145; compared to Canada, 142–46; extent of bitumen oil resource, 140–41; history of control of oil in, 140, 148, 153–59; move of oil workers to Alberta, 159–60; recent political history of, 141

visual arts: Alberta government response to critical, 337–39; censorship of critical art, 351; challenges and possibilities for, 352–53; democratic role of, 333, 334–35; funded by oil industry, 334, 340–43; oil industry use of, 337, 340, 344, 349; and protest against oil industry, 336, 343, 345–52; response to critical art, 351

Walker, Michael, 301, 302, 308

water: consumption of in bitumen extraction, 108n8, 206–7; monitoring regulatory body, 207–9; quality, 202–4, 210

whistle-blowing legislation, 378–79, 386n8

Wildrose Alliance Party of Alberta: corporate support for, 374; election of 2012, 145–48; formed, 82–83; and migrant workers, 263; support of oil industry for, 83, 307; in 2015 election, 85

Wilkinson, Neil, 379–82

Wise Wood, Henry, 72–73

Workers' Compensation Board (WCB), 237, 238

Zapatistas, 106

A book in the Campus Alberta Collection, a collaboration of Athabasca University Press, the University of Alberta Press and the University of Calgary Press.

Alberta Oil and the Decline of Democracy in Canada (2015)
Edited by Meenal Shrivastava and Lorna Stefanick
978-1-77199-029-5 (paperback)
Athabasca University Press • aupress.ca

So Far and Yet So Close: Frontier Cattle Ranching in Western Prairie Canada and the Northern Territory of Australia (2015)
Warren M. Elofson
978-1-55238-794-8 (paperback)
University of Calgary Press • ucalgary.ca/ucpress

Upgrading Oilsands Bitumen and Heavy Oil (2015)
Murray R. Gray
978-1-77212-035-6 (hardcover)
University of Alberta Press • uap.ualberta.ca